DISCARDED

# MID-AMERICAN
# ★ FRONTIER ★

*This is a volume in the Arno Press collection*

# MID-AMERICAN ★ FRONTIER ★

**Advisory Editor**
Jerome O. Steffen

**Editorial Board**
Richard S. Brownlee
William W. Savage, Jr.

*See last pages of this volume
for a complete list of titles*

# Johnson's
# History of Nebraska

HARRISON JOHNSON

ARNO PRESS
A New York Times Company
New York — 1975

Editorial Supervision: ANDREA HICKS

Reprint Edition 1975 by Arno Press Inc.

Reprinted from a copy in The State
 Historical Society of Wisconsin Library

THE MID-AMERICAN FRONTIER
ISBN for complete set: 0-405-06845-X
See last pages of this volume for titles.

Manufactured in the United States of America

Publisher's Note: The foldout map at the
beginning of this book has been deleted in
this edition.

Library of Congress Cataloging in Publication Data

Johnson, Harrison.
 Johnson's history of Nebraska.

 (The Mid-American frontier)
 Reprint of the 1880 ed. published by H. Gibson, Omaha.
 1. Nebraska--History. I. Title. II. Title:
History of Nebraska. III. Series.
F666.J67 1975        978.2       75-106
ISBN 0-405-06873-5

# Johnson's
# History of Nebraska

OLD TRADING POST, BELLEVUE, IN 1854.

# JOHNSON'S

# HISTORY OF NEBRASKA,

BY

HARRISON JOHNSON.

OMAHA.

---

OMAHA, NEB.:
PUBLISHED BY HENRY GIBSON.
HERALD PRINTING HOUSE,
1880.

Entered according to an Act of Congress in the Year 1879, by HARRISON JOHNSON, in the office of the Librarian of Congress, at Washington, D. C.

*Stereotyped
By Henry Gibson.*

# CONTENTS.

## CHAPTER I.—HISTORICAL.

| | PAGE. | | PAGE. |
|---|---|---|---|
| The Province of Louisiana, | 33 | Nebraska admitted as a State, | 47 |
| First settlement | 39 | U. S. Senators—Delegates and Members of Congress | 49 |
| Treaties with the Indians, | 40 | Officers—Territory and State | 50 |
| Nebraska admitted | 41 | Popular vote for Congressmen, | 51 |
| Apportionment of House and Council—First general election | 45 | Popular vote for Governor, | 52 |
| Judicial Districts—Territorial Governors, | 46 | | |

## CHAPTER II.—INDIANS.

The Omahas and other Tribes, .................................................53–59

## CHAPTER III.—GEOGRAPHY—TYPOGRAPHY—MINERALS.

| | | | |
|---|---|---|---|
| Geographical position, | 62 | Timber, | 71 |
| Rivers | 63 | Topography, | 72 |
| Minerals, | 69 | | |

## CHAPTER IV.—NATURAL ADVANTAGES.

| | | | |
|---|---|---|---|
| Soil, | 76 | Fruit culture, | 83 |
| Agriculture, | 79 | Stock Raising, | 86 |

## CHAPTER V.—PUBLIC LANDS.

| | | | |
|---|---|---|---|
| Lands received from the U. S. | 93 | Union Pacific land grant, | 99 |
| State University—College lands, | 95 | B. & M. R. R. R. lands, | 101 |
| Common school lands, | 96 | Government lands, | 104 |
| Saline lands, | 97 | Homestead and timber laws, | 105 |
| Penitentiary and other lands, | 98 | | |

## CHAPTER VI.—RAILROADS.

| | | | |
|---|---|---|---|
| American Railways, | 107 | Capital and funded debt, &c., | 109 |

## CHAPTER VII.—RAILWAYS IN NEBRASKA.

| | | | |
|---|---|---|---|
| Miles of road in operation, | 114 | Details of Roads, | 115–131 |

## CHAPTER VIII.—CLIMATE OF NEBRASKA.

| | | | |
|---|---|---|---|
| Altitude, | 133 | Rainfall, | 136 |
| Temperature, | 135 | | |

## CHAPTER IX.—EDUCATIONAL ADVANTAGES.

| | | | |
|---|---|---|---|
| Free Schools—School Revenues, | 137 | Normal School—Deaf and Dumb, | 141 |
| State University, | 140 | Institution for the Blind, | 142 |

## CHAPTER X.—THE CHURCHES.

Church Interests, &c., .................................................... 143

## CHAPTER XI.—MILITARY MATTERS.

| | | | |
|---|---|---|---|
| First Nebraska Volunteers | 150 | Curtis' Horse, | 157 |
| Officers of First Regiment Nebraska Cavalry, | 153 | Indian outbreak of 1864, | 159 |
| | | Militia Companies, | 160 |
| Second Regiment Neb. Cavalry, | 155 | State Militia, | 162 |
| First Battalion Neb. Cavalry | 156 | | |

## CHAPTER XII.—IMMIGRATION.

| | | | |
|---|---|---|---|
| The Character of Immigration, | 163 | Destination of Immigrants, | 165 |

## CHAPTER XIII.—POPULATION.

Population of Nebraska by Counties,..................................169

## CHAPTER XIV.—ASSESSED VALUATION.

Taxable property,................172　　State Indebtedness,..............174
Farm Animals, by Counties,....173

## CHAPTER XV.—THE PRESS OF NEBRASKA.

Pioneer Journalists..............175　　List of Newspapers,.............176

## CHAPTER XVI.—NEBRASKA—1879.

Commerce,........................181　　Grasshoppers,..................183
Manufactures,...................182　　The people of Nebraska,........184

## CHAPTER XVII.—ORGANIC ACT AND CONSTITUTION.

Organic Act of the Territory,...187　　Constitution adopted in 1875,...189
Constitution adopted in 1866,...188

## NEBRASKA IN COUNTIES.

| | PAGE. | | PAGE. |
|---|---|---|---|
| Adams, | 193 | Jefferson, | 399 |
| Antelope, | 199 | Johnson, | 404 |
| Boone, | 204 | Keith, | 413 |
| Burt, | 207 | Kearney, | 415 |
| Butler, | 217 | Knox, | 425 |
| Buffalo, | 226 | Lincoln, | 431 |
| Cass, | 230 | Lancaster, | 436 |
| Cedar, | 246 | Madison, | 451 |
| Colfax, | 250 | Merrick, | 466 |
| Cuming, | 254 | Nemaha, | 456 |
| Clay, | 264 | Nuckolls, | 475 |
| Cheyenne, | 270 | Nance, | 478 |
| Chase, | 273 | Otoe, | 481 |
| Custer, | 273 | Platte, | 494 |
| Douglas, | 274 | Pawnee, | 502 |
| Dodge, | 311 | Pierce, | 511 |
| Dawson, | 320 | Polk, | 514 |
| Dixon, | 328 | Phelps, | 520 |
| Dakota, | 332 | Richardson, | 521 |
| Dundy, | 334 | Red Willow, | 529 |
| Fillmore, | 335 | Saunders, | 533 |
| Franklin, | 340 | Sarpy, | 542 |
| Frontier, | 345 | Saline, | 550 |
| Furnas, | 346 | Seward, | 556 |
| Gage, | 350 | Sherman, | 560 |
| Greeley, | 358 | Stanton, | 563 |
| Gosper, | 361 | Sioux, | 566 |
| Hall, | 363 | Thayer, | 566 |
| Hamilton, | 375 | Valley, | 569 |
| Harland, | 381 | Wayne, | 571 |
| Hitchcock, | 386 | Washington, | 574 |
| Holt, | 389 | Webster, | 585 |
| Howard, | 393 | Wheeler, | 588 |
| Hayes, | 399 | York, | 588 |

# DEDICATION.

*To the People of the State of Nebraska:*

Through whose large enterprise, indomitable energy and great liberality, in the brief space of twenty-five years, an unorganized Territory has developed into a prosperous Commonwealth, that now occupies a proud and important position, politically and commercially, in the Union of States, this volume is respectfully dedicated by the author.

## PREFACE.

In presenting this work to the public, the author recognizes the widespread demand throughout this country, as also in the different sections of Europe, for a more reliable and comprehensive description of the great State of Nebraska, than has yet been issued from the press. This work not only embraces a full and complete description of every County, City and Town in the State, in which the advantages and disadvantages offered to immigration are impartially set forth, but includes a reliable history of the State and the territory from which it was organized, from 1803 up to the present time. While much time and labor has been expended on the historical portions of the work, the primal object of the author has been to obtain by personal observation, correct information relative to the topography, climate, soil, productions, rainfall, temperature, water supply, amount of timbered and prairie lands, and their value per acre, educational advantages and prospects, religious privileges, character of the people, railway advantages and market facilities, and other valuable and interesting facts connected with a State that the moving millions, both of this country and Europe, are making the most earnest inquiry for. In a condensed, reliable and readable form this material and important information is now presented to the public.

# INTRODUCTION.

Our work is done. The volume is completed, and only awaits the Introduction. The printers are clamoring for this, and only a few more lines and the History of Nebraska, on which we have spent so many anxious hours, will be in type for the use of our numerous friends and subscribers, who are found all over the State, and, indeed, all over the country. The work has been no sinecure. It covers the history of sixty-five counties, extending over a State of 80,000 square miles, and illustrates a period of time—the most eventful of the Nation's existence—of a quarter of a century. Stirring times have these been that have witnessed the throes of a mighty nation for existence, and have brought peace and quiet and life throughout our borders instead of anarchy and misrule and terror and death. The closing of the war brought many of the citizen soldiers to the broad fertile fields of this new State to claim their land privileges and make for themselves and their children a name and a home. And these have not come unattended, but from the four quarters of the globe the swelling thousands have come to settle with those that have made their way hither from the older States; and of these there are representatives from every State from Maine to Texas and from every Territory of the Rocky Mountains. More than 50,000 have come in during the present year to people the vast prairies that stretch in such wonderful extent and beauty through the eastern and middle portions of Nebraska. And the immigration has just commenced. Only some of the salient points are yet taken, and there is still room for an empire to occupy the fruitful lands that yet lie, in their virgin soil, waiting for the coming of the husbandman. The streams are waiting to turn the busy spindles and move the machinery that shall give bread to the millions and clothing to the masses.

Nothing in this age of wonders is so wonderful as this western civilization that is measuring a score of miles every year into the unbroken wilderness, and making it literally "bud and blossom as the rose." Before the days of the present century are numbered, and many think some years before, the center of wealth and power and political influence for the whole country will be in the Mississippi Valley, and Nebraska will do her full share to change this center of civilization to the banks of the Father of Waters.

It seems but yesterday that the painted savage called this State his home. He was "monarch of all he surveyed." His tepees were reared on the banks of the streams and his council-fires blazed on the sites of our cities and towns. He followed in the chase with his bow and arrow, the buffalo and deer, the antelope and the elk; and the wolf and bear followed his steps to gather up the remnants of the slaughtered buffalo and those of the moving camp. The war-whoop rang out on the clear morning air, and if time had not erased nearly all their rude records, there would be strange tales of many a well fought field, of lurking foes, of savage cruelty, and, doubtless, of manly courage and magnanimity creditable to these untutored sons of Nature, whose only light was that of heathenish darkness.

This volume has been the outgrowth of a desire, not only of myself, as an individual, once an actor in all these scenes of frontier life, but as a cherished feeling of the people of the State, and particularly the old settlers, that a permanent record should be made of the early days. The men who left their eastern homes and came to build up a new State in the great sisterhood of States were men of no ordinary stamp. There might be, as there always are in such new settlements, mere adventurers, reckless speculators, and selfish persons, but the rank and the file, the bone and the muscle, were men who came to stay. Men who counted the cost, who measured the sacrifices, who knew that they were coming to the wilderness, to the abodes of savage life, that they would leave for a time the comforts and luxuries of civilization, that they with their wives and children in founding a new basis of civilization would endure suffering and exposure, if not actual want; but these men had the vision of to-day before them; they saw with prophetic eye the oncoming thousands; they saw the fields blossoming for the harvest, they heard the songs of harvest home, they saw the smoke of rising cities, the highways of commerce, and some of them saw the highway of nations, so long a fable to the American people, stretching up through their valleys to the everlasting mountains and on to the broad Pacific. They saw it more clearly than Brigham Young, the Mormon prophet, saw the "Jordan" and the great lake, and the busy city, and the fruit and grain and "cattle on a thousand hills," for the people that he was leading. They believed fully in the future possibilities of the new commonwealth, and they determined to bear an active, generous and enterprising part in the mighty development of the coming civilization.

How well their dreams have been realized and their sacrifices been repaid may be seen by looking over this immense State. It has laid aside its territorial dependence—become one of the States of the Union. Its cities and towns crown the hill-tops and nestle by the winding streams. The iron horse not only sweeps through the State from east to west, bearing the wealth of China and Japan and the products of the Atlantic coast and the Golden Gate, but the State is gridironed with railroads that bear the millions of surplus bushels of grain and herds of cattle and flocks to distant markets in the east, west and south.

The dug-out and log-cabin and modest frame house of one room have given place to the elegant mansion or the comfortable farm house, surrounded by the thousands of groves that have sprung up almost by magic all over the prairies, until Nebraska from an open prairie begins to look like a wooded country. The church spire and the school house, in true Puritan style, have become the institutions of freedom and progress, and they are found on every hand as the beacon lights of a free, progressive civilization; and all this has come from the rude beginnings of worship in the open air or in humble dwellings.

These tasks of the early settlers have been well performed, and under a pressure and through obstacles and discouragements that those who are inexperienced in frontier life and trials can neither understand nor appreciate. Many of these facts and experiences that would soon have been but traditions have been rescued from oblivion in these pages. Much more could have been told by many lips that are now sealed in death, and the story of their trials and successes lost forever, if from the first a faithful record had been kept of the early days. And the object of this book has been to save from oblivion as much as possible of the early history of the pioneers of each county in the State.

Of course it would not require a miracle alone but a good many miracles to give an entirely correct account of the work of a quarter of a century of busy western life. This cannot be done, and the author only hopes to approximate to the truth. His efforts have been to give a full, impartial, accurate statement of current events, and for years he has been taking notes, consulting with old settlers, gathering statistics, getting facts and incidents and illustrations for his work. He has, as intimated in the commencement of the introduction, traveled thousands of miles by rail and stage, and private conveyance, and frequently through the entire Platte Valley to the Mountains. He has been brought face to face with many of the men of the early days and has gathered his information from their lips.

For the later information with regard to the Counties he has been obliged to depend in a great measure upon the reports of judicious, careful men, residents of the Counties. In most of the Counties some of the first pioneers are found who remember with more or less distinctness the occurrences of the early days, and who have a vivid recollection of their experiences in the wilderness. From these men the most reliable information has been received. And the author desires to make his acknowledgments, not only to these, but to numerous persons that cannot be named in various parts of the State. Some Counties and individuals have responded promptly to requests for information, while others have given no attention to the subject whatever. The author also desires to say that his aim has been to be wholly impartial in his history and representations, and he has not received one penny from any corporation or individual for the insertion of any article or cut in this volume.

The author has prepared with great care the statistical matter contained in the work, so as to give the reader a correct estimate of the resources and the development of all the industries of the State. Reliable information is also given of the topography of the State, its rivers, timber, minerals and all its material resources. The vast fields are spread out so that those who contemplate settlement here may judge of the attractions, compare the localities and decide as to the best place for them to locate. That Nebraska is destined to become one of the richest and most populous States of the Union can no longer be doubted.

But this subject is almost too vast for human thought. It comprises the progress of the age and the race. But few live but would be glad to re-visit these scenes when a century, or half that time, has rolled away. When Nebraska will be numbered not by hundreds of thousands but by millions, when her cities will vie with the largest of the olden States, when the sound of the loom and the spindle will be heard beside all her waters, when, not only the genius of agriculture, but that of manufactures, shall be developed throughout the commonwealth, and when science and art shall be enthroned with their handmaids, education and religion, and with free institutions shall be the crowning glory of a great State.

It is an inspiring thought that we, the first settlers in this then far off country, are laying the foundations of a mighty empire. They should be laid broad and deep. They should be built upon virtue and truth, morality and pure religion, and with such a foundation and with such material prospects, there can be no doubt of the future of Nebraska.

It could hardly be expected that a work of the magnitude of this—where the subject matter changes many times on a single page, and the names of cities, towns and persons occur so often, that some mistakes would not occur. We have discovered a few, which are given below:

Page 129. In Eleventh line from top, should read 100,384.08 acres, instead of 10,184,448.

Page 187. In Seventh line from top, the word *pensions* should be *pardons*.

Page 257. In Sixth line from bottom, *the* Germans should be *two* Germans.

Page 291. In Second line from bottom it should read *Daniel S.*, instead of *David S.*

Page 296. In Third line from bottom, Farnam and *Ninth* should read Farnam and *Tenth*.

Page 309. In Ninth line from bottom, it should read *Kuhns* instead of *Kountze*.

Page 312. Physical *culture* should read physical *features*.

# LIST OF ILLUSTRATIONS.

|  | PAGE. |
|---|---|
| Frontispiece — Old Trading Post, Bellevue, 1854 | |
| Late Map of Nebraska | |
| Union Pacific Transfer Depot | 124 |
| State University | 140 |
| Catholic Cathedral, Omaha | 149 |
| High School Building, Fremont | 168 |
| High School Building, Tekamah | 211 |
| High School Building, Plattsmouth | 241 |
| Old Territorial Capitol, Omaha | 286 |
| Union Pacific Headquarters, Omaha | 296 |
| Grand Central Hotel, Omaha | 301 |
| High School Building, Omaha | 303 |
| U. S. Postoffice Building, Omaha | 307 |
| Gage County Court House, Beatrice | 357 |
| Hall County Court House, Grand Island | 371 |
| Public School Building, Grand Island | 374 |
| Hamilton County, Court House, Aurora | 380 |
| Johnson County Court House, Tecumseh | 406 |
| Public School Building, Tecumseh | 409 |
| Public School Building, Sterling | 411 |
| Elk Creek, in the Nemaha Valley | 412 |
| Farm View near Shelton, Buffalo County | 424 |
| Junction of North and South Forks of Platte River, Lincoln County | 432 |
| View One Mile Southwest of Lincoln | 450 |
| Normal School Building, Peru | 463 |
| View near Central City, Merrick County | 474 |
| View in the Beaver Valley near Albion, Boone County | 480 |
| Public School Building, Pawnee City | 510 |
| Court House Building, Wahoo, Saunders County | 537 |
| High School Building, Wahoo, Saunders County | 539 |
| Ashland High School Building | 541 |
| Blair High School Building, Washington County | 582 |
| Bell Creek School Building | 584 |

## CITIES AND TOWNS IN NEBRASKA.

| | PAGE. |
|---|---|
| Ayr | 199 |
| Albion, C. S. | 207 |
| Arapahoe | 349 |
| Adams | 358 |
| Aurora, C. S. | 379 |
| Alma City, C. S. | 385 |
| Atkinson | 392 |
| Aspinwall | 464 |
| Arago | 528 |
| Ashland | 540 |
| Alexandria | 568 |
| Arborville | 591 |
| Bloomington, C. S. | 343 |
| Beaver City, C. S. | 348 |
| Burton's Bend | 349 |
| Beatrice, C. S. | 356 |
| Blue Springs | 357 |
| Blyville | 430 |
| Bazille Mills | 431 |
| Bennett | 451 |
| Battle Creek | 455 |
| Brownville, C. S. | 462 |
| Bellevue | 550 |
| Beaver Crossing | 559 |
| Belvidere | 568 |
| Blair, C. S. | 581 |
| Bell Creek | 583 |
| Custer, C. S. | 274 |
| Cozad | 323 |
| Covington | 334 |
| Culbertson, C. S. | 388 |
| Coatesfield | 399 |
| Centoria | 423 |
| Creighton | 430 |
| Central City, C. S. | 473 |
| Clarksville | 473 |
| Chapman | 475 |
| Columbus, C. S. | 501 |
| Clear Creek | 542 |
| Cuming City | 579 |
| Crete | 554 |
| Camden | 559 |
| Carleton | 568 |
| Decatur | 211 |
| David City, C. S. | 225 |
| Dixon | 332 |
| Dakota City, C. S. | 333 |
| Daviesville, C. S. | 363 |
| Dannebrog | 398 |
| Denton | 451 |
| Dunbar | 493 |
| Dawson's Mill | 528 |
| De Witt | 555 |
| Dorchester | 554 |
| De Soto | 578 |
| Elm Creek | 230 |
| Edgar | 270 |
| Elkhorn Station | 310 |
| Exeter | 339 |

| | PAGE. |
|---|---|
| Elk Creek | 413 |
| Eaton | 425 |
| Fairfield | 270 |
| Florence | 309 |
| Fremont, C. S. | 319 |
| Fairmont | 339 |
| Fillmore | 340 |
| Farmer's Valley | 380 |
| Fairbury, C. S. | 408 |
| Fredericksburg | 425 |
| Firth | 451 |
| Fullerton | 479 |
| Falls City, C. S. | 527 |
| Friendville | 555 |
| Fort Calhoun | 576 |
| Fontenelle | 577 |
| Gibbon | 229 |
| Greenwood | 245 |
| Geneva, C. S. | 338 |
| Grafton | 339 |
| Grand Island, C. S. | 373 |
| Genoa | 379 |
| Gilmore | 550 |
| Guide Rock | 588 |
| Hastings, C. S. | 197 |
| Harvard | 270 |
| Hooper | 319 |
| Halifax | 361 |
| Hamilton | 379 |
| Helena | 413 |
| Howard | 465 |
| Hopeville | 521 |
| Humboldt | 527 |
| Hebron, C. S. | 568 |
| Herman | 585 |
| Inland | 198 |
| Irvington | 311 |
| Ionia | 332 |
| Indianola, C. S. | 533 |
| Juniata | 198 |
| Jackson | 333 |
| Jackson U. P. | 501 |
| Kenesaw | 198 |
| Kearney, C. S. | 229 |
| Keene | 423 |
| Kemma | 430 |
| Lyons | 212 |
| Linwood | 225 |
| Louisville | 244 |
| Logan | 320 |
| Lamartine | 360 |
| Lincoln Valley | 380 |
| Lowell | 423 |
| Lincoln, C. S. | 448 |
| Leslie | 573 |
| London | 465 |
| La Platte | 550 |
| Loup City, C. S. | 562 |
| La Porte, C. S. | 573 |

## CITIES AND TOWNS IN NEBRASKA.

| | PAGE. |
|---|---|
| Millard | 309 |
| Martinsburgh | 331 |
| Minden, C. S. | 423 |
| Mirage | 425 |
| Millersboro | 431 |
| McPherson | 435 |
| Madison, C. S. | 455 |
| Milford | 559 |
| Neligh | 204 |
| Newton | 213 |
| North Bend | 319 |
| Nickerson | 320 |
| New Castle | 381 |
| Naponee | 344 |
| New Era | 349 |
| Niobrara, C. S. | 430 |
| North Platte, C. S. | 434 |
| Newton | 451 |
| Norfolk | 455 |
| Newman's Grove | 456 |
| Nemaha City | 464 |
| Nelson, C. S. | 477 |
| Nebraska City, C. S. | 492 |
| North Loup | 570 |
| Oakdale, C. S. | 203 |
| Oakland | 213 |
| Omaha, C. S. | 299 |
| Overton | 324 |
| Omadi | 334 |
| O'Conner, C. S. | 361 |
| Orville City | 379 |
| Orleans | 386 |
| O'Neil City | 391 |
| Ogalalla | 416 |
| Osco | 425 |
| Osceola, C. S. | 519 |
| Ord, C. S. | 570 |
| Plattsmouth, C. S. | 237 |
| Pebble | 320 |
| Plum Creek, C. S. | 323 |
| Ponca, C. S. | 331 |
| Paddock, C. S. | 592 |
| Plum Valley | 431 |
| Peru | 463 |
| Palmyra | 493 |
| Platte Center | 501 |
| Pawnee City, C. S. | 509 |
| Pierce, C. S. | 513 |
| Plainview | 514 |
| Papillion, C. S. | 549 |
| Pleasant Hill | 555 |
| Riverside | 213 |
| Rock Bluffs | 245 |
| Rogers | 255 |
| Richland | 255 |
| Riverton | 344 |
| Richmond | 350 |
| Republican City | 386 |
| Rose Creek City | 404 |

| | PAGE. |
|---|---|
| Reidsville | 431 |
| Rulo | 528 |
| Red Willow | 533 |
| Red Cloud, C. S. | 587 |
| St. Edwards | 207 |
| Savannah | 224 |
| Shelton | 230 |
| South Bend | 245 |
| St. Helena, C. S. | 249 |
| St. James | 250 |
| Strahmsburg | 250 |
| Schuyler, C. S. | 253 |
| Sutton, C. S. | 269 |
| Sidney, C. S. | 272 |
| Scribner | 320 |
| Summit | 334 |
| Stockville, C. S. | 345 |
| Scotia | 360 |
| St. Paul, C. S. | 398 |
| Steele City | 404 |
| Sterling | 411 |
| Saltillo | 451 |
| Silver Creek | 473 |
| Sheridan | 465 |
| St. Deroin | 465 |
| Superior | 477 |
| Syracuse | 493 |
| St. Barnabas | 502 |
| Strohmsburg | 519 |
| Sherwood | 521 |
| Salem | 528 |
| Sarpy Center | 550 |
| Seward, C. S. | 558 |
| Stanton, C. S. | 565 |
| Tekamah, C S | 210 |
| Tecumseh, C. S. | 410 |
| Table Rock | 510 |
| Ulysses | 225 |
| Unadilla | 493 |
| Utica | 559 |
| Valley | 310 |
| Vesta | 413 |
| Valparaiso | 541 |
| Weeping Water | 244 |
| West Point, C. S. | 263 |
| Wisner | 263 |
| Waterloo | 310 |
| Webster | 320 |
| Willow Island | 324 |
| Wilsonville | 349 |
| Warsaw | 399 |
| Walnut Grove | 431 |
| Waverly | 451 |
| Williamsburg | 521 |
| Wahoo, C. S. | 540 |
| Wilber, C. S. | 554 |
| Waco | 591 |
| York, C. S. | 591 |

# CHAPTER I.

Lewis and Clarke's Expedition—Nebraska as a Territory—Nebraska Admitted as a State—Popular Vote for Governor and Members of Congress.

## HISTORICAL.

About the middle of the seventeenth century Canadian traders visited the Indian tribes then inhabiting the northern part of the country now embraced within the limits of Nebraska, and established a profitable trade with them for their rich robes and furs, which was continued for long years thereafter. In 1673, Marquette, the famous French missionary among the Indians, visited this part of the country and explored and mapped out the principal streams. At that time all of this Northwestern country was claimed by Spain, and formed part of the great Province of Louisiana; but in 1683, La Salle took possession of the country in the name of the King of France, and the French held it until formally ceded to Spain in 1762. It was ceded back to the French in 1800, and was by them sold to the United States for $15,000,000.

The purchase was accomplished during the administration of President Jefferson, by treaty at Paris, April 30th, 1803, and ratified by the United States Senate on the 31st of October of the same year. An act was immediately passed by Congress by which the President was authorized to take possession of the Territory, in conformity with the treaty; on the 20th of December, 1803, the formal transfer was made to William C. C. Claiborne and James

Wilkinson, commissioners of the United States, by M. Laussat, the colonial prefect, at New Orleans, of the French Republic. On the 26th of March, 1804, Congress passed an act dividing the province into two Territories, denominating the southern "The Territory of Orleans," and the northern "The District of Louisiana." The latter included within its boundaries all of the Territory now embraced by the States of Arkansas, Missouri, Iowa, Nebraska and Oregon, and the largest parts of Minnesota, Kansas and Colorado, also the Territories of Washington, Montana, Idaho, Dakota, and parts of Wyoming and Indian, containing altogether, about 1,122,975 square miles.

The District of Louisiana, thus defined, was regularly organized as the Territory of Louisiana, by an act of Congress passed on the 3rd of March, 1805, and President Jefferson immediately appointed General James Wilkinson, Governor, and Frederick Bates, Secretary. The Governor, with Judges Return J. Meigs and John B. C. Lucas, of the Superior Court, constituted the Legislature of the Territory. St. Louis was made the Capital.

#### LEWIS AND CLARKE'S EXPEDITION.

Shortly after the acquisition of this vast Territory, an expedition for the exploration of the Missouri and Columbia Rivers, and to ascertain the most practicable route across the Continent to the Pacific Ocean, was organized under the auspices of President Jefferson and placed in command of Captains Merriweather Lewis and William Clarke, both young and intelligent officers in the army.

The corps consisted of forty-three men, including the officers, and was made up of regular soldiers, who had volunteered for the enterprise, several Kentuckians, two French interpreters, some hunters, and a colored servant belonging to Captain Clarke.

On Monday, May 14th, 1804, the expedition left its encampment on the Mississippi River, one mile below the mouth of the Missouri, and, embarking on board of three boats, proceeded up the latter stream on their world-famed tour of discovery. The largest boat was a Keel boat, fifty-five feet long, carrying a large square sail and twenty-two oars, and having a deck of ten feet each in the bow and stern, while the covering of the middle was so arranged that it could be raised for breastworks in case of attack. The two smaller boats were open, carrying six and seven oars respectively. The stores consisted mainly of Indian goods, such as knives, tomahawks, gaily colored cloths, paint, beads, etc.; besides a large quantity of clothing, provisions, tools, powder, balls, gun-flints and other articles for use of the officers and men.

The expedition reached the mouth of the Platte River, Saturday, July 21st, where they encamped for the night, and proceeded on their journey early the following morning, making a distance of about ten miles that day, and going into camp near the present townsite of Bellevue, Sarpy County. Five days were spent at this camp in making necessary repairs to the outfit, dressing skins, and airing the provisions, baggage and stores; and from here two men were sent to the Indians then living up the Platte river to notify them of the recent change in the Government, and of the desire of the commanding officers to meet their Chiefs in council for treaty. July 27th the expedition proceeded up the river, and on the 30th it reached the point which had previously been agreed upon for holding a council with the Indians. This is the exact spot where, in 1819, the Government established Fort Atkinson—afterwards called Fort Calhoun—which was abandoned as a military post in 1827. The old town of Fort Calhoun, Washington County, now occupies the site. It is about sixteen miles in a straight line above Omaha, or forty by the river. The place is described as follows in the *Journal* of Lewis and Clarke:

"The land here consists of a plain, above the high water level, the soil of which is fertile and covered with a grass from five to eight feet high, interspersed with copses of large plums and a currant like those of the United States. It also furnishes two species of honeysuckle, one growing to a kind of a shrub common about Harrisburg, Kentucky, and the other not so high. The flowers grow in clusters, are short and of a light pink color. The leaves, too, are distinct, and do not surround the stem as do those of the United States. Back of this plain is a woody ridge about seventy feet above it, at the end of which we formed our camp. This ridge separates the lower from a higher prairie of a good quality, with grass of ten or twenty inches in height, and extending back about a mile to another elevation of eighty or ninety feet, beyond which is one continuous plain. Near our camp we enjoy from the bluffs a most beautiful view of the river and the adjoining country. At a distance varying from four to ten miles, and of a height between seventy and three hundred feet, two parallel ranges of high land afford a passage to the Missouri, which enriches the low grounds between them. In its winding course it nourishes the willow islands, the scattered cottonwood, elm, sycamore, lynn, and ash; and the groves are interspersed with hickory, walnut, coffeenut, and oak. The hunters supplied us with deer, turkeys, geese, and beaver. Catfish are abundant in the river, and we have also seen a buffalo-fish. One of our men brought in yesterday an animal called by the Pawnees, chocantoosh, and by the French, blairvau, or badger."

Of the council with the Indians held at this camp the report says:

"We waited with much anxiety the return of our messenger to the Ottoes. Our apprehensions were at last relieved by the arrival of a party of about fourteen Ottoe and Missouri Indians who came at sunset on the second of August, accompanied by a Frenchman who resided among them and interpreted for us. Captains Lewis and Clarke went out to meet them and told them that we would hold a council in the morning. In the meantime we sent them some roasted meats, pork, flour and meal, in the return for which they made us a present of watermelons.

"The next morning, the Indians, with their six Chiefs, were all assembled under an awning formed with the mainsail, and in the presence of all of our party, paraded for the occasion. A speech was then made announcing to them the change in the Government, our promises of protection, and advice as to their future conduct. All the six Chiefs replied to our speech, each in his turn, according to rank. They expressed their joy at the change in the government, their hopes that we would recommend them to their great father (the President) that they might obtain trade and necessaries. They wanted arms as well for hunting as for defence, and asked our mediation between them and the Mahas (Omahas), with whom they are now at war. We promised to do so, and wished some of them to accompany us to that nation, which they declined, for fear of being killed by them. We then proceeded to distribute our presents. The Grand Chief of the nation, not being of the party, we sent him a flag, a medal and some ornaments for clothing. To the six Chiefs who were present we gave a medal of the second grade to one Ottoe Chief and a Missouri Chief, and a medal of the third grade to two inferior Chiefs of each nation; the customary mode of recognizing a Chief being to place a medal around his neck, which is considered among his tribe a proof of his consideration abroad. Each of these medals was accompanied by a present of paint, garters and cloth ornaments of dress, and to this we added a canister of powder, a bottle of whisky, and a few presents to the whole, which appeared to make them perfectly satisfied. The air gun, too, was fired and astonished them greatly. The absent Grand Chief was an Ottoe, named Wahrushhah, which, in English, degenerates into Little Thief. The two principal Chiefs present were Shongolongs, or Big Horse, and Wethea, or Hospitality; also, Shosguscan, or White Horse, an Ottoe. The incidents just related induced us to give to this place the name of Councilbluff. The situation of it is exceedingly favorable for a fort and trading factory, as the soil is well calculated for bricks, and there is an abundance of wood in the neighborhood, and the air being pure and healthy. It is also central to the chief resorts of the Indians, being one day's journey to the Ottoes; one and a half to the great Pawnees; two days from the Mahas; two and a quarter from the Pawnee Loups village; convenient to the hunting grounds of the Sioux, and twenty-five days' journey to Sante Fe. The ceremonies of the council being concluded, we set sail in the afternoon and encamped at the distance of five miles on the south side, where we found the musquitoes very troublesome."

On August 19th, at a point on the river a few miles below where Sioux City, Iowa, now stands, Sergeant Floyd, one of the party, was taken violently ill with colic, and notwithstanding every effort possible was made by his comrades to save his life, he died on the following day. His remains were interred on the high bluffs overlooking the river, on the Iowa side, which have ever since been known as Floyd's Bluffs. After the burial the party proceeded a mile further to a small stream on the same side, and encamped. The commanding officers named this stream Floyd's

River, to perpetuate the memory of the first man who had fallen in this important expedition.

On Tuesday, the 4th day of September, the expedition reached the mouth of the Rapidwater, or Niobrara River, as now called, which was their last camping place on Nebraska soil, on their outward course.

Here we will leave the voyagers to pursue their long and hazardous journey across the continent, which was so successfully accomplished, notwithstanding the great difficulties, privations and dangers which they had to endure and overcome. The computed distance traveled by the expedition, from its starting point at the mouth of the Missouri River, to the farthest point of discovery on the Pacific ocean, is four thousand, one hundred and thirty-three miles, and the time consumed in making the journey was two years, four months and ten days, reaching St. Louis, on its return on the 23d day of September, 1806.

Clarke and Lewis found the country inhabited by numerous tribes of Indians, of whom the Pawnees, Otoes, (then called Ottoe), Missouris, and Omahas, (or Mahas), are spoken of as the principal nations living within what are now the limits of Nebraska. The Pawnees at that time occupied the country south of the Platte, with their principal villages along the Republican river, and are mentioned as being a very powerful and warlike nation, and the most skillful horsemen of the plains. The Otoes and Missouris lived in the eastern part of the Territory, with their villages on the south bank of the Platte River, while the Omahas, with whom they were at war, were located still further north, near the mouth of the Niobrara River.

At the time the territory was opened for settlement by the whites, all of these tribes had become greatly reduced in numbers by disease, privation and incessant warfare. The Sioux—of which tribe there were several branches—dominated the plains, being by far the most numerous and savage. They resided chiefly in the northwestern part of the Territory and were almost constantly at war. They frequently extended their hunting expeditions to the villages of the weaker tribes in the eastern part of the Territory, especially those of their hereditary enemy, the Pawnees, whom they fell upon and slaughtered without mercy. The Pawnees came next, in point of numbers, to the Sioux, then the Omahas, Otoes and Missouris, but all were mere remnants of the once powerful tribes they represented.

The first to encroach upon the Indian sovereignty were the traders, who dealt with the Indians for their furs and skins.

The first white settlement in the Territory was made at Bellevue, Sarpy County, where, in 1810, the American Fur Company established a trading post. At its head, at the time of the organization of the Territory, was Col. Peter A. Sarpy, a French gentleman, well known on the frontier, and distinguished for his enterprise, sagacity and courage. In 1834 a Baptist mission was established near the trading post, but discontinued the following year on account of the death of the missionary, Rev. Moses Merrill. In 1847 the Presbyterian Board of Foreign Missions erected buildings at Bellevue for a Mission House and School, which was kept up until the removal of the Indians. In 1848, the Government established Fort Kearney, on the site now covered by Nebraska City, but soon afterward removed it to Fort Childs, then established on the Platte River, in the present Kearney County, the name of Fort Childs being changed to Kearney. With the exception of the few persons living at these posts, there were no white settlements in the Territory until the passage of the organic Act.

General John C. Fremont's surveying expedition passed up the Platte Valley in 1842, and in 1847 the Mormons made a large trail across the State in their march to Salt Lake, but it was not until about 1850, after the great tide of emigration had set in to California, and people had traveled over and seen the rich and beautiful country lying between the Missouri River and the Rocky Mountains, which had hitherto been thought only a barren waste, that schemes for its organization into a Territory began to be agitated.

A bill was shortly afterwards introduced into Congress providing for the organization of one large Territory, embracing all of Kansas as at present bounded, and extending as far north as the Platte River. This, however, did not meet the wishes of the people of Iowa, who were desirous of having the country lying immediately west of them speedily opened up for white settlement, also; neither did it suit the thousands of emigrants who had flocked to the eastern banks of the Missouri, and were anxiously waiting the permission of the General Government to cross over and settle in the new Territory. And to that end, in the fall of 1853, a considerable number of persons crossed the Missouri from Iowa, and assembling at Bellevue and Old Fort Kearney, proceeded to hold an election for a delegate to represent their interests at Washington in securing a territorial organization. Said election was held on the 11th day of October, 1853, and resulted in the unanimous choice of Hon. Hadley D. Johnson, a prominent lawyer and leading citizen of Council Bluffs, Iowa.

When Mr. Johnson reached Washington, about the first of January, 1854, he found that a bill was then in the hands of the Committee on Territories, providing for the organization of the single Territory of Nebraska, embracing, as before stated, all of present Kansas, and that portion of Nebraska lying south of the Platte river; and although Mr. Johnson was not entitled to a seat on the floor of the House, it was chiefly through his instrumentality and cogent arguments before the Committee on Territories, that a substitute for the original bill was reported, which substitute provided for the organization of two Territories instead of one, and which, with amendments, became the famous Kansas-Nebraska bill.

As a preliminary measure to the opening up of the country to white settlement, Colonel Manypenny, Commissioner of Indian Affairs, and Major James M. Gatewood, Indian Agent, held a council at Bellevue, in February, 1854, with the Chiefs of the Omahas, and the confederate tribes of Otoe and Missouri Indians, in reference to selling their lands to the United States. Logan Fontenelle, Chief of the Omahas—a half-breed Indian, who was educated at St. Louis, and understood the English language perfectly—was chosen by the different tribes as head Chief in the negotiation of the treaty, and a delegation of Chiefs, headed by Fontenelle, proceeded to Washington. A treaty was made with the Otoes and Missouris on the 15th, and with the Omahas on the 16th day of March, 1854, and ratified June 21, following, which extinguished the Indian title to a large portion of the lands bordering on the west bank of the Missouri River. A proclamation of these treaties was made by President Pierce on the 24th of June, 1854.

## NEBRASKA AS A TERRITORY.

Nebraska was organized as a Territory on the 30th day of May, 1854, at which time it contained 351,558 square miles, extending from the fortieth parallel of north latitude to the British Possessions, and from the Missouri River west to the summit of the Rocky Mountains. On February 28, 1861, 16,035 square miles were set off to the Territory of Colorado; and on March 2d, 228,907 square miles to Dakota. At the latter date Nebraska received from Washington and Utah Territories a triangular tract of 15,378 square miles, lying on the southwest slope of the Rocky Mountains, north of the forty-first parallel, and east of the one hundred and tenth meridian. This, however, was included in the 45,999 square miles taken from Nebraska, March 3d, 1863, to form the Territory of Idaho. Nebraska was thus reduced to its present limits.

The first Territorial officers appointed by President Pierce, were as follows: Francis Burt, of South Carolina, Governor; Thomas B. Cuming, of Iowa, Secretary; Fenner Furguson, of Michigan, Chief Justice; James Bradley, of Indiana, and Edward R. Hardin, of Georgia, Associate Justices; Mark W. Izard, of Arkansas, Marshal, and Experience Estabrook, of Wisconsin, Attorney.

Governor Burt reached the Territory in ill-health, on the 6th day of October, 1854, and proceeded to Bellevue, where he was the guest of Rev. Wm. J. Hamilton, at the old Mission House. His illness proved of a fatal character, and he sank rapidly until on the morning of Wednesday, October 18th, 1854, he died.

With the death of Governor Burt the duties of organizing the Territorial government devolved upon Secretary Cuming, who, by virtue of his office, became the Acting Governor.

THE FIRST OFFICIAL ACT IN THE TERRITORIAL GOVERNMENT—PROCLAMATION OF GOVERNOR CUMING.

EXECUTIVE DEPARTMENT, NEBRASKA TERRITORY, }
October 18th, 1854. }

It has seemed good to an Allwise Providence to remove from the Territory by the hand of death, its Chief Magistrate, Governor FRANCIS BURT. He departed this life this morning, at the Mission House, in Bellevue, after an illness protracted since his arrival, during which he received the most faithful medical aid and assiduous attention. His remains will be conveyed, on Friday next, to his home in Pendleton, South Carolina, attended by a suitable escort.

In this afflictive dispensation, as a mark of respect and affection for the lamented and distinguished Executive, and a sign of the public sorrow, the national colors within the Territory will be draped in mourning, and the Territorial officers will wear crape upon the left arm, for thirty days from date.

Given under my hand, at Bellevue, Nebraska Territory, this 18th day of October, A. D., 1854.

T. B. CUMING,
*Acting Governor of Nebraska.*

The Territory was divided into eight Counties, viz: Burt, Washington, Dodge, Douglas, Cass, Pierce, Forney and Richardson.

BURT COUNTY was bounded as follows: Commencing at a point on the Missouri River, two miles above Fort Calhoun, thence westwardly, crossing the Elkhorn River, 120 miles, to the west boundary of lands ceded to the United States, thence northerly to Mauvaise River, and along the east bank of the same, to the Eau Qui Court, or Running Water, thence easterly to the Aaoway River, and along the south bank of it, to its mouth, and thence southerly along the Missouri River to the place of beginning.

*Precincts*—There were two precincts or places of voting in Burt County, viz: One in Tekamah Precinct, at the house of General John B. Robinson; and the second, in Blackbird Precinct, at the Blackbird House. J. B. Robinson, W. N. Byers and B. R. Folsom were appointed judges of the first election precinct, and W. W. Maynard and H. C. Purple clerks of the same; Frederick Buck, Dr. Shelley and John A. Lafferty judges of election in the second election precinct, and Lorenzo Driggs and William Sherman clerks of said precinct.

WASHINGTON COUNTY was bounded as follows: Commencing at a point on the Missouri River, one mile north of Omaha City, thence due west to the dividing ridge between the Elkhorn and Missouri Rivers, thence northwestwardly twenty miles to the Elkhorn River, thence eastwardly to a point on the Missouri River, two miles above Fort Calhoun, and thence southerly along said River, to the place of beginning.

*Precinct*—There was one precinct or place of voting in said County, viz: At the Postoffice at Florence. Anselam Arnold, Charles How and William Bryant were appointed judges of election, and Henry Springer and William More clerks of same.

DODGE COUNTY was bounded as follows: Commencing at a point on the Platte River, twenty miles west of Bellevue, thence westwardly, along the said Platte River, to the mouth of Shell Creek, thence north twenty-five miles, thence east to the dividing ridge between the Elkhorn and Missouri rivers, and thence southerly, to the place of beginning.

*Precinct*—There was one precinct or place of voting in said County, viz: At the house of Dr. M. H. Clark, in Fontenelle precinct. William Kline, Christopher S. Leiber and Wm. S. Estley were appointed judges of election, and Wm. Taylor and E. G. McNeely, clerks of same.

DOUGLAS COUNTY was bounded as follows: Commencing at the mouth of the Platte River, thence north along the west bank of the Missouri River, to a point one mile north of Omaha City, thence west along the south boundary of Washington County, twenty miles, thence south ten miles, more or less, to the Platte River, and thence east to the place of beginning.

*Precincts*—There were two precincts or places of voting in said County, viz: One at the brick building at Omaha City and one at the Mission House at Bellevue. David Lindley, T. G. Goodwill and Chas. B. Smith were appointed judges of election in the Omaha precinct, and M. C. Gaylord and Dr. Pattee, clerks of same. Isaiah Bennet, D. E. Reed and Thos. Morton were appointed judges of the Bellevue precinct, and G. Hollister and Silas A. Strickland, clerks of the same.

CASS COUNTY was bounded as follows: North by the Platte River, east by the Missouri, south by the Weeping Water River to its head waters, thence westwardly to the west boundary of lands ceded to the United States, and thence by said boundary, north to the Platte River.

*Precincts.*—There were two precincts or places of voting in said County, viz.: one at the house of Colonel Thompson, in

Kanosha precinct, and one at the house of Samuel Martin, in Martin's precinct. J. S. Griffith, Thomas B. Ashley and L. Young were appointed judges of election in Kanosha precinct and Benjamin B. Thompson and Wm. H. Davis, clerks of the same. James O'Neil, Thos. P. Palmer and Stephen Willes were appointed judges of election in Martin's precinct, and T. S. Gaskill and Levi G. Todd, clerks of the same.

PIERCE COUNTY was bounded as follows: Commencing at the mouth of the Weeping Water River, on the Missouri River, thence westwardly, along the south bank of the same, to its head waters, thence due west, to the west boundary of lands ceded to the United States, (100 miles,) thence south twenty miles, to the north line of Forney County, thence due east, along the north line of said Forney County to Camp Creek, and along the north bank of said Creek, to the Missouri River, and thence northwardly along said River to the place of beginning.

*Precinct.*—There was one precinct or place of voting in said County, viz.: at the house of Major H. P. Downs. Wm. C. Fowlkes, Simpson Hargous and Henry Bradford were appointed judges of election, and James H. Cowles and James H. Decker, clerks of the same.

FORNEY COUNTY was bounded as follows: Commencing at the mouth of Camp creek, thence to the head waters of the same, thence due west to a point sixty miles from the Missouri river, thence due south twenty miles, thence east to the head waters of the Little Nemaha River, thence along the north bank of said River to the Missouri River, and thence along the Missouri River north to the place of beginning.

*Precinct.*—There was one precinct or place of voting in said County, viz.: at the place known as Brownville, at the house of Richard Brown. Richard Brown, Allen L. Coate and Israel Cuming were appointed judges of election, and A. J. Benedict and Stephen Sloan, clerks of same.

RICHARDSON COUNTY was bounded as follows: Commencing at the northwest corner of the half breed tract, thence westwardly along the south bank of the Little Nemaha River, thence westwardly to a point sixty miles west of the Missouri River, thence south to the 40th parallel, the boundary between Kansas and

Nebraska, thence east along said boundary, to the Missouri River, thence north along the Missouri River and west ten miles to the southwest corner of the half breed tract, and thence northerly, along the boundary of said tract to the place of beginning.

*Precincts.*—There were two precincts or places of voting in said County, viz.: one at the house of Wm. Level, in precinct No. 1; the second at the house of Christian Bobst, in precinct No. 2. John Purket, Robert, T. Archer and James M. Roberts were appointed judges of election of the first precinct, and Wm. W. Soper and John A. Singleton, Clerks of the same; and Henry Shellhorn, Henry Abrams and Wm. J. Burns, judges of election in precinct No. 2, and Christian Bobst and W. L. Soper, clerks of the same.

An enumeration of the inhabitants of the Territory was made in accordance with a proclamation of the Acting Governor, dated October 21, 1854, and the following apportionment of Councilmen and Representatives was made in accordance with the census returns of November 20th:

BURT COUNTY.—One Councilman, two Representatives.
WASHINGTON COUNTY.—One Councilman, two Representatives.
DODGE COUNTY.—One Councilman, two Representatives.
DOUGLAS COUNTY.—Four Councilmen, eight Representatives.
CASS COUNTY.—One Councilman, three Representatives.
PIERCE COUNTY.—Three Councilmen, five Representatives.
FORNEY COUNTY.—One Councilman, two Representatives.
RICHARDSON COUNTY.—One Councilman, two Representatives.

The first general election for members of the Legislature and a delegate to Congress, was held on December 12th, 1854, in pursuance of a proclamation dated November 23d, and by proclamation of December 20th, the Legislative Assembly was convened at Omaha on the 16th day of January, 1855.

The following gentlemen composed the first Legislature:

COUNCIL.

RICHARDSON COUNTY.—J. L. Sharp, *President.*
BURT COUNTY.—B. R. Folsom.
WASHINGTON COUNTY.—J. C. Mitchell.
DODGE COUNTY.—M. H. Clark.
DOUGLAS COUNTY.—T. G. Goodwill, A. D. Jones, O. D. Richardson, S. E. Rogers.
CASS COUNTY.—Luke Nuckolls.

PIERCE COUNTY.—A. H. Bradford, H. P. Bennet, C. H. Cowles.
FORNEY COUNTY.—Richard Brown.
OFFICERS OF THE COUNCIL—Dr. G. L. Miller, Omaha, Chief Clerk; O. F. Lake, Brownville, Assistant Clerk; S. A. Lewis, Omaha, Sergeant-At-Arms; N. R. Folsom, Tekamah, Doorkeeper.

#### HOUSE OF REPRESENTATIVES.

DOUGLAS COUNTY.—A. J. Hanscom, Speaker; W. N. Byers, Wm. Clancy, F. Davidson, Thomas Davis, A. D. Goyer, A. J. Poppleton, Robt. Whitted.
BURT COUNTY.—J. B. Robertson, A. C. Purple.
WASHINGTON COUNTY.—A. Archer, A. J. Smith.
DODGE COUNTY.—E. R. Doyle, J. W. Richardson.
CASS COUNTY.—J. M. Latham, Wm. Kempton, J. D. H. Thompson.
PIERCE COUNTY.—G. Bennet, J. H. Cowles, J. H. Decker, W. H. Hail, Wm. Maddox.
FORNEY COUNTY.—W. A. Finney, J. M. Wood.
RICHARDSON COUNTY.—D. M. Johnson, J. A. Singleton.
OFFICERS OF THE HOUSE.—J. W. Paddock, Chief Clerk; G. L. Eayre, Assistant Clerk; J. L. Gibbs, Sergeant-At-Arms; B. B. Thompson, Doorkeeper.

Hon. Napoleon B. Giddings, was elected as Nebraska's first delegate to Congress.

The Territory was divided into three Judicial Districts, which was made public by proclamation on December 20th, 1854. Hon. Fenner Ferguson, Chief Justice of the Supreme Court, was assigned to the First Judicial District, embracing the Counties of Douglas and Dodge; Hon. Edward R. Hardin, Assistant Justice Supreme Court to the Second Judicial District, embracing all that portion of the Territory lying south of the Platte River; and Hon. James Bradley, Assistant Justice Supreme Court, to the Third Judicial District, embracing the Counties of Washington and Burt.

Judges of Probate, Justice of the Peace, Sheriffs, Constables, and Clerks of the Court, were also designated for the several Counties.

The erection of a Capitol building was commenced at Omaha in the fall of 1855, and completed by January, 1858. It was a commodious brick structure, and occupied a commanding position on Capitol Hill.

Hon. Mark W. Izard, of Arkansas, the second Governor, relieved Acting Governor Cuming, in February, 1855. He was succeeded in 1857, by Hon. William A. Richardson, of Illinois, who resigned in April, 1858. Hon. J. Sterling Morton, Secretary of the Territory, acted in the interim, and was relieved by Hon. Samuel Black, appointed by President Buchanan, in 1859, who served until succeeded by Hon. Alvin Saunders, of Mount Pleasant, Iowa, in 1861, appointed by President Lincoln. Governor Saunders continued in office until the admission of the State in 1867.

### NEBRASKA ADMITTED AS A STATE.

In March, 1860, the question of forming a State Government was submitted to the people and disapproved by a vote of 1,877 to 1,987. On April 19th, 1864, an enabling act was passed by Congress providing for the admission of Nebraska into the Union, but the necessary action for admission was not taken at that time by the Territory. The continuance of the war and the prevalence of Indian hostilities checked the growth of Nebraska; but prosperity came with the return of peace. Early in 1866 the Territorial Legislature framed a Constitution, which was ratified by the people on June 21st. The first Legislature under the new Government assembled July 4th. On the 28th a bill for the admission of Nebraska as a State was passed by Congress, but did not receive the signature of the President. In January, 1867 another bill for this purpose was passed, but was vetoed by the President on the ground that it embraced conditions not contained in the enabling Act, that the proceedings attending the formation of the Constitution were different from those prescribed, and that the population of the Territory did not justify its becoming a State. The bill, however, was passed over the executive veto by a vote of thirty to nine in the Senate, February 8th, and one hundred and twenty to forty-four in the House on the following day. The act was not to take effect " except upon the fundamental condition that within the State of Nebraska there shall be no denial of the elective franchise, or of any other right, to any person by reason of race or color, except Indians not taxed; and upon the further fundamental condition that the legislature of said State by a solemn public act shall declare the assent of said State to the said fundamental condition." This act was ratified by the Legislature which assembled at Omaha on February 20th for that purpose, and compliance with the Congressional conditions was announced by proclamation of the President of the United States, March 1st, 1867.

Immediately after the admission of the State the Legislature decided to move the Capitol from Omaha to some other point. Commissioners were appointed to determine where this should be. In October, 1867, LANCASTER, a town of half a dozen houses, in Lancaster County, was selected, and this selection was approved by the Legislature. The new Capitol was named LINCLON, in honor of the President.

David Butler, the first Governor, was elected in 1866, but did not commence the duties of his office until the admission of the State into the Union, in 1867. He was re-elected October 8th, 1868, and October 13th, 1870. He was impeached and removed from office June 2d, 1871, the vacancy being filled by the Secretary, William H. James, until the inauguration of Governor Robert W. Furnas, on January 13th, 1873, Hon. Silas Garber was elected Governor in October, 1874, and re-elected in October, 1876.

Governor Albinus Nance, the present incumbent, was inaugurated January 9, 1879.

On May 2d, 1871, delegates were elected to a Convention to frame a new State Constitution. This Convention was in session from June 5th to August 19th, and completed a Constitution which was rejected by the people September 19th. However, the need for a new fundamental law being urgently felt, a second Constitutional Convention was convened at the Capitol during the summer of 1875, and the new instrument submitted by it was approved by the people at the general election held in October, 1875. The first Legislature under the new Constitution met on the first Monday in January, 1877. The Constitution provides that the House of Representatives shall consist of eighty-four members, and the Senate of thirty members, until the year 1880, after which time the number of members of each House shall be regulated by law; but the number of Representatives shall never exceed one hundred, nor that of Senators thirty-three.

The first United States Senators from Nebraska were John M. Thayer and Thomas W. Tipton, and the first Representative, after its admission into the Union, was John Taffe.

JOHNSON'S HISTORY OF NEBRASKA. 49

The following is a list of United States Senators from Nebraska since its admission.

JOHN M. THAYER, 1867–73.  THOMAS W. TIPTON, 1867–75.
PHINEAS W. HITCHCOCK, 1871–77.  ALGERNON S. PADDOCK, 1875–81.
ALVIN SAUNDERS, 1877–83.

### DELEGATES AND MEMBERS OF CONGRESS.

Napoleon B. Giddings, Dec. 12, 1854.  Phineas W. Hitchcock, Oct. 11, 1864.
Bird B. Chapman, Nov. 6, 1855  John Taffe, Oct. 9, 1866.
Fenner Ferguson, Aug. 3, 1857.  Lorenzo Crounse, Oct. 8, 1872.
Experience Estabrook, Oct. 11, 1859.  Frank Welch, (a) Nov. 7, 1876.
Samuel G. Daily, Oct. 9, 1860.  Thomas J. Majors (b) Nov. 5, 1878.
E. K. Valentine, Nov. 5, 1878.

### SENATORS AND REPRESENTATIVES FROM NEBRASKA IN THE FORTY-SIXTH CONGRESS.

SENATORS.—Algernon S. Paddock, Alvin Saunders.
REPRESENTATIVE.—E. K. Valentine.

### LIST OF THE FEDERAL OFFICERS OF THE TERRITORY AND STATE—JUDGES OF THE SUPREME COURT—CHIEF JUSTICES.

Fenner Ferguson, Oct. 12, 1854.  Wm. A. Little, (a) 1866.
Augustus Hall, March 25, 1858.  Oliver P. Mason, (c) 1867.
Wm. Pitt Kellogg, May 27, 1861.  George B. Lake, (d) Jan. 16, 1873.
William Kellogg, May 8, 1865.  Daniel Gantt, (e) Jan. 3, 1878.
Samuel Maxwell, (f) May 29, 1878.

### ASSOCIATE JUSTICES OF THE SUPREME COURT.

Edward R. Hardin, Dec. 4, 1854.  Joseph E. Streeter, Nov. 18, 1861.
James Bradley, Oct. 25, 1854,  Elmer S. Dundy, June 22, 1863.
Samuel W. Black, ——  Geo. B. Lake, Feb. 21, 1867.
Eleazer Wakley, April 22, 1857.  Lorenzo Crounse, Feb. 21, 1867.
Joseph Miller, April 9, 1859.  Daniel Gantt, Jan. 16, 1873.
Wm. F. Lockwood, May 16, 1861.  Samuel Maxwell, Jan. 16, 1873.
Amasa Cobb, May 29, 1878

### UNITED STATES CIRCUIT AND DISTRICT COURTS.

Hon. John F. Dillon, Circuit Judge.  James Neville, District Attorney.
Hon. Elmer S. Dundy, District Judge.  William Daily, U. S. Marshal.
Watson B. Smith, Clerk.

---

(a) Died in office.
(b) Elected for unexpired term.
(c) Appointed to fill vacancy.
(d) Re-elected, October 12, 1875, under provisions of Constitution.
(e) Chief Justice under provisions of Constitution. Died May 19th, 1878.
(f) Chief Justice under provisions of Constitution.

### UNITED STATES MARSHALS.

Mark W. Izard, Oct. 28, 1854.
Eli R. Doyle, April 7, 1855.
Benj. P. Rankin, March 29, 1856.
P. W. Hitchcock, Sept. 19, 1861.
Casper E. Yost, April 1, 1865.
J. T. Hoile, July 1, 1869.
William Daily, ———, 1871.

### OFFICERS OF THE TERRITORY AND STATE OF NEBRASKA SINCE ITS ORGANIZATION.

#### GOVERNORS.

Francis Burt, (*a*) Oct. 16, 1854.
Mark W. Izard, Feb. 20, 1855.
Wm. A. Richardson, (*b*) Jan. 12, 1858.
Samuel W. Black, May 2, 1858.
Alvin Saunders, May 15, 1861.
David Butler, Feb. 21, 1867.
Robert W. Furnas, Jan. 13, 1873.
Silas Garber, (*c*) Jan. 11, 1875.
Albinus Nance, Jan. 9, 1879.

#### SECRETARIES.

Thomas B. Cuming, (*d*) Aug. 13, 1854.
John B. Motley, (*e*) Mar. 23, 1858.
J. Sterling Morton, (*f*) July 12, 1858.
Algernon S. Paddock, (*g*) May 6, 1861.
Thomas P. Kennard, Feb. 21, 1867.
Wm. H. James, (*h*) Jan. 10, 1871.
John J. Gosper, Jan. 13, 1873.
Bruno Tzschuck, (*i*) Jan. 11, 1875.
S. J. Alexander, Jan. 9, 1879.

#### AUDITORS.

Chas. B. Smith, Mar. 16, 1855.
Samuel S. Campbell, Aug. 3, 1857.
Wm. E. Moore, June 1, 1858.
Robt. C. Jordan, Aug. 2, 1858.
Wm. E. Harvey, Oct. 8, 1861.
John Gillespie, Oct. 10, 1865.
J. B. Weston, (*i*) Jan. 13, 1873.
F. W. Leidtke, Jan. 9, 1879.

#### TREASURERS.

B. P. Rankin, Mar. 16, 1855.
Wm. W. Wyman, Nov. 6, 1855.
Augustus Kountze, Oct. 8, 1861.
Henry A. Koenig, Jan. 10, 1871.
J. C. McBride, (*i*) Jan. 11, 1875.
Geo. M. Bartlett, Jan. 9, 1879.
James Sweet, Jan. 11, 1869.

---

(*a*) Died October, 1854, the office being filled by T. B. Cuming, Secretary, until the appointment of Governor Izard.

(*b*) Resigned, the office being filled by J. Sterling Morton, Secretary, until the arrival of Governor Black.

(*c*) Re-elected November 7, 1876.

(*d*) Acting Governor from Oct., 1854, to Feb. 20, 1855, and from Oct. 25, 1857, to Jan. 12, 1858. Died March 12, 1858.

(*e*) Acting Secretary until the arrival of J. Sterling Morton.

(*f*) Acting Governor from Dec. 5, 1858, to May 2, 1859, and from Feb. 24, 1860, to 1861.

(*g*) Acting Governor from May 15, 1861, and during a greater portion of the period to 1867.

(*h*) Acting Governor upon impeachment and removal of Governor Butler, and until Jan. 13, 1873.

(*i*) Re-elected Nov. 7, 1876.

## LIBRARIANS.

James S. Izard, Mar. 16, 1855.
H. C. Anderson, Nov. 6, 1855.
John H. Kellom, Aug. 3, 1857.
Alonzo D. Luce, Nov. 7, 1859.

Robt. S. Knox, ———, 1861.
Thos. P. Kennard, June 22, 1867.
Wm. H. James, Jan. 10, 1871.
Guy A. Brown, Mar. 3, 1871.

## ATTORNEY GENERALS.

Seth Robinson, ———, 1869.
Geo. H. Roberts. Jan. 10, 1871.

Geo. H. Roberts (a) Jan. 11, 1375.
C. J. Dilworth. Jan. 9, 1879.

J. R. Webster, Jan. 13, 1873,

## SUPERINTENDENTS OF PUBLIC INSTRUCTION (b).

Seth W. Beals, ———, 1869.
J. M. McKenzie, Jan. 10, 1871.

S. R. Thompson, (c) ———, 1877.
S. R. Thompson, ———, 1878.

## COMMISSIONER OF PUBLIC LANDS AND BUILDINGS (d).

F. M. Davis, (c) 1877.

---

THE POPULAR VOTE OF NEBRASKA FOR MEMBERS OF CONGRESS SINCE 1855.

TOTAL

1855—Bird B. Chapman, 380; Hiram P. Bennett, 292; Scattering, 18.. 690
1857—Fenner Ferguson, 1,642; Bird B. Chapman, 1,559; Benjamin P.
 Rankin, 1,241; John M. Thayer, 1,171; Scattering, 21......... 5,634
1859—Experience Estabrook, 3,100; Samuel G. Daily, 2,800........... 5,900
1860—J. Sterling Morton, 2,957; Samuel G. Daily, 2,943.......... 5,900
1862—Samuel G. Dally, 2,331; John F. Kinney, 2,180............... 4,511
1864—Phineas W. Hitchcock, 3,241; Geo. L. Miller, 2,399; Scattering, 2.. 5,822
1866—John Taffe, 4,820; Algernon S. Paddock, 4,072; George Francis
 Train, 30..................................................... 8,922
1868—John Taffe, 8,724; Andrew J. Poppleton, 6,318.................15,042
1870—John Taffe, 12,375; George B. Lake, 7,967....................20,342
1872—Lorenzo Crounse, 17,124; Jesse F. Warner, 10,412..............27,536
1874—Lorenzo Crounse, 22,532; James W. Savage, 8,386; James G.
 Miller, 4,074; James W. Davis, 972.........................35,964
1876—Frank Welch, (Rep.) 30,900; Joseph Holman, (Dem.) 17,206; M.
 Warren, (Greenb'k), 3,579; Scattering, 89....................51,774
1878—E. K. Valentine, (Rep.) 28,341; J. W. Davis, (Dem. and Grenb'k),
 21,752; Scattering, 21........................................50,247

---

(a) Re-elected Nov. 7, 1876.
(b) Office created by act, Feb. 15, 1869.
(c) Chosen at election, Nov. 7, 1876.
(d) Office created by Constitution of 1875.

POPULAR VOTE FOR GOVERNOR SINCE FIRST ELECTION IN 1866.

                                                                                                                              TOTAL

1866—David Butler, 4,093; J. Sterling Morton, 3,948.................. 8,041
1868—David Butler, 8,576; J. R. Porter, 6349..........................14,925
1870—David Butler, 11,126; John H. Croxton, 8,648..................19,774
1872—Robert W. Furnas, 16,543; Henry G. Lett, 11,227.............27,770
1874—Silas Garber, 21,568; Albert Tuxbury, 8,046; J. F. Gardner, 4,159; J. S. Church, 1,346......................................36,019
1876—Silas Garber, 31,947; Paren England, 17,219; J. F. Gardner, 3,022; Scattering, 86.........................................52,234
1878—Albinus Nance, 29,469; W. H. Webster, 18,417; Levi G. Todd, 9,475.....................................................52,417

# CHAPTER II.

## INDIANS.

The Omahas—The Pawnees—The Otoes—The Santee Sioux—The Winnebagos—The Poncas—The Iowas and Sacs and Fox.

In 1854, when Nebraska was admitted into the Union, there were, as nearly as can be estimated, 10,000 Indians on reservations in the Territory, the greater portion of them living in the eastern part, in permanent villages, along the Missouri and Platte Rivers, and their tributaries, while in the northwestern part there were several roving bands of the great Sioux nation, of whom those in the eastern part stood in mortal fear.

### THE OMAHAS,

Numbering between 900 and 1,000 at that time, occupied the country lying along the Missouri, extending from the mouth of the Platte River, northward to the old Council Bluffs of Lewis and Clarke, in Washington County, and westward some forty miles. Their main villages were at Bellevue (Sarpy County) and Saling's Grove, on the Big Papillion, eight miles distant, where they had lived most of the time since 1830.

The Omahas are a tribe of the Dakota family. Marquette represents them on his map in 1673, and about 1766 Cover found them on the St. Peter's, where they formed two tribes—the Hongashanos and the Ishbanondas, or Grey Eyes—divided into thirteen clans, one of which preserved a sacred shell in a rude temple, constantly guarded. They cultivated corn, beans and melons.

Among their customs was one preventing a man from speaking with his father-in-law or mother-in-law. Just what length of time this tribe was known on the Missouri is difficult to ascertain, but somewhere about the year 1780, they crossed over the country from the Upper Lakes and settled on the Missouri, at or near the mouth of the Big Sioux River, in Iowa, at which time there was a band of Cheyennes with them. Shortly afterward they crossed to the west side of the Missouri and settled on the Niobrara, near its mouth, at which place Lewis and Clarke found them in June, 1804, numbering about 600. Being pursued relentlessly by the Sioux, and greatly reduced in numbers by small-pox, they burned their village on the Niobrara and removed to the Blackbird hills, about 100 miles further down the Missouri, where they have resided at times for more than half a century. Treaties were made with them on July 20th, 1815, September 23d, 1825, and July 15th, 1830, ceding lands at Council Bluffs for an annuity, blacksmith shop and agricultural implements. After this last treaty they formed their villages at Bellevue, near the trading post of Colonel Peter A. Sarpy, and at Saling's Grove, where they remained until June, 1855. The Sioux frequently drove them to the Elkhorn River, but in 1843 they returned to their villages and made peace with certain bands of the Sioux. A mission begun in 1839 failed, and one established in 1846, had but little success. By treaty of March 16, 1854, more of their lands were ceded, and in the following year they were removed to their present reservation of 345,000 acres in the northeastern part of the State, between the Missouri and Elkhorn Rivers. Since then they have devoted themselves to agriculture, and their condition has rapidly improved. In 1879 they numbered about 1,050. Their Great Chief, Logan Fontenelle, was killed by the Sioux while on a hunting expedition, in July, 1855.

### THE PAWNEES,

In 1854, lived on the south bank of the Platte River, their main village being a few miles east of where Fremont now stands. They numbered then between 4,000 and 5,000. They had been residents of Nebraska for a century or more, and are spoken of by both Spanish and French explorers as being a warlike and powerful nation, and the most numerous of any west of the Missouri. They were first heard of through the Illinois, and the name is of that language. Marquette noted several bands on his map in 1673. They were hostile toward the Spaniards but have always been friendly toward the Americans. Their first stopping place on the west side of the Missouri River seems to have been at the confluence of the Republican, which place they soon abandoned, however, moving a considerable distance up the latter stream, where they established a large permanent village of earth-covered lodges, and cultivated corn, beans and melons, frequently going off to the buffalo lands to hunt and meet their enemies in warfare. They claimed the country south to the Kansas River and north to the Platte. Pike, in 1806, estimated the population of three villages at 6,223, with two thousand warriors. They were divided into four bands— Tswa (Grand Pawnee), Tskithka Petower Kattahankies (Republican Pawnee), Tapage Pawnee and Sker Pawnee, Mahas or Loups. They were constantly at war with the Sioux and other tribes. From time to time they sacrificed prisoners to the sun to obtain good crops and success in warfare. Anyone was at liberty to offer up a prisoner that they had captured in warfare. The victim was clothed in the gayest apparel and fed and feasted on the best that could be had, and when sufficiently fattened for their purpose, a suitable day was appointed for the sacrifice, so that the whole nation might attend. The unfortunate victim was then bound to a cross in the presence of the assembled multitude, after which a solemn dance and other ceremonies were performed, and at their conclusion the warrior whose prisoner he had been, stepped forward and cleaved his head with a tomahawk, the other warriors filling his body with arrows. This barbarous custom, however, was finally stopped in 1820, through the influence of the missionaries.

The removal of the Delawares to lands between the Platte and Kansas Rivers led to a war with that tribe, who, in 1832, burned the great Pawnee village on the Republican River. They then removed to the Platte, in the present Butler County, where small-pox carried off large numbers of them. By treaty of October 9th, 1832, they sold lands south and agreed to remain north of that river and west of the Loup River. Provisions were then made for education and they were soon possessed of comfortable homes, good farms and schools, but all this was checked by the Sioux, who attacked them in their hunts, killing many, and finally invading their villages, burning them and killing men, women and children, and driving them south to the Kansas River. The Government regarded this as a violation of their treaty and stopped their annuities, their missionaries and farmers left them, cholera and smallpox swept off hundreds, and in three or four years they had lost one half of their number. Returning again to the Platte, they resided for many years at the junction of Salt Creek with that stream near where Ashland now stands.

By treaty of September 4th, 1857, they sold more of their lands and were soon afterward removed to their reservation in the valley of the Loup Fork River, containing 288,000 acres. In June, 1861, they numbered 3,414, and furnished the government a sufficient number of scouts for the Indian war of 1864, on the plains. This increased the hostility of the Sioux, who, after making peace with the government, turned again on the wretched Pawnees, slaughtering them without mercy, and effectually stopping their progress and improvements. By act of Congress June 10th, 1872, 118,424 acres were sold for their benefit, the grasshoppers having destroyed their crops. On October 8th, 1874, the Pawnees in general council agreed to remove to a reservation in the Indian Territory, where they were taken in the following year. They have a perpetual annuity of $30,000, with an appropriation for education, farming, etc., of $22,600 more. There is no grammer or vocabulary of their language.

## THE OTOES,

In 1854, occupied the south eastern portion of the State, south of the Platte River, their hunting grounds extending as far west as the Blue. They numbered at that time between 800 and 1,000, all told, and their principal village was a few miles below the present Nebraska City.

The Otoes belong to the Dakota family and were originally a part of the Missouris, with whom they have been for years united, forming one village. They were known to the French in 1673 under the name of Attanka, and calling themselves Wahoohtahta. Major Long, who explored this country in 1819-20, says the Otoes were a band from a great nation living at the head of the Mississippi River, from whom they separated in about 1724, coming west to the Missouri, their first settlement in Nebraska being near the mouth of the Great Nemaha River. Their next camping ground was on the Platte, fifteen or twenty miles from its mouth, and it was from this camp that several of their Chiefs and warriors went to visit and hold a council with Lewis and Clarke in the summer of 1804, at the latter's camp on the bluffs of the Missouri sixteen miles above Omaha, from which incident the place derived its name of Council Bluffs. From the Platte they came to the Missouri and established villages on the plateau now occupied by the city of Omaha, where they were living in 1820, but removed shortly afterward again to the Platte, near their old homes. Abandoning this place they established permanent villages of earth-covered huts on the Missouri a few miles south of the present location of Nebraska City, where they were living at the time of the opening up of the Territory to settlement. Treaties were made with them on June 24th, 1817, and September 26th, 1825, and by treaty on March 15th, 1854, the confederated tribes of Otoes and Missouris ceded their rights to the lands lying along the Missouri, and were removed to a reservation of 16,000 acres on the southeastern border of the State, where they still remain; both tribes, together, in 1879, numbering less than five hundred souls. The western half of their reservation has been appraised for sale.

### THE SANTEE SIOUX,

About eight hundred in number (1879), are located in Knox County on the Missouri River, near the mouth of the Niobrara, on a reservation of 115,200 acres, of which one-fourth is adapted to tillage, and nearly all the rest suitable for grazing. These Indians wear citizens' dress and are the most civilized of all the Sioux. They have five schools under the care of the Episcopalians.

### WINNEBAGOES.

The Winnebagoes, a tribe of the Dakota family, live on a reservation of 128,000 acres at the Black Bird hills, on the Missouri River, in the northeastern part of the State, north of and adjoining the Omaha reservation, and numbered, in 1879, about 1,650. They lived in Wisconsin and Minnesota in 1793. After being defeated by Wayne they made peace with the Government, but in the war of 1812 took sides with the English. After several treaties being made with them at different times, they were removed in April, 1863, to Crow Creek, in Dakota, above Fort Randall. The place was entirely unsuited to them, affording no means of livelihood or support, and surrounded by hostile tribes of Indians. Deaths were so numerous from disease, war and famine, that out of 1,985 but 1,222 were left. They left and succeeded in reaching the Omaha reservation, and appealed for shelter. In May, 1866, they removed to Winnebago where all had to commence anew. In June, 1869, they were assigned to the care of Friends. They are a quiet, peaceable people, wearing citizens' clothing, electing Chiefs annually, and preserving order by means of an Indian Police. Lands were allotted to such as wanted to take up farms, and in 1874, they numbered 1,445, with farms, cottages, stock, and three day schools. On their removal from Minnesota, 160 half-breeds, who had taken land, remained, and these received as tribal share $800, but many have lost this and lands, and have joined the tribe in Nebraska. In the winter of 1874 they numbered nearly 1,000. Most of these were removed to a small tract purchased for them near the Winnebago reservation, but many of them left almost as soon as they reached it. Attempts by the Catholics and Presbyterians to bring them back met with little success.

### PONCAS.

The Poncas resided for many years on a reservation near the mouth of the Niobrara River, in Dakota Territory. They were originally a branch of the Mahas or Omahas, and resided on the Red River of the North. Here they were attacked by the Sioux, and after losing greatly, removed to the opposite side of the Missouri and built a fortified village on the Ponca River. They united with the Omahas but have generally kept apart. Their constant pursuit by the Sioux kept them wandering until reduced to a wretched condition. At the beginning of this century their number was very small, but after the coming of Lewis and Clarke and the treaty of June 28, 1817, and June 9, 1825, they improved rapidly, and in 1832 they numbered 750, a large majority of which were women. On March 12, 1858, they sold their lands to the Government and went on a reservation near the Yanktons, the compensation to be in installments of $185,000, with the support of schools and agricultural aid. But their crops failed and they were harassed and killed by the Sioux. A new treaty March 10th, 1865, gave them a reservation of 576,000 acres of bottom land near the junction of the Niobrara, in Dakota, where they formed three villages. In the distribution of Agents the Poncas were assigned to the Protestant Episcopal Church, and soldiers were sent in 1874 to protect them. They then numbered 730, and 132 half-breeds. They are an inoffensive, agriculturally disposed people, speaking the same language as the Omahas.

In 1877, the Poncas were removed to a reservation in the Indian Territory.

In 1879, thirty of these Indians, with Standing Bear, their Chief, left their Reservation, and returned to the Omaha Reservation, where they remained until a detachment of soldiers were ordered to take them back. On arriving at Omaha, under arrest, by order of the Interior Department, in charge of soldiers, a writ of *habeas corpus* was sued out, and heard before Judge Dundy, of the United States Court, where Hon. A. J. Poppleton and J. L. Webster, volunteered their services on behalf of the Indians, which came on in Court May 2d, and after a careful hearing, they were released from custody. They returned to the Omaha Reservation. The question, however, is still pending in the U. S. Courts.

On June 3d, U. S. Court, Prosecuting Attorney presented the case before Judge Miller, who decided he had no jurisdiction over the Ponca prisoners released by Judge Dundy, on a writ of *habeas corpus*, as they were not in Court, but would continue the case in order to give Prosecuting Attorney Lambertson time to investigate further. The Indians, however, are at liberty.

### IOWAS, AND SACS AND FOX.

The Iowas, and Sacs and Fox Indians occupy a reservation of 32,000 acres in the south-eastern corner of the State, extending over into Kansas.

In 1879 the Iowas numbered about 250, and the Sacs and Fox 100.

The Iowas are a tribe of the Dakota family, and were called Pahucha—dirty nose,—and by some, Grey Eyes, or Iowas. Marquette, in 1673, lays them down as the Pahoutet, living back of the Des Moines River, and consisting of eight clans—the Eagle, Wolf, Bear and Buffalo, which are still in existence, and the Pigeon, Elk, Beaver and Snake, now extinct,—each clan being distinguished by a peculiar way of cutting the hair. The Iowas, numbering 992 in 1824, were removed by treaty of September 17, 1836, and placed on the Missouri, above Wolf River, but a part broke off the next year and became vagrants, living by theft and hunting on grounds of other tribes. A Presbyterian mission and labor school earnestly maintained from 1835 to 1866, failed to save this people, and in 1846 they had declined to 706. By treaty of March 6, 1861, the tribe, reduced to 305 souls, ceded all but a reservation of 16,000 acres; in 1869 they agreed to sell this and remove, but retracted, giving part to the Sacs, who actually sold their reservation. In 1872 they numbered 225, and were quite favorable to the school, which had sixty-three pupils. They dress in civilized garb, have a number of good frame and log houses, and cultivate several hundred acres of land, while the value of their stock is about $8,000. The United States holds $57,500 in trust for them, the interest of which is paid annually to heads of families.

The Sacs and Fox have long been united, forming one band. In 1822 they lived on the Mississippi River, near Fort Armstrong, and are spoken of as being expert hunters and canoemen. They cultivated corn, beans and melons, and a few were employed in the lead mines near Galena, Ill. Treaties were made on August 4, 1824, and July 15, 1830, in which they ceded lands. They were to some extent involved in the BLACK HAWK war of 1831, at the close of which the two tribes made a treaty at Ft. Armstrong with General Scott and Governor Reynolds, ceding lands for an annuity of $20,000 for twenty years, and by a subsequent treaty at Rock Island, a part reserved in the last embracing 256,000 acres, for $192,000. They then settled on the Des Moines River, Iowa, on an irregular square tract about 140 miles each way; the Foxes at this time numbering 2,446. Government removed them again by treaty in 1842, and in 1849 they were chiefly on the Osage. Since then in spite of the Government's efforts to civilize and improve them, they have declined in numbers very rapidly, rejecting with a steady persistency missionaries and schools. The united Sacs and Fox in 1822 numbered 8,000, but were reduced in 1874 to 1,135, of whom 500 were in the Indian Territory, 338 in Iowa, 200 in Kansas, and ninety-seven on their reservation of 16,000 acres in the southeastern part of Nebraska, adjoining that of the Iowas. They have an annuity of $10,506.

# CHAPTER III.

### NEBRASKA, ITS GEOGRAPHY—MINERALS—TOPOGRAPHY.

Nebraska is included between latitude 40° and 43° north, and longitude 95° 25' and 104° west from Greenwich.

It is bounded on the north by Dakota, east by Iowa and Missouri, from which it is separated by the Missouri River, south by Kansas and Colorado, and west by Colorado and Wyoming, containing an area of 75,995 square miles, or over 48,000,000 acres of land. The width from north to south is two hundred and eight miles, and the length in the central part is about four hundred and twenty miles, extending from the Missouri River westward to the base of the Rocky Mountains.

Geographically, Nebraska is not far from the center of that portion of North America which may properly be called temperate in climate. The most aggressive and prosperous States of the Union lie chiefly between the same parallels. It is in the direct line of the great tidal wave of emigration to the gold fields of the Territories and the Pacific Coast.

Nebraska is altogether a prairie State, having no mountains nor any hills of magnitude. Its surface consists of undulating prairies, rich alluvial valleys and table lands, stretching away into extensive level plains, with a gradual ascent from the Missouri River westward, reaching an altitude on its western border of about five thousand feet above the level of the sea, and yet the incline is so gradual that in the construction of the Union Pacific Railroad up the Platte Valley, not a tunnel, trestle or fill of any importance were required, nor a single difficulty encountered from the Missouri River to the foot of the Rocky Mountains.

## THE MISSOURI RIVER.

This, the only navigable river in Nebraska, forms the eastern line of the State, being the boundary between it and the States of Iowa and Missouri. It is an exceedingly crooked, treacherous stream, and yet it has been, and is to some extent, an important avenue for both travel and freight to the more distant northwest. Its source is in latitude 45 north, and longitude 110:30 west, high up in the Rocky Mountains, and the distance it flows from the Great Falls to its junction with the Mississippi River is 2,575 miles. Its course is nearly north to the Great falls, and thence to the northeast until it joins the White Earth River, from whence its course to its confluence with the Mississippi is generally southeast. Below the mouth of the Kansas River, the Missouri runs almost a due east course through the State of Missouri, emptying into the Mississippi in latitude 38:50 and longitude 90:45 west. Its chief tributaries between its mouth and Fort Leavenworth are the Osage, Grand and Kansas Rivers, the first two being navigable from 150 to 200 miles. North from its confluence with the Kansas it receives the Nodawa, Little Tarkio, Big Nemaha, Nishnabatona, Little Nemaha, and Platte Rivers before the city of Omaha is reached, while further to the north it receives the Boyer, Little Sioux, Big Sioux, James, Niobrara, White Earth and Yellowstone Rivers, besides a large number of less important streams. From the point where the Platte empties into it, to the mouth of the Yellowstone, the Missouri varies from 400 to 1,000 yards in width. The Missouri seems to hold a mortgage on the lands that flank it on either side, and it often takes such lands by force, only to return them when some other change in its ever shifting course is developed.

Previous to the exploration made by Lewis and Clarke, the impression prevailed among the Spanish and French residents in what was then known as the Northwestern Territory, that the source of the Missouri was near the point where it joins the Niobrara, and most of the maps in use previous to the exploration referred to, locate its source at or near the point mentioned.

## THE FIRST STEAMER ON THE MISSOURI.

The *Western Engineer*, built at Pittsburgh in 1818, by the

United States Government, was the first steamboat to navigate the Missouri.

She left her moorings at Pittsburgh on the 3d of May, 1819, having on board an exploring expedition, sent out by order of the Government to explore the Missouri river and the country west of it to the Rocky Mountains. The expedition was under the command of S. H. Long, Major in the United States Engineer Corps, and arrived in St. Louis on the 20th of June, one month and seventeen days after starting. The mouth of the Platte was reached on the 17th of September following, and on the 19th of the same month the expedition cast anchor near the mouth of Boyer River, on the Iowa side, about five miles below Council Bluffs, mentioned by Lewis and Clarke, where it went into winter quarters. The point of encampment was known as Fort Lisa, and was occupied by the Missouri Fur Company as a trading post. Here the explorers remained during the winter of 1819-20, Major Long in the meantime returning to Philadelphia, the then seat of Government, with the reports of the expedition. On the 20th of June, 1820, Major Long returned to Fort Lisa, with orders from John C. Calhoun, then Secretary of War, for the expedition to proceed overland to the headwaters of the Arkansas and Red Rivers for the purpose of exploring those streams and the country contiguous to them, and in accordance therewith the expedition left the boat at this point and proceeded up the valley of the Platte, holding councils with the numerous Indian tribes through which they passed.

The *Western Engineer*, after the departure of the expedition, received a new commander and was employed for many years thereafter in transporting Government supplies to the forts and trading posts along the Missouri river.

The Platte, the principal interior river of the State, is a broad, shallow stream, with low banks, about 1,200 miles in length, and is formed in the western part of the State by the confluence of the North and South Forks which have their sources in the Rocky Mountains, the former in Wyoming and the latter in Colorado. The course of the Platte is eastwardly through the central portion of the State, dividing it into two nearly equal portions, and emptying into the Missouri River on the line between Sarpy and Cass Counties. It has many large fertile islands, valuable at present for their timber and fine grasses for hay. The great valley of the Platte, famous for its beauty and productiveness, extends through the State from east to west, and is from three to fifteen miles wide.

The Platte has a large number of important tributaries flowing into it from the north, though none of any size from the south, with the exception of Salt Creek, in the eastern part of the State. The principal streams on the north are the Elkhorn, Loup and Wood Rivers, Shell and Prairie Creeks.

The Elkhorn is about 300 miles in length, and a remarkably crooked stream. Its source is in the north-central part of the State in a number of sloughs or lakes, which cover an area of fifteen or twenty miles square, and its course is south-easterly, passing through the Counties of Holt, Antelope, Madison, Stanton, Cuming, Dodge, Washington, Douglas, and Sarpy, emptying into the Platte River in the last named County. The Elkhorn is a beautiful River, narrow, but deep and rapid, and furnishes unlimited water-power for manufacturing purposes, as do also some of the larger creeks which join it on either side. The bottoms, varying in width from three to six miles, are composed of a sandy alluvium impregnated with carbonates and phosphate, and produce a large yield of the cereals and vegetables.

The Loup River, the largest of the tributaries, is formed in Howard County by the junction of the North, Middle and South Forks, which rise in unorganized territory in the northwestern part of the State, each being a stream of considerable size. The general course of the Loup is easterly, passing through the Counties of Nance and Platte to the south-east corner of the last named where it joins the Platte. It is a swift running stream with fertile bottoms composed of a sandy loam, varying from three to five miles in width.

Wood River rises in Custer County and flows easterly through the Counties of Dawson, Buffalo and Hall, emptying into the Platte in the southwestern part of Merrick County. It is a small stream, has a slow current, and seldom overflows its banks. The bottoms are comparatively narrow but rich and productive.

Shell Creek is a sparkling stream rising in the northern part of Boone County, and flowing in a southeasterly course through Platte and Colfax Counties, joins the Platte in the southeastern part of the last named County. It affords some excellent mill privileges, and the valley through which it passes is remarkable for its beauty and fertility. The bluffs which skirt it rise in places to a height of from 75 to 100 feet above the Platte bottoms on the south.

Prairie Creek rises in Buffalo County, flows northeasterly through the Counties of Hall, Merrick and Nance, and empties into the Platte in Platte County. It is a slender stream, about 80 miles in length, and its course lies through an undulating, sandy prairie of average productiveness.

Salt Creek, the most important tributary of the Platte from the south, rises in the southern part of Lancaster County, flows northeasterly through that County and empties into the Platte near the town of Ashland. It is a very fine stream, supported by numerous creeks and springs, and passes through a beautiful and fertile region of country. It also furnishes unusually good mill privileges.

The Republican, one of the finest and most important rivers in the State, waters the southern tier of Counties, as far east as Nuckolls County. It rises in the mountains of Colorado, flows in an easterly course, entering Nebraska at the southwest corner, passes through the Counties of Dundy, Hitchcock, Red Willow, Furnas, Franklin, Webster and Nuckolls, and thence into Kansas. The water of this river is clear and has a fall of about seven feet to the mile. The Valley of the Republican, varying in width from two to six miles, is famed for its magnificent scenery and rich bottoms. The Republican has a large number of very fine tributaries in this State, of which the most important are the Stinking Water, Blackwood, Red Willow, Medicine, Muddy, Turkey, Spring, Thompson, Center and Rock Creeks, on the north, and Driftwood, Beaver, Sappa and Prairie Dog Creeks on the south. The majority of these streams furnish an ample volume of water for mills, and with their branches, nourish and drain a large extent of country.

The Niobrara River, the largest stream in the State north of the Platte, rises in Wyoming, flows eastwardly through the northern part of the State, forms part of the boundary line between Nebraska and Dakota, and empties into the Missouri on the northeastern boundary of the State. It has a rapid current and extensive alluvial bottoms similar to other large streams of Nebraska. In places contiguous to the stream, however, there are considerable areas covered with a loose, shifting sand, yet the greater part of the bottom land is fertile and beautiful as any one could wish. The Niobrara passes through a country 300 miles on the west, almost wholly unsettled, and there are greater bodies of timber along its course and on its tributaries than in any other part of the State. The principal tributaries of the Niobrara are Snake River, the Pines, Willow, Eagle, Red Bird, and Verdigris Creeks, on the south and the Keya Paha River, Antelope, Clay and Reunion Creeks on the north. The Keya Paha River forms a small section of the boundary between Nebraska and Dakota.

White River, a direct tributary of the Missouri, rises in the northwestern part of this State, and flows northeasterly through Dakota.

The Big Blue River, one of the most beautiful streams in the State, rises in Hamilton County and flows in a general southeasterly course into Kansas, passing through the Counties of Polk, Butler, Seward, Saline and Gage. The Big Blue has a rocky bed, and is famous as a mill stream, also for the lovely scenery of its valley, and dry, rich bottoms and table lands. The principal tributaries are the North and West Blue Rivers and Lincoln Creek, or Middle Blue, each furnishing sufficient water for mills.

The Little Blue River rises in Adams County and flows southeasterly, nearly parallel with the Big Blue, passing through the Counties of Adams, Clay, Nuckolls, Thayer and Jefferson, and joining the Big Blue in Kansas. It is a stream scarcely inferior to the Big Blue in size and importance, in the grandeur and fertility of its valley and its splendid mill advantages. The principal tributaries are Big and Little Sandy Creeks on the north, and Morehouse, Elk and Muddy Creeks on the south. These also have volume of water sufficient for mills.

The Great Nemaha River, in southeastern Nebraska, rises in Lancaster County, flows southeasterly through the counties of Gage, Johnson, Pawnee and Richardson, and discharges its waters into the Missouri in the southeast corner of the State. Its course lies through one of the most thickly populated and prosperous sections of the State, celebrated for its fine fruits and general productiveness. The Great Nemaha also affords fine advantages for manufacturing purposes, more than a dozen mills being already located upon it. It is supported by numerous creeks and rivulets on either side, of which Muddy and Long Branch Creeks are the principal on the north, and the South Fork on the south. Muddy Creek extends through both Nemaha and Richardson Counties, and has several flouring mills upon it.

The Little Nemaha River rises in Cass County, flows southeasterly through Otoe and Nemaha Counties, running parallel with and from ten to fifteen miles north of the Great Nemaha, and empties into the Missouri. There are several first class flouring mills located on this stream, with plenty of room for more. The lands adjoining are composed of a deep, rich loam, and compare, for productiveness, with any in this part of the State. The principal tributaries are the North and South Forks, which, with their numerous branches, extend over and drain a large scope of country.

Taken as a whole, Nebraska is remarkably well supplied with water, having, besides the rivers, many clear running creeks and brooks supported by never-failing springs. There are large portions of the State where running water can be found on each quarter section of land, and where such is not the case good water can be had by digging or boring at a depth of from thirty to sixty feet. Water is usually found in the lacustrine deposits at a depth of from twenty to forty feet, but sometimes it is necessary to go beneath these deposits before a good supply can be had. At the bottom of the lacustrine deposits there is generally a stratum of sand and gravel which is a great reservoir of water, and from which it flows in unlimited quantities, and frequently water is not found until this stratum is reached. In some sections of the State, in the vicinity of the larger water-courses south of the Platte, on the high divides between the Loup and Niobrara Rivers, and in the northeastern portions along the Missouri, where the lacustrine deposits are very thick, this stratum of sand and gravel is struck at a depth varying from sixty to one hundred and thirty feet. In many localities this underlying bed of sand and gravel lies on clay or rock, and in such places water is unusually plentiful. On all of the flood plains, valleys and undulating prairies, water is of easy access. It is found by chemical analysis that the water of the State is above the average in purity, the most common foreign ingredient being the carbonate of lime.

MINERALS.

There has been no thorough geological survey yet made of Nebraska. Prof. F. V. Hayden, however, has made a careful examination of the southeastern part of the State, and Prof. Samuel Aughey, of the Nebraska State University, of different localities further west, and from these investigations enough has been discovered to demonstrate the presence of considerable mineral wealth. Coal, salt, peat, marl, limestone of several varieties, sandstone, fine clays and mineral paint have been discovered.

*Coal* exists in considerable quantities in Cass, Otoe, Nemaha, Richardson, Johnson and Pawnee Counties, in the southeastern part of the State. The coal is of good quality, and in Cass and Nemaha Counties the seams vary from eighteen inches to two feet in thickness. Several miles below Plattsmouth, in Cass County, a shaft has been sunk to a seam eighteen inches thick; also at Aspinwall, Nemaha County, and at various other points. The coal from the mine in Pawnee County is preferred in many places to any other in the market. Thin seams of lignite coal exist in Dodge, Burt, Dixon, Dakota and other Counties in the northern part of the State. Near Ponca, in Dixon County, a bed eighteen inches thick supplies fuel to the farmers and people of the neighborhood.

The surface indications in several of the Republican Valley Counties are very favorable for coal. The veins already found are light, though the coal is of a fine bituminous quality, free from sulphur.

It is believed that the coal measures underlie the greater portion of the State, and that there are thick, workable beds at a greater depth than has yet been reached, but they remain to be developed by larger capital than has thus far been employed.

*Salt* is found in great abundance at Lincoln, the Capital of the State. The great salt basin, three miles from that city, covers an area of twelve by tewnty-five miles, in which innumerable salt springs rise to the surface, forming an extensive marsh, through the length of which, partially draining it, flows Salt Creek, a tributary of the Platte River. The water from these springs contains by weight 29 per cent. of pure salt, and a very considerable amount of that useful article is manufactured here by solar evaportion.

*Building Stone*, of several varieties and various qualities, is abundant. Magnesian and common blue limestone of an excellent quality, suitable for building, is found in large quanties in the southeastern Counties, and in all of the Counties bordering on the Missouri, south of the Platte River, good building stone is plentiful. In Cass and Sarpy Counties, along the Platte, large quarries have been opened, and the stone extensively used at Omaha for building, macadamizing the streets, and rip-rapping the river banks. The elegant U. S. postoffice building at Lincoln was constructed of Sarpy County limestone. On the Republican, the Nemahas and Blues, and some of their tributaries, magnesian limestone of the finest quality is abundant. Extensive quarries are being worked in Lancaster County, south of Lincoln, and in Gage County, near Beatrice. The major part of the stone used in the construction of the State buildings at Lincoln was taken from these quarries. Valuable quarries have also been opened in some of the northeastern Counties, extensive beds of fine magnesian limestone having been discovered on Logan Creek, and at other points. On the Elkhorn and Loup Rivers, and in other sections north of the Platte, a fair quality of building stone is found, but in smaller quantities. An excellent brown sandstone is abundant in a number of the eastern Counties. It is extensively used for building and in walling wells and cellars. A superior coarse red sand, valuable as a building material, is found in abundance in many of the Counties.

*Peat* exists in great quantities in various parts of the State. On the Blue Rivers, the Elkhorn, Calamus, Logan, on Elk Creek in Dakota County, and on many other streams, there are extensive deposits of peat, which, if properly prepared, would supply the State with fuel for many years. No use has yet been made of these deposits, but such treasures cannot remain long undeveloped.

*Marl Beds* are abundant, especially in the western sections of the State, but no use of it has yet been made, the richness of the soil preventing any demand for fertilizers. The beds, however, remain in store against the future demands of agriculture.

*Clay* of many varieties and degrees of fineness abound. Good common clay for the manufacture of brick can be found in almost any County. Clay for fire brick, said to equal the celebrated Milwaukee fire clay, is found at different points in the bluffs of the Missouri, and a superior quality of potters' clay is abundant in the southeastern and northeastern sections of the State. In Jefferson and Cass Counties there is a fine, valuable clay resembling Kaolin.

*Mineral Paint.* Along the Missouri River, in the southeastern part of the State, there are immense deposits of ochre of a quality equal to any in the market. It is of various colors—red, brown, yellow and other shades, according to the amount of iron that is present. A company has recently been organized for the purpose of working these mines.

### TIMBER.

Timber is one of the natural deficiencies of the State. Yet whilst there are no dense forests nor large bodies of native timber, the supply is sufficient for the wants of the people for some years to come, and the rapid growth of the artificial groves will, in a few years, furnish an abundance. On the Niobrara and Keya Paha Rivers, and their tributaries, in the north-central and western portions of the State, there is a considerable tract of pine, cedar, ash, oak, walnut and other varieties of timber, which will shortly be opened up, and a cheap conveyance to the markets afforded by the Columbus, Covington & Black Hills R. R. and other lines now in course of construction through this sparsely settled region. All of the Counties bordering on the Missouri still have sufficient native timber to supply the present demands for fuel. The Elkhorn, Loup and other large streams north of the Platte, and the Nemahas, the Blues and Republican, and their tributaries south of it, are tolerably well skirted with timber. In the early settlement of the State there were a number of fine groves of hardwood scattered throughout the eastern portion, but these were the first to be claimed by the settlers, and many of them have long since disappeared, but are fast growing up again; yet there are many beautiful native groves still standing in several of the Counties. In the canons and along the streams in the western part of the State there is still a considerable quantity of good timber, and formerly there was a great deal of fine cedar, which was extensively used in building forts, and in the construction of railroads.

There are about fifty species of native forest trees growing in the State, embracing two varieties of cottonwood, ten of oak, six of hickory, four of elm, three of maple, four of ash, two of locust, three of cedar, two of pine, several of willow, and one each of hackberry, sycamore, mulberry, coffee-bean, ironwood, box elder and linn.

The deep interest taken by the people in tree planting has greatly increased the quantity, and wherever the sweeping prairie fires have been kept in check the native timber is extending its limits and growing up finely. Many of the artificial groves already furnish sufficient fuel for the farmer. Cottonwood, soft maple and box elder are the most rapid growth native trees. Experience has shown that a farmer can raise his own fuel within five years, from the seed.

## TOPOGRAPHY.

The surface of Nebraska consists chiefly of valley, table and beautifully rolling prairie land, there being no mountains, nor any hills, lakes, or swamps of magnitude within her borders. Fully one-sixth of the whole State is valley and bottom land; twenty per cent. is table land, and fifty per cent. gently rolling prairie, while the bluffs cover, perhaps, ten per cent.

The extensive and magnificent valleys of the Platte, Republican, Elkhorn, the Loups, Niobrara, the Blues, Nemahas, and other large streams, are among the most attractive on the Continent, and have gained a national renown for the grandeur of their scenery, their unsurpassed fertility and general adaptability to agricultural purposes. The streams are most generally fringed with a luxuriant growth of native timber, while on one side, and sometimes both, a range of low, rounded hills, rising in places to precipitous bluffs, mark the dividing line between the valley and upland.

The table lands which occupy so large a per cent. of the area, are elevated considerably above the bottoms, and lie in beautiful level plateaus, varying in width from half a mile to a mile and a half, rising in a succession of gradations, one above another, until the upland is reached. In the South Platte country, west of the Blues, there are extensive table lands, or plains, which appear to the eye almost perfectly level, yet having a gradual ascent to the westward; and the same may also be said of many sections north of the Platte, especially in the vicinity of the Loup Forks.

The rolling lands, of which the surface of the State so largely consists, particularly the east half, are everywhere visible, from the bluffs of the Missouri to the western border. In nearly all of the Missouri River Counties, for several miles into the interior, the lands are considerably rolling, and somewhat broken in occasional places, yet it is very rarely so steep or broken as to prevent easy tillage, except in the bluffs themselves; and further westward the high, rolling land is gradually succeeded by low, gently undulating prairies which sweep in graceful outlines across the wide divides till lost to view in the distance. In the western part of the State, now used as stock ranges, there are large tracts, embracing millions of acres, of almost monotonously level prairie. Near the western border, south of the Platte, the surface is more rolling and rugged, and is frequently cut through by deep ravines and long, winding canons; and the same is also the case in some localities bordering on the Forks of the Platte, and in the vicinity of the Loups and other streams in the northern part of the State.

Many glowing tributes have been paid to the charming landscape of Nebraska by eminent visitors and distinguished writers, during the past several years. The following is from the pages of *The North American Review*, volume CIX:

"The most perfect display of the prairies is found in the eastern parts of Kansas and Nebraska. It is no exaggeration to pronounce this region, as left by the hand of Nature, the most beautiful country in its landscape upon the face of the earth. Here the forest is restricted to narrow fringes along the rivers and streams, the courses of which are thus defined as far as the eye can reach, whilst all between is a broad expanse of meadow lands, carpeted with the richest verdure and wearing the appearance of artistically-graded lawns. They are familiarly called the rolling prairies, because the land rises and falls in gentle swells, which attain an elevation of thirty feet, more or less, and descend again to the original level, within the distance of one or more miles. The crest-lines of these motionless waves of land intersect each other at every conceivable angle, the effect of which is to bring into view the most extended landscape, and to show the dark green foliage of the forest trees skirting the streams in pleasing contrast, with the light green of the prairie grass. In their spring covering of vegetation these prairies wear the semblance of an old and once highly cultivated Country, from the soil of which every inequality of surface, every stone and every bush has been carefully removed, and the surface rolled down into absolute uniformity. The marvel is suggested, how Nature could have kept these verdant fields in such luxuriance after man had apparently abandoned them to waste."

Prof. Samuel Aughey thus writes of the "Bad Lands" of Nebraska:

"In the extreme western part of the State, between Spon Hill Creek and the Niobrara River, there is a remarkable region, extending down from the White Earth River in Dakota Territory. The surface deposits here are miocene tertiary. This region is known as the Bad Lands, Mauvaises Terres, or in the Dakota language, Ma-kao-si-tcha, which means a difficult country to travel, because, while the surface is broken, there is little, if any, good water, wood or game. Here are some of the most curious remains in the world, and the Geologist never tires of investigating them. The almost vertical sections of white rock have been chisseled by water agencies into unique forms. Indeed, as viewed from a distance, they remind the explorer of one of those old cities which only exhibit their ruins as reminders of their ancient greatness. Among these grandest desolations, the weird, wild, old stories of witchery appear plausible and possible. It is in the deepest canons, at the foot of the stair-like projections, that the earliest of those wonderful fossil treasures are found which have done so much to revolutionize our notions of the life of tertiary times. Here are found the remains of rhinoceri, some with horns and some without, titanotheriums, and hyopatami, which were river horses much like the hippopatami of modern times. Higher up in the deposits are found countless numbers of turtles mingled with the remains of land animals. Among these are the wonderful oreontidae, which Leidy calls ruminating hogs, because their cutting teeth and canines and their feet are like those of the swine family, while their molars were patterned after those of the deer, and the upper portions of the head much like that of the camels.

"Several species of fossil monkeys have also been found in these sediments. The vast numbers of these animals were kept within proper bounds by gigantic carnivorous animals, such as sabre-toothed tigers, hyænodons, wolves, etc. Though this region is unattractive to the utilitarian, I doubt whether any portion of Nebraska will be of so much benefit to mankind, simply because here we have outlined so marvelously the old life of miocene times and it must ever be a stimulus to geological studies. A State that contains within its borders such a wealth of fossil treasures ought to give in the future illustrious diciples to science."

The sand areas, or hills, so often spoken of, are also found in the western portion of the State, chiefly along the Upper Loups and the Niobrara, and some of their tributaries; also on the south side of the Platte, where they run parallel with the stream, and are from one to six miles wide. In the northern part of the State, however, they cover much larger areas. These hills are composed of fine sand, pebbles and gravel, and in some places are covered with nutricious grasses, and are stationary, while in other places, again, they are entirely barren, and the sand so loosely compacted that the wind is ever changing their form.

This sand region has never been thoroughly explored nor properly investigated. Some scientists have undertaken to account for these hills by the theory that the winds in the course of ages have blown the sand from the bars on the rivers; but there are many difficulties in the way of this theory, as in many places the hills are composed of pebbles and stones that could not well have been moved by the wind.

Numerous important streams rise in this sand region of the northern part of the State, among which are the Loups, the Elkhorn, Cedar and Calamus flowing southwardly, and the Pines, Evergreen, Plum and Fairfield Creeks, flowing northwardly to the Niobrara.

# CHAPTER IV.

SOIL—AGRICULTURE—FRUIT—STOCK RAISING AND SHEEP HUSBANDRY.

### SOIL.

The unrivalled fertility of her soil, places Nebraska in the front rank among the great grain producing States of the Union. The soil of the table and up-land is composed of what is known as the Lacustrine or Loess deposit, which is the most valuable for agricultural purposes. This deposit prevails over more than three-fourths of the surface of the State, and is of uniform color, It ranges in thickness from 5 to 150 feet, and in some places in the northeastern Counties it is even 200 feet thick.

Prof. Samuel Aughey, State Geologist, recently made an analysis of this soil, taken from different parts of the State, for the purpose of showing the chemical properties and homogenous character of the lacustrine deposits, which is given in the following table, with accompanying remarks from the Professor's pen. No. 1 is from Douglas County; No. 2 from the bluffs near Kearney, in Buffalo County; No. 3 is from the Loup; No. 4 from Clay County, and No. 5 from Harlan County, in the Republican Valley.

| COMPOSITION OF SOIL. | No. 1. | No. 2. | No. 3. | No. 4. | No. 5. |
|---|---|---|---|---|---|
| Insoluble (silicious) matter | 81.28 | 81.32 | 81.35 | 81.30 | 81.32 |
| Ferric Oxide | 3.86 | 3.87 | 3.83 | 3.85 | 3.86 |
| Alumina | .75 | .75 | .74 | .73 | .74 |
| Lime, Carbonate | 6.07 | 6.06 | 6.03 | 6.05 | 6.09 |
| Lime, Posphate | 3.58 | 3.59 | 3.58 | 3.57 | 3.59 |
| Magnesia, Carbonate | 1.29 | 1.28 | 1.31 | 1.31 | 1.29 |
| Potassa | .27 | .29 | .35 | .34 | .33 |
| Soda | .15 | .16 | .14 | .16 | .16 |
| Organic Matter | 1.07 | 1.06 | 1.05 | 1.06 | 1.06 |
| Moisture | 1.09 | 1.08 | 1.09 | 1.08 | 1.09 |
| Loss in Analysis | .59 | .54 | .53 | .55 | .47 |
| Totals | 100.00 | 100.00 | 100.00 | 100.00 | 100.00 |

"From the above it is seen that over eighty per cent. of this formation is silicious matter, and so finely comminuted is it that the grains can only be seen under a good microscope. So abundant are the carbonates and phosphates of lime, that in many places they form peculiar rounded and oval concretions, vast numbers of these concretions, from the size of a shot to a walnut, are found almost everywhere by turning over the sod, and in excavations. When first exposed they are soft enough to be rubbed fine between the fingers, but they gradually harden by exposure to the open air. The analysis show the presence of a comparatively large amount of iron, besides alumina, soda, potash, etc.

"As would be expected from its elements, it forms one of the richest and most tillable soils in the world. In fact, in its chemical and physical properties, and the mode of its origin, it comes nearest to the Loess of the Rhine and the Valley of Egypt. It can never be exhausted until every hill and valley which composes it is entirely worn away. Owing to the wonderfully finely comminuted silica of which the bulk of the deposit consists, it possesses natural drainage in the highest degree. However great the floods of water that fall, it soon percolates through this soil, which in its lowest depths, retains it like a sponge. When drougths come, by capillary attraction, the moisture comes up from below, supplying the needs of vegetation in the dryest seasons. This is the reason why all over this region, where this deposit prevails, the native vegetation and cultivated crops are seldom either dried out or drowned out. This is especially the case on old breaking and where deep plowing is practiced.

"This deposit is a paradise for fruits, especially the apple, plum, grape, and all the small fruits of the temperate zone. They luxuriate in a soil like this, which has perfect natural drainage and is composed of such materials."

The alluvium deposits are the next most important after the Loess or Lacustrine. From an analysis made of the bottom lands, it appears that, chemically, alluvium differs from the lacustrine cheifly in having more organic matter and alumina and less silica. The following analysis of bottom soils, by Prof. Aughey, will give an idea of their physical character. The first is from the

Elkhorn, the second from the Platte, the third from the Republican, the fourth from the Blue, and the fifth from an exceptionally wet and sticky soil near Dakota City:

| BOTTOM SOILS. | No. 1. | No. 2. | No. 3. | No. 4. | No. 5. |
|---|---|---|---|---|---|
| Insoluble (silicious) matter | 63.07 | 63.70 | 63.01 | 62.99 | 61.03 |
| Ferric Oxide | 2.85 | 2.25 | 2.40 | 2.47 | 2.82 |
| Alumina | 8.41 | 7.76 | 8.36 | 8.08 | 10.52 |
| Lime, Carbonate | 7.08 | 7.99 | 8.01 | 7.85 | 7.09 |
| Lime, Phosphate | .90 | .85 | .99 | .94 | .98 |
| Magnesia, Carbonate | 1.41 | 1.45 | 1.39 | 1.40 | 1.38 |
| Potash | .50 | .54 | .61 | .67 | .60 |
| Soda | .49 | .52 | .54 | .58 | .57 |
| Sulphuric Acid | .79 | .79 | .71 | .79 | .69 |
| Organic Matter | 14.00 | 13.45 | 13.01 | 13.27 | 13.40 |
| Loss in Analysis | .50 | .79 | .97 | .96 | .92 |
| Totals | 100.00 | 100.00 | 100.00 | 100.00 | 100.00 |

The depth of this soil varies greatly, it often being twenty feet or more in thickness, then again the sand of the sub-soil is reached at a depth of two or three feet. Most of the bottom lands are well drained and are dry and warm, while some are low and cold, and in wet seasons, difficult to work. The bottom lands are the richest in organic matter, and are generally preferred for the raising of corn and vegetables, while the table and rolling lands are selected as the best adapted to small grain, fruits, etc. Yet after many years' experience in the cultivation of these lands the question of the superiority of the one over the other, for general farming purposes, remains undecided. Bottom lands are so well distributed throughout the State, that in the choice of a farm, usually a portion of both bottom and upland is selected.

Alkali lands are to be found in different sections of the State, but chiefly in the western portion. In the east half there are scarcely any such lands, the majority of the Counties having none at all, while in others there may be only a small spot in a township so affected. These alkali lands, however, are often renovated and eventually made productive for the cereals, by thorough drainage, deep cultivation, and seeding with wheat, especially in the wet seasons.

The following analysis of these alkali soils, by Prof. Aughey, shows how variable they are. The first was taken from the Platte Bottom, south of North Platte; the second from near Fort Kearney, and the third two miles west of Lincoln:

| ALKALI SOILS. | No. 1. | No. 2. | No. 3. |
|---|---|---|---|
| Insoluble (silicious) matter | 74.00 | 73.10 | 73.90 |
| Ferric Oxide | 3.80 | 3.73 | 3.69 |
| Alumina | 2.08 | 2.29 | 2.10 |
| Lime, Carbonate | 6.01 | 4.29 | 3.90 |
| Lime, Phosphate | 1.70 | 1.40 | 1.49 |
| Magnesia, Carbonate | 1.89 | 1.29 | 1.47 |
| Potash | 1.68 | 1.80 | 3.69 |
| Soda, Carbonate and Bicarbonate | 5.17 | 7.33 | 4.91 |
| Sodium, Sulphate | .70 | .89 | .89 |
| Moisture | .99 | .88 | .98 |
| Organic Matter | 1.20 | 2.10 | 2.10 |
| Loss in Aanalysis | .78 | .80 | .88 |
| Totals | 100.00 | 100.00 | 100.00 |

## AGRICULTURE.

Nebraska is essentially an agricultural State, the bountiful soil, mildness of the climate, and the long seasons of growth, are especially favorable to the cereal crops, and, in fact, to all of the products of the temperate zone, nearly all of which are grown here to perfection, and attain a size and quality seldom found in the older States.

With the exception of the Republican River Counties, agriculture is confined as yet almost wholly to the east half of the State, the 100th meridian being the dividing line; but there are many large districts west of this which will become, in the near future, valuable as farming lands.

*Wheat* is always a sure crop, with proper cultivation, the average yield per acre being about eighteen bushels, although in many of the western Counties the yield is frequently from twenty-five to thirty bushels per acre, and seldom less than twenty. The grain is of a superior quality, with a full, plump berry, usually weighing from sixty-two to sixty-seven pounds per bushel.

The following table will show the wheat crops for the past nine years, as reported by the Assessors:

| Year. | No. Bushels. | Year. | No. Bushels |
|---|---|---|---|
| 1870 | 1,848,000 | 1875 | Not reported. |
| 1871 | 1,829,000 | 1876 | 4,330,900 |
| 1872 | 2,560,000 | 1877 | 8,759,319 |
| 1873 | 3,584,000 | 1878 | 10,349,333 |
| 1874 | 3,619,000 | | |

The Assessors' returns for 1878 are very incomplete, several of the leading wheat growing Counties not reporting at all, so that it would be safe to estimate the wheat crop for that year at 12,000,000 bushels.

The figures for 1879 cannot be given, as no returns have yet been received from the Counties for that year; but the acreage in wheat was much larger than in preceding years, and the yield uniformly large.

The following are a few of the leading wheat growing Counties for 1878, according to reports made to the State Board of Agriculture:

| County. | Acres. | Bushels. |
|---|---|---|
| Saunders | 65,095 | 728,265 |
| Lancaster | 58,120 | 535,428 |
| York | 60,177 | 711,927 |
| Dodge | 39,279 | 471,623 |
| Fillmore | 49,882 | 620,253 |
| Hamilton | 42,338 | 470,931 |
| Cass | 47,822 | 593,783 |
| Boone | 37,291 | 453,406 |
| Saline | 48,001 | 585,102 |
| Adams | 36,252 | 421,873 |

The climate of Nebraska is better adapted to spring wheat, and very little winter wheat is grown on account of the open character of the winters.

*Corn* grows to perfection on the bottoms, tables, or uplands, and is one of the most profitable crops to the farmer. The yield for 1879 will average at least forty bushels to the acre throughout the State, and the quality is of the very highest grade. No State in the Union excels Nebraska in the production of corn, the soil and climate alike being well adapted to its growth.

In some localities, or where the cultivation has been more than common, the yield often runs from fifty to one hundred bushels per acre.

The following statement will show the acreage in corn and the number of bushels raised during the past three years:

| Year. | Acres. | Bushels. |
|---|---|---|
| 1876 | 850,000 | 25,500,000 |
| 1877 | 1,132,595 | 38,817,000 |
| 1878 | 780,721 | 26,687,860 |

More than a dozen of the older Counties have failed to report to the Board of Agriculture for 1878, hence the small returns for that year.

The following Counties show the largest corn crop for 1878:

| Counties. | Acres. | Bushels. |
|---|---|---|
| Cedar | 72,133 | 2,826,259 |
| Richardson | 61,182 | 2,215,810 |
| Lancaster | 54,659 | 1,997,993 |
| Saunders | 59,794 | 1,578,366 |
| Johnson | 38,742 | 1,549,697 |
| Saline | 35,101 | 1,491,850 |
| Washington | 34,084 | 1,308,486 |
| Dodge | 39,726 | 1,415,538 |
| Sarpy | 27,786 | 1,016,210 |
| Gage | 29,789 | 938,956 |

It is estimated that the corn crop for 1878 will reach 45,000,000 bushels, and for the present year, 1879, in the neighborhood of 50,000,000 bushels.

*Oats* are a successful and profitable crop. The yield usually ranges from thirty to seventy bushels per acre, according to culture and location, the average being about forty bushels.

The following Counties return the largest oat crop for 1878:

| Counties. | Bushels. |
|---|---|
| Lancaster | 294,935 |
| Seward | 275,845 |
| Dodge | 271,351 |
| Sarpy | 266,633 |
| Wayne | 225,264 |
| York | 176,482 |
| Saline | 138,403 |
| Red Willow | 151,118 |
| Platte | 150,639 |

| Counties. | Bushels. |
|---|---|
| Gage | 154,297 |
| Cedar | 163,582 |
| Boone | 175,048 |

*Barley* is largely cultivated and is a paying crop. The grain is of fine quality, and the average yield about thirty bushels per acre.

The barley crop from 1871 to 1877, inclusive, is reported as follows:

| Year. | Acres. | Bushels. |
|---|---|---|
| 1871 | 8,673 | 252,000 |
| 1872 | 12,117 | 309,000 |
| 1873 | 11,837 | 355,000 |
| 1874 | 14,549 | 355,000 |
| 1876 | 21,363 | 470,000 |
| 1877 | 153,764 | 2,401,420 |

The Counties showing the largest crops of barley for 1878 are:

| Counties. | Acres. | Bushels. |
|---|---|---|
| Saline | 7,648 | 189,573 |
| Cedar | 6,384 | 181,260 |
| Cass | 5,438 | 133,687 |
| York | 5,153 | 132,931 |
| Fillmore | 6,602 | 160,881 |
| Hamilton | 6,016 | 99,496 |

*Rye* is grown in almost every County in the State and is an important and valuable crop, the yield ranging from eighteen to thirty-five bushels per acre. It makes an excellent winter pasturage, and farmers with a large lot of stock frequently sow it as much on that account as for the grain.

The following eight Counties show the largest yield of rye for 1878.

| Counties. | Acres. | Bushels. |
|---|---|---|
| Dodge | 4,825 | 66,324 |
| York | 2,995 | 46,970 |
| Johnson | 2,957 | 44,485 |
| Colfax | 2,853 | 44,536 |
| Furnas | 2,080 | 42,004 |
| Saunders | 3,790 | 39,598 |
| Polk | 2,817 | 37,692 |
| Merrick | 2,503 | 36,485 |

*Flax* is rapidly becoming an important product in Nebraska. The soil is admirably adapted to its culture, and the yield averages about twelve bushels per acre. Extensive establishments for the manufacture of oil and oil cake from flax seed have long been in existence at Omaha and other points in the State.

Buckwheat, sorghum, broom corn, tobacco, beans, etc., are cultivated to a more or less extent, and all do finely.

Potatoes, onions, beets, cabbage, melons, and in fact, all of the root crops and garden vegetables produce abundantly and attain a great size and excellence. The yield of potatoes generally ranges from one to three hundred bushels per acre.

*Hops* grow luxuriantly and are a sure and remunerative crop. They are also found in the wild state growing in profusion on many of the streams, and are said to equal the best cultivated ones.

### FRUIT.

Much attention has been given in the past several years to fruit culture, and the question as to the adaptability of Nebraska soil to fruit growing is no longer a matter of doubt.

The hundreds of thrifty young orchards throughout the eastern portion fully attest this fact. The apple, pear, plum, grape, cherry, and the berries are now successfully and profitably produced. The cultivation of the apple has met with marked success. Fine, heavy-bearing orchards of this excellent fruit, embracing all the choice and delicate varieties, are numerous in almost all of the older settled Counties, and some of them already afford a handsome return.

Pears grow to great perfection. The trees are very productive, and the fruit highly flavored.

The cultivation of the peach has not met with the same success which has attended the cultivation of the apple and pear, although there are quite a number of fine peach orchards growing in the State, especially in the southeastern portion, which bear more or less fruit every year, and at least one year in three the yield is very large. The peaches thus far grown are usually of extra size, finely flavored, and rich in all the valuable properties of this delicious fruit. No doubt in process of time, as timber becomes more plentiful in the State—as it soon will be, in the eastern portions especially, thus affording better protection to the orchards—the peach will also be profitably raised.

The cultivation of the grape has been attended with remarkable success. The soil is naturally adapted to its growth, and it flourishes and does well almost anywhere. Many farmers have made a specialty of grape culture, and have fine, prolific vineyards. The grapes are very rich and finely flavored, and are equal, if not superior to those of California.

At the annual meeting of the American Pomological Society, convened at Richmond, Virginia, in September, 1871, Nebraska exhibited 146 varieties of apples, fifteen of peaches, thirteen of pears, one of plums, and one of grapes, and was awarded the first premium of $100 for the best collection of different species of fruit. A similar success has since been achieved for Nebraska fruit at each annual meeting of this Society.

There are a number of flourishing nurseries in the State, some of which are exceptionably large and fine, and the business is rapidly growing in proportions by the constantly increasing demand for fruit and shade trees, shrubbery and evergreens.

### WILD FRUITS.

Probably no State in the Northwest is better supplied with wild fruits than Nebraska:

The plum grows in great profusion, along almost all the watercourses, and on the outskirts of the timber belts. The bushes are from six to twelve feet high, and when in bloom the thickets present a vast sea of white flowers, whose fragrance is wafted on the breezes a long distance.

There is an endless variety of plums, ranging in size from half an inch to an inch in diameter, and of various colors, from almost white to many shades of yellow, and red tinged with blue. They are finely flavored, and make most excellent preserves and table-sauce. Delicious as some of these wild plums are, their size and flavor are much improved by cultivation and pruning. It is easy to produce an early and fruitful growth from the seed.

The sand-hill cherry, so famous on our western plains, is really, botanically, a dwarf plum. It grows in thick clusters on a shrub from one to two feet in height, and is found over the greater part of the western half of the State, on the sand-hills and very sandy land. It is a prolific fruit, about the size of the domestic cherry, and is very finely flavored.

Choke cherries are also abundant. They grow on a small shrub or bush from four to eight feet high, and are much used for making jelly and in pastries.

The Buffalo berry is found along the banks of the Missouri, Platte, Elkhorn and Loup Rivers, and their tributaries, in the northern part of the State, and on the Republican, Nemahas and Blues, and some of their tributaries in the southern part. The Buffalo tree is usually from eight to twelve feet in height, and rather scrubby, the branches rusty white and quite thorny, with numerous small, thorn-like limbs. The leaves are oblong and silvery white in color. The berry grows in bunches in the forks of the branches, close to the main stem, and is about the size of a currant, round, red-colored, and slightly tartish. It ripens in early autumn, and if not disturbed hangs until winter. Wherever this berry becomes known it is at once a favorite, and is highly prized for the manufacture of jellies and canning.

Gooseberries of the largest and finest qualities grow in great abundance all over the State. There is scarcely a brook but what has a plentiful growth of this delicious fruit along its banks, and in the timber adjacent. There are four varieties of this berry growing wild. They are easily domesticated, and grow wherever set out without any difficulty, their qualities being much improved by cultivation.

Currants, of two species, abound mostly in the western portion of the State, but are not plentiful. The fruit is much like the black currant of the garden.

Strawberries are abundant in the eastern portion of the State, but scarce in the western portion. They grow in the valleys, on the sides of the hills, and near the timber belts, and are almost equal to the tame strawberry in size and flavor.

Black raspberries are plentiful, in the eastern Counties especially. These berries are very large and fine, and are among the choicest of the wild fruits. Large quantities are gathered annually and marketed, and put up in cans for winter use They bear profusely, and are found on the wood and brush land, and on the banks of streams.

Blackberries are plentiful in the southeastern portion of the State, and rather scarce in other sections.

The Grape is the most abundant of all the wild fruit. It is hardy and very prolific, and a failure of the crop is an unheard of thing. It is found in great profusion along the Missouri and almost all the other water-courses. Some of the timber belts are almost impassable from the number and length of the vines, which form a complete net work from tree to tree, in many instances climbing to the very tops, and when the fruit is ripe the tree will be black from the ground to the top. In other places the vines run over the tops of the brush for many rods, and frequently straggling vines are found far out on the prairies. Where deprived of any other support they creep along the ground over the weeds and grass. There are several varieties of these grapes; some ripen in the summer, others in the fall, frequently not until after frost. There are large quantities of this fruit gathered, canned and dried for winter use. In many places along the Missouri and other large streams, they are gathered by the wagon loads and made into native wines, which is used at home and sold abroad.

### STOCK RAISING AND SHEEP HUSBANDRY.

One of the most important industries of this country is that of stock raising and sheep husbandry, and the State of Nebraska, and more especially its northwestern and western portions, is fairly entitled to the first position among the Western States and Territories as a stock producing and a stock sustaining region. Its vast prairies; abundant, luxuriant and nutritious grasses; its rivers, creeks, and springs of clear and sparkling waters; and still more, its uniform and delightful climate, in which the rounding season gives not only a simple promise, but the full protection of a genial clime—these are a few of the more substantial reasons why Nebraska excels all other Western States in the profitable industries referred to. While it is true, that almost every County in the State is adapted to these industries, as before stated, it is in the western sections where a wider range, and larger opportunities are offered for prosecuting the business successfully that stock men must look as the future great grazing fields of the Continent.

Less than twenty years ago, a very large per cent. of the herds and flocks shipped to the seaboard markets, were the products of the States lying east of the Mississippi River; Illinois, Indiana, Kentucky, Ohio and Michigan, being the chief sources of supply. As those States became more densely populated, and the lands divided up into smaller farms, stock raising was crowded westward where wider and more profitable ranges were offered; hence Iowa, Eastern Nebraska, Missouri, Kansas, Texas, and the Territories, from 1862 until the present time, have been the chief source of supply. But as these sections of country, like those to the East of the Mississippi, became more densely settled, cattle raising has been forced still further west, to more extended fields. As in all other industries, men engaged in stock raising and sheep husbandry, will naturally seek such sections of country as offer the largest advantages in the way of economical production. These advantages are in a great measure confined to such sections of country as require the smallest expense in winter feeding. There are but two species of natural grass upon which stock can be successfully pastured during the more inclement season of the year;—the Buffalo grass of western Nebraska, and the Musquite, or bunch grass, as it is known here, of Texas and New Mexico—these retain a large portion of their nutritious properties during the winter months, and it is on these that flocks and herds can be successfully pastured the year round. In the way of water and marketing facilities, Nebraska affords advantages for stock raising not found even in Texas, a State that produces more meat cattle than any other five States of the Union. Then again, the present grazing fields of Texas are largely adapted to the culture of cotton and grain, and it is only a question of time when they will be more exclusively employed in the cultivation of those products. In Nebraska, however, that vast section of country west of the 100th meridian, embracing nearly one-half of the State, also portions of Colorado, Dakota and Wyoming, are non-productive grain sections; and yet, producing as they do, an abundance of Buffalo grass, they offer advantages not to be found elsewhere, for stock raising, including cattle, sheep and horses. It has been contended in some quarters that these grazing fields are too far north to be economically employed in raising cattle; that the per cent. of loss during the winter seasons would prove so alarmingly large as to discourage the industry. The past ten years' experience, however, have proved all such predictions to be entirely groundless, as the average loss of cattle from inclement weather and other causes, has been much less north of the thirty-eighth parallel of latitude during the past few years than it has south. This is especially the case in the losses suffered in Texas, as compared with those in Western Nebraska, Wyoming and Colorado.

It is to the grazing fields of Western Nebraska that the attention of stock growers is especially directed at the present time. They have discovered the almost immeasurable advantages it offers over other sections of the country.

To note the progress made in the industry of stock raising in this State during the past ten years is truly marvelous. On ranges employed for that purpose, the grasses support the stock the year through, hence the cost of raising a steer of 1,200 pounds, so far as the feed is concerned, is less than that of raising a yearling calf in the Eastern States.

While Western Nebraska offers almost unlimited facilities for stock raising, the industry is by no means confined to that part of the State, as it is most extensively carried on in nearly all of the eastern and middle Counties, and large droves of the better grades of beef cattle, hogs and sheep are annually shipped to the East from the older settled portions of the State. On many of the larger farms one can see thoroughbred bulls, and droves of from twenty to one hundred head of cattle, either mixed or graded. In fact, many of the farmers have made fine stock breeding a specialty and have met with uniform success. A large number of fine blooded stallions and Kentucky jacks have been introduced, as also the Norman breed of horses, which have greatly improved the size and class of the draught horses. The fine appearance of the horses and graded stock is a subject of remark by strangers while passing through the State or visiting at the Agricultural Fairs.

Sheep raising throughout the eastern Counties receives a large share of attention, and is attended with very favorable results. The winters are so short and dry, and the green feeding so plentiful during the greater portion of the year, that sheep raising is rapidly becoming a prominent industry. The sheep are remarkably free from the diseases so common among them in the older States. The flocks now in the eastern and western portions of the State are numbered by the thousands. The breeds are being constantly improved by the introduction of the best blooded animals, and the result is that Nebraska wool ranks very high in the market.

SWINE.

In a great corn producing State like this, where it can be profitably raised and readily bought at from fifteen to twenty-five cents per bushel, and where the price of pork ranges from three to four and one-half cents per pound, hog raising must necessarily yield handsome returns. This industry is increasing so rapidly that in a few years more Nebraska must be ranked among the greatest of the pork-producing States. During the years of the grasshopper invasion, 1874-75, a check was given to the hog crop, especially in the western Counties. In these years the corn was almost entirely destroyed, and farmers having none to feed their hogs they were obliged either to kill or sell them. However, the abundant crops of the succeeding years have given a new impetus to hog raising, and immense numbers of these animals are now shipped to the Eastern markets, while the extensive pork packing establishments at home furnish a ready market for tens of thousands more.

But, as before stated, it is in the unorganized and unsettled territory in the western part of the State that the great stock region is to be found. Here the land costs the ranchman nothing for its use, and the expense required for buildings and herding is so trifling when compared with that attending the business further east, where the cost of land and winter feeding is a great item, and all other expenses proportionately high, that it enables the western stockmen to successfully compete in the markets with the higher grade stock of the East. The ranche buildings are generally rude and inexpensive, consisting of corrals, hay-covered sheds and a cheap house for the use of the herders, and men employed in marking, branding and shipping the stock. Hay is put up at an expense of $1.00 a ton. Many of the ranches are so admirably located, with a broad stream circling around on one side, and deep-cut canons on the other, as to require only a few rods of fencing to complete an enclosure of thousands of acres; others again, are on peninsulas at the junction of two streams, the open ends only requiring a fence, thus making the task of herding very light. The most advantageous and desirable locations have been pretty generally taken, although thousands of choice sites yet remain where stock raising could be carried on with convenience and profit, especially in the Niobrara country. The amount of stock on the plains is increasing very rapidly, and new herds are being started each year. Thousands upon thousands of Texas and Cherokee cows and heifers are annually driven to these ranches and bred to fine blooded bulls, which are carefully selected from the best stock farms of Kentucky, Missouri and other Eastern States, and Canada. The stock is thus being constantly improved, and commands in the markets very nearly as much as the native cattle of the East.

A number of the leading and most successful stockmen of to-day are old plainsmen, who have grown up to the business, and are conversant with its every detail; men of ability and energy who, from a very small beginning, have seen their herds increase to thousands of head. The profits attending the business, when judiciously and understandingly handled, are usually from forty to sixty per cent. above all expenses; therefore it will be seen that stock raising, notwithstanding the losses that occur from mismanagement and other causes, is a profitable business, although requiring a large capital, great care and attention.

For the purpose of better showing the profits of stock raising we append the following:—

Estimate for a herd of 6,000 Texas cattle, to be bought there, say in April, 1878, and driven to the western plains of Nebraska, with the result of the investment, under good management and ordinary success, at the end of three years and a half, allowing for an annual loss through death or straying, of three per cent., and assuming that eighty per cent. of the cows will have calves that mature.

```
1,000 Beef steers, 4 years old and upwards, at $20 each..$ 20,000
1,000 Three-year-old steers, at $15 each ................  15,000
1,000 Two-year-old steers, at $11 each..................  11,000
1,000 Cows at $15 each..................................  15,000
1,000 Two-year-old heifers at $10.50 each...............  10,500
1,000 Yearling heifers at $7 each.......................   7,000
                                                        $ 78,500
```

### EXPENSES.

| | |
|---|---:|
| Wages of drovers, provisions, etc., including all incidental expenses in bringing herd from Texas—four months' time—at the rate of $1.50 per head........$ | 9,000 |
| Eight months' expenses on range, herding, branding, etc., at the rate of $1.50 per head per year......... | 6,000 |
| Thirty horses bought in Texas, at $40 each, and kept for herding on range................................. | 1,200 |
| Mower, hay-rake, wagon, plow, saddles, ranche buildings, etc............................................ | 1,000 |
| 100 bulls, fair to fine grades, bought in the North, at an average price of $50 each...................... | 5,000 |
| | $100,700 |
| Interest at 10 per cent. for one year................... | 10,070 |
| Amount of investment at the end of one year..........$ | 110,770 |
| Expenses six months' herding, etc., to Oct. 1, 1879...... | 4,500 |
| Interest half year, at 10 per cent..................... | 5,763 |
| | $121,033 |

| | | |
|---|---:|---:|
| October 1, 1879, net returns for sale of 2,465 beef steers, averaging 1,100 pounds each, at 3c per pound.................................$81,345 | | |
| 200 old cows, averaging 900 pounds each, at 3c per pound................................. | 5,400 | 86,745 |
| | | $ 34,288 |

### STOCK INVENTORY AFTER SALES, OCTOBER 1879.

| | | |
|---|---:|---:|
| Beef steers......................................... | 400 | |
| Cows............................................... | 1,710 | |
| Heifers, two-year-olds.............................. | 955 | |
| Calves.............................................. | 1,528 | |
| Bulls............................................... | 100 | |
| | | 4,693 |

### OCTOBER 1, 1880.

| | | |
|---|---:|---:|
| Expenses one year............................$ | 7,039 | |
| One year's interest at 10 per cent.............. | 4,132 | |
| Bought 50 bulls, at $50 each................... | 2,500 | $ 13,671 |
| | | $ 47,959 |

### SALES ACCOUNT IN OCTOBER, 1880.

| | | |
|---|---:|---:|
| 388 beef steers, averaging 1,100 pounds each, at 3c per pound.............................$12,804 | | |
| 400 old cows, averaging 900 pounds each, at 3c per pound........................................ | 10,800 | 23,604 |
| Net capital account........................... | | $24,355 |

## STOCK INVENTORY AFTER SALES OCTOBER, 1880.

| | | |
|---|---:|---:|
| Cows (926 last year's two-year-olds), | 2,185 | |
| Yearlings | 1,482 | |
| Calves | 2,068 | |
| Bulls | 150 | |
| | | 5,885 |

### OCTOBER 1, 1881.

| | | |
|---|---:|---:|
| Expenses one year | $8,827 | |
| One year's interest at 10 per cent | 3,318 | $ 12,145 |
| | | $36,500 |

### SALES ACCOUNT IN OCTOBER, 1881.

500 old cows, averaging 900 pounds each, at 3c per ℔....$13,500

Net capital account.................................$23,000

### INVENTORY OF STOCK AND APPURTENANCES AFTER SALES IN OCT., 1881.

| | |
|---|---:|
| 30 horses, worth at least $30 each......$ | 900 |
| Wagons, mower, hay rake, plows, saddles, ranche buildings, etc | 1,000 |

#### GRADED STOCK.

| | |
|---|---:|
| 1,619 cows, valued at $27 each | 43,713 |
| 719 two-year-old heifers, valued at $16 each | 11,504 |
| 719 two-year-old steers, valued at $16 each | 11,504 |
| 1,003 yearling steers, valued at $10 each | 10,030 |
| 1,003 yearling heifers, valued at $10 each | 10,030 |
| 1,695 calves, valued at $5 each | 8,475 |
| 150 bulls, valued at $50 each | 7,500 |
| | $104,656 |
| Deduct outstanding capital account | 23,000 |
| Balance to profit, exclusive of 10 per cent. interest.....$ | 81,656 |

This makes an admirable exhibit and will be encouraging to those who think of investing their money in cattle; but to succeed one must have patience, shrewdness and self-reliance, with any amount of energy and capacity.

The plains of Nebraska have been the natural grazing grounds through untold ages of millions of buffalo and other grass-feeding animals, and they are rapidly becoming the great meat producing lands of the nation. In a few years it will be a difficult matter to find a vacant range in the State suitable or capable of sustaining 5,000 head of cattle. The rivers and creeks are all being rapidly taken up by small herders or branches of large herds.

## CHAPTER V.

### PUBLIC LANDS.

Lands Received from the Interior Department—State University Lands—Common School Lands—Saline Lands—Penitentiary Lands—Public Building Lands—State Normal School Endowment Lands—Union Pacific R. R. Lands—Burlington & Missouri River R. R. Lands—Government Lands—The Homestead Law—Pre-Emption Law—Timber Culture Act.

As stated in another portion of this work, the State of Nebraska contains an area of 75,995 square miles, or over 48,500,000 acres of land, and it is the purpose of the writer to show in this Chapter, as nearly as possible, what portion of this vast domain has been disposed of, and for what purposes, as also what remains undisposed of, at the commencement of the year 1879.

The State of Nebraska has received from the General Government grants of lands amounting in the aggregate to upwards of 3,370,000 acres, as follows:

| | |
|---|---:|
| For Internal Improvement | 500,000 |
| " Agricultural College | 90,000 |
| " University | 46,080 |
| " Public Buildings | 12,800 |
| " Penitentiary | 32,000 |
| " Saline purposes | 46,080 |
| For Common School purposes, sections 16 and 36 in every township, which will amount in the aggregate, as estimated, to | 2,643,080 |
| Making the total grant to the State | 3,370,040 |

The 500,000 acres for internal improvement purposes, were granted to the State upon its admission to the Union, under the provisions of an Act of Congress, approved September 4th, 1841. These lands were selected through agents appointed for that purpose, and disposed of in pursuance of the provisions of an Act of the Legislature, approved February 15th 1869.

The following exhibit is taken from the report of the Commissioner of Public Lands, as published for the year 1878. It shows when these lands were received from the General Government, the amount, and how they were disposed of:

ACCOUNT OF LANDS RECEIVED FROM THE INTERIOR DEPARTMENT.

| | | |
|---|---|---|
| March 29th, 1870, received | 359,708.06 | acres. |
| October 13th 1871 " | 94,232.96 | " |
| June 17th, 1872, " | 18,441.22 | " |
| May 27th, 1873, " | 22,213.01 | " |
| January 7th, 1874, " | 880.00 | " |
| February 24th, 1874 " | 8,656.61 | " |
| Making a total of | 504,131.86 | acres |
| Deduct from the above the difference between short and full sections—short sections being charged in the above list as full sections | 3,319.86 | acres |
| Which leaves a real total of | 500,812.00 | acres |

HOW DISPOSED OF—TO WHOM.

| | | |
|---|---|---|
| Deeded to Saline County for Bridges | 1,000.00 | acres |
| Deeded to Gage County for Bridges | 1,000.00 | " |
| Deeded to Elkhorn & Mo. Valley R. R. | 100,030.32 | " |
| Deeded to Midland Pacific R. R. | 100,384.08 | " |
| Deeded to Brownville & Fort Kearney R. R. | 19,989.12 | " |
| Deeded to Burlington & Missouri River R. R. | 50,104.77 | " |
| Deeded to Sioux City & Pacific R. R. | 47,327.10 | " |
| Deeded to Omaha & Southwestern R. R. | 100,010.00 | " |
| Deeded to Omaha & Northwestern R. R. | 80,416.24 | " |
| Deeded to Burlington & Southwestern R. R. | 20,000.00 | " |
| Deeded to Atchison & Nebraska R. R. | 12,841.54 | " |
| | 533,103.17 | acres |
| Disposed of in excess of grant | 32,291.17 | acres |

The amount deeded in excess of grant occurred in deeding the same parcel of lands to the Burlington & Southwestern on June 20th, 1870, that were deeded to the Omaha & Southwestern Road on October 10th, 1862, viz.: 20,000 acres. There are, however, 12,291 acres that was deeded in excess of the 500,000 acres as granted by the Act of Congress referred to, that ar note accounted for in the above statement.

## STATE UNIVERSITY LANDS.

By an Act of Congress, approved April 19th, 1864, seventy-two sections of the unappropriated lands in the State of Nebraska were donated to the State for the use and support of a State University. The selection of these lands was made by the authorized agents of the State, which were confirmed by the Interior Department, on the 17th of February, 1874. The lands were located as follows:

| County. | No. of Acres. | County. | No. of Acres. |
|---|---|---|---|
| Webster | 17,803.48 | Knox | 4,800.00 |
| Nuckolls | 4,916.68 | Dakota | 320.00 |
| Cedar | 1,600.00 | Dixon | 640.00 |
| Pierce | 3,197.67 | Holt | 8,322.10 |
| Madison | 2,240.00 | Antelope | 1,280.00 |

45,119.93
Total amount donated by Congress............46,080.00

Amount due from the United States.............. 960.07

## AGRICULTURAL COLLEGE LANDS.

Under an Act of Congress, approved July 2d, 1862, donating public lands to the several States and Territories which may provide Colleges for the benefit of agriculture and the mechanic arts, military tactics, etc., a tract of land equal to thirty thousand acres for each Senator and Representative in Congress, to which Nebraska was entitled by the apportionment under the census of 1860, was selected by the State, and confirmed by the Interior Department as follows:

September 20th, 1871, selections made and confirmed for.................................................11,504.96 acres.
December 8th, 1871, selections made and confirmed for.................................................77,947.82 "

Making a total of......................89,452.78 acres
Located as follows:

JOHNSON'S HISTORY OF NEBRASKA.

| County. | Amount of Land. | County. | Amount of Land. |
|---|---|---|---|
| Knox | 33,490.64 | Stanton | 320.00 |
| Cedar | 27,677.96 | Burt | 640.00 |
| Wayne | 15,648.98 | Dixon | 2240.00 |
| Pierce | 7,835.20 | Cuming | 960.00 |
| Dakota | 640.00 | | |

Total selections..............................89,452.78
Amount donated by Congress........................90,000.00

Amount due from the U. S.................... 547.22

COMMON SCHOOL LANDS.

The following statement shows the number of acres of Common School lands belonging to the State on the 30th day of November, 1878, and the Counties in which such lands are located:

| County. | Acres. | County. | Acres. |
|---|---|---|---|
| Adams | 20,000 | Lancaster | 27,881 |
| Antelope | 31,400 | Madison | 24,311.88 |
| Boone | 23,040 | Merrick | 15,033.53 |
| Burt | 16,997.88 | Nuckolls | 20,440 |
| Buffalo | 29,700.59 | Nemaha | 10,801.11 |
| Butler | 21,480 | Otoe | 19,986.88 |
| Cuming | 19,740 | Pawnee | 16,610 |
| Colfax | 14,225.28 | Pierce | 19,200 |
| Clay | 21,040 | Phelps | 20,247.85 |
| Cass | 16,242.18 | Platte | 24,029.08 |
| Cedar | 27,499.14 | Polk | 16,508.94 |
| Dakota | 5,989.14 | Red Willow | 25,574.01 |
| Dixon | 15,689 | Richardson | 8,830 |
| Dodge | 16,408.83 | Saline | 18,349 |
| Douglas | 8,444.72 | Sarpy | 7,087.65 |
| Filmore | 20,308.51 | Saunders | 25,253.25 |
| Franklin | 20,471.85 | Seward | 19,350 |
| Furnas | 24,654.15 | Sherman | 20,752.20 |
| Hamilton | 20,480 | Stanton | 14,730 |
| Hall | 19,635.26 | Thayer | 20,036.72 |
| Harlan | 20,433.93 | Valley | 20,484 |
| Howard | 23,299.30 | Wayne | 15,360 |
| Gage | 22,028.31 | Washington | 12,300.26 |
| Greeley | 20,555.20 | Webster | 20,480 |
| Jefferson | 14,419.53 | York | 20,480 |
| Johnson | 12,158 | Pawnee | * 2,240 |
| Kearney | 16,830.70 | Lancaster | * 320 |
| Knox | 26,238.82 | | |
| | | Total | 1,026,067.68 |

* Deeded to the State by A. J. Cropsey.
* "    "    "    " Esther L. Warren.

Estimated number of acres of Common School land in Counties established but not organized, as also in Counties organized, but not having a complete record of their lands, and the amount of indemnity school lands therein:

| COUNTIES. | ESTIMATED NO OF ACRES | NO. OF ACRES OF INDEMNITY LAND. | TOTAL. |
|---|---|---|---|
| Lincoln | 92,160 | 1,172.70 | 93,332.70 |
| Cheyenne | 211,200 | 5,853.20 | 217,053.20 |
| Gosper | 15,360 | ....... | 15,360 |
| Hitchcock | 25,600 | ....... | 25,600 |
| Keith | 71,680 | 1,012.03 | 72,692.03 |
| Dawson | 35,840 | 1,162.40 | 37,002.40 |
| Frontier | 35,840 | ....... | 35,840 |
| Holt | 81,920 | ....... | 81,920 |
| Chase | 30,600 | ....... | 30,600 |
| Dundy | 15,360 | ....... | 15,360 |
| Custer | 92,160 | ....... | 92,160 |
| Wheeler | 20,480 | ....... | 20,480 |
| Hayes | 25,600 | ....... | 25,600 |
| Sioux | 126,720 | ....... | 126,720 |
| Total | 880,520 | 9,200,33 | 889,720.33 |

Estimated number of acres of Common School lands in the unorganized territory of the State on the 30th of November, 1878....................527,360

Making a grand total of two million, four hundred and forty-three thousand, one hundred and forty-eight acres of Common School land owned by the State at the close of the year 1878.

Number of acres of Common School lands sold prior to
 January 1st, 1877......................................110,362.08
Number of acres leased prior to 1877.................... 80,381.79
Number of acres of indemnity land in the State.......... 25,845.21
Number of acres of Common School land deeded during
 1877 and 1878....................................... 6,770.83
Number of acres of Common School land sold on time
 during 1877 and 1878................................. 26,819.16
Number of acres of Common School land leased during
 the years 1877 and 1878..............................100,918

### SALINE LANDS.

By an Act of Congress, approved April 19th, 1864, seventy-two sections of land were granted to Nebraska for Saline purposes. These lands were selected by the agents of the State and confirmed by the Interior Department, as follows:

Dec. 23d, 1872, selections made and confirmed for....35,849.91 acres
June 21st, 1873,    "     "     "    .... 7,663.34   "
April 12th, 1878    "     "     "    .... 1,880.13   "

                                        45,393.38   "
Deduct error in selecting same land..................  280.00   "

Total confirmed to date.............................45,113.38   "
Amount awaiting confirmation......................  966.62   "

Amount of grant...................................46,080.00   "
Amount of Saline lands reserved for State Normal
   School (confirmed)..............................12,722.36   "
Amount of Saline Lands reserved for Model Farm.. 1,115.35   "
  "    "    "    "    " Asylum.......  154.51   "
  "    "    "   sold......................17,516.16   "
  "    "    "   unsold...................13,605.00   "

                                          45,113.38

All unsold Saline lands are located in Lancaster County.

### PENITENTIARY LANDS.

By an Act of Congress, approved April 19th, 1864, fifty sections of land were donated to Nebraska for a penitentiary or State prison. The land was selected by the State and confirmed by the Interior Department, as follows:

February 17th, 1870, selections made and confirmed for..32,044,01 acres.

### PUBLIC BUILDING LANDS.

By the act of Congress above cited, twenty sections of land were granted the State for the erection of Public Buildings. This land was selected by the agents of the State, and, by Act of the Legislature, approved February 10th, 1871, was transferred to the Penitentiary lands, and are included in that account. The Interior Department has confirmed list of Public Building lands dated February 17th, 1870, for twenty sections or.......12,751.05 acres

Total public building and Penitentiary lands.........44,795.06   "

Amount sold............................43,438.35
  "    unsold......................... 1,356.71—44.795.06   "

### STATE NORMAL SCHOOL—ENDOWMENT LANDS.

Under an Act of the State Legislature, approved June 20th,

1867, twenty sections of the Saline lands were selected and set apart for the purpose of endowing the State Normal School, at Peru, in Nemaha County, which are reported as follows:

| | | |
|---|---:|---:|
| Set apart for endowment of State Normal School, 20 sections............................ | | 12,800 acres. |
| Sold and deeded of the above lands... | 3,200 | |
| Remaining unsold at the close of the year 1878........................ | 9,602 36 | |
| Excess in survey..................... | | 2.36 |
| | | 12,802 36 |

The unsold Normal School lands are all located in Lancaster County.

## RECAPITULATION.

| | | |
|---|---:|---:|
| Amount received by the State for internal improvements...................... | 500,812 | |
| Amount deeded by the State........... | 533,103 17 | |
| Error in deeding same lands........... | | 32,291 17 |
| Agricultural College grant............. | | 90,000 acres. |
| None of this land has been disposed of. | | |
| State University grant................. | 46,080 | |
| Amount sold of the above............. | 1,270 97 | 44,809 03 |
| Saline grant.......................... | 46,080 | |
| Amount sold.......................... | 17,516 16 | |
| Reserved for State purposes and unsold. | | 28,563 84 |
| Penitentiary grant (amount received).. | 32,044 01 | |
| Public buildings (amount received).... | 12,751 05 | |
| | 44,795 06 | |
| Amount sold.......................... | 43,438 35 | |
| Amount unsold....................... | | 1,356 71 |
| | | 164,729 58 |
| Common School lands belonging to the State, December 1, 1878............ | | 2,443,148 01 |
| Total.............................. | | 2,607,877 59 |

### THE UNION PACIFIC LAND GRANT.

The aggregate amount of lands in Nebraska, received by the Union Pacific Railway from the Government, was 5,926,400 acres, of which about 4,000,000 acres are unsold. All are contiguous to their line of road, being distributed through the following Counties.

| Counties. | Acres. | Counties. | Acres. |
|---|---|---|---|
| Douglas and Sarpy | 5,000 | Buffalo | 200,000 |
| Washington | 5,000 | Hamilton | 75,000 |
| Dodge | 20,000 | York | 20,000 |
| Colfax | 25,000 | Adams | 15,000 |
| Saunders | 25,000 | Kearney | 40,000 |
| Butler | 20,000 | Phelps | 100,000 |
| Polk | 25,000 | Gosper | 250,000 |
| Platte | 80,000 | Sherman | 9,000 |
| Merrick | 40,000 | Dawson | 225,000 |
| Hall | 120,000 | Lincoln | 690,000 |
| Howard | 80,000 | | |

About 2,000,000 acres of the above mentioned lands are in the Platte Valley, nearly 1,000,000 acres being in Eastern Nebraska, and hence are among the best lands of the State, for grain and fruits. So much has been said and written about the beautiful and fertile valley of the Platte, that it seems unnecessary in these pages to say more than that it is all the human heart could desire, for he that could desire more in the way of soil, climate and water, would exhibit a most inexcusable ingratitude to his Creator, who spoke into existence such a gardenlike section of country for his children. A few years ago this beautiful valley, extending westward from the Missouri River through the entire length of the State, was the home of the Indian and the trapper, while a little later it became the great overland trail to the Pacific. To-day it is the richest agricultural district to be found in the West. The soil has been proved, as have also the climate and water, and nothing has been found wanting. To such as may contemplate buying homes in the West, the Author—who, as stated in another portion of this work, has been a citizen of this State for the past twenty-five years—can conscientiously say, no better lands, on more advantageous terms, can be obtained in any other portion of the Union than in the great Platte Valley of Nebraska.

The Union Pacific lands are all placed at prices, and on terms that bring them within the means of any man who is possessed of energy and industry, and desires to secure a home. The range of prices for these lands are wide in the extreme, and are fixed according to location, quality and soil, water and general surroundings. The buyer can find lands as low as $2, $3, $4, $5, or even up to $10 per acre. To illustrate: in Douglas, Washington,

Saunders, Hamilton and Kearney Counties, at from $5 to $10 per acre, while in most of the other Counties it ranges from $2 to $10. Considering their location, relating to railway and market facilities and school and church privileges, these lands are certainly selling at a low price.

The lands are sold on ten years' time, with one tenth down, and the remainder in annual payments, at six per cent. interest, and where parties prefer to pay cash down, a discount of ten per cent. is made. A large per cent. of the lands sold by the Company are now under a good state of cultivation, and in many instances the products of the soil has paid for the lands, leaving the purchaser a large margin for his labor. The Company extend the most liberal facilities to all who desire to examine their lands. Land exploring tickets are sold at greatly reduced rates, while the actual buyer is transported free of charge. Liberal reductions are also made in the transportation of freight for settlers. Immigrant houses, as they are called, are provided at a moderate cost, to such as are not able to immediately settle on their purchases.

### THE BURLINGTON & MISSOURI RIVER R. R. LANDS.

This Company received from the Government a land grant in Nebraska amounting to 2,382,208 acres; they received from the State of Nebraska, 50,104 acres, and when they took possession of the Omaha & Southwestern Road they acquired the land grant made to that line by the State, of 100,010 acres, making their total land possessions in Nebraska, originally, 2,532,322 acres. Of this amount 1,423,598 acres have been sold up to June, 1879, leaving over a million acres yet to be disposed of, and which are offered at such low figures and reasonable terms as to place them within the reach of all persons of moderate means desiring farms in the West.

The B. & M. Lands are situated chiefly in the north-central and south-central portions of the State, and are designated as the "North Platte" and "South Platte" lands. They are sold for cash, or on the two, six or, ten years' credit plan.

On the *Ten Years' Credit Plan*, only the interest, at six per cent. is required at the time of purchase. At the commencement of the second, third and fourth years, the same payment is required, and not until the beginning of the fifth year is any part of the principal to be paid. At this time one-seventh part of the principal is required, with interest at six per cent. on the balance, and one-seventh with interest on the balance each year thereafter, until the whole is paid.

On the *Six Years' Credit Plan*, a discount of twenty per cent. is allowed, and only the interest at six per cent. for the first three years required, after which equal yearly payments of principal, with interest at six per cent.

On the *Two Years' Credit Plan*, a discount of $32\frac{1}{2}$ per cent. is allowed, one-third of the principal being paid down and the balance in equal payments the second and third years, with interest at six per cent.

On the *Cash Plan*, a discount of thirty-five per cent. is given.

In the South Platte Country the B. & M. Company has remaining for sale about 350,000 acres of choice prairie lands, situated in one of the best settled portions of the State, where towns, churches, schools, railroads, bridges, orchards, etc., are already established.

The following is a list of the Counties in which these lands are located, as also the number of acres in each, and price per acre:

| Counties. | Acres. | Price per Acre. |
|---|---|---|
| Adams | 10,000 | $ 2.00 to $ 7.00 |
| Clay | 5,000 | 4.00 to 8.00 |
| Cass | 25,000 | 7.00 to 10.00 |
| Franklin | 50,000 | 2.00 to 5.00 |
| Fillmore | 5,000 | 5.00 to 9.00 |
| Gage | 9,000 | 5.00 to 8.00 |
| Hamilton | 8,000 | 4.00 to 7.00 |
| Jefferson | 5,000 | 5.00 to 8.00 |
| Kearney | 10,000 | 2.00 to 6.00 |
| Lancaster | 75,000 | 4.00 to 10.00 |
| Otoe | 10,000 | 6.00 to 10.00 |
| Saline | 40,000 | 4.00 to 10.00 |
| Seward | 40,000 | 5.00 to 10.00 |
| Saunders | 10,000 | 3.00 to 7.00 |
| Webster | 10,000 | 2.00 to 5.00 |
| York | 30,000 | 4.00 to 8.00 |

The North Platte lands, comprising over 650,000 acres, well

adapted to farming and stock purposes, are located in the following Counties, with the amount in each and price:

| Counties. | Acres. | Price per Acre. |
|---|---|---|
| Antelope | 90,000 | $1.50 to $6.00 |
| Boone | 150,000 | 2.00 to 6.00 |
| Cedar | 12,000 | 1.25 to 6.00 |
| Dixon | 12,000 | 1.25 to 6.00 |
| Dakota | 5,000 | 1.25 to 6.00 |
| Greeley | 130,000 | 1.00 to 5.00 |
| Howard | 40,000 | 2.00 to 4.00 |
| Madison | 60,000 | 2.00 to 6.00 |
| Platte | 10,000 | 1.25 to 6.00 |
| Pierce | 13,000 | 1.25 to 6.00 |
| Sherman | 80,000 | 1.00 to 5.00 |
| Valley | 120,000 | 1.00 to 5.00 |
| Wayne | 20,000 | 1.25 to 6.00 |

The B. & M. land sales during the year 1878, were 511,609 acres, for which they realized $2,616,870; or, in other words, their land sales for 1878 averaged about 42,000 acres per month, at an average price of $5.11 per acre. These lands were sold to 4,000 purchasers, who are rapidly improving them.

The land grants to other railroads in the State are very small compared to the grants made to the Union Pacific and the Burlington & Missouri roads. These lands are located mostly in the northeastern and southeastern portions of the State, and are now nearly all sold, the unsold being in the market at prices corresponding with other railroad land of those sections.

The lands of the Pawnee Reserve—now embraced by Nance County—which contained 288,000 acres, have been appraised for sale, and are now on the market at from $2.50 to $10.00 per acre. The terms of sale are one-third down and the balance in two deferred payments.

The west half of the Otoe Reserve, in the southeastern part of the State, has also been appraised for sale, and is now open to buyers, at prices ranging from $2.50 to $10.00 per acre, the terms of sale being the same as in the Pawnee lands.

The Indian reserve lands in the State amount in the aggregate to several hundred thousand acres, all of which is admirably adapted to farm and stock purposes.

A large per cent. of the wild lands in the eastern and older settled Counties of the State, is owned by speculators and non-residents, who hold it merely for speculative purposes. Owing to the stringency of the times, however, much of this land has been forced upon the market within the past few years, and may be purchased at from $4.00 to $12.00 per acre, the price varying according to location, quality of the soil and general surroundings.

### GOVERNMENT LANDS.

To the immigrant and all those seeking homes in the West, Nebraska undoubtedly offers the most inviting field for the location of homestead, pre-emption and timber culture claims, it having the largest acreage of desirable Government lands now untaken of any State or Territory in the Union, the amount being estimated in round numbers, at 24,000,000 acres.

The NORTH PLATTE Land Office, in Lincoln County, having jurisdiction over the Counties of Lincoln, Cheyenne, Keith, Dawson, Chase, Dundy, Hitchcock, and portions of Buffalo, Phelps, Gosper and Frontier, also a large portion of unorganized territory of the State, has upwards of 20,000,000 acres yet unclaimed and subject to entry under the homestead, pre-emption and timber culture laws.

The NIOBRARA Land Office, at Niobrara, in Knox County, has about 900,000 acres within its jurisdiction subject to entry, which are located mainly in the northeastern portion of the State.

The NORFOLK Land Office, at Norfolk, in Madison County, has some 500,000 acres within its jurisdiction yet unclaimed, which are located chiefly in the Counties of Madison, Stanton, Antelope, Pierce, Boone and Wheeler.

The GRAND ISLAND Land Office, at Grand Island, Hall County, has upwards of 1,000,000 acres of Government land yet unclaimed, which is situated mostly in the Counties of Hall, Howard, Merrick, Platte, Wheeler, Greeley, Valley, Custer, Sherman, Buffalo and Dawson.

The BLOOMINGTON Land Office, at Bloomington, Franklin County, having jurisdiction over Government land in the southwestern part of the State, has about 1,000,000 acres yet of unclaimed land.

The LINCOLN and BEATRICE Land Offices have disposed of nearly all the desirable land under their jurisdiction.

## THE HOMESTEAD LAW.

Under the provisions of the Homestead Law every person who is the head of a family, or who has arrived at the age of twenty-one years, and is a citizen of the United States, or who has filed his declaration to become such; any soldier or sailor who served ninety days, or upwards in the Union army during the war of the Rebellion, and the widow or orphan children of any soldier or sailor is entitled to 160 acres of unappropriated public lands anywhere outside of the limits of a railroad land grant. Soldiers and sailors of the Union Army, or their widows and orphan children, however, are entitled to a full quarter section within the limits of a railroad land grant, all other parties being entitled to only eighty acres therein. Six months' time is allowed from the date of filing a homestead claim in which to begin actual settlement; and five years' continuous occupation and improvement of a homestead entitles the claimant to a patent therefor. Soldiers and sailors of the late war may have the period of their service in the army or navy deducted from the five years' occupation required to perfect title; but no patent will be issued to any homestead settler who has not resided upon, improved and cultivated his homestead for a period of at least one year from the date of beginning said improvements.

## THE PRE-EMPTION RIGHT.

Any person entitled to the benefits of the homestead law, may pre-empt any number of acres, not exceeding 160, except such as already own 320 acres, or have abandoned a residence on lands of their own in the same State or Territory where they seek to make such pre-emption. Actual settlement must be made on lands pre-empted within sixty days from the date of filing the claim, and a patent may be secured for the same at the expiration of thirty months from the time of filing, on payment of $1.25 per acre, where the land is located outside the limits of a railroad land grant, and $2.50 per acre where it is within said limits.

## THE TIMBER CULTURE LAW.

Under this law, any homesteader, pre-empter, or any citizen of the United States may file a claim upon 160 acres, or less, for the purpose of timber culture. The ratio area required to be broken, planted, etc., under the amended law of 1878, is one-sixteenth of the land embraced in the entry. The party making an entry of 160 acres is required to break or plow five acres of the same, during the first year, and five acres in addition during the second year. The five acres broken or plowed during the first year he is required to cultivate by raising a crop or otherwise, during the second year, and to plant in timber, seeds or cuttings, during the third year. The five acres broken or plowed during the second year, he is required to cultivate by raising a crop or otherwise, during the third year, and to plant in timber, seeds or cuttings, during the fourth year.

Entries of less than 160 acres are required to be broken or plowed, cultivated and planted, in trees, during the same periods, and to the same extent, in proportion to their total areas, as for entries of a quarter section. At the expiration of eight years from the date of filing a patent may be secured for the land embraced in the entry. Not more than 160 acres in any one section can be entered as a timber claim. No residence upon the land is required.

# CHAPTER VI.

## RAILROADS.

### AMERICAN RAILWAYS.

The American Railway System is the marvel of the age, and the most significant expression of American enterprise. To epitomize the subject, it is like the arterial currents of the human body, and no less important for the development of commercial life, than the blood for the complete growth of man. From an abstract theorem it has become the complex machinery that weaves all interests and productions into a commercial and social web. It may be termed the revolutionary agency of the Nineteenth Century, and yet, the strongest conservative power in the nation.

To trace the history of the railway system from the first crude experiment to the completed lines now in operation, extending a distance of eighty-two thousand, nine hundred and sixty-eight miles in every section of this country, would require immense labor and research, hence, for the purpose of this Chapter, to generalize the subject will afford greater interest, leaving the more specific and detailed aspect of the subject, to be referred to under the heads of particular railways.

Although steam as a motive power had been discovered and used in propelling vessels, and although in 1784 the first locomotive engine was patented by Watts, the first railway was not constructed until 1825, extending from Stockton to Darlington, and operated with a stationary engine. Four years after the opening of the Stockton and Darlington road, George Stephenson built a locomotive called the "Rocket," and in 1829 it dashed along the track of the Liverpool and Manchester road at the rate of *twelve* miles an hour.

The first American locomotive was built by the Kimble engineers in New York, in 1830, and was used upon the South Carolina Railway, which, in 1833, was the longest road in the world, extending a distance of 136 miles.

In 1830 the Mohawk and Hudson Railway was commenced, and in 1831 the construction of the Harlem road and the Camden and Amboy road began.

The Baltimore and Ohio road was the first passenger railway projected in this country, and up to the fall of 1831 was operated by horse-power. In that year it was completed sixty-one miles, and operated with an engine of American make. At the present time —1879—it operates a line of 1,489 miles and notwithstanding it had to construct thirteen tunnels—one of which is one mile in length, in passing the Cumberland Mountains—its cost per mile has been less than any other road in the United States, having a uniform gauge.

In 1830, a little less than fifty years ago, there was only twenty-three miles of railway in this country, which was increased to 1,273 miles in 1836, and to 4,026 miles in 1842. From 1842 to 1849 the increase per annum was a little over three hundred miles. Since that date, however, the increase has been about 2,050 miles per annum.

The following statement shows the total miles of road operated with the annual increase, from 1830 to 1879, commencing with twenty-three miles, and ending on the 31st of July, 1879, with 82,968 miles:

| YEAR. | Miles in operation | Annual increase of miles. | YEAR. | Miles in operation | Annual increase of miles. | YEAR. | Miles in operation | Annual increase of miles. |
|---|---|---|---|---|---|---|---|---|
| 1830 | 23 | ........ | 1846 | 4930 | 297 | 1862 | 32120 | 884 |
| 1831 | 95 | 72 | 1847 | 5598 | 668 | 1863 | 33170 | 1050 |
| 1832 | 229 | 134 | 1848 | 5996 | 398 | 1864 | 33908 | 738 |
| 1833 | 380 | 151 | 1849 | 7365 | 1369 | 1865 | 35085 | 1177 |
| 1834 | 633 | 253 | 1850 | 9021 | 1656 | 1866 | 36801 | 1742 |
| 1835 | 1098 | 465 | 1851 | 10982 | 1961 | 1867 | 39250 | 2449 |
| 1836 | 1273 | 175 | 1852 | 12908 | 1926 | 1868 | 42229 | 2979 |
| 1837 | 1497 | 224 | 1853 | 15360 | 2452 | 1869 | 46544 | 4315 |
| 1838 | 1913 | 416 | 1854 | 16720 | 1360 | 1870 | 52914 | 6070 |
| 1839 | 2302 | 389 | 1855 | 18374 | 1654 | 1871 | 60283 | 7379 |
| 1840 | 2818 | 516 | 1856 | 22016 | 3647 | 1872 | 66171 | 5878 |
| 1841 | 3535 | 717 | 1857 | 24503 | 2647 | 1873 | 70278 | 4107 |
| 1842 | 4026 | 491 | 1858 | 26968 | 2465 | 1874 | 72383 | 2105 |
| 1843 | 4185 | 159 | 1859 | 28789 | 1821 | 1875 | 74098 | 1712 |
| 1844 | 4377 | 192 | 1860 | 30635 | 1846 | 1876 | 76808 | 2712 |
| 1845 | 4633 | 256 | 1861 | 31286 | 651 | 1877 | 79147 | 2339 |
|  |  |  |  |  |  | 1878 | 81841 | 2694 |
| Total number of miles on July 30th 1879............ | | | | | | | 82968 | 1127 |

The following statement shows the number of miles of railway operated from 1871 to 1879, their capital and funded debt, gross earnings, and net earnings:

| YEAR. | MILES OPERATED. | CAPITAL AND FUNDED DEBT. | GROSS EARNINGS. | NET EARNINGS. |
|---|---|---|---|---|
| 1878 | 81,841 | $4,580,048,793 | $490,103,361 | $187,515,177 |
| 1877 | 79,147 | 4,568,597,248 | 472,909,272 | 170,976,697 |
| 1876 | 76,808 | 4,468,591,935 | 497,257,959 | 186,452,752 |
| 1875 | 74,094 | 4,415,631,630 | 503,065,505 | 185,506,438 |
| 1874 | 72,383 | 4,221,763,594 | 520,466,016 | 189,570,958 |
| 1873 | 70,278 | 3,784,543,034 | 526,419,935 | 183,810,562 |
| 1872 | 66,171 | 3,159,423,057 | 465,241,055 | 165,764,373 |
| 1871 | 60,283 | 2,664,627,645 | 403,329,208 | 141,746,404 |

The following table shows the marvelous development of the railway system in the States and Territories named, taken in periods of ten years, commencing in 1841, and ending July 31st, 1879.

| STATES & TERRITORIES. | 1841. | 1851. | 1861. | 1871. | 1879. |
|---|---|---|---|---|---|
| *New England States.* | | | | | |
| Maine | 11 | 293 | 472 | 871 | 989 |
| Vermont | | 413 | 562 | 675 | 873 |
| Massachusetts | 373 | 1,088 | 1,264 | 1,606 | 1,872 |
| Rhode Island | 50 | 68 | 108 | 136 | 208 |
| Connecticut | 102 | 451 | 630 | 820 | 922 |
| New Hampshire | 53 | 537 | 661 | 790 | 10,18½ |
| *Middle States.* | | | | | |
| New York | 538 | 1,623 | 2,700 | 4,470 | 5,884½ |
| New Jersey | 186 | 303 | 587 | 1,265 | 1,663 |
| Pennsylvania | 74 | 1,297 | 2,802 | 5,113 | 6,023¼ |
| Delaware | 39 | 39 | 127 | 227 | 280 |
| Maryland | 259 | 274 | 386 | 820 | 962 |
| West Virginia | 61 | 159 | 361 | 480 | 669 |
| Ohio | 36 | 588 | 2,974 | 3,740 | 5,180 |
| Indiana | | 558 | 2,175 | 3,529 | 4,234½ |
| Michigan | 138 | 379 | 810 | 2.235 | 3,621 |
| *Southern States.* | | | | | |
| Virginia | 223 | 520 | 1,379 | 1,490 | 1,646 |
| North Carolina | 87 | 283 | 937 | 1,190 | 1,445 |
| South Carolina | 204 | 378 | 973 | 1,201 | 1,419 |
| Georgia | 271 | 795 | 1,420 | 2,108 | 2,428 |
| Florida | | 21 | 402 | 466 | 487 |

| STATES & TERRITORIES. | 1841. | 1851. | 1861. | 1871. | 1879. |
|---|---|---|---|---|---|
| *Southern States—Contin'd.* | | | | | |
| Alabama | 46 | 183 | 743 | 1,671 | 1,839 |
| Mississippi | 14 | 75 | 862 | 990 | 1,126 |
| Louisiana | 40 | 80 | 335 | 539 | 500 |
| Texas | | | 392 | 865 | 2,502 |
| Kentucky | 28 | 44 | 549 | 1,123 | 1,600 |
| Tennessee | | 112 | 1,253 | 1,520 | 1,681 |
| Arkansas | | | 38 | 258 | 786 |
| *Western States.* | | | | | |
| Illinois | 22 | 271 | 2,917 | 5,904 | 7,506 |
| Wisconsin | | 50 | 933 | 1,725 | 2,850 |
| Minnesota | | | | 1,612 | 2,536½ |
| Iowa | | | 701 | 3,160 | 4,324 |
| Kansas | | | | 1,760 | 2,513 |
| Nebraska | | | | 1,129 | 1,384½ |
| Missouri | | | 838 | 2,580 | 3,420 |
| Colorado | | | | 392 | 1,215 |
| *Pacific States & Territories.* | | | | | |
| California | | | 23 | 208 | 2,149 |
| Oregon | | | | 248 | 283 |
| Nevada | | | | 627 | 627 |
| Washington | | | | 197 | 212 |
| Dakota | | | 62 | 290 | 320 |
| Wyoming | | | | 465 | 472 |
| Utah | | | | 506 | 580 |
| Arizona | | | | | 152 |
| Idaho | | | | | 127 |
| New Mexico | | | | | 124 |
| Indian Territory | | | | 275 | 275 |
| GRAND TOTAL | 3,538 | 10,982 | 31,286 | 60,283 | 82,968 |

That all of this stupendous work has been accomplished in less than fifty years at an expenditure on an average of $43,476 per mile, swelling the grand total outlay to something over four billion dollars, must convince the world, that the American railway system is indeed the marvel of the age, and excels that of the remainder of the world combined, both in the number of miles of road in operation, as also in the general equipment.

In the four billions mentioned above, no account is made of what is known as "watered stock," nor fictitious valuations, but is approximately as close to the actual cost of all our railway lines as can be obtained, after the most rigid investigation.

The average dividends of roads for a series of years were nearly as follows: New England roads, 6 21-100 per cent.; roads in the Middle States, 5 71-100 per cent.; Pacific States, 3 92-100, and Southern States 50-100 per cent. Thus it will be seen, through the magnificent railway system of our country, in less than fifty years the great problem of transportation has been solved, and the distance across the continent has been abridged in time from three months to six days, and a territory more extensive than all civilized Europe has been opened up to cultivation and to the arts and sciences of a vigorous life. It is the American railway system that has brought under successful husbandry over 4,627,860 square miles of fertile lands which are now exclusively devoted to the production of corn, and 15,9436,40 square miles of wheat fields. This only in part shows the magnitude of the result, and affords a satisfactory estimate of the value of roads, even if every dollar of their original cost were a total loss to the stockholders.

From the most reliable returns, we find that the product of grain in the western states for 1840 was about 100,000,000 bushels. In 1850 this product was increased to 250,000,000 bushels, in 1875 to 1.250,000,000, in 1877 to 1,400,000,000, and in 1879 to 1,600,-000,000, while the future, under the large flow of immigration to the fruitful fields of the west, warrants the prediction that the increase in productions for the next decade, will largely exceed that of the past ten years.

Before the construction of railways it cost 20 cents per ton per mile to transport grain, which absorbed the full value of corn at a distance of 125 miles, while wheat would bear transportation only 250 miles. Hence the area of a corn producing circle being 49,087 square miles, determined the limited extent of territory that could be profitably cultivated. What a change! We now see over 40,000 miles of railways traversing the Western and Middle States, and the rates of transportation such as to enable the producer to ship his cereal crop a distance of from 1,000 to 4,000 miles to the Atlantic seaboard, leaving him a fair compensation for the products of his fields. Nor is this the only benefit derived from railways. They bring to the very door of the western farmer, at a nominal cost, all the manufactured articles of the east, supplying his want of agricultural implements and his domestic comforts with all he may need or require. Those who have given this subject a careful and exhaustive study, estimate the actual benefit of railways to the the country at not less than $90,000 to each mile of road in operation. Yet, in the face of all these facts, notwithstanding the reduction in transportation, from 20 cents per ton per mile to one cent per ton, there is ample room for a still further reduction and yet leave the railways a comparatively larger margin for their services than is realized by the producer for his products. Hence, while urging the great benefits that flow directly from our system of railways, and which has given a new birth to the commerce of this country during the past forty years, there is much to be written relative to their mismanagement. This opens a wide field for suggestion and criticism, which it would be entirely vain to attempt to traverse in these pages. Eminent publicists and statesmen have given much time and study to the general management of railroads, and while some are advocates of consolidating the management of long lines, others can only see monopoly and extortion in such a policy.

The real remedy, however, can only be reached through a healthy competition. That inevitable law of supply and demand which regulates commercial values throughout the world, will in time regulate railway transportation, and cure whatever extortion and abuses there may exist in the present system. For it must be conceded that when railways are operated with the same honesty, prudence and economy which characterize the management of private business affairs, and the integrity that is demanded in mercantile circles, there will be less to complain of on the part of the public, and stockholders would receive larger dividends.

The future of our railway system is what now engages public attention, and the revival of the work of railway building, which a few years ago was almost at a standstill, is a matter of universal comment throughout the nation. The country having safely emerged from all financial dangers, the contemplated Southern and Northern routes to the Pacific, a considerable portion of both of which lines are now in operation, and the full completion of which the commercial prosperity of the country imperatively demands, will in all probability be rapidly pushed forward.

Then the vast trade this country enjoyed with China and Japan previous to the rebellion, through a healthy competition in transportation to and from the Pacific Coast, will be retrieved and advanced to an importance that will make the cities of the Pacific the rivals of the great cities upon the Atlantic. And to our progressive railway system, with all its magnificent equipment, and grand lines of steel rail, the means will be secured to reconstruct and rebuild our commercial marine until it shall again whiten every sea, and trade in every port in the world.

Having said this much upon railways in general, it seems eminently proper to devote a chapter to a review of some of the more prominent lines of the country, and to that end the Nebraska lines will claim our attention.

## CHAPTER VII.

### RAILWAYS IN NEBRASKA.

UNION PACIFIC—OMAHA & REPUBLICAN VALLEY—UTAH & NORTHERN—COLORADO DIVISION—ST. JOE & DENVER CITY—BURLINGTON & MISSOURI RIVER IN NEBRASKA—THE NEBRASKA RAILWAY—OMAHA & SOUTHWESTERN—OMAHA & NORTHERN NEBRASKA—SIOUX CITY & PACIFIC—FREMONT, ELKHORN & MISSOURI VALLEY—ATCHISON & NEBRASKA—COVINGTON, COLUMBUS & BLACK HILLS.

On the 31st of July, 1879, there were in operation in the State of Nebraska one thousand, four hundred and seventy-nine miles of railway, all of which has been constructed since the spring of 1865. Although not in reality one of the railways of the State, the Chicago & Northwestern was the first line from the East to salute the people of Omaha with the screech of the engine whistle, the first train on that road entering the city on Sunday, January 17th, 1867. The Missouri River was crossed on a pile bridge, which, for several years, was used during the winter months for crossing the river, it being removed during the months of navigation, and a ferryboat employed in its place, to transfer passengers and freight.

The second road to reach the State was the St. Joe & Council Bluffs line, now known as the Kansas City, St. Joe & Council Bluffs road. The Burlington & Missouri, or the Chicago, Burlington & Quincy, was completed to the city of Omaha in 1868. The first road built on Nebraska soil was the eastern portion of the Union Pacific, the first fifty miles of which was completed on the first day of January, 1866. The Omaha & Northwestern was built to Herman, a distance of forty miles, in October, 1871, and during the same year the Omaha & Southwestern was completed to the Platte River. But as each of these lines, as also all other lines in operation in the State, will be reviewed at length in another portion of this Chapter, the reader's attention is now called to the

## UNION PACIFIC RAILWAY.

That popular and important transportation route which spans that fertile portion of the great west lying between the Missouri River and the Rocky Mountains, connecting with the Central Pacific midway between Omaha and the Pacific coast, was the first railway enterprise commenced in Nebraska; and while its early history abounds with incidents of deep interest to the people of the State, to the general reader a careful and impartial review of its present and prospective advantages to the State, as also to the whole country, will prove of much greater value.

Although the project of building a railway to the Pacific Coast was agitated in railroad circles and among prominent men of the nation, as far back as 1846, the enterprise assumed nothing like a definite shape until 1853, when a commission was appointed by the government to investigate the practicability of the undertaking, and after discharging the duties of the appointment, by reporting favorably, Congress, in 1862, passed an act authorizing the construction of a trunk line from the one hundredth meridian, a point some two hundred miles west of Omaha, to San Francisco. The act provided for a trunk line and two branches, the one to start from some central point on the western boundary of Iowa, the second from Sioux City, in the same State, and the third from the western boundary of Missouri, all to connect at the point of location, on the one hundredth meridian. In 1863, however, the Act was modified, by changing the Sioux City and Missouri branches, and empowering the President of the United States to designate the point where the eastern terminal should be located. On the 17th of November, 1863, after a careful consideration of the subject, President Lincoln decided the question as follows:

"At a point on the western boundary of Iowa, opposite section ten, in township fifteen, north of range thirteen, east of the sixth principal meridian in the Territory of Nebraska,"

The Act authorizing the construction of the road, provided that the branch reaching the one hundredth meridian first, should build the remainder of the line west. The Act also authorized a land donation of 13,875,200 acres to be located on each side of the line. Subsequent legislation also provided a subsidy to aid in building the line, to the extent of $16,000 per mile between the Missouri River and the base of the Rocky Mountains; $48,000 per mile for one hundred and fifty miles across the Rocky Mountains; $32,000 per mile for the distance between the Rocky and Sierra Nevada Range, and $48,000 per mile for one hundred and fifty miles over the Sierra Nevadas.

The stimulating effect of such a liberal offer on the part of the General Government, resulted in the organization of a company for carrying out the stupendous enterprise, and on the afternoon of December 3d, 1863, amid great enthusiasm, and in the presence of a large gathering of people from Omaha and Council Bluffs, the great undertaking was formally dedicated, as it were, by "breaking gound" on the west bank of the river near the old telegraph crossing, with all the pomp and ceremony that the importance of the event demanded.

After invoking a divine blessing for the success of the enterprise, Governor Saunders stepped forward, grasped a spade, and amid the thunder of artillery and the deafening cheers of the enthusiastic assembly, removed the first spadefull of earth. Such was the birth scene of the greatest and, in many respects, the most important railway project ever conceived by man. Ground having been formally broken, the interesting ceremony closed with addresses of a most eloquent and enthusiastic character, from Governor Saunders, George Francis Train, Mayor Kennedy, A. J. Poppleton, Dr. C. C. Monell, A. V. Larimer and others.

Early in the spring of 1864 the work of grading the road bed commenced, on a line running due west from the City of Omaha, which line, after having expended on it nearly or quite one hundred thousand dollars, proving too heavy to allow a completion to the one hundredth meridian, in time to comply with the terms of the charter, was abandoned.

One might suppose that such a disastrous beginning would have disheartened the projectors. Such was not the case, however, as all echoed the words of "Jacob Faithful," "Better luck next time." Two new lines were immediately surveyed, the first running in a northwesterly course from Omaha, while the second started from a point at or near Bellevue, on the Missouri River, and ran a northwesterly course. This last line, owing to some of its beautiful windings, was called the "Ox Bow," yet its apparent innocence of ever having been subjected to the surveyor's art, and the violent opposition it encountered from the people of Omaha, who had their fears aroused at the danger to Omaha of locating the eastern terminus of the line at Bellevue, did not prevent its being chosen by the company. The people of Omaha, however, were equal to the emergency, and by a donation of $250,000 secured the coveted prize, which, in 1876. was wrested from them, through a decision of the United States Supreme Court, which awarded the eastern terminal of the line to Iowa, in accordance to the location made by President Lincoln.

The "Ox Bow" route having been harmoniously adopted, grading was pushed forward with great vigor, while track laying followed as fast as the road bed was finished. Every twenty miles completed was inspected by commissioners appointed for that purpose, and on the 1st day of January, 1866, the first fifty miles was completed and in operation. The line was extended during the year 1866, two hundred and sixty miles, and in 1867 an additional two hundred and forty miles was built, while from January 1st, 1868, to May 10th, 1869, the remainder of the line—five hundred and fifty-five miles—was completed and in operation.

Thus it will be seen that the great work was finished in just three years, six months and ten days from the time it was commenced. Some of the most rapid track laying in railway history was done on this line, the average being often as high as five miles per day. The ties used on the road between Omaha and the Platte Valley were chiefly from the Missouri River bottoms, and were mostly cottonwood. They were, however, subjected to the "charring" process, which rendered them very durable. The ties and timber for the remainder of the line were of hardwood, and were procured chiefly from Michigan and other distant sections of country, and the cost was often as high as $2.50 per tie, when delivered at Omaha.

There being no rail communication between Omaha and Des Moines, at that time, nearly all of the material used in building the Union Pacific road, had to be transported either up the Missouri River by steamers, or from Des Moines by teams, a distance of one hundred and fifty miles. Even the seventy horse-power engine employed in the railroad shops at Omaha, was hauled on wagons from Des Moines. And in this connection it may be stated that the Company commenced building their extensive machine shops during the latter part of 1864, and they were fully completed during the fall of 1865. These shops include a dozen or more of large, substantial brick buildings, and their importance to Omaha will be readily appreciated when it is stated that they furnish employment to some eight hundred persons. Besides which the Company, in its various other departments at Omaha, employ some five hundred men.

The books of the Company show that there was used in the construction of the Union Pacific road, 300,000 tons of rail; 1,700,000 fish plates, 6,800,000 bolts, 23,505,500 spikes, and 6,126,375 ties. Within the past three or four years the road bed has been well ballasted, hence, at the present time it will compare favorably with the better class of roads at the East.

As before stated, the line was completed to Ogden, on the 10th of May, 1869, the event being observed in Omaha by a grand celebration. It was a general gala-day for everybody, and from early dawn until late at night enthusiasm ruled the hour. The city was dressed in an old-fashioned Fourth of July costume; flags, banners, festoons, and mottos decorated the town from end to end. Telegraphic communication was had with Promontory, where the "golden spike" which united the two great ribs of steel, was being driven into that highly finished tie of laurel wood, with a silver hammer; and when the last blow was given to that spike of precious metal, the instrument on Capitol Hill said, "IT IS FINISHED!" and one hundred guns in thunder tones echoed the glad news, "IT IS FINISHED!" Yes, the stupendous work of uniting the two great oceans of this Continent with bands of steel was finished, and the glad tidings was not confined to Omaha, but was wafted o'er hill and dale, to city, village and hamlet, throughout the Union.

The afternoon of the 10th of May, after the reception of the news that the last spike had been driven, was devoted to processions, street parades, speech making and a general hour of rejoicing. Even the shades of evening did not check the enthusiasm, for as the twilight deepened into darkness, the city was most brilliantly illuminated, while the liberal display of pyrotechnics lent the scene a beauty and grandeur never before witnessed in the West.

UNION PACIFIC RAILROAD BRIDGE.

The iron bridge spanning the Missouri River at Omaha was not commenced until the early part of 1869, or about the time the Union Pacific road was completed, although an Act had been passed by Congress in 1866, authorizing the work at or near Omaha. When the question was finally taken under consideration, a division of opinion arose as to the most advantageous point of crossing the river. A majority of the Company favored a crossing at "Child's Mill," some four miles below Omaha. Here was a new danger to the interests of the city, to ward off which, and secure the bridge, a second quarter of a million dollars was donated towards its construction by the city. This last donation was made in consideration that the main transfer depots, machine shops and general offices of the Company should be located at Omaha.

In September, 1868, the Boomer Bridge Company, of Chicago, secured the contract of building the bridge for $1,089,500, the time of its completion to be November 10th 1869. They were greatly delayed in the work, however, and did not get the first cylinder ready for sinking until March, 1869; and in July of that year their contract with the U. P. Company was annulled, the latter Company taking hold of the work and completing the bridge on the 25th of March, 1873.

The bridge is composed entirely of iron, and is two thousand seven hundred and fifty feet in length, fifty feet above high water mark, and consists of eleven spans of two hundred and fifty feet each. The superstructure is supported by one stone masonry abutment and eleven piers, each pier being formed of two iron pneumatic tubes, eight feet six inches in diameter, and sunk in sections of ten feet each to the solid rock in the bed of the river, then filled with stone and cement. The least time in which a column was sunk to bed rock from the commencement of the process was seven days. The greatest depth below low water mark reached by any column at bed rock was eighty-two feet. About five hundred men were constantly employed in the construction of the bridge, and ten steam engines were used in hoisting material, driving piles, etc. The bridge is approached from the Iowa side by a grade about one and a half miles long, thirty-five feet rise to the mile, and on the Nebraska side there is a trestle work, now filled in with earth, about fifty feet in height and seven hundred feet long. The Company claims that the bridge cost $2,500,000.

At an early hour on the morning of August 25th, 1877, two spans at the eastern terminus of this great bridge were carried away by a tornado and entirely destroyed. As the tornado struck the bridge it lifted the massive superstructure from the piers, strewing the span which had rested on the Iowa shore along the embankment, while the other was carried into the deep water of the river. The piers were uninjured. A temporary Howe truss bridge was erected immediately after the catastrophe, and before the close of 1877 the iron spans were replaced.

The Union Pacific Railroad, in 1879, owned and operated the following lines:

Union Pacific, main line, from Omaha to Ogden.... 1033 miles.
Omaha & Republican Valley road, from Valley to Osceola................................................. 85 "

| | |
|---|---|
| Utah Northern, from Ogden to Beaver Canon...... | 274 miles. |
| Colorado Division, from Cheyenne to Denver...... | 138 " |
| Colorado Division Narrow Guage, from Golden to Central City................................... | 23 " |
| Colorado Division Narrow Gauge, from Forks of Clear Creek to Georgetown..................... | 24 " |
| St. Joseph & Denver City, from St. Joseph to Grand Island......................................... | 292 " |
| ............................................... | 1869 |

Their contemplated lines include the following:

| | |
|---|---|
| Jackson to Norfolk (now building)................. | 47 miles. |
| Jackson to Osceola............................... | 18 " |
| Jackson to Albion................................ | 45 " |
| Grand Island to St. Paul.......................... | 22 " |
| Valparaiso, Neb., to Marysville, Kansas........... | 100 " |
| Total........................................... | 232 |
| Grand Total.................................... | 2101 |

### THE OMAHA & REPUBLICAN VALLEY RAILWAY,

A branch of the Union Pacific, extending from Valley Station, on the Union Pacific, to Osceola, the County Seat of Polk County, eighty-five miles, was commenced in 1876 and completed to its present terminal point in 1879. It traverses Saunders, Butler and Polk Counties, Wahoo, David City and Osceola being the chief towns on its line. It enters Saunders County at the northeast corner and leaves it at or near the extreme southwest corner, from whence it bends quite abruptly to the north until David City is reached, when it again turns to the southwest to Osceola, describing in its course the letter S. It is a most important transportation route for that section of the State, and when completed further up the Republican Valley it will assume still greater importance.

### THE UTAH & NORTHERN

Is another branch of the Union Pacific road. This branch has a three feet gauge, extends from Ogden to Beaver Cannon, Idaho, 274 miles, and is being pushed rapidly northward. Its objective terminal point to the north is Helena, Montana. Although traversing a thinly populated portion of the West, its net earnings during the past three or four years has been from $60,000 to $220,000.

### THE COLORADO DIVISION,

(Commonly known as the Colorado Central Railway), another limb of the mammoth Union Pacific body, extends from Cheyenne, Wyoming, to Denver, Colorado, a distance of 138 miles. This is a most important transportation route to the mineral portions of the country to the south and west, and is as profitable in a financial aspect as it is convenient to travel and commerce.

The Narrow Gauge, from Golden to Central City, a distance of twenty-three miles, also the Narrow Gauge from the forks of Clear Creek to Georgetown, twenty-four miles, are also branches of the Union Pacific. This is the most direct route to Leadville, and for the past six months its traffic in both travel and freight has been very large.

### THE ST. JOSEPH & DENVER CITY RAILWAY,

Extending from St. Joseph, Missouri, to Grand Island, Nebraska, came under the control of the Union Pacific in the Spring of 1879, and is now their prominent outlet to St. Louis, and other points to the southeast.

The St. Joseph and Denver road was chartered by the legislature of Kansas, February 17th, 1857, by the title of the Marysville, Palmetto & Roseport Railroad Company, with authority to build a line from either of the above named places to a connection with the Hannibal & St. Joseph Railroad, at or near Roseport. The corporate name was changed to St. Joseph & Denver City Railroad, April 17th, 1862. The authority to build a road from the Nebraska State line to Fort Kearney was obtained under the general law of Nebraska, on the 11th of August, 1866. The Northern Kansas Railroad Company was consolidated with this Company, and the right to lands granted by Act of Congress, July 23d, 1866, of one million, seven hundred thousand acres, was thereby obtained. The capital stock was also increased to $10,000,000. Subscriptions from municipal corporations to the amount of $1,025,000, and from individuals to the extent of $1,400 were secured in aid of building the road. On these subscriptions work was commenced, and eighty miles of the line was completed and in operation in October, 1870, at a cost of about $1,500,000. In 1871 the line was extended forty-eight miles, and on the following year it was completed to Hastings, its western terminus, when it passed into the hands of the Union Pacific, who extended it to Grand Island on their line of road during the summer of 1879. The total cost of the line from St. Joseph to Hastings, was $5,449,620.77, of which stockholders paid $1,400; $782,727.10 from State and municipal aid, and the remainder $4,665,493.67 from the proceeds of mortgage bonds. In 1874 the road passed into the hands of a Receiver, who operated it until the 29th of March, 1877, when it was re-organized under its present title. While in the hands of the Receiver the road was sold under foreclosure, and that portion in Kansas was re-organized under the name of the St. Joseph & Pacific, and that part in Nebraska, as the Kansas & Nebraska Railroad.

The gross earnings, operating expenses and net earnings of the U. P. road, per mile, for the years named, were:

| Year. | Gross Earnings. | Operating Expenses. | Net Earnings. | Proportion of Expenses. |
|---|---|---|---|---|
| 1870 | $ 736,386 | $ 451,706 | $ 284,680 | 61.34 per ct. |
| 1871 | 726,381 | 344,713 | 378,668 | 48.87 " |
| 1872 | 858,774 | 463,599 | 395,175 | 53.98 " |
| 1873 | 991,415 | 480,353 | 511,062 | 48.46 " |
| 1874 | 1,019,785 | 468,827 | 509,580 | 45.97 " |
| 1875 | 1,158,264 | 481,225 | 677,139 | 41.54 " |
| 1876 | 1,244,506 | 508,760 | 735,746 | 40.88 " |

The net earnings more than doubled during the first six years that the line was operated, and nearly doubled during the past six years.

Statement of operations, yearly, for seven years:

| Year. | Total Gross Earnings. | Operating Expenses. | Net Earnings. |
|---|---|---|---|
| 1870 | $ 7,625,277.11 | $ 4,667,414.84 | $ 2,947,862.27 |
| 1871 | 7,521,682.16 | 3,600,566.86 | 3,921,115.30 |
| 1872 | 8,892,605.53 | 4,800,573.48 | 4,092,032.05 |
| 1873 | 10,266,103.66 | 4,974,861.02 | 5,291,242.64 |
| 1874 | 10,559,880.12 | 4,854,703.87 | 5,705,176.25 |
| 1875 | 11,993,832.09 | 4,982,047.95 | 7,011,784.14 |
| 1876 | 12,886,858.84 | 5,268,211.20 | 7,618,211.29 |

The following is a comparative statement of passenger and freight earnings, including Omaha bridge:

|  | 1877. | 1878. | Increase. | Decrease. |
|---|---|---|---|---|
| Passenger earnings... | $3,672,173.47 | $3,190,369.72 | .......... | $492,100.52 |
| Freight earnings...... | 7,995,813.00 | 8,500,955.76 | $572,935.94 | .......... |

The equipment of the road in 1879 was as follows:

Locomotives, 172; snow plows, 17; passenger coaches, first class, 15; second class, 19; emigrant, 63; sleepers, 27; mail, 9; express, 9; baggage, 11; dinky-baggage, 12; officers' cars, 2; pay car, 1.

Freight—Box cars, 1,548; flat cars, 164; coal cars, permanent, 287; coal cars, temporary, 593; coal hoppers, 394; coal, dumpers, 20; charcoal, 45; way cars, 11; hay cars, 96; water cars, 15; outfit cars, 10; ferry cars, 5; derrick, 4; derrick caboose, 4; oil tank, tubular, 1. Total passenger and freight equipment, 3,384.

UNION PACIFIC TRANSFER DEPOT.

In accordance with the decision of the Supreme Court, as before me tioned, the Company have located their transfer depot at Dillonville, on the Iowa side, about midway between Council Bluffs and the river.

### THE BURLINGTON & MISSOURI RIVER RAILROAD,

The main line of which extends from the City of Plattsmouth, on the Missouri River, to Kearney Junction, where connections are made with the Union Pacific, a distance of 190 miles. This Company was organized under a liberal charter in 1869, with a capital stock of $7,500,000, which was divided into 75,000 shares, funded debt, first mortgage eight per cent. convertable bonds, dated July 1st, 1869, with semi-annual interest payable in January and July, and principal payable July 1st, 1894. On the 1st of May, 1871, the capital stock of the Company was increased to $12,000,000.

The Company received a land grant from the Government amounting to 2,382,208 acres, also a grant from the State of Nebraska of 50,000 acres, and when they took possession of the Omaha & Southwestern road they acquired the land grant made to that line by the State, to the extent of 100,010 acres. It may be proper to state here that the Omaha & Southwestern road, although chartered from Omaha to Lincoln, was only built to the Platte River where it formed a junction with the B. & M. road, over which it secured track service into Lincoln until its transfer by lease to the latter line.

On the 1st of August, 1879, the Company owned and operated in the State of Nebraska 443 miles, as follows: from Plattsmouth, via Lincoln, to Kearney Junction, 190 miles, where connections are made with the Union Pacific road; from Plattsmouth to Omaha, twenty-one miles, where connections are made with the U. P., O. &. N. W., C. & N. W. and Chicago Rock Island & Pacific roads. In brief, at Omaha connections are made with lines radiating east, west, and north. From Lincoln to York, fifty-five miles; from Lincoln to Brownville, on the Missouri, sixty-five miles; from Crete to Beatrice, thirty miles; from Hastings to Bloomington, sixty-nine miles. The lines above mentioned traverse the following Counties, making connections with other lines at the points named: Douglas, Sarpy, Cass, Otoe, Nemaha, Lancaster, Seward, York, Saline, Fillmore, Clay, Adams, Kearney, Buffalo, Webster, Franklin, and Gage; while their projected lines, some of which are under construction, traverse Hamilton, Hall, Merrick, Jefferson, Thayer, Nuckolls, Harlan, Furnas, Red Willow, Hitchcock, Dundy and Johnson Counties. The projected lines are as follows: From York to Aurora, in Hamilton County, twenty miles; from Aurora to Hastings twenty-two miles; from Aurora to Grand Island, sixteen miles; from Aurora to Central City, sixteen miles; from Beatrice to Red Cloud, 100 miles; from Bloomington to State Line, west, 150 miles; from Beatrice to Nemaha, sixty-five miles. These lines completed, the B. &. M. will operate 832 miles of road in the State; roads that traverse and open up to vigorous commerce much of the richest and most beautiful and inviting portion of Nebraska. Nearly every mile of their line from Plattsmouth to Kearney Junction, passes through one of the richest farming countries to be found in the West.

In brief, the B. & M. lines occupy the garden, as it were, of the Platte and Republican Valleys. This corporation has adopted and pursued from the date of its organization, a most liberal and comprehensive policy towards the country through which its lines of road are constructed. To a much larger extent than is usual in railway corporations, it has exhibited a disposition to make its interests and that of the country through which it passed, identical. In fact, the history and development of the Burlington & Missouri River road is most intimately interwoven with the development and prosperity of the great South Platte country; and the writer only echoes the popular voice, when he makes the statement that every movement of this corporation has tended directly towards the material advancement of that beautiful portion of the State occupied by its lines, which has made it one of the most prosperous as well as popular roads in the west.

Their lines are well and safely built; their bridges and culverts are constructed upon the most approved system; their rolling stock is ample, and their passenger equipment combines all of the more modern improvements for the speed, comfort and safety of passengers.

The equipment of the B. & M. road in 1879 consisted in part of the following rolling stock: Sixteen locomotives, twelve passenger coaches, seven baggage and express cars, one hundred and fifty box cars, eighty-six platform cars, and forty-three coal cars; total two hundred and ninety-eight.

The Company's general office is at Omaha, where they own a

fine new brick building, and give employment to a large number of persons. Their machine shops are at Plattsmouth, in which they employ some three hundred men. At Plattsmouth this line connects with the Chicago, Burlington & Quincy road.

The following is a statement of articles forwarded from, and received at stations on the Burlington & Missouri River Railway, in the South Platte country, for five years, ending December 31st, 1878:

WEIGHT IN POUNDS OF ARTICLES FORWARDED.

| YEAR. | MERCHAN-DISE. | MILL PRODUCTS. | GRAIN. | LIVE STOCK. | STONE AND BRICK. |
|---|---|---|---|---|---|
| 1874 | 5,446,340 | 3,628,186 | 94,204,000 | 10,820,000 | 2,208,000 |
| 1875 | 4,098,439 | 4,915,287 | 122,872,000 | 6,059,500 | 2,304,000 |
| 1876 | 6,248,104 | 8,296,986 | 208,732,000 | 16,455,100 | 384,000 |
| 1877 | 17,104,996 | 11,317,170 | 273,621,000 | 28,980,000 | 9,264,000 |
| 1878 | 22,385,693 | 8,447,250 | 422,746,000 | 56,647,500 | 8,832,000 |

WEIGHT IN POUNDS OF ARTICLES RECEIVED.

| YEAR. | MERCHAN-DISE. | EMIGRANT MOVABLES. | LUMBER. | COAL. | STONE AND BRICK. |
|---|---|---|---|---|---|
| 1874 | 30,921,541 | 6,480,000 | 47,736,000 | 11,928,000 | 2,784,000 |
| 1875 | 31,875,754 | 4,600,000 | 38,040,000 | 24,000,000 | 2,472,000 |
| 1876 | 34,069,915 | 6,680,000 | 41,088,000 | 27,096,000 | 4,992,000 |
| 1877 | 51,277,825 | 6,380,000 | 90,363,000 | 46,080,000 | 6,288,000 |
| 1878 | 82,323,429 | 19,020,000 | 102,074,000 | 44,294,000 | 10,320,000 |

THE BURLINGTON & MISSOURI RIVER RAILWAY BRIDGE AT PLATTSMOUTH.

The construction of the above mentioned bridge, spanning the Missouri River at Plattsmouth, was commenced in 1879, under the supervision of Geo. S. Morrison, Chief Engineer of that Company.

The channel of the river, at the point where the bridge crosses it, is only 344 feet, a narrowness that was secured by many years of rip-rapping, by the Railroad Company, who have constructed formidable piers and dikes of stone, on the Iowa side, in order to turn the channel permanently in the direction of the rocky bluffs on the Nebraska shore. These improvements, although attended by an enormous outlay of money, has so securely hemmed in the channel as to make the enterprise of bridging the stream an easy and comparatively cheap undertaking.

The bridge is constructed of steel spans, of three hundred feet in length each. These spans are supported in the center and at the ends, by piers of great solidity, constructed of stone and iron. The substructure of these piers is the bed rock, which at that point is reached at fifty feet below low water mark. This work will be effected by compressed air, the machinery for which was procured at a large cost. The pier on the Nebraska shore, however, rests on the bed of the rock bluff which is at about low water mark. This bridge is approached from the Iowa side by a high grade of considerable length, while on the Nebraska side it is approached through a deep cut in the bluffs. The bridge is fifty feet above high water mark, thus doing away with the necessity of a draw.

### THE NEBRASKA RAILWAY,

Now owned and operated by the Burlington & Missouri River Road, which extends from Nemaha City, in Nemaha County, on the Missouri, to York, in York County, a distance of 136 miles, passing in its course through Brownville, Nebraska City, Syracuse, Palmyra, Bennett, Lincoln and Seward, was organized in 1871, under the title of the Midland Pacific Railroad. The line was built from Nebraska City, to Lincoln, a distance of fifty-eight miles, in 1871, and extended to Seward, eighty-three miles from Nebraska City, in 1874. It was the intention of the original Company to build the line to Fort Kearney, or to some point further east on the Union Pacific road. A branch line was also projected from the main line, at some point in Otoe County, to Fort Riley in Kansas. The line was, however, sold under foreclosure, and a company re-organized under the title of the Nebraska Railway, and was operated as such until it passed into the hands of the B. & M. Company, in 1876, who extended the line west from Seward to York, its present terminus, and from Nebraska City to Nemaha City, its present southeastern terminus. This line passes through the rich farming Counties of Nemaha, Otoe, Lancaster, Seward and York, connecting at Brownville, on the Missouri River, with the Kansas City, St. Joseph and Council Bluffs road, and at Lincoln with the entire system of railways radiating from that center.

The original Company were the recipients of a land grant to aid in the construction of their line from Nebraska City to Seward, of 10,184,448 acres. By an Act of the State Legislature, approved February 22d, 1875, the Company were also granted a certain amount of *Saline* lands, but as it did not comply with the conditions of the grant, such lands reverted back to the State.

### THE OMAHA & SOUTHWESTERN RAILWAY,

Operated since 1872 under a perpetual lease by the Burlington and Missouri River Road, was built from Omaha to Lincoln, a distance of sixty-eight miles, by rail, in 1869, and was the second railway projected in the State. Among the original stock-holders were S. S. Caldwell, President; John Y. Clopper, Clinton Briggs, Henry Gray, Frank Murphy, A. S. Paddock, and Frank Smith.

This branch of the B. &. M in connection with the Atchison & Nebraska, and the Missouri and Pacific, forms a through line from Omaha to St. Louis, on the west side of the Missouri River.

### THE OMAHA & NORTHERN NEBRASKA RAILWAY,

Formerly *The Omaha & Northwestern* was commenced in 1869, and completed to Herman, a distance of forty miles, in 1871. In 1876 it was extended to Tekamah, the County Seat of Burt County, a distance of fifty-two miles, from Omaha. This line traverses the eastern portions of Douglas, Washington and Burt Counties, and is a most important outlet for the produce of the highly cultivated and prosperous country through which it runs. It is being extended during the present year to Oakland, in the famous Logan Valley, a flourishing little town, situated near the west line of Burt County, about sixteen miles from Tekamah.

This line will in all probability be extended north and west through the rapidly developing Counties of Cuming, Black Bird,

Wayne, Pierce, and Knox to Niobrara, a thriving little city situated at the junction of the Niobrara and Missouri Rivers. At Blair, the County Seat of Washington County, the O. & N. W. crosses the Sioux City and Pacific road, which connection furnishes an outlet both east and west for passengers and freight, while at Omaha it connects with the railway system of Nebraska. The road is of great value to the country through which it passes, and when pushed forward to a river terminal point, opening up the fertile Logan Valley and the country further north, it must become both a profitable and an important line.

Among the original stock-holders and projectors of the O. & N. W. road, was James. E. Boyd, its first President; William A. Paxton, John A. Morrow, John I. Redick, Herman Kountze, Edward Creighton, Jonas Gise, John A. Horbach, C. H. Downs, Frank Smith, G. M. Mills, and Joseph and Ezra Millard.

### THE SIOUX CITY & PACIFIC,

In connection with the Union Pacific, and the Chicago & Northwestern roads, forms a direct and short transportation route from Fremont, Neb., to Chicago; also in connection with the Iowa Division of the Illinois Central, Sioux City & St. Paul lines, it affords a direct route to St. Paul, Duluth and Milwaukee. The Sioux City & Pacific road runs from Sioux City along the east bank of the Missouri River to a point about two miles west of Missouri Valley Junction, Iowa, where it connects with the Chicago & Northwestern, over which Council Bluffs and the entire system of railways radiating from that point and Omaha are reached. Leaving the C. & N. W. road it bends to the west, crossing the Missouri River by a steam ferry, about three miles east of the city of Blair, where it crosses the Omaha & Northwestern road. From Blair it bends a little to the southwest until Fremont, a thriving little city situated on the east bank of the Platte River, on the Union Pacific, is reached. There, connections are made with the Elkhorn Valley road, which runs up the Elkhorn Valley to Stanton, the County Seat of Stanton County.

From Fremont to points east and north, the Sioux City & Pacific has the advantage of being the quickest and most direct route, and to St. Paul and other northern points, it is the most popular route.

### THE FREMONT, ELKHORN & MISSOURI VALLEY ROAD,

Operated by the Sioux City & Pacific, extends from Fremont on the Union Pacific, to Stanton, the County Seat of Stanton County, which latter point it reached in 1879. The first ten miles of the road was completed by December 31st, 1869.

This line follows the Elkhorn Valley northward, through one of the loveliest, richest and fast-settling regions of the State, and has a profitable and rapidly increasing traffic.

There are several prosperous and growing towns along the line, the principal of which are Fremont, West Point, Scribner, Hooper and Stanton. The extension of this road through Madison and Antelope Counties is now progressing.

### THE ATCHISON & NEBRASKA RAILWAY

Is a link of the important transportation route from Omaha to St. Louis, *via* Lincoln. One hundred and ten miles of its line is in Nebraska, passing in a southeasterly direction from Lincoln, through the rich grain growing Counties of Lancaster, Gage, Johnson, Pawnee and Richardson. The extension of the Atchison & Nebraska road from Lincoln to Columbus, where a junction is formed with the Union Pacific, was commenced in 1879. As a transportation route for produce to St. Louis, this line has advantages that no amount of competition can wrest from it. This company was organized in 1870, and the line completed from Atchison to Lincoln, a distance of 148 miles, in 1872. The equipment of the road includes ten locomotives, six passenger cars, three mail and express cars, ninety-five box cars, fifty-five flat, sixteen stock, and fifty-five combination cars.

The Nebraska connections of the A. & N. are the Burlington & Missouri River, Omaha & Southwestern, and Nebraska Railways, at Lincoln, and the Union Pacific, at Columbus.

### THE COVINGTON, COLUMBUS & BLACK HILLS R. R.

Was built in 1876-7, and is twenty-six miles in length, extending from Covington on the Missouri River opposite from Sioux City to Ponca, the County Seat of Dixon County. This line traverses a rich and rapidly developing section of the State, and is well patronized and profitable, and when extended further west, as it eventually will be, it will prove a most important avenue for commerce and travel, in that portion of the State. The principal towns along the line of the road are Covington, Dakota City, Jackson, Summit and Ponca; and at Sioux City connections are made with the Dakota Southern, Sioux City & St. Paul, Illinois Central, and Sioux City & Pacific roads.

There are a large number of projected railway lines in different parts of the State, and under the present era in railway building it is more than probable that before another five years have passed that Nebraska will have a net work of rail lines equal to that of Illinois or Indiana.

# CHAPTER VIII.

## CLIMATE OF NEBRASKA.

Its Altitude—Temperature—Rainfall.

It must be borne in mind that Nebraska is comprised within the forty and forty-third degrees of latitude, and between the ninety-sixth and one hundred and fourth degrees of longitude west from Greenwich, or between the nineteenth and twenty-seventh degrees west from Washington; thus giving it a diversified climate throughout its extended area.

The average elevation above the sea level being about 2,500 feet, with a range of mountains to the west, spanning the Continent from the Gulf of Mexico to the British Possessions, gives a pure, invigorating air, and hence is witnessed an almost entire absence of fevers and other malarial diseases so common in some sections of the West where low lands and marshy swamps are encountered. Perhaps no State in the Union, outside of New England, has less stagnant waters within its borders, or more pure springs and running streams than are to be found in Nebraska; and it is a matter susceptible of proof from the records, that no Western State can show a smaller death rate than this.

The rare, clear atmosphere gives wonderful range of vision, tone and vitality to every form of animal and vegetable life, and the most enjoyable climate upon the Continent. Take the seasons as they come and go, and average them, and no State can make such goodly promises as this for health, development and longevity.

Mr. L. D. Burch, Western Editor of the Chicago *Commercial*

*Advertiser*, who spent some years in traveling over Nebraska, has recently published a very valuable work on the State, from which the following in regard to climate is taken:

"The entire State has a southwestern exposure, the downward slope or incline from the northwest to southeast, being about 2,600 feet, or nearly seven feet to the mile. The influence of this warm exposure upon the climate and vegetable growth is of incalculable advantage. The Nebraska summer is a long, and genial warm season, with delightful, breezy days and cool refreshing nights. The hottest days of July and August are tempered by the almost constant southerly and southwest winds. The high tone and stimulus of the atmosphere of this region are proverbial. The cool still nights are a restful and refreshing pleasure experienced in but few regions of the world. The Nebraska winter, as compared with the rigorous, snowy, frost-bound winter of New England, New York and Wisconsin, is a very mild and pleasant season. Nine-tenths of the cold season is made up of bright, dry, mild weather. February and March give an occasional severe storm of short duration. The best commentary upon the winter of this country is the grazing of cattle and sheep upon the ranges in the west half of the State, the year round, their only shelter from the storms being the native groves, gulches and ravines.

"The soft blue haze, subdued mellow sunshine, and gorgeous red sunsets of autumn in Nebraska, make that season a benediction. The cold winds are the only unpleasant feature of the cold season, but the settler easily gets accustomed to these and they are known to be the most effective conservators of health. They sweep away any possible malarial influence and leave the climate with every needed condition to normal health. The rare, invigorating, life-inspiring atmosphere gives remarkable brilliancy to the climate and leaves its impress upon every form of life. Men and animals move with quick, elastic step, and even the vegetable kingdom expresses the presence of these vitalizing forces in a wonderful degree. The streams are rapid; the plow runs to the water's edge; there are no stagnant pools to give off poisonous exhalations; the southwest winds sweep down from the snow-clad *sierras* across an ocean of sweetest verdure, and the country is as healthful as any upon the green earth. There are no local conditions to generate or foster disease in men, animals or plants. Only life and health and the spirit of divine youth is evoked from the bright skies, clear atmosphere and pure water, of this superb climate. It is but simple justice to Nebraska to say that it is a poor country for doctors and physic, and comes very near to being a paradise for invalids. While it may not have the mildness or softness of the more humid climates of Florida, South Texas and Southern California, it has vastly more tone and vitalizing force. If the Gileads of the older lands have no value for the great army of their invalids, afflicted with incipient consumption, bronchial affections, asthma, dyspepsia and kindred ills, and will send them out to Nebraska, to camp out, ride in the saddle, hunt deer, antelope, prairie chickens and water-fowls, live upon their broiled flesh, drink sweet milk and grow sunbrowned and happy-hearted, the writer will warrant nine-tenths of them salvation from their ills in a dozen moons."

The following tables, reported by Charles Dill, Sergeant in the U. S. Signal Service, will show the mean monthly temperature, highest and lowest temperature in each month, and monthly range, and amount of rainfall, at Omaha, Nebraska, for the period of years stated:

MEAN MONTHLY TEMPERATURE.

| DATE. | JANUARY. | FEBRUARY. | MARCH. | APRIL. | MAY. | JUNE. | JULY. | AUGUST. | SEPTEMBER. | OCTOBER. | NOVEMBER. | DECEMBER. |
|---|---|---|---|---|---|---|---|---|---|---|---|---|
| 1874 | 22.3 | 23.4 | 33.8 | 45.1 | 66.6 | 73.2 | 80.0 | 77.3 | 63.0 | 54.0 | 36.0 | 28.4 |
| 1875 | 11.1 | 13.8 | 30.5 | 45.4 | 63.2 | 71.1 | 74.4 | 70.2 | 62.9 | 49.6 | 32.6 | 33.5 |
| 1876 | 26.8 | 30.1 | 29.3 | 51.3 | 63.6 | 68.6 | 75.1 | 75.4 | 60.0 | 50.3 | 33.2 | 19.2 |
| 1877 | 20.2 | 37.3 | 33.7 | 50.5 | 60.7 | 69.1 | 76.0 | 73.2 | 66.6 | 51.1 | 36.3 | 39.2 |
| 1878 | 28.9 | 36.9 | 48.1 | 55.0 | 58.5 | 68.4 | 79.1 | 77.9 | 64.3 | 52.5 | 44.0 | 21.8 |
| 1879 | 21.8 | 27.1 | 41.6 | 54.2 | 67.0 | 72.7 | 78.7 | 75.5 | ..... | ..... | ..... | ..... |

## MONTHLY AND ANNUAL AMOUNT OF RAINFALL, OR MELTED SNOW.
### INCHES AND HUNDREDTHS.

| Date. | January. | February. | March. | April. | May. | June. | July. | August. | September. | October. | November. | December. | Total. |
|---|---|---|---|---|---|---|---|---|---|---|---|---|---|
| 1874 | 0.32 | 0.92 | 1.49 | 2.01 | 1.24 | 6.93 | 0.54 | 2.08 | 7.18 | 1.45 | 1.05 | 0.54 | 25.75 |
| 1875 | 0.26 | 0.51 | 1.24 | 3.06 | 4.25 | 10.95 | 10.01 | 7.77 | 2.55 | 1.16 | 0.13 | 1.00 | 42.89 |
| 1876 | 0.22 | 0.40 | 3.18 | 2.65 | 2.07 | 3.47 | 7.30 | 6.27 | 4.93 | 0.69 | 1.17 | 0.16 | 32.51 |
| 1877 | 0.53 | 0.44 | 1.26 | 6.24 | 8.62 | 8.36 | 0.96 | 3.13 | 2.05 | 5.86 | 1.36 | 2.14 | 40.95 |
| 1878 | 1.13 | 0.14 | 3.09 | 5.97 | 5.77 | 8.48 | 7.66 | 2.48 | 3.22 | 0.55 | 0.29 | 0.27 | 37.05 |
| 1879 | 0.07 | 0.93 | 2.17 | 1.77 | 5.53 | 4.09 | 3.17 | 1.51 | .... | .... | .... | .... | .... |

## HIGHEST AND LOWEST TEMPERATURE IN EACH MONTH, AND MONTHLY RANGE.

| Date. | 1874. | | | 1875. | | | 1876. | | | 1877. | | | 1878. | | | 1879. | | |
|---|---|---|---|---|---|---|---|---|---|---|---|---|---|---|---|---|---|---|
|  | High. | Low. | Range. | High. | Low. | Range. | High. | Low. | Range. | High. | Low. | Range. | High. | Low. | Range. | High. | Low. | Range. |
| Jan....... | 47 | 9 | 56 | 43 | 19 | 62 | 58 | 2 | 60 | 59 | 16 | 75 | 51 | 0 | 51 | 62 | 22 | 84 |
| Feb...... | 45 | 6 | 51 | 40 | 16 | 56 | 65 | 10 | 75 | 61 | 12 | 49 | 61 | 9 | 52 | 60 | 9 | 69 |
| March.... | 57 | 10 | 47 | 75 | 1 | 76 | 64 | 4 | 68 | 74 | 1 | 73 | 80 | 22 | 58 | 82 | 3 | 79 |
| April..... | 85 | 21 | 64 | 81 | 21 | 60 | 81 | 29 | 52 | 77 | 22 | 55 | 82 | 34 | 48 | 80 | 14 | 66 |
| May...... | 90 | 39 | 51 | 90 | 28 | 62 | 88 | 37 | 51 | 82 | 36 | 46 | 82 | 33 | 49 | 91 | 35 | 56 |
| June..... | 93 | 48 | 45 | 94 | 48 | 46 | 94 | 43 | 51 | 92 | 42 | 50 | 89 | 46 | 43 | 93 | 45 | 48 |
| July...... | 105 | 57 | 48 | 97 | 58 | 39 | 94 | 55 | 39 | 99 | 53 | 46 | 96 | 57 | 39 | 96 | 60 | 36 |
| August... | 105 | 55 | 50 | 86 | 54 | 32 | 92 | 54 | 38 | 93 | 49 | 44 | 97 | 57 | 40 | 93 | 55 | 38 |
| Sept...... | 92 | 36 | 56 | 90 | 37 | 53 | 85 | 33 | 52 | 86 | 44 | 42 | 89 | 36 | 53 | .. | .. | .. |
| Oct....... | 78 | 18 | 60 | 77 | 22 | 55 | 78 | 23 | 55 | 73 | 30 | 43 | 82 | 15 | 67 | .. | .. | .. |
| Nov...... | 74 | 7 | 67 | 69 | 6 | 75 | 68 | 1 | 67 | 61 | 2 | 63 | 71 | 18 | 53 | .. | .. | .. |
| Dec...... | 58 | 2 | 60 | 66 | 5 | 71 | 57 | 7 | 64 | 61 | 5 | 56 | 59 | 8 | 67 | .. | .. | .. |

## CHAPTER IX.

### EDUCATIONAL ADVANTAGES.

FREE SCHOOLS—STATE UNIVERSITY—STATE NORMAL SCHOOL—INSTITUTE FOR THE DEAF AND DUMB—INSTITUTE FOR THE BLIND.

It is no more patent to the human mind that the prosperity, stability and perpetuity of a State are matters of supreme concern, than that liberal and judicious provisions for fostering and building up public instructions, for both political and economical reasons, are matters of supreme concern. Public education in this country is the most effective means yet devised to promote general intelligence and morality.

It also removes much of the friction in society in the way of crime, and hence becomes a public and practical necessity in every State. The greater the degree of education in any community or State, the greater the security of life and property; or in other language, general intelligence resulting from popular education is effective in preserving life and property, and hence, of increasing wealth by productive industry.

This is the substructure on which the free school system of Nebraska is based. Money expended under this system is not a gift in charity, but a most profitable investment to the State, simply because the wealth and prosperity of a self-governing State is entirely dependent on the intelligence of its citizens.

Profiting by the experience of the older States, Nebraska has incorporated into her Common School system what has been proved by experiment as the most advantageous and economical methods.

The school revenues of the State are classed under two heads, temporary fund, and permanent fund.

During the two years ending December 31, 1878, there was placed to the credit of the temporary school fund, and distributed to the Counties, and by them to the school districts, the sum of four hundred and thirty-eight thousand, three hundred and fifteen dollars and twelve cents, derived from the following sources: Interest on land sold $129,033.50; interest on leased lands, $62,633,93; private loans, $2,540; State and County bonds, $73,572.25: school tax collected, $170,185.81; from all other sources, $349.63; total, $438,315.12.

Of this sum there was disbursed in 1877, $169,281.88; and in 1878, $205,637.88, an increase of $36,356. The rate per pupil in 1877 was, $1.83; and in 1878, $1.99.

There is a great difficulty in the way of arriving at a correct statement of the permanent fund, owing to the fact that its productive value is constantly changing. The whole amount of land leased prior to 1877, was 80,381 acres, and since that date up to December 31, 1878, 100,918 acres, making a total of 181,299 acres, at an average price of $4.45 per acre. Prior to 1877, 110,362 acres were sold at an average price of $9.26 per acre, and since that date, up to December 31, 1878, 26,819 acres, at an average price of $7.54.

One hundred and eighty-one thousand, two hundred and ninety-nine acres at $4.45 gives a valuation of $806,758, which is at eight per cent. The income in 1878 from unpaid principal on school lands, was $46,635.43, which indicates a valuation on which such interest was paid, of $777,257.16. The total productive school fund on the 31st of December, 1878 was as follows:

| | |
|---|---:|
| Invested in State bonds...........................$ | 426,267.35 |
| Invested in County bonds..................... | 52,500.00 |
| Invested in School District bonds............. | 7,800.00 |
| Invested in private securities.................. | 49,600.00 |
| Unpaid principal of school lands.............. | 777,257.16 |
| Leased lands (valuation)....................... | 806,758.00 |
| Total ........................................ | $2,120,182.51 |

By a constitutional provision this is made a trust fund, and if any part is lost, the State is obligated to replace it. The interest can be used for the payment of teachers and for no other purpose whatsoever. The interest on the State bonds is eight per cent., and six per cent. on school bonds, the interest prior to 1877 being ten per cent.

The following is a summary of the school statistics of Nebraska, from 1870 to 1879. It will prove of more value in showing the progress and healthy condition of the educational system of the State than would be a volume of remarks by the author.

| | 1870 | 1871 | 1872 | 1873 | 1874 | 1875 | 1876 | 1877 | 1878 | 1879 |
|---|---|---|---|---|---|---|---|---|---|---|
| Number of organized counties | 31 | 35 | 48 | 59 | 60 | 60 | 60 | 61 | 62 | 63 |
| Number of school districts | 797 | 1028 | 1410 | 1863 | 2215 | 2405 | 2513 | 2496 | 2690 | 2776 |
| Number of school houses | 298 | 558 | 787 | 1138 | 1516 | 2018 | 2195 | 2212 | 2231 | 2409 |
| Children of school age | 32789 | 41071 | 51123 | 63108 | 72991 | 80122 | 86191 | 92161 | 104030 | 123411 |
| Average number in each district | 41 | 40 | 36 | 33 | 33 | 33 | 33 | 37 | 38 | 44 |
| No. of children attending school | 12791 | 23265 | 29786 | 37872 | 47718 | 55423 | 59996 | 56774 | 62785 | 76856 |
| Per cent. of attendance | 39 | 56 | 56 | 60 | 60 | 69 | 70 | 61 | 60 | 63 |
| Number of male teachers | 267 | 560 | 773 | 1046 | 1252 | 1504 | 1468 | 1571 | 1609 | 1607 |
| Number of female teachers | 269 | 520 | 739 | 1176 | 1483 | 1587 | 1893 | 2153 | 2121 | 2221 |
| No. of days taught by male teachers | 18931 | 41411 | 55996 | 75996 | 90430 | 111393 | 109577 | 121403 | 109347 | 125332 |
| No. days taught by female teachers | 18436 | 36024 | 55901 | 82796 | 106472 | 121723 | 135971 | 160011 | 145546 | 173962 |
| Av. No. days taught by each teacher | 70 | 72 | 74 | 72 | 72 | 96 | 95 | 88 | 85 | 78 |
| Number of graded schools | | | | 21 | 32 | 38 | 56 | 61 | 47 | 60 |
| Total wages paid male teachers | $ 26650 13 | $ 81264 73 | $107818 69 | $ 149511 13 | $ 171776 86 | $ 222994 49 | $ 219420 00 | 220962 42 | $ 208957 13 | $ 208642 23 |
| "   "   female teachers | 31088 30 | 65992 74 | 93677 75 | 140341 77 | 171029 40 | 210748 51 | 230140 00 | 236085 28 | 235542 97 | 258058 78 |
| Average wages per month, males | 28 16 | 39 24 | 38 50 | 39 36 | 37 98 | 38 60 | 37 14 | 35 46 | 34 65 | 33 25 |
| "   "   "   females | 33 72 | 36 64 | 33 40 | 33 90 | 32 12 | 33 10 | 32 84 | 31 80 | 25 75 | 29 55 |
| Value of all school property | 178604 34 | 420936 66 | 817163 59 | 1167103 87 | 1553926 15 | 1848239 00 | 1585736 60 | 1862385 88 | 1805466 66 | 1810288 27 |
| Total receipts | 167597 95 | 371888 73 | 537630 39 | 901189 94 | 988740 20 | 928188 00 | 1093275 39 | 1026583 34 | 849300 45 | 1069007 23 |
| Total expenditures | 163930 84 | 365520 36 | 534095 97 | 915076 39 | 1094857 03 | 1054817 09 | 1098974 75 | 1027192 21 | 936931 98 | 1067569 18 |
| Total indebtedness | 31657 09 | 73469 63 | 176075 85 | 649307 77 | 918055 01 | 1054817 09 | 1048058 66 | 1039546 68 | 1036245 02 | 1010607 60 |
| Am't apportioned from State fund | 57982 50 | 1388 40 | 157495 11 | 167493 11 | 176461 98 | 292471 49 | 241167 53 | 183025 80 | 169281 88 | 205622 50 |

## GROWTH OF THE NEBRASKA SCHOOL SYSTEM.

The following statement shows the rapid expansion of the educational advantages of Nebraska, during the past nine years:

| YEARS. | AV'GE NO. OF DAYS OF SCHOOL. | DISTRICTS | CHILDREN | TEACHERS | VALUE OF SCHOOL PROPERTY. |
|---|---|---|---|---|---|
| 1870 | 46  | 797   | 32,789  | 536   | $ 178,604 |
| 1872 | 79  | 1,410 | 51,123  | 1,512 | 817,163   |
| 1874 | 88  | 2,215 | 72,991  | 2,735 | 1,553,926 |
| 1876 | 90  | 2,513 | 86,191  | 3,636 | 1,585,736 |
| 1878 | 92  | 2,690 | 104,030 | 3,730 | 1,806,466 |
| 1879 | 107 | 2,776 | 123,411 | 3,828 | 1,810,288 |

Total number of School Districts in the State, 2,776; number of graded schools, 60; number of ungraded schools, 2,716; school age of pupils, from five to twenty-one years.

### THE STATE UNIVERSITY,

Located at Lincoln, was established by Act of the Legislature in 1869, and opened in 1871. Rev. E. B. Fairfield, D. D., L. L. D., Chancellor; Professors, eight; Tutors, six; legislative appropriation, $25,000 per year.

By Act of the Legislature five Colleges are authorized to be established as follows;
1. A College of Literature, Science and the Arts.
2. An Industrial College embracing Agriculture, Practical Science, Civil Engineering, and the Mechanic Arts.
3. A College of Law.
4. A College of Medicine.
5. A College of the Fine Arts.

As yet only the first two have been established. Fourteen instructors devote their time to the University; Military and Preparatory departments have been added; the library contains 2,100 well selected volumes, and the cabinet consists of many thousand specimens of the various departments of Natural History; tuition is free to all, except for music, painting and drawing; both sexes are admitted. Two hundred and eighteen students were enrolled for 1879. The University has an endowment of 46,080 acres, and the Agricultural College an endowment of 90,000 acres donated to the State by the General Government for their permanent support.

### THE STATE NORMAL SCHOOL,

Located at Peru, Nemaha County, was opened in 1867, Robert Curry, A. M., Ph. D., Principal. Assistant teachers, eight; students enrolled in 1879, 242; legislative appropriation $12,000 per year; tuition free.

This school, designed principally for the education of young ladies and gentlemen as teachers, has been remarkably successful, it being necessary during the two years just passed to employ assistant teachers to meet the wants of the increased attendance. The studies pursued are an elementary normal course of two years; an advanced English normal course of three years, and an advanced classical normal course of three years. By an Act of the Legislature, approved June 20th, 1867, twenty sections of the Saline lands of the State were set apart as an endowment for this school.

### THE NEBRASKA INSTITUTE FOR DEAF AND DUMB,

Located at Omaha, was opened in 1869. J. A. Gillespie, Principal; assistant teachers, three; pupils, fifty-two; legislative appropriation, $6,000 per annum.

This institution aims to give its pupils a good common school education, and especially to give them a command of the English language. The highest branches now taught are Physiology, Universal History, Geography and Arithmetic.

The Principal in a recent letter says: "We teach articulation as a branch of our work. We do this by means of Bell's Visible Speech, a system founded upon the positions the vocal organs assume to produce sounds. As to trades we have but one, —printing. We have now thirteen boys learning this. They print the *Mute Journal of Nebraska*, a monthly publication. The smaller boys are trained in gardening and farm work. The girls are taught house-work and sewing."

The Institute building is a commodious brick structure, located on the outskirts of the City of Omaha, and was erected in 1871, at the expense of the State.

### THE NEBRASKA INSTITUTION FOR THE BLIND,

Located at Nebraska City, was opened in 1875. Principal, J. B. Parmlee; assistant teachers, three; pupils December, 1878, twenty-one; legislative appropriation, $5,450.00 per annum.

This Institution is admirably conducted, and is doing excellent service. The school is divided into three departments, viz.: The literary, musical, and industrial, separate in themselves, yet forming one complete course of instruction. The studies pursued are arithmetic, algebra, grammar and analysis, physical and descriptive geography, rhetoric, physiology, history, reading spelling and penmanship.

The musical department has made rapid advancement under the efficient management of Jacob Niermeyer, who is himself blind. The choir and band meet every afternoon on alternate days. Two pianos, an organ, flutes, and violins make up the equipment of instruments.

In the industrial department the boys and young men are required to spend a certain number of hours each day at the trades taught, which at present are limited to broom making, cane seating, etc.

The girls and young ladies are instructed in all kinds of sewing, knitting, crocheting, bead-work, etc.

# CHAPTER X.

## THE CHURCHES.

PRESBYTERIAN—CONGREGATIONAL—METHODIST EPISCOPAL—EPISCOPAL—CATHOLIC—LUTHERAN—BAPTIST—UNITARIAN—CHRISTIAN.

There is, perhaps, no interest in the State that has received such universal and hearty indorsement as have the Churches of all denominations. From the first settlement of the Territory there has been a constant spirit of sacrifice to lay deep the foundations of all the different Christian denominations. It has been less a spirit of strife, or rivalry, than a recognition of the great fundamental law that neither new nor old communities can long exist and prosper, without the softening, chastening and refining influences of Christianity; and the zealous labor of Christians in all the history of the State has been marked, as they have made education and Christianity the corner-stone of all their institutions. There is no State in the Union, with the same number of inhabitants, that has so many and so good Churches and school houses, nor one that gathers more to the services of the various Churches, considering that the State is yet comparatively in its infancy.

Many are swift to conclude that in a new frontier State but little will be done in this direction, and they hesitate about leaving their Church associations and privileges, and coming to a new country, but these fears are groundless. The pioneer denominations, as usual, have occupied the frontier. They have gathered the people for worship in groves in the open air, in dug-outs, in school houses and private dwellings. All denominations have done this, the Bishop and the Priest, and the Minister and Preacher; and almost invariably as soon as a passable home has been provided for the family, and a room, however humble, for the school, the next thought has been for the Church in which to worship God; and this has been built, sometimes rudely and cheaply at first, but always in keeping with, and often beyond, the means of the inhabitants.

And in this action there has been a singular unanimity of all classes in the community. Men who have belonged to no Church, who have expressed no particular religious convictions, who have identified themselves with no creed, have been just as anxious for these privileges for themselves and their children as those connected with the Churches. They have recognized the great power and benefit of the Christian Church in the formation of morals and the dissemination of virtuous principles in the communities where they have lived.

There is another peculiarity that has been marked in the progress of the Christian Churches of this State, and that has been the conspicuous absence of denomination rivalries and disputes. Bigotry has seemed to have no place in the denominational work. There have been few or no angry discussions or denunciations of different religious beliefs or theories.

Men have accorded to each other the best intentions, and while disseminating widely different doctrines and usages, they have done this in a spirit of Christian charity, manly forbearance, that recognizes the fact that there is room for all of every faith; that each Church or organization must stand or fall on its own merits, and while the most zealous work has been done, often calling for severe labor and constant sacrifice to build up these institutions in their own way, according to early habits and influences, and in accordance with their peculiar views, there has been but little effort to pull down others and build on their ruins. It is the freedom of our Churches from this sectarian strife, the willingness to give every man the unrestrained right of opinion, and of practice that has made the Churches of all denominations so great a power throughout the State. Men are not to be trammelled. Their religious convictions, and the expression of them, is free as the air they breathe on our vast prairies. It is the genuine freedom of thought and action that is found in all the history of the world in the settlement of new countries, and developed peculiarly here from the influence of our free institutions, that make every man, however humble, a sovereign in his own right in all matters of opinion.

In all our prominent cities and large towns, comfortable, and spacious, if not elegant Churches, are found with their heaven-pointing spires, showing that God is honored, and that men acknowledge this by building temples in which to worship according to the dictates of their own consciences. And in the more remote settlements the people are not behind the large towns in the erection of suitable places of worship. And these results of Church building, Church going and educational facilities are produced by the character of many of the settlers on the frontier. Said a clergyman a short time since who preached in the most sparsely populated and distant portion of the State, "I have for my hearers here three College graduates, with families of the best educational and Christian culture; and the leader of my choir is a lady who has delighted thousands of metropolitan ears in fashionable Churches." This is the character of many, very many of our settlers. They have come from the best homes and purest associations of the East; they are cultivated, educated and refined, and they demand, and will have around them that which will satisfy the cravings of their natures for spiritual and intellectual and moral food. High intellectual attainments and moral and religious culture are confined to no localities. They flourish as surely on the prairie, in the humble home, by the fireside of comparative poverty, as in the abode of wealth and metropolitan influence. Nebraska can point with pride to the record of the Churches and schools. The men who have molded and controlled, and fashioned them, amid their arduous labors, their isolation, and their long and wearisome journeys, have found time to become men of letters, scientific men and authors, who have made themselves famous, and who have ranked first in the work they have undertaken and in the books they have published.

The right-arm of the Churches—the Sabbath schools of the State—have no superiors anywhere, whether we consider their management, their progress or their numbers. They have been complimented by experts in Sabbath school work, from the great educational centers of the country, as fully up to the best standards, and equal to any in the front rank of schools in the world. This of course commenced in the cities. Men were found who had peculiar adaptation to this work, men who had the ability and who were not satisfied to be behind the very best of self-sacrificing Sunday school workers in any land; and they have accomplished all and much more than they promised. And this work has spread by individual effort and by united influence until there is no better system, and none more carefully and conscientiously and intelligently followed than that of this new State.

It follows then that we have all the agencies, appliances, and zeal in this great work that is necessary to carry it forward and give the Church, the universal Church, a place in the hearts and homes and the institutions of our State. We are laying the foundations broad and deep for an universal acknowledgement of the claims of the Christian Church, and for its firm establishment in the minds and hopes of the people, and as a bulwark against bigotry, fanaticism and indifference, and as a perpetual acknowledgement of the enduring truths of Christianity.

The following statistics of our Churches show that our estimate is in keeping with the facts as they exist throughout our borders:

### PRESBYTERIAN.
#### Furnished by Rev. Wm. McCandlish, Omaha.

The State of Nebraska had, on the 1st of May, 1879, one Synod in connection with the General Assembly of the Presbyterian Church; three Presbyteries—Omaha, Nebraska City and Kearney; sixty ordained ministers; one licentiate and four candidates for the ministry; 101 organized Churches; 3,573 members; 501 members added on profession last year; 446 members added on certificate last year; 4,250 scholars in Sunday schools; $710 contributed to Home Mission last year; $507 contributed to Foreign Mission last year; $33,385 contributed to congregation purposes, including pastors' salary, Church buildings, &c., and $1,544 contributed to miscellaneous causes.

### CONGREGATIONAL.
#### Furnished by Rev. A. F. Sherrill, Omaha.

The first Society was organized at Omaha, on the 3d of May,

1856, by Rev. Reuben Gaylord, with six members. Their first Church, a brick, was commenced in 1856 and finished in 1857. A second house of worship, a frame, was built in 1866.

The present number of Congregational organizations in the State is 112; houses of worship, thirty-six; ministers, seventy-four; membership, about 3,000; value of Church edifices, $80,000; college and school property, $55,000; parsonages, (four) $5,000; total value of Church property $140,000.

Doane College, located at Crete, Saline County, founded in 1872 by Colonel Doane, is a flourishing and rapidly growing institution, conducted under the auspices of the Congregationalists. It has an attendance of about one hundred and fifty students, of both sexes. It has an endowment of six hundred acres of valuable land adjoining Crete.

### METHODIST EPISCOPAL.

The first class of this Society was organized at Omaha, in the summer of 1855, by Rev. Isaac F. Collins, and in the following year their first house of worship, a brick, was erected at Omaha.

The present membership in the State is 8,039; probationers, 1,156; local preachers, 136; Churches, fifty-seven, estimated value, $124,250; parsonages, forty-two, estimated value, $25,025; Sabbath Schools, 172; officers and teachers, 1,478; scholars, 8,745.

### EPISCOPAL.
Furnished by Rt. Rev. Bishop Clarkson, Omaha.

Number of baptized members, 3,340; teachers and officers of Sunday Schools, 202; Sunday School scholars, 1,830; Churches, thirty-two, value, $117,500; educational institutions, five, value of buildings, $54,500. The first Church was organized in the spring of 1856, by Bishops Lee and Kemper.

### CATHOLIC.
Furnished by Rev. John F. Quinn.

The first Catholic mission was organized by Rev. T. Tracy, in 1854. There was not a dozen Catholic familes at Omaha at that date. Rt. Rev. James O'Gorman was the first Bishop, and made Omaha his See in 1859. He died July 4, 1874. When he arrived at Omaha there were only two Churches in the State, and only two priests. When he died there were fifteen Churches and thirty-five missions, attended by thirteen priests. The Catholic population was 10,500. The present Bishop, Rt. Rev. James O'Connor, came to Omaha in 1876. There are now in Nebraska sixty Churches and ninety-five missions, cared for by forty-nine priests. There is one free college, three female academies, three convents and a number of parochial schools.

### LUTHERAN.
#### Furnished by Rev. W. A. Lipe.

Number of members, 4,000; Sunday school children, 6,000; congregations, 175; ministers, eighty; Church buildings, thirty; value of Church property, $60,000.

### BAPTIST.
#### Furnished by Rev. E. H. E. Jameson.

The first organization was effected in 1856, at Florence, under the direction of Rev. G. W. Barnes. During the past three years the Baptist Church has increased more rapidly than for any previous period. The last annual report shows 138 Churches, with a total membership of about 5,000. These Churches do not all sustain independent Sunday schools, but unite largely with other denominations. There are, however, about sixty Sunday schools, with an average attendance of 3,600 scholars. The houses of worship are generally small, but the Church at Omaha has recently finished a magnificent building, the total cost of which will not be far from $32,000. The Nebraska City Church is a model of neatness and comfort. The Lincoln Church, besides having a neat house of worship, has recently built an elegant parsonage, at a cost of $2,500.

### UNITARIAN.
#### Furnished by Rev. W. E. Copeland.

The Unitarians have six Societies in Nebraska, and one clergyman the first Unitarian Church of Omaha was formed in 1869. Its first pastor was Rev. H. F. Bond. In 1870 a house of worship was erected worth about $6,000. The Society of North Platte was formed in 1869, and in 1871 a wooden Church was erected valued at $4,000. Societies were organized in Crete and Beatrice in 1875; no Church buildings. The Society of Lincoln was formed in 1874, with Rev. W. E. Copeland as pastor. Societies were formed at Fremont and Hastings in 1875, a wooden Church building being erected at the latter place in 1878, valued at $4,000. Rev. W. E. Copeland since moving to Nebraska in 1874, has acted as State Missionary under the auspices of the American Unitarian Association of Boston.

### CHRISTIAN.

Furnished by Rev. R. C. Barrow, Tecumseh.

Organized Societies, seventy-two; membership, 3,530; ministers, 40; Sunday school children, about 2,402; houses of worship, eighteen; value of church property, $28,900.

Rev. R. C. Barrow has been a traveling missionary of the Church in Nebraska during the past fifteen years, and for ten years "State Evangelist."

We have not been able to gather statistics relating to the other denominations represented in the State, some of whom have a very large membership.

CATHOLIC CATHEDRAL, OMAHA.

# CHAPTER XI.

## MILITARY MATTERS.

### THE CIVIL WAR—THE INDIAN WAR—STATE MILITIA.

#### THE CIVIL WAR.

At the commencement of the Civil War in 1861, Nebraska, then only a Territory, had a population numbering between 28,000 and 29,000 souls, of whom, probably, not more than one-fourth were males of the age required for military service, and yet she furnished during the war of the Rebellion, three thousand three hundred and seven officers and men, or about twelve per cent. of her entire population.

The following is a list of the organizations raised, and the number composing each:

| | |
|---|---|
| First Nebraska Cavalry, rank and file | 1,370 |
| Second    "    "    "    "    " | 1,384 |
| The Curtis Horse    "    "    " | 341 |
| " Pawnee Scouts    "    "    " | 120 |
| " Omaha    "    "    "    " | 92 |
| Total | 3,307 |

The First Regiment of Nebraska Volunteers was organized in June, 1861, as Infantry, and so served until November, 1863, when they were changed, by order of the Secretary of War, to the cavalry branch of the service.

The Regiment, under command of Col. John M. Thayer, embarked at Omaha for the field of action on the 30th of July, 1861, and for the remainder of that year were stationed in Missouri, where they participated in numerous skirmishes and hard marches, going into winter quarters at Georgetown. On February 2d, 1862, they left Georgetown for Tennessee, reaching Fort Henry, in that State, on the 11th of the same month, and immediately proceeded to Fort Donaldson, then under siege by Gen'l Grant, at which place they arrived on the night of the 13th; were ordered to the battle-field the next morning and sustained a creditable part in the battle until the surrender of the Fort two days afterward. This was the first regular engagement participated in by the Regiment; the next was the great battle of Pittsburgh Landing, in April of the same year, where they were thrown into the hottest of the fight, and the men all acted so nobly, that their Division Commander, General Lew Wallace, in his report of the battle, spoke in the highest praise of their bravery and gallantry. In this battle, as also that of Fort Donaldson, General Thayer commanded the Brigade to which his Regiment was attached.

The Regiment next participated in the battle of Corinth, and during the remainder of the year, 1862, were engaged in innumerable skirmishes and scouting expeditions in different Southwestern States. On the 26th of April, 1863, while they were stationed at Cape Girardeau, Missouri, the enemy, under command of General Marmaduke, attacked that post, and were repulsed after a hotly contested fight, with great loss, the First Nebraska taking a prominent part in the battle, and also in the pursuit of the enemy, whom they overtook and had another fight with at Chalk Bluffs, on the St. Francois River.

In the fall of 1863 the Regiment was stationed at St. Louis, doing guard duty and scouting in the adjoining country. By Special Orders No. 278, from Head Quarters Department of the Missouri, dated St. Louis, October 11th, 1863, the First Nebraska was mounted as a cavalry Regiment, and in the following month were ordered to duty in Arkansas where they were engaged in scouting and had numerous heavy skirmishes with the enemy. January 18, 1864, they assisted in the capture of a squad of Rebels on Black River, and a few days later a detachment of the Regiment, under Lieut. Col. Baumer, had a three day's fight with the Rebels under Col. Freeman, at Sycamore Mountains, whom they completly routed. At Jacksonport, April 20, they were attacked in their camp by the enemy, who were driven back with considerable loss in killed and wounded. At Duvall's Bluffs the Regiment was separated, the veterans, under command of Col. Livingstone, going to St. Louis, and the non-veterans, in Command of Lieut. Col. Baumer, remaining at the Bluffs. In St. Louis the veteran Regiment were furloughed until August 13, 1864, at which date they rendezvoured at Omaha, and were assigned to duty in Nebraska. During the summer and fall of 1864, particularly, and up to the time they were mustered out of service, July 1, 1866, the Regiment rendered most valuable and efficient service on the plains in quelling the Indian disturbances of those years; in protecting the lives and property of the settlers, guarding the overland mail routes, and performing other hazardous and arduous duties. The headquarters of the Regiment during the greater portion of the time were at Fort Kearney. In July, 1865, Col. Livingston was mustered out of service under the provisions General Orders No. 83, War Department, leaving Lieut. Col. Wm. Baumer in command; and in this month, also, the First Battalian, Nebraska Veteran Cavalry was consolidated with the First Regiment Nebraska Veteran Cavalry.

It is to be regretted that the records are so incomplete that the number of killed, wounded and taken prisoners, in the different engagements in which the Regiment participated, cannot be given.

They served faithfully for upwards of five years, took an active part in many of the leading battles of the South, and when their presence was no longer needed to assist in crushing the Rebellion, they nobly came to the protection of their own frontier, then being invaded by the Sioux and other hostile Indians, and it was mainly through the valor displayed by them in many sharp contests with these savages that the Territory was saved from being over-run and desolated.

The following is a list of the field officers of the First Regiment of Neb., Vet. Volunteer Cavalry:

JOHNSON'S HISTORY OF NEBRASKA. 153

| RANK. | NAME. | RESIDENCE. | MUSTERED INTO SERVICE. | REMARKS. |
|---|---|---|---|---|
| Colonel | John M. Thayer | Omaha | June 15, '61 | Promoted to Brig. Gen., Oct. 4. 1862. |
| " | Robt. R. Livingston | Plattsmouth | Oct. 4, '62 | Must'ed out, July 1, 1865. |
| Lieut. Col. | Hiram P. Downs | Nebraska City | June 15, '61 | Resigned, Dec. 31, 1861. |
| " | Wm. D. McCord | Plattsmouth | Jan. 1, '62 | Resigned, April 22, 1862. |
| " | Robt. R. Livingston | " | Apl. 22, '62 | promoted Colonel, Oct. 4. 1862. |
| " | Wm. Baumer | Omaha | Oct. 4, '62 | Must'ed out, July 1, 1866. |
| Major. | Wm. D. McCord | Plattsmouth | June 15, '61 | Promoted Lieut. Col., Jan. 1, 1862. |
| " | Robt. R. Livingston | " | Jan. 1, '62 | Promoted Lieut. Col., Apl. 22, 1862. |
| " | Wm. Baumer | Omaha | Apl. 22, '62 | Promoted Lieut. Col. Oct. 4, 1862. |
| " | Allen Blacker | Nebraska City | Oct. 4, '62 | Resigned, March 13, 1865. |
| " | Geo. Armstrong | Omaha | Sept. 24, '64 | Tr'f'd 1st Bat. Nb. Cv. Must'd out July 1, '66. |
| " | Thos. J. Majors | Brownville | July 19, '65 | Must'ed out, July 1, 1866. |
| Adjutant. | Silas A. Strickland | Bellevue | July 3, '61 | Resigned, Apl. 22, 1862. |
| " | Francis L. Cramer | Iowa | Apl. 26, '62 | Dis'ged for promotion, Oct. 24,6'3. |
| " | F. A. McDonald | " | Jan. 1, '64 | Resigned, Apl. 22, 1865. |
| R. Q. M. | J. N. H. Patrick | Omaha | July 13, '61 | Resigned, Fed. 5, 1862. |
| " | Jno. E. Allen | " | Feb. 5, '62 | Resigned, May 9, 1862. |
| " | Chas. Thompson | " | May 9, '62 | Must'ed out, July 10, 1865. |
| Reg. Com. | John Gillespie | Brownville | Jan. 1, '64 | Must'ed out, July 10, 1865. |
| Surgeon. | Enos Lowe | Omaha | June 15, '61 | Tr'fed to Custer's Horse, Jan. 5, '62. |
| " | Jas. H. Seymour | " | Jan. 5, '62 | Died at Helena, Ark., Sept. 6, 1862. |
| " | Wm. McLelland | " | Sept. 7, '62 | Must'ed out, July 1, 1866. |
| Asst. Sur. | Wm. McLelland | " | July 25, '61 | Promoted to Surgeon, Sept. 7 1862. |
| " | N. B. Larsh | Nebraska City | Oct. 25, '62 | Resigned, Nov. 28, 1864. |
| " | G. W. Wilkinson | Omaha | Nov. 28, '62 | Must'ed out, July 10, 1865. |
| Chaplain. | Thos. W. Tipton | Brownville | July 23, '61 | Must'ed out, July 10, 1865. |

## LINE OFFICERS.

*Company A*—Captains : R. R. Livingston, A. F. McKinney, Lee P. Gillette; First Lieutenants : A. F. McKinney, N. J. Sharp, John W. Haygood, Martin B. Cutler; Second Lieutenants: N. J. Sharp, John W. Haygood, John G. Whitlock.

*Company B*—Captains : William Bumer, Chas. E. Provost ; First Lieutenants : Peter Walter, E. Bimmeman, Theo. Leubben; Second Lieutenants: Henry Keonig, E. Bimmeman, Theo. Leubben, A. Althaus.

*Company C*—Captains : J. D. N. Thompson, Thomas J. Majors, Thos. H. Griffin; First Lieutenants: Thomas J. Majors, Ruben J. Beyer, Thomas H. Griffin, David W. Smith ; Second Lieutenants: Ruben J. Beyer, Thomas H. Griffin, Wm. A. Pollock, Wilson E. Majors.

*Company D*—Captains : Allen Blacker, John C. Potts, First Lieutenants : Lee P. Gillette, John C. Potts; Second Lieutenants: Chas. E. Provost, Elias M. Lowe.

*Company E*—Captains : W. G. Hollins, S. M. Curran; First Lieutenants: S. M. Curran, W. S. Whitten, W. H. B. Stout; Second Lieutenants, J. N. H. Pa.rick, W. S. Whitten, Geo. W. Reeves, A. S. Jackson, Lewis J. Boyer.

*Company F*—Captains : Thos. M. Bowen, G. W. Burnes, Lyman Richardson, Henry Kuhl, E. Donovan ; First Lieutenants: Alex. Scott, J. P. Murphy. Wm. M. Alexander ; Second Lieutenants Alex. Scott, Jno. P. Murphy, Fred. Smith, Merril S. Tuttle, Wm. B. Raper.

*Company G*—Captains : John McConihe, Thos. J. Weatherwax; First Lieutenants: J. Y. Clopper, T. J. Weatherwax, Morgan A. Hance; Second Lieutenants: M. A. Hance, Jno. S. Seaton.

*Company H*—Captains : Geo. T. Kennedy, Wm. W. Ivory ; First Lieutenants: L. W. Sawyer, Silas A. Strickland, W. T. Clark, W. R. Bowen; Second Lieutenants: W. T. Clark, S. A. Strickland, S. W. Moore, Jas. M. Noster.

*Company I*—Captains : Jacob Butler, Henry H. Ribbel, J. P. Murphy; First Lieutenants : H. H. Ribbel, F. D. Cramer, E. Peck, J. Talbott ; Second Lieutenants: F. L. Cramer, E. Peck, Francis A. McDonald, Geo. P. Belden.

*Company K*—Captains: Jos. W. Paddock, Ed. Lawler, H. F.

C. Krumme, Lewis Lowry ; First Lieutenants : Robt. Howard, E. Lawler, E. Donovan, Jas. Steele; Second Lieutenants: E. Lawler, E. Donovan, Lyman Richardson, Lewis Lowry.

### THE SECOND REGIMENT NEBRASKA CAVALRY.

Was organized in the fall of 1862, as a nine months Regiment, and served about one year.

During the greater part of the time it was attached to General Sully's command, and participated in the campaigns of that General against the hostile Indians in Western Nebraska and Dakota, who, fresh from the great massacre of whites in Minnesota, were retiring southward, threatening the lives of the settlers on the frontier, hundreds of whom were abandoning their homes and fleeing for safety to the older settlements.

At the battle of White Stone Hill, in Dakota, in September, 1863, the causualities in the Second Nebraska, were seven men killed, fourteen wounded and ten missing ; besides the loss of five horses killed, nine wounded and nine missing. The enemy were composed of the Upper and Lower bands of Yanktonai Sioux, the Black feet Sioux, and the Brule, Sans-Arc and Cathead bands of Sioux, numbering about 2000 warriors, under the command of the celebrated Yanktonai Chief, Two Bears, who, with his forces, was completely routed. In their flight they abandoned their tents, clothing, cooking utensils, and valuables of all kinds, even leaving behind many of their children.

The following is a list of the commissioned officers of the Second Nebraska Cavalry:

#### FIELD AND STAFF.

Colonel, R. W. Furnas....................Brownville.
Lieutenant Colonel, W. F. Sapp...............Omaha.
Major, George Armstrong......... ...........Omaha.
Major, John Taffe.............................Omadi.
Major, John W. Pearman...............Nebraska City.
Surgeon, Aurelius Bowen............ ......Nebraska City.
Assistant Surgeon, W. S. Latta............Plattsmouth.
Assistant Surgeon, H. O. Hanna......... ....———
Adjutant, Henry M. Atkinson..............Brownville.
Reg. Quarter Master Josiah S. McCormick......Omaha.
Reg. Commissary, John Q. Goss.............Bellevue.

### OFFICERS OF THE LINE.

*Company A*—Captain, Peter S. Reed; First Lieutenant, Silas E. Seeley, Second Lieutenant, Elias H. Clark.

*Company B*—Captain, Roger T. Beall; First Lieutenant Charles D. Davis; Second Lieutenant, Chas. F. Porter.

*Company C*—Captain, Theodore W. Bedford; First Lieutenant, Jas W. Coleman; Second Lieutenants, H. M. Atkinson, Jacob B. Berger.

*Company D*—Captain, Henry Edwards; First Lieutenant, Henry Gray; Second Lieutenant, Wilbur B. Hugus.

*Company E*—Captains, Robert W. Furnas, Lewis Hill; First Lieutenants Lewis Hill, John H. Maun; Second Lieutenants, John H. Maun, Alex. S. Stewart.

*Company F*—Captain, Dominick Laboo; First Lieutenants, Chas. W. Hall, R. Mason; Second Lieutenants, R. Mason, H. R. Newcomb.

*Company G*—Captain, Oliver P. Bayne; First Lieutenant, Chauncey H. Norris; Second Lieutenant, Joseph F. Wade.

*Company H*—Captain, John W. Marshall; First Lieutenant, Isaac Wiles; Second Lieutenant, Abraham Deyo.

*Company I*—Captains, John Taffe, Silas T. Leaming; First Lieutenants, Silas T. Leaming, Moses H. Deming; Second Lieutenants, Moses H. Deming, Jacob H. Hallock.

*Company K*—Captain Edwin Patrick; First Lieutenant, Wm. B. James; Second Lieutenant, Philip P. Williams.

*Company L*—Captain, Daniel W. Allison; First Lieutenant John J. Baiyne; Second Lieutenant, Daniel Reavis.

*Company M*—Captain, Stearns Cooper; First Lieutenant, Obadiah B. Hewitt; Second Lieutenant, Francis B. Chaplin.

#### FIRST BATTALION NEBRASKA VETERAN CAVALRY.

When the Second Nebraska Cavalry was mustered out of service in September, 1863, Major George Armstrong was commissioned by Governor Saunders to raise an independent battalion of cavalry from the veterans of the Second Regiment, to serve during the war. This battalion, consisting of companies A, B, C and D, was mustered into service as the First Battalion, Nebraska Veteran Cavalry, and assigned to duty on the Plains.

## JOHNSON'S HISTORY OF NEBRASKA. 157

In July, 1865 this battalion was consolidated with the First Regiment Nebraska Veteran Cavalry, and one year later was mustered out of service.

The following is a list of officers of the First Battalion Nebraska Veteran Cavalry.

*Company A*—Captains, Geo. Armstrong, Chas. F, Porter; First Lieutenants, Chas. F. Porter, John Talbot; Second Lieutenants, H. F. C. Krumme, Merril S. Tuttle.

*Company B*—Captain, Z. Jackson; First Lieutenants, Jos. N. Tuttwiler, W. H. B. Stout; Second Lieutenant Jas. M. Nosler.

*Company C*—Captain, Henry Kuhle; First Lieutenant, Martin B. Cutler; Second Lieutenant, Geo. P. Belden.

*Company D*—Captain, Henry F. C. Krumme; First Lieutenant, Wm. R. Bowen; Second Lieutenant, Samuel A. Lewis.

### CURTIS' HORSE.

The four Companies, A, B, C and D, composing the first battalion of this Cavalry Regiment, which was afterwards united with the Fifth Iowa Cavalry, were mainly recruited in Nebraska.

*Company A*, was recruited at Omaha by M. T. Patrick, and was composed chiefly of men from Nebraska. It was mustered into the U. S. service at Omaha September 14, 1861, by Lieut. J. N. H. Patrick; M. T. Patrick, of Omaha, Captain.

*Company B*, was recruited at Omaha by J. T. Croft, and was composed of men from Nebraska and a few from Iowa. It was mustered into service at Omaha, September 21, 1861, by Lieut. J. N. H. Patrick; John T. Croft, of Omaha, Captain.

*Company C*, was recruited at Nebraska City and in Page County, Iowa, by Captain J. M. Young and Alfred Matthias, and was mustered into service at Omaha, September 19, 1861, as a half Company, and October 3, 1861, as a full Company, by Lieut. J. N. H. Patrick; J. Morris Young, of Page County, Iowa, Captain.

*Company D*, commenced recruiting at Omaha, and was mustered into service as a half Company, with Wm. Curl as First Lieutenant, at St. Louis, October 30, 1861. Here it was joined by a detachment of Missouri Volunteers, and was mustered in as a full company at St. Louis, November 13, 1861, with Harlan Beard, of Nebraska, as Captain.

The following is a list of the Field Officers of the Curtis Horse Cavalry Regiment at the completion of its organization, February 1, 1862:

W. W. Lowe, Colonel; M. T. Patrick, Lieut-Colonel; W. B. McGeorge, Adjutant; Enos Lowe, Surgeon; B. T. Wise, Assistant Surgeon; Jerome Spillman, Chaplain.

### OFFICERS OF THE NEBRASKA BATTALION.

*Company A.*—Captains— M. T. Patrick, promoted Lieutenant Colonel, November 13, 1861; Wm. Kelsey, promoted Major, February 1, 1862; John J. Lower, resigned December 19, 1862; Samuel Paul, promoted from Q. M. Sergeant.

First Lieutenants—Wm. Kelsay, promoted Captain, November 13, 1861; John J. Lower, promoted Captain February 1, 1862; Horace Wallers, resigned June 1, 1862.

Second Lieutenants—John J Lower, promoted First Lieutenant, November 13, 1861; Horace Wallers, promoted First Lieutenant February 1, 1862; F. A. Williams, resigned June 8, 1862; Marion A. Hinds, promoted from First Sergeant.

*Company B.*—Captain—John T. Croft.

First Lieutenants—Milton S. Summers, wounded and died August 29, 1862; Erastus G. McNeely, promoted from Second Lieutenant.

Second Lieutenants—Jere. C. Wilcox, promoted Captain of Company H; Erastus G. McNeely, promoted First Lieutenant September, 1, 1862; Douglas H. Stephens, promoted from First Sergeant.

*Company C.*—Captains—Morris J. Young, promoted Major, November 1, 1862; Alfred Matthias, promoted from First Lieutenant.

First Lieutenants—Alfred Matthias, promoted Captain, December 22, 1862; Chas Langdon, promoted from Second Lieutenant.

Second Lieutenants—Charles Langdon, promoted First Lieutenant December 22, 1862; Wm. T. Wilhite, promoted from First Sergeant.

*Company D.*—Captains—Harlan Beard, promoted Major, November 1, 1862; Wm. Curl, promoted from First Lieutenant.

First Lieutenants—Wm. Curl promoted Captain November 1, 1862; W. C. McBeath,

Second Lieutenants—Wm. Aston, promoted Bat. Adjt. January 9, 1862; Wm. C. McBeath, promoted First Lieutenant November 1, 1862; Wm. Buchanan, promoted from First Sargeant.

The Curtis Horse served their time in the Southwestern Army, where they fought heroically in some of the most prominent battles and saw much hard service generally. They were almost constantly on the go, being engaged in many of those great raids which so crippled the enemy and gained for the Cavalry Branch of the service such deserved fame, especially during the latter part of the Rebellion.

## THE INDIAN OUTBREAK OF 1864.

During the summer of 1864 Nebraska was again invaded by the Sioux, Cheyennes and other powerful bands of hostile Indians, who threatened the annihilation of the frontier settlements.

Fears had been entertained for a long time prior to the date mentioned that an Indian outbreak would occur unless the Government did something to check it, and in response to the calls of the settlers for protection, the Seventh Iowa Volunteer Cavalry was ordered out in the summer of 1863, and assigned to duty along the line of the overland stage route, from Fort Kearney westward to the frontier of the Territory.

The officer directly in command of these troops in the locality named, was Major George M. O'Brien, (afterwards General O'Brien) who, being a skillful civil and military engineer, at once commenced constructing fortifications and putting the country occupied by his command in a thorough defencible position. He selected a site for a new Post at Cottonwood Springs, and constructed the same, naming it Fort Cottonwood, which name was subsequently changed to that of Fort McPherson, and became one of the most important posts on the frontier.

In the summer of 1864 the First Nebraska Veteran Volunteer Cavalry was also assigned to duty in this locality, which, with a few Companies of Regulars, constituted the force on the plains at the time the outbreak commenced.

This force, however, was deemed entirely inadequate to keep in check or afford protection to the settlers against the immense numbers of savages who were swarming down the valleys and on the overland roads, capturing the mail stages and emigrant trains, murdering the emigrants and ranchmen, taking captive the women and children, destroying stock and crops, and threatening general destruction to the whole Western border.

The settlers from the valleys of the Blues, the Platte, and at all the unprotected points, were abandoning their homes and fleeing with their stock and household goods as best they could, in one continuous stream toward the older Counties, or to some place of rendezvous, where a few of the more courageous threw up breastworks and made other hasty preparations to meet and give battle to the invaders. The excitement in the Territory was most intense, and not without good cause. Hundreds of the settlers and their families had already been butchered and their homes laid waste, and the Indians flushed with success were advancing rapidly toward the Missouri River, in greater numbers than had ever before threatened the Territory.

In this emergency Governor Saunders promptly called out additional troops to aid those already in the field.

The following militia Companies were hastily organized and sent to the front:

*Company A*—First Regiment, Second Brigade, fifty-three men, rank and file, mustered into service August 12, 1864; served four months and nine days; Thos. B. Stevenson, Captain; F. J. Bruner, M. B. Corbin, First Lieutenants; R. Andrews, Second Lieutenant.

*Company B*—First Regiment, Second Brigade, fifty-three men, rank and file, mustered into service August 13, 1864; served six months; Isaac Wiles, Captain; Henry J. Straight, First Lieutenant; Leslie C. Johnson, Second Lieutenant.

*Company C*—First Regiment, Second Brigade, fifty-seven men, rank and file, mustered into service August 24, 1864; served five months and thirteen days; Alvin G. White Captain; Wm. B. Rapier, First Lieutenant; Levi Anthony, Second Lieutenant.

*Company A*—First Regiment, First Brigade, forty-seven men, rank and file, mustered into the service August 30, 1864; served two months and twelve days; John R. Porter, Captain; Allen T. Riley, First Lieutenant; Martin Dunham, Second Lieutenant.

A detachment of artillery militia under command of Captain Edward P. Childs, numbering thirteen men, rank and file, was mustered into the service August 30, 1864, and served two months and twelve days.

August 31, 1864, a Company of Pawnee Indians was called into service by authority of the Provost Marshal General, for the term of one year. They were organized and commanded by Captain Frank North. They were known as Company "A," Pawnee Scouts, numbering ninety men, rank and file, and were mustered into the United States service, January 13, 1865.

By an order of the War Department, a Company consisting of eighty-five men, rank and file, of Omaha Indians, was called into the United States service for the term of one year, with Edwin R. Nash, Captain. They were mustered out of service, July 16, 1866.

The timely and valuable services rendered by these troops connot be too highly estimated. Their prompt assistance in checking the onward march of the savage foe no doubt saved the inhabitants of the Territory from a fate similar to that visited upon the settlers in north western Minnesota in 1862, when several hundred of them were massacred, and by these same Indians.

11

## STATE MILITIA.

The following is a list of the militia Companies in Nebraska, organized since 1875:

| NAME OF COMPANY. | NO. OF MEN. | DATE OF OR'ZATION | STATION. | COUNTY. | NAME OF CAPTAIN. |
|---|---|---|---|---|---|
| Co. A, 1st Reg. Mil'a In'ty | 68 | 1876 | Lincoln | Lancaster | Julius Pfisterer |
| Co. B. " Kearney Guards. | 40 | Nov. 5, '75 | Kearney Junction | Buffalo | E. C. Calkins |
| Co. C, 1st Reg. Paddock Guards. | 59 | June 9, '75 | Beatrice | Gage | A. W. Conlee |
| Co. D, 1st Reg. Mil'a In'ty | 29 | Aug. 23, '76 | Papillion | Sarpy | E. A. Sexon |
| Co. E, " " " | 45 | Sept. 26,'76 | New Castle | Dixon | L. H. Smith |
| Co. F, " " " | 55 | Sept. '76 | Sidney | Cheyenne | Thos. Kane |
| Co. G, " " " | 44 | Sept. 1, '76 | Plum Creek | Dawson | Thos. J. Hewitt |
| Co. H, " " " | 61 | Sept. 18, '76 | Orleans | Harlan | Horace Cole |
| Co. I, " " " | 68 | Sept. 1, '76 | O'Neil City | Holt | M. H. McGrath |
| Co. J, " " " | 39 | Sept. 1. '76 | Cozad | Dawson | T. A. Taylor |
| 1st Neb. Light Artillery. | 30 | June 10, '75 | Blue Springs | Gage | C. M. Murdock |
| Ceder Rangers. | 40 | June 19, '76 | Doublin | Greeley | Robt. Gardiner |
| Greeley Co. Home Guards | 40 | June 15, '76 | Lamartine | Greeley | Joseph Conway |
| Garber Co. Rangers. | 67 | June 3, '76 | Douglas Grove | Wheeler | W. H. Comstock |
| Howard Co. Guards. | 49 | Nov. 28, 76 | St. Paul | Howard | O. M. Gold berry |
| Indian Home Guards. | 44 | Nov. '76 | Danbury | R'd Willow | S. W. Stilgeboner |
| Taylor Co. Mta. Rangers. | 45 | May 29, '76 | The Forks | Wheeler | R. P. Alger |
| Red Willo.. Co. Guards. | 41 | Nov. '76 | Red Willow | R'd Willow | W. D. Wildeman |
| Sherman Co. Guards. | 38 | Dec, 5, '76 | Loup City | Sherman | J. H. Gardner |
| Valley Co. Rangers | 97 | Dec. '76 | Ord | Valley | Frank Chubbuck |
| Victoria Guards. | 14 | May 25, '76 | New Helena | Custer | C. R. Mathews |
| Co. K., 1st Reg, State Mil. | 44 | May 21, '78 | Juniata | Adams | S. J. Shirley |
| Co. A., 2d " " " | 51 | June 21, '78 | Red Cloud | Webster | Joseph Garber |
| Stevenson Battery. | 45 | May 10, '78 | Nebraska City | Otoe | T. B. Stevenson |
| Garber State Guards. | 55 | May 8, '77 | Nebraska City | Otoe | Brock'y Kinney |
| North Platte Guards. | 89 | Nov. 14, '78 | North Platte | Lincoln | Frank North |
| Otoe Rifles. | 65 | Nov. 7, '77 | Nebraska City | Otoe | A. S. Cole |

# CHAPTER XII.

## IMMIGRATION.

The character of immigration to this country, and its usual routes from East to West, is a subject deserving of more than a passing notice in this connection. It is a matter of surprise to many that there is such a pronounced difference between the class of immigration to the Western States, and that to the southwestern sections of our country. All comprehend the fact that there is a wide difference in the general characteristics and habits, in enterprise and industry between the two classes, even when immigration is from the same general source, yet, they do not understand why it is that settlers in Nebraska, Iowa, or any other of the more immediate Western States should bring with them those habits of industry, economy and enterprise, while those starting from the same point and settling in the south or southwest—south of the thirty-fourth degree of north latitude—should, in a brief space of time, lose those habits entirely, and become imbued with that same inertia, indolence or lassitude witnessed in those of the manor born. This indolence is a habit of an entirely different birth from slothfullness and improvidence. It is one of the legitimate results of climate; results that it is impossible to escape, simply because there is an absence of that metalic element in the air, so necessary in infusing vigor and animation to animal life. Under this influence the body becomes torpid and inactive, and indeed, the most active, enterprising and vigorous soon succumb to the influences of the climate in this respect. Nor is this effect confined to animal life. It takes within its scope vegetables, which, after their maturity, cannot be kept for any length of time—as at the North—without their decaying. This is also the case with fruits, which, like potatoes, turnips, cabbage, onions, etc., cannot be carried through the fall and winter months. Neither can meats be cured in salt or brine there as at the North. This is one of the chief obstacles encountered by settlers south of the thirty-fourth degree of north latitude, and this obstacle is too serious to be overcome even by the numerous other advantages the more southern section of this country offers to immigration.

Then, again, the flow of immigration from East to West has, as a rule, been over the two great parallel lines—natural routes—from the Atlantic to the Pacific, the one known as the great central route, which traverses east and west, the States of Massachusetts, New York, northern Ohio and southern Michigan, Illinois, Iowa, Nebraska, Wyoming, Nevada, and California, to the Pacific, and the other known as the great valley or plateau of the Chattanooga, which commences at the Atlantic in North Carolina, traversing in its westerly course, the States of Tennessee, Georgia, Mississippi, Arkansas, Texas, New Mexico, Southern Arizona, ending at San Diego, on the Pacific. It was over these two great parallel lines that the early pioneer, with his pack upon his shoulders, first wended his way, only to be followed at a later day by the pack horse, wagon and stage coach, and lastly by the railway engine, the great representative of American enterprise, the chief factor in developing the many resourses of this country.

Confining its movement to these two great routes, seldom resorting to latteral lines, immigration to the immediate Western States and Territories on the central route has been chiefly from the Eastern and Middle States, as also from the larger portion and better class of Europeans landing at New York, Boston and Philadelphia. While on the other hand, immigration over the southern line has been and is still largely composed of people from the eastern and middle portions of what are called the Southern States, or to States east of the Mississippi River and south of the thirty-seventh parallel of north latitude.

The total immigration to the United States, from 1820 to March 31, 1879, was 9,794,264, of which 5,848,423 were males, 3,810,944 females and 134,897 sex not stated.

JOHNSON'S HISTORY OF NEBRASKA. 165

The following statement shows the immigration to this country from August 1, 1855, to December 31, 1878, as also the States and Territories chosen by the immigrants:

| DESTINATION OF IMMIGRANTS. | FROM AUG. 1, 1855, TO DEC. 31, 1873. | 1874. | 1875. | 1876. | 1877. | 1878. | TOTAL. |
|---|---|---|---|---|---|---|---|
| Minnesota | 51,045 | 4,448 | 3,186 | 2,507 | 1,962 | 4,092 | 67,240 |
| Mississippi | 1,233 | 21 | 20 | 38 | 16 | 21 | 1,349 |
| Missouri | 61,214 | 2,602 | 1,780 | 1,274 | 1,232 | 1,267 | 69,369 |
| Montana | 214 | 15 | 22 | 20 | 13 | 34 | 318 |
| Nebraska | 10,292 | 3,027 | 1,219 | 1,251 | 1,326 | 2,613 | 19,728 |
| Nevada | 588 | 344 | 302 | 204 | 166 | 291 | 1,895 |
| New Hampsh'e. | 3,698 | 147 | 140 | 101 | 83 | 75 | 4,244 |
| New Jersey | 103,261 | 5,350 | 3,840 | 2,356 | 1,496 | 2,260 | 118,563 |
| New Mexico | 85 | | 3 | 2 | 22 | 9 | 121 |
| New York | 1,346,906 | 52,444 | 35,560 | 27,068 | 24,992 | 34,586 | 1,521,556 |
| North Carolina. | 942 | 8 | 18 | 17 | 22 | 26 | 1,033 |
| Ohio | 175,881 | 7,142 | 4,171 | 2,976 | 2,505 | 2,932 | 195,607 |
| Oregon | 483 | 92 | 72 | 70 | 51 | 78 | 846 |
| Pennsylvania.. | 344,807 | 17,167 | 8,813 | 5,925 | 4,764 | 5,554 | 387,030 |
| Rhode Island.. | 30,529 | 1,678 | 1,155 | 641 | 526 | 551 | 35,080 |
| South Carolina. | 2,317 | 122 | 116 | 54 | 51 | 64 | 2,724 |
| Tennessee | 5,789 | 257 | 168 | 116 | 120 | 122 | 6,572 |
| Texas | 2,873 | 214 | 156 | 172 | 229 | 600 | 4,244 |
| Utah | 30,355 | 2,075 | 1,575 | 1,325 | 1,522 | 1,940 | 38,792 |
| Vermont | 5,738 | 194 | 158 | 108 | 55 | 73 | 6,326 |
| Virginia | 9,800 | 266 | 149 | 113 | 78 | 120 | 10,526 |
| Washingt'n Ty. | 59 | 20 | 43 | 13 | 11 | 28 | 174 |
| West Virginia.. | 1,132 | 217 | 78 | 47 | 52 | 57 | 1,583 |
| Wisconsin | 167,288 | 7,611 | 4,161 | 3,172 | 2,445 | 2,878 | 187,555 |
| Wyoming | 120 | 56 | 35 | 28 | 26 | 35 | 300 |
| Alabama | 812 | 30 | 21 | 36 | 16 | 42 | 957 |

*Continued from page 165.*

| DESTINATION OF IMMIGRANTS. | FROM AUG. 1, 1855, TO DEC. 31, 1873. | 1874. | 1875. | 1876. | 1877. | 1878. | TOTAL. |
|---|---|---|---|---|---|---|---|
| Arizona | 5 | | | 2 | | 1 | 8 |
| Arkansas | 450 | 38 | 93 | 114 | 5 | 28 | 728 |
| California | 35,619 | 4,022 | 3,848 | 2,879 | 2,787 | 2,708 | 51,863 |
| Colorado | 1,078 | 334 | 247 | 148 | 209 | 340 | 2,356 |
| Connecticut | 59,441 | 3,016 | 2,470 | 1,419 | 1,044 | 1,336 | 68,726 |
| Dakota | 885 | 1,930 | 544 | 471 | 588 | 888 | 5,300 |
| Delaware | 3,170 | 113 | 48 | 42 | 44 | 41 | 3,458 |
| Dist. Columbia | 10,603 | 314 | 173 | 103 | 112 | 123 | 11,428 |
| Florida | 554 | 30 | 70 | 53 | 29 | 36 | 772 |
| Georgia | 2,696 | 122 | 132 | 45 | 69 | 40 | 3,104 |
| Idaho | 78 | 52 | 17 | 8 | 5 | 12 | 172 |
| Illinois | 318,934 | 10,217 | 8,399 | 6,135 | 5,395 | 5,723 | 354,803 |
| Indiana | 42,727 | 1,676 | 1,188 | 796 | 547 | 753 | 47,687 |
| Iowa | 66,668 | 3,965 | 3,735 | 2,842 | 2,059 | 2,686 | 81,955 |
| Kansas | 12,527 | 2,098 | 1,173 | 3,137 | 1,133 | 1,940 | 21,738 |
| Kentucky | 15,235 | 458 | 304 | 301 | 243 | 222 | 16,763 |
| Louisiana | 5,733 | 232 | 191 | 123 | 151 | 268 | 6,698 |
| Maine | 5,526 | 220 | 153 | 117 | 115 | 145 | 6,276 |
| Maryland | 24,483 | 1,215 | 753 | 397 | 266 | 392 | 27,506 |
| Massachusetts | 154,952 | 6,982 | 4,349 | 2,791 | 2,581 | 2,741 | 174,396 |
| Michigan | 91,429 | 4,851 | 3,122 | 2,180 | 1,730 | 1,910 | 105,222 |
| Total to United States | 3,209,984 | 147,432 | 97,970 | 73,737 | 62,887 | 82,681 | 3,764,691 |
| Total to other Countries | 90,372 | 2,330 | 1,933 | 1,298 | 963 | 1,120 | 98,016 |
| Grand total | 3,300,356 | 149,762 | 99,903 | 75,035 | 63,850 | 83,801 | 3,772,707 |

The tide of immigration commenced its flow towards points west of the Missouri River as early as 1847, the Mormons being the *avaunt courier* of the moving thousands that were attracted towards the Pacific coast by the gold excitement that began in 1849. And it was in a great measure due to that excitement that the vast, fertile country stretching away from the Missouri River to the base of the Rocky Mountains, was so rapidly developed into productive and vigorous life. Yes, it was owing to the constant and enormous flow of travel to California, Utah and Oregon, from 1849 to 1854 that the grand enterprise of a transcontinental railway was conceived in 1853, and matured by provisions for its construction in 1862. A chain of events, beginning with the date that California was acquired by this Government, were not only fruitful in their results so far as pertains to the development of the various latent resources of the Great West, but were the chief factor in the construction of a railway from ocean to ocean, a work which stands as the marvel of the age.

The towering ranges of the Rocky and Sierra Nevada Mountains, which like grim sentinels stand guard over the mines of wealth that lie buried in the slopes beyond, have been overcome and converted into a steel ribbed railway, and along their bleak and rugged sides, which before, could only be passed after weeks of the most arduous toil, are now avenues over which travel and commerce passes at the rate of twenty miles an hour,

The change wrought in the past dozen years is truly wonderful. A country rich in agricultural productiveness, traversed by railways, and doted all over with thriving towns and cities, marks the route, along whose toilsome trails, but a few short years ago, moved countless thousands who turned their footsteps westward in search of fickle fortune or homes in the New West. Immigration then moved upon parallel lines, those coming from the East and Southeast, via St. Louis, followed the south bank of the Platte, while those from the East and Northeast, moving via Chicago, followed the north valley of the Platte, the two routes forming a junction at Fort Kearney, those north of the Platte crossing over to the south side, and the whole again crossing to the north side at a point near old Julesburgh.

In this ever moving human caravan, one would see many hardy gold-seekers making the journey on foot, with their outfit strapped on their backs, while further on in the line of march would be seen hand carts and wheelbarrows vigorously propelled by human strength; and still further on were carriages and vehicles of all description, from a light sulky to ponderous freight wagons, many of which were covered and well arranged for cooking and sleeping apartments. Some were propelled by horses or mules, some by oxen some by cows, while other of the lighter class, employed as motive power, goats and even dogs. Vast droves of cattle and sheep were also to be seen moving towards the west. Such were the active, ever changing scenes that met the eye during the palmy days of the over-land route to California. But the march of civilization and steam has wrought the change we see to-day, and abridged the time between the two oceans from three months to one week, railways now being the pioneers and the locomotive whistle the great tocsion of prosperity and civilization.

HIGH SCHOOL BUILDING, FREMONT.

# CHAPTER XIII.

## POPULATION.

The following statement shows the population of Nebraska, by Counties, as taken from the census returns, from 1855—one year after the organization of the Territory—to 1879.

| COUNTIES. | 1855. | 1856. | 1860. | 1870. | 1874. | 1875. | 1876. | 1878. | 1879. |
|---|---|---|---|---|---|---|---|---|---|
| Adams | | | | 19 | 2,694 | 3,093 | 3,940 | 5,583 | 8,162 |
| Antelope | | | | | 1,387 | 1,289 | 1,303 | 1,575 | 2,178 |
| Boone | | | | | 798 | 965 | 1,099 | 1,503 | 2,626 |
| Buffalo | | | 114 | 193 | 2,106 | 2,861 | 4,396 | 4,819 | 6,878 |
| Burt | 89 | 146 | 338 | 2,847 | 3,866 | 4,041 | 4,354 | 4,992 | 5,165 |
| Butler | | | 27 | 1,290 | 4,027 | 4,440 | 4,730 | 6,025 | 7,310 |
| Cass | 712 | 1,251 | 3,369 | 8,151 | 10,397 | 10,452 | 10,787 | 11,936 | 13,435 |
| Cedar | | | 246 | 1,032 | 1,817 | 1,979 | 2,421 | 2,400 | 2,775 |
| Chase | | | | | | | | | |
| Cheyenne | | | | 190 | 449 | 457 | 476 | 899 | 1,218 |
| Clay | | | 165 | 54 | 3,622 | 4,183 | 4,787 | 7,012 | 9,373 |
| Colfax | | | | 1,424 | 3,458 | 3,651 | 4,187 | 5,080 | 5,960 |
| Cuming | | 8 | 67 | 2,964 | 3,644 | 6,152 | 6,402 | 7,744 | 9,095 |
| Custer | | | | | | | | 371 | 696 |
| Dakota | 86 | 646 | 819 | 2,040 | 2,759 | 2,759 | 3,006 | 3,107 | 3,208 |
| Dawson | | | 16 | 103 | 800 | 1,407 | 2,133 | 2,581 | 3,871 |
| Dixon | | | 247 | 1,345 | 2,842 | 2,886 | 3,263 | 3,512 | 4,061 |
| Dodge | 139 | 313 | 309 | 4,212 | 6,893 | 7,534 | 8,465 | 98,55 | 11,579 |
| Douglas | 1,028 | 3,465 | 4,328 | 19,982 | 22,670 | 24,698 | 25,722 | 31,113 | 36,557 |
| Dundy | | | | | | | | | |
| Fillmore | | | | 238 | 4,380 | 4,731 | 5,373 | 6,556 | 8,760 |
| Franklin | | | | 26 | 1,821 | 1,807 | 1,953 | 2,756 | 4,137 |
| Frontier | | | | | 128 | 139 | 243 | 313 | 626 |
| Furnas | | | | | 1,342 | 1,482 | 1,550 | 1,810 | 2,982 |
| Gage | | | 421 | 3,359 | 5,290 | 5,714 | 6,021 | 7,486 | 9,629 |
| Greeley | | | | | 209 | 229 | 194 | 473 | 753 |
| Gosper | | | | | 100 | 261 | 250 | 313 | 622 |
| Hall | | | 116 | 1,057 | 3,842 | 4,414 | 4,615 | 5,119 | 6,375 |
| Hamilton | | | | 130 | 3,186 | 3,526 | 6,253 | 5,026 | 6,478 |
| Harlan | | | | | 1,847 | 2,027 | 2,140 | 2,388 | 4,193 |
| Hayes | | | | | | | | 300 | 600 |
| Hitchcock | | | | | | 95 | 90 | 132 | 264 |
| Howard | | | | | 1,339 | 1,708 | 1,680 | 2,329 | 3,246 |
| Holt | | | | | | | | 1,300 | 1,839 |
| Jefferson | | | 122 | 2,440 | 3,375 | 3,814 | 4,075 | 5,016 | 6,280 |
| Johnson | | | 528 | 3,429 | 4,644 | 4,862 | 4,908 | 5,338 | 6,302 |
| Kearney | | | 474 | 58 | 327 | 560 | 803 | 1,517 | 2,840 |
| Keith | | | | | 95 | 124 | 108 | 137 | 274 |
| Knox | | | 152 | 261 | 1,133 | 1,524 | 1,248 | 1,446 | 2,088 |
| Lancaster | | 125 | 153 | 7,074 | 14,308 | 15,224 | 15,407 | 15,658 | 18,675 |
| Lincoln | | | 117 | 16 | 2,555 | 2,855 | 1,327 | 1,658 | 2,017 |

## Continued from page 169.

| COUNTIES. | 1855 | 1856. | 1860. | 1870. | 1874. | 1875. | 1876. | 1878. | 1879. |
|---|---|---|---|---|---|---|---|---|---|
| Madison | | | | 1,133 | 3,335 | 3,171 | 3,245 | 3,683 | 4,280 |
| Merrick | | | 109 | 557 | 3,092 | 3,101 | 3,139 | 3,786 | 4,625 |
| Nemaha | 604 | 1,281 | 3,139 | 7,593 | 8,202 | 9,131 | 8,276 | 9,017 | 10,504 |
| Nuckolls | | | 22 | 8 | 942 | 1,104 | 1,381 | 2,159 | 2,964 |
| Nance | | | | | | | | | 1,000 |
| Otoe | 1,188 | 1,862 | 4,211 | 12,345 | 12,380 | 13,270 | 11,756 | 12,411 | 13,863 |
| Pawnee | 142 | 301 | 882 | 4,171 | 5,057 | 4,881 | 4,783 | 5,164 | 5,899 |
| Phelps | | | | | 101 | 110 | 151 | 326 | 1,275 |
| Pierce | | | | 152 | 557 | 606 | 631 | 565 | 684 |
| Platte | | 35 | 782 | 1,899 | 3,944 | 4,378 | 4,689 | 6,045 | 7,587 |
| Polk | | | 19 | 136 | 2,764 | 3,031 | 3,356 | 3,931 | 5,023 |
| Red Willow | | | | | 545 | 694 | 663 | 536 | 963 |
| Richardson | 299 | 532 | 2,385 | 9,780 | 15,000 | 15,000 | 11,327 | 12,509 | 13,433 |
| Saline | | | 39 | 3,106 | 7,718 | 8,163 | 9,227 | 10,453 | 12,417 |
| Sarpy | | | 1,201 | 2,913 | 3,164 | 3,385 | 3,735 | 4,196 | 4,392 |
| Saunders | | | | 4,547 | 8,754 | 10,382 | 10,462 | 12,514 | 13,528 |
| Seward | | | | 2,953 | 7,429 | 6,601 | 6,875 | 7,991 | 9,389 |
| Sherman | | | | | 460 | 496 | 561 | 594 | 1,120 |
| Stanton | | | | 636 | 1,135 | 1,158 | 1,223 | 1,410 | 1,486 |
| Sioux | | | | | | | | 275 | 550 |
| Thayer | | | | | 1,781 | 2,139 | 2,410 | 3,391 | 4,535 |
| Valley | | | | | 264 | 287 | 749 | 1,075 | 1,540 |
| Washington | 207 | 751 | 1,249 | 4,452 | 5,304 | 6,114 | 6,286 | 7,116 | 8,361 |
| Wayne | | | | 182 | 272 | 431 | 299 | 386 | 481 |
| Webster | | | | 16 | 2,250 | 2,590 | 2,962 | 4,341 | 5,947 |
| Wheeler | | | | | | | | 350 | 700 |
| York | | | | 604 | 4,593 | 5,266 | 5,921 | 7,348 | 9,112 |
| Unorg'd Ter'y | | | 2,371 | 1,660 | 1,600 | 3,000 | 4,000 | 15,000 | 17,625 |
| TOTAL | 4,494 | 10,716 | 28,841 | 122,993 | 230,007 | 246,280 | 257,747 | 313,748 | 386,410 |

The increase in population, as will be seen by the foregoing statement, has been constant and remarkably rapid. From 1855 to 1860 the increase was 541 per cent.; from 1860 to 1870, it was 326 per cent.; from 1870 to 1875, 100 per cent., and from 1875 to 1879, nearly fifty-seven per cent., or an increase in the last nine years of 214 per cent., and probably 50,000 will be added in 1879.

### TABLE OF POPULATION—1879.

| COUNTIES. | MALES. | FEMALES. | TOTAL. | COUNTIES. | MALES. | FEMALES. | TOTAL. |
|---|---|---|---|---|---|---|---|
| Adams | 4,492 | 3,670 | 8,162 | Cheyenne | 788 | 430 | 1,218 |
| Antelope | 1,199 | 979 | 2,178 | Clay | 5,112 | 4,261 | 9,373 |
| Boone | 1,462 | 1,164 | 2,626 | Colfax | 3,078 | 2,882 | 5,960 |
| Buffalo | 3,711 | 3,167 | 6,878 | Cuning | | | 9,095 |
| Burt | 2,865 | 2,300 | 5,165 | Custer | 415 | 281 | 696 |
| Butler | 3,956 | 3,354 | 7,310 | Dakota | 1,717 | 1,491 | 3,208 |
| Cass | 7,305 | 6,130 | 13,435 | Dawson | | | 3,871 |
| Cedar | 1,517 | 1,258 | 2,775 | Dixon | 2,129 | 1,832 | 4,061 |

*Continued from page* 170.

| COUNTIES. | MALES. | FEMALES. | TOTAL. | COUNTIES. | MALES. | FEMALES. | TOTAL. |
|---|---|---|---|---|---|---|---|
| Dodge | | | 11,579 | Nemaha | | | 10,504 |
| Douglas | | | 36,557 | Nuckolls | 1,615 | 1,349 | 2,964 |
| Dundy | | | | Nance | | | 1,000 |
| Fillmore | 4,766 | 3,994 | 8,760 | Otoe | 7,412 | 6,451 | 13,863 |
| Franklin | 2,245 | 1,892 | 4,137 | Pawnee | 3,102 | 2,797 | 5,899 |
| Frontier | | | 626 | Phelps | | | 1,275 |
| Furnas | 1,711 | 1,271 | 2,982 | Pierce | 357 | 327 | 684 |
| Gage | 5,196 | 4,433 | 9,629 | Platte | 4,125 | 3,462 | 7,587 |
| Greeley | 436 | 317 | 753 | Polk | 2,725 | 2,298 | 5,023 |
| Gosper | 354 | 268 | 622 | Red Willow | 544 | 419 | 963 |
| Hall | 3,465 | 2,910 | 6,375 | Richardson | 7,227 | 6,206 | 13,433 |
| Hamilton | 3,527 | 2,951 | 6,478 | Saline | 7,271 | 5,146 | 12,417 |
| Harlan | | | 4,193 | Sarpy | 2,431 | 1,961 | 4,392 |
| Hayes | | | 600 | Saunders | 7,119 | 6,409 | 13,528 |
| Hitchcock | | | 264 | Seward | | | 9,389 |
| Howard | 1,712 | 1,534 | 3,246 | Sherman | 652 | 468 | 1,120 |
| Holt | 1,063 | 776 | 1,839 | Stanton | 788 | 698 | 1,486 |
| Jefferson | 3,377 | 2,903 | 6,280 | Sioux | | | 550 |
| Johnson | 3,391 | 2,911 | 6,302 | Thayer | | | 4,535 |
| Kearney | | | 2,840 | Valley | 838 | 702 | 1,540 |
| Keith | | | 274 | Washington | | | 8,361 |
| Knox | 1,157 | 931 | 2,088 | Wayne | 269 | 212 | 481 |
| Lancaster | 10,092 | 8,583 | 18,657 | Webster | 3,233 | 2,714 | 5,947 |
| Lincoln | 1,130 | 887 | 2,017 | Wheeler | | | 700 |
| Madison | 2,288 | 1,992 | 4,280 | York | 4,944 | 4,168 | 9,112 |
| Merrick | 2,480 | 2,145 | 4,625 | Unorg'ized ter'y | | | 17,625 |
| | | | | | | | 386,410 |

# CHAPTER XIV.

## ASSESSED VALUATION.

### TAXABLE PROPERTY.

Statement showing the total valuation of taxable property in the State as returned by the County Clerks, for 1879.

| | |
|---|---:|
| Land, 13,429,308.05 acres value | $38,378,509.80 |
| Town lots, value | 9,013,371.90 |
| Money used in merchandise | 2,483,864.47 |
| Money used in manufactures | 525,576.00 |
| Sheep, number 131,787, value | 123,358.20 |
| Swine, number 562,790, value | 515,715.70 |
| Mules and asses, number 15,412, value | 493,401.75 |
| Horses, number 157,619 value | 4,116,069.00 |
| Neat cattle, number 513,668, value | 4,185,533.50 |
| Vehicles, number 57,289, value | 909,692.00 |
| Moneys and credits | 842,546.50 |
| Mortgages | 679,524.00 |
| Stocks | 500,250.05 |
| Furniture | 902,822.35 |
| Libraries | 54,018.00 |
| Property not enumerated | 2,432,351.33 |
| Railroads | 9,154,476.87 |
| Telegraph | 48,717.45 |
| Total | $75,359,798.87 |

Statement showing the total Assessed Valuation of all Taxable Property in the State for each year since its Organization:

| YEAR. | VALUE. | YEAR. | VALUE. | YEAR. | VALUE. |
|---|---|---|---|---|---|
| 1867 | $20,069,222.00 | 1871 | $55,513,658.00 | 1875 | $75,467,398.91 |
| 1868 | 32,632,550.00 | 1872 | 69,873,318.68 | 1876 | 74,178,645.48 |
| 1869 | 42,123,595.55 | 1873 | 78,239,692.64 | 1877 | 71,311,578.90 |
| 1870 | 53,709,828.82 | 1874 | 80,754,044.17 | 1878 | 74,389,535.97 |
| | | | | 1879 | 75,359,798.87 |

## JOHNSON'S HISTORY OF NEBRASKA. 173

| COUNTIES. | HORSES | MULES | CATTLE | SHEEP | SWINE | COUNTIES. | HORSES | MULES | CATTLE | SHEEP | SWINE |
|---|---|---|---|---|---|---|---|---|---|---|---|
| Adams....... | 2,510 | 572 | 4,071 | 977 | 8,166 | Kearney...... | 1,205 | 173 | 1,483 | 581 | 2,723 |
| Antelope..... | 1,079 | 94 | 2,361 | 502 | 1,477 | Keith........ | 192 | 6 | 19,094 | ....... | 24 |
| Boone........ | 1,276 | 105 | 2,223 | 583 | 1,630 | Knox......... | 813 | 78 | 2,972 | 447 | 596 |
| Buffalo....... | 1,837 | 237 | 5,523 | 4,059 | 2,383 | Lancaster.... | 7,390 | 695 | 15,330 | 5,406 | 31,487 |
| Burt......... | 3,033 | 271 | 9,765 | 6,385 | 17,246 | Lincoln...... | 1,351 | 69 | 40,364 | 5,307 | 146 |
| Butler....... | 3,398 | 268 | 5,705 | 480 | 7,804 | Madison...... | 2,707 | 116 | 5,156 | 789 | 6,316 |
| Cass......... | 7,311 | 729 | 18,305 | 307 | 41,043 | Merrick...... | 2,434 | 189 | 7,340 | 1,189 | 3,621 |
| Cedar........ | 1,201 | 63 | 6,245 | 2,452 | 1,412 | Nance........ | 153 | 20 | 1,134 | 1,011 | 124 |
| Cheyenne.... | 1,166 | 147 | 57,679 | 331 | 88 | Nemaha...... | 4,892 | 630 | 13,630 | 591 | 34,739 |
| Clay......... | 4,248 | 494 | 5,006 | 558 | 12,752 | Nuckolls..... | 1,862 | 211 | 2,945 | 999 | 7,776 |
| Colfax....... | 2,308 | 171 | 6,255 | 4,611 | 8,273 | Otoe......... | 5,994 | 724 | 18,460 | 5,659 | 31,742 |
| Cuming...... | 2,298 | 173 | 5,772 | 5,694 | 8,902 | Pawnee....... | 3,282 | 162 | 8,216 | 6,604 | 10,246 |
| Custer....... | 835 | 20 | 23,900 | 4,161 | 138 | Phelps....... | 496 | 111 | 916 | 190 | 315 |
| Dakota...... | 2,140 | 92 | 8,520 | 123 | 4,411 | Pierce........ | 421 | 22 | 1,323 | 685 | 926 |
| Dawson...... | 643 | 48 | 5,155 | 3,068 | 295 | Platte........ | 3,313 | 288 | 9,123 | 3,173 | 7,206 |
| Dixon........ | 2,122 | 72 | 6,782 | 158 | 2,496 | Polk......... | 2,423 | 290 | 3,696 | 217 | 10,284 |
| Dodge........ | 4,350 | 377 | 11,552 | 3,424 | 14,927 | Red Willow.. | 544 | 51 | 2,817 | 1,375 | 284 |
| Douglas...... | 4,078 | 409 | 8,847 | 792 | 11,873 | Richardson... | 7,221 | 696 | 18,091 | 3,162 | 34,690 |
| Fillmore..... | 4,329 | 465 | 5,429 | 2,765 | 18,162 | Saline........ | 5,527 | 412 | 8,397 | 2,029 | 26,289 |
| Franklin..... | 1,659 | 176 | 3,276 | 1,325 | 4,516 | Sarpy........ | 2,734 | 165 | 7,176 | 438 | 11,013 |
| Frontier..... | 527 | 18 | 8,672 | 1,471 | 86 | Saunders..... | 6,379 | 599 | 11,847 | 2,979 | 29,512 |
| Furnas....... | 1,674 | 135 | 4,229 | 2,267 | 1,434 | Seward....... | 4,740 | 453 | 6,648 | 1,855 | 19,611 |
| Gage......... | 5,070 | 490 | 10,359 | 13,377 | 20,994 | Sherman..... | 382 | 65 | 1,283 | 169 | 658 |
| Greeley...... | 307 | 33 | 1,272 | 78 | 395 | Stanton...... | 775 | 27 | 1,833 | 2,440 | 1,830 |
| Gosper....... | 275 | 31 | 819 | 2,313 | 234 | Sioux*....... | ....... | ....... | ....... | ....... | ....... |
| Hall......... | 2,736 | 360 | 8,668 | 1,409 | 5,134 | Thayer....... | 2,076 | 186 | 3,733 | 3,156 | 8,921 |
| Hamilton..... | 3,567 | 405 | 4,258 | 720 | 7,027 | Valley........ | 681 | 68 | 1,909 | 54 | 522 |
| Harlan....... | 1,630 | 184 | 3,401 | 1,007 | 2,050 | Washington.. | 3,666 | 469 | 10,656 | 1,313 | 18,408 |
| Hitchcock.... | 312 | 12 | 13,312 | ....... | 14 | Wayne....... | 288 | 10 | 675 | 1,439 | 878 |
| Howard...... | 1,083 | 220 | 2,420 | 1,250 | 1,786 | Webster...... | 2,681 | 413 | 5,032 | 3,922 | 12,450 |
| Holt......... | 630 | 56 | 3,344 | 215 | 494 | Wheeler*..... | ....... | ....... | ....... | ....... | ....... |
| Hayes*...... | ....... | ....... | ....... | ....... | ....... | York......... | 4,755 | 434 | 5,647 | 1,383 | 17,262 |
| Jefferson..... | 3,116 | 309 | 6,197 | 5,029 | 11,247 | | | | | | |
| Johnson...... | 3,494 | 344 | 7,280 | 1,334 | 14,257 | Total..... | 157,619 | 15,412 | 513,668 | 181,787 | 562,790 |

* Returned with adjoining Counties.

## RECAPITULATION OF NUMBER AND VALUE OF FARM ANIMALS.

| FARM ANIMALS. | NUMBER. 1875. | VALUE. 1875. | NUMBER. 1879. | VALUE. 1879. | INCREASE IN NUMBER. | INCREASE IN VALUE. |
|---|---|---|---|---|---|---|
| Horses...... | 94,637 | $3,678,528.00 | 157,619 | $4,116,069.00 | 62,982 | $ 437,541.00 |
| Mules and Asses.... | 8,785 | 428,817.00 | 15,412 | 493,401.75 | 6,627 | 64,584.75 |
| Neat Cattle. | 242,659 | 2,852,162.00 | 513,668 | 4,185,533.50 | 271,009 | 1,333,371.50 |
| Sheep ...... | 36,014 | 44,689.00 | 131,787 | 123,358.20 | 95,773 | 78,669.20 |
| Swine...... | 146,933 | 182,308.00 | 562,790 | 515,715.70 | 415,857 | 333,407.70 |

### INDEBTEDNESS.

The excellent condition and wise and economical manner in which the finances of the State are managed is a matter upon which the citizens may be congratulated. The bonded indebtedness of the State is very small, amounting at present to only $599,267.35. Of this amount $50,000 are in bonds issued for the relief of the grasshopper sufferers, and the balance, $549,267.35 is in bonds issued to fund the State debt, $426,267.35 of which is held by the permanent School Fund of the State, and $123,000 by private parties. The balance of money in the treasury, on the 30th of November, 1878, was 460,181.99, which, with the delinquent taxes, will more than balance all outstanding claims against the State, thus leaving it practically free of debt.

The assessment rolls of the State show a notable increase from year to year in taxable property, in the addition of acres of taxable land, miles of railroad constructed, and of various descriptions of personal property. The total assessed valuation of taxable property for 1879—which is hardly one-half of its real value—was $75,359,798.87, against $20,069,222 in 1867, the year in which the State was organized, thus showing a constant and enormous ncrease in its material wealth. During the past several years liberal appropriations have been made for the establishment and maintenance of Asylums for the Deaf, Dumb and Blind, a Hospital for the Insane, the Normal School, Penitentiary, for the support of the University, and for charitable purposes.

# CHAPTER XV.

## THE PRESS OF NEBRASKA.

Too much cannot be said in praise of the newspapers of Nebraska for the important and influential part they have taken in the development of the State, in promoting immigration and building up its interests from the earliest settlements. Journalists of ability were among the foremost of our pioneers, and helped to lay the foundations of many of our most flourishing towns, and who, as soon as settlement was fairly begun, started lively little newspapers to herald the advantages and beauties of the new country to the people of the East; and as the settlements were developed and the towns increased to cities, so were the newspapers enlarged to keep pace with their general surroundings. To-day the *Press* of the State is the pride of the people, and will compare favorably for journalistic ability and influence with that of any Western State. Several of our dailies are among the foremost journals of the West, and are well patronized and influential at home and abroad; while almost every village in the State of a few hundred inhabitants, has a well-sustained weekly newspaper, many of them models of neatness and conducted with marked ability, which render the State and their localities great service.

To residents of older States who inquire after the growth and prosperity of Nebraska, no fact is more surprising and none more gratifying, than the remarkable number of neat and able papers published, patronized and read in the State. We need no better evidence of the average intelligence of the people who come west of the Missouri to make permanent homes.

We are sometimes told by cynical philosophers, that common papers are in no sense public teachers, and that really intelligent people get their knowledge from books; that the newspaper of the day is little better than a bundle of trash, designed to amuse the people no matter how low their tastes, and to further the schemes of ambitious politicians. We leave the public to judge how much truth is contained in such a remark, enforcing the thought, however, that if it is true, such truth reflects directly upon popular taste and intelligence, and should be a matter for radical reform on the part of both journalist and reader.

View it as we may, the newspaper bears the same relation to great libraries, that the common school does to the university. The masses cannot yet defray the expense of valuable books in large numbers, and have not the time to winnow wheat from chaff, either of current events or of standard history and philosophy. Newspaper subscribers may be regarded as a vast co-operative association, each member of which contributes to employ the editor to select and condense for him. This, when rightly considered, places the editor in the position of an important public servant, with grave responsibilities. He may be in position to use his judgment to the highest and noblest ends; the demands of his employers may force him to the unwilling task of furnishing light idle matter, when his own inclinations might lead him to furnish none but the brightest grains which the great harvests of the world afford.

We are glad to believe that every paper in Nebraska has a place in its history, and that no other agency—not even the great corporations with all their wealth and far-seeing enterprise, not even the governing men and statesmen who have labored to give Nebraska position, influence and fame,—has wielded a greater influence for the prosperity and importance of the State, than the cloud of news prints which every week settles down among its busy population.

## LIST OF NEWSPAPERS IN NEBRASKA,
*Arranged by Counties.*

It will be seen that they number: Daily, eleven; Weekly, 139; Monthly and Semi-monthly, seven.

### ADAMS.

| | | | |
|---|---|---|---|
| Hastings | Journal | Hastings | Gazette |
| " | Nebraskian | Juniata | Herald |

## JOHNSON'S HISTORY OF NEBRASKA. 177

**ANTELOPE.**

Neligh..................Republican     Oakdale..........Pen and Plow

**BUFFALO.**

Kearney......................Press     Kearney..........….Nonpareil
"      ...............True Citizen     "   ..(semi-mon.) Lit. Notes

**BURT.**

Tekamah.................Burtonian      Tekamah.............Advocate
Decatur..................Vindicator

**BUTLER.**

David City....................Press    David City..........Republican

**BOONE.**

Albion.......................................Argus

**CASS.**

Plattsmouth................Herald      Plattsmouth...........Sentinel

**CUMING.**

West Point.............Republican      West Point........….Progress
"      ...........Staats Zeitung

**CLAY.**

Harvard....................Phoenix     Harvard..............Sentinel
Fairfield......................News     Sutton............ .........Globe
Sutton............. .............Mirror

**CHEYENNE.**

Sidney...................Telegraph     Sidney..............Plaindealer

**COLFAX.**

Schuyler........................Sun    Schuyler.............Democrat

**CEDAR.**

St. Helena...............................Bulletin

**DIXON.**

Ponca................... ...Courier    Ponca.................Journal

**DAWSON**

Plum Creek................Pioneer      Cozad.....Hundredth Meridian

**DAKOTA.**

Dakota City..................Eagle     Jackson............. ....Herald

**DOUGLAS.**

Omaha....(daily and weekly) Herald     Omaha......(d & w) Republican
"      .......(daily and weekly) Bee     "     ..... ......(daily) News
"      ............... Agriculturist     "     .............Watchman
"      ..........(monthly) Guardian      "     (tri-w'k'y)Danske Pioneer
"      .............(tri-weekly) Post    "     ..........Pokrok Zapadu
"      .(monthly) Western Magazine       "     .........Folkets Tiding
"      .......Commercial Exchange        "     (m) High School Journal
"      ........Journal of Commerce       "     .......Rural Nebraskian
"      ...............Mute Journal       "     .............Die Vestern
Waterloo...................Sentinel      "     ................Portfolio
12

### DODGE.
Fremont............(d. & w.) Herald    Fremont...............Tribune
"         ........(monthly) Bulletin

### FILLMORE.
Exeter...................Enterprise    Fairmount.............Bulletin
Friendville...............Telegraph    Geneva................Review

### FRANKLIN.
Riverton..................Reporter     Bloomington............Guard
Naponee ...................Banner

### FURNAS.
Beaver City................................Times

### GAGE.
Beatrice....................Courier    Beatrice..............Express
Blue Springs..............Reporter

### GREELEY.
Scotia......................................Tribune

### HAMILTON.
Aurora..................Republican     Aurora..................News

### HALL.
Grand Island...........Independent     Grand Island............Times
"            .............Democrat

### HARLAN.
Orleans.....................Sentinel   Republican City..........News
Alma.......................Standard

### HOWARD.
St. Paul...................Advocate    St. Paul............Phonograph

### JOHNSON.
Tecumseh................. Chieftain    Tecumseh..............Journal
Sterling......................News

### JEFFERSON.
Fairbury..................Telegraph    Fairbury..............Gazette

### KNOX.
Niobrara................................Pioneer

### KEARNEY.
Mindon.................................... Bee

### LINCOLN.
North Platte............Nebraskian     North Platte........Republican

### LANCASTER.
Lincoln............(d. & w.) Journal   Lincoln.........(d. & w.) Globe
"              ..............(d. & w.) World      "     .....(d. & w.) Democrat
"              ....................Register      "........(monthly) Farmer
"              ..........(monthly) Student

### MERRICK.
Central City...............Courier  Clarkesville............Messenger
### MADISON.
Norfolk..................Journal  Madison................Chronicle
### NEMAHA.
Sheridan......................Post  Brownville............Advertiser
Brownville...............Granger  Peru......................Herald
### NUCKOLLS.
Nelson....................Herald  Superior...................Guide
### OTOE.
Nebraska City......(d. & w.) Press  Nebraska City.............News
Syracuse..................Journal
### PAWNEE.
Pawnee City...........Enterprise  Pawnee City..........Republican
### PLATTE.
Columbus..................... ....Era  Columbus................Journal
" ............Independent  " ..............Democrat
### POLK.
Osceola..................... .................Record
### PIERCE.
Pierce...........................................Call
### RICHARDSON.
Falls City................ ...Press  Falls City.........Globe-Journal
Humboldt................ .......Sentinel  Salem.................Advertiser
### SAUNDERS.
Wahoo................Independent  Wahoo....................Times
Ashland.................. .........Reporter
### SALINE.
Crete......................Union  Crete...................Democrat
De Witt................Free Press  Wilber....................Record
Friendville..............Telegraph
### SEWARD.
Seward...................Reporter  Seward.................Advocate
### STANTON.
Stanton..................................Register
### SARPY.
Papillion.......................................Times
### SHERMAN.
Loup City.................................Times
### THAYER.
Hebron....................Journal  Hebron..................Sentinel
Alexandria..................News

### VALLEY.
Ord City..............................Journal

### WASHINGTON.
Blair..........................Pilot    Blair....................Times

### WEBSTER.
Red Cloud....................Chief    Red Cloud..............Argus

### WAYNE.
La Porte........................ .........Review

### YORK.
York....................Republican    York...................Tribune

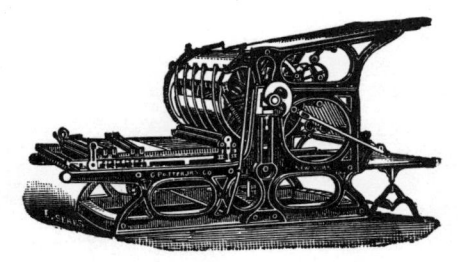

# CHAPTER XVI.

## NEBRASKA—1879.

COMMERCE—MANUFACTURES—THE GRASSHOPPERS—THE PEOPLE OF NEBRASKA.

### COMMERCE.

The central position occupied by Nebraska, between the great markets of the East and the extensive mineral and stock regions of Colorado, Wyoming, Utah, Montana and Idaho, on the West, give her rare advantages in a commercial point of view, which are being rapidly developed into an immense and profitable trade.

The railroads of the State are freighted with merchandise of all descriptions, implements, lumber, flour, pork, butter, cheese, eggs, grain and other farm products, going westward to the people of this vast mining and non-agricultural region, where the demand is always equal to the supply, and who in return load the cars with precious metals and ores for our smelting and refining works, and with stock for the Eastern markets.

There were 57,809,535 pounds of gold and silver-bearing ores received at Omaha during the year 1878, over the railways from the west, the greater part of which was handled by the Omaha Smelting and Refining Works. The amount of gold and silver coin, gold dust and bullion arriving at Omaha from the West during 1878, was $35,452,000. The gold and silver product of the country lying immediately west of Nebraska is steadily increasing, and the greater part of these productions pass into and through Omaha.

The beef and pork packing industry in Nebraska is increasing to vast proportions, these establishments employing thousands of men and slaughtering hundreds of thousands of hogs and cattle yearly. New houses for this purpose, of double the capacity are being built each year, and the old ones enlarged. Nebraska beef is now being packed and shipped to the English markets. With the splendid advantages afforded by the plains of Nebraska for the rearing and fattening of stock cheaply, our packing establishments will, in a very short period of time, no doubt, assume proportions second to none other in the country.

The trade and commerce of Nebraska is expanding at a marvelous rate, that of Omaha alone is placed at $30,000,000 for 1878. The wholesale business is increasing at the rate of thirty to forty per cent. yearly, and within the past five years the volume of trade and number of merchants may be safely said to have doubled. Several of our other cities have an annual jobbing trade reaching into the millions, and whose business relations extend beyond the limits of the State. Retail houses doing a yearly business of $10,000 to $25,000 are common, while the sales of a large number range from $50,000 to $100,000 per annum.

## MANUFACTURES.

In the way of manufactures Nebraska has made commendable progress, considering the age and essentially agricultural character of the State. At Omaha there are extensive white lead works, a nail factory, oil works, one of the largest distilleries in the country, several breweries, the largest smelting and refining works on the continent, several foundries, carriage, wagon, cigar, broom and file manufactories, soap works, safe and vault manufactory, cabinet ware, agricultural implements, flouring mills and many smaller manufacturing establishments. At West Point, in Cuming County, on the Elkhorn River, there is a large paper mill and furniture factory; at Lincoln large numbers of wagons are made, and of a quality and appearance equal to any imported; at Nebraska City, Fremont and other large towns, plows and various other agricultural implements and minor articles are manufactured. Steam and water-power flouring mills, employing all modern improvements and of large capacity, are located throughout all the settled portions of the State. Cheese factories are springing up rapidly in the Western Counties, and the manufacture of cheese will, ere long, form an important element in our industries.

No State offers a more inviting field for the location of the manufacturer or man of capital than this, and there is none where he would be received with heartier welcome, or where the investment of his means would yield larger returns. The resources of the country are inexhaustible, the manufacturing advantages unsurpassed, water power abundant and well distributed, and to men of capital and skill the field for manufacturing enterprises, of the kind to suit the wants of the country, is unlimited. A more advantageous location for woolen mills, paper and flouring mills, tanneries, and factories of various kinds, is not presented in any other western country. The State is settling up at an unprecedented rate; hundreds of immigrants are arriving each day, and every season thousands of new farms are opened out. In no agricultural country is the demand for machinery so great as in this, and no establishment for the manufacture of all the different farming implements would be better patronized and pay handsomer profits on the money invested.

### THE GRASSHOPPERS.

During the growing seasons of 1874 and '75 the Rocky Mountain locust, or grasshopper, visited Nebraska and did incalculable damage by devouring the crops in a large portion of the State. In many sections—more particularly in the western and middle Counties—the destruction of the crops by these insects was most complete, not a vestage of anything green being left untouched by them; and as many of the farmers living in the sections so afflicted were new settlers, the total loss of their crops, upon which they were dependent for the support of their families, was a great calamity and caused much distress and suffering. The destitution was so widespread and so great in some localities, that public aid was asked, for the relief of the sufferers. The prompt and generous responses to the call by the people of the East and other localities not so afflicted, in fowarding provisions, clothing and money, saved many a poor family from actual want, if not starvation.

While it is true that the damage done by the grasshoppers was very great, and caused much genuine distress among the people in several of the Counties, yet the whole matter was grossly exaggerated and enlarged upon by a certain busy class of persons who somehow always come to the front on such occasions, actuated, generally, more by a desire to further their own selfish ends than by any kindly, true feeling for the distressed. This blatant, noisy class, with their loud demonstrations and universal begging, not only disgusted the more sensible people, but did the State an injury next to that of the grasshoppers themselves.

Yet it is a stubborn fact that the timely succor sent to the settlers in the devastated districts saved much suffering among the poorer portion; and the people of Nebraska owe a lasting debt of gratitude to the noble men and women of the East, who contributed so willingly and bountifully to their aid in time of need, and by whose generosity the miseries of want were alleviated and the hearts made glad in many an humble prairie home.

By an Act of the Legislature of Nebraska, $50,000 were donated as a relief to the grasshopper sufferers, which amount was judiciously expended and distributed for that purpose.

But the grasshopper scares have passed away, we hope, forever; the seasons have come and gone, leaving us with bountiful crops of all kinds to enrich and supply the wants of all, and prosperity reigns supreme throughout the length and breadth of the State.

### THE PEOPLE OF NEBRASKA.

The population of Nebraska is made up largely of people from the Eastern, Middle and Northwestern States, although, of course, all sections of the Union are well represented in the grand total, as are also all of the European countries, to a large extent, with a few from nearly every nationality in the civilized world.

They come here from all points of the compass, and are usually men and women above the average in ambition, energy and brains —people who have outgrown the circumscribed life in older lands and have followed the tide of emigration westward to the grand prairies and broad rich bottoms of Nebraska, and there have laid the foundations for lasting and comfortable homes for themselves and children, transforming a wilderness, as it were, into thousands of waving grain fields, flourishing orchards and beautiful gardens, who have established schools, churches and colleges, founded a moral and refined society, and built railways which transport the commerce of nations to their numerous, wide-awake and prosperous cities and villages.

Of this spirited, enterprising and ambitious class of people the great bulk of Nebraska's population consists—where the pure, bracing atmosphere infuses a vigor and activity in the people never witnessed in the older States. People of the very highest attainments and social qualities are settled in all parts of the State. Many of our most cultered and refined citizens, who have done so much to mould and improve our society and institutions, have been glad to exchange the uncertainties of vocation and extravagance of fashionable life in the more crowded States, for the security and comforts of a prairie home in Nebraska.

The average intelligence of the people of Nebraska will reach a higher standard than is generally found in agricultural countries; their habits and customs are also peculiarly suited to the condition of things; and in business matters, religion, politics, and in social life there is infinitely more freedom here than in Eastern society.

Very many of the pioneers who came here almost penniless, have to-day comfortable homes for their families and a goodly share of this world's goods, while others are possessed of valuable, well-stocked farms, who, had they remained in the East, would probably never have owned an acre of ground.

The author has traveled through nearly every County in the State, from the Missouri River to the western frontier; he has watched with zealous pride the onward march of civilization during the past quarter of a century, and has seen the vast rolling prairies, which only a few short years ago were in their virgin glory, just as the hand of the Great Architect of the Universe had fashioned them, rapidly developed into a populous State, dotted with enterprising cities and towns, and ribbed with great railways reaching to all points.

It seems more like a dream as he looks back over these fleeting years, and recalls the scene then, as compared with the wonderful changes and progress civilization has made to-day. Many of the old acquaintances—pioneers—who bore him happy company over the trackless plains in the days gone by, have long since faded from view, some wandering to other lands in search of new adventure when this grew old, while others, and by far the greater number, alas! have gone to that bourne whence no traveler returns.

There are innumerable hardships, privations and dangers which the pioneers of a new country must contend with and surmount, that the later settlers know but little of. The pioneer goes before, braves the dangers, and makes settlement practically easy and safe for those who follow in his footsteps. Great honor is due to his bravery and courage, and yet everything depends upon the character and intelligence of the class of settlers who follow in the wake of the pioneer, and who lay the foundations of a solid and substantial government; and in this respect Nebraska has every reason to be proud.

# CHAPTER XVII.

## ORGANIC ACT AND CONSTITUTION.

### THE ORGANIC ACT OF NEBRASKA TERRITORY.

By the provisions of the Act of Congress organizing the Territory of Nebraska, the executive power in and over said Territory was vested in a Governor, whose term of office was for four years, or until his successor was appointed and qualified, unless sooner removed by the President of the United States. The Governor was made Commander-in-Chief of the militia of the Territory; was empowered to grant pensions and respites against the laws of the Territory, and reprieves for offences against the laws of the United States, and it was his duty to commission all officers appointed under the laws of the Territory, and to take care that the laws were faithfully executed.

A Secretary of the Territory was appointed who was required to reside therein, and whose term of office extended for five years, unless sooner removed by the President. In case of death, removal, resignation or absence of the Governor from the Territory, the Secretary was authorized and required to act in his stead, and execute and perform all the duties of the Governor during his absence or vacancy in the office.

The legislative power of the Territory was vested in the Governor and Legislative Assembly, the latter consisting of a Council and House of Representatives.

The judicial power of the Territory was vested in a Supreme Court, District Courts, Probate Courts and Justices of the Peace. The Supreme Court consisted of a Chief Justice and two Associate Justices, any two of whom constituted a quorum, and they were required to hold a term at the Capital of the Territory annually. The Territory was divided into three judicial districts, and a district court held in each, presided over by one of the justices of the Supreme Court.

An Attorney and Marshal for the Territory were appointed, whose term extended for four years, and whose salary and fees were the same as that allowed the Attorney and Marshal of the Territory of Utah.

The salary of the Governor was $2,500 per annum, that of the Secretary $2,000, and the Chief Justice and each of the Associate Justices $2,000.

The pay of the members of the Assembly was $3.00 each per day, during their actual attendance at the sessions, and $3.00 each for every twenty miles traveled in going to and returning from the sessions; and an additional allowance of $3.00 per day was paid the presiding officer of each house.

The Act also provided for the election of a delegate to the House of Representatives of the United States, for the term of two years, who was entitled to the same rights and privileges as exercised and enjoyed by the delegates from the several other Territories of the United States.

### CONSTITUTION OF NEBRASKA, ADOPTED JUNE 2, 1866.

LEGISLATIVE.—It provided that the legislative authority was vested in a General Assembly, which shall consist of a Senate and House of Representatives. The Senate consisted of thirteen members, and the House of Representatives consisted of thirty-nine members, which could not be increased for the term of ten years after the adoption of the Constitution.

EXECUTIVE.—The Executive Department consisted of Governor, Secretary and Treasurer, who held their offices for the term of two years, and the Auditor for four years, and in case of death, resignation or removal from office of the Governor, the duties of that office was performed by the Secretary of State.

JUDICIARY.—The judicial powers was vested in a Supreme Court, District Courts, Probate Courts and Justices of the Peace. The Supreme Court consisted of a Chief Justice and two Associate

Justices, any two of whom constituted a quorum for the transaction of business. Said Judges were elected by the people, and held their offices for six years. The State was divided into three judicial districts, and the Supreme Judges held the District Courts in the three judicial districts, the Legislature assigning the judges to their respective districts.

FINANCE.—The credit of the State could not be given to any individual or corporation in the construction of improvements, neither could the State be a party to any works of internal improvements, or contract any debt beyond fifty thousand dollars.

EDUCATION.—The principal of all funds arising from the sale of lands or other property granted to the State for educational or religious purposes, shall forever be preserved inviolate and undiminished; and all incomes arising therefrom shall be faithfully applied to the specific object of the original grant or appropriations, and all school lands or University lands shall not be sold for a less sum than five dollars per acre.

## CONDENSED SYNOPSIS OF THE CONSTITUTION OF THE STATE OF NEBRASKA. ADOPTED 1875,

DISTRIBUTION OF POWERS.—The powers of the Government of this State are divided into three distinct departments: the Legislative, Executive, and Judicial, and no person, or collection of persons, being one of these departments shall exercise any power properly belonging to either of the others, except as hereinafter expressly directed or permitted.

LEGISLATIVE.—The Legislative authority is vested in a Senate and House of Representatives. The House of Representatives shall consist of eighty-four members, and the Senate shall consist of thirty members, until the year eighteen hundred and eighty, after which time the number of members of each House shall be regulated by law; but the number of Representatives shall never exceed one hundred, nor that of Senators thirty-three. The sessions of the Legislature shall be biennial, except as otherwise provided in the Constitution. The Senate and House of Representatives in joint convention shall have the sole power of impeachment, but a majority of the members elected must concur therein. The Legislature shall not pass local or special laws granting to any corporation, association, or individual, any special or exclusive privileges, immunity, or franchise whatever. Lands under control of the State shall never be donated to railroad companies, private corporations, or individuals

EXECUTIVE DEPARTMENT.—The Executive Department shall consist of a Governor, Lieutenant-Governor, Secretary of State, Auditor of Public

Accounts, Treasurer, Superintendent of Public Instruction, Attorney General, and Commissioner of Public Lands and Buildings, who shall each hold his office for the term of two years, from the first Thursday after the first Tuesday in January next after his election, and until his successor is elected and qualified. The Governor, Secretary of State, Auditor of Public Accounts, and Treasurer, shall reside at the Seat of Government during their terms of office, and keep the public records, books, and papers there, and shall perform such duties as may be required by law. No person shall be eligible to the office of Governor or Lieutenant-governor, who shall not have attained the age of thirty years, and been for two years next preceding his election a citizen of the United States and of this State. All civil officers of this State shall be liable to impeachment for any misdemeanor in office. The supreme executive power shall be vested in the Governor, who shall take care that the laws be faithfully executed. The Governor shall be Commander-in-Chief of the military and naval forces of the State (except when they shall be called into the service of the United States), and may call out the same to execute the laws, suppress insurrection and repel invasion. In case of death, impeachment and notice thereof to the accused, failure to qualify, resignation, absence from the State, or other disability of the Governor, the powers, duties and emoluments of the office, for the residue of the term, or until the disability shall be removed, shall devolve upon the Lieutenant-Governor. The Lieutenant Governor shall be President of the Senate, and shall vote only when the Senate is equally divided. The salaries of the Governor, Auditor of Public Accounts, and Treasurer shall be two thousand five hundred dollars ($2,500) each, per annum, and of the Secretary of State, Attorney General, Superintendent of Public Instruction, and Commissioner of Public Lands and Buildings, two thousand dollars ($2,000) each per annum. The Lieutenant-Governor shall receive twice the compensation of a Senator.

THE JUDICIAL DEPARTMENT.—The judicial power of this State shall be vested in Supreme Court, District Courts, County Courts, Justices of the Peace, Police Magistrates, and in such other Courts inferior to the District Courts, as may be created by law for cities and incorporated towns. The Supreme Court shall consist of three Judges, a majority of whom shall be necessary to form a quorum or to pronounce a decision. It shall have original jurisdiction in cases relating to the revenue, civil cases in which the State shall be a party, mandamus, quo warranto, habeas corpus, and such appelate jurisdiction as may be provided by law. At least two terms of the Supreme Court shall be held each year at the Seat of Government. The Judges of the Supreme Court shall be elected by the electors of the State at large, and their terms shall be six years. The State shall be divided into six Judicial Districts, in each of which shall be elected by the electors thereof, one Judge, who shall be Judge of the District Court therein, and whose term of office shall be four years. Until otherwise provided by law, said Districts shall be as follows:

*First District*—The Counties of Richardson, Johnson, Pawnee, Gage, Jefferson, Saline, Thayer, Clay, Nuckolls, and Fillmore.

*Second District*—The Counties of Nemaha, Otoe, Cass, and Lancaster.

*Third District*—The Counties of Douglas, Sarpy, Washington and Burt.

*Fourth District*—The Counties of Saunders, Dodge, Butler, Colfax, Platte, Polk, Merritt, Hamilton, York, Seward, Hall, and Howard.

*Fifth District*—The Counties of Buffalo, Adams, Webster, Franklin, Harlan, Kearney, Phelps, Gosper, Furnas, Hitchcock, Dundy, Chase. Cheyenne, Keith, Lincoln, Dawson Sherman, Red Willow, Frontier, and the unorganized territory west of said District.

*Sixth District*—The Counties of Cuming, Dakota, Dixon, Cedar, Wayne, Stanton, Madison, Boone, Pierce, Knox, Antelope, Holt, Greeley, Valley, and the unorganized territory west of said District.

The Judges of the Supreme and District Courts shall each receive a salary of $2,500 per annum, payable quarterly. No Judge of the Supreme or District Courts shall receive any other compensation, perquisite, or benefit for or on account of his office in any form whatever; nor act as attorney or counsellor-at-law, in any manner whatever; nor shall any salary be paid to any County Judge.

EDUCATION.—The Governor, Secretary of State, Treasurer, Attorney-General, and Commissioner of Public Lands and Buildings, shall, under the direction of the Legislature, constitute a Board of Commissioners for the sale, leasing, and general management of all lands and funds set apart for educational purposes, and for the investment of school funds in such manner as may be prescribed by law. All funds belonging to the State for educational purposes, the interest and income whereof only are to be used, shall be deemed trust funds held by the State, and the State shall supply all losses thereof that may in any manner accrue, so that the same shall remain forever inviolate and undiminished; and shall not be invested or loaned except on United States or State securities, or registered County bonds of this State; and such funds, with the interest and income thereof, are hereby solemnly pledged for the purposes for which they are granted and set apart, and shall not be transferred to any other fund for other uses. No sectarian instruction shall be allowed in any school or institution supported in whole or in part by the public funds set apart for educational purposes; nor shall the State accept any grant, conveyance, or bequest, of money, lands, or other property, to be used for sectarian purposes. The Legislature may provide by law for the establishment of a school or schools for the safe keeping, education, employment, and reformation of all children under the age of sixteen years, who for want of proper parental care, or other cause, are growing up to mendicancy or crime.

COUNTIES.—No new County shall be formed or established by the Legislature which will reduce the County or Counties, or either of them, to a less area than four hundred square miles, nor shall any County be formed of a less area. No County shall be divided, nor have any part stricken therefrom without first submitting the question to a vote of the people of the County, nor unless a majority of all the legal voters of the County voting on the question shall vote for the same.

RAILROAD CORPORATIONS.—Railways heretofore constructed, or that may hereafter be constructed in this State, are hereby declared public highways, and shall be free to all persons for the transportation of their persons and property thereon, under such regulations as may be prescribed by law. And the Legislature may from time to time pass laws establishing reasonable maximum rates of charges for the transportation of passengers and freight on the different railroads in this State. The liability of railroad corporations as common carriers shall never be limited.

MUNICIPAL CORPORATIONS.—No City, County, Town, Precinct, Municipality, or other sub-division of the State shall ever become a subscriber to the capital stock, or owner of such stock, or any portion or interest therein, of any railroad or private corporation or association.

# NEBRASKA IN COUNTIES,

ALPHABETICALLY ARRANGED.

## ADAMS COUNTY.

Adams County was organized on the 12th day of December, 1871. It is located in the south-central part of the State, in the sixth tier of Counties west of the Missouri, and second north of the Kansas line, and is bounded on the north by Hall, east by Clay, south by Webster, and west by Kearney County, containing 576 square miles, or 368,640 acres, at an average elevation of 1,850 feet above the sea level.

Population of the County in 1870, nineteen; in 1875, 3,093; in 1879, 8,162; increase in four years, 5,069.

WATER COURSES.—The Little Blue River, with its source in the northeast of this County, is the principal stream. It flows southeasterly through the central portion, having numerous tributaries on either side reaching through nearly every township, the most important being Thirty-two Mile Creek, a very fine stream, affording a volume of water sufficient for mill purposes. Pawnee Creek waters the southeastern part of the County, while the northern townships are watered by innumerable springs and rivulets, which rise in this County and flow north-eastwardly toward the West Blue River. The Platte River cuts across the northwest corner, and altogether, Adams is a well-watered County. Soft, sweet water can be found almost anywhere, by boring, at a depth of from twenty-five to seventy-five feet.

TIMBER.—Considerable native timber yet remains in the vicinity of the Little Blue, while nearly all of the streams have more or less along their banks. The principal varieties of native trees are the box-elder, cottonwood, soft maple, elm, ash and oak. Large quantities of timber have been planted throughout the County by the settlers, and already flourishing artificial groves may be seen dotting the prairie in every direction. Each year the amount of planting is largely increased, and as the cottonwood, box-elder and other varieties grow very rapidly, it will not be long before Adams County will have plenty of timber for fuel of her own growing.

FRUIT.—Planting of fruit trees of various kinds has received a large share of attention from the people, and their efforts in this line have fine promises of reward. In 1879 there were 17,627 apple, 529 pear, 1,814 cherry, 9,839 plum and 18,364 peach trees under cultivation in the County, besides 3,514 grape vines, and many other varieties of fruits. The plum and grape, in the wild state, are found in great abundance along the streams.

CHARACTER OF THE LAND AND SOIL.—The surface of the country in the vicinity of the Little Blue and other streams in the Western part of the County, is broken with occasional deep-cut ravines; but this forms only a very small per cent. of the whole, by far the greater part consisting of beautiful undulating table land, intersected with the fine valleys of the numerous streams. On the Blue, Thirty-two Mile Creek and many smaller streams, there are long stretches of bottom land that cannot be surpassed for fertility and beauty. Immediately next to the Platte River there is a narrow strip of sandy land, to the south and east of which the surface rises in a succession of plateaus, of a mile or so in width, and terminating in high, undulating table land.

The soil almost everywhere is of the best quality, consisting of a deep, rich mould, impregnated with lime, clay and sand, and resting on a gravelly bed. It will stand any amount of drougth or moisture, and when properly cultivated yields bountiful crops.

THE CROPS.—The number of acres under cultivation in the County, by the Assessors' returns for March, 1879, was 62,848. In winter wheat, seventy-five; yield, 837 bushels. Spring wheat, 36,177 acres; yield, 421,036 bushels. Corn, 11,403 acres; yield,

284,762 bushels. Barley, 2,146 acres; yield, 40,714 bushels. Oats, 3,193 acres; yield, 90,432 bushels. Potatoes, 301 acres; yield, 17,195 bushels. Broom corn, 3,839 acres; yield, 574 tons. Hungarian, 216 acres; yield, 5,232 bushels.

FIRST SETTLEMENTS.—In 1870 the population was nineteen, composed of a few settlers on the Little Blue. Several years previous to this, however, a few ranches had been established, and other efforts made at settlement, on the old over-land road to Pike's Peak, but the Indians were unusually troublesome in this part of the country, and destroyed many of the ranches, killing the inmates and compelling others to leave, through fear. The graves of a number of the pioneers may yet be seen on the banks of Thirty-two Mile Creek and the Blue. The first actual settlement north of the Little Blue, was made by Mr. T. Babcock, April 24, 1871, on the present town site of Juniata. John Stark, and his son Isaac W., with their families, came on the 5th day of May of the same year and located on the same section. Soon after homesteads were taken by other settlers near by and during the month of May, along and adjacent to the survey for the B. & M. Railroad, some twenty-five or thirty settlements were made. Settlements continued to increase rapidly, mainly under the patronage of Messrs. Bowen & Brass, agents of the Michigan Emigration Company, who themselves became permanent residents. Over one hundred families, mainly from Michigan, settled in the County during the year 1871 and the Spring of 1872, and the tide of emigration has continued steadily up to the present time.

COUNTY ORGANIZATION.—The election for County officers and location of the County Seat was held December, 12, 1871, at the residence of T. Babcock, and resulted in the unanimous choice of section twelve, town seven, north, range eleven west—the present location of Juniata—for the County Seat, and the election of the following County officers, viz.: Commissioners, Samuel L. Brass, Edwin M. Allen, and W. W. Selleck; Probate Judge, Titus Babcock; County Clerk, Russel D. Babcock; Sheriff, Isaac W. Stark; Treasurer, John S. Chandler; Assessor, W. W. Camp; Superintendent of Schools, Adna H. Bowen.

RAILROADS.—Prior to 1871 the trial line for the B. & M. road had been run near the line now used. The road runs nearly east and west through the County, entering at a point about eight miles south of the northeast corner, and passing out about four miles south of the northwest corner. During the summer of 1871 the road bed was constructed through the County and west to its junction with the Union Pacific. By the first of September the rails were laid to within three miles of the east line of the County when work was suspended for the season. In June, 1872, the road was completed to Juniata, and continued thence west to its present terminus. Length of road in County, 24.06 miles.

The St. Joe & Denver City Railway was completed to its present junction with the B. & M., in 1873. It enters the County near the middle of the eastern line, and runs northwesterly, joining the B. & M. at Hastings. Length of road so far completed in County, 7.20 miles.

The Hastings & Republican Valley R. R., running from Grand Island, on the Union Pacific, through this County, via Hastings, to points in the Republican Valley, was completed in 1879. Length of road in County about twenty-eight miles.

PUBLIC SCHOOLS.—The number of school districts in Adams County in 1879 was sixty-two; school houses, fifty-eight; children of school age, 2,678; average number of days taught by each teacher, ninety-six; districts having six months school or more, twenty-five; total number of children in the County between the ages of five and twenty-one years, 2,678—males, 1,377; females, 1,301; number of qualified teachers employed—males, twenty-eight, females, forty-eight; value of school houses, $35,866; value of school house sites, $1,751; value of books and apparatus, $375.85; wages paid teachers for the year, males, $3,919.7; females, $6,593.29; total, $10,312.36.

TAXABLE PROPERTY.—Statement of the taxable property of the County, as returned by the Assessors, for 1879: Acres of land, 267,495; average value per acre, $3.11; value of town lots, $114,750; money used in merchandise, $90,422; money used in manufactures, $25,592; number of horses, 2,510; value, $86,838; number of mules, 572, value, $19,579; number of cattle, 4,071; value, $37,065; number of sheep, 977, value, $994; number of swine, 8,166, value, $6,732; number of vehicles, 1,296, value, $22,973; moneys and credits, $18,821; mortgages, $24,392; stocks, etc., $805; furniture, $42,351; libraries, $1,010; property not enumerated, $94,914; railroads, $316,649.17; total, $1,734,848.17.

LANDS.—There is no desirable Government land remaining in this County. The Burlington & Missouri River Railroad Company owns 10,000, and the Union Pacific Company several thousand acres of well located and desirable land here which they offer for sale at prices ranging from $2.00 to $10.00 per acre.

PRECINCTS.—The County is divided into eight precincts. We give the name and population of each for 1879: Denver, 3,026; Little Blue, 548; Silver Lake, 518; Kenesaw, 542; Cottonwood, 610; Pawnee, 1,017; Juniata, 1,125; West Blue, 776. Total for County, 8,162.

FLOURING MILLS.—There are three flouring mills in this County—one located at Gilson, on the Blue, one at Millington, and one at Juniata. The Juniata Mills are propelled by steam; the building is four stories high, has three run of stone, with a capacity of one hundred barrels of flour every twenty-four hours.

### HASTINGS,

The County Seat, is one of the most enterprising and rapidly developing cities in Nebraska. Scarcely more than half a dozen years old, it already has a population of 3,500, and the increase has been greater in the last two years than at any other period. The admirable location of Hastings, at the junction of three leading railway lines—the Burlington & Missouri, St. Joe & Denver, and Hastings & Republican Valley—gives her great commercial advantages and is the main cause of her remarkable and substantial growth. She is the center of trade for a large portion of the Republican Valley and northern Kansas, and transacts an immense business in the handling and shipment of grain, in the sale of agricultural implements, lumber and merchandise of all description. The wholesale and retail houses do a thriving business, and generally have commodious, well-stocked stores, while all the minor branches of trade and mechanics are well represented. The hotel accommodations are ample; the schools are graded and have a large attendance; the school houses are models of beauty and are furnished with all the modern improvements in desks and apparatus; Churches of the leading denominations have erected houses of worship, several of them very neat in appearance and costly, and all the prominent secret societies—Masons, Odd Fellows, Good Templars and Temple of Honor—have flourishing lodges. There are three newspapers published at Hastings—the *Adams County Gazette* and *Hastings Journal*, weeklies; and the *Central Nebraskian*, a semi-monthly and weekly paper—all well patronized and able papers.

In September, 1879, Hastings was visited by a most destructive fire, which destroyed nearly two blocks in the business portion of the city, causing a loss estimated at from $75,000 to $100,000. This happening during the busy opening of the fall trade, was severely felt; but the citizens, with their characteristic energy and business enterprise, set to work immediately to clear away the debris, and larger and more substantial brick blocks will occupy the places of those destroyed, before the present year is out.

### JUNIATA,

The next town of size and importance in the County, is located on the line of the B. & M. Railway, six miles west of Hastings. It was laid out as a town in 1872, and at present has some 400 inhabitants.

Juniata is the oldest town in the County, and was, until quite recently, the County Seat. It is surrounded by a magnificent and fertile country, dotted with large and highly cultivated farms, many of them supplied with groves of fruit and forest trees. A brisk business is transacted here in grain, implements, lumber and general merchandising. They have a good school house costing $3,500; several Churches, two hotels, and one of the best flouring mills in the West. The *Juniata Herald* is published here weekly, and is a journal of influence in the County.

### KENESAW

Is a thriving little town on the line of the B. & M. road, eight miles west of Juniata, and was laid out soon after that place. It has a very fine, large school house, a hotel and several business houses.

### INLAND

Is a small village on the B. & M., five miles east of Hastings. It was laid out in 1872, and bids fair to become a prosperous town. It has several business establishments and is a good market for grain and stock.

### AYR

Is the name of a town laid out within the past year, on the line of the Republican Valley branch of the B. & M. R. R. It is located in the midst of an excellent agricultural section, and business is already well represented in the town.

POSTOFFICES.—The postoffices in the County, outside of the towns named, are: Millington, Gilson, Kingston, Little Blue, Mayflower, Silver Lake, North Blue, Roseland and Rosedale.

## ANTELOPE COUNTY.

ANTELOPE COUNTY was organized in accordance with an Act of the Legislature, in June, 1871. It is located in the northeastern part of the State, in the fifth tier of Counties west of the Missouri River, and is bounded on the north by Knox, east by Pierce, and Madison, south by Boone, and west by Holt County and unorganized territory, and contains 864 square miles, or 552,960 acres of land.

WATER COURSES.—The Elkhorn River is the principal stream, flowing diagonally through the central portion, and by its tributaries draining the entire country, except the northern townships, which are nourished by the numerous branches of Verdigris and Bazile Creeks that flow northward to the Missouri. The Elkhorn at this point is about twenty-five yards wide, with an average depth of eighteen inches, has a rapid current, clear, pure water, and sandy bottom. On the south side are two tributaries, Clear Water and Cedar Creeks, both large enough for mill purposes. There are also seven smaller streams within the limits of the County tributary to the Elkhorn, and two or three that water the southern townships and flow southward into the Loup. Springs are abundant along most of the small streams throughout the County, and a few are to be found along the Elkhorn.

TIMBER.—There is enough native timber in this County, especially in the western part, to supply all fuel for many years to come. Well seasoned oak wood can be bought for $3.50, and cottonwood for $3.00 per cord. The timber found along the Elkhorn is chiefly cottonwood, ash, white elm, willow and oak. The tributaries are timbered with the above named varieties, with the addition of red elm, hackberry, basswood, and box elder. Cottonwood is more abundant along the Elkhorn than any other wood, and oak is more plentiful on most of the smaller streams, and in the timbered gulches.

Artificial groves have been set out by almost every farmer.

WILD FRUITS.—Many kinds of shrubs grow either among the timber or in thickets by themselves, the most common of which are the plum, and choke cherry. Wild fruits are very abundant in a favorable season, the most plentiful being plums, grapes and gooseberries.

CHARACTER OF THE LAND, SOIL, ETC.—The greater portion of this County is embraced in the beautiful valley of the Elkhorn River, which drains a country about thirty miles wide. The valley of the Elkhorn is here generally about two miles wide, but is in some places from three to five, and nearly always undulating, with small level tracts, and many smooth, long slopes from the adjacent foot hills toward the river. The bottom lands have an average elevation of about twenty feet above the river, with sufficient fall to carry off all surplus water from heavy rains. Near the river there are some small tracts of low land known as first bottoms, which produce a heavy grass, and are subject to occasional overflow. The valley of the Elkhorn is skirted on either side by a range of hills varying from about twenty to one hundred and fifty feet above the bottom lands, and broken through every two or three miles by small streams tributary to the Elkhorn. These hills are in some places steep and broken, in others low and rounded, and susceptible of cultivation. The uplands are gently rolling, and are intersected with small valleys each from one to four miles wide and drained by a tributary of the Elkhorn. There are no large tracts of level land in the County. There are only a few small tracts along the Elkhorn too low, and a few on the divides between the streams too rough and broken, to admit of cultivation. As a whole the surface of the country is rolling, with one large valley running diagonally through the center, and nine or ten smaller valleys running in a direction nearly at right angles with the larger one. About three-fourths of the land in the County has a first-class clay loam soil, the remaining fourth a sandy soil, varying in quality from a rich sandy loam to a worthless yellow sand. The usual depth of the soil on the uplands is about eighteen inches, and on the bottoms, two-and-a-half to three feet. There are exceptional places on the narrow ridges where the soil is but a few inches deep, while at the foot of steep hills, where decayed vegetable matter has accumulated for ages, it may be eight or ten feet in depth. A large portion of the sandy land is rolling or hilly, and is almost worthless for any purpose except grazing. It produces a tolerably good growth of grass, and will be of value in the future when stock raising becomes a leading business. Wherever the sandy tracts are level, the soil is fair in quality, and in some places rich and black, producing equally as well as the clay loam soil. Water can be had by digging or boring, on the Elkhorn bottom, at the depth of from ten to twenty-five feet; on the bottoms of the smaller streams at the depth of from twenty to forty feet, and on the uplands from sixty to ninety feet.

FIRST SETTLEMENTS, &c.—The first settler in the County was Crandall Hopkins, of Wisconsin, who located with his family on a claim in the Elkhorn Valley, in November, 1868. He was followed by Thomas Mahan, in February, 1869, and early that spring by J. H. Snider and family, Mr. Timms, William Clark, A. M. Salnave and A. J. Leach. The settlement of the County once begun, proceeded rapidly. The summer of 1869 was a productive one, and the settlers who were there early enough to do any breaking, raised excellent crops; prosperity smiled upon them, new settlers came weekly, sometimes daily, and before fall the choicest tracts of the Elkhorn bottom were settled as far west as the Upper Yellow Banks, within two or three miles of the west limit of the County.

In 1870 the settlers suffered from the first Indian raid. A party of ten Indians visited the new settlement, appearing friendly at first, but in two or three instances becoming extremely insolent, firing a number of shots into the house of Louis Patras, and finally stealing nine horses and hurrying off toward the Sioux reservations in the northwest.

In November of this year, the Indians made a second raid upon the settlements, breaking into the house of Robert Horne, living on the head of Cedar Creek, and carrying off or destroying all his household goods. These Indians were followed by fourteen of the settlers, overtaken and severely punished, within sight of where James McFarland now lives, in Holt County, a few miles below O'Neil City. Two of their number were killed, and two or three known to be wounded. The whites also suffered in this battle, two of the men receiving severe arrow wounds, and one horse was killed and three wounded. Since that time the settlers have not been molested by Indians.

These raids did not stop the settlement of the County. During the summer of 1870 the Elkhorn bottom continued to fill up with new settlers, and the valleys of the smaller streams, at least as far west as Cedar Creek, were tolerably well settled by fall. By the first of November there were not less than 150 voters within the limits of the County. The pioneers were subject to many privations and inconveniences. The nearest postoffice, store or mill was at Norfolk, distant from thirty to fifty miles. Mr. A. J. Leach, before there was a postoffice in the County, frequently brought the mail from Norfolk for the entire community, in his overcoat pockets, leaving it at Judge Snider's for distribution.

The organization of the County was effected by the election of a full board of County officers, at the first general election, held in June, 1871, in pursuance of an Act of the Legislature. At this election 202 votes were polled, and OAKDALE designated as the County Seat.

In 1879 there were thirty school districts in Antelope County; school houses, twenty-seven; children of school age, 914; males, 511; females, 403; number of qualified teachers employed, males, nine; females, twenty-two; value of school houses, $3,923; value of school house sites, $772.

The Assessors' returns for 1879 show the following amount of taxable property in the County: Number of acres of land, 127,395; average value, $1.62 per acre; value of town lots, $22,340; money used in merchandise, $8,120; money used in manufactures, $300; horses, 1,079; value, $30,362; mules and asses, ninety-four, value, $4,088; neat cattle, 2,361, value, $22,136; sheep, 502, value,

$645; swine, 1,477, value, $1,179; vehicles, 364, value, $6,800; moneys and credits, $2,425; mortgages, $2,698; furniture, $1,353; libraries, $50; property not enumerated, $9,528; total, $319,119.

The County is divided into six voting precincts. The following is the name and population of each, in 1879: Center, 599; Twin Grove, 467; Elm Grove, 341; Cedar, 372; Mills, 282; Sherman, 117; total population of County, 2,178.

There is yet some Government land in this County subject to homestead and pre-emption, but it is being rapidly taken up, and in a year or two more none will be left. The Burlington & Missouri River Railroad Company also owns between 80,000 and 90,000 acres, for which they ask from $1.50 to $6.00 per acre.

There is an unlimited supply of nutritious prairie grass in Antelope County, both for pasturage and hay, and the raising of cattle and sheep must become, and is fast becoming, one of the leading industries in this part of the country. At the present time there is not stock enough in the County and adjacent territory to consume one hundredth part of the grass during the grazing season, nor one tenth of the hay that could be put up for winter use.

Two railroads are projected through this County, and the surveys and preliminary work is already accomplished. The Fremont and Elkhorn Valley R. R., now in running order to Stanton, in Stanton County, will more than likely be extended to and through Antelope before the close of another year.

There are two saw mills in the County, also two good flouring mills that are kept running to their full capacity, the settlers coming fifty to one hundred miles to mill.

## OAKDALE,

The County Seat, has a fine location on the Elkhorn River, in the southeastern part of the County. It is favorablely situated for business, and enjoys a large trade from the country adjacent. The town is keeping pace with the growth of the County, and to-day has a population of 300 ; has a number of good stores, a hotel and other business establishments ; a fine school house, and several church organizations. The *Pen and Plow*, a weekly newspaper, established here in 1876, continues to prosper, and has done, and is doing excellent service for the County.

### NELEIGH,

One of the brightest little towns in the valley, is located on the Elkhorn, five miles above the County Seat. Its present population is about 450, and it is growing very rapidly. Churches, schools and business have been established on a firm basis, and all are prospering wonderfully. The *Republican*, a weekly newspaper, is issued here and is well patronized.

Several young towns, with a postoffice, general store, school, blacksmith shop, etc., have been started in different parts of the County.

## BOONE COUNTY.

The first settlements in Boone County were made early in the Spring of 1871 by people chiefly from Massachusetts, Wisconsin and Minnesota, among the more prominent of whom were S. P. Bollman, Harvey Maricle, L. H. Baldwin, N. G. Myers, Albert Dresser, Richard Evans, T. T. Wilkenson, John Hammond, Stephen D. Avery and Elias Atwood, senior, who settled mostly in the valley of the Beaver.

The County was organized by a special Act of the Legislature, approved March 28, 1871. It is located in the northeastern part of the State, and is bounded on the north by Antelope, east by Madison and Platte, south by Nance, and west by Greeley and Wheeler Counties, and embraces about 672 square miles or 430,080 acres.

The surface of the country consists mainly of high rolling and gently undulating prairie, almost every portion of which is susceptible of easy tillage. The valley of Beaver Creek, extending from northwest to southeast through the central portion of the County, is exceedingly beautiful and fertile, the bottoms ranging from one to two miles in width. The valley of Cedar Creek on the west, and running parallel with the Beaver, is also very fine, and nearly as extensive. Plum, Timber, Shell and the smaller creeks, each afford considerable excellent bottom land. The soil throughout the County is uniformly good and well adapted to the growth of all the cereals, vegetables and fruits. On the table land wheat will average twenty bushels to the acre. The natural grasses are abundant, affording fine advantages for the rearing of cattle or sheep. On the uplands a constant supply of fresh water can always be had at the light expense of boring wells for windmills.

Beaver Creek, a tributary of the Loup, is the principal stream of the County. It is a beautiful creek, affording sufficient water power for mills, and flows in a southeasterly course through the central portion of the County, supported by a number of creeks and brooks.

Cedar Creek, the next stream in point of size, waters the southwestern townships, flowing in the same general direction of the Beaver, Timber Creek being its principal support.

Plum Creek flows in a southeasterly course about midway between the Beaver and Cedar. Shell Creek and a number of small streams flowing into it, water the upper portions of the County, and flows into the Platte River.

Native timber is scarce in the County and is confined to the margins of the streams and ravines. Small quantities of Cedar are found in occasional places along the creek bearing that name.

Tree planting has been generally well attended to. The first plantings were greatly injured by the grasshoppers, but through the perseverence of the settlers many thrifty young groves may now be seen.

The number of acres of timber reported under cultivation in the County in 1879, was 450, and the number of trees planted, 424,360.

The number of fruit trees reported under cultivation, was pear, thirty-three; peach, 521; plum, 478; cherry, 185; and grape vines, 509.

The organization of the County was effected by commissioners appointed for that purpose by the Probate Judge of Platte County, in accordance with the provisions of a special Act of the Legislature, approved March 28, 1871. The Commissioners were: S. P. Bollman, John Hammond, and Harvey Maricle.

The valuation of taxable property in the County, as reported for 1879, is as follows: Number of acres of land, 220,110; average value per acre, $1.06; value of town lots, $8,583.00; money used in merchandise, $3,813.00; number of horses, 1,276, value, $35,004.00; number of mules and asses, 105, value, $3,687.00; cattle, 2,223, value, $17,047.00; sheep, 583, value, $583.00; swine, 1,630, value, $764.00; vehicles, 529, value, $8,680.00; moneys and credits; $3,281.00; mortgages, $1,349.00; furniture $3,325.00; property not enumerated, $16,557; total, $330,054.00.

The school interests of Boone County are in a flourishing condition. The number of school districts in 1879, was thirty-one; school houses, seventeen; children of school age, 926; males, 504; females, 422; number of qualified teachers employed—males, six; females, nineteen; amount paid male teachers, $235.40; paid female teachers, $1,405.87; value of school houses, $3,897.50; value of school house sites, $140.

The Government land in this County has all been taken up, with the exception of a few odd parcels or small tracts, not desirable for farming purposes. The Burlington & Missouri River Railroad Company, however, owns a large amount of very fine land here—about 150,000 acres—for which two to six dollars per acre is asked

At present the nearest railroad point to Boone County is on the Union Pacific, about twenty-five miles distant. A railway has been projected through this County and the grading has already been made. In a few years' time all this country will be opened to railway travel and traffic. Silver Creek, on the Union Pacific is connected with Albion and other towns in Boone County, by a graded, air-line wagon road, built by Adam Smith, Esq., and other citizens interested in the welfare of the County.

The County is divided into nine precincts, the following being the population of each: Manchester, 421; Cedar, 396; Shell Creek 376; Plum Creek, 240; Boone, 307; Ashland, 122; Oakland, 266 Beaver, 381; Dublin, 117. Total population of the County in 1879 2,626. Of the above 1,462 are males, and 1,164 females.

According to the crop returns made in March, 1879, Boone County had 65,549 acres under cultivation. The number of acres planted and yield of the principal crops, is as follows: Winter wheat, 390 acres, 5,080 bushels; rye, 1,643 acres, 24,619 bushels spring wheat, 36,901 acres, 448,326 bushels; corn, 21,371 acres 689,780 bushels; barley 1,943 acres, 34,408 bushels; oats, 5,32 acres, 175,048 bushels, and potatoes 105 acres, 10,327 bushels.

### ALBION,

The County Seat, is a very promising town of 300 inhabitants. It was laid out in 1871, and was the first town platted and recorded in the County. It is centrally located on the west bank of the Beaver, on the S. one-half, N. W. one-fourth, Sec. twenty-two, town twenty north, range six west. The business of the place is represented by three grocery and dry goods stores, a drug store, two harness shops, an extensive wagonmaker's and blacksmith shop, a hotel, livery stable, grain warehouses, lumber, feed, implement and other stores. It has a neat frame Court House 22x30 feet, a large frame school house, and a weekly newspaper—*The Argus*. A substantial bridge spans the creek in front of the town, and an excellent flouring mill is close at hand. Several of the religious societies have organizations and hold regular services.

### WATERVILLE,

On the graded road, in the southeastern part of the County, has recently been laid out and is fast assuming the importance of a town, having at present about 150 inhabitants, several stores and other places of business.

### ST. EDWARDS,

On the Beaver, a few miles southeast of the County Seat, has a fine new flouring mill, good assortment stores, a hotel, blacksmith shops, school house, &c.

DAYTON, DUBLIN, MYRA, RAVILLE, OXFORD, ROSELMA, BOONE and COON PRAIRIE are names of postoffices throughout the County. at some of which are located a general store and school house.

---

## BURT COUNTY.

Adjoining Washington County on the north, flanked on the east by the Missouri River, on the south by the Omaha Indian reservation, and on the west by Dodge and Cuming Counties, is situated Burt County, containing about 441 square miles, or 282,240 acres.

It was named in honor of Francis Burt, Nebraska's first

Governor, and was organized by an Act of the Territorial Legislature, approved February 18, 1855, the present boundaries of the County being defined by an Act of the Legislature of 1872-3. Outside of the valleys flanking the different water courses, the surface of the County is rolling, the soil, with a few exceptions, being a dark loam, easily tilled and of great productiveness for all descriptions of grain, vegetables and fruits. The higher hills in many portions of the County are most admirably adapted to the cultivation of grapes and other small fruits. The average yield of wheat in this County for some years past has ranged from fifteen to twenty-three bushels per acre, the estimated average yield for the present year, 1879, being fifteen bushels. Spring varieties of wheat are usual y cultivated, although, by deep drilling in, large yields of winter varieties are produced.

The second bottom lands, as they are called, succeeding the narrow flood plains along the Missouri, rise in gentle undulations towards the high table lands, which range from three to eight miles distant from the river. As a rule, this beautiful stretch of prairie bottom is dry, extremely fertile, and especially adapted to the culture of corn and vegetables. In some instances quite extensive sloughs intervine, as is the case between Tekamah and the river; yet, by a proper system of ditching, these wet lands can be entirely redeemed and converted into the most productive corn lands. The bluffs, as they are commonly termed, are generally low and sloping, and, as a rule, susceptible of tillage; those not adapted to grain, as before stated, being excellent for grapes, small fruits and sheep raising. It is estimated that about one-eighth of the land in Burt County is under cultivation, the larger portion of the uncultivated being held by non-residents and speculators. Unimproved land ranges from four to twelve dollars per acre, according to quality and location, while improved farms are valued all the way from fifteen to forty-five dollars per acre, improvements, railway and market facilities governing values.

Traversing the western portion of the County, from north to south, is the wide, fertile and beautiful valley of Logan Creek. Here one sees on every hand large, well improved farms with neat farm houses and well-constructed barns and other outbuildings. The beauty and richness of the valley has earned for it the name of the Gennesee Valley of Nebraska, and certainly it is to northern Nebraska what the famed Gennesee Valley is to the State of New York. A few miles to the east of Logan Valley, and running nearly parallel with it, is the Valley of Bell Creek, much smaller than the Logan, yet equally fertile and beautiful. Valleys varying in width and importance border nearly every water course to be found in the County.

WATER COURSES.—It may be stated in the outset that Burt County is abundantly watered; the Missouri flowing along its eastern border, while Logan Creek, a swift running, beautiful stream, with bold banks, passes through the western tier of townships, from north to south. This stream is fed by brooks and springs on either side, thus affording a volume of water entirely sufficient for driving any amount of milling and other manufacturing machinery during all seasons of the year.

Bell Creek has its source in the northern portion of the County, and flowing in a southeasterly direction empties into the Elkhorn River, in Washington County. The northeastern part of the County is watered by Blackbird, and several other creeks which empty into the Missouri River while the more central sections of the County are drained by Elm, Silver, Tekamah and several smaller streams which have their source within the borders of the County, their flow being generally in a southeasterly direction, to a lake or lagoon, about five miles long by half a mile in width, situated in the southeastern portion of the County, some four or five miles from the Missouri River.

Besides these creeks, there are many fine springs in the County, prominent among which may be mentioned Golden Spring, situated about eight miles north of Tekamah. This spring flows from a rock, and for the purity of its waters and the beauty of its surroundings it is unequalled in the State.

TIMBER —While the Missouri bottoms, as also the banks of the different streams in the County, furnish an abundance of natural timber for fuel, there is little or none suitable for lumber, and very little that could be converted into building timber. The varieties found are chiefly cottonwood, ash, elm, oak, hickory, walnut, box elder, and coffee bean.

Farmers have usually turned their attention to the cultivation of timber, and as a result, a large number of fine groves are to be seen in the settled portions of the County. Even at this time, these groves are sufficiently developed to supply their owners with fuel.

FRUIT.—The soil and climate of Burt County are well adapted to all descriptions of fruit growing in northern latitudes, as the large number of bearing orchards in the County attest. At the present time there is an abundance of wild fruits, along the streams and especially on the Missouri bottoms, such as grapes, plums, gooseberries and raspberries. The number of fruit trees under cultivation in the County in 1879, is as follows: Apple, 61,617; pear, 643; peach, 1,638; plum, 9,559; cherry, 2,919.

BUILDING MATERIAL.—As before stated there is an absence of building timber, and a large per cent. of the lumber used in the County is procured at other points to the East and North. There is, however, an abundance of good sand-stone in the bluffs along the Missouri River, and also an abundance of fine clay from which a good quality of brick are manufactured.

POPULATION.—This County is divided into eight precincts, the population in each in 1879 being as follows: Arizona, 618; Decatur, 804; Oakland, 954; Silver Creek, 409; Bell Creek, 50; Eeverett, 576; Riverside, 260; Tekamah, 1,033. Total population of the County 5,165, of which 2,865 are males, and 2,300 females.

## TEKAMAH,

The County Seat, located in the southeastern part of the County, is a prosperous and well laid out city of 800 inhabitants. Being situated on the Omaha & Northern Nebraska Railway gives it fine commercial advantages, and it is the chief shipping point and business center of the County. Elevators, warehouses and stock yards have been erected to facilitate the extensive shipments of grain and stock.

The town contains many fine stores and business establishments of various kinds; good hotel accommodations, a commodious Court House, beautifiul High School building, several Church organizations and neat houses of worship, and two old established weekly newspapers—*Burtonian* and *Advocate.*

Tekamah is located in the midst of a prosperous, well settled country, and is consequently a thriving, busy town, one of the largest and most enterprising in Northern Nebraska.

SCHOOL BUILDING, TEKAMAH.

### DECATUR,

On the Missouri River, in the northeast corner of the County, was located in the Fall of 1855, by the "Decatur Town and Ferry Company," the principal members of which were Stephen Decatur, Peter A. Sarpy, B. R. Folsom and W. B. Beck. During the Summer of 1856, Mr. Decatur, assisted by Mr. Schemousky, surveyed and platted the townsite. In 1857 town shares were valued at $1,000 each. The first hotel erected was known as the Porter House.

The mercantile interests in 1857 were represented by Col. P. A. Sarpy C. Lambert, John Chase, Dr. Horner, and Brown & Co., their stock consisting principally in Indian goods, whiskey and tobacco. The Congregationalists organized the first Church Society in the town. The Episcopal Church was next organized and soon after erected a house of worship. The first birth in the town was that of Margueretta Decatur, daughter of O. F. Wilson, born in the Fall of 1857. The first death occured the same Fall, and was that of John Gardner. The first physician was Dr. McDougall, the next, Dr. Whittacre. Capt. S. T. Leaming was the first Mayor, and Hon. Frank Welch. (afterwards Member of Congress from Nebraska, and now deceased,) the first City Clerk. C. Lambert, of Kit Karson fame, and Rev. J. F. Mason, were among the first settlers.

At the present time Decatur has about 500 inhabitants. It has an elegant large, new school house, and the business of the town is represented by half a dozen general merchandise stores, two drug, two hardware, several grocery, feed, and boot and shoe stores, lumber yards, carpenters', wagon-makers', and blacksmith shops, etc. A weekly newspaper—the *Vindicator*—is also published here.

## LYONS,

Situated on the east bank of Logan Creek, in the northwestern part of the County, is a pretty little village of some seventy-five inhabitants, containing several stores, a church, carpenter shop, wagon and blacksmith shop, an excellent flouring mill, and a fine school building, costing about $1,900. Josiah Everett, the pioneer of this part of the County, located here with his family in 1867. Mr. Waldo Lyon built a small house and barn in the summer of 1868, and in the following fall brought his family here. Warner & Freeland put up a store building, and stocked it with goods, in 1869. In the summer of 1870 a grist mill and the Presbyterian Church was completed. The Methodists and several other denominations have organized Societies and hold services regularly. Some of the best farmers in the county are in the vicinity of Lyons, and the extension of the Omaha and Northern Nebraska Railroad has given a new impetus to business, which will add largely to its inhabitants.

## OAKLAND.

About fifteen miles to the west of Tekamah, on the Logan in the famous Logan Valley, is situated Oakland, a fine little country town of about 150 inhabitants. Besides the different mercantile industries, an excellent flouring mill, and the different trades usual to a small town, religious and educational interests are well represented in Oakland. As in most other portions of Burt County, the town is flanked on every side by as rich and beautiful farming country, as can be found in the State. The Omaha & Northern Nebraska Railway, was extended from Tekamah to Oakland in the year 1879.

## NEWTON.

Some four miles east of Tekamah, in Arizona precinct, is situated Newton postoffice, where will be found a good country store, with a church, school and other advantages. Newton is the home of Senator Beck, brother of United States Senator Beck, from Kentucky, and is surrounded by a rich farming country.

## RIVERSIDE

Is situated on the Missouri River, about five miles north of Newton, where will be found a fine steam saw mill, postoffice, country store, etc. The logs that are converted into lumber at the Riverside Mill, are procured chiefly from a fine body of timber on the Iowa side of the river.

HOMESTEAD postoffice is about six miles south of Newton, where will be found a country store, blacksmith shop, etc. This little centre is also in the midst of a highly productive farming country.

GOLDEN SPRING postoffice is about eight miles to the north of Tekamah. These springs flow from a rock of peculiar formation, and for the purity of its waters, or the beauty of its surroundings, is not excelled in the State.

There are also what is known as Clarke's postoffice, on Bell Creek, near the center of the County, Alder Grove postoffice, situated about ten miles southwest of Tekamah, and Bertram, the last postoffice organized in the County, and situated about ten miles northwest from Tekamah.

FIRST SETTLEMENTS.—On the 2d of October, 1854, a party of nine men, consisting of B. R. Folsom, W. N. Byers, J. W. Pattison, H. C. Purple, John Young, Jerry Folsom. Wm. T. Raymond, a Mr. Maynard, and a Mr. White, crossed the Missouri River at Council Bluffs, Iowa, for the purpose of exploring the interior of Nebraska, with a view to permanent settlement therein. The first night in the new Territory the party camped at the old Mormon town of Winter Quarters, now called Florence, a village six miles above Omaha, and from here they took a westerly course crossed the Elkhorn River, and examined the country as far west as the present town of North Bend, on the Platte River; from here they returned to the Elkhorn, re-crossed that stream, and followed it up to the mouth of Logan Creek, thence up that stream to a point nearly west of the present town of Decatur. Not finding the country and timber such as they wished, they changed their course to a southeasterly direction, finally arriving at a fine, large body of cottonwood timber, on the Missouri, and all being favorably impressed with the advantages of the situation for a town site, they decided upon its selection. Accordingly, on the 6th day of October 1854, the town site of Tekamah was located, after which the party returned to Council Bluffs for supplies, and to make preparations for surveying, &c., returning to Tekamah again in a few days with an accession to their number of twenty-three men, making in all thirty-two.

In the meantime contracts had been made by the Town Company and settlers for the erection of a Town House and ten other buildings in Tekamah, before winter set in, but owing to the difficulty of obtaining the material, and the annoyances from Indians, they were not fulfilled, and no adequate shelter being provided for man or beast, the whole party returned to Iowa, where they remained during the winter.

Early in the Spring of 1855 John R. Folsom, in company with W. N. Byers, F. W. Goodwill, Miles Hopkins, Z. B. Wilder, and N. R. Folsom, returned to Tekamah and commenced getting out logs for two houses. The timber was divided with a whip-saw for the walls and floor, the roof being covered with cottonwood bark, and by the first of July following, the houses were finished and occupied.

A week or two after the return of Mr. Folsom and others to Tekamah, they were joined by Dedrick Face and wife, F. E. Lange and W. B. Beck. Mrs. Face has the honor of being the first white woman in the County.

On the 28th of July of this year, a colony from La Salle County, Illinois, consisting of G. M. Peterson, Thomas Thompson, John Oak and George Erickson, with their families and household goods, twenty-four souls in all, arrived at Tekamah. These were the first families to locate upon claims in the County. They located north of Silver Creek, and at once began cutting and hauling logs for building permanent homes; but they had scarcely commenced work before a messenger was sent to them with the terrifying news that two white men had just been killed and scalped by the Santee Sioux near Fontenelle, and that a general Indian attack was apprehended. Their fond dreams of peace and prosperity were thus suddenly changed to consternation and disappointment; and gathering up their effects, they hastily left for Tekamah, where preparations for a defense were being made.

Hon. B. R. Folsom made a requisition upon the Governor for arms and ammunition for the settlers, which were readily supplied. In the meantime Major Olney Harrington and family, and a few others, had arrived at Tekamah, which increased the number of inhabitants to about fifty. A military company was organized with B. R. Folsom as Captain, W. B. Beck, Lieutenant, and N. R. Folsom, First Sergeant. Eighteen names were enrolled, and the men drilled twice a day. A great number of logs were cut and hauled from the grove on the Missouri bottom, and a fort or block house, partially erected as a better means of defense, (now a hotel and is called the Astor House, kept by C. Astor—resident fourteen years). But the summer wore away without any more Indian disturbances occurring, the scare gradually died out, and the settlers returned to their claims to make preparations for the coming winter.

The first election for County organization was held on the 6th of November 1855, at which the following officers were elected, viz: William Bates Judge of Probate; John Newett, Sheriff; Peter Peterson, Register; Lewis Peterson, Treasurer; Wm. F. Goodwill. Surveyor; Olney Harrington, and Adam Olinger, Justices of the Peace.

Tekamah had been incorporated as a city by an Act of the Legislature, approved March 14, 1855, and was made the seat of justice.

During the Spring and Summer of 1856 a large number of claims were taken throughout the County and Tekamah improved rapidly. The terrible winter following, which caused such widespread suffering among the young settlements of Nebraska, was also severely felt by the pioneers of Tekamah and vicinity. Cut off for a time by the deep snows from all supplies, they suffered greatly for provisions, especially flour. Most of the stock perished from exposure and starvation. However elk, deer, and all kinds of small game was abundant, and formed the chief article of food for the settlers.

The first marriage in the County was that of Lewis P. Peterson to a daughter of Thomas Thompson, in the Fall of 1855.

The first death was that of Mrs. Thomas Thompson, in the Fall of 1855, who died in child-birth, the child dying shortly afterward, also making it the first birth and death in the County.

Rev. L. F. Stringfield, of the Methodist Episcopal Church, organized a Society in Tekamah in August, 1856. In the Fall following, Rev. J. M. Taggart, of the Baptist Church, organized a Society with eight members. From this time onward religious meetings were regularly held at Tekamah and at other points in the County.

B. R. Folsom was appointed Judge of Probate for Burt County, by the Governor, his commission dating May 16, 1855.

Very little progress was made in the settlement of the County during the year 1857, but in the following Spring claims were taken in all parts of the County, farms were opened out, buildings erected and other substantial improvements made, and from this date the real prosperity of the County commenced and continued steadily up to the present time.

The Omaha & Northwestern Railroad, now the Northern Nebraska, was completed to Tekamah in the Fall of 1876, which remained its terminus until the present year, 1879, when it was extended to Oakland, in the western part of the County.

SCHOOLS.—Good schools were among the first institutions opened at Tekamah and Decatur, and as the County developed, comfortable school houses were erected in all the most convenient centers.

The number of school districts in the County in 1879, was fifty-two; school houses, fifty-one; children of school age, 2,010; —males, 1,067; females, 943; whole number of children that attended school during the year, 1,445; number of qualified teachers employed—males, thirty-five, fiemales, forty-nine; wages paid teachers—males, $3,977.39, females, $5,156.35; value of school houses, $30,610.00; value of school house sites, $1,073.00; value of books and apparatus, $1,107.00.

CROPS.—The reports for 1879 give the number of acres of land under cultivation in the County at 22,515. The acreage sown and the yield of the principal crops, is as follows: Winter wheat, eighty-three acres, 784 bushels; rye, 1,088 acres, 16,790 bushels; spring wheat, 10,175 acres, 138,293 bushels; corn, 2,494 acres, 61,861 bushels; barley, 612 acres, 14,246 bushels; oats, 1,614 acres, 56,318 bushels; potatoes, 238 acres, 18,303 bushels.

TAXABLE PROPERTY.—The total valuation of taxable property in the County, as returned by the Assessor for 1879, is as follows: Acres of land, 278,979, average value per acre, $3.75; value of town lots, $53.287.00; money used in merchandise, $30,061; money used in manufactures, $7,885.00; number of horses, 3,033, value $65,481.00; mules and asses, 271, value, $5,316.00; neat cattle, 9,765; value, $82,544.00; sheep, 6,385, value, 6,434.00; swine, 17,246, value, $10,788.00; vehicles, 967, value, $11,788.00; moneys and credits; $5,511.00; mortgages, $12,837.00; stocks, etc., $613.00; furniture, $17,863.00; libraries, $796.00; property not enumerated, $16,173.00; railroads, $24,129.00; total, $1,406,160.00.

## BUTLER COUNTY.

Butler County lies in the great Platte Valley about fifty-one miles west of the Missouri River. It has an area of 594 square miles, or 351,360 acres of land, and is bounded on the north by the Platte River, which separates it from Platte and Colfax Counties east by Saunders, south by Seward, and west by Polk County, having an average elevation above the sea level of 1,500 feet. It was organized June 26, 1856, by a proclamation of Governor Cuming, and was named in honor of Wm. O. Butler, of Kentucky, who was appointed by President Pierce to be Territorial Governor of Nebraska, but who, however, declined.

WATER SUPPLY.—The Platte River washes the northern, boundary of the County, Wilson, Elm, Deer, Bone and Skull creeks have their source in the central portions of this County, and flow northwardly into the Platte, the last two being very fine streams. The central and southwestern portions of the County are watered by the Blues, and the southeastern townships by Plum Creek and the Oaks.

Good well-water is generally attainable at a depth of ten to sixty feet.

TIMBER.—Native timber is scarce, although considerable is yet found along the Platte and Blue Rivers, on Oak Creek and the other streams. Small quantities of cedar and hardwood are found in the bluffs. Large quantities of artificial timber have been planted throughout the County, and thriving groves may be seen on many farms; and where cultivation has kept the prairie fires from the brush-land young native timber is springing up rapidly.

In 1879 there were 2,514 acres of timber under cultivation in the County, and 1,400,505 trees planted.

FRUIT.—The people of Bultler County have long enjoyed choice fruit from their own orchards and vines, and in the past year or two the number of fruit trees has been nearly doubled. In 1879 there were 6,454 apple, 322 pear, 3,634 peach, 1,411 plum and 3,981 cherry trees, and 214 acres of grape vines under cultivation in the County.

CHARACTER OF THE LAND, ETC.—The surface of the country consists for the most part of gently rolling prairie or upland, which is almost everywhere susceptible of easy tillage, and possesses a rich dark soil well adapted to the growth of cereals. The valley of the Platte averages about five miles in width in this County, and is level and beautiful, with a gradual rise towards the bluffs. The Valley of the Big Blue, in the southwestern part of the County although much narrower, is generally smooth with wide fertile bottoms. Splended well-drained bottom lands are found on the North Blue, Skull, Bone and other streams.

In an irregular line from four to six miles south from the Platte River bank, the bluffs or breaks rise suddenly and boldly up from the floor-like plain, affording a landscape spectale of surpassing beauty, and one peculiarly different from any view east of the Missouri. After pitching and tossing about promiscuously, these ridges which constitute natural winding turnpikes or highways, and the interjacent ravines, abruptly cease, blending all at once in the perfectly level and beautiful tableland. The contrast thus presented is most enchanting to one just arrived from the timbered countries of the east.

Away to the southward and eastward, lie the valleys of the Big Blue and the Oaks, marked in summer time by a thread-like continuation of green groves and plum thickets winding through the nude plain. Approaching these, after crossing the table land proper, you behold a moderately rolling surface stretching away to the southward, a region most admirably adapted to pasturage and agriculture.

FIRST SETTLEMENTS.—In 1857 the Waverly Town Company, from Plattsmouth, arrived upon the banks of Skull Creek—so named from the surprising number of Pawnee skulls found strewn about—near the ruins of an ancient village of that tribe, which once flourished near the spot where Linwood now stands. This was the first *bona fide* attempt to settle in this region, which was still really in possession of the murderous Pawnee, not to speak of an occasional visit by marauding bands of Sioux.

Huttsizer, Barker, Garrison and nine others were the members of this pioneer company, which, however, was short-lived, owing to the Pike's Peak excitement of the next year (1858-9). These erected the first house in Butler County, about a half mile above the Linwood mills, on the west bank of Skull Creek. At this date no white man had broken a permanent trail through the grass upon the Platte bottoms, (south side) but the Mormon trail, and old Government road had wound their lonely lengths in dusty majesty along the table lands for many years prior.

Soon after the advent and exodus of the Waverly Company, the families of Solomon Garfield and James Blair followed, and took up their lonely abode in the house alluded to. Both families still reside in the County.

In 1859 an attempt was made to effect a County organization, in which the following persons participated, viz: John Beecroft, Thompson Bissel, William Bissel, James Blair, Solomon Garfield, William Earl, J. W. Seeley, Simpson, Beardsley and McCabe; but this organization was never perfected.

These, then, were the videttes, the outposts of civilization, who, with a few persons subsequently arriving, held lonely possession of this County from 1858 to 1868—ten years. The skirmish line of permanent settlers penetrated this region about the latter date. As is usual with first comers, they avoided the high, broad prairie, tables and benches, preferring to distribute themselves along the valleys of the various streams, settling in the little groves and nooks under the protection of the hills, in the vicinity of these prime necessities of frontier life—water and wood—each new arrival venturing a little further up the stream, to the next thicket or shelter.

Thus such portions of the valleys and bottoms along the Platte, the Blues, Oaks, etc., as are within this County, were first selected and occupied, while the highlands were yet entirely unsettled.

In August, 1868, Butler County was permanently oraganized and the first election held, showing a poll of seventy votes, indicating a population of about two hundred souls; for it must not be forgotten that at this early day a large per centage of the inhabitants were unmarried young men. The County Seat was located at Savannah, on the banks of the Platte.

In 1869-70 the advance columns of the great army of occupation swarmed in, entirely absorbing the valleys, and soon after the table and rolling lands beyond the Platte bluffs and breaks. The immediate cause of this remarkable influx of immigrants was, of course, the completion of the Union Pacific Railroad, affording both an outlet and an inlet to this heretofore isolated territory.

During the summers of 1869-70-71-72, inclusive, rather more than 2,500 persons pitched their tents and settled in the County, transforming it, as if by magic, into a very garden, with a population containing all the elements and conditions found in communities which have been generations growing up to their present estate. More than 40,000 acres of prairie sod were overturned by the plow, and hundreds of dwellings and school houses erected.

Twenty years ago all this country was a blank—a lonely, silent region of grass-covered hills, hollows and plains, whose time-old solitude had been forever unbroken save by the whistling of the winds, the tramp of the bison, or the twang of the red man's bow string.

Five or six years later, a dozen or so persons had straggled hither, scattered along the old wagon trails to the mountains; in 1868 the number had increased to about 200; in 1870 to 1,280; in 1873, to 3,800; in 1874, to 4,440; in 1876, to 4,695, and in 1879, by the census, to 7,310.

The Bohemians are congregated in the northeast, among the hills and ravines of Skull and Bone Creeks, and are industrious and economical. They number several hundred in the County, many of whom have opened up and improved fine farms.

The first white child born in the County was Amanda Simpson, November, 1860.

There are sixteen voting precincts in the County, the following being the population of each in 1879:

Linwood, 1,008; Bone Creek, 515; Savannah, 339; Alexis, 410; Summit, 343; Olive, 410; Franklin, 1,082; Skull Creek, 621; Oak Creek, 397; Center, 456; Union, 386; Reading, 622; Read, 305; Ulysses, 304; Spurk, thirty-six; Richardson, seventy-five. Total, 7,310, of whom 3,956 are males, and 3,354 females.

The origin of the several names of the precincts are generally apparent. Three of them are in commemoration of old residents; three are named for streams passing through them; Linwood from the presence of linn or basswood—very rare in this vicinity; Savannah for an Eastern town of that name; Summit for the former Wisconsin residence of C. C. Cobb, Esq., who established a mercantile business here in 1872; Center from geographical position; Reading for a Michigan town of that name, and Ulysses for Gen. U. S. Grant.

The first public house of any description was erected in the Summer of 1867, on section four, township, sixteen, range three. The materials used for its construction were small, unhewn logs; the roof—as was the custom in those days—was of poles and long slough or bottom grass, covered with sod; its dimensions about ten feet by twelve. In this unpretending edifice the first Commissioners' meeting was held and the first school taught, Miss Ada Vanderkalk being the teacher, and the juvenile members of the families of D. R. Gardner, James Blair, Wm. Butler, Jas. Green and Mrs. Solomon Garfield, pupils. This was a "subscription school," the wages paid were $20.00 per month.

Ranche life in Butler County covered a period of ten years, beginning with 1858 and ending about 1868, when the County was organized, and freighters' customs and road laws gave way to legislative enactments.

Gardner's Ranche was established in 1859, by David R. Gardner, on the site now occupied by the town of Savannah. McCabe's Ranche, on Deer Creek, Thomson Bissel's, on Elm Creek, and Simpson's Ranche a few miles further west, were all established in 1859. Thomson Bissel broke the first land in the County and raised the first crop.

Several graves of "Forty-niners" may yet be seen on the hill points near McCabe's Ranche, but of the ranche itself little is visible beyond a profuse growth of gigantic weeds.

The first session of the District Court held in Butler County was at Savannah, on May 20, 1871. As may be supposed, the docket was not cumbered to any great extent with the names of litigants and attorneys. One case only was brought on for trial. This was in reference to the murder of one Edward McMurty, (a citizen of what is now known as Pepperville precinct) by some Pawnee Indians. For some fancied insult to certain members of their tribe, who were in the habit of begging and pilfering among the settlers on the south side of the Platte, a party of the red-skinned assassins laid in wait for their victim at a secluded spot on the Stage Company's Island, two miles south of Columbus, and upon his appearance riddled him with bullets and arrows; dragged his body to an out-of-the-way place, and anchored it out of view in a water-hole, by means of a forked stick.

A change of venue was had on account of some supposed unfriendliness of the deceased's relatives and neighbors, and the culprits were placed in the Omaha jail. They were finally liberated and sent to their reservation above Columbus.

Much shorter and more satisfactory were the proceedings in the case of one Robert Wilson, who killed Ransal B. Grant, proprietor of Grant's ranch, a year or so previous, Wilson being hung to a neighboring tree, and his body dropped into the Platte by way of burial.

April 10, 1871, and April 14, 1872, are remembered as the days of the great snow storms, the like of which has not been known in this locality before or since. The former was the more tempestuous of the two but of only twenty-four hours duration, hence no considerable losses were sustained. The latter raged and "screamed" during three days and nights. Cattle and horses were led into dwelling houses, and thus saved to the owners, which otherwise must certainly have perished. In many cases farmers found it impossible to go to their stables, but ten or twelve rods distant, and upwards of two hundred head of stock perished from suffocation and exposure.

The most notable prairie fire occured in October, 1872. It came into Buttler from Polk County, sweeping everything before it jumping hedge-rows and fire lines a hundred feet wide, devouring hundreds of acres of standing corn, demolishing grain and hay stacks without number, and in several instances burning graineries, stables and houses, with their contents. Many horses cattle and hogs were burned to death in the fire. The loss in the County is variously estimated at from $15,000 to $20,000.

Next came the grasshopper plague of 1874, which marked an era in the hisiory of the County, and in the lives of its inhabitants. long to be remembered. Of course its sad effects are fresh in the minds of all the people, how the countless millions of lean and hungry insects came down in great black clouds upon the growing crops without a moments warning, devouring every green thing raised by the hand of man, even stripping the leaves from the trees, both great and small; how the generous-hearted, noble people of the East responded to their wants with clothing and provisions ; how eagerly upon the approach of Spring the first appearance of the tender grass was watched and waited for in behalf of the starving horses and cattle, and the first fruits of the garden and field, by their expectant masters. And then followed the abundant rains, the luxurious grass, and the marvellous prodigality of vegetable growth, insomuch that corn in six months, fell from two dollars to fifteen cents per bushel, etc.

During the year 1878 the Omaha & Republican Valley Railroad was extended west through Butler County, giving it direct railway connection with Omaha and the East, and enhancing values greatly.

A considerable portion of the land here is owned by speculators and non-residents. The Union Pacific Railroad Company owns about 20,000 acres, ranging in price from $3.00 to $7.00 per acre. The Government land is all occupied by settlers.

PUBLIC SCHOOLS.—In 1869 the present school system was inaugurated by blocking out nine school districts. At the first enumeration there were found to be 153 children of school age. In 1879 there were sixty-eight school districts; sixty school houses; 2,689 children of school age, 1,458 being males, and 1,231 females; and ninty-three qualified teachers employed. Amount of wages paid teachers, males, $6,666.42 females, $4.852.24; value of school houses, $27,487.00 school house sites, $693.00 ; of books and apparatus $2,010 25.

TAXABLE PROPERTY.—The following statement will show the taxable property in the County in 1879: Acres of land, 324.657, average value $3.81; value of town lots, $50,049.00; money used in merchandise, $33,186.00; money used in manufactures, $3,735.00; horses, 3,398, value, $105,040.00 ; mules and asses, 268, value, $8,900.00 neat cattle, 5,795, value, $60,667.00; sheep, 480, value, $202.00; swine, 7,804, value, $8,129.00; vehicles. 1,383, value, $23,451 ; moneys and credits, $5,426.00 ; mortgages, $11,671.00 ; stocks, etc., $5,033.00; furniture, $13,886; libraries, $580,00; property not enumerated, $33,389.00, railroad; $123,651.00; total valuation, $1,726,163.00.

## SAVANNAH,

Located on the Platte Bottom, in the center of the County from east to west, was the first County Seat, and during the years from 1869 to 1872, was a thriving village, containing twenty-five or thirty houses, a Court House, stores, &c. The site was owned by D. R. Gardner and Samuel Woodward. Among the residents were B. O. Perkins, H. Pepper, Captains Samuel W. and Andrew B. Roys, merchants; Dr. D. H. Dickson, Dr. J. F. Gilbert, E. G. Paige, D. Bresee, blacksmith, and M. Porter, shoemaker. Here the Courts and Councils were held during the above specified years ere its dismantlement and removal to its successor, David City.

### DAVID CITY,

The County Seat, located on the Omaha & Republican Valley Railroad, in the central part of the County, is an active and remarkably prosperous city. It was laid out in 1872 and two years later was legally incorporated. Three years ago its population was a little over two hundred, to-day it has seven hundred and fifty inhabitants, and is well built up with tasteful dwellings and substantial business blocks; has three neat Churches, a bank, High School building, Court House, two weekly newspapers—the *Press* and the *Republican*—and all the stores, trades and business establishments usual to a live, growing city like this.

Since the advent of the railroad, which reached here September, 24, 1877, David City has doubled in size, and its business has extended to all parts of the County. Larger hotels, business houses, warehouses, elevators and other conveniences have been erected to meet the demand of the largely increasing business of which this is the centre, and is in the midst of one of the prettiest and richest sections of country in the State.

### LINWOOD

Was begun in 1870-71, on the old Waverly townsite, in the northeast part of the County. It is beautifully located on the east bank of Skull Creek, on a little bench or plain under the bluffs which lie to the south, and is a flourishing village of about 200 inhabitants, containing a fine school house, grist mill, several stores, groceries, etc. Among the older settlers of the place are Fred Johnson, John L. Smith, J. P. Brown, S. O. Crawford, Jehiel Hobart, Gilbert Hobart, William Spring and James McBride.

### ULYSSES,

In the south central part of the Connty, contains about 300 inhabitants and is the second place in size and importance. It was laid out in June, 1868, in a romantic little nook among the trees, on the south bank of the Big Blue River, and has steadily improved during each succeeding year. J. M. Palmer was the original owner of the town site. Ulysses is well situated for business, and almost all the different branches are represented. An excellent grist mill has been in operation here for several years. J. N. Batty, H. Ellsworth, F. H. Daws, Godfrey Reyhart, Dr. S. W. Thrapp, J. M. Palmer, Tom. Shields, P. G. Dobson, George and Robert Reed are among the earlier inhabitants in this vicinity.

## BUFFALO COUNTY.

Buffalo County lies between the Valleys of the Platte and South Loup Rivers, in the central part of the State from east to west. It was organized in 1864, and is bounded on the north by Custer and Sherman, east by Hall, south by the Platte River, which separates it from Kearney and Phelps, and west by Dawson County, containing about 900 square miles, or 576,000 acres

WATER COURSES.—It is well watered by the Platte, Loup and Wood Rivers, and their numerous branches. The Platte washes the entire southern border, and the South Loup flows from west to east, through the upper tier of townships, having several small tributaries which extend through and water the central portions of the County. Wood River flows from west to east through the southern portion of the County, running nearly parallel with, and from three to five miles north of the Platte—the last half of its course. There is an abundance of water power. Well water can be had at a depth varying from twenty to sixty feet.

CHARACTER OF THE LAND AND SOIL.—About forty per cent of the area consists of valley and bottom, the remainder of fine rolling prairie with a small amount of Bluff and broken land in the vicinity of some of the water courses. On the wide bottoms of the Platte and along the entire length of Wood River the land cannot be surpassed for agricultural purposes. On the Loup and many of the tributary streams also, there are beautiful tracts of wide, rich bottom.

The soil is a rich, black loam varying from one to three feet in depth. When properly cultivated the uplands produce handsome returns of small grain, while the valleys are well adapted to the growth of all classes of crops. Wheat will average about twenty bushels per acre ; corn, thirty to seventy ; barley, twenty-five to forty; oats, thirty-five to sixty.

TIMBER AND FRUIT.—Buffalo is better supplied with native timber than most Nebraska Counties, the Platte, Wood, Loup and several of the streams being tolerably well timbered. Many of the ravines are thickly timbered also; the varieties most abundant being cottonwood, ash, elm, hackberry, box-elder and soft maple.

Besides the native growth there are many thrifty artifical groves throughout the settled portions of the County. The number of trees reported under cultivation in 1879 was 225,000.

Wild fruits of various kinds grow here in profusion along the streams and in the timber gulches. There are many fine orchards under cultivation. The number of fruit trees planted up to 1879 was: Apple, 2,199; pear, thirty-three; plum, 506; peach, 470, and cherry, thirty-two.

LANDS.—There is a considerable amount of Government land in this County remaining untaken which is open to the homesteader or pre-empter. The Union Pacific Railway Company also owns in the neighborhood of 150,000 acres here for which they ask from $3.00 to $6.00 an acre.

The prairies and hills produce an abundance of nutritious grasses affording splendid advantages, in connection with the plentiful supply of running water, for the raising of cattle and sheep.

The County is traversed by two lines of railway—the Union Pacific and Burlington & Missouri River—which form a junction at Kearney City, thus offering fine facilities for the shipment of stock and grain to the Eastern markets.

TAXABLE PROPERTY.—The amount and valuation of all taxable property in the County, as reported for 1879, was as follows: Number of acres of land, 330,521; average value per acre, $1.28; value of town lots, $100,403.40; money used in merchandise, $46,523; money used in manufactures, $9,410.00; number of horses, 1,837; value, $43,322.00; mules and asses, 237; value, $6,943.00; neat cattle, 5,523; value, $36,506.00; sheep, 4,059; value, $3,060.00; swine, 2,383; value, $1,705.00; vehicles, 822; value, $13,009.00; moneys and credits, $9,379.00; mortgages, $6,597.00; stocks, etc., $110.00; furniture, $17,863; libraries, $696.00; property not enumerated, $44,549.00; railroads, $448,736.32; telegraph, $3,264.00; total, $1,217,106.74.

CROPS.—The number of acres under cultivation reported in 1879 was 45,836. The acreage planted and yield of the principal crops was as follows: Winter wheat, 28½ acres, 337 bushels; rye 723 acres, 7,989 bushels; Spring wheat, 14,827 acres, 170,367 bushels; corn, 26,412 acres, 935,115 bushels; barley, 365 acres, 8,162 bushels; oats, 4,505 acres, 126,667 bushels; buckwheat, 16½ acres, 387 bushels; sorghum, thirty-four acres, 3,212 gallons; flax, fifty-six acres, 383 bushels.

EDUCATIONAL ADVANTAGES.—The number of school districts in the County in 1879 was fifty-one; school houses, twenty-nine; children of school age, 1,771; males, 931; females, 840; whole number of children that attended school during the year, 1,044; number of qualified teachers, fifty-five; nineteen males and thirty-six females; wages paid male teachers during the year, $3,343.76; paid female, $4,732.35; value of school houses, $22,010.74; value of school house sites, $772.00; value of books and apparatus, $700.05.

POPULATION.—Buffalo County is divided into twelve precincts; the population of each in 1879 being as follows:

Shelton, 930; Gibbon, 794; Center, 1,048; Kearney, 1,920; Odessa, 182; Western, 300; Buffalo, 135; Grant, 313; Divide, 386; Loup, 285; Cedar, 163, Schneider, 426. Total population of the County in 1879, 6,878. In 1860 the population was 114; in 1870, 193; and in 1875, 2,861, showing an increase in four years of 4,017.

The County was first settled in 1857 by a band of Mormons who broke up and cultivated a small tract of land in what is now Shelton precinct, but their stay was of short duration, the greater part of them moving on to Salt Lake City, after remaining here a year or two. Joseph E. Johnson, one of their number, who had formerly been connected with the newspapers called the *Council Bluffs Bugle*, at Council Bluffs, Iowa, also the *Omaha Arrow* at Omaha, in 1854, and was an able writer. He started a paper here called *The Huntsman's Echo*, which, however, was short-lived.

The settlement of the County progressed very slowly before the construction of the Union Pacific and B. & M. Railways, since which time its development has been wonderfully fast, as will be seen by the foregoing statements of population and taxable property.

## KEARNEY CITY.

The County Seat was laid out in 1872, and organized as a city in 1873. It is located on the Platte Bottom, in the center of the County from east to west, at the junction of the Union Pacific and B. & M. Railroads, and at present has a population of 1,500. The city is advantageously situated in a business point of view, and is growing rapidly, having a number of elegant brick business blocks and many handsome residences. A fine Union Depot has been erected here. The Methodists, Presbyterians, Catholics, Congregationalists, Christians and Baptists, each have neat and comfortable houses of worship, and the several prominent secret societies have flourishing organizations. Three school buildings adorn the town, and there is a good system of graded schools. Five papers are published here, *The Central Nebraska Press*, *Nonpareil*, *True Citizen*, *Greenback Journal*, and *Literary Notes*, all weeklies except the latter, which is a monthly, devoted to literature and the school interests.

A good bridge across the Platte at this point connects Kearney with the South Platte and Republican Valley Counties. There are between fifty and sixty business establishments in the city, among which are real estate, lawyers' and doctors' offices, two banks, three hotels, two lumber yards, and a first-class steam flouring mill, having three run of burrs and all modern improvements.

## GIBBON,

Containing 200 inhabitants, is located on the U. P. Railway thirteen miles east of the County Seat. It was laid out in 1871, and was first settled by a colony from Ohio. For a short period it was the County Seat, and a splendid brick court house, costing about $20,000, erected during that time, is now used as an Academy. Wood River passes within a mile and a half of the town. The Presbyterians have a neat brick church; the Methodists, Catholics, Baptists, and other denominations have organizations. A good flouring mill, with three run of burrs is in operation here. There is one drug, one hardware, one harness, and several general merchandise stores, a hotel, lumber yard, and large elevators for the accommodation of the grain trade.

#### SHELTON

Is located on the Union Pacific road near the east line of the County, and has a population of about 200. Wood River runs close by, on which there is located a good flouring mill. The town is improving rapidly. It has a good hotel, school house, elevators, and several general merchandise stores and places of business.

#### ELM CREEK

Is a station on the U. P. near the west line of the County, containing about 100 inhabitants, general stores, grain warehouses, school houses, etc.

STEVENSON, ODESSA, PRAIRIE, CENTER, SHELBY, STANLEY, CENTENNIAL, AMADA, BERG and SWEETWATER are names of postoffices in the County, at which will be found a general assortment—store and school house, blacksmith shop, and other branches of industries represented.

## CASS COUNTY.

Cass County was organized in 1855 by an Act of the first Territorial Legislature. It is located on the southeastern border of the State, and is bounded on the north by the Platte River and Saunders County, east by the Missouri, south by Otoe, and west by Lancaster County, and embraces about 550 square miles, or 352,000 acres, at an average elevation of 1,000 feet above the sea level.

WATER COURSES.—The Missouri River washes the eastern border of the County, and the Platte nearly the entire northern border. The Weeping Water is the principal interior stream. It heads in the northwestern part of the County, and flows southeasterly through the central portion, supported by numerous branches from ten to twelve miles in length, and empties into the Missouri. Salt Creek cuts across the northwest corner and receives two important tributaries from this County, which waters the northwestern townships. Several small creeks, varying from five to fifteen miles in length, rise in the central portions of the County and flow northwardly into the Platte, among which are Pawnee, Cedar, Turkey and Four Mile. Branches of the little Nemaha

River water the southwestern townships, and Rock Creek, a tributary of the Missouri, flows through the middle eastern part of the County.

CHARACTER OF THE LAND.—The surface of the County consists of bottom, table and undulating prairie land, the latter comprising about three-fourths of the whole. The bottoms of the Missouri are here quite narrow. In the western part of the County the bluffs of the Platte run close to the river, the bottoms gradually widening as they approach the Missouri. The bluffs of the Missouri are generally high and cut through with frequent draws or hollows, but the table lands, or level plain, is usually reached at from one to three miles back. The uplands stretch away in wave-like undulations as far as the eye can reach, and are intersected with rich, wide-spreading valleys traversed by clear running streams, flowing over hard, gravelly beds, and fringed along their margins with a fine growth of native timber. These valleys are natural meadows, yielding a luxuriant growth of fine grasses for hay, and when put under cultivation, produce bountiful crops of grain and vegetables. The soil throughout the County is of great durability and excellence.

TIMBER.—In the early settlement of the County, timber was quite plentiful on the bottoms of the Missouri and adjacent bluffs, consisting principally of cottonwood, ash, elm and hackberry. A considerable quantity was also found in the bluffs and on the large islands of the Platte, the latter furnishing fine cedar for posts. In the eastern and middle portions of the County there is still a number of native groves, mostly of hardwood. Besides the native timber there is a large number of artificial groves in the County which furnish their owners with fuel. In 1879 Cass County had 2,176½ acres, or 899,730 forest trees under cultivation, and 302½ miles in hedging.

FRUIT.—Cass is one of the best fruit growing Counties in the State, and for several years past has had an abundance of the choicest varieties of her own raising. In 1879 there were 105,687 apple, 1,279 pear, 49,373 peach, 3,572 plum, and 13,578 cherry trees, and 6,221 grape vines under cultivation, and all in a prosperous condition.

BUILDING STONE.—A superior quality of magnesian limestone

is abundant in several localities. Extensive quarries have been opened on the line of the B. & M. Railway in the northwestern part of the County, and at Rock Bluffs, a few miles below Plattsmouth. On the Weeping Water, near the Falls, there is an abundance of excellent building stone, and at other points good stone for building and making lime is found.

COAL.—Bituminous coal has been discovered at several different points in the County. On the banks of the Missouri, fourteen miles below Plattsmouth, a shaft of forty feet has been sunk to an eighteen inch seam. It is of good quality. This same seam crops out five miles further northwest. It is estimated that miners can bring out from one to ten tons of coal per day from these mines.

OCHRE.—Along the Missouri below Plattsmouth, there are extensive deposits of mineral paint, or ochre. Some of the beds are from three to five feet thick, and of as fine quality as any in the market.

FIRST SETTLEMENTS.—Mr. Samuel Martin has the honor of being the first settler in Cass County. He obtained a special permit from the Secretary of War to establish a trading post on the Missouri River, below the mouth of the Platte. Under this permit Mr. Martin, assisted by James O'Neil and others, early in the spring of 1853, built a two story log house, at the foot of Main street, on the north side, on lots six and seven, block thirty-one of the present town site of Plattsmouth. The "Old Barracks" as this was more generally called, was subsequently used for different purposes—stores, offices, postoffice, etc.,—till it was removed, in 1864, to make room for a brick building. In the fall of 1853 James O'Neil also built for the same Samuel Martin, a smaller log house, a little north and west of the first, which, in later days was largely used for County offices.

On the extinguishment of the Indian title to the lands bordering on the west bank of the Missouri River, on June 24, 1854, a rush was made for the most valuable claims, and but a few days passed before most of the more desirable lands in Cass County, near the Missouri River, were staked and marked with the claimant's names. Before the legal organization of the Territory, some 250 men had penciled their names on claim stakes within what is now Cass County.

Before the organization of the Territorial Government it was found necessary to have some tribunal for the settlement of disputes, and each settlement, defining its own boundaries, formed itself into a "Club" for this purpose. These clubs varied much in character, according to location. The earlier settlements near the river were largely composed of speculators, who often equaled, if they did not outnumber, the real settlers; while further back from the river the number of pioneers largely predominated. Of course the different clubs varied in character. On the one extreme, self-interest ruled largely in most of the proceedings; while on the other, the general interest and welfare of the settlement was the ruling principle.

An offender against the laws or decisions of the club was generally summarily dealt with. There was no machinery for assessing fines; no jails or prisons; hence little or no attempt was made to grade the punishment according to the offense. In the clubs controlled by real settlers the offender had a fair trial and was informed what he *must do* to retain his membership, and the penalty of refusal to conform at once to the judgment of the club. The penalty of obstinate and unyielding disobedience was "Removal from the Territory," or, in the language of the day, to be "Put over the River." Very few had the hardihood to resist the judgment of the club, for it was well known that persistent offenders would be so effectually *removed* that they could cause no more trouble.

There was probably but one case in Cass County when it became necessary to resort to this extreme penalty. The one, but too vividly remembered yet by many citizens of Plattsmouth, when four unhappy men were started on their last voyage *over* the river, but their arrival on the other side has never been reported, nor have they ever been seen or heard from since.

Following are the names and time of settlement of a few of the pioneers. Many of the first on the ground in several of the precincts were merely speculators, or of a transitory character, selling out their claims and passing on, and their names are therefore omitted:

In MARTIN'S PRECINCT, now Plattsmouth, are found in 1854, Samuel Martin, Jacob Adams, Wm. H. Shafer, J. W. O'Neill, W.

Mickelwait, C. H. Wolcott, Levi Walker, Stephen Wiles, A. J. Todd and William Gullion.

Rock Bluffs—N. R. Hobbs, Wm. Young, F. M. Young, Sr., Wm. Gilmour, Sr., Abram Towner, Benj. Albin, J. McF. Haygood, 1854.

Four Mile Creek—Lorenzo Johnson, 1855; Thomas Thomas, Wm. L. Thomas, Samuel Thomas, Peter Beaver, Capt. D. L. Archer, 1856.

Eight Mile Grove—John Scott, 1855; John Mutz, Geo. S. Ruby, J. P. Ruby, 1856.

Louisville—Adam Ingram, James Ingram, 1856; A. L. Child, 1857; Wm. Snyder, Conrad Ripple, Pat. Blessington, Fred Stohlman, 1858.

Avoca—John Kanoba, J. G. Hanson, 1856; Amos Teft, Sr., Amos Teft, Jr., Orlando Teft, 1857; Geo. W. Adams, 1859.

Liberty—Joseph Van Horn, 1854; Samuel Kirkpatrick, 1855; L. Sheldon, J. F. Buck, Stephen Hobson, 1856.

On March 30, 1855, the Governor appointed Abram Towner Probate Judge, and Thos. J. Palmer Register of Deeds, as also Thomas B. Ashley Justice af the Peace for Kanosha Precinct.

On the same day Judge Towner opened his Court, and by order, divided Cass County into two precincts, viz: Plattsmouth and Rock Bluffs. He also ordered the first County election to be held on April 10, 1855, and appointed James O'Neill, Elias Gibbs and Stephen Wiles as Judges, and Charles Wolcott and P. Shannon as Clerks of Plattsmouth Precinct, and Thomas B. Ashley, Frank McCall and Curtis Rakes, Judges, and Wm. H. Davis and John Griffith Clerks of Rock Bluffs Precinct. No returns or poll books are to be found of this election, but it appears that L. G. Todd and Allen Watson were elected as Justices of the Peace for Plattsmouth Precinct, and Thomas B. Ashley and Thomas Thompson for Rock Bluffs, and Bela White, County Treasurer.

The first session of the District Court was held in Cass County in April of 1856, Judge Edward Hardin presiding; A. C. Towner, Sheriff.

On March 3, 1856, Rock Bluffs Precinct was divided into Cassville and Kanosha; and on September 10, on petition of several citizens of Clay and Lancaster Counties, the Probate

Judge created the Precinct of Chester, and on the same day divided Cass County into three Commissioners' Districts, named Plattsmouth, Kanosha and Cassville, preparatory to the election of County Commissioners, which occurred at the general election of November, 4, 1856.

The choice of lands in 1854 was confined almost entirely to the vicinity of the Missouri River ; few if any were taken at any considerable distance from it. In 1855 a few settlers reached out to Four Mile Creek, Eight Mile Grove and a short distance up the valley of the Weeping Water. But in 1856 there was a more general extension. The several earlier settlements were much enlarged, and in addition, the Weeping Water, up to and above the Falls, Cedar, Thompson, Fountain, and Salt Creek, had considerable settlements.

At the general election of November 4, 1856, as before stated, J. Vallery, Jr., R. Palmer and W. D. Gage were elected as the first Board of County Commissioners.

The pioneers of Cass County suffered but little from the Indians. In the early days they were in the habit of roaming through the settlements, from the single individual up to fifteen or twenty in number, but there is nothing on record to show that they ever attempted personal injury to any settler of the County. They were always a source of great terror to the women and children, and also to husbands and fathers lest they should attack the family in their absence, but beyond a few raids made for the purpose of stealing, and the intolerable annoyance caused by their continual begging for food, they committed no serious depredations.

The first death in the County was that of Samuel Martin, on December 15, 1854. Mr. Martin was not only the first white settler in the County, but the first to fill a settler's grave.

The first marriage was that of Elza Martin to Sarah Morris, on November 16, 1854, by Abram Towner, Probate Judge.

The first white child born in the County was Nebraska Stevens, son of Wm. Stevens, in December, 1854, or January, 1855.

The first sermon preached in the County was in October, 1854, at the house of Thos B. Ashley, by Abram Towner.

During several years preceeding 1864 a number of citizens of this County suffered much loss and hardship from horse thieves.

About the first of June of that year, 1864, (some say 1863) two horses were taken from Capt. Isaac Wiles, and one from John Snyder, of this County. Pursuit was immediately made. A quarrel between the thieves, about the division of the horses induced one of the three to betray the other two. The informer was secured, and on the information given the two were followed and found secreted in a loft at "Mullen's Ranch," on the divide south of South Bend. They were secured, and the party returned with them to Eight Mile Grove. In the trial of the men which followed before the self-constituted court, there was not, nor could there be, any denial of guilt. They were horse-thieves taken in the very act. No possible mistake in their identity, design or act. A plea was offered for the one who betrayed the other two. But it was considered that, as no repentance or better feeling had induced this action, but only revenge and malice toward his fellow criminals, it gave no shadow of an excuse for sparing him, perhaps to repeat the offense before another day, and without a dissenting voice, sentence was passed and followed by immediate execution ; and death then and there closed the career of three miserable men.

The Burlington & Missouri River R. R. runs across the northern portion of the County, from the city of Plattsmouth westward. This Company owns 25,000 acres of land in Cass County, the price ranging from $7.00 to $10.00 per acre.

POPULATION.—Cass County is divided into sixteen voting precincts, the population of each, in 1879, being as follows: Plattsmouth, 2,692; Rock Bluffs, 1,251; Liberty, 1,215; Plattsmouth, 975; Greenwood, 729; Stove Creek, 721; Weeping Water, 687; Eight Mile Grove, 664; Elmwood, 629; Center, 594; Tipton, 575; South Bend, 573; Salt Creek, 558; Avoca, 554; Louisville, 544; Mount Pleasant, 474. Total population of County in 1879, 13,435 —males, 7,305; females, 6,130.

EDUCATIONAL ADVANTAGES.—There are eighty-four school districts in the County and eighty-six school houses; seventy-two are frame, ten brick, and two stone. The total value of school property in the County is $78,120; number of teachers employed in 1879, was males, sixty-six, and females, sixty-eight; average wages paid teachers monthly, males, $35.61; females, $28.90; the number of children of school age in the County, in 1879, was, males, 2,724;

females, 2,430; total, 5,154; the attendance during the year mentioned was, males, 1,973; females, 1,671; total, 3,644.

CROPS.—The reports for 1879 give the number of acres under cultivation in the County at 95,078. The yield of the principal crops, was as follows: Winter wheat, 392 acres, 5,968 bushels; rye, 1,501 acres, 20,927 bushels; spring wheat, 47,440 acres, 587,815 bushels; corn, 17,028 acres, 552,292 bushels; barley 5,438 acres, 133,687 bushels; oats, 4,313 acres, 127,933 bushels; sorghum, sixty acres, 1,982 gallons; flax, 165 acres, 1,382 bushels; millet and Hungarian, 329 acres, 1,325 tons; potatoes, $612\frac{1}{2}$ acres, 65,519 bushels; tobacco, two acres, 2,060 pounds; beans, $19\frac{3}{4}$ acres, 107 bushels; onions, 6 8-10 acres, 1,004 bushels.

The Assessors' returns for 1879 show the total value of land in the County to be $1,624,683; average value per acre, $4.90; total value of town lots, $207,792; money invested in manufacturing including buildings and material, $38,585; money invested in mercandising, $55,055; number of horses, 7,311, average value, $29.00; total, $22,068; number of mules and asses, 729, average value, $31.63; total, $23,068; number of cattle, 18,305, average value, $10.14; total, $185,691; number of sheep, 307, average value, $1.17; total $359; number of swine, 41,043, average value, $1.09; total, $42,485; number of vehicles, 2,199, average price, $19.31; total value, $424,629; mortgages, stocks, bonds and other securities, $180.64; household furniture not exempt, including gold and silver plate, musical instruments, watches and jewelry, $70,557; private libraries, $21.41; all other property not enumerated, $171,369; railway property, $288,030; total value of property in the County, $3,058,135.

## PLATTSMOUTH.

Twenty-one miles south of Omaha, on the west bank of the Missouri, about one and a half miles south of where the Platte empties into the first named river, deriving its name from its location near the mouth of the Platte, is situated the City of Plattsmouth, the County Seat of Cass County, which was platted, laid out and christened on the 15th day of August, 1855, which entitles it to a place among the oldest cities of the State. In 1879 the city contained a population of 3,300, about forty per cent. of which were foreign born. Although too near to Omaha and Lincoln, to acquire more than a local importance as a commercial centre, its railway advantages and the rapid development of the rich agricultural country that flanks it to the west and south, has served to make it a solid business town, and to somewhat increase its patronage, both as a receiving and distributing market. The business portion of the city is built very compact and includes some really attractive structures, although as a rule, the business houses are of wood and rather ancient in their general aspect. The streets are laid out at right angles, and are broad and pleasant, and under a fine system of natural drainage towards the river; the town is kept comparatively clean with little labor. The city is situated on a strip of table land, about fifty feet above the level of the river, which slopes gently towards the stream, while to the south, west and northwest, rises a range of high hills, which are well wooded with both natural timber and artificial groves. The residence portion of the town is somewhat rolling and occupies the space between the range of hills mentioned, and the business center of the place. There the streets are adorned on either side with luxuriant shade trees, and one sees numerous beautiful residences that are surrounded with fine shaded yards, so that whatever the town lacks in the way of attractiveness in its business portion, is nearly or quite compensated for in the inviting appearance of its resident streets.

A view of the city from the river is indeed charming. Passing over the portion of town devoted to trade, the eye rests on the stately mansion of the opulant, and the neat cottage of the less pretentious citizen, the one standing out in bold relief, and the other nestling in the cooling shade of tree and vine, all speaking in the most unmistakable language, "We are the homes of wealth, contentment and virtue."

The religious and educational advantages, as in most other cities throughout the State, are excellent and ample. There are eight church buildings in the city—some of which have attractive exteriors and finely finished interiors—including one Methodist, one Episcopal, one Lutheran, one Christian, one Baptist, one Catholic and one African Methodist. There are four good Common School buildings, 26x40 feet, constructed of brick, and one High School building, which stands on a commanding elevation and is very fine structure. Among the more prominent public buildings is the post office and custom house, Court House and opera house, all of which, except the Court House, are of a character that would reflect credit on a much larger town.

Society organizations include one Masonic Lodge, one Odd Fellows, one Knights of Honor, one Good Templars, one Temple of Honor, one Red Ribbon Club and one Ladies' Christian Temperance Union. The various industries are represented as follows: B. & M. Railway Shops, employing five hundred men; three newspapers, the *Sentinel* (weekly), *Herald* (weekly), and *Enterprise* (daily); nine dry good stores, three hardware, three clothing, three millinery, three jewelry, four drug, three farming implements, four hotels, one flouring mill, one saw mill, one bank, one loan agency, three grocery stores, four confectionery shops, two tin shops, four blacksmith shops, six carpenter shops, two carriage and wagon shops, three harness shops, one shoe store, two shoe shops, one foundry and machine shop, two lumber yards, four paint shops, four meat markets, two wood yards, three coal dealers, two undertaker's stores, three elevators, four warehouses, one pork house, eight grain merchants and numerous others, such as billiard halls, saloons, barber shops, laundries, etc. The B. &. M. R. R. bridge, now in course of construction across the Missouri River at this point, is to be finished early in 1880.

EARLIER HISTORY OF PLATTSMOUTH.—Samuel Martin, with his two log houses commenced the settlement of both city and County. Club law ruled supreme from June, 1854, to September, 1855, when it was weakened some from the presence of the two Justices of the Peace, Allen Watson and L. G. Todd, but still exerted a controlling power for a year or so later.

The first movement on record looking towards the "City of Plattsmouth," was the organization of the "Plattsmouth Town Company," October 26, 1854.

The first members of this Company were Samuel Martin, James O'Neil, J. L. Sharp, C. and L. Nuckolls and Manly Green. Other members subsequently joined them. In November, 1854, this Company proceeded to lay out and plat the City of Plattsmouth.

O. N. Tyson was the surveyor of the Company, and surveyed

and platted the future city. On March 16, 1855, the Company obtained from the first Legislature an Act of Incorporation of the City of Plattsmouth. The town site was entered January 22, 1859.

In the order for a County election issued by Judge Towner for April 10, 1855, he changed the name of the Precinct from "Martins" to Plattsmouth, so that Martin's name now remains only as a name in history. Meantime he had finished his work in the settlement and was laid away with so few attending spectators that when active search and inquiries were instituted a few years since by his relatives for his remains, they failed to find any clue to them.

Mr. Martin's two log houses, built in 1853, were followed by the third, a log house, built by T. G. Palmer; the fourth, also of logs, by W. Mickelwait, and the fifth, of logs, also, by Wm. Garrison.

The first frame building erected was on the south side of Main street, just above where the Platte Valley House now stands. It was built for and used as the first hotel in the city. It was called the "Farmer's Hotel." The foregoing log houses and this hotel were built during the fall of 1854 and spring of 1855.

Three good frame houses were built in 1856 by W. Mickelwait, among which was the "Nebraska House," or City Hotel, built for the Plattsmouth Town Company. During the same summer, Messrs. Slaughter and Worley built the old New York store. The first brick was probably built by Judge A. L. Sprague, in 1858 or 1859, now used as the Surveyor General's office; the second about the same time or a little later, by J. Krouth; and the third, in 1859 and 1860, by W. B. Warbritton. In 1863 and 1864 three or four more brick houses were erected. Tootle & Hanna's store, the Masonic Block, in 1865, and John Fitzgerald's block on the corner of Main and Sixth streets, are structures of which no city need be ashamed. The second hotel was built in 1856 and named the "Farmers' Home;" the third was the "Platte Vallley," built in the spring and summer of 1857.

Wheatley Mickelwait was the first postmaster of Plattsmouth. He was appointed in the fall of 1855.

A saw mill was erected by C. Heisel early in 1856; an attachment was added by which some flour was made in the fall of the same year. It was subsequently moved, rebuilt, and by August, 1857, was doing a good business as a saw and flouring mill. Sarpy's flouring mill was built in the summer of 1862.

PLATTSMOUTH PUBLIC SCHOOL.

"A ferry across the river at Plattsmouth," was one of the Acts of incorporation of the first legislature. The parties included in this Act were W. Mickelwait, J. O'Neil, J. L. Sharp, J. G. Palmer and L. Nuckolls and their associates. The charter was dated March 1, 1855. A flat-boat was run up to August, 1857, when the

"Emma" was put on; followed by the "Survivor," in 1858, the "Paul Wilcox," in the fall of 1859, and later by the present "Mary McGee."

Under the charter of March 16, 1855, a city government was organized by an election, on December 29, 1856, at which Wheatley Mickelwait was elected Mayor, and Enos Williams, W. M. Slaughter and Jacob Vallery, Aldermen. This City Council met and proceeded to business January 29, 1857.

At a special election held in Plattsmouth on April 24, 1869, $50,000 in bonds were voted by the city, and donations made by individual citizens of a large number of city lots to the B. & M. Railway Company, on condition that the Company should erect there, and maintain depot, shops, and general fixtures, making and continuing Plattsmouth the headquarters of the Company in Nebraska; putting the road through to the west end of the County, all in good running order and actual operation, within sixteen months after June 3, 1869. These conditions were accepted by the company, and the contract closed by W. Thielson, the authorized agent of the Company, and the City Council, June 15, 1869. Early in July, in the presence of a large crowd of spectators, John Fitzgerald, at the foot of Main street, in Plattsmouth, displayed his strength and skill in "breaking ground" for the railroad track. In September, 1869, in a still larger and more excited crowd, the first locomotive, the "American Eagle," was landed and gave her first scream on Nebraska soil. The long wished, and long listened for whistle was now a matter of unquestionable fact upon the streets of Plattsmouth.

The first newspaper published in the city was the Plattsmouth *Jeffersonian*, by L. D. Jeffries, assisted by J. D. Ingalls, who finally succeeded Jeffries as publisher. The *Jeffersonian* was first issued early in 1857.

Late in 1858, or early in 1859, the Platte Valley *Herald* was started by Alfred Thompson.

A few months after the establishment of the *Herald*, E. Giles moved the Cass County *Sentinel* from Rock Bluffs to Plattsmouth. The *Sentinel* died out or was sold out to Joseph I. Early, who for a short time issued the Democratic *Times*.

In February, 1865, H. D. Hathaway started the Nebraska

*Herald*, and continued it till it passed into the hands of the present publisher, John A MacMurphy.

In November, 1870, Fox & Fullilove issued the Cass County *Democrat*, which was succeeded by the Nebraska *Watchman*, F. M. MacDonough, editor.

The *Deutsche Wacht* was started in the fall of 1875, but after a few months was sold out to John A. MacMurphy.

For short periods some of these papers have appeared as dailies, but the support has not justified a long continuance.

The Methodist Episcopal Church organized June 29, 1857, with twenty members, and the Rev. Hiram Birch, as first pastor.

The Congregational Church was organized in 1870, with five members and Rev. Frederick Alley, pastor. A Church was erected and finished clear of debt.

The Protestant Episcopal Church erected a Rectory in 1865, and a church in 1866 and 1867. The first Church services held in the building were on May 12, 1867.

The Presbyterian Church, Rev. Mr. King, in the summer of 1857, preached the first sermon. Rev. Mr. Hughes succeeded in an organization of the Society in May, 1858, with sixteen members.

The Catholic Church. The first Church building was erected in 1861, but there was no regular Priest or services until 1862, when Father Teckachet came and remained until 1864. In the fall and winter of 1875-6, the new church building was erected.

The Baptist Church was constituted October 17th, 1856, with ten members. The Society owns a Church building, erected in 1872, at a cost of $1,800.

The Christian Church was organized in May, 1859, by Elder T. J. Todd, with fourteen members.

The first session of District Court held in the city was in April, 1856, by Judge Edward Harden; A. C. Towner, Sheriff, and M. W. Kidder, Clerk.

The first birth in the city was Fred Mickelwait, on March 9, 1855.

Company "A" of the First Nebraska Volunteers was raised in Plattsmouth.

The Company was mustered into the United States service,

June 11, 1861, Robt. R. Livingston, Captain; A. F. McKinney, First Lieutenant; N. J. Sharp, Second Lieutenant; and J. G. Whitelock, First Sergeant.

### WEEPING WATER

Is located on a stream of that name twenty miles west from Plattsmouth. It was laid out in December, 1870, and in 1879 its population was 350, mostly Americans of high culture and refinement. With the exception of a tract from five to eight miles wide, south of the town, that is held by speculators, the country surrounding Weeping Water is well settled and very productive. Along the river west of the town at a distance of ten or twelve miles, are some of the finest limestone quarries to be found in the West. The following includes some of the business industries of the place : Two general merchandise stores, two hardware stores, one millinery store, two drug stores, three flouring mills, one in the town, and one above, and the other below the town, one mile distant; one hotel, one livery stable, one harness shop, two blacksmith shops, two shoe shops, one wagon shop, one fine school house, one Methodist and one Congregational organization, each occupying a good stone Church. In brief, it is a pleasant, thriving little town.

### LOUISVILLE.

Eighteen miles northwest from Plattsmouth, on the B. & M road, is located the thrifty little town of Louisville. Organized and settled on March 1, 1872, its population in 1879 being about 300. The different industries are represented as follows : Four general merchandise stores, one grocery, two drug, one furniture, one agricultural implement depot, three hotels, two wagon and blacksmith shops, two harness shops, two livery and feed stables, one millinery store, one steam flouring mill, one extensive pottery works, one fire-brick factory, one brick yard, shipping stock yards, two grain warehouses, one elevator, one lumber yard, one butcher shop, two doctors, and two lawyers, three religious organizations, viz., one Methodist, one Baptist, one Congregational, all of which hold there meetings in the school house. To the south of Louisville, the farmers are chiefly intelligent, thrifty and well to do Germans.

Near the town there is a large deposit of kaolin, which will some day afford the material for a large manufacture of pottery. The depot and a large freight train was totally destroyed by fire on the night of August 20, 1879. The depot has been rebuilt.

## SOUTH BEND.

Twenty-three miles west of Plattsmouth on the B. &. M, Road, in the heart of a well-cultivated, rich farming country, is South Bend, which was laid out in 1870 by a company consisting of B. M. Smith, Thomas Doane and others. But little improvement was made, however, until 1876, when it became quite a little business centre. The Platte River at this point has been spanned by a good pile wagon bridge, built by a stock company. The country to the South is well settled by enterprising and thrifty farmers, chiefly Americans and Germans. Two miles to the South of the town is James Romne's Fishery, one of the largest and most complete enterprises of the kind in the State. Fine salmon, trout, pickeril and many other choice varieties of the finny family are raised there in abundance. The town has one good school, one Methodist and one Baptist Church, two grain elevators, one warehouse, three hotels, two general merchandise stores, two drug stores, two blacksmith shops, one wagon shop, one lumber yard, one livery and feed stable and four boarding houses.

In the Southeastern portion of the County is Rock Bluff and Liberty Precincts, in which there is a large belt of fine timber, and also an abundance of fine lime stone. A very good quality of bituminous coal has been discovered at seven different points in that part of the country, and it is more than probable that extensive coal beds will be developed in that section in the immediate future.

The following is a statement of the cities and towns in Cass County, the date of their organization and their population in 1879:

Plattsmouth, August 15, 1855, 3,300; Rock Bluffs, June 10, 1856, 150; Weeping Water, December 19, 1870, 350; Louisville, March 1, 1872, 250; South Bend, August 17, 1870, 200; Greenwood, October 7, 1870, 300.

Besides the above there were nearly or quite a dozen towns

laid out and platted and afterwards abandoned. We note the following:

Cedar Creek City, date of filing, July 20; platted, 1871; Elgin, October 27, 1857; Clay City, November 18, 1856; Avoca, November 10, 1857; Troy, January 1, 1857; Saline, March 10, 1857; Cladonia, June 22, 1857; Capital City, August 3, 1857; Carlisle, October 21, 1856; Bluffdale, March 9, 1857; Centerville, February 27, 1857; Kanosha, August 11, 1858; Eldorado, January 8, 1857.

## CEDAR COUNTY.

Cedar County was organized by an Act of the Territorial Legislature, approved February 12, 1857. It lies on the Northern border of the State, and is bounded on the North by the Missouri River, East by Dixon, South by Wayne and Pierce, and West by Pierce and Knox Counties, embracing an area of about 792 square miles.

WATER.—The Missouri River washes the entire Northern boundary, flowing in a general Southeasterly direction. Its principal tributaries in this county are East, Middle and West Bow, and Beaver Creeks. The water runs over gravel and is very pure. The main Bow is an excellent mill stream, and has three first-class flouring mills on its banks, aggregating ten run of burrs.

Logan and Middle Creeks and several branches of the north fork of the Elkhorn River water the Southern portion of the County. There are numerous springs. Well water is obtained at a depth of from twelve to seventy feet.

TIMBER AND FRUIT.—In the Missouri Bottoms elm, bass, hackberry, box elder, soft maple, ash, hickory, black walnut, coffee tree, red cedar and red and white willow are to be found. All the creeks are tolerably well skirted with timber, and occasionally fine groves are to be met with. Wild grapes and plums grow luxuriantly on the banks of all the streams. Of late years much attention has been given to forest tree planting, especially on the upland, and all the choice varieties of fruit trees have been tried and found to thrive well. In 1879 851,437 forest trees, 1,310 apple, twenty-six pear, 159 peach, 130 plum, sixty-one cherry, three acres of grape vines and five and three eighth miles of hedging were reported under cultivation in the County.

STONE.—A soft chalk rock is abundant in the bluffs of the Missouri. It hardens some by exposure, and is used to a considerable extent for building purposes and making lime.

CHARACTER OF THE LAND, ETC.—In the Southern part of the County the land is exceedingly fine, being nearly as level as a house floor, and yet well drained, in consequence of the peculiar nature of the soil. In the Northern part the surface of the upland is more rolling and somewhat hilly, yet very little of it too much so for cultivation.

The soil is rich and highly productive almost everywhere. About forty per cent. is valley and bottom land. The valleys of the Bows and Beaver Creeks are exceedingly rich and beautiful, and splendid crops are always gathered.

FIRST SETTLEMENTS.— During the year 1857 the first settlers arrived in the County and located in the neighborhood of the present town of St. James, among whom were C. C. Van, James Hay, O. D. Smith, Saby Strahm, Hanson Wiseman, John Andres and Henry, Ernest, Gustavus and Herman Ferber, with their venerable father, Paul Ferber, who still reside in the County. This colony emigrated from Harrison County, Iowa.

In the Spring of 1858 the settlements of Waucapona and St. Helena were commenced. Among the first settlers of Waucapona, who are still residents of the County, are Warren Saunders, George A. Hall and Amos S. Parker. L. E. Jones Surveyed and platted the town site of St. Helena, in July. C. B. Evens and sons, of Council Bluffs, Iowa, located there that Summer, and in the Spring of 1859, Henry Felber and sons, Henry, Jacob and William, Peter Jenal, Sr., Peter Jenal, Jr., and Mr. Jones and family arrived by boat from St. Louis.

Immediately after the settlement of St. Helena, Saby Strahm and a few others began the present prosperous settlement of Strahmburg, in the northwest corner of the County, nearly opposite the now flourishing town of Yankton, the Capital of Dakota.

The first meeting of the County Commissioners took place at St. James, October 4, 1858.

The first County Clerk was George L. Roberts; the first Treasurer, George A. Hall.

In the Spring of 1858, L. E. Jones commenced publishing a weekly newspaper called the *St. Helena Gazette*, the first nine numbers of which were printed at St. Louis, and dated ten days later than the day of publication, as it usually took that length of time for the mail to reach St. Helena. After the removal of the publishing office from St. Louis to St. Helena, in July, it was conducted for a few months by A. Nette, when it died a natural death for want of support.

The first saw mill in the County was a steam mill brought by the colonists who located at St. James in 1857. By the same power they also run a small corn grinder, which was highly appreciated by the settlers, as corn bread was their main sustenance in those days. Wheat flour could not be got nearer than Sioux City.

In the Summer of 1858 L. E. Jones located another steam saw mill at St. Helena. In the Spring of 1860 this mill was nearly destroyed by fire, but it was rebuilt at once, and has been running ever since.

There are at present one water and four steam saw mills, and three flouring mills in the County.

Three chartered ferries are in operation between this County and Dakota Territory. The steam ferry between Strahmburg and Yankton does a large and lucrative business.

In 1872 the County authorities purchased a pile driver and up to the present time about two hundred pile bridges have been constructed over the numerous streams at all the principal crossings,

At a general election held on the 8th of April, 1876, the citizens of the County voted bonds to the amount of $150,000 to aid in the construction of the Covington, Columbus & Black Hills Railroad through the County. Work on the road is being pushed with vigor, and it is now completed to within a few miles of the east line of this County.

Educational matters were almost entirely neglected by the early settlers, and it was not until 1867 that the first public schools were opened—one at St. Helena, and one at St. James. Private schools, however, had been taught at both of these places in 1860-61, by George L. Roberts, T. C. Bunting and P. Clark. In 1879 the number of school districts in the County was twenty-nine; number of school houses, twenty-eight; children of school age, 1,096—males, 569; females, 527; whole number of children that attended school during the year, 727; number of qualified teachers employed, forty-three—males, twenty-seven; females, sixteen; amount of wages paid male teachers, $4,763.24; paid female, $1,480; value of school houses and sites, $15,824.75; of books and apparatus, $779.

The number of acres of land under cultivation in the County, reported in 1879, was 13,568. The acreage in cultivation and yield of the leading crops was as follows: Winter wheat, 283¾ acres, 6,432 bushels; rye, 2,677 acres, 35,453 bushels; spring wheat, 36,235 acres, 375,943 bushels; corn, 72,133 acres, 2,826,259 bushels; barley, 6,384 acres, 181,260 bushels; oats, 19,028 acres, 163,582 bushels; buckwheat, forty-five and three-fourths acres, 339 bushels; flax, sixty-one acres, 400 bushels; broom corn, fifty acres, eighteen and one-half tons; potatoes, 148¼ acres, 19,163 bushels; onions, eight and seven-eights acres, 2,636 bushels.

The taxable property of the County as reported by the Assessors for 1879, is as follows: Number of acres of land, 329,946; average value per acre, $2.26; value of town lots, $17,547.00 ; money used in merchandise, $11,530.00 ; money used in manufacture, 11,500.00; number of horses, 1,201, value, $38.992; mules and asses, 63, value, $1,935.00; neat cattle, 6,245, value, $48,301.00; sheep, 2452, value, $1,937.00; swine, 1,412, value, $1016.00; vehicles, 544, value, $7,948.00 ; moneys and credits ; $14,265.00 ; mortgages, $2,000.00; furniture, $2,654.00; libraries, $45; property not enumerated, $8,791 ; total valuation, $912,469.00.

The voting precincts is numbered from one to eleven, inclusive, the population of each in 1879 being as follows: No. 1, 335; No. 2, 611; No. 3, 478; No. 4, 194; No. 5, 348; No. 6, 101; No. 7, 143; No. 8, 117; No. 9, 67; No. 10, 131; No. 11, 260.

Total population of County, 2,775, 1517 being males, and 1,258 females.

### ST. HELENA,

the County Seat, is situated on the banks of the Missouri in the center of the County from east to west. The County Seat was removed to this place from St. James, by vote of the citizens, in the fall of 1869. It has a population of 300, and is gradually improving in size and importance as a business point, being now the center of trade for the County. Business is represented by a weekly newspaper—the *Bulletin*, a bank, dry goods, clothing, grocery, boot and shoe, drug, implement, and several general stores, a lumber yard, carpenter and blacksmith shops, lawyer and doctors' offices, etc. It has a convenient Court House and good school and church advantages.

### ST. JAMES,

Located on the Missouri, six miles east of St. Helena, was the first County Seat and while it remained such was a very promising town. Latterly its progress has been slow. It contains about two hundred inhabitants, a Methodist Church, school house, hotel, several stores, etc.

### GREEN ISLAND, OR STRAHMBERG,

Is situated about eight miles west of the County Seat, on the banks of the Missouri, opposite the city of Yankton. An excellent steam ferry connects it with the latter place and attracts to it a large trade. It is a prosperous village and now numbers 200 inhabitants.

SMITHLAND, LOGAN VALLEY, ST. PETERS, CENTER BOW, BOW VALLEY and MENOMINEE are Postoffices in the County having a store, school, etc.

## COLFAX COUNTY.

Colfax County was organized by Act of the Legislature, in February, 1869, and was named in honor of Schuyler Colfax, at that time Vice President of the United States. It is located in the middle-eastern part of the State, in the third tier of Counties west of the Missouri River, and is bounded on the north by Stanton and Cuming Counties, east by Dodge County, south by the Platte River which separates it from Butler County, and west by Platte County, and contains about 414 square miles, or 264,960 acres, at an average elevation of 1,335 feet above the sea level.

WATER COURSES.—The Platte River washes the entire southern border of the County, flowing in a general northeasterly direction.

Shell Creek, a large beautiful tributary of the Platte, and a splendid mill stream, flows from west to east across the southern portion of the County. It already furnishes power for three very large first-class flouring mills, and has available sites for dozens more. North and South Maple Creeks are fine, clear streams, having numerous branches, which meander through and drain the central and northern townships. There is not a township in the County without running water, and springs are abundant.

TIMBER AND FRUIT.—At the time of the first settlement of the County the streams were all tolerably well wooded, and there is yet considerable cottonwood, box elder, ash, elm, etc., along the Platte Bottom, and on Shell and Maple Creeks. The artificial timber is far advanced, and as every farmer planted more or less at an early day, beautiful groves now dot the country in every direction. Fuel is no longer a scarcity. Of late years many orchards of choice fruit trees have been planted also, and are promising finely. In 1879 there were 961 acres of forest trees under cultivation in the County; also 4,683 apple, ninety-five pear, 788 peach, 444 plum, and 868 cherry trees, besides 1,053 grape vines and eight miles of hedging.

PHYSICAL FEATURES.—The uplands are gently rolling, with but few breaks or untillable places. The southern portion of the County is embraced within the famous Platte Bottom, which reaches to the northward in fine undulations for a width of several miles; then comes the beautiful Valley of Shell Creek, and to the north and east a few miles further, the smaller valleys of the Maples. The bottoms of Shell Creek have an average width of two miles, with a gentle slope toward the stream; and those of the Maples, though narrower, are very fine.

SOIL.—The soil of the upland is a deep, black, rich loam, and of the bottoms a deep alluvial. All crops common to the latitude are grown to perfection. Large quantities of hay are annually put up on the meadows and prairies, and finds a ready market at the railroad towns.

HISTORY.—Isaac Albertson has the honor of being the first settler within the present limits of the County, locating, where he still resides, near the mouth of Shell Creek, on the 26th of April, 1856. Daniel Hashburger was the next permanent settler. For the next year or two very few settlements were made, but in 1859 and 1860, when the Pike's Peak excitement was at its height, the travel through the County was very great; ranches were established along the Platte Bottom, and many claims were taken in the northeastern part of the County, especially along and near the mouth of Shell Creek. It was in these palmy days that Col, Loren Miller, General Estabrook, a Mr. McField and several other gentlemen from Omaha, established a town near the mouth of Shell Creek, which they named Buchanan, in honor of the then Chief Magistrate of the nation, but its existence was brief, and soon no trace of it remained.

For many years Omaha, over seventy-five miles away, was the nearest point for obtaining supplies, and Fort Calhoun, on the Missouri, the nearest mill. The settlers who passed the memorable winter of 1856-7 on their claims were reduced to the severest trials, the whole country being covered with snow to the depth of three feet on the level for over two months and the weather keeping intensely cold. Their flour, and in fact, provisions of all kinds, were exhausted long before the snow melted; but fortunately game was abundant, and by that means they were saved from starving.

Daniel Harshburger was the first Postmaster in the County.

The first general election was held on the 12th of October, 1859, at which time a full board of County officers were elected, and the County Seat permanently located.

In 1871 a substantial bridge was built over the Platte, at Schuyler, costing $65,000. At present good bridges span all the streams at the principal crossings.

The *Schuyler Register*, the first newspaper in the County, was established on the 30th of September, 1871. The name has since been changed to the *Schuyler Sun*.

The Western Union Telegraph was built through the County in 1860, and the Union Pacific Railroad in 1868.—Length of road in the County, eighteen miles.

There are three flouring mills in the County, located on Shell Creek, which do a large amount of business.

LAND.—The government land is all taken, but the Union Pacific Railroad Company owns 20,000 acres in this County, for which from $3.00 to $10.00 an acre is asked.

SCHOOLS.—The number of school districts in the County in 1879 was fifty-one; school houses, forty-eight; children of school age, 2,169—males, 1,017, females, 1,152; whole number of children that attended school during the year, 1,302; wages paid teachers during the year, $9,797.74; value of school houses, $22,913.88; value of school house sites, $604,00; value of books and apparatus, $1,484.85,

CROPS.—The crop returns for 1879 show the number of acres under cultivation in the County to be 54,595. The acreage sown and the yield of the principal crops was as follows: Spring wheat, 25,297 acres, 307,847 bushels; rye, 2,853 acres, 44,556 bushels; corn, 13,484 acres, 414,392 bushels; barley, 913 acres, 22,192 bushels; oats, 4,987 acres, 160,085 bushels; sorghum, twenty-six acres 1,763 gallons; flax, 1,787 acres, 13,328 bushels; potatoes, 323 acres, 23,345 bushels.

TAXABLE PROPERTY.—The taxable property of the County, reported for 1879, was as follows: Number of acres of land, 319,378; average value per acre, $3.84; value of town lots, $98,-895.00; money used in merchandise, $41,214; money used in manufacture, $2,050.00; number of horses, 2,308, value, $69,479.00; mules and asses, 171, value, $5,215.00; neat cattle, 6,255; value, $56,600.00; sheep, 4,611, value, $5,335.00; swine, 8,273, value, $6,177.00; number of vehicles, 843, value, $13,566.00; mortgages, $17,599.00; furniture, $3,997.00; libraries, $800.00; property not enumerated, $25,375.00; railroads, $186,588.00; telegraph, $1,530,-00; total, $1,376,724.00.

POPULATION.—There are eleven Precincts in Colfax County, the population of each in 1879 being as follows: Richland, 362; Shell Creek, 455; Wilson, 340; Stanton, 213; Schuyler, 1,160; Grant, 539; Midland, 603; Adams, 383; Colfax, 523; Maple Creek, 500; Lincoln, 512. Total population of the County in 1879, 5,960. In 1875 the population was 3,651, showing an increase in four years of 2,309.

## SCHUYLER,

The County Seat, is the chief town in the County. It was laid out in April, 1869, and is located in the south-central part of the County, on the line of the Union Pacific Railroad, and has 900 inhabitants. It is a prosperous town and does an immense shipping business, having large elevators, warehouses, stock yards and all the conveniences for the handling of grain and stock. Since the completion of the splendid wagon bridge over the Platte River at this place, it has also been the shipping point for the grain and farm products of the northern part of Butler County. Business is generally well represented. It has some very fine stores, good hotels, real estate offices, lumber yards, agricultural implement warehouses, various mechanics' shops, etc. Two weekly newspapers are published here, the *Sun* and the *Democrat*, and both are well supported, the *Sun* being the first paper published in the County. A brick Court House, costing $20,000, was erected in 1871. The High School building is an elegant and commodious structure. The Methodists, Congregationalists, Presbyterians and Episcopalians each have a house of worship.

Rogers and Richland are shipping stations on the Union Pacific Road, the former east and the latter west of the County Seat.

Several small villages, with a postoffice as a nucleus, have sprung up in different parts of the County.

## CUMING COUNTY.

Cuming County was established and the boundaries defined by an Act of the first Territorial Legislature, approved March 16, 1855. The same Act also located the County Seat at Catharine. By an Act approved February 12th, 1857, the boundaries were re-defined and the name of the County Seat changed to Manhattan. By a special Act approved February 12, 1866, the boundaries were fixed as they exist at present.

The County was named in honor of Thomas B. Cuming, the first Secretary and Acting Governor of Nebraska. It is located in the northeastern part of the State, and is bounded on the north by Wayne County and Omaha Indian Reserve, east by Omaha Indian Reserve and Burt County, south by Dodge and Colfax, and west by Stanton County, embracing 576 square miles, or 368,640 acres of land.

WATER COURSES.—The principal stream in the County is the Elkhorn River, which flows southeasterly through the central portion, furnishing an abundance of water power and many superior sites for the location of flouring mills and other manufacturing enterprises. Logan Creek, with its branches, waters the eastern portion of the County. It is next in size, and is also an excellent mill stream. Plum Creek enters the County from the northwest and joins the Elkhorn in the central portion. Rock, Cuming, Fisher and Pebble Creeks, tributaries of the Elkhorn, meander through different portions of the County, and are all clear, beautiful streams. Springs are abundant. Well water can be had anywhere at a depth of from ten to fifty feet.

TIMBER AND FRUIT.—There is a moderate supply of natural timber on the Elkhorn River, Logan and Plum Creeks, and an occasional small grove is met with. An immense amount of artificial timber was set out at an early day, and thrifty groves, now sufficiently grown to supply all the fuel needed, adorn a great many farms. Grapes, plums and other wild fruit grow in profusion along the streams. There are a number of orchards of choice fruit trees under cultivation in the County, but no report has been made of the kind or quantity of trees planted.

CHARACTER OF THE LAND.—At least thirty per cent. of the land in this County consists of valley, and the balance of rolling prairie, with very little bluff or waste. The Valley of the Elkhorn is from three to seven miles wide, rich and beautiful. Logan Valley, at this point, is scarcely inferior to the Elkhorn. Plum and the larger creeks all have fine wide bottoms, on which from one to three tons of hay are put up to the acre. Timothy and blue-joint grass grow luxuriantly. The soil on the uplands is a black loam, from one to four feet in depth. There is an abundance of the finest grasses for pasturage. Sheep raising is carried on to a considerable extent. In 1878, 34,561 acres were cultivated in the County; 52,855 bushels of wheat and 69,920 bushels of corn were raised. No crop reports for 1879.

HISTORICAL.—In the summer of 1856, Benjamin B. Moore left Hillsdale, Michigan, with his wife, daughter Kate, and three sons, Abram, George and Oscar, and coming to Nebraska, located a claim, and made the first settlement in Cuming County at Catharine, or Dead Timber, where they immediately erected a cabin.

The winter following was an unusually severe one, the snow falling to such a depth that it was impossible to drive a team, and Mr. Moore and his sons were compelled to haul their provisions from Fontenelle, a distance of twenty-five miles, on a hand sled. But fortunately wild game was abundant that winter, the Elkhorn Valley being literally alive with deer, antelope and elk. These animals flocked to the friendly shelter of the timber on the bottoms, and during that winter Mr. Moore and his sons killed not less than seventy-five of them close to their home.

In March, 1857, Uriah Bruner, John J. Bruner, Henry A. Kosters, William Sexaner, Andrew J. Bruner, Peter Weindheim, Henry Eike, Charles Beindorf and others of Omaha, associated themselves together under the name and style of "The Nebraska Settlement Association," and appointed a committee to go up the Elkhorn Valley and select a town site. Uriah and John J. Bruner, with several others of the company, immediately started up the valley on a prospecting tour, and arriving at the present site of the town of West Point, they were so favorably impressed with the general appearance of the country, the apparent richness of the soil, with the beautiful stream that so gracefully wound its way down the broad undulating valley, and the excellent facilities it afforded for manufacturing purposes, that they determined to locate their town there. Returning at once to Omaha they reported to the Association, who approved of the selection they had made, and measures were immediately taken to establish and lay out a town thereon. A steam saw mill was purchased by the Company which arrived at the town site in June of that year. Log houses were erected, and during the summer the town site was surveyed by Andrew J. Bruner. The town was christened Philadelphia, but the name was soon changed to West Point.

In March, 1858, John D. Neligh and James C. Crawford, of Pennsylvania, and Josiah and John McKirahan, of Ohio, took claims near West Point, built houses and commenced breaking prairie as soon as the season opened. Messrs. Neligh and Crawford that summer bought and put in running order the saw mill of the "Nebraska Settlement Association," and also its claim to the town site. A postoffice was established at West Point, with J. C. Crawford as postmaster.

Mrs. John Gaul died early in 1858, being the first death in in the County.

The first election for County officers occured at West Point on the 12th of October, 1858, and resulted as follows: W. R. Artman, Probate Judge ; James C. Crawford, Treasurer ; G. W. Houser, Clerk; John D. Neligh, Register ; Henry Cline, Sheriff, A. A. Arlington, John Bromer and J. McKirahan, Commissioners.

At this election West Point was chosen as the County Seat, and an old log house became the official headquarters.

The following persons voted at the first election : Aron Arlington, Henry Cline, J. D. Neligh, J. C. Crawford, George W. Houser, John McKirahan, Josiah McKirahan, W. R. Artman, John Roggansock, Jergen Roggensock, George Weikel, B. B. Moore, A. L. Ward, Amasa Babbit, John Bromer, E. C. Dallon, J. S. Walters, John Freeburg and Mr. McCrea. Nineteen votes were cast.

In the latter part of June, 1859, about three thousand Pawnee Indians came up the Elkhorn Valley, ostensibly on their way North on a hunting expedition, but, as the sequel proved, their main errand was to plunder the whites. They seemed to be in a half starved condition, and, in order to satiate their hunger, commenced a systematic warfare upon the settlers' pigs, poultry, and stock, whenever a favorable opportunity offered. They made their appearance in the vicinity of West Point on the 29th of June, and butchered a heifer belonging to Mr. Clemens. The Indians having committeed numerous depredations further down the valley, the citizens organized and started in pursuit. About sundown on the 29th, a Company of volunteers from Fontenelle and vicinity, commanded by Captain Kline, arrived at West Point. The next day a number of Indians made their appearance across the river, opposite the saw mill, and the Germans, seeing their approach, concealed themselves between the saw mill and river, with a view of sending some of them to their " happy hunting grounds." Their guns, however, missed fire, and the Indians, discovering that danger was brewing, retreated. Upon discovering that a strong force was rendezvoused at West Point, the Indians moved up the river, and a party of thirty men, commanded by Captain Patterson, a young lawyer of Fontenelle, started up the river on the east side in order to protect the few settlers in the vicinity of De Witt, where B. B. Moore resided. The whites saw eleven Indians approaching, and conceived the idea of taking them prisoners. Accordingly the party moved into the kitchen, where Mrs. Moore and daughter were preparing dinner, with a view of decoying the Indians into the sitting room, which was divided from the kitchen by a light board partition. The Indians came to the house and entered the sitting room, whereupon a part of the whites passed out of the kitchen and took a position near the south door to prevent their escape. Soon after, firing commenced, by which party is unknown, and then followed a scene which beggers description. With a wild war whoop the Indians rushed out of the house, dashed through the lines of the whites, and ran towards their camp on the opposite side of the river, followed by a deadly shower of leaden hail. The battle cry sounded by the retreating Indians was answered by their comrads across the Elkhorn (a distance of two miles or more), and as the echo and re-echo of the terrible war whoop found its way along the river and over the prairie, consternation filled the breasts of all who heard it, and many of the settlers were panic-stricken. Just how many Indians were killed is not known, but members of the tribe afterwards admitted that only three reached their camp, and that one of them was mortally wounded. One Indian was left dead at Moore's house, and two others were left badly wounded. They were put in a wagon when the party started for West Point; one died on the way, and the other was supposed to be dead and thrown into the river at the Dupray place. He proved, however, to have been playing "possum," and struck out for the shore, but never reached it. An ounce or two of lead caused him to sink to rise no more. The only white man wounded was a Mr. Peterson, of Fontenelle.

Immediately after the fight everybody left for West Point. A rumor being started that several hundred Indians were preparing to swarm down upon the little band of settlers to avenge the death of their fallen braves, caused a panic such as the citizens of West Point have never witnessed since. During the excitement a consultation was held, and the majority determined to abandon West

Point and go to Fontenelle. Messrs. Neligh, Crawford, McClellan, Babbitt, Schadaman and Thomas, who were opposed to the move, remained behind to secret what goods they could. There were only two persons left in the County, A. L. Ward and Casper Eberline, both of whom were several miles above DeWitt at the time of the fight, in blissful ignorance of the stirring scenes being enacted.

On the 4th of July a party was organized at Fontenelle to go to DeWitt, consisting of J. D. Neligh, J. M. McKirahan, J. C. Crawford, Jno. McClellan, A. Clemens, J. B. Robinson, Thos. Parks, Jno. Shoer, Wm. Keys and others for the purpose of seeing what the Indians had been doing. Arriving at Moore's house they found a dead Indian lying on the kitchen floor with a bucket of water beside him, a pan of unbaked biscuit on the stone hearth, dishes broken, feathers strewn on the floor, and bureau drawers broken and contents strewn about. While the party was viewing this picture of disolation and death, from without came the startling cry of, "Indians! Indians! Indians!" and in an instant all was in commotion. A general rush was made for the wagons in which their arms were lying, and in the excitement which followed, a gun was accidently discharged, its contents lodging in Mr. Shoer, killing him instantly. The alarm was discovered to have been a false one, and soon after the sad accident the party started for Fontenelle, where they arrived the same evening, bearing with them the lifeless body of their unfortunate comrade.

A month or so later peace was made with the Indians, and a majority of the settlers returned to their claims. Late in the Fall (1859) J. D. Neligh and J. C. Crawford erected a frame building, which has since been remodeled into a hotel, known as the West Point House.

Early in the Summer of 1860, seven families, with nine teams, under the escort of J. D. Neligh, arrived at West Point.

The first patent issued upon land in Cuming County, was to Patrick Murry, on the 3d day of July, 1860, giving a title to the northeast quarter of section twenty-one, township twenty-two, range six, east.

The first marriage license was issued by the Probate Judge in the Summer of 1861, the parties being John Pilger and Miss Harriet Arlington.

The valuation of all taxable property in the County in the Spring of 1863, was—personal, $4,654; real estate, $2,635; total, $7,289.

The first homestead entry was made by Benjamin B Moore, February 16, 1863.

A. E. Fenske opened a small store at West Point in the Summer of 1865. This was the first mercantile establishment in the County.

Father Erlad, a Catholic missionary, organized the St. Antonius Church at St. Charles, in 1866. In April, of this year, Rev. Louis Janney, of the M. E. Church, was sent to the DeWitt Mission. The first Quarterly Meeting was held on June 29 and 30, at Mr. Moore's residence, at which time the first Methodist Society in the County was formed.

The first warranty deed recorded in the Clerk's Office was given December 17, 1867, to Catharine B. Neligh by Mattias Schmacker.

On the 24th of July, 1870, Rev. Sheldon Jackson perfected the organization of the Presbyterian Church at West Point. Rev. Mr. Peebles, of the Presbyterian Church of Decatur, had preached here in the Spring of 1867.

The Catholic Church at St. Charles, erected in the Spring of 1867, was the first Church building in the County.

In 1868 Bruner & Neligh completed a grist mill at West Point, and people came here to mill from fifty miles around. In the Summer of this year the organization of the German Evangelical Church was effected.

West Point was incorporated on the 17th of May, 1869. In June, of this year, the U. S. Land Office was located here, and in the fall a splendid bridge was completed over the Elkhorn. In the spring of 1870 the town site of West Point was re-surveyed. In June a Masonic Lodge was organized. The Fremont, Elkhorn and Missouri Valley Railroad was completed to West Point on the 25th of November, of this year, and on the 28th trains commenced running regularly. The value of improvements at West Point from December, 1869 to December, 1870, was estimated at $129,-000, exclusive of the depot and other improvements made by the Railroad Company. The first number of the West Point *Repub-*

*lican* was issued November 18, 1870; E. N. Sweet, editor, M. S. Bartlett, publisher.

Early in the Spring of 1871 a Company was organized by the stockholders of the Fremont, Elkhorn and Missouri Valley Railroad, known as the Elkhorn Land and Town Lot Company. A tract of land was purchased in Elmont Precinct, on the line of this road, upon which a town site was surveyed, platted and named Wisner—in honor of S. P. Wisner, at that time Vice President of the F., E. & M. V. R. R. Company. On or about the 20th of July, the railroad was completed to this point, and on the 26th following, town lots were sold at auction, the proceeds netting $8,130. Immediately after the sale of lots the erection of business houses and dwellings was begun. The first work commenced was by George Canfield, upon the Wisner House, and the first building completed in the town was a warehouse and office, by John W. Pollock. A depot was built by the Railroad Company, and during the summer and fall, several business houses were opened.

In the meantime improvements were being rapidly made in and around West Point. In 1871 a brick Evangelical Church was erected; Bruner, Neligh and Kipp built a brick bank building; a Teachers' Institute was organized; a Lutheran Church was erected in Bismarck precinct; a hook and ladder company was organized, and also a County Medical Association, of which Dr. Alex. Bear was chosen President, and R. J. Mulhern, Secretary. In 1872 the contract for the building of a brick Court House was let, and in 1874 the building was finished at a cost of about $40,000. January 9, 1873, the brick hotel, known as the Neligh House, at West Point, was completed. In March, of this year, the West Point Land Office was removed to Norfolk. September 11, the Second Annual Fair of the Cuming County Joint Stock Agricultural Society was held at the Fair Grounds at West Point.

In the spring of 1874 an iron bridge was constructed over the Elkhorn, at West Point, at a cost of $7,000; an Odd Fellows Lodge and a Fire Company was organized. On November 4 of this year, the West Point Manufacturing Company was organized. The business to be transacted by this Company was the manufacture of flour, paper, woolen goods, agricultural implements, etc. In 1875 machinery for a furniture factory arrived and a two story building was erected in which to put up and operate the same. In May, 1876, machinery for a paper mill and a foundry arrived from the East, and work was commenced on a race at West Point, capable of operating immense manufacturing establishments, During the Summer of 1876 the structure for the paper mill. 60x120 feet, two stories high, of brick, was completed, and the machinery set up in the furniture factory. These enterprises are now in successful operation. In 1876 a lodge of the Knights of Pythias, and a Literary Club were organized at West Point, and a very fine Catholic Church erected.

SCHOOLS.—The first school district was organized on the 11th day of April, 1864, and embraced all the territory in the County on the east side of the Elkhorn River. Sixty dollars was voted at the same time toward building a school house. Mrs. J. C. Crawford taught a private school at her residence in Bismarck precinct, in the Winter of 1865, and had fourteen scholars. This is said to have been the first school opened in the County.

The number of school districts in the County, in 1879, was forty-five; number of school houses, forty-two; children of school age, 1,836—males, 983; females, 853; total number of children attending school during the year, 1,137; number of qualified teachers, fifty-seven—males, thirty; females, twenty-seven; wages paid male teachers, $6,174.55; paid female, $3,633.62; value of school houses, $24,308; value of school house sites, $2,259; value of books and apparatus, $1,225.50.

TAXABLE PROPERTY.—The taxable property, as returned for 1879, was as follows: Number of acres of land, 300,053; average value per acre, $2.12; value of town lots, $120,942; money used in manufactures, $2,854; money invested in merchandise, $120,942; number of horses, 2,298, value, $43,524; mules and asses, 173, value, $3,969; neat cattle, 5,772, value, $33,559; sheep, 5,694, value, $4,032; swine, 8,902, value, $4,739; number of vehicles, 714, value, $6,461; moneys and credits, $12,345; mortgages, $3,225; furniture, $1,467; libraries, $205; property not enumerated, $9,188; railroads, $76,048; telegraph, $855; total valuation, $987,286.50.

POPULATION.—In 1856 the County had a population of eight; in 1860 it had increased to sixty-seven; in 1875 it was 6,152; in 1878, 7,744, and in 1879 it was 9,095.

## WEST POINT,

The County Seat, is beautifully located on the Elkhorn River, and is a fast growing, brisk business place of 1,000 inhabitants. The Elkhorn affords it unusually fine manufacturing advantages, and various enterprises, such as flouring mills, paper mills, furniture factory, etc., as before stated, are now in successful operation here, and others will soon follow. Being situated on the Fremont & Elkhorn Valley Railroad gives it direct communication with Omaha, and makes it a shipping point of a large grain and stock region. It has neat Churches and splendid school houses, good hotels, large lumber yard, brewery, carriage and wagon manufactory, several grocery and dry goods stores, and all the business places and trades usual to a place of its size. Three weekly newspapers are published here—the *Republican*, *Progress* and *Staats Zeitung*, all well sustained, prosperous sheets. A fine iron bridge spanning the Elkhorn at this point, attracts the trade from the western part of the County.

## WISNER,

Containing about 850 inhabitants, is located on the Elkhorn in the northwestern part of the County, and was for several years the terminus of the Fremont & Elkhorn Valley Railroad, which gave it a substantial growth and large trade. It was incorporated on the 14th of May, 1873. Among the first to locate in the town were John W. Pollock, E. M. Clark, (deceased) and George W. Canfield. In June, 1873, an excellent iron bridge was completed across the Elkhorn at this place, which added greatly to its business. The Elkhorn River is here capable of propelling mammoth manufactories and is susceptible of easy control. During the present season the railroad was extended from Wisner westward to the County Seat of Stanton County. Wisner is certainly one of the best business points in this part of the State, and has enjoyed for several years past the almost exclusive shipping trade of the adjoining Counties to the north and west. Business in every line is well established and the school and Church advantages are all that could be desired.

## CLAY COUNTY.

Clay County was established in 1867 and organized in October, 1871, by proclamation of Acting Governor William H. James. It is located in the southeastern part of the State, in the fifth tier of Counties west of the Missouri River, and is bounded on the north by Hamilton, east by Fillmore, south by Nuckolls, and west by Adams County, and embraces 576 square miles, or 368,640 acres, at an average elevation of 1,775 feet above the sea level.

WATER COURSES.—The Little Blue River is the most important stream in the County. It waters the southwestern townships and furnishes ample water-power for flouring mills and other manufacturing enterprises. School Creek, a fine large tributary of the West Blue River, flowing from west to east, waters, with its numerous branches, the central and northern portions of the County, and also furnishes a sufficient volume of water for mills. Big Sandy Creek, a fine tributary of the Little Blue, waters the southeastern townships. Springs are abundant along the Little Blue and School Creek.

TIMBER.—There is very little native timber in the County. The Little Blue River and School Creek are tolerably well timbered in places. Few Counties in the State, if any, excel Clay in the matter of tree planting. In 1879 she had 2,160 acres or 3,114,828 forest trees under cultivation, many of the groves being from three to twenty acres in extent, and well developed. There are forty-six miles of hedge fence in the County.

FRUIT.—In 1879 there were 14,249 apple, 652 pear, 36,416 peach, 10,640 plum, and 3,074 cherry trees, and 2,643 grape vines under cultivation in the County, promising in the near future an abundance of the choicest fruits.

STONE.—A good stone for building and lime abounds on the Little Blue.

PHYSICAL FEATURES.—The surface of the country consists almost entirely of nearly level prairie, a small portion being rolling, but none is too rough to prevent tillage, except, probably, in occasional places bordering the Little Blue and at the sources of the creeks. There is a gradual slope all through the County, west by north; thus while the eastern border is a little over 1,670 feet above the sea level, the western border is 1,835 feet, the rise being gradual all the way. The Little Blue has a very fine, wide valley, as have also School and Sandy Creeks, although smaller.

SOIL.—The surface soil of the uplands is a rich, black vegetable mould, generally ranging from eighteen inches to two feet in depth; on the bottoms the soil is often several feet in depth. Corn, wheat, rye, oats, barley, flax, broom-corn and vegetables of all kinds do well. Corn yields from thirty-five to seventy and wheat from fifteen to twenty bushels per acre. The area in cultivation in 1878, was 73,776 acres; in 1879, 95,078 acres; increase, 21,302 acres. Spring wheat raised in 1877, 472,528 bushels; in 1878, 600,000 bushels. Yield of corn in 1877, 645,239 bushels; in 1878, 725,000 bushels.

HISTORICAL.—The first settlement within the present limits of the County was made in 1857, by J. B. Weston, who built a house at Pawnee Ranche, on section sixteen, township five, range eight, in Spring Ranche Precinct. He was succeeded at the ranch by Fred and George Roper, who held it until 1864, at which time they were driven off by the Indians, and two of George Roper's daughters captured, they being restored to their friends again in 1872 or 1873.

The general uprising of the Indians in 1864 greatly retarded the settlement of this County, and it was not until about 1870 that emigration was renewed to any extent. The settlements are here given by precincts:

SCHOOL CREEK PRECINCT.—Peter O. Norman, and brother, natives of Sweden, settled in this precinct in 1870, and built themselves a "dug-out" on the banks of the creek.

LINCOLN PRECINCT.—F. M. Davis, Ezra Brown, and Samuel Slote were the first to settle in this precinct about the year 1870. Mrs. Add Horsington taught the first school in the spring of 1872.

HARVARD PRECINCT was first settled in the fall of 1871, by Isaac Dawson and John Hackenthaler.

LYNN PRECINCT was first settled in May, 1871, by W. H. Chadwick, J. D. Moore, L. J. Starbuck and B. F. Hocket.

LEWIS PRECINCT was first settled in the Spring of 1870, by A.

D. Peterson, Lewis Peterson and Jonas Johnson, natives of Sweden. John S. Lewis, after whom the precinct was named, settled in April, 1872.

SUTTON PRECINCT was first settled in 1870, by Luther French, of Ohio. The first neighborly call after the completion of his house, was by Captain Charley White, of Indian fame, and Miss Nellie Henderson, who came on horseback from the West Blue, eight miles off, and had chased down and caught an antelope on the way.

SHERIDAN PRECINCT was settled in February, 1872, by John Yates. He was followed closely by others. A school house was erected in this precinct in December 1872, the first school being taught by Joseph Trout, with sixteen scholars. In February, 1873, a Methodist Episcopal Society was organized, and in June a Union Sunday School was started.

LOGAN PRECINCT was first settled by Albert Curtis, on the 7th of March, 1871. In August following, a school was organized, with Josephine Reed, as teacher—salary, twenty-five dollars per month.

MARSHALL PRECINCT was first settled in July, 1872, by Flavius Northrup, from Buffalo County, Wisconsin. Mr. Northrup brought with him a flock of about seventy-five sheep, which were the first sheep brought into the County for permanent rearage.

LEISCESTER PRECINCT was first settled in the Winter of 1871, by William Woolman, A. Woolman, Joseph Rowe and Stephen Brown. Miss Truelove Tibbles, an adopted daughter of Rev. Wm. Woolman, was drowned in April, 1876, while attempting to cross one of the Creeks in this precinct.

SCOTT PRECINCT was first settled by G. W. Briggs and George McIntyre. The B. & M. R. R. passes through the northern part, and the St. Joe & Denver City R. R. across the northwest corner of this precinct.

LONE TREE PRECINCT was first settled in 1871 by John P. Scott, who located near the "Lone Tree," from which the precinct derives its name. The St. Joe & Denver R. R. crosses the southwest corner of this precinct.

FAIRFIELD PRECINCT.—The settlement of this precinct commenced at Liberty Farm Ranche, at the mouth of Liberty Creek, on the Little Blue. This ranche was for a long time an important station for the overland mail and Wells, Fargo & Co.'s Pony Express. It was kept in 1858 by James H. Lemon, who was succeeded, in 1867, by Benjamin and John Royce, from Illinois.

EDGAR PRECINCT was first settled in November, 1871, by J. K. Sanborn, who built himself a good log house. The flourishing town of Edgar is in this precinct.

The pioneers of the County were more or less harassed by Indians up to as late as 1868, especially in the valley of the Little Blue, on the overland stage road, where the ranches were repeatedly destroyed, and the inhabitants driven from the country or murdered.

James Bainter, who succeeded a Mr. Metcalf at Spring Ranche, in 1862, had a store stocked with about $5,000 worth of provisions and merchandise. A friendly Pawnee brought him the news one day that the Sioux were coming in force, and had attacked the ranches above him. Bainter immediately sent his family to Pawnee Ranche, about a mile to the east of his, then kept by the Ropers, and mounting a fast horse rode up the river to reconnoiter. He met the Indians about nine miles off, coming rapidly toward his place, so hurrying back he loosed his stock, and hastened to his family at Pawnee Ranche. In a short time he saw the smoke ascending from his store and dwelling, and very soon thereafter Pawnee Ranche was attacked by about 200 Sioux. Pawnee Ranche was a strong sod building, with pallisade around it, and contained at the time of the attack, four men and several women and children. This courageous party, small as it was, managed to keep the enemy at bay, the women assisting the men in watching and loading their guns ; and for three days the attack was continued till finally Bainter succeeded in killing the Sioux Chief, when the Indians withdrew from their immediate vicinity. A large party of friendly Pawnees came up at this juncture, and with their assistance the Sioux were driven off for the time. Not long after this however, the Sioux again attacked the ranches all along the Little Blue, and Bainter and all the settlers were compelled to leave the country, the stage line was broken up, and many of the drivers and passengers killed. A large wagon train was captured at the crossing of the overland road on Big Sandy Creek, and about sixty persons slaughtered.

The organic election was held on the 14th of October, 1871, at the house of Alexander Campbell, on section six, town seven, range six. Eighty-nine votes were polled, fifty-six of which were cast for Sutton, making it the County Seat. The following County officers were elected : Commissioners, A. K. Marsh, P. O. Norman, and A. A. Cory ; Probate Judge, John R. Maltby ; Clerk, F. M. Brown; Treasurer, J. Hollinsworth; Sheriff, P. T. Kearney ; Surveyor, R. S. Fitzgerald; Superintendent of Public Instruction, J. S. Schermerhorn; Coroner, J. Steinmetz.

The first session of the Board of Commissioners was held on the 4th of November, 1871, at which time the County was divided into three equal districts, designated as Commissioner and voting precincts, and named respectively, Harvard, Little Blue and School Creek. The Commissioners' precincts remain, but the voting precincts were increased to sixteen, in 1875.

The Burlington and Missouri River R. R. was built through the northern portion of the County in 1871. Length of the road in the County, twenty-four and eighty-seven one-hundredths miles.

The St. Joe and Denver City R. R. was built through the southwestern portion of the County in the spring of 1872. Length of road in the County, twenty-two and fifty one-hundredths miles.

The Clay County Agricultural Society was organized on the 15th of April, 1872. A fair is held regularly every year at Sutton.

The people of Clay County were great sufferers by the grasshopper invasion of 1874. In July, of that year, these insects came from the northwest in such countless numbers as to make the sunlight dim; and so swiftly did they destroy the crops that a forty or an eighty acre corn field would not last more than two hours. The rank, growing corn would literally bend to the ground with the weight of the insects. Potatoes, vegetables and crops of all kinds, except wheat and barley, which had already been harvested, were swept out of existence all over the County in the short space of two days. Not a bushel of corn was gathered in the County, whereas the year before settlers burned corn, it being worth only fifteen cents a bushel.

PUBLIC SCHOOLS.—In 1870 there were sixty-nine School Districts in the County, sixty-seven school houses and 3,041 children of school age, 1,553 being males, and 1,488 females; total number of children that attended school during the year, 2,089; number of qualified teachers employed, 117—males, forty-two; females, seventy-five; wages paid teachers for the year—males, $4,486.35, females, $7,289.95; total, $12,776.30; value of school houses, $36,347.89; value of school house sites, $2,684.00; value of books and apparatus, $1,712.35.

TAXABLE PROPERTY.—The following statement will show the amount and valuation of the taxable property in the County for 1879: Number of acres of land, 284,143; average value per acre, $3.10; value of town lots, $82,198.00; money invested in merchandise, $67,260; money used in manufactures, $6,948; number of horses, 4,248, value, $120,005; mules and asses, 494, value, $15,628; neat cattle, 5,006, value, $41,880; sheep, 558, value, $624.00; swine, 12,752, value, $12,432; vehicles, 1,765, value, $27,550; money and credits, $15,182; mortgages, $17,272; stocks, $330.00; furniture, $18,788; libraries, $1,276; property not enumerated, $94,111; railroads, $297,188; total, $1,700,704.10.

LAND.—The Burlington & Missouri River R. R. Company owns 5,000 acres of land in this County, for which they ask from $4.00 to $8.00 an acre. The Government land is all taken.

POPULATION.—The following is the population of the County, in 1879, by precincts: Logan, 339; Edgar, 830; Fairfield, 722; Spring Ranche, 419; Glenville, 428; Lone Tree, 348; Marshall, 379; Sheridan, 330; Sutton, 1,391; Lewis, 411; Lynn, 474; Scott, 447; Leiscester, 440; Harvard, 1,176; Lincoln, 516; School Creek, 723; total population of the County, 9,373—males, 5,112; females, 4,261. In 1875 the population of the County was 4,183, and in 1878 it was 7,012, showing an increase in the last year of 2,361.

## SUTTON,

The County Seat, is situated in the Valley of School Creek, on the B. & M. Railroad, in the northeastern part of the County. Its present population is 800, having doubled in size in the last three years. It has a bank and two weekly newspapers—the *Globe*, an old established paper, and the *Mirror*. The Court House is a commodious two-story building, and the school house is an elegant and convenient structure, costing $4,000. The Congregationalists built the first Church in the County here, in 1875, at a cost of $1,500; the Methodists followed next with a brick house of worship, costing $2,000. Several denominations are now represented.

Sutton is a beautiful town. A tract of twelve acres has been laid off as a public park, through which School Creek makes a horse-shoe bend, its banks being heavily timbered with rock elms.

### HARVARD,

Located on the line of the B. & M. R. R., thirteen miles west of Sutton, was incorporated in 1873, and at present has 650 inhabitants. Two weekly newspapers are published here, the *Sentinel* and *Phœnix*. In 1873, a $4,000 school house was erected. It has several hotels, Churches, elevators, brick and lumber yards, and business houses representing almost every line of trade. The surrounding country is well settled up by thrifty, prosperous farmers, the German element predominating.

### EDGAR,

Is a very promising town of 550 inhabitants, located on the St. Joe & Denver City Railroad, in the southeastern part of the County. It was incorporated on the 15th of March, 1875, and is improving very rapidly. It is well situated for business, being the shipping point for a large, well-settled agricultural country.

### FAIRFIELD,

On the St. Joe & Denver Railroad, several miles west of Edgar, is an enterprising town of about 350 inhabitants. It has excellent school and Church advantages, and a weekly newspaper—the *New*—to advance its interests. It commands the shipping trade of the southwestern portion of the County.

## CHEYENNE COUNTY.

Cheyenne County is located on the extreme western border of the State, bounded on the north by Sioux County, east by unorganized territory and Keith County, south by Colorado and west by Wyoming. It was organized in 1867, and contains about 7,224 square miles, or 4,623,360 acres.

Water power is unlimited. The principal stream is the North Fork of the Platte River, which enters at the northwest corner and flows southeasterly through the County, leaving it in the southeastern portion. Its main tributaries are Blue River and Rush, Cold Water, Pumpkinseed, Red Willow, Wild and Kiowa Creeks. Lodge Pole Creek, a tributary of the South Platte, which flows from west to east almost entirely across the southern portion of the County, and through whose valley the Union Pacific Railroad extends, is the most important stream. It has a large number of tributaries, the largest being Dry Creek, which waters the southwestern portion of the County.

The majority of the streams and many of the canyons are well timbered.

Cheyenne County lies in the great grazing belt of Nebraska, and its territory is almost exclusively devoted to the rearing and fattening of stock, agriculture receiving only a very limited share of attention, being confined to the valley of Lodge Pole Creek, along the line of the railroad, and small patches about the ranches.

Outside of Sidney the inhabitants of the County number less than 300, and these are all engaged in the cattle business, with the exception of the few permanently located at the shipping stations on the railroad.

The surface of the country consists of vast rolling prairies, gulches and canyons, which furnish an abundance of the richest grasses in the world for pasturage. The buffalo grass, the most common variety here, cures on the ground, retaining all its wonderfully nutritious elements, and upon which cattle live and thrive the year 'round. The timbered canyons afford excellent shelter for the stock during the winter months, and in most cases none other is provided.

There is a large amount of government land in this County. Food crops can be raised in the valleys.

The crop reports for 1879 show the number of acres under cultivation in the County to be 17,326½: Rye, forty acres, 753 bushels; spring wheat, 7,740¼ acres, 116,480 bushels; corn, 3,784 acres, 145,820 bushels; barley, 778 acres, 23,161 bushels; oats, 2,513 acres, 100,982 bushels; sorghum, eleven acres, 1,491 gallons.

There is but one school district in the County and one school house; children of school age, 219—males, 117, females, 102.

The amount and valuation of taxable property in the County returned for 1879, was as follows; Number of acres of land, 3,539, average value per acre, $1.00; value of town lots, $58,275; money invested in merchandise, $31,300; number of horses, 1,166, value, $23,320; mules, 147, value, $5,880; neat cattle, 57,679, value, $461,432; sheep, 331, value, $331; swine, eighty-eight, value, $176; vehicles, 193, value, $3,860; moneys and credits, $19,510; mortgages, $12,572; furniture, $4,717; libraries, $375; property not enumerated, $20,753; railroad, $1,015,868; telegraph, $8,840; total, $1,670,748.

The County is divided into six voting precincts, the population of each in 1879 being as follows: Sidney, 935; Big Spring, twenty-two; Lodge Pole, seventy; Court House, eighty-seven; Potter, fifty-two; Antelope, fifty-two.

Total population of the County, 1,218—males, 788, females, 430. In 1875 the County had a population of only 457; increase in four years, 761.

### SIDNEY,

The County Seat, is located on the north bank of Lodge Pole Creek, and on the Union Pacific Railroad, 414 miles west of Omaha. It is a lively, business place of 950 inhabitants, and has attained considerable importance as a point of outfitting and departure for the Black Hills' gold fields. Fine Concord coaches, carrying mails and express leave daily, and land passengers at Deadwood, 267 miles distant, in about fifty hours. It has two newspapers—the *Plaindealer* and *Telegraph*, an $1,800 school house, two excellent hotels, large outfitting and forwarding houses and other necessary auxilaries to the Black Hills trade. One firm of freighters shipped two and a half million pounds of goods to the Hills in one year. The roads from Sidney to the Hills are first-class, and lined with ranches and stopping places, Fort Robinson being on the route.

The stations on the U. P., in this County, are Big Springs, Barton, Chappel, Lodge Pole, Colton, Brownson, Potter, Bennett, Antelopeville, Adams, Bushnell and Pine Bluffs.

## CHASE COUNTY.

Chase County, located on the southwestern border of the State, was established in 1873. It is bounded on the north by Keith, east by Hayes, south by Dundy, and west by the State of Colorado, and contains 936 square miles, or 599,040 acres.

It is watered by Whiteman's Fork, Stinking Water and other tributary streams of the Republican River.

The County is yet unorganized and very sparsely settled, cattle raising being the chief pursuit of the inhabitants. There are no towns in the County, and no reports have been made of population or taxable property.

---

## CUSTER COUNTY.

Custer County was established by an Act of the Legislature, approved February 17, 1877. It is located in the central part of the State, bounded on the north by unorganized territory, east by Valley and Sherman, south by Buffalo and Dawson, and west by Lincoln County and unorganized territory, containing 2,592 square miles, or 1,658,880 acres.

The Middle Loup River and its branches, water the northeastern portion of the County. Clear and Mud Creeks water the central, and the South Loup and branches, the southeastern portion of the County. The Loups are good mill streams, and furnish a moderate supply of timber.

The surface of the country consists largely of high, rolling prairie, about ten per cent. being bluff and five per cent. valley. Very little is done in the way of agriculture as yet, although the soil is generally well adapted to the growth of small grain. Stock raising—for which the country affords every advantage—is the leading industry.

The County was organized in the spring of 1877, by Commissioners appointed by the Governor for that purpose.

The taxable property in the County reported for 1879, was as follows: Number of acres of land, 1,308, average value per acre,
18

$1.50; money used in manufactures, $250; number of horses, 835, value $14,395; number of mules twenty, value, $536; number of neat cattle, 23,900, value $150,231; number of sheep, 4,161, value $4,161; number of swine, 183, value $218.25; number of vehicles, 171, value, $3,401; moneys and credits $425; mortgages $685; furniture $1,958; property not enumerated, $2,723.50; total, $180,-746.25.

In 1879 there were two school districts, two school houses, and sixty-one children of school age in the County.

The population of the County in 1879, was 696, of whom 415 were males, and 281 females.

There is plenty of Government land in this County, suitable either for stock raising or farming.

### CUSTER,

The County Seat, is located on the South Loup River, about twenty-eight miles north of the town of Plum Creek, on the Union Pacific Railroad. It is the supply depot for the numerous cattle ranches in the vicinity, and at certain seasons of the year is a very busy place.

TUCKERVILLE, GEORGETOWN, DOUGLAS GROVE, NEW HELENA, and LENA are Postoffices in the County.

## DOUGLAS COUTNY.

Douglas County was created in the fall of 1854, by proclamation of Acting Governor Cuming, and the boundaries were re-defined by an Act of the first Territorial Legislature, approved March 2, 1855. By an Act approved February 7, 1857, Sarpy County was formed out of the southern part of Douglas County, and the boundaries of the latter fixed as they exist at present. It is located on the middle-eastern border of the State, and is bounded on the north by Washington and Dodge Counties, east by the Missouri River, south by Sarpy County, and west by the Platte River, which separates it from Saunders County, and contains about 321 square miles, or 195,440 acres, at an average elevation of 1,000 feet above the sea level.

WATER COURSES.—The Missouri River washes the eastern and the Platte River the western border of the County. The Elkhorn River, the principal interior stream, flows from north to south through the western portion of the County, affording some excellent mill privileges. A cut-off from the Platte, some five or six miles long, unites with the Elkhorn in the southwestern part of the County. Rawhide Creek is a beautiful stream emptying into the Elkhorn in the northwestern part of this County. Big Papillion Creek, a fine stream with numerous branches, furnishing sufficient water power for light manufacturing purposes, rises in Washington County, and flows in a general southeasterly direction through the eastern portion of this County. Little, or West Papillion Creek, draining the central portion of the County, and East Papillion Creek, draining the eastern tier of townships, are tributaries of the Big Papillion, and flow in the same general direction. Mill Creek is a small stream in the northeastern part of the County, emptying into the Missouri, at Florence.

CHARACTER OF THE LAND.—The second bottoms or table lands of the Missouri are generally from one to two miles wide, and rise in gentle undulations from the low flood plains toward the bluffs, which are usually low and rounded from the northeast corner of the County down to Omaha, below which they are quite steep and broken, and the bottoms narrower. From the bluffs of the Missouri westward to the Papillions, the uplands are considerably rolling, with long sloping knolls, but nowhere, scarcely, is the surface so broken as to prevent plowing. The three Papillion Creeks, running from north to south, and from two to four miles apart, the first one about five miles west of the Missouri, have beautiful valleys, with a great deal of rich, level bottom land. The central portion of the County consists principally of gently undulating prairie, while the western portion is taken up with the wide, level bottoms of the Elkhorn and Platte Rivers, a tract of country reaching from the northern to the southern boundary, and from six to twelve miles wide, comprising some of the finest and most desirable agricultural lands in the State. A coast-like range of bluffs, rising from seventy-five to one hundred feet above the bottoms, extend along the east bank of the Elkhorn, from the heights of which a magnificent view of the beautiful level valley country can be had as far as eye can reach.

The soil is a very deep, rich alluvial in the valleys, and on the uplands it is a rich, black vegetable mould, ranging from eighteen inches to two feet in depth. Wheat, rye, barley, oats, flax, corn, etc., are profitably grown, and Irish and sweet potatoes, melons and garden vegetables of all kinds are raised to perfection, both as regards to quality and quantity.

The number of acres under cultivation in the County in 1878 was 44,150. Of the principal crops planted 7,425 acres were in wheat, the average yield being fourteen bushels per acre; rye, 745 acres, average seventeen bushels; oats 6,596 acres, average thirty-three bushels; barley 1,445 acres, average twenty-one bushels; corn 25,709 acres, average forty bushels; and potatoes 560 acres, yielding from 100 to 250 bushels per acre. Grasses are abundant and nutritious. Immense quantities of hay are annually put up on the meadows of the Papillions and their tributaries, and on the prairie, which always finds a ready market at Omaha.

FOREST AND FRUIT TREES.—Formerly there were a number of fine groves of hardwood in the eastern portion of the County and along the bottoms of the Missouri, not much of which, however, is now left standing; but there is considerable natural timber yet along the Platte, Elkhorn and the Papillion, and where the original groves were cut off fine young timber is springing up. The artificial timber is well grown, and in proportion to the number of farms opened out, it will compare favorably as to quantity with any County in the State.

There are thrifty orchards in the County that have been in bearing for some years past, and each year an increased quantity of fruit trees are planted, promising at an early day an abundance of the choicest fruits. Wild plums, grapes, gooseberries, and raspberries are plentiful along the streams.

HISTORY.—Lewis and Clarke's famous expedition up the Missouri camped on the Omaha Plateau, as appears from their Journal, on the 27th of July, 1804. At that time the ever-shifting channel of the Missouri ran close up to the high bank at the foot of Farnam street, covering the level bottoms which, until within a year or two, reach out a half mile or more from the bank, and upon which have been erected the Union Pacific Company's machine shops, the smelting works, railroad tracks, warehouses, a large distillery, extensive lumber and coal yards, and various other business establishments.

The next white person to visit this locality appears to have been a man named T. B. Roye, who established an Indian trading post with the Otoes, on the plateau where Omaha now stands, in 1825.

The first attempt at permanent settlement by the whites, within the present boundaries of the County, was made by the Mormons, in 1845. Several thousand of these people, driven from Nauvoo, Illinois, crossed the Missouri from Iowa, during the years 1845 and 1846, and made a settlement on the banks of the river six miles north of Omaha, which was called "Winter Quarters," the name of the place being afterwards changed to Florence. Here they broke up and cultivated a large tract of land, long afterwards known as "the old Mormon field," which yielded them a bountiful crop of sod corn, potatoes and vegetables, and timber being plentiful, substantial log houses were built, and their prospects for the future looked encouraging. Their numbers were constantly increased by new arrivals, and before many months had elapsed, "Winter Quarters" was considerable of a town.

The Indians, however, objecting to the Mormons cutting their timber, the Indian Agent ordered them to quit the reservation, which they did, in 1847, by recrossing the Missouri and settling in the bluffs on the Iowa side, where they established the town of Kanesville, named in honor of a Mormon Elder named Kane, the name of the town being changed, in 1853, to Council Bluffs.

Early in the Spring of 1847, before abandoning Winter Quarters, the Mormons fitted out an expedition, consisting of one hundred and eight wagons, with from four to six men to each wagon, which was sent West under the leadership of Brigham Young, to look up a favorable location for the permanent settlement of the main party. This expedition arrived at the top of the hill overlooking the now famous Salt Lake City, on the 24th day of July of the same year, and on the 28th the ground for the Temple was selected and a city two miles square laid off. A number of this pioneer party, after planting crops, returned and took back their families the same year.

The largest emigration of Mormons that left Kanesville was

in the year 1853, but they continued to emigrate in large bodies for several years later, some with cattle trains, others with hand carts. The cattle trains were made up principally of cows, which were worked as oxen, thus doing the double service of pulling the loads and supplying the emigrants with milk on the way. The hand-cart trains consisted of small carts loaded with provisions, clothing, bedding, &c., which were pushed or pulled along by the men and women, none but the smaller children, or sick, riding.

To William D. Brown, of Mt. Pleasant, Iowa, it is generally conceded, belongs the honor of being the first white settler to stake a claim on the plateau now occupied by the City of Omaha. Mr. Brown was one of the many who started for the gold fields of California in 1849 and 1850, and stopping on his way at Council Bluffs, then called Kanesville, he established a ferry across the Missouri for the accommodation of the large California and Oregon emigration of that day. In 1852 he equipped a flat boat for this purpose, which received the name of the "Lone Tree Ferry," from a solitary tree that stood at the landing of the boat on the west bank of the river, just east of where the Union Pacific machine shops now stand.

In the Spring of 1853, Mr. Brown staked off a claim which embraced most of the original town site of Omaha, and on the 23d day of July of the same year, a new ferry company was organized, taking in Mr. Brown as a member, under the title of "The Council Bluffs and Nebraska Ferry Company," whose object was to increase the ferrying facilities and to establish a town on the west side of the river.

The new Company consisted of Dr. Enos Lowe, President; William D. Brown, Tootle & Jackson, S. S. Bayliss, Joseph H. D. Street, Henn & Williams, Samuel R. Curtis, Tanner & Downs, and others.

A substantial steam ferry boat, named the "General Marion," was purchased by Dr. Lowe in Cincinnati, Ohio, which arrived at Council Bluffs in September, and commenced running regularly as a ferry boat across the river from that point, in May, 1854.

Months before this, however, and before the passage of the organic act opening up Nebraska for settlement, crowds of hungry land speculators and sharpers had congregated in and around

Council Bluffs anxiously waiting when they could pounce upon the choice sites bordering on the river, especially in the vicinity of the contemplated town, and notwithstanding the Indians had forbidden the whites from settling on their lands, a number of men crossed the river on the ice in January and February, 1854, and staked off claims along the river within the present limits of the County. But as soon as the ferry boat commenced running, an immense rush was made for the west side of the river, and in a month or two a large portion of the County was staked out in claims, but not one in ten of these claims was ever settled upon or improved by the claimant, who held the lands merely for speculative purposes.

Immediately after the passage of the bill admitting Nebraska as a Territory, May 23, 1854, the Ferry Company proceeded to lay out their contemplated town. The beautiful plateau upon which Omaha now stands was selected for the town site, and Mr. A. D. Jones, assisted by C. H. Downes, surveyed the same, which occupied the greater part of June and July. Omaha was the name given to the new town by the Company, at the suggestion, it is said, of Jesse Lowe, now dead.

The city was laid out in 320 blocks, each being 264 feet square; the streets 100 feet wide, except Capitol avenue, which was made 120 feet wide, but which was given no alley in the blocks on each side of it. The lots were staked out sixty-six by 132 feet, with the exception of business lots which were made only twenty-two feet wide. Three squares were reserved—Capitol Square, 600 feet; Jefferson Square, 264 by 280 feet, and Washington Square 264 feet square. A park of seven blocks, bounded by Eighth and Ninth, and Jackson and Davenport streets, was laid out, but was afterwards given up to business purposes.

In 1856 another town company was organized under the title of "The Omaha Town Company," which included in its members most of the members of the "Ferry Company." This Company secured lands lying contiguous to Omaha, which they laid out as additions to the city, the survey being known as "Scriptown."

The first house in Omaha was commenced sometime in January or February, 1854, by Mr. Tom Allen for the Ferry Company. It was a large log house, and was used when finished, as a hotel, store, and for the accommodation of the public in general.

It stood in Jackson street, opposite Twelfth, and was known by the high-sounding name of St. Nicholas, Mr. and Mrs. Wm. P. Snowden were its first tenants.

The second house in the city was built by M. C. Gaylord, a carpenter, about the first of July, 1854. It was made of pine flooring, and stood on the hill near the present site of Creighton College. In this house Mrs. Gaylord gave birth to a son in November following, which was the first child born in the city. Mr. Gaylord who was sick at the time, died shortly after the birth of his son, and his was the first death among the settlers. He was buried on the ridge a short distance from the house, and in June, 1877, while excavating for the Creighton College, his remains were taken up and re-buried.

The "Big 6," was the name given to the third house on the town site, which was built by William Clancy, in the forepart of July. It was a large shanty, built of Cottonwood boards, banked on the outside with sod, and stood on the north side of Chicago street, between thirteenth and fourteenth. Mr. Clancy opened here a general assortment of merchandise suitable to the times and place, and the "Big 6" soon became a very popular resort.

William P. Snowden, in the fall, built a log house on the west side of Tenth street, between Howard and Jackson. This was the fourth house erected on the town site, and upon its completion, a grand "house-warming" sociable was given by Mr. and Mrs. Snowden, which was attended by all the settlers, and many from Council Bluffs.

P. G. Peterson, the first Sheriff of the County, built the fifth house, a small, one-story frame structure, which then stood at the southwest corner of Farnam and Tenth streets.

S. E. and Wm. Rogers built the next house, on the south side of Douglas street, between Tenth and Eleventh.

In the latter part of 1854, Mr. A. D. Jones built himself a residence in the south part of town, in a lovely grove, known as "Park Wilde."

About the same time Cam Reeves built a residence near the large spring south of town, near where now stands the Cold Spring Brewery. Mr. Reeves opened the first stone quarry in the County, near his claim, and supplied the stone for the foundation of the old State House, Capitol and other prominent buildings.

The frame residence, still standing on the south side of St. Mary's avenue, between Twenty-first and Twenty-second streets, was built in the fall of 1854, by the author, and was occupied by him for fifteen years.

The old State House, built by the Ferry Company for the meeting of the first Territorial Legislature, was the first brick building erected in the city. It stood on Ninth street, between Farnam and Douglas, and was used as a State House until the completion of the Capitol building, in the Winter of 1857-8. The brick for this building was hauled from Council Bluffs.

The Douglas House, a large frame building, which stood on the southwest corner of Thirteenth and Harney streets, was the first regular hotel opened in the city. It was commenced in the fall of 1854 and opened to the public on the evening of January 14, 1855, with a grand ball. This house was headquarters for the politicians and speculators for a long time, and for several years did an immense business. In 1879 the old building was removed to make room for a fine brick, containing five large store rooms.

The City Hotel, a frame building, still standing on the southwest corner of Eleventh and Harney streets, built by Ed. Burdell, was opened as a hotel next after the Douglas House. In this house a ball, or reception was given, in January, 1855, in honor of Mark W. Izard, the second Governor of the Territory, on his arrival in the city.

The Western Exchange Bank building, a fine brick, on the corner of Twelfth and Farnam streets, was built in 1855, by Jesse Lowe. The Western Exchange Bank, the first banking house in the city, opened in this building early in 1856, and was a flourishing institution until the fall of 1857, when it went under in the great money crisis, with the rest of the wild-cat banks of the day. The building is now occupied by the banking house of Caldwell, Hamilton & Company.

The Pioneer Block, on Farnam, between Eleventh and Twelfth streets, built in 1856, by Dr. Henry, H. H. Visscher and A. Root, was the first brick block in the city. This block was destroyed by fire in the spring of 1877, and replaced the same year by much finer buildings.

The frame residence at the southwest corner of Dodge and Eighteenth streets, was built by Secretary Cuming, in 1855-56, and his widow, a most respected lady, still resides there.

The first lumber yard was opened by the Hon. William A. Gwyer, his lumber arriving by steamboat, July 10th, 1856. Mr. Gywer, this year, built the Farnam House, now called the Donovan, on Harney street, between Thirteenth and Fourteenth.

The second lumber yard was opened in the spring of 1857, by J. N. H. and N. T. Patrick.

Dr. Lowe's brick residence, at the southwest corner of Harney and Sixteenth streets, was built in 1857.

The Herndon House—built by Dr. G. L. Miller, Lyman Richardson and others—at the corner of Farnam and Ninth streets, the largest brick hotel in the city, until the Grand Central was built, was commenced early in the spring of 1857 and finished in 1859, as a company enterprise. It was a commodious house, elegantly furnished and fitted up with all the conveniences of a first class hotel, and when opened to the public it at once became the fashionable resort of the city. In 1870 the building was rented to the Union Pacific Railroad Company for offices, and in 1875, the Company purchased it for $42,000.

Several other brick houses had been erected in the city by this time, also a large number of frame dwellings, hotels and business houses.

Among the places of note in the early days of the city was the "Apex" saloon, on Harney street, been Twelfth and Thirteenth. In the summer of 1856, two horse thieves were tied to a liberty pole in front of this saloon and soundly whipped, previously having had their heads shaved, after which they were kindly permitted to leave for parts unknown.

The first general merchandise store in the city and County was opened by Tootle & Jackson, on Farnam street, early in the spring of 1855.

Shields & Carr opened another general store the same spring, as did also Megeath, Richards & Co., John R. & H. B. Porter and others. The Messrs. Porters' store was destroyed by fire in the Winter of 1856, being the first building burned in the city.

Dr. C. A. Henry opened a small drug store in 1855. Dr. James K. Ish, the same year, opened the first drug store, keeping a full assortment of drugs and fancy articles.

O. D. Richardson, and A. J. Poppleton, both from Michigan, were the first practicing lawyers, both arriving at Omaha early in the fall of 1854. Mr. Richardson is now dead, and Mr. Poppleton is the attorney for the Union Pacific Railroad Company.

Dr. George L. Miller was the first physician in Omaha, he arriving in the fall of 1854. Dr. B. Y. Shelly also arrived at an early date.

Rev. Peter Cooper, of the Methodist Church, delivered the first sermon in the city, at the St. Nicholas Hotel—Mr. Snowden's residence—on the 13th of August, 1854.

Rev. Mr. Koulmer, of the United Brethren Church, was the next minister to arrive. He preached a while at Omaha, Fontenelle and Bellevue, in 1855.

Rev. Isaac F. Collins, of the Methodist, Rev. Reuben Gaylord, of the Congregational, and Rev. Wm. Leach, of the Baptist Church, each held services in Omaha during 1855.

Rev. Moses F. Shinn was the first Presiding Elder in Nebraska. He was appointed by the Iowa Conference, in 1855. His district was known as the Nebraska and Kansas district, with stations at Omaha, Old Fort Kearney, Waukaressa and Fort Leavenworth.

The first marriage in the County was that of John Logan to Miss Caroline Mosier, at Omaha, November 11, 1855, by Rev. Isaac F. Collins. Mr. Logan was one of the first grocerymen of the city; both he and wife still reside at Omaha.

The first grave dug upon the town site was by Wm. P. Snowden, in the summer of 1854, where Turner Hall now stands, to bury an old Omaha squaw, who had been abandoned by her tribe.

The second death among the settlers—Mr. M. C. Gaylord's being the first—was that of a Mr. Todd, who died in the fall of 1854, and was buried on the south side of the creek, between Thirteenth and Fourteenth streets, the Union Pacific Railroad now passing over his grave. Mr. Todd came to Omaha in August,

1854, and erected a cottonwood shanty on Jackson street, near the St. Nicholas, where he kept a small store.

The first white woman to die in the city was Rev. Isaac F. Collins' wife, in the summer of 1855, in child-birth; the next was a Mrs. Driscoll, who died in February, 1856. She was the first person buried in the old burying ground, southwest of the city, now Shull's Addition.

The second birth in the city was that of Margaret, daughter of James Ferry, in November, 1854.

Mr. A. D. Jones, who surveyed the town site in June and July, 1854, was the first practical surveyor to locate in the city, being one of its very first settlers.

W. N. Byers and Col. Loren Miller, both practical surveyors, came in the fall of 1854. Mr. Byers sectionized a large portion of the County, and was one of Omaha's most active business men. He and Thos. Gibson, of Fontenelle, left in 1859 for Pike's Peak, with a printing press, type and material for a newspaper, with which they established the *Rocky Mountain News*, in Denver City, Colorado, in the spring of 1859—the first newspaper of that Territory. Col. Miller surveyed Scriptown during the spring and summer of 1855, also several other towns in the eastern part of the Territory. He is still a resident of Omaha, and has held the office of Mayor and several other prominent positions within the gift of the people.

The Omaha *Arrow* was the first newspaper of the city. It was a four-page, six-column paper, printed in the *Bugle* office, at Council Bluffs, and was ably edited by J. W. Pattison and Joe. E. Johnson. It had a brilliant but brief career, the first number appearing July 28, 1854, and the last—the twelfth—on the 10th of November following.

The *Nebraskian*, established in the fall of 1854, was the first paper printed at Omaha. Its first editor was John Sherman. The press and material for the paper were brought from Ohio, by Hon. Bird B. Chapman. The *Nebraskian* ceased as a paper in 1864.

The *Times*, established in 1857, by W. W. Wyman, and the *Democrat*, established in 1858, by Hon. Hadley D. Johnson, were both short-lived.

The first saw mill in the County was a steam mill built at

Omaha in the fall of 1854, by Samuel Bayliss and Alexander Davis. On the 25th of November, 1860, the boiler of this mill exploded, instantly killing Mr. Sperry, the engineer, and injuring several others.

Saulsbury & Smith built the second steam saw mill at Omaha in 1856. It was located on the bottom, above where the Union Pacific Railroad machine shops now are.

The first grist mill in the County was a steam mill, located on the Missouri, four miles below Omaha, built in 1855, by E. L. Childs. The mill was destroyed by fire in the fall of 1859. Mr. Childs has the credit of manufacturing the first flour in the County.

There are at present in the County six water and two steam flouring mills, and several steam and water power saw mills.

OMAHA MADE THE CAPITAL OF THE TERRITORY.—Acting Governor Cuming having designated Omaha as the place for holding the first Territorial Legislature, that body met in the old State House, on Ninth street, on the 16th day of January, 1855. The session lasted till the 17th day of March following. It being the duty of the first Leglstature to locate the Capitol, the greater part of the session was taken up with this important question; and excitement ran at fever heat all the time the Capitol contest was being fought. The contestants for the prize were Omaha, Fontenelle, Florence, Bellevue, Plattsmouth, Nebraska City, Brownville, and several other towns south of the Platte; but Omaha finally came out victorious. The joint resolution locating the Capitol at Omaha was passed February 22, 1855.

The first County officers were appointed by Governor Cuming, and were as follows: Probate Judge, William Scott; Register of Deeds, Lyman Richardson; Treasurer, T. G. Goodwill; Sheriff, P. G. Peterson.

The first regular election was held on the 8th of October, 1855, and resulted in the election of the following County officers, viz: Commissioners, Jesse Lowe, Thomas Davis, and James H. McArdle; Treasurer, George Forbes; Register of Deeds, Thomas O'Connor; Sheriff, Cam Reeves.

Omaha was chartered as a city by the Legislature in February, 1857, the first city election occurring on the first Monday of March following, with the following result: Jesse Lowe, Mayor;

L. R. Tuttle, Recorder; J. A. Miller, City Marshal; Charles Grant, Solicitor; Lyman Richardson, Assessor; A. S. Morgan, Engineer; A. Chappel, Health Officer; A. D. Jones, T. G. Goodwill, G. C. Bovey, H. H. Visscher, Thomas Davis, W. N. Byers, W. W. Wyman, Thomas O'Connor, C. H. Downs, J. H. Kellom, and James Creighton Councilmen. On the 5th of March the Council was organized.

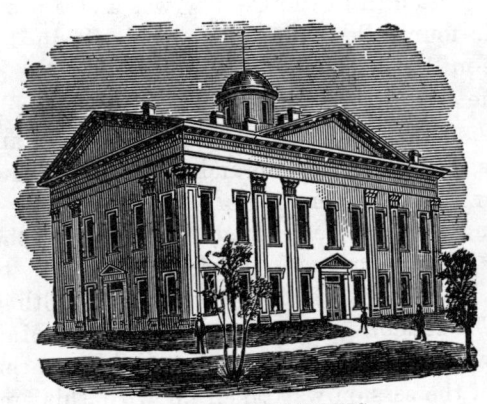

OLD CAPITOL BUILDING.

The old Territorial Capitol, which stood on Capitol Hill, on the spot now covered by the High School building, was a large, handsome brick building and from its commanding position could be seen for many miles from the city. The contract for its erection was awarded to Messrs. Bovey & Armstrong, of Omaha, who commenced work on the building in November, 1855, and the structure was completed by January, 1858, sufficiently for the meeting of the Legislature. The cost of the building was $150,000.

Upon the admission of Nebraska as a State, March 1, 1867, and the removal shortly afterwards of the Capitol to Lincoln, the old Capitol building was donated by an Act of the Legislature to the City of Omaha for educational purposes, and in 1870 it was torn down to make room for the present High School building.

On the 9th of February, 1869, by Legislative enactment, Omaha became a city of the first class; and on May 15th following, the Council, by an ordinance, divided the city into six wards.

CLAIM CLUB.—The Omaha Claim Club was an institution

established with the first settlement of the County, and for three or four years, or till the opening of the United States Land Office, it held absolute sway over all matters pertaining to claims.

Before the public lands in the Territory had been surveyed, the laws afforded the settlers no protection against land sharpers and jumpers, and the only title they could get to the land upon which they were located was what was called the "claim," or "squatters'" title; therefore, for their mutual benefit and protection, and for the adjustment of all disputes arising in regard to claims, the settlers of the County formed themselves into a Club, electing a Judge, Clerk, Recorder, and Sheriff, and enacting a code of laws for the government of all claim matters.

The first meeting of the Omaha Club, for the purpose of organizing, was held on the afternoon of July 22, 1854, under a large elm, known as the "lone tree," which stood on the bank of the river at the landing of the ferry boat. Samuel Lewis was chosen Chairman, and M. C. Gaylord, Secretary. A constitution and by-laws were prepared and adopted, after which a full sett of officers were elected, as follows: A. D. Jones, Judge; S. Lewis, Clerk; M. C. Gaylord, Recorder, and R. B. Whitted, Sheriff.

The Club was the recognized high tribunal of the land. There was no stay of execution or appeal from its decrees. Although some injustice was undoubtedly done under its workings, the community was in the main benefited by it, as claim-jumping and claim quarrels were of daily occurrence, and it was only through the arbitrary power wielded by the Club that much bloodshed was prevented.

Claim clubs were a necessity as long as squatter titles existed, but as soon as government title to land could be obtained, there were no further use for such organizations, and accordingly the Omaha Claim Club, as well as all other similar associations in Nebraska, disbanded in 1857–8.

The land in Douglas County was surveyed by the Government during the year 1856.

The United States Land Office was opened at Omaha for the entry of land on the 17th day of March, 1857. Col. A. R. Gilmore was the first Receiver, and Col. J. A. Parker the first Register of the Land Office.

The first entry of land made in Nebraska was on the day of the opening of the Land Office, March 17, by Jesse Lowe, Mayor, who entered 320 acres as the town site of Omaha.

The land covered by the site of Omaha was granted in two patents—one to John McCormick, dated May 1, 1860, the land having been bid off by him at the public sale of July 5, 1859, acting as trustee, and deeded by him to David D. Belden, Mayor of the City, in trust for the owners, and the other to Jesse Lowe, Mayor, dated October 1, 1860, on the entry made March 17, 1857.

STEAMBOATING DAYS.—Before the advent of the railroad connecting Omaha with the eastern markets, the steamboat played the most prominent part in the matter of transportation. Stage coaches were also run across the State of Iowa, but the steamboat brought the great bulk of the emigrants, provisions, lumber, and in fact everything needed in the way of building up a new country.

The first steamboat of the season was hailed with the greatest joy by the settlers, who looked upon its arrival as the opening again of another busy season after a dreary, tedious winter. Men, women and children, merchant, mechanic and Indian, all flocked to the levee at the first sound of the whistle to greet its arrival and welcome the emigrants. Frequently gay cotillion parties were held on board while the cargo was being discharged.

During the busy season often seven and eight boats a week would arrive, filling the levees from end to end with all manner of merchandise, and presenting a scene of bustle and business not witnessed since then.

The levee where the greater part of the business was done has since been nearly all washed away by the river. Steamboating died out gradually as the railroads advanced, and it is now confined principally to the Upper Missouri.

FIRST MURDERS, EXECUTIONS, ETC.—One of the first homicides that occurred in the County was the killing of Jesse Wynn, a brick mason, who was shot near the old California crossing on the Elkhorn River, in the winter of 1855, by a man from Council Bluffs. The shooting was the result of a quarrel over a claim. The man was arrested in Council Bluffs, tried and discharged.

On the 4th of July, 1857, a Mr. Kingsley was stabbed and killed at Florence, by a blacksmith named Biggs, who accused Kingsley of being too intimate with his wife. Biggs was confined in jail at Omaha, and being allowed considerable liberty while awaiting trial, he took advantage of it and made his escape.

In the latter part of March, 1858, two men named Braden and Dailey were captured with some horses that had been stolen near Rockport, a village several miles above Omaha. The men were confined in the Omaha jail, and a couple of evenings afterwards a party of disguised men took them from the jail by force and placing them in an open wagon drove rapidly to a point about two miles north of Florence and there hung them to a large tree. Public sentiment, however, was so strongly against this proceeding that four men, suspected of being implicated in it, were subsequently arrested and tried on the charge, but were acquitted.

One night in April, 1861, two men named Bouve and Iler went to a stable near the military bridge in Omaha, and taking a horse apiece, rode twelve miles into the country to a Mr. Geo. C. Taylor's place, on Big Papillion Creek, at the crossing of the old California road. Tying their horses, they entered the house, the lower part of which was used as a bar-room, in which they found the hired man, sleeping. This man they bound securely with a lariat, and then helping themselves to what liquor they wanted, they proceeded up stairs, cocked revolvers in hand, to Mrs. Taylor's room (Mr. Taylor being absent) of whom they demanded the money and valuables of the house.

Bouve was very abusive and ugly, threatening several times to take Mrs. Taylor's life, and was only prevented from doing so by his comrade, Iler. After securing all the booty they could find— some ten or twelve hundred dollars in gold, a watch, revolver and some silverware—the robbers jumped on their horses and were back again to Omaha before daylight, returning the horses to the stable from which they had taken them.

The authorities at Omaha being notified of the robbery the next day, Bouve and Iler, who were strangers in the city, and spending money very lavishly, were arrested on suspicion of being the perpetrators, and placed in jail to await the arrival of Mrs. Taylor, who was immediately sent for to identify them. When she came she readily picked out Bouve and Iler from amongst a room full of men in which they had been placed, although they had in the meantime been shaved and otherwise altered in appearance. The identification of the thieves being complete, they were returned to the jail to await trail. A meeting of the citizens was held that night in front of the Pioneer Block, in regard to the matter, and on the following night about twelve o'clock, a vigilance committee took the prisoners from their cells and hung Bouve to the bridging of the upper floor of the building, and liberated Iler on account of his intercessions for the life of Mrs. Taylor. Iler, it is said, afterwards enlisted in a Nebraska regiment and made a good soldier for the Union.

The first legal execution in Nebraska was that of Cyrus H. Tator's, who was hung at Omaha, in August, 1863, for the murder of Isaac Neff. Neff was engaged in the freighting business, and had returned from Denver, Colorado, a short time before the murder, accompanied by Tator. In June, 1863, Neff's body, with two log chains wrapped around it, was found by some boys, lying in the shallow water of the river, near the sulphur springs, at Omaha. It was evident that he had been murdered. It was also discovered that Tator had sold some of Neff's cattle and effects, and that he had gone West with a wagon load of goods and team of horses formerly owned by Neff. He was pursued and arrested at Shinn's Ferry, in Colfax County, by Thomas L. Sutton, Sheriff of Douglas County, who brought him back and lodged him in the Omaha jail. The Court being then in session a special Grand Jury was impanneled, which found a bill of indictment against Tator, and he was tried and convicted of the murder, and was sentenced to be hanged on the 28th of August, on which day he was executed, at precisely one o'clock, the scaffold being erected on the high ground near the sulphur springs. Tator was a native of New York, thirty years of age, was a lawyer by profession, and had lived in Kansas for several years, where he had been a Judge of Probate and a member of the Legislature. The evidence in his case was purely circumstantial, but so clear and positive that it left no doubt in the minds of the public as to his guilt.

The second legal execution in the County was that of Ottway G. Baker, for the murder of Woolsey D. Higgins, on the night of

November 21, 1866. Mr. Higgins was the bookkeeper and Baker the porter of the wholesale grocery store of Will R. King & Co., of Omaha, then kept in the brick building which stands on the southeast corner of Twelfth and Farnam streets. On the evening of the murder, Mr. Higgins received fourteen or fifteen hundred dollars, after banking hours, which he placed in the safe of the store, Baker being aware of the fact. Higgins and Baker slept together in the store, and that night, while Higgins was asleep, Baker got up stealthily and struck him two fearful blows on the head with an axe, killing him instantly, after which he unlocked the safe, took out the money, then dressed himself, went out the back door, and walked to the west side of Eleventh street, between Harney and Howard, where he hid the money under the board sidewalk. Returning again to the store, he undressed himself, then collecting a lot of combustible material together in the cellar, he set fire to it, hoping thus to destroy the building and all traces of his crime. Before the fire had made much headway, however, it was discovered by the night watchman of the block, who gave the alarm, which soon brought the fire department and a large number of citizens to the scene. Baker, at the proper time, rushed out of the building in his night clothes, yelling fire, murder and thieves, having previously shot himself in the arm with his revolver, making a slight flesh wound. The fire was extinguished before any considerable damage was done. Baker protested that the store had been entered by burglars who had set fire to the building, and that after a desperate fight with them, Mr. Higgins had been killed and himself wounded in the arm. His story received little credence, and at the inquest over Higgins' body, he was held for the murder. After a long and tedious trial, he was convicted and sentenced to be hanged on the 14th of February, 1868, the execution taking place on the day appointed, at a spot about a half mile west of the High School building. Sometime before his execution, Baker confessed his guilt, and also to the firing of Hellman's warehouse previously, by which half a block of buildings were destroyed.

On Saturday, December 10, 1874, Thomas Keeler, a farmer living a few miles north of Elkhorn Station, in the western part of the County, was killed by David S. Parmelee, a grain merchant at the Station, who also owned a farm in the neighborhood of Keeler's.

An ill-feeling had arisen between the two men in regard to the trespassing of Keeler's cattle on Parmelee's land, and it appears that Keeler had threatened to shoot Parmelee on sight, and on account of his threats against him, Parmelee was in the habit of going armed. On the afternoon of the shooting, they met with their teams on the outskirts of the town, and when they came within shooting range, both men jumped from their wagons and fired at each other—Parmelee with a Winchester rifle and Keeler with a double-barreled shot-gun—so nearly together that the reports of their guns were barely distinguishable. Keeler was killed outright, but Parmelee escaped unhurt. Immediately after the shooting, Parmelee surrendered himself to a deputy sheriff and was taken to Omaha, where he gave bail for his appearance at court; but he was never indicted by the Grand Jury. Mr. Parmelee still resides at Elkhorn, and has been three times elected to the Legislature.

INDIAN TROUBLES.—The Pioneers of this County were exceedingly fortunate in their dealings with the Indians, and never experienced any real trouble from them, although they had "scares" innumerable, and suffered their full share of annoyance. When danger threatened the outer settlements, the citizens of the County always promptly rallied a strong force for their protection; and in every Indian campaign of those early days the Douglas County troops were conspicuous alike for their valor and their numbers.

One of the most horrible occurrences in the annals of Indian barbarism happened within the limits of this County, being no less an event than the skinning alive of a white man by the Pawnees.

In 1849, a party of gold-seekers left Wisconsin for California, by the overland route. Among their number was a young man named Rhines, who, it appears, had made a foolish boast that he would shoot the first Indian he saw. One morning, shortly after their arrival in Nebraska, when the party were about breaking camp on the banks of the Elkhorn, near the old California crossing, some Indians came strolling along the banks of the river, and one of Rhines' comrades jocularly reminding him of his boast, he raised his rifle and shot one of the Indians dead—a young squaw. The train then moved hastily on, but just as they had reached a small stream about five miles distant, they were met by a large band of Pawnee warriors on horseback, who demanded the surrender of the murderer, which had to be done, or the whole party would have been massacred. Rhines was taken by the Indians, stripped of his clothing, and fastened to the ground with a lariat, after which they deliberately commenced skinning him alive, his companions being formed in a circle around him while the operation was being performed. The skinning process being completed, the Indians appeared perfectly satisfied, and left for their village on the Platte, without harming any of the other emigrants. Rhines survived the operation but a few minutes. His body was interred on the bank of the stream, which has ever since been known as the Rawhide.

The first Indian scare participated in by the citizens of this County, occurred in the month of July, 1855, when two white men were killed at Fontenelle at one shot by a Santee Sioux Indian. The news of this tragedy created the wildest excitement throughout the settlements, and forces were immediately raised in all of them to send against the Indians, as a general attack was apprehended.

Omaha raised a company for this purpose, which was commanded by Captain Wm. E. Moore; and the troops from the several towns were formed into a battalion under the command of Colonel John M. Thayer, which proceeded to Fontenelle and made that place its headquarters. The campaign was a short one, no hostile Indians being found; and after spending several weeks in scouting along the Elkhorn and reconnoitering the country in the vicinity of Fontenelle, the expedition was disbanded.

In what was known as the "Pawnee War" of 1859, Douglas County was represented by a mounted company under command of Capt. Wm. E. Moore, and a gun squad, commanded by Capt James Ford, making together about 100 men.

In the summer of 1864, a large band of Indians appeared on the Elkhorn, in the western part of this County, which so frightened the settlers of that neighborhood that they left everything and fled precipitately to Omaha.

A few days before this, several suspicious looking strangers had arrived in the city, and a rumor was started that they were a part of Quantrell's band that had just previously destroyed Lawrence, Kansas, and who were here looking over the grounds preparatory to raiding Omaha; so when the settlers of the Elkhorn came flocking into the city before daylight, it caused the most intense excitement. Business was entirely suspended that day. A meeting was called at the Court House at two o'clock in the afternoon, and before sunset every able-bodied man in the city was fully armed, equipped, and prepared for anything that might occur. A strong guard was organized and stationed that night at all the approaches to the city, and this vigilance was continued for about two weeks. These precautions, no doubt, prevented an attack on the city from either bushwhackers or Indians. The settlers of the Elkhorn lost some of their cattle and valuables, which were appropriated by the Indians as soon as they had gone.

At the breaking out of the Indian disturbances in Nebraska in 1864, Governor Alvin Saunders made a call for the militia for self-protection, and under this call companies of mounted infantry were organized for four months' service, among them being the following from Omaha:

*Company A.*—R. T. Beall, Captain; George C. Yates, First Lieutenant; J. H. Barlow, Second Lieutenant.

*Company B.*—John Taffe, Captain; Edwin Patrick, First Lieutenant; Abraham Deyo, Second Lieutenant.

*Company C.*—Charles S. Goodrich, Captain; Martin Dunham, First Lieutenant; David T. Mount, Second Lieutenant.

*Company D.*—Jesse Lowe, Captain; E. Estabrook, First Lieutenant; O. B. Selden, Second Lieutenant.

These companies were organized during the latter part of August, and were intended more as a home guard than anything else, being composed principally of the business men of the city. Captain Beall was placed in command of all the militia forces at Omaha, and kept the city under guard at night.

THE CIVIL WAR.—At the commencement of the great rebellion, Douglas County promptly responded to the call of the general Government with troops for the preservation of the Union.

Recruiting depots were immediately opened at Omaha and other points in the County, and volunteers by the hundreds hastened to place their names on the roll of honor.

The First Regiment Nebraska Volunteers, the First Battalion,

Second Regiment Nebraska Volunteers, the First Nebraska Veteran Cavalry and four companies of Curtis' Horse, were mainly recruited at Omaha, and did noble service in the southwestern army during the rebellion, and on the western plains fighting hostile Indians.

Besides the above mentioned troops, Captain John R. Porter, organized at Omaha, Company A, First Nebraska Militia Cavalry Regiment for home service against "confederate tribes of Indians," and Captain E. P. Childs, of Omaha, raised an artillery attachment.

THE TELEGRAPH.—The first telegraph line to reach Omaha, was the Missouri & Western, in 1860, built from St. Louis, by the late Edward Creighton, of Omaha.

Mr. Creighton shortly afterwards built the Pacific line across the plains which triumph gained for him a national fame and princely fortune. Before the close of the year 1860, he had extended the Missouri & Western from Omaha to Julesburg, Colorado, and early in the following spring he renewed the work with a large force of men and teams, and reached Salt Lake City with his line on the 17th day of October, 1861, where he was joined one week later by a line from California, where the lines were connected and the Atlantic and Pacific oceans were united by the electric current.

The second telegraph line to reach Omaha was the Illinois & Mississippi Valley, from Chicago, in 1861.

In 1863, Omaha had three wires—one from St. Louis, one from Chicago, and one to San Francisco.

In 1870, the Great Western Telegraph was built from Chicago to Omaha, connecting with the Pacific coast over the Union Pacific and Central Pacific Railroad wires.

The Atlantic & Pacific Telegraph Company established their lines west from Omaha to San Francisco, in 1869, and in 1873, constructed a line between Omaha and Chicago, to connect their Western and Eastern systems.

Twenty-three wires now enter Omaha, each one terminating here. There are now in Omaha fifteen telegraph offices, of which the Union Pacific has nine, located at their headquarters, train dispatchers' offices, depots, shops, bridge offices, etc. The others are those of the Western Union and Atlantic & Pacific Telegraph Companies, the Chicago, Burlington & Quincy, the Chicago & Rock Island, Chicago & Northwestern, B. & M. in Nebraska, and the Kansas City, St. Joe & Council Bluffs Railroad Companies.

The American Union Telegraph Company reached Omaha with their line, and opened an office in Union Block, on November 15, 1879.

UNION PACIFIC HEADQUARTERS.

RAILROADS.—The ceremony of "breaking ground" for the Union Pacific Railroad, took place at Omaha, December 3, 1863.

The Headquarters of the Union Pacific Railroad Company have been maintained at Omaha ever since the road was projected., In 1876, the Company purchased the property known as the Herndon House, which was reconstructed at an expense of $58,000, and is now one of the handsomest and most substantial buildings of the kind to be found west of Chicago.

The B. & M. Headquarters, located on Farnam and Ninth Streets, is also a very fine brick building, erected 1878, and is a magnificent building for which it is used.

The Chicago & Northwestern was the first railroad to reach Omaha from the East, the first train arriving on Sunday, January 17, 1867. Next came the St. Joe & Council Bluffs road—now called the Kansas City, St. Joe & Council Bluffs.

The Chicago & Rock Island road reached Omaha in the spring of 1868, and was followed, the same year, by the Burlington & Missouri, now called the Chicago, Burlington & Quincy.

The Omaha & Southwestern, and the Omaha & Northwestern —now called the Omaha & Northern Nebraska—were both commenced in 1869.

The Omaha & Republican Valley road, a branch of the Union Pacific, was completed to Wahoo, Saunders County, in 1876.

The Omaha & St. Louis Railroad was completed in the fall of 1879.

Omaha has now six passenger trains to and from Chicago, five to and from St. Louis, besides the Union Pacific trains, and those of the Burlington & Missouri River, and Omaha & Northern Nebraska roads. The Sioux City & Pacific road also gives Omaha direct communication with St. Paul, and cities in northwestern Iowa and Dakota.

A more complete history of the railroads of Nebraska will be found in another Chapter.

PUBLIC SCHOOLS.—The first school taught in the County was opened in the basement of the Congregational Church, at Omaha, in the fall of 1856. It was a private school.

In 1879 the number of school districts in the County was forty-nine; number of school houses, fifty-seven; number of children of school age, 8,490—males, 4,141; females, 4,349; whole number of children that attended school during the year, 4,280; number of qualified teachers employed, 140—males, forty; females, 100; wages paid teachers for the year—males, $6,780.80; females, $39,721.25; total, $45,502.08; value of school houses, $332,938; value of school house sites, $98,711; value of books and apparatus, $2,003.

TAXABLE PROPERTY.—The following is a statement of the taxable property of the County, as returned for 1879: Acres of land, 199,963; value, $1,501,879; average value per acre, $7.59; value of town lots, $3,682,785; money invested in merchandise,

$536,111; money used in manufactures, $121,150; number of horses, 4,078, value, $127,249; mules and asses, 409, value, $15,260; neat cattle, 8,847, value, $99,983; sheep, 792, value, $1,386; swine, 11,873, value, $18,755; vehicles, 2,220, value, $70,142; moneys and credits, $105,157; mortgages, $81,047; stocks, etc., $230,760; furniture, $109,791; libraries, $8,284; other personalty, $414,288; railroad and telegraph property, $425,325,14; total valuation, $7,549,352.14.

LAND.—A large portion of the land in this County is held for speculative purposes, and is unimproved. The Union Pacific Railroad Company owns several thousand acres in the western part of the County, for which they ask from $5.00 to $10.00 per acre. Good unimproved upland can be bought at an average price of ten dollars an acre.

POPULATION.—No census returns have been made. The estimated population of the County, January 1, 1879, was 36,557.

OLD SETTLERS OF THE COUNTY.—The following is a partial list of the old settlers of the County, many of whom located at Omaha in 1854: William D. Brown, Dr. Enos Lowe, Jesse Lowe, A. D. Jones, M. C. Gaylord, William P. Snowden, Lorin Miller, Dr. George L. Miller, A. J. Poppleton, Hadley D. Johnson, Harrison Johnson, E. Estabrook, James G. Megeath, C. H. Downs, J. W. Paddock, S. E. Rogers, H. H. Visscher, Allen Root, John Davis, John Logan, Edwin Patrick, John Withnell, Rev. Reuben Gaylord, W. W. Wyman, J. W. Pickard, A. J. Hanscom, Herman Kountze, S. A. Orchard, D. C. Sutphen, the Creightons, J. G. Chapman, Ezra Millard, Dr. J. K. Ish, John Green, Cam Reeves, J. H. Millard, Dr. Plummer, the Durnalls, Tom Murray, O. F. Davis, M. Hellman, A. Cahn, John R. Horbach, G. M. Mills, Wm. Sexauer, Judge George B. Lake, H. R. A. Pundt, the Patricks, Gen. John M. Thayer, F. A. Schneider, Hon. James M. Woolworth, John R. Porter, Dr. Peck, John McCormick, Harry Deuel, Edwin Loveland, Josiah S. McCormick, John M. Sheely, J. R. Merideth, Fred. Davis, J. I. Brown, A. J. Simpson, P. W. Hitchcock, A. S. Paddock, Byron Reed, J. W. Tousley, Joel T. Griffin, Major George Armstrong, Rev. W. A. McCandlish, Judge Briggs, Levi Kennard, Ignace Scherb, Tom Riley, Hon. John I. Redick, John Riley, W. A. Gwyer, James E. Boyd, James M.

Winship, William A. Paxton, Frank Dellone, Fred. Dellone, G. W. Doane, S. A. Strickland, Father Curtis, Thomas O'Connor, A. J. Harmon, Milton Rogers, Dr. William McClelland, J. W. Van-Nostrand, W. J. Kennedy, James McArdle, John Kennedy, E. F. Cook, S. R. Brown, Randall Brown, Fred. King, A. N. Ferguson, George I. Gilbert, John Kennedy, Thomas Swift, E. V. Smith, C. W. Koenig, C. W. Hamilton, D. Whitney, A. R. Gilmore, J. S. Gibson, Fred Krug, Frank Kleffner, D. S. Parmelee, Michael Connolly, Luke McDermot, Patrick Dinan.

OMAHA,

The County Seat, had at the beginning of the year 1879, a population of 26,500. Laid out in the summer of 1854, its growth has been constant and of the most substantial character, so that to-day it is not only the leading city of Nebraska, but is one of the most prosperous and beautiful cities in the West.

The fine plateau—nearly a mile broad, and elevated some fifty or sixty feet above the Missouri—embraced by the original town site, is now occupied by the chief business portions of the city, while the low-rounded, tree-covered hills, forming a semi-circle on the west and south, are thickly dotted with tasteful and elegant residences and buildings of note.

On the elevated ground at the southwestern boundary of the city limits, is Hanscom Park, containing sixty acres, covered with a fine natural grove, which has been laid out and beautified by the city for the benefit of the public. Immediately west of the city is the Poor Farm on which has been erected a commodious brick Almshouse. Northwest of the city, about two miles distant, is situated the State Deaf and Dumb Institute; and further to the north, on a high hill, adorned with shade trees and evergreens, in plain view of the city, is Prospect Cemetery. The Douglas County Fair Grounds, the Omaha Driving Park, and the Omaha Barracks, lie just beyond the northern limits of the city.

Omaha, owing to her splendid geographical position—being the half-way station across the continent, and the gateway leading to the rich mining districts of the Rocky Mountains and Pacific coast—has become an important railroad and commercial center. Her railroads reach out in every direction, aud her wholesale trade, now amounting to twelve or fifteen million dollars annually, is constantly on the increase, while her manufactures are rapidly developing into an important interest.

Being at the head of the Union Pacific Railroad, the principal machine shops and general offices of that great company are located here. The machine shops were completed in 1865. They are located on the Missouri bottoms, in front of the city, and consist of a dozen or more large and substantial brick structures, covering an extensive area of ground. They give employment to between six and seven hundred men, among whom over half a million dollars is paid out annually. A large amount of money has been expended in the past year by the Government and Union Pacific Railroad Company in rip-rapping the banks of the river above the machine shops.

Omaha has one linseed oil mill, manufacturing annually millions of pounds of oil cake and thousands of gallons of oil; one distillery, which pays a government tax of more than $300,000 per year; six large breweries, a white lead works, nail works, extensive stock yards, several large pork-packing establishments, two steam flouring mills, two steam saw mills, two planing mills, two immense grain elevators, two machine shops and foundries, a safe factory, one large carriage factory and several smaller ones, a cracker factory, soap, brush and broom factories, ten brick yards, agricultural implement and numerous smaller manufacturing and industrial establishments.

There are four sound banking houses in the city—the First National, the Omaha National, Caldwell, Hamilton & Co., and the State Bank of Nebraska.

The hotel accommodations of Omaha, since the destruction of the Grand Central by fire, in 1878, are entirely inadequate.

The Grand Central was a magnificent brick structure, with stone facings, one hundred and thirty-two feet square, five stories and basement. It was finished in 1873, at a cost of $300,000, and was considered the finest hotel between Chicago and San Francisco. The fire originated through the carelessness of a workman, who, on the evening of September 4, 1878, while the hotel was undergoing repairs, and unoccupied, left a candle burning on a piece of board, in the elevator-way, near the roof, when he quit work in the evening. The hotel was totally destroyed, and five of the Omaha firemen, John Lee, Asst. Chief, Wm. McNamara, Henry Lockfeld, Fred. Wilson and A. D. Randall perished in the ruins.

GRAND CENTRAL HOTEL.

The Withnell House, corner of Harney and Fifteenth streets, is a new and first-class house, opened in the fall of 1878, by the Kitchen Brothers, who were the lessees of the Grand Central, and heavy losers by the fire.

The Metropolitan Hotel, corner of Twelfth and Douglas streets, is a first class house.

The Canfield House, corner of Ninth and Farnam streets, is a new and very fine hotel.

The Atlantic, Donovan, St. Charles, Planters' and Omaha House are among the flourishing hotels of the city.

The *Nebraskian* was the first newspaper printed at Omaha. It was established in the fall of 1854 and lived until 1864. The *Weekly Times*, established in 1857, by W. W. Wyman, was the second paper printed in the city. It was short-lived, as was also the *Democrat*, established the following year by H. D. Johnson.

The *Republican* was started as a weekly paper on the 5th of May, 1858, by Ed. F. Schneider and Harrison J. Brown. In 1863 it was changed to a daily, and in 1871 it was consolidated with the Omaha *Tribune*, an opposition paper which had been started in

January, 1870, by J. B. Hall and others. It then became a joint stock company, and was issued under the name of *Tribune and Republican* until 1873, when it resumed its old name of *Republican*. It has long been the leading Republican organ of the State.

The *Telegraph* was the first daily paper published in Omaha. the first number appearing in December, 1860. It did not last more than a year.

The Omaha *Daily Herald* was established in 1865 by Dr. George L. Miller and D. W. Carpenter, the former being the editor. Lyman Richardson and John S. Briggs published the *Herald* for a short time in 1868, and upon Mr. Briggs retiring, the firm became Miller & Richardson, Dr. Miller retaining the editorial pen. In 1874 Miller & Richardson built and moved the *Herald* into the fine brick structure now occupied by it, on Farnam, near Fifteenth street. The *Herald* is to-day the leading Democratic paper of the Northwest.

The Daily *Evening Times*, independent, was started in 1868, and shortly afterwards removed to Sioux City, Iowa.

The *Daily Bee* was established in June, 1871, by Edward Rosewater. It is Republican in politics, and has grown step by step from a small sheet to a large and influential paper, publishing two editions daily—morning and evening.

The *Daily Dispatch*, established in 1873, by J. C. Wilcox, died out in two or three months.

The *Daily Union*, established in January, 1874, ceased to exist in the following Fall.

The *Center-Union Agriculturist*, Geo. W. Brewster, editor and proprietor, was established several years ago, and is at present a very prosperous and neat weekly.

The *Daily Evening News*, Fred Nye, editor, was established in 1878, and has met with splendid success, being now one of the leading papers of the city.

The *Nebraska Watchman*—"Little Mac's" paper—F. M. MacDonagh, editor, was removed from Council Bluffs to Omaha in the spring of 1879. It is a weekly, devoted to " colonization, immigration and the interests of the working man," and is a most excellent and successful family newspaper.

The *Portfolio*, issued weekly by the Portfolio Printing Company, was established in 1879, and is a very able and successful journal, advocating the National Greenback doctrine.

Besides the foregoing there are several other papers and periodicals published at Omaha, as follows: *High School Journal, Guardian, Danske Pioneer, Pokrok Zapadu, Falkets Tidning, Post* (tri-weekly), *Western Magazine, Commercial Exchange, Rural Nebraskian, Journal of Commerce, Die Vestern* and *Mute Journal.*

PUBLIC SCHOOLS.—The educational advantages of Omaha are unsurpassed by any city in the West. There is one high and eleven fine ward school buildings. The value of school property is as follows: Sites, $101,000; buildings, $324,000; furniture, $9,150; apparatus, $950; total, $485,100.

HIGH SCHOOL BUILDING.

The High School building, occupying the site of the old Territorial Capitol, is, in point of architectual beauty, convenience of construction and commanding location, without a rival among public school buildings on the continent. It was completed in

1872, at a cost of $250,000. Its spire is 390 feet above the Missouri river, and from its cupola it commands a view of the whole city, and other points in the Missouri Valley, for fifteen miles.

The North Omaha, Third Ward, South Omaha, Hartman's Addition and Hascall's Addition school houses are of brick, the balance being handsome frame structures.

The Board of Education, in whom is vested the government of public schools, is composed of twelve men, two from each Ward.

Creighton College, a handsome brick building with stone facings, erected on an elevated site in the northwestern portion of the city, is one of the institutions of Omaha. It was completed in 1878, at a cost of $55,000, which sum, with a further amount of $100,000 as a permanent endowment, was bequeathed for that purpose by the late Mrs. Edward Creighton. The school is under the supervision of the Jesuits, and will accommodate 480 pupils. It is free to all. The building is 54x126 feet, three stories and a basement.

St. Catharine's Academy, at the corner of Cass and Eighteenth streets, is a substantial brick structure, erected in 1877, at a cost of $17,000. It was built and is managed by the Sisters of Mercy, and is exclusively a girls' school.

Brownell Hall, a young ladies' Seminary and school for boys, is a flourishing private institution, under the auspices of the Episcopal Church.

Mt. St. Mary's Academy is a well-sustained Catholic school.

The Great Western Business College, established in 1873, by Prof. G. R. Rathbun, has become a popular institution with those seeking a thorough business training.

Omaha, in 1879, had twenty-eight churches, representing all the different denominations.

Rev. Peter Cooper, of the Methodist Church, preached the first sermon in the city in the Summer of 1854, at the old Ferry Company's house—the St. Nicholas.

The Roman Catholics built the first church edifice in the city —a brick structure still standing on Ninth street, between Harney and Howard.

The Catholic Cathedral, on Ninth street, was commenced in 1864 and finished in 1866. It possesses the largest and finest organ in the city—a gift by the late Mrs. Edward Creighton, who also furnished the means for building its superb altar.

The First Methodist Episcopals built the second church in the city in 1856, on Thirteenth street, between Farnam and Douglas, which was converted into a business block, the Society building a brick Church on Seventeenth street, between Dodge and Capitol Avenue. This building was turned over to the bondholders in June, 1877, the Society, in the Fall following, erecting a commodious frame structure on Davenport street, which was dedicated on the 9th of June, 1878, by Mrs. Van Cott, the Evangelist.

The Congregationalists commenced the erection of a brick Church on Sixteenth street early in 1856, and finished it in 1857, chiefly through the indefatigable exertions of Rev. Reuben Gaylord, its first pastor. This Society at present has a neat frame house of worship, corner of Nineteenth and Chicago streets.

The Episcopal congregation was organized in 1856, by Rev. G. W. Watson, and in 1859 Trinity Church, a small brick edifice at the corner of Ninth and Farnam, was built on leased ground. In 1867 Trinity Society erected a frame church at the corner of Capitol Avenue and Eighteenth streets, which was destroyed by fire in 1872, and their present house of worship was immediately erected on the site of the old one. It is now contemplated to erect a new edifice at a cost of $25,000.

The Lutheran Church, on Douglas street, between Twelfth and Thirteenth, was built in 1861, and dedicated February 16, 1862. It is a large brick edifice, and its erection is mainly due to the persistent efforts of Rev. A. Kountze, who organized the first Lutheran Society in the city.

The German Catholic Church, a frame structure on Douglas street, between Sixteenth and Seventeeth, was erected in 1869.

The Presbyterian Church, at the corner of Seventeenth and Dodge streets, built in 1869, is a handsome and spacious brick structure.

St. Mark's Church (Episcopal), in South Omaha, is a frame building and was erected in 1869.

20

The United Presbyterian Church, a frame, at the corner of Eighteenth and Webster streets, was erected in 1869.

The Unitarian Church, a brick, on Seventeenth street, between Cass and Davenport, was built in 1869.

St. Barnabas Episcopal Church, a frame, on Nineteenth street, between Cass and California, was erected in 1870.

The Baptist Church, a brick, on the corner of Davenport and Fifteenth streets, was built in 1870.

The M. E. Church, on Eighteenth street, a frame, was moved to its present location from North Omaha and re-constructed in 1873.

The Lutheran Church (Swedish) a frame, on Cass street, between Eighteenth and Nineteenth, was moved to its present location in 1875.

The M. E. Church (African), a small frame, at the corner of Eighteenth and Webster streets, was erected several years ago.

The Baptist Church (African), a frame, at the corner of Eleventh and Harny streets, was moved to its present location in 1875.

The Lutheran Church (Scandinavian), a frame, on Jackson street, between Twelfth and Thirteenth, was finished in 1875.

The Lutheran Church (German), on St. Mary's Avenue, is a brick, and was finished in 1876.

The Catholic Church, a frame, at the corner of Cuming and Eighteenth streets, was erected in 1876.

The North Mission Church (Episcopal), a frame, in Shinn's Addition, was erected in 1876.

The Union Mission Church, a small frame on Twenty-third street, between Saunders and Cuming, was built in 1877.

The Latter Day Saints, or Mormon Church, a small frame near the corner of Cass and Sixteenth streets, was built several years ago.

The Odd Fellows are the oldest of the Secret Societies in Omaha, the first Lodge having been organized in January, 1856. There are now several Lodges of this Order in the city. Odd Fellows' Hall, a splendid three-story brick building at the corner of Dodge and Fourteenth streets, was completed in 1874, at a cost of $18,000.

Capital Lodge, A. F. and A. M., was established in 1857. The Masonic fraternity is very strong in the city, numbering several Lodges, including the higher orders of Royal Arch and Knights Templar. Masonic Hall, a handsome three-story brick structure at the corner of Sixteenth street and Capitol Avenue, was commenced in 1876 and finished in the Spring of 1877, at a cost of $15,000.

The Knights of Pythias is also a strong Order; and there are besides numerous German and Irish Orders, Temperance and Benevolent Societies.

U. S. POST OFFICE BUILDING.

The Postoffice, fronting on Fifteenth and Dodge streets, completed in 1873, is one of the handsomest Government buildings in the country. It is built of a fine free stone from Ohio, is four stories high, occupying two lots, and cost, with the furniture, $450,000. The first floor is occupied exclusively by the postoffice, and the upper floors by the United States Courts and Government officers, while the basement is fitted up as a prison, with quarters for janitor and attendants.

The Court House, on Farnam street, is a two-story brick building, which was commenced in 1857 and finished in 1859. Its dimensions were then considered ample, but are now entirely inadequate and inconvenient. A plot of ground has been selected and a Court House more in accord with the needs of the city, will, no boubt, be erected during the coming year.

The Omaha jail is one of the handsomest buildings and most secure institutions of the kind in the West. It was erected in 1879. The walls are of brick and the cells of hardened steel.

DEPARTMENT OF THE PLATTE.—Since 1865 Omaha has been the headquarters of a military division, known as the Department of the Platte, which includes Nebraska, Wyoming, Utah and a portion of Dakota. A large share of the commercial and financial supremacy of Omaha in the Missouri Valley, is due to the heavy purchases and distribution of military supplies at this point, and the handling of the Quartermaster, Commissary and Paymaster funds of the department by the city banks. In 1872 the National Government acquired eighty-two and a half acres of land on the plateau two miles north of this city. Upon this tract was established what was known as Omaha Barracks, which has recently been re-christened as Ft. Omaha. Over $100,000 has been expended in buildings and upon improvements of these grounds. The quarters for soldiers have accommodated from two to fourteen companies of troops each winter. During the past year about $60,000 has been expended at Ft. Omaha, for an elegant brick residence for the Department Commander, brick storehouses and the re-construction of officers' residences. The grounds are tastefully laid out. The present Commander of the Department of the Platte is Brigadier General Crook.

During the present year, 1879, the telephonic system of communication has been introduced in the city. The Telephone Company, with general offices in Union Block, corner of Fifteenth and Farnam streets, has erected lines through the principal streets of the city, and almost every prominent business house, and many private dwellings, have connecting wires.

Water works—of which the city stands badly in need—have engrossed the attention of the City Fathers during the past several months. Rival companies have made propositions to the city for the construction of works, and much discussion has followed over the merits and demerits of the different systems. The matter is not yet fully settled, but that Omaha will have water-works before another year is assured.

Omaha has a most exellent steam fire department, which is, at present, under the efficient management of Chief John Galligan.

Horse railways traverse the principal streets, leading from the Union Depot, in the southeastern portion of the city, to the northwestern boundary line. During the past three years the growth of the city has been greater, and more permanent and substantial improvements have been made than at any period heretofore in its history. The improvements reported in 1877 footed up $800,000; for 1878 they amounted to $1,000,000, and for the present year the increase has been at least twenty-five per cent. greater. Omaha is also a port of entry, and has the privilege of importing goods in bond, by rail or river.

### FLORENCE,

Located on the Missouri, six miles north of Omaha, is now a small village of less than one hundred inhabitants. The place was first settled by the Mormons, in 1845, and was called by them Winter Quarters. They, however, made Florence the chief outfitting point for their emigrant trains to Salt Lake, and for several years it was a lively business place.

The Florence Town Company was organized in 1856, and the same year the town was chartered as a city. Up to 1858 it grew very rapidly and was a good business point, several of the Omaha merchants opening branch stores there.

At an election in August, 1857, for delegate to Congress, Florence gave 700 votes for Fenner Ferguson. During the same year a newspaper called *The Courier*, was published there, and a theater was in operation; but the great financial crisis of that year crippled those mostly interested in the city's growth, and it began to recede. At present Florence has a couple of general merchandise stores, a hotel, blacksmith shop, school house, and a water-power grist mill.

### MILLARD,

A station on the Union Pacific Railroad in the south-central part of the County, was laid out in the sprimg of 1870, by Ezra Millard, of Omaha, after whom it is called. It contains several neat dwellings, an excellent school house, a blacksmith shop, two general stores, two hotels, a grain warehouse, large corn cribs, and a large water-power grist mill, on Little Papillion Creek, which runs past the town. Millard is twelve miles southwest of Omaha, by wagon road.

### ELKHORN STATION,

On the Union Pacific Railroad in the western part of the County, is a flourishing village, pleasantly located on the high ground about two miles east of the Elkhorn River. It contains a Catholic Church, school house, two general stores, a hotel, blacksmith shop, and large grain warehouses. The surrounding country is a well-settled excellent farming section, making this an extensive shipping point for grain and stock.

### WATERLOO

Is a small town in the western part of the County, situated on the west bank of the Elkhorn River, and on the line of the Union Pacific Railroad. It contains a hotel, two stores, a school house, blacksmith shop, and one of the best water-power flouring mills in the County. An excellent wagon bridge spans the Elkhorn here, also.

### VALLEY STATION,

At the junction of the Omaha & Republican Valley with the Union Pacific Railroad, in the northwestern part of the County, is situated on the fertile bottoms, midway between the Platte and Elkhorn Rivers, about three miles from each. Since the Omaha & Republican Valley road commenced operation in 1876, Valley Station has improved very rapidly, and it now bids fair to become an important business center. It has a school house, hotel, good general store, grain warehouses, etc., and the surrounding country is admirably adapted to farming and stock raising.

### ELKHORN CITY,

On the old Military Road, twenty-five miles northwest of Omaha, was a flourishing village in the early days of the County, but is almost entirely deserted. It was surveyed and platted in the spring of 1856, and while staging and freighting across the plains lasted, it was a lively business point. The largest cheese factory in the County is located here.

### IRVINGTON,

Is a small village on the Military Road, eight miles west of Omaha. It has a general store and school house. The Congregationalists have erected a neat Church here, and hold regular services.

## DODGE COUNTY.

Dodge County, named in honor of Augustus Cæsar Dodge, a United States Senator from Iowa, was organized by an Act of the first Territorial Legislature, approved March 6, 1855, which also fixed the County Seat at Fontenelle.

The Legislature, March 2, 1858, re-defined the eastern boundary of the County, and December 22, 1859, the southern boundary was changed to where it still remains, on the south bank of the Platte River. In January, 1860, the eastern boundary was again changed and placed upon the Elkhorn River, which cut off Fontenelle, the County Seat, and left Dodge County without a Capital. In February, 1867, a portion of the territory lost by the Act of 1860, known as Logan Creek, was re-annexed to Dodge. In March, 1873, some slight changes were made in the boundaries, and in February, 1875, the Legislature described the limits of the County as they exist at present.

Dodge County is located in the middle-eastern part of the State, in the second tier of Counties west of the Missouri River, and is bounded on the north by Cuming and Burt Counties, east by Burt and Washington Counties, and the Elkhorn River, which is the dividing line about one-half the distance; south by Douglas County and the Platte River, which separates it from Saunders County, and west by Colfax County, containing 540 square miles, or 345,600 acres, at an average elevation of 1,176 feet above the sea level.

WATER COURSES.—The Platte River washes nearly the entire southern border of the County. The Elkhorn River, affording magnificent manufacturing advantages, flows in a southeasterly direction through the eastern portion of the County, being joined in the northeastern part by Logan Creek, also a fine mill stream. Maple Creek, a clear, beautiful stream, and tributary of the Elkhorn, flows from west to east through the central portion of the County. Pebble and Cuming Creeks water the northern townships, and Rawhide Creek, a sluggish stream, with low banks, flows from west to east through the southern portion of the County, all being tributaries of the Elkhorn. There is not a township without running water.

TIMBER.—There is considerable native timber in the valleys and skirting all the streams. Well developed artificial groves now adorn almost every farm, and furnish plenty of fuel. In 1879 there were 2,152 acres, or 59,457 forest trees, and 124 miles of hedging under cultivation in the County.

FRUIT.—The number of fruit trees under cultivation in 1879, was reported as follows: Apple, 20,082; pear, 544; peach, 10,359; plum, 11,271; cherry, 2,696, and grape vines, 1,310.

PHYSICAL CULTURE.—At least one-third of the area is valley, and the balance gently rolling upland. Extending across the southern portion of the County are the wide bottoms of the Platte; in the eastern portion are the fertile valleys of the Elkhorn and Logan, here from four to seven miles in width; and through the central portion extends the beautiful Valley of the Maple. The Rawhide, Pebble and Cuming Creeks, each have fine reaches of dry bottom. The surface is almost everywhere tillable, the only exception being in occasional places on the ridge dividing the valley and upland.

CROPS.—The following is a statement of the crops reported in 1879: Acres under cultivation, 102,195; winter wheat, 209 acres, 3,701 bushels; rye, 4,825 acres, 66,324 bushels; spring wheat, 39,070 acres, 467,923 bushels; corn, 39,726 acres, 1,415,538 bushels; barley, 2,094 acres, 46,989 bushels; oats, 8,962 acres, 271,351 bushels; buckwheat, thirty-one acres, 529 bushels; sorghum, thirteen acres, 621 gallons; flax, seventy acres, 406 bushels; broom corn, six acres, one ton; millet and Hungarian, fourteen acres, twenty-five tons; potatoes, 393 acres, 37,206 bushels.

HISTORICAL.—The first election in the County was held on the 12th day of December, 1854, at Fontenelle, at which Dr. M. H.

Clark was elected to the Territorial Council, and J. W. Richardson and Col. E. R. Doyle to the House of Representatives. Only eight votes were polled at this election.

Dr. Clark, on the 16th of February, 1855, made a most exhaustive report to the Legislature upon the subject of a Pacific Railroad, advocating the Platte Valley route as the one most practicable, and predicting " that before fifteen years have transpired, the route to India will be opened, and the way across this continent will be the common way of the world." Viewed in the light of to-day, it seems almost prophetic, and indicates largely what must have been the character of the man.

Arthur Bloomer, of Platte precinct, is the oldest settler of continuous residence, in the present County of Dodge. There are others, such as J. H. Peters, John Batie, and John Cramer, of Maple, and Samuel Whittier, of Fremont, who came to Fontenelle previous to Mr. Bloomer coming into Dodge, but none who have lived so many years continuously, in this County, as he. J. H. Peters, Samuel Francis, John Evans, Thos. Gibson and several others made claims in 1855, near Fontenelle, and did some plowing during that year. John and Arthur Bloomer made their claims, near the mouth of Maple Creek, early in April, 1856, and broke on the first of May following, twenty-five acres of prairie.

Mrs. Wealthy Beebe, with her minor children, and her son-in-law, Abram McNeal, and family, located in the Platte Valley, two miles west of where Feemont now stands, on the 25th of May, 1856. Twin daughters born to Mr. and Mrs. McNeal on August 8, 1856, were the first children born in the County.

George Emerson made the first settlement west of the Beebe's, in the following month.

On the 4th of July, 1856, the settlement at North Bend was begun by a colony of ten adults and ten children, viz; Geo. Young and wife, Robert Miller and wife, John Miller and wife, Miss Ezra Miller (now Mrs. W. H. Ely), William and Alexander Miller and George McNaughton. Their numbers increased very rapidly, and soon North Bend was a flourishing town. A steam saw mill was brought here from Cleveland, Ohio, in July, 1857, by M. S. Coterell, J. M. Smith, Jas. Humphries and Alex. Morrison. Seth Young, son of Geo. Young, born November 30, 1856, was the first birth at the Bend, and his mother dying a few days after, was the first death. Rev. J. Adriance, of the Methodist Church, organized a class here in September, 1858.

On the 23d of August, 1856, E. H. Barnard and John A. Kountz located claims on the site of the present city of Fremont, setting their claim stakes on the swell ground near what is now "D" and First streets, after which they proceeded to the cabin of Seth P. Marvin, about two miles off, on the California road, where they were hospitably entertained. Three days later—the 26th— a Town Company was organized under the name of Pinney, Bernard & Co., which consisted of E. H. Bernard, John A. Kountz, Seth P. Marvin, George M. Pinney, James G. Smith, Robert Kittle and Robert Moreland, the last named four having arrived immediately after Messrs. Bernard and Kountz.

James G. Smith was elected President of the Company, Robert Kittle, Vice President, John A. Kountz, Secretary, Geo. M. Pinney, Treasurer and E. H. Bernard, Surveyor. A plot of ground one mile square was immediately laid off for a town site, and on the 3d of September the company adopted the name of Fremont for their new town, in honor of Gen. John C. Fremont, who was at that time the candidate of the Republican party for the Presidency of the United States.

On the evening of the organization of the Town Company the Platte Claim Club was organized, with Seth P. Marvin as President, J. W. Peck, Vice President, E. H. Barnard, Secretary and George M. Pinney, Recorder.

All the members of the Town Company, except Mr. Pinney, either remained or soon returned, and by their united efforts contributed to form the nucleus of the future city.

The first shanty erected was upon the lot now owned and occupied by the Congregational Church, which was completed and used for the first time by its owners, Messrs. Bernard & Kountz, on the 10th day of September, 1856; Robert Kittle, James G. Smith and Wm. E. Lee were the boarders, and Leander Gerard, now banker at Columbus, cook of the establishment.

That cabin, insignificant as it was, broke the solitude of the wilderness; it was a station upon the Great American Desert, a hotel, boarding house, and a wonder to the Pawnees, whose village,

1,500 strong, was upon the high bank of the Platte, three miles south.

In October, 1856, the Pawnees notified the settlers that they must leave within three days or they would kill them and destroy their property. A council of the settlers was called, and James G. Smith dispatched to Governor Izard for assistance. The Governor gave him a box of muskets and some ammunition, and re-enforced the settlers with eight men, which, added to the inhabitants of Fremont and surrounding country, made a total grand army of twenty-five, who, by marching and counter-marching, by bon-fires and torch-light processions and the burning of hay stacks, produced the impression upon the Pawnees that it was a vast army, and had the effect of over-awing them, and at the end of three days they sent a flag of truce, saying that the chiefs had re-considered the matter and concluded to let them go unmolested for the present.

The Pawnees, however, continued to be a great annoyance to the settlers during the succeeding winter, demanding pay for the timber that had been cut upon their lands, and making all sorts of threats to compel payment; but the settlers pursued a pacific policy toward them, which resulted, finally, in a lasting peace. In the Summer of 1859, when the Pawnees started on the war-path against the whites of the Elkhorn Valley, they made no hostile demonstrations until several miles beyond Fremont, although the war party passed through the town on their way out.

It is a mooted question as to who built the first permanent house in Fremont, that honor lying between Robert Kittle and Wm. G. Bowman; but there were but a few days' interval between the completion of each. Rev. Isaac E. Heaton's was the first family in the place, and he was the first clergyman. The first blacksmith was John Homel, who was induced to remain by the offer of a town share (nine lots) and material for a shop. James G. Smith was the first merchant, John C. Flor the first hotel keeper, and S. B. Colson the first shoemaker. E. H. Rogers and William Cartney made the first brick. The first male child born in the town was Fred Kittle, and the first female child, Alice Flor. The first post office in the County was established here in the Summer of 1857, with James G. Smith, P. M. The first marriage in the town and County was that of Luther Wilson to Eliza Turner, August 25, 1858.

A re-organization of the County took place in accordance with an Act of the Legislature, approved January 13, 1860, which provided for an election to be held on the first Monday in February, following. At this election Fremont was made the County Seat, and the following County officers elected, viz: E. H. Barnard, Probate Judge; Wm. S. Wilson, Sheriff; H. C. Cambell, Treasurer; J. Reynolds, Clerk, and George Twiner, George Tutton, and Thomas Fitzsimmons, Commissioners.

The County, at this time, was divided into the three precincts of Fremont, North Bend and Maple Creek.

The Western Union Telegraph was built through the County in 1860.

The Union Pacific Railroad was built through the County in 1866. Length of road in the County, twenty-five miles.

The Sioux City & Pacific Railroad made a junction with the Union Pacific, at Fremont, on the 12th of February, 1869. Length of road in the County, seven and three-sixths miles.

The Fremont, Elkhorn & Missouri Valley Railroad had the first ten miles of their road completed by December 31, 1869. Length of road in the County, twenty-nine miles.

Henry J. Robinson is the proprietor and builder of the three water-power flouring mills in the County, viz: one on Maple Creek, erected in the summer of 1859; one on Logan Creek, built in 1863, and one on Pebble Creek, built in 1867-68. There are now several mills running in the County.

Dodge County, out of a total population of less than four hundred, furnished twenty-five volunteers, during the rebellion, for frontier protection.

RELIGIOUS MATTERS.—The first sermon preached in the County was by Rev. I. E. Heaton, November 2, 1856, at Fremont; text, Psalms, 111, 10—"The fear of the Lord is the beginning of wisdom." On the following Sabbath, services were held at the house of Robert Kittle, and from that time onward public worship was continued regularly at Fremont. A Congregational Society was organized at Fremont on the 2d of August, 1857, with Rev. F. E. Heaton as pastor.

The second minister in the County was Rev. Mr. Cooley, a Baptist, who located near Timberville, in February, 1857.

In September, 1858, Rev. J. Adriance, of the Methodist Episcopal Church, organized Societies in Fremont and North Bend.

The first Church building was fitted up by the Congregationalists, in Fremont, in 1861. They dedicated a second and larger one on the 2d of August, 1868, and enlarged it in the spring of 1874. Until 1875, this Church contained the only bell in Fremont, 1,118 pounds, which was used for Church, school, public meetings, fire alarms, and for all purposes of a general public nature.

The St. James P. E. Church, of Fremont, was erected during the summer of 1867, and consecrated on the 15th of September, of same year, by Bishop Clarkson.

The Methodist Episcopal Church, of Fremont, was erected in the summer of 1866, and dedicated in December following.

Rev. Father Ryan, of the Roman Catholic Church, held services in Fremont in 1868. Their Church building was erected and dedicated in 1869.

The Baptist Church, of Fremont, was dedicated in December, 1871.

The Evangelical German Church, of Fremont, was erected and dedicated in 1872.

The Presbyterian Church, of Fremont, was organized in 1873, and their Church building dedicated January 3, 1875.

The United Presbyterians organized two Societies in the County early in its history—one at Fremont and the other at North Bend, and erected a Church at the latter place.

The Universalists have had occasional services at Fremont, by different ministers, for years past.

SCHOOLS.—Miss Charity Colson taught a private school at Fremont in the summer of 1858, which was the first school opened in the County. In the summer of 1859 a public school was opened at Fremont, Miss McNeal, teacher, and at North Bend, Miss Mary E. Heaton, teacher.

The number of school districts in the County in 1879, was sixty-seven; school houses, sixty-five; number of children of school age, 3,278—males, 1,548; females, 1,730; whole number of children that attended school during the year, 2,383; number of qualified teachers employed, 123—males, forty-three; females, eighty; wages paid male teachers for the year, $6,770.75; female, $12,676.87; total, $19,447.62; value of school houses, $42,615; value of sites, $3,138; value of books and apparatus $2,827.97.

TAXABLE PROPERTY.—The following statement will show the taxable property of the County, as returned for 1879: Acres of land, 315,299; average value per acre, $3.30; value of town lots, $298,249; money invested in merchandise, $95,527; money used in manufacture, $14,761; number of horses, 4,350, value, $125,784; mules, 377, value, $12,399; cattle, 11,552, value, $104,000; sheep, 3,424, value, $3,424; swine, 14,927, value, $13,025; vehicles, 1,426, value, $21.330; moneys and credits, $11,402; mortgages, $25,246; stocks, etc., $25,000; furniture, $30,051; libraries, $2,602; other personalty, $42,248; railroads, $390,262.06; telegraph, $3,925; total, $2,261,010.06.

LANDS.—There are no vacant Government lands in the County. Those of the Union Pacific Railroad Company amount to 15,000 acres, and are offered at prices ranging from $5 to $10 per acre.

In the summer of 1877 the wife of Dr. St. Louis, a physician of Fremont, died after a brief illness and was buried. Friends of the deceased suspicioned foul play and had the remains disinterred for *post mortem* examination. Portions of the stomach and bowels were submitted to chemical tests in Chicago, and were found to contain arsenic in large quantities. Dr. St. Louis was thereupon arrested upon the charge of poisoning his wife, and lodged in the Fremont jail. At his trial in the District Court in Fremont, he was found guilty and sentenced to be hanged. A new trial, however, was granted and a change of venue taken to Saunders County, where he was again convicted and sentenced to death. The case was then taken to the Supreme Court of the State, which sustained the decisions of the lower courts. Dr. St. Louis was to have been executed at Wahoo in April, 1879, but on the morning of the day set for his execution, he committed suicide in the jail at Fremont, where he had beed incarcerated, by shooting himself through the head with a small pocket pistol.

POPULATION.—In 1879 the population of the County was 11,579; in 1875 it was 7,534; increase in four years, 4,045.

## FREMONT,

The County Seat, is on the Union Pacific Railroad, forty-six miles west of Omaha, at the junction of the Sioux City & Pacific and Fremont, Elkhorn & Missouri Valley Railroads. It is located on a beautiful site at the junction of the Platte and Elkhorn Valleys, which are here nearly ten miles wide. The population of the city in 1879 was 3,000. A fine wagon bridge across the Platte River connects Fremont with Saunders County, from which a large trade is drawn.

It has two banks, agricultural implement, furniture and wagon manufactories, large elevators for the large shipping trade, brick yards, lumber and coal yards, and a good assortment of stores, some of the houses doing a wholesale business amounting to over a million dollars a year. It has three newspapers, the *Tribune*, weekly, established July 24, 1868, the *Herald*, daily and weekly, established August 2, 1871, and the *Bulletin*, a monthly; a $12,-000 brick Court House, a $15,000 jail, an $18,000 school house, and several handsome Church buildings. Three well organized fire companies furnish protection against the devouring element. Elegant private residences grace the suburbs, and a large park set in blue grass and adorned with shade trees, is the fashionable resort in pleasant weather. Close to the city are the Fair Grounds, with a splendid mile track.

## NORTH BEND,

On the Union Pacific Railroad, sixteen miles west of Fremont, is situated on a bend in the Platte River, from which it takes its name. Within the past two years the town has greatly improved, and several new stores and other business houses have been opened. It contains 300 inhabitants, an excellent weekly newspaper, the *North Bend Independent*, two Churches, a good school, two hotels, lumber yard, large grain elevator, and immense corn cribs, just erected this season. A wagon bridge over the Platte makes it a convenient shipping point for the farmers of Saunders County.

## HOOPER,

On the Fremont, Elkhorn & Missouri Valley Railroads, in the middle-eastern part of the County, is the second town of size, having a population of 500. It is a brisk business point and is growing rapidly.

### SCRIBNER,

Situated on the line of the Fremont, Elkhorn & Missouri Valley Railroad, several miles northwest of Hooper, has 360 inhabitants, and is a very flourishing place, having a large shipping and general merchandising trade.

### LOGAN,

Is a small village situated on the east bank of the Elkhorn, near the mouth of Logan Creek, and has a good flouring mill, store, and an excellent school house.

### WEBSTER,

Is a thriving village located in the middle-western part of the County, and has two Churches, good general stores and a fine school building.

### NICKERSON,

Is the first important station on the line of the Fremont, Elkhorn & Missouri Valley Railroad, north of Fremont. It does an excellent grain business and is rapidly developing.

### PEBBLE,

Is a growing village, situated near the mouth of Pebble Creek, in the north-central part of the County.

There are twenty odd Postoffices in the County.

## DAWSON COUNTY.

Dawson County was organized July 11, 1871, by proclamation of Acting Governor Wm. H. James. It is situated in the southwestern portion of the State, 231 miles west of the Missouri River, and is bounded on the north by Custer, east by Buffalo, south by the Platte River, Gosper and Frontier Counties, and west by Lincoln County, containing 1,008 square miles, at an average elevation above the sea level of 2,370 feet.

WATER COURSES.—The Platte River flows in a southeasterly

direction through the southwestern portion of the County. Wood River and its numerous branches water the northeastern townships; Elm, Buffalo, Plum and several smaller streams water different portions of the County.

TIMBER.—This County has about 950 acres of forest trees under cultivation. The streams are all tolerably well timbered, as are also many of the gulches and canyons.

PHYSICAL FEATURES.—Nearly one-half of the County lies in the fertile valley of the Platte. The uplands consist mostly of smooth, beautiful prairies, probably five per cent. being broken, untillable land. The prairies yield an abundance of the richest grasses for hay and pasturage, making this an admirable region for the stock-grower. The grass cures on the ground, furnishing rich food for cattle the winter through.

FIRST SETTLEMENTS.—The first permanent settlements in the County were made in what is now Plum Creek Precinct, by Daniel Freeman, J. W. Delahunty and a few others, in 1867–68, or about the time of the completion of the Union Pacific Railroad. On April 9th, 1872, a colony from Philadelphia, Penn., consisting of sixty-five men, women and children, arrived. This colony took up their quarters in four empty box-cars, which the Railroad Company placed on the side-track for their use until they could build themselves permanent houses. The first post office in the County was established at Plum Creek, in this Precinct, in 1872, and was kept in the U. P. depot, by J. A. McDonald, deceased.

MELLOTT Precinct was settled in April, 1872, by H. Clay Stuckey, Jeremiah Smith, Simon Fetters, and others.

WILLOW ISLAND Precinct was settled in March, 1873, by Josiah Huffman.

WOOD RIVER Precinct was settled in April, 1873, by James B. Mellott.

CAYOTE Precinct was settled in April, 1873, by S. S. Baldwin.

OVERTON Precinct was settled in 1873, by James N. Patton and Prof. D. B. Worley. Mr. Patton built the first house and Geo. Slocum the second.

PLATTE Precinct was settled early in the spring of 1873.

COZAD Precinct was settled in December, 1873, by Samuel Atkinson, who was soon followed by a small colony. In February,

1874, a much larger colony arrived, and the population of the Precinct was 333.

COUNTY ORGANIZATION.—The first general election was held on the 11th day of July, 1871, at the store of Daniel Freeman, at Plum Creek, in accordance with Acting Governor Wm. H. James' proclamation of June 26, 1871, which also named J. W. Delahunty, R. O'Keefe and Otto Hansen as Judges, and John Kehoe and E. Delahunty, Clerks of said election.

A full board of County officers was chosen at this election, as follows: J. W. Delahunty, Joseph Smith and Otto Hansen, Commissioners; Daniel Freeman, Clerk, and Superintendent of Public Schools; Richard O'Keefe, Probate Judge; Patrick Delahunty, Treasurer; John Kehoe, Sheriff; David Meek, Surveyor, and Patrick Gaffney, Coroner.

CHURCH MATTERS.—As early as 1867, Father Ryan, of the Catholic Church, held services at the old Plum Creek stationhouse, which have been regularly continued.

In the fall of 1872, Rev. William Wilson organized the first Methodist Society in the County. It has largely increased and now has regular appointments at Plum Creek and other towns.

In April, 1864, Rt. Rev. Bishop Clarkson organized Plum Creek Parish, and through the untiring perseverance of W. Tudor Tucker and family, a neat brick house of worship was erected at Plum Creek, in April, 1875, being the first Church building in the County.

In 1874, the Missionary Baptist Society was organized, and now holds stated services in the several towns.

The Presbyterian congregation of Plum Creek was organized in 1873, and during the same year a Society organized at Overton.

Flourishing Sunday Schools are now in operation at Plum Creek, Overton, Cayote, Cozad, Willow Island, and Smith's school house.

PUBLIC SCHOOLS.—The first school district was formed in 1872, and embraced the entire County. In 1879 there were twenty-four districts, fourteen school houses, 291 male, and 259 female children of school age in the County. Number of qualified teachers employed, nineteen—males, eleven, females, eight; total wages paid teachers for the year, $1,282.50; value of school houses, $19,400; value of sites, $1,085; value of books and apparatus, $327.50.

TAXABLE PROPERTY.—The amount and valuation of the taxable property of the County returned in 1879, was as follows: Acres of land, 145,180.10, average value per acre, $1; value of town lots, $15,876, money used in merchandise, $6,335; number of horses, 643, value, $8,414.50; mules, forty-eight, value, $907.75; neat cattle, 5,155, value, $23,971; sheep, 3,068, value, $2,035; swine, 295, value, $277.50; vehicles, 240, value, $2,089.50; moneys and credits, $6,163, furniture, $3,128; libraries $50; other personalty, $2,544; railroad, $456,104; telegraph, $3,740; total, $676,-805.

LAND.—There is a large amount of both Government and railroad land in this County which is admirably adapted to stock raising and agriculture. The price of the Union Pacific lands is from $2 to $6 per acre.

POPULATION.—In 1879 the County had a population of 3,871.

RAILROAD.—The Union Pacific traverses the County from east to west, a distance of forty-four miles.

## PLUM CREEK,

The County Seat, is a flourishing town of 750 inhabitants. It is located on the Union Pacific Railroad, 231 miles west of Omaha, and was incorporated March 7, 1874. J. W. Ayers erected the first building in the town, and T. Martin, the first hotel—called the "Alhambra," now the Union Pacific. A very fine stone and brick Court House, and an imposing school house adorn the town. A substantial wagon bridge crosses the Platte at this point, and draws a large trade from the Republican Valley towns.

Plum Creek is the headquarters of a large district, and is a lively business center. It has a number of well-stocked general merchandise stores, good hotels, a hardware, two drug, jewelry, and furniture stores, lumber yards, grain warehouses, etc., and an excellent weekly newspaper—the *Pioneer*.

## COZAD,

Is a village on the Union Pacific Railroad, about twelve miles west of Plum Creek. It was founded by J. J. Cozad, of Ohio, in December, 1873, a number of very fine brick houses were erected.

On the night of April 29, 1876, the town was nearly destroyed by fire. At present it has seventy-five inhabitants, and is gradually improving. A weekly newspaper is published here, called the *One Hundredth Meridian.*

### WILLOW ISLAND,

On the Union Pacific Railroad, twenty miles west of Plum Creek, was laid out in March, 1873, by Josiah Huffman. It has two stores, a blacksmith shop, telegraph office, etc.

### OVERTON,

On the Union Pacific railroad, in the southeastern portion of the County, was laid out in June, 1873. It has an elegant school house, costing $2,100, and a number of stores and business places. A splendid iron bridge has been erected over Buffalo Creek at this point, adding greatly to the business of the town.

JEWELL and TRAPPER'S GROVE, are Postoffices in the northern part of the County.

INCIDENTS OF THE EARLY SETTLEMENT.—While the railroad was being built through Dawson County, the engineers, graders and track-layers were frequently driven from their work by the Indians. Not only then, but after the track was laid and trains running, it was sometimes torn up and trains ditched, causing the loss of lives and the destruction of property. One of these attacks took place near Plum Creek. In July, 1867, a train was ditched about four miles west of the above named station. It was by a band of Southern Cheyennes, under a Chief called TURKEY LEG. He was a vicious-looking fellow, his appearance naturally suggesting him as a fit subject for a hanging bee. At a small bridge or culvert, over a dry ravine, they had lifted the iron rails from the ties—raising only one end of each rail—about three feet, piling up ties under them for support, and firmly lashing the rails and ties together by wire cut from the adjoining telegraph line. They were pretty cunning in this arrangement of the rails, and evidently placed them where they thought they would penetrate the cylinder on each side of the engine. But not having a mechanical turn of mind exactly, and disregarding the slight curve in the road at this point, they missed their calculations, as the sequel shows, as one of the rails did no execution whatever, and the other went straight into and through the boiler. After they had fixed the rails in the manner described, they retired to where the bench or second bottom slopes down to the first, and there concealed themselves in the tall grass, waiting for the train. Before it left Plum Creek, a hand-car with three section men was sent ahead as a pilot. This car encountered the obstacle, and ran into the ravine, bruising and stunning the men and frightening them so that they were unable to signal to the approaching train. As soon as the car landed at the bottom of the ravine, the Indians rushed up, when two of the men, least hurt, ran away in the darkness of the night—it was little past midnight—and hid in the tall grass near by. The other, more stunned by the fall of the car, was scalped by the savages, and as the knife of the savage passed under his scalp, he seemed to realize his condition partly, and in his delerium wildly threw his arms out and snatched the scalp from the Indian, who had just lifted it from his skull. With this he, too, got away in the darkness, and was afterward in the employ of the Company at Omaha.

But the fated train came on without any knowledge of what had transpired in front. As the engine approached the ravine, the head-light gleaming out in the darkness in the dim distance, fast growing less and less, the engineer, Brooks Bowers by name, but familiarly called "Billy Brooks," by the railroad men, saw that the rails were displaced, whistled "down brakes," and reversed the engine, but all too late to stop the train. The door of the fire-box was open, and the fireman was in the act of adding fuel to the flames within, when the crash came. That fireman was named Hendershot, and the boys used to speak of him as "the drummer boy of the Rappahannock," as he bore the same name, and might have been the same person whose heroic deeds, in connection with Burnside's attack on Fredericksburg, are now matters of history. He was thrown against the fire-box when the ravine was reached. and literally roasted alive, nothing but a few of his bones being afterwards found.. The engineer was thrown over the lever he was holding in his hands, through the window of the cab, some twenty feet or more. In his flight the lever caught and ripped open his abdomen, and when found he was sitting on the ground holding his protruding bowels in his hands. Next to the engine were two flat-cars loaded with brick. These were landed, brick and all, some thirty or forty feet in front of the engine, while the box cars, loaded with freight, were thrown upon the engine and around the wreck in great disorder. After a time these took fire, and added horror to the scene. The savages now swarmed about the train and whooped and yelled in great glee. When the shock first came, however, the conductor ran ahead on the north side of the track to the engine, and there saw Bowers and Hendershot in the position we have described them. He told them that he must leave them and flag the second section of the train following after, or it, too, would be wrecked. He then ran back, signaled this train, and with it returned to Plum Creek. Arriving there about 2 o'clock in the morning, in vain did he try to get a force of men to proceed at once to the scene of the disaster. No one would go. In the morning, however, they rallied, armed themselves and went out to the wreck. By this time it was near ten o'clock. The burning box cars had fallen around the brave engineer, and while the fiery brands had undoubtedly added to his agony, they had also ended his earthly existence. His blackened and charred remains only told of his suffering. The rescuing party still found the train burning—the Indians had obtained all the plunder they could carry, and left in the early morning. In the first gray dawn of the morning they manifested their delight over the burning train in every possible way, and their savage glee knew no bounds. From the cars not then burned they rolled out boxes and bales of merchandise, from which they took bright-colored flannels, calicos and other fancy goods. Bolts of these goods they would loosen, and with one end tied to their ponies' tails or the horn of their saddles, they would mount and start at full gallop up and down the prairie just to see the bright colors streaming in the wind behind them. But the end of this affair was not yet.

Major North, in command of a company of Pawnee scouts, assisted by a few white soldiers stationed in the neighborhood, hastened to the scene of the late disaster. He followed the trail of the Indians far enough to ascertain that they were southern Cheyennes, and then returned and went into camp at Plum Creek, believing if not pursued, the Indians would soon return on another raid. Subsequent events proved this belief to be true, and they had not long to wait. In about ten days one of the scouts came running into camp from the bluffs south of Plum Creek, and reported that the Indians were coming. He had discovered them in the distance, making their way in the direction of the overland stage station, which they soon after reached. Arriving here, they unsaddled their horses and turned them loose in an old corral to feed and rest. They then began preparations to remain all night. The scouts, however, proposed to find out who and what they were before the evening approached. There were in the command two white commissioned officers—Captain James Murie, and Lieutenant Isaac Davis—two white sergeants and forty-eight Pawnees. The company marched from their camp striaght south to the Platte River, which they crossed; then turning to the left, followed down its banks under the bushes to within about a mile-and-a-half of the creek. Here they were discovered by the Cheyennes. Then there was mounting in hot haste—the Cheyennes at once preparing for the fray. There were one hundred and fifty warriors to be pitted against this small band of fifty-two, all told. As the order to charge was given, the Pawnees set up their war-whoop, slapped their breasts with their hands and shouted "Pawnee!" The opposing lines met on the banks of the creek, through which the scouts charged with all their speed. The Cheyennes immediately broke and fled in great confusion, every man for himself. Then followed the chase, the killing and the scalping. The Indians took their old trail for the Republican Valley, and put their horses to utmost speed to escape the deadly fire of the Pawnees. Night finally ended the chase, and when the spoils were gathered, it was found that fifteen Cheyenne warriors had been made to bite the dust, and their scalps had been taken as trophies of victory. Two prisoners were also taken, one a boy of sixteen, the other a squaw. The boy was a nephew of Turkey Leg, the Chief. Thirty-five horses and mules were also taken while not a man of the scouts was hurt. A company of infantry, under command of Captain John A. Miller, had remained in camp guarding Government and company property, and knowing that a battle had been fought, were intensely anxious to learn the result. When the Pawnees came near, it was with shouts and whoops, and songs of victory. They exhibited their scalps and paraded their prisoners with great joy, and spent the whole night in scalp-dances and wild revelry.

This victory put an end to attacks on railroad trains by the Cheyennes. The boy and the squaw were kept in the camp of the Pawnees until late in the season, when a big council was held by the Brule Sioux, Spotted Tail's band, at North Platte, to make a new treaty. Hearing of this council, Turkey Leg, Chief of the Cheyennes, sent in a runner and offered to deliver up six white captives held in his band for the return of the boy and the squaw. After the necessary preliminaries had been effected, the runner was told to bring the white captives, that the change might be made.

The captives were two sisters by the name of Thompson, who lived south of the Platte River, nearly opposite Grand Island, and their twin brothers; a Norwegian girl, taken on the Little Blue River, and a white child, born to one of these women while in captivity. They were restored to their friends as soon as possible.

## DIXON COUNTY.

Dixon County was organized by Act of the Territorial Legislature, in December, 1858. It lies on the northeastern border of the State, and is bounded on the north by the Missouri River, east by the Missouri River and Dakota County, south by Omaha Indian Reservation and Wayne County, and west by Wayne and Cedar Counties, containing about 450 square miles, or 288,000 acres.

WATER COURSES.—The Missouri River washes the northeastern border of the County. The principal streams of the interior are the Powder, Turkey and Lime Creeks, in the northern part, and Silver, West Branch, Daily, South, and Ayoway Creeks, in the central and southern part of the County. These are all beautiful, clear streams. Ayoway Creek, especially, being a large and superior mill stream, already furnishing power for three flouring mills, with excellent sites for twenty more. Altogether, the County is well watered, every township having one or more living streams passing through it. Springs are abundant.

TIMBER.—On the Missouri bottoms and skirting all the creeks, there is a fine natural growth of timber, the varieties consisting principally of cottonwood, willow, ash, elm, maple, basswood, ironwood, walnut and oak. Dry cottonwood can be bought in the markets at $2.50 per cord. The number of forest trees under cultivation in the County in 1879 was 285,155; hedge fencing seven miles.

FRUIT.—Grapes, plums and several other varieties of wild fruit grow in profusion along the streams. There are at present 3,663 apple, twenty-four pear, twenty-seven peach, 743 plum, and 544 cherry trees, and 267 grape vines under cultivation, and in a thrifty condition.

PHYSICAL FEATURES.—Twenty-five per cent. of the area is fertile bottom land. Ayoway and several of the creeks have very fine valleys. The bluffs of the Missouri are frequently very high and precipitous, but the greater part of the upland is gently rolling prairie, with a good soil, well adapted to agriculture or stock raising.

CROPS.—Number of acres under cultivation in the County, 30,146. The yield of the principal crops was as follows: Winter wheat, three and one-half acres, seventy-five bushels; rye, $189\frac{1}{2}$ acres, 2,514 bushels; spring wheat, 9,480 acres, 404,883 bushels; corn, 6,053 acres, 197,200 bushels; barley, 588 acres, 13,180 bushels; oats, 2,250 acres, 76,719 bushels; sorghum, eighty-one acres, 6,362 gallons; flax, forty-seven acres, 542 bushels; hungarian, eight acres, sixty-five tons; potatoes, 155 acres, 17,945 bushels.

MINERALS.—A fair quality of coal has been taken from the bluffs of the Missouri, in small quantities, for several years past, and recently more extensive beds have been discovered and preparations made for their immediate development.

Lime and building stone, marl, kaolin, and fire-clay, are found in the County.

FIRST SETTLEMENT.—The County was first settled in the spring of 1856, by a small Irish colony who took claims in the valley of South Creek. The steady tide of emigration that at once set in received an unexpected check toward the close of 1857 by the great financial panic of that year and the consequent prostration of all branches of industry. Many of the settlers of this County returned to the East, or removed to localities where the prospect of obtaining immediate employment was better, and but few of them ever returned to their claims. The few who returned and succeeded in tiding over the difficulties of their situation, are to-day the possessors of fine, well-stocked farms.

The first election for County officers took place on the second Monday in December, 1868. The following officers were elected: Commissioners, H. A. Fuller, John Cavanaugh, and John Messinger; Probate Judge, J. B. Denton; Clerk, Edward Arnold; Sheriff, C. F. Putnam.

The first flouring mill in the County was erected on Ayoway Creek, in 1859, by Stough Brothers; but owing to the non-arrival of the machinery, it did not begin operations until 1860.

The first death in the County was that of Mrs. Robert McKenna, in January, 1857.

The first marriage was celebrated in the winter of 1856–7, and was that of Charles Buckman.

The first birth took place in June, 1857—a son to Mrs. Burcham Buson.

The first term of the District Court was held at the County Seat on the 16th day of May, 1859; Hon. Eleazer Wakeley, presiding Judge.

There are five Churches in the County, viz: one Presbyterian, two Roman Catholic, one Lutheran and one Methodist.

Three grist mills and five saw mills are now in operation in the County.

The Covington, Columbus and Black Hills Railroad is now in running order to the County Seat, and soon will be extended westward.

It is estimated that at least 25,000 acres in this County are enclosed by substantial post and rail fences.

LAND.—The Burlington and Missouri River Railroad Company owns 12,000 acres of land in this County, the price ranging from $1.25 to $6.00 per acre; and there are, besides, several thousand acres of desirable Government land yet untaken.

TAXABLE PROPERTY.—The amount and valuation of all taxable property of the County, returned for 1879, was as follows: Acres of land, 235,538; average value per acre, $2.41; value of town lots, $51,677; money invested in merchandise, $15,341; money used in manufactures, $9,521; number of horses 2,122, value, $44,974; mules 72, value, $1,587; neat cattle, 6,782, value, $43,323; sheep, 158, value, $153; swine, 2,496, value, $2,372.75; vehicles, 646, value, $7,102; moneys and credits, $8,755; stocks, etc., $3,000; furniture, $3,019; property not enumerated, $11,722; railroads, $11,107; total, $782,388.84

POPULATION.—The following is the population of the County in 1879, by Precincts: Logan, ninety-nine; North Bend, 118; Hookers, 320; Spring Bank, 389; New Castle, 441; Otter Creek, 177; Summer Hill, 201; Galena, 177; Ponca, 1,170; Daily, 299; Ionia, 241; Silver Creek, 414; Clark, eighty-five; South Creek, 130. Total, 4,061.—males, 2,129; females, 1,832.

PUBLIC SCHOOLS.—In 1879, the County had fifty-four school districts, forty-nine school houses and 1,643 children of school age, 832 being males, and 811 females; number of qualified teachers employed, eighty-two—males, thirty-two, females, fifty; total wages paid teachers for the year, $7,127.30; value of school houses, $16,030; value of sites, $525; value of books and apparatus, $471.

### PONCA,

The County Seat, is situated at the confluence of the west and south branches of Ayoway Creek, in the northeastern part of the County, and is at present the terminus of the Covington, Columbus and Black Hills Railroad. It derives its name from the Ponca Indians, who, in recent years, roamed over the hills and plains in this vicinity. Since the advent of the railroad, in 1877, the town has made wonderful improvement, and its business has more than doubled. Three years ago it was a village of three or four hundred inhabitants; to-day it has eight hundred, and is the largest and most flourishing town in this part of the State. It has two good weekly newspapers, the *Courier* and *Journal*, a commodious Court House, excellent school and Church advantages, and business houses representing the various lines of trade.

### NEW CASTLE,

On the west branch, and

### MARTINSBURG,

On the south branch of Ayoway Creek, **are** flourishing villages, with stores, postoffice, schools, etc.

### IONIA AND DIXON

Are bright villages, on the Missouri, besides which there are a number of other close settlements in the County, having a general assortment store, postoffice, etc.

## DAKOTA COUNTY.

Dakota County was created by the first Territorial Legislature, in 1855. It is located on the northeastern border of the State, and is bounded on the north by Dixon County and the Missouri River, east by the Missouri River, south by the Omaha Indian Reserve, and west by Dixon County, containing about 250 square miles, or 160,000 acres.

It is well watered by the Missouri River, Omaha, Elk, and Pigeon Creeks. Omaha Creek is a fine mill stream, with numerous branches, and waters the southeastern portion of the County. Elk Creek, a tributary of the Missouri, waters the western townships and furnishes sufficient power for mills. Pigeon Creek waters the central portion of the County. Every township has running water, and the majority of the streams are well timbered. No returns have been made of the number of forest and fruit trees under cultivation, or of crops.

The bluffs of the Missouri are here very bold. About ten per cent. of the area is bluff, twenty per cent. bottoms, and seventy per cent. rolling prairie. The soil is deep and rich almost everywhere, and is well adapted to the growth of cereals.

Building stone is abundant in this County, and on Elk Creek there are extensive peat beds.

PUBLIC SCHOOLS.—The present number of school districts in the County is thirty-three, school houses, thirty, and children of school age 1,304, of whom 637 are males, and 667 females; qualified teachers employed, fifty-one,—males, twenty-six, females, twenty-five; total wages paid teachers for the year, $2,378.60; value of school houses, $19,375.00; value of sites, $1,655.00; value of books and apparatus, $540.

TAXABLE PROPERTY.—The amount and valuation of the taxable property of the County is as follows: Acres of land, 140,010, average value per acre, $3.33; value of town lots, $47,000; money invested in merchandise, $8,066; money used in manufactures, $3,501; number of horses, 2,140, value $34,095; mules, ninety-two, value, $2,061; neat cattle, 8,520, value, $59,686; sheep, 123, value, $123; swine, 4,411, value, $2,581; vehicles, 522, value, $4,926; moneys and credits, $2,734; mortgages, $13,879; stocks, $204; furniture, $1,753; libraries, $50; property not enumerate $7,954; railroads, $65,904.50; total, $720,780.50.

LAND.—There is a small amount of Government land remaining untaken, and the Burlington & Missouri River Railroad Company owns 5,000 acres here, the price ranging from $1.25 to $6.00 per acre.

RAILROADS.—The Covington, Columbus & Black Hills Railroad traverses the northern portion of this County from east to west, a distance of twenty miles.

POPULATION.—The County is at present divided into six Precincts, the population of each in 1879, being as follows: Omadi, 873; St. Johns, 696; Covington, 805; Summit, 297; Dakota, 262; Pigeon Creek, 295; total population of County, 3,208, of whom 1,717 are males, and 1,491 females.

### DAKOTA CITY,

The County Seat, is situated on a fine plateau overlooking the Missouri, and is also on the line of the Covington, Columbus & Black Hills Railroad. It is a prosperous town of several hundred inhabitants, and commands the shipping trade of an extensive, well-settled agricultural country to the south and west. The *Eagle*, a weekly newspaper, is published here. The Court House is a commodious building, the schools excellent, Church facilities good, and stores and other business places are increasing rapidly.

### JACKSON,

On the Covington, Columbus & Black Hills Railroad, situated several miles west of the County Seat, is the second town of size and importance in the County. It supports a weekly newspaper, the *Herald*, has good schools, neat Churches, a number of fine stores, grain warehouses, etc. The town has grown very rapidly since the railroad reached it three years ago, and the improvements are substantial and permanent.

### COVINGTON,

Situated on the banks of the Missouri, opposite Sioux City, Iowa, is at the head of the Covington, Columbus & Black Hills Railroad, and is improving very rapidly under the patronage of that corporation. It already enjoys a large trade from the surrounding country, and through its advantageous location, promises to become the leading city and business center of the County.

### SUMMIT,

Is a small village and shipping station on the railroad in the northeastern part of the County.

### OMADI,

Is an old settled and flourishing town, situated on Omaha Creek, in the southeastern part of the County. It is a prosperous, growing town, located in the midst of an excellent farming section, the Precinct having a population of 873.

HOMER, RANDOLPH, LODI, and ELK VALLEY are Postoffices in the County.

## DUNDY COUNTY.

Dundy County was created by an Act of the Legislature, in 1873. It is located on the southwestern border of the State, bounded on the north by Chase, and east by Hitchcock County, south by Kansas and west by Colorado, containing 936 square miles, or 599,040 acres.

It is watered by the Republican River and several large tributaries.

County unorganized and sparsely settled. It lies in the great grazing range of the State, and is admirably adapted to stock-raising. It is nearly all Government land.

No report of property, crops, schools, or population.

## FILLMORE COUNTY.

Fillmore County was created in 1855 and organized in the spring of 1871. It is located in the southeastern part of the State, in the fifth tier of Counties west of the Missouri River, and is bounded on the north by York, east by Saline, south by Thayer, and west by Clay County, containing 576 square miles, or 368,640 acres, at an average elevation of 1,600 feet above the sea level.

WATER COURSES.—The West Blue River and its fine tributary, School Creek, water the northwestern townships of the County, the Blue being an excellent mill stream. The north fork of Turkey Creek flows from west to east through the central portion of the County, being supported on either side by numerous rivulets and never-failing springs. Indian Creek waters the northeastern townships, and Little Sandy, South Turkey and Walnut Creeks flow through the southern portion of the County.

TIMBER.—There is a moderate amount of native timber along the streams, the varieties consisting of cottonwood, maple, elm, willow, ash, walnut and oak. Though the early settlers cut down much wood, there are now more timber in the County than on the day when the first white man set foot within its borders. There are now 2,822 acres, or 1,181,134 forest trees under cultivation, besides 108 miles of hedging.

FRUIT.—Small fruits are being successfully grown here, answering the largest anticipations. In 1879, there were 14,037 apple, 509 pear, 24,954 peach, 11,727 plum, and 5,372 cherry trees, and 2,932 grape vines reported under cultivation.

PHYSICAL FEATURES.—The surface of the country consists mostly of gently rolling table lands, having a gradual rise to the westward, the elevation above sea level on the eastern border being 1,550, and on the western border 1,570 feet. There are no sloughs and scarcely any waste land. Along the West Blue River and Turkey Creek there is fine valley lands.

SOIL AND CROPS.—The soil produces all the grains which grow anywhere in the same latitude, and produces them in great abundance. In 1879 there were 98,372 acres reported under cultivation in the County, the yield of the principal crops being as follows:

Winter wheat, 205 acres, 3,205 bushels; rye, 2,144 acres, 31,363 bushels; spring wheat, 49,677 acres, 617,048 bushels; corn, 25,865 acres, 870,244 bushels; barley, 6,062 acres, 160,881 bushels; oats, 4,980 acres, 168,973 bushels; sorghum, thirty-one acres, 410 gallons; flax, 326 acres, 3,301 bushels; hungarian, 470 acres, ninety-four tons, and potatoes 470 acres, 53,391 bushels.

HISTORICAL.—William Bussard and William Whitaker located homesteads in this County as early as June, 1866, several months in advance of any other settlers. In the autumn of this year Nimrod Dixon, J. A. Werts, James Whitaker, and J. H. Malick arrived and secured claims, but Werts and Malick were the only ones who stuck to their claims during the succeeding winter, the others returning to the older settlements in hopes of finding employment while waiting for spring to permit them to commence work upon their claims. They all returned early in the spring, bringing with them the pioneer lady settler of the County, Mrs. E. A. Whitaker, a lady over seventy years of age, who also took a homestead. The first land was broken in May, 1867, by N. G. Dixon. In the spring of 1868 this settlement was strengthened by the arrival of several others, among whom was H. L. Badger, the pioneer surveyor; and during the summer and fall, D. H. Dillon, and a number of others settled on Turkey Creek, in the eastern part of the County. In the spring and summer of 1869, Charles Eberstine, J. F. Snow and others, located in the southeastern part of the County, and in 1870, E. L. Martin settled on the West Blue, in the northwestern part, where he laid off the town of Fillmore, the first town started. Here the first stock of dry goods and groceries were opened by J. E. Porter, and the first Postoffice in the County was established here in March, 1871, with E. L. Martin as postmaster. In April, 1871, Elder E. R. Spear, of the Methodist Church, settled on Turkey Creek, and he was for a long time the only regular minister in the County. His first sermon was preached at the residence of Colonel McCalla, on the second Sabbath in May, 1871. During the year 1871, C. H. Bane and J. W. Eller, the first attorneys, and Dr. H. F. King, the first physician, settled in the County, and before the close of that year settlements had been made so rapidly that all the valuable claims were taken, and much of the Burlington & Missouri Railroad land sold.

Franklin Precinct, in the southeastern part of the County, not being covered by a railroad land grant, settled up more rapidly than any other precinct, and at the organic election it was found to contain more voters than all the remainder of the County; yet, strange as it may appear, the citizens of that precinct voted the seat of justice at the center of the County.

The organic election was held at the residence of N. McCalla, on the 21st day of April, 1871, at which time the seat of justice was established at the geographical center of the County, and the following County officers were elected, viz: Commissioners, E. L. Martin, C. H. Bassett, and Jesse Lee; Clerk, H. L. Badger; Treasurer, Wilber Duel; Sheriff, J. F. Snow; Judge, William H. Blain; Superintendent Public Instruction, G. R. Wolfe; Surveyor, H. L. Badger; Coroner, T. E. Burnett.

PUBLIC SCHOOLS.—Number of school districts in the County in 1879, seventy-seven; number of school houses, seventy-four; number of male children of school age, 1,649; female 1,440; total 3,089; total number that attended school during the year, 2,138; number of qualified teachers employed, 115—males, forty, females seventy-five; wages of male teachers for the year, $5,021.66; wages of female teachers, $7,376.30; total, $12,397.96; value of school houses, $36,733.00; value of sites, $1,311.25; value of books, etc., $921.50.

TAXABLE PROPERTY.—The following is a statement of the taxable property of the County as returned for 1879: Acres of land, 314,285, average value per acre, $3.02; value of town lots, $77,750; money invested in merchandise, $67,885; money used in manufactures, $2,185; number of horses, 4,329, value, $113,895; mules, 465, value, $14,373; neat cattle, 5,429, value, $49,489; sheep, 2,765, value, $2,064; swine, 18,162, value, $7,213; vehicles, 1,615, value, $23,629; moneys and credits, $15,121; mortgages, $23,634; stock, $300; furniture, $14,356; libraries, $1,894; property not enumerated, $47,528; railroad property, $193,169.60; total, $1,603,470.60.

RAILROADS AND LANDS.—The only railroad at present traversing this County is the Burlington & Missouri River, which passes from east to west through the upper tier of townships, and was constructed in 1871. The Burlington & Missouri Company owns

5,000 acres of land here, its price ranging from $5 to $9 per acre. Government land all occupied.

POPULATION.—The County is divided into sixteen voting Precincts, the population of each in 1879 being as follows: Exeter, 728; Glengary, 474; Fairmount, 1,126; Chelsea, 427; West Blue, 575; Stanton, 367; Grafton, 612; Momence, 396; Bennett, 443; Bryant, 369; Geneva, 855; Hamilton, 399; Madison, 497; Belle Prairie, 355; Liberty, 622; Franklin, 515; total, 8,760—males, 4,766, females, 3,094. The population of the County in 1870, was 238; in 1875, 4,731; increase in last four years, 4,029.

IMPROVEMENTS.—The following is a statement of the value of buildings erected and other improvements made in each Precinct during the year 1878: Exeter, $42,986; Glengary, $10,057; Fairmount, $43,838; Chelsea, $10,880; West Blue, $10,275; Stanton, $11,970; Grafton, 23,050; Momence, $10,675; Bennett, $16,775; Bryant, $8,975; Geneva, $24,285; Hamilton, $8,270; Madison, $10,950; Belle Prairie, $6,170; Liberty, $17,030; Franklin, $5,630; grand total for the County, $261,816; total number of buildings reported for 1878, 682.

It will be seen from the above that building has been general all over the County. Four and five hundred dollar houses comprise the bulk of the buildings, and very comfortable dwellings can be erected, at the present low price of building material, for either of these given amounts.

## GENEVA,

The County Seat, within a mile of Turkey Creek, occupies one of the prettiest sites for a town in this part of the State. It now has 700 inhabitants. In 1873 a neat frame Court House and jail, combined, was erected at a cost of $4,000. During the past year the town has grown amazingly, and now has some of the largest and most costly buildings in the County, over $7,000 having been expended here in improvements in 1878, and for the present year the increase will be much greater. A railroad to run through this town is now in prospect, and as soon as the same assumes a more definite shape, building will be more rapid and brisk than ever. The *Review*, published here by M. M. Neeves, has been the principal factor in the development of the town, always the leader in every enterprise, always public-spirited, and always the last to desert any scheme calculated to be of importance to Geneva.

### FAIRMONT,

Situated on the line of the Burlington & Missouri R. R., about the center of the County, from east to west, is the largest town in the County, having at present 1,000 inhabitants. It is surrounded by a fine country, and all branches of industry are represented. There are large grain houses, a steam elevator, flouring mills, machine shops, lumber yards, good hotels, merchandise stores, a bank, etc., and an excellent paper, the Fairmont *Bulletin*, published by Mr. L. D. Calkins. It has a graded school, well patronized by town and country, and there are several Church organizations and comfortable houses of worship. Fairmont is one of the most promising towns in south-central Nebraska, and is growing rapidly, the buildings and other improvements made in 1878 amounting to nearly $26,000.

### EXETER,

On the line of the Burlington & Missouri, seven miles east of Fairmont, was laid out in November, 1871, and has 500 inhabitants. Dr. H. G. Smith brought the first stock of goods to Exeter in December, 1871. There are now a number of general merchandise stores, lumber yards, grain warehouses, a fine school house, and several Church organizations. The town has prospered during the year beyond measure. The *Enterprise*, a weekly paper, is published here, by Mr. W. J. Waite.

### GRAFTON,

On the Burlington & Missouri, eight miles west of Fairmont, was laid out in 1875, and now has 400 inhabitants. The first building erected in the town was a large warehouse, by C. M. Northrop. During the past year new business houses, new residences and new public buildings have been erected, giving the town a busy air, and making it one of the best trading and shipping points, for its size, on the road. It has excellent Church and school privileges, several flourishing Societies, and all its town appointments are first class.

#### FILLMORE,

Located on the West Blue River, was laid out in 1870, by Mr. J. L. Martin. It has an excellent water-power flouring mill, but has not made much progress as a town.

## FRANKLIN COUNTY.

Franklin County was created by the Legislature in 1867, and organized in 1871. It is located on the middle-southern border of the State, and is bounded on the north by Kearney, and east by Webster County, south by Kansas, and west by Harlan County, containing 576 square miles, or 368,640 acres.

WATER COURSES.—The Republican River flows from west to east through the southern portion of the County, having a large number of tributaries on either side, the most prominent being Thompson, Cottonwood, Center, Turkey and Lovely Creeks, which have their rise a dozen miles or so back in the prairie, and are fed by innumerable springs and small branches. Water power is abundant.

TIMBER.—The Republican River and tributaries are all skirted with a fine growth of native timber, a large portion of it being hardwood, especially that along the streams on the south side. The uplands are now dotted with large, thrifty artificial groves, sufficiently grown to supply all the fuel needed. In 1879 there were 719,703 forest trees, and sixteen and one-half miles of hedging reported under cultivation.

FRUIT.—This County has made great advancement in fruit-culture and now has many fine orchards in bearing. In 1879 there were 2,130 apple; eighty-nine pear, 5,079 peach, 8,549 plum, 312 cherry trees, and 252½ acres of grape vines in the County.

BUILDING STONE.—A good quality of limestone is found in different parts of the County, and is abundant on the south side of the Republican.

PHYSICAL FEATURES.—About fifteen per cent. of the area is valley, the remainder rolling prairie and occasional bluff. South of the Republican the surface is considerably broken, in the vicinity of the streams. The north half of the County consists of broad tables and gently undulating prairie. The valley of the Republican varies in width from four to eight miles.

SOIL AND CROPS.—The soil is a rich, black vegetable mould, varying from eighteen inches to three feet thick, on the uplands. Franklin County was awarded the champion prize medal at the Nebraska State Fair, in 1876, 1877, and 1878, for the best display agricultural and garden products of all kinds. The acreage under cultivation reported for 1879 was 32,136, the yield of the principal crops being as follows: Winter wheat, $424\frac{1}{2}$ acres, $4,701\frac{1}{2}$ bushels; rye, 1,130 acres, 14,868 bushels; spring wheat, 8,647 acres, 85,545 bushels; corn, 7,557 acres, 199,067 bushels; barley, 423 acres, 7,276 bushel; oats, 1,105 acres, 24,254 bushels; sorghum, thirty-nine and one-fourth acres, 3,140 gallons; broom corn, 356 acres, forty-six and one-half tons; millet and hungarian, 577 acres, 3,124 tons; potatoes, 470 acres, 53,391 bushels.

FIRST SETTLEMENT.—On the 14th of September, 1870, James W. Thompson, W. C. Thompson, Richard Beckwith, John Corbin, Isaac Chapel, and Barnett Ashburn started from Omaha to explore the Republican Valley country with a view to settlement. They crossed the Platte River on the 15th, and passed through Beatrice on the fourth day out, where they crossed the Big Blue. Entering the Republican Valley at Elm Creek, Webster County, they proceeded to a creek within two miles of the east line of Franklin County (now known as Thompson Creek) where they encamped. J. W. Thompson explored this creek to its forks, found it to be a good mill stream and well timbered, with fine bottoms on either side. After inspecting the country as far west as Turkey Creek, they returned and selected claims near the mouth of Thompson Creek, where the town of Riverton now stands, and then started on their return to Omaha, arriving there the latter part of October, of the same year.

About the time the foregoing party were making their explorations, another party, known as the "Knight Colony," were sent out from Omaha by the Republican Land Claim Association to look up a favorable location for settlement. This company selected a site about a mile northwest of the mouth of Center Creek, where they laid out and surveyed Franklin City.

On the first of November, 1870, several families were sent out to the new city by the Association, under the charge of its Vice President, C. J. Van Laningham.

Another company, organized in Plattsmouth, selected a location one mile east of Franklin City, where they laid out the town of Waterloo—the name afterwards being changed to Franklin.

The first claim on Thompson Creek was entered at the Land Office, at Beatrice, in September, 1870, by Burnett Ashburn, on his return to Omaha from his first exploration of the country. William C. Thompson entered the adjoining claim. In March, 1871, the first log house was finished, and in April, the breaking-plow was started.

On Lovely Creek, Thomas Shoemaker, John Hanna. and a Mr. Roberts were among the first settlers. Center Creek was first settled by Messrs. Van Laningham, Van Etten, Thompson, Hagar, Haines, Buster, Ashby, Hunt, Harman, Chapman, Hutchison and Pury. On Vining Creek, Messrs. Vining, Bass, Durant, Blackledge, Hammond, Betts, and Kave were among the first. On Turkey Creek, among the first were Messrs. Sprague, Healy, Marston, Young, Walter Brown, J. M. Brown, Burley, Lloyd, Streets, Ray, Mrs. Wadkins, Bush, Edgerton, Walter Brothers, and Phillips. On Crow Creek, Mr. Stanlow settled in 1871, and Messrs. Gage, Brown, Novinger, Stover, Hawks, Kent and Chalfance, in 1872. Rebecca Creek was first settled by G. L. Thompson, L. M. Moulton, J. F. Zediker, Mrs. Douglas, Albert Dowd, James Douglas, Elam Douglas, Dr. N. L. Whitney, and the Johnson brothers. On Cottonwood Creek the first were the Pugsley family, Messrs. Nixon, Enos J. Haynes, E. Haynes, Pilgers, Bass, Shaffer, J. W. and Jacob Dearey, O. and W. Davis, Harold, and J. Kezer, and brother. J. F. Pugsley, Sr., came out from Omaha in the fall of 1870, and selected claims for himself and sons near the mouth of Cottonwood and Pugsley Creeks, and in May, 1871, he brought out his wife, two sons and two daughters. He has now one of the best improved, well-stocked farms in the County. The first settlers on Pugsley Creek were Gideon Pugsley, Pogle, Morton, Steward, Rev. C. R. Townsend, and Charles H. Townsend.

The first County Fair was held in 1873, with great success.

RAILROADS.—Early in the present year the Republican Valley

branch of the Burlington & Missouri Railroad, was completed through the County from Hastings, and is now in running order.

LANDS.—All the desirable Government land is taken. The Burlington & Missouri River Railroad Company owns 50,000 acres of land in this County, for which they ask from $2 to $5 per acre. The tide of emigration is now very strong, and the broad acres of the County are fast being taken up by sturdy settlers from the eastern States.

This is an excellent country for the stock business. Several stock farms are located on the south side of the Republican, and many on the north side, having from 100 to 300 head of cattle.

PUBLIC SCHOOLS.—The present number of school districts in the County is forty-three; number of school houses, thirty; children of school age—males, 755, females, 697, total, 1,452; qualified teachers employed, forty-four—males, nineteen, females, twenty-five; total wages paid teachers for the year, $3,353.50; value of school buildings, $4,535.00; value of sites, $313.00; value of books, etc., $153.50.

TAXABLE PROPERTY.—The amount and valuation of all taxable property in the County, is as follows: Acres of land, 181,354; average value per acre, $1.04; value of town lots, $18,447; money invested in merchandise, $21,839; money used in manufactures, $5,490; number of horses, 1,659, value, $57,364; mules, 176, value, $7,505; neat cattle, 3,276, value, $32,188; sheep, 1,325, value, $1,088; swine, 4,516, value, $3,700.65; vehicles, 743, value, $13,046; moneys and credits, $6,469; mortgages, $8,209; stocks, etc., $ 788; furniture, $9,495; libraries, $184; property not enumerated, $17,889; total, $392,013.89.

POPULATION.—The population of each Precinct in 1879, was as follows: Grant, 911; Salem, 194; Buffalo, 204; Oak Grove, 247; North Franklin, 387; Turkey Creek, 279; Franklin, 621; Bloomington 523; Macon, 369; Ash Grove, 407; total population of County, 4,137—males, 2,245, females, 1892. Population in 1875, 1,807; increase in four years, 2,330.

BLOOMINGTON,

The County Seat, is the principal town in the County. It is pleasantly located on a southern slope facing the Republican, and has a fine view of the valley for miles in either direction.

The United States Land Office for the Republican Valley is located here. An iron bridge spans the river at this point and brings in a large Kansas trade. Among the different branches of business represented are a bank, nine attorneys, three real estate offices, three hotels, three restaurants, three bakeries, two drug stores, three dry goods, grocery and general merchandise stores, two tin shops, two millinery shops, five lumber yards, two agricultural implement and two furniture stores, three blacksmith, one wagon and two paint shops, five contractors and builders, etc. The religious element is well represented, there being three congregations—Methodist, Presbyterian and Baptist. The Methodists will have a Church building completed this fall. The *Guard*, is a well-sustained weekly paper published here. The town is in a healthy, growing condition, it having about doubled its population and number of buildings since the railroad reached it several months ago.

## RIVERTON,

On the line of the Republican Valley Railroad, near the east line of the County, is a flourishing town of about 500 inhabitants. It is beautifully situated on the Republican, at the mouth of Thompson Creek, and has the best water-power of any town in the valley. The business of the place is represented by one newspaper, the *Reporter*, six general merchandise stores, two hardware, and two drug stores, two millinery and two farm machinery establishments, four restaurants, four meat markets, three blacksmith and wagon shops, one harness shop, one furniture store, three large livery and feed stables, four attorneys, one grain elevator, and two first-class flouring mills. There is a good school house, and the citizens are about to erect a Church.

## NAPONEE,

Is situated two miles from the western line of the County, on the eastern side of Turkey Creek, near its confluence with the Republican. The town was laid out in February, 1879, since which time one hotel, one livery stable, several business houses, and a large number of dwellings have been erected. At present it is a flourishing town and already has a good weekly newspaper, the Naponee *Banner*. The track of the Republican Valley Railroad is completed to this place and trains are now running.

Naponee Mills, containing three run of burrs, are situated here. A wagon bridge across the Republican at this point is now in course of construction.

MACON, MOLINE, ASH GROVE, WEST SALEM, STOCKTON, AMAZON and LANGDON are villages in different parts of the County, with school house, general store, Postoffice, etc.

FRANKLIN and MARION are stations on the railroad, and have promising futures.

## FRONTIER COUNTY.

Frontier County was organized in 1872. It lies in the southwestern part of the State, bounded on the north by Lincoln and Dawson, east by Gosper, south by Gosper, Furnas and Hitchcock, and west by Hayes County, containing 972 square miles, or 622,080 acres.

It is watered by Medicine and Red Willow Creeks, two very prominent tributaries of the Republican, and numerous smaller streams, all flowing in a southeasterly direction. There are some good mill privileges.

This County is chiefly devoted to the stock business and is sparsely settled, the number of its inhabitants being estimated at 626. No report of crops or improvements for this year.

Taxable property reported for 1879 was as follows: Acres of land, 5,722, average value per acre, $1.25; money used in manufacture, $300.00; number of horses, 529, value, $12,541.00; number of mules, eighteen, value, $480.00; number of cattle, 8,672, value $60,704.00; number of sheep, 1,471, value, $1,102.25; number of swine, eighty-six, value, $107.00; vehicles ninety-seven, value, $1,576.00; moneys and credits, $1,810.00; mortgages, $350; property not enumerated, $653.00; total, $86,472.75.

There are two school districts in the County, and one hundred and thirty children of school age.

County nearly all Government land. As a stock region it cannot be excelled, and much of it is fine agricultural land.

### STOCKVILLE,

Situated on Medicine Creek, near the geographical center of the County, is the County Seat.

## FURNAS COUNTY.

Furnas County was organized in April, 1873, by proclamation of Governor R. W. Furnas, in honor of whom it was named. It is located on the southern border of the State, bounded on the north by Frontier and Gosper, east by Harlan County, south by Kansas, and west by Red Willow County, containing 720 square miles, or 460,800 acres.

WATER COURSES.—The County is well watered by the Republican River and its several large tributaries. The Republican flows from west to east through the upper portion of the County, being supported on the north by Medicine, Deer, Elk, Muddy and Turkey Creeks, all fine large streams. Through the central and southern portion of the County flow Beaver and Sappa Creeks, magnificent streams, tributaries of the Republican, which are supported by innumerable small creeks and springs. Water-power in great abundance.

TIMBER.—The Republican, Beaver, Sappa and several of the smaller streams are well timbered. In 1879 there were 102,093 forest trees under cultivation.

FRUIT.—The number of fruit trees under cultivation at present is as follows: Apple, 573; pear, seventy-six; peach, 1,212; plum 289; cherry forty-nine. Grapes and plums grow in profusion on all the streams.

BUILDING STONE is abundant.

PHYSICAL FEATURES.—About thirty per cent. of the area is valley, five per cent. bluff, and the balance rolling prairie. The Valley of the Republican varies in width from two to five miles, and the valleys of the Beaver and Sappa are here also very wide, fertile and beautiful.

SOIL AND CROPS.—The soil is everywhere mellow and rich, the uplands yielding splendid crops of small grain. The area under cultivation reported for 1879 was 12,630 acres. The yield of the principal crops was as follows: Winter wheat, 581 acres, 10,181 bushels; rye, 2,080 acres, 42,004 bushels; spring wheat, 3,472 acres, 49,429 bushels; corn, 3,662 acres, 80,687 bushels; barley, 554 acres, 16,380 bushels; oats, 394 acres, 13,953 bushels; sorghum, fifty-three and five-eighths acres, 4,138 gallons; broom corn, twenty and one-fourth acres, twelve tons; hungarian, $381\frac{1}{2}$ acres, 108 tons; potatoes, ninety-two acres, 10,844 bushels.

FIRST SETTLEMENTS.—In September, 1870, Galen James, alone, made his way up the valley of Beaver Creek from the stockade on the Republican River, where the town of Melrose is now situated, to the junction of Sappa Creek with the Beaver, in what was then called James County, and there built himself a "dug-out." Here he lived alone for a year and a half, seeing no white persons, except when in rare instances he visited the stockade, or some of the early settlers on the Republican.

In the spring of 1871, Theodore Phillips, with his family, settled on the Republican, at the mouth of Turkey Creek, being the first of a large settlement now known as New Era.

Shortly after this, John and Ben Arnold located near the mouth of Dry Creek, and were the first settlers upon that stream. About this time J. B. Burton pitched his tent at Burton's Bend, in the western part of the County, where he soon gathered around him a number of families, and in the fall of 1872 obtained the establishment of a Postoffice. In July, 1871, G. W. Love and family settled near where the town of Arapahoe is situated. Early in the spring of 1872, a company consisting of Captain E. W. Murphy, Charles Brown, and G. W. Calvin, arrived and surveyed the town site of Arapahoe.

In April, 1872, Eugene Dolph and John Mitchell settled upon Beaver and Sappa creeks respectively, and were the first settlers in the County south of the Republican, after Galen James. In May and June of the same year, the greater part of the most valuable land in the Beaver valley as far west as Beaver City, and in the Sappa valley as far west as Richmond, was taken up as homesteads by a good class of settlers, mainly from the North-Western States. H. W. Brown located a claim upon the present town site of Richmond, on the 15th of June, 1872, and in November following had a Postoffice established there for the accommodation of the settlers —this being the first Postoffice in the County south of the Republican.

In May, 1872, C. A. Wilson, James A. Gibson, J. R. Johnson,

and George Soper passed up the Beaver, and began a settlement in the western part of the County, which was at first known as Wild Turkey, but is now called Wilsonville. This settlement increased rapidly, and in the spring of 1873 a Postoffice was established, with Miss Jennie Plumb as postmistress.

During the year 1872, settlers arrived in rapid succession, several towns were laid out, and Postoffices established in various parts of the County.

The first general election for County officers was held on April 8, 1873, at which a full board of County officers were elected, and the County Seat located at Beaver City.

PUBLIC SCHOOLS.—The number of school districts in 1879 was 35; school houses, 19; children of school age—males, 538; females, 431, total 969; number of qualified teachers employed—males 18, females 15; amount of wages paid teachers for the year, $1,262; value of school houses, $2,619; value of sites, $254.54.

TAXABLE PROPERTY.—The following is a statement of the taxable property of the County for 1879: Acres of land, 78,067, average value per acre, $2.15; value of town lots, $14,799; money invested in merchandise, $19,435; money used in manufactures, $5,928; number of horses 1674, value $46,342; number of mules 135, value $5,393; neat cattle 4,229, value $38,265; sheep 2,267, value $2,267; swine 1434, value $1,397; vehicles 555, value $9,031; moneys and credits, $11,392; mortgages, $11,873; furniture, $4,948; libraries, $226; property not enumerated, $17,701; total, $356,659.

LANDS.—There is a small amount of good government land left. The price of wild lands ranges from $1.25 to $5.00 per acre. The Republican Valley Railroad is now in running order to the west line of Franklin County, twenty-four miles distant, and is being rapidly pushed toward Furnas.

POPULATION.—The following are the names of the Precincts and the population of each in 1879: Burton's Bend, 288; Arapahoe, 449; New Era, 426; Beaver City, 998; Wilsonville, 230; Spring Green, 203; Richmond, 288. Total population of County, 2,982—males 1,711; females 1,271.

BEAVER CITY,

The County Seat, is the largest town in the County, about 500 population, and is an excellent business center. It is beautifully situated on the north bank of Beaver Creek, which is here spanned by a good wagon bridge, facilitating trade with the southern portion of the County and Northern Kansas. The first store was opened in October, 1873, by McKee & Denham. In June, 1873, the town site was surveyed, and in the fall of the following year Monell & Lashley's grist and saw mills were completed. Since, the town has been constantly improving, and now has several well-stocked stores, lumber yards, grain warehouses, hotels, good school and court-house, and a weekly newspaper, the *Times*.

### ARAPAHOE,

Situated on the Republican, near the mouth of Muddy Creek, in the north-central part of the County, is an excellent business point. The town site was surveyed in the spring of 1872, and the first house completed on the 9th of August of that summer, by G. W. Calvin. It now has several stores and other business establishments, a good grist-mill, and a newspaper. It is the nearest point in the County to the Union Pacific Railroad, about thirty miles distant, and the greater part of the freighting passes through it.

### NEW ERA

Is a thriving village, situated on the Republican, about ten miles northeast of the County Seat. Mr. Theodore Philips and family came here in the spring of 1871, and were the first settlers. It has an excellent school house, and several lines of business are represented.

### BURTON'S BEND

Is a village on the Republican, five miles west of Arapahoe. It was started by J. B. Burton in 1871, and in the following year a Postoffice and store was established. The town is gradually improving.

### WILSONVILLE

Is a rapidly growing town, located on the north side of Beaver Creek, in the western part of the County. The first settlements were made here in 1872; a Postoffice was established in the spring of 1873, and in August of the same year Mr. L. M. Wilson, after whom the town is named, opened a general merchandise store.

### RICHMOND

Is located on the Sappa, directly south of the County Seat. Mr. H. W. Brown was the first settler, he locating here on the 15th of June, 1872. A Postoffice was established here in November, 1872.

LYNDEN, SPRING GREEN, ROCKTON, PRECEPT, MIDWAY, WILMOT, CARRISBROOKE, WHITNEY and BUFFALO, are Postoffices in the County.

## GAGE COUNTY.

Gage County was created by the Legislature, in 1855, and organized in July, 1857. It lies in the southeastern part of the State, in the third tier of Counties west of the Missouri, and is bounded on the north by Lancaster, and east by Johnson and Pawnee Counties, south by Kansas and Otoe Indian Reserve, and west by Jefferson and Saline Counties, containing 680 square miles, or 435,200 acres.

WATER COURSES.—The Big Blue River is the principal stream of the County. It flows diagonally through the central portion, from the northwest to the southeast corner, and has a large number of tributaries on either side, which, with their branches, extend through and drain nearly every township in the County. Its principal tributaries are Bear, Indian, Mud, and Cub Creeks. The Blue furnishes unlimited water-power, and is not excelled in the State as a mill-stream.

The Great Nemaha River and branches water the northeastern townships.

TIMBER.—Native timber is more than ordinarily plentiful in this County, the Blue and many of its tributaries being well skirted with forest trees and an occasional beautiful grove. In 1879 the County had 603,682 forest trees and 115 miles of hedging under cultivation.

FRUIT.—Like in all the southeastern Counties of Nebraska the settlers of Gage gave early attention to fruit culture, and now possess many fine orchards bearing the choicest varieties. The kinds and quantity under cultivation in 1879 were: Apple trees, 27,641; pear, 647; peach, 42,865; plum, 2,496; cherry, 7,360; grape vines, 2,572.

BUILDING MATERIAL.—Magnesian limestone of the finest quality is found in abundance on the Blue. Extensive quarries have long been in operation at Beatrice, and large quantities of the stone taken therefrom were used in the construction of the public buildings at Lincoln. Good brick clay is plentiful, and potter's clay of a superior quality is also found here.

CHARACTER OF THE LAND.—The wide and magnificent valley of the Big Blue, with the smaller valleys of its tributaries, comprise about twenty-five per cent. of the area, the balance consisting of rolling prairie table and a very small per cent. bluff. The hills skirting the larger streams are generally low and rounded and easily tilled. The soil is described as a rich, dark vegetable mould, intermixed with sand and lime, and ranging in depth from one and a half to three feet.

CROPS.—Area under cultivation, 75,496 acres. Winter wheat, 1,356 acres, 26,812 bushels; spring wheat, 24,118 acres, 208,412 bushels; rye, 1,649 acres, 22,824 bushels; Corn, 29,789 acres, 938,956 bushels; barley, 2,495 acres, 52,271 bushels; oats, 4,636 acres, 154,297 bushels; buckwheat, sixteen acres, 742 bushels; sorghum, seventy-six acres, 10,168 gallons; flax, ninety-three acres, 446 bushels; hungarian, 136 acres, 287 tons; potatoes, 234 acres, 28,984 bushels; onions, 952 bushels.

HISTORICAL.—On the morning of the 3d of April, 1857, the steamer Hannibal, then plying up and down the Missouri, left the levee at St. Louis, bearing on board a numerous collection of western-bound immigrants, representing almost every State in the Union. Old men and women, the middle-aged and young, the rich and the poor, the learned and unlearned, mechanics, artisans, farmers, laborers, and professional men, some seeking homes in the then Territories of Kansas and Nebraska, others looking still farther on toward the shores of the Pacific coast.

Among this promiscuous gathering were the first settlers of the now beautiful and flourishing town of Beatrice, some of whom have held honorable positions in the State, some have wandered beyond their comrades' visions, and others sleep in honored graves.

Thirty-five persons on board the steamer organized themselves into a company or colony, bound together by a written constitution and by-laws. Among the signers were J. B. Weston, who has filled the office of State Auditor for three successive terms; Judge John F. Kinney, of Nebraska City; G. T. Loomis, J. R. Nelson, and Albert Towle, prominent citizens of Beatrice; the lamented Dr. H. M. Reynolds, Bennett Pike, and the late John McConihe.

An exploring committee, consisting of J. B. Weston, Bennett Pike, H. F. Cook, Dr. Wise, and Judge Kinney, was sent out to select a favorable location for the colony. They chose the present town site of Beatrice (so named in honor of Judge Kinney's daughter), as the most desirable; and at a meeting of the company at Omaha, on the 22d of May, it was adopted as the future home of the colony.

After the spot was decided upon, a portion of the company started at once to commence operations on the town site, which was then four days' journey from Nebraska City, with only a few scattered settlements intervening over what is now a thickly-settled and wealthy country.

David Palmer, who lost his life in the latter part of June, 1876, by drowning, while swimming in the Big Blue, settled in the County some time before the arrival of the thirty-five constituting the Beatrice Town Company, and is generally supposed to have been the first settler.

There is no uncertainty, however, as to who was the first woman that came into the County, for all agree that it was Mrs. J. P. Mumford.

Mr. Mumford, with his wife and two men, had crossed the Missouri in search of a suitable location for settlement, and entering Gage County, were seen by one of the Beatrice people, who carried the news to camp. The presence of a woman so near the camp caused great excitement; and eager to gain so valuable an acquisition to the little colony, all hands turned out to welcome the party and induce them to stop at Beatrice, which was readily accomplished.

Mrs. Mumford shortly afterward opened a boarding-house for

the accommodation of the members of the Town Company, who made it a paying business during the summer of 1857.

The Fourth of July was celebrated in grand style. A number of persons came out from Nebraska City, among whom were Judge Kinney and his daughter, Beatrice. The national colors were presented to the Town Company, by Miss Beatrice, in a neat and appropriate speech, which was responded to by Bennett Pike, on behalf of the company, in a very felicitous manner.

The first election was held on July 16, 1857, and resulted as follows: Albert Towle and Dr. H. M. Reynolds, Commissioners; O. B. Hewett, Probate Judge; and P. M. Favor, Sheriff.

At the time of holding the first election, the total population of the County was thirty-three men and one woman, and each candidate received just thirty-three votes.

The Sheriff never made an arrest during his two-years' term; neither did "His Honor" have a case in that time. J. P. Mumford, the first Treasurer, served two years without collecting a cent or paying a warrant. Lawrence Johnson served one year as County Clerk for fifty cents.

The town of Beatrice was pretty well deserted by its inhabitants during the winter of 1857-8. The few who remained and braved the hardships of that first winter experienced much suffering for food before the dawning of spring.

Settlements were made on Bear, Indian and Cub Creeks, and at Blue Springs, in the latter part of 1857 and spring of 1858. The names of a few of those who located on Bear and Indian Creeks, near Beatrice, are Joseph Proud, Ira Dixon, Samuel Jones, John Pethoud, John Wilson, George Mumford, a family by the name of Austin, M. C. Kelley, J. H. Butler, and Orr Stevens, whose names appear upon the records of the County, in connection with the organization of Beatrice. Samuel Kilpatrick, familiarly known as "Uncle Sammy," whose death occurred in 1875, together with L. Y. Coffin, Thomas and Joseph Clyne, William Webb, Charles Buss, F. R. Roper, J. B. Roper, and others, settted on Cub Creek. James H. Johnson, Jacob Poff, R. A. Wilson, Ruel Noyes, Jacob Chambers, and a family named Elliott, settled at Blue Springs. William Tyler and C. C. Coffinberry settled in the vicinity. S. M. Hazen and F. H. Dobbs settled on Mud Creek.

The extreme northern part of the County was not settled until about 1862, with the exception of a few who had located on the Great Nemaha, in Adams Precinct. John Adams, John Hillman, John Shaw, George Gale, John Lyon, Joseph Stafford, Frank Proudfit, S. P. Shaw, William Silvernail, William Shaw, L. Silvernail, John Stafford, Lewis Hildebrand, Val. Kebler, J. Fisk, and Frank Pillmore, are a few of the first settlers in this locality.

David Palmer, Mr. Dewey, Jonathan Sharp, N. D. Cain, and others, settled on Plum Creek, in the southeastern part of the County, at a very early date.

The first death in the County was that of M. W. Ross, one of the original Town Company, which occurred at Beatrice in the winter of 1857.

The first birth occurred early in 1858, was a son to a Mr. Cross, who lived in a "dug-out" on Indian Creek.

Miss Katie Towle was the first female child born in the County.

The first school house was built at Beatrice, on the property known as the "School Block;" and the first teacher was a Mrs. Francis Butler.

The first mail route through the County was established in 1860, from Nebraska City *via* Beatrice, to Marysville, Kansas. Joseph Sanders was the first mail carrier. He brought the first mail into Beatrice on the 3d day of October.

The *Blue Valley Record*, established at Beatrice in 1867, was the first newspaper published.

On the 5th of July, 1857, after the inhabitants had exhibited their patriotism by celebrating the national anniversary, they assembled together for religious devotion, the Rev. D. H. May, Pastor of the M. E. Church at Nebraska City, officiating, who then delivered the first sermon preached in the County.

The Presbyterian Church of Beatrice was organized in 1869, by the Presbytery of Nebraska City. The building is a commodious and elegant edifice.

In April, 1871, the Episcopal Church of Beatrice was organized as a Mission Station, and two years thereafter it was organized as a Parish, under the name of Christ Church. In the summer of 1874 a neat edifice was erected, at a cost of $3,000.

The Christian Church of Beatrice was organized in October, 1872. In the summer of 1874, an edifice was erected at a cost of $2,500.

The First Baptist Church of Beatrice was organized in the fall of 1873, and in the following year a neat edifice was erected, at a cost of $1,400.

The United Brethren Church of Beatrice was organized on the 14th of December, 1874, and have since erected a commodious house of worship.

The German Baptists, or "Dunkards," organized a Church in the County on the 9th of June, 1875, which is in a flourishing condition.

The German Methodist Church, in Clatonia Precinct, was organized in 1870, and an edifice erected in the following year, at a cost of about $1,000. In 1875, the Lutherans organized a Society here, and have secured land for an edifice, cemetery, school house, and parsonage. Religious services are also held by the Congregationalists, Methodists, and the Church of God, in the several school houses in the Precinct.

The M. E. Church of Blue Springs was organized in 1859, and an edifice of stone erected in 1869. The Evangelical Association and Adventists also hold regular services at this place.

The M. E. Church in Adams Precinct was organized in 1867, and in 1874 built a parsonage at a cost of $500. A Baptist Society was organized in the same Precinct in 1870.

A Society of the Church of God was organized in the northwestern part of the County in 1874. Services are held every Sabbath.

The Baptists have a Church on Plum Creek, in Liberty Precinct.

RAILROADS.—There are at present 22.16 miles of railroad in the County; the Burlington & Missouri River having thirteen, and the Atchison & Nebraska 9.16 miles. The B. & M. reached Beatrice through the valley of the Big Blue, in November, 1871. The Atchison & Nebraska road passes up the valley of the Great Nemaha, across the northeast corner of the County, and was built in 1872.

PUBLIC SCHOOLS.—Districts in the County, eighty-seven;

school houses, seventy-five; children of school age—males 1,854, females 1,614, total 3,468; qualified teachers employed—males, seventy-one, females, sixty-seven, total, 138; wages paid teachers for the year—males, $10,082.33, female, $7,777, total, $17,859.33; value of school houses, $36,858; value of sites, $3,277; value of books and apparatus, $1,787.26.

TAXABLE PROPERTY.—Acres of land, 414,196; average value per acre, $2.13. Value of town lots, $216,489. Money invested in merchandise, $63,141; money used in manufactures, $3,430; horses 5,070, value $110,504; mules and asses 490, value $12,820; neat cattle 10,359, value $74,244; sheep 13,377, value $12,528; swine 20,994, value $22,286; vehicles 1,616, value $20,051; moneys and credits, $20,461; mortgages, $14,576; stocks, etc., $500; furniture, $3,950; other personalty, $30,000; libraries, $1,745; railroad, $149,879.05; total valuation, $2,054,574.05.

LANDS.—The price of wild lands ranges from $4 to $12, and improved $7 to $25 per acre, The B. & M. Company owns 9,000 acres in this County, for which they ask from $5 to $8 per acre.

MILLS.—There are four flouring and several saw-mills in the County, with excellent sites for many more.

POPULATION.—The County is divided into sixteen Precincts, the population of each in 1879 being as follows: Beatrice, 2,606; Blue Springs, 896; Clatonia, 645; Paddock, 598; Blakeley, 540; Cicily Creek, 541; Liberty, 526; Rockford, 507; Grant, 463; Highland, 460; Mud Creek, 437; Adams, 385; Nemaha, 339; Holt, 327; Bear Creek, 191; Hooker, 171. Total 9,629, of whom 5,196 are males, and 4,433 females. Population of County in 1875, 5,714; increase in last four years, 3,915.

### BEATRICE,

The County Seat, is beautifully located in the valley of the Big Blue, near the geographical center of the County, and is at present the terminus of a southeastern branch of the B. & M. Railroad. It is handsomely built up, and is one of the largest and most attractive towns in Southeastern Nebraska. Its present population is 1,700. Among the buildings of note are a neat $16,000 court-house, an $18,000 school house, a $15,000 flouring mill, and several Churches, ranging in cost from $2,000 to $8,000 each. There are many elegant brick business blocks and beautiful private residences surrounded with shade trees and shrubbery. Beatrice, being the terminus of a railroad, is the shipping point for the stock and grain of a large scope of country on the south. It also has three excellent newspapers, the *Courier*, *Express*, and *Leader*. Good bridges span all the streams in the vicinity. The U. S. Land Office is located here.

BEATRICE COURT HOUSE.

### BLUE SPRINGS

Is a thriving village of several hundred inhabitants, located on the Blue. about eight miles southeast of Beatrice. It was first settled in 1857. The surrounding country is a fertile agricultural region, and well settled. The town commands a large trade, and is improving rapidly. It has excellent school and Church privileges, and a weekly newspaper, the *Reporter*.

#### ADAMS,

On the Atchison & Nebraska Railway, is the shipping point for the northern portion of this and the adjoining Counties of Johnson and Otoe. It has a splendid location, and is a good business center.

Besides the above, there are eighteen other villages in the County, each having a Postoffice, stores, good school and Church advantages.

## GREELEY COUNTY.

Greeley County, named in honor of Hon. Horace Greeley, was organized in 1872. It is located in the sixth tier of Counties west of the Missouri River, in the central part of the State from north to south, and is bounded on the north by Wheeler, east by Boone, south by Howard, and west by Valley County, containing 576 square miles, or 368,640 acres, at an average elevation of 2,000 feet above the sea level.

WATER COURSES.—The County is watered by the North Fork of the Loup River and several large tributaries. The North Fork flows through the southwestern portion, and is a good mill stream. Its principal branches in this County are Fish, Wallace, Babcock, Shepard, Stewart, Willow and Davis Creeks, the latter stream having a flouring mill upon it. Spring Creek waters the central portion, and Cedar Creek the northeastern portion of the County.

TIMBER.—The natural timber is confined to the small quantities along the streams, cottonwood and elm being the most abundant. Some very fine cedar timber is found along the stream bearing that name, and in the bluffs. Thrifty artificial groves surround almost every farm house.

STONE.—A good building stone is found in the bluffs of the North Fork.

TOPOGRAPHY.—About one-fourth of the County is valley—the balance rolling prairie and bluff. The valley of the North Fork is here from two to four miles wide, and is usually skirted on both sides with a high range of bluffs. Cedar Valley varies in width from one and a half to three miles. The uplands possess a dark, rich soil, and produce excellent crops of small grain. Nutritious grasses and running water are abundant, affording fine advantages for sheep and cattle raising.

CROPS.—Acres under cultivation, $4,685\frac{1}{4}$. Rye 177 acres, 2,323 bushels; spring wheat $1,992\frac{3}{4}$ acres, 24,302 bushels; corn $1,005\frac{1}{2}$ acres, 19,670 bushels; barley 143 acres, 3,402 bushels; oats $418\frac{3}{4}$ acres, 13,673 bushels; sorghum $6\frac{7}{8}$ acres, 851 gallons; potatoes $52\frac{1}{4}$ acres, 6,737 bushels.

HISTORICAL.—The first permanent settlements in the County were made in August, 1871, by S. C. Scott, A. Shepard and J. G. Kellog, who came from Illinois and located on Shepard Creek, on the north side of the Loup.

November 1, 1871, Messrs. A. P. Fish, L. E. Gaffy and J. M. Talmadge located claims on Fish Creek. Mr. Gaffy built the first house in the County, into which he and Mr. Fish moved in February, 1872, Mr. Fish's family arriving in May following.

Claims were taken on Cedar Creek in 1872, Mr. William Shaw being one of the first to locate here.

In 1874, O. M. Harris, T. McKernan, and others, located on Spring Creek, and soon afterwards the town of Eldorado was laid out and a Postoffice established.

The first woman in the County was Mrs. James Wallace, of Virginia, who came in 1872. She shortly afterwards, however, returned to her home in the East. Mrs. Gray, who still resides in the County, was the first permanent lady settler.

The first sod was turned in May, 1872. The first Postoffice was established at Lamartine, on the Loup, in 1873, with Mr. A. P. Fish postmaster. The first marriage occurred in April, 1874, and was that of Mr. A. N. Bradt to Miss Clara Harlow. The first birth was a son to Mr. and Mrs. John Sheldon, in July, 1873. The first death in the County occurred in September, 1875, and was that of Job Skay, an old gentleman over seventy years of age, who was thrown from a load of hay and instantly killed.

The first general election for County officers was held at the house of Mr. A. P. Fish, on the 13th of October, 1872, and resulted as follows: A. P. Fish, A. Shepard, and T. C. Davis, Commissioners; E. B. Fish, Clerk; S. C. Scott, Treasurer; M. Davis, Surveyor; J. G. Kellog, Superintendent Public Instruction; George Hillman, Probate Judge; G. W. Babcock, Sheriff; C. Wellman, Coroner.

PUBLIC SCHOOLS.—Number of school districts, thirteen; school houses, four; children of school age—males 129, females 141; total, 270; whole number of children that attended school during the year, 139; number of qualified teachers employed—males four, females ten; total, fourteen; wages paid teachers for the year—males $176.75, females $796; total, $972.75; total value of school property, $1,865.

TAXABLE PROPERTY.—Acres of land, 184,673; average value per acre, $0.83. Value of town lots, $910. Money invested in merchandise, $605; money used in manufactures, $720; number of horses 307, value $11,821; number of mules 33, value $1,461; neat cattle 1272, value $11,237; sheep 78, value $98; swine 395, value $617; vehicles 160, value $3,641; moneys and credits, $745; mortgages, $406; furniture, $1,763; libraries, $140; property not enumerated, $6,028. Total valuation, $194,866.

LANDS.—There is considerable fine government land in this County subject to entry under the homestead and pre-emption laws. The value of improved lands ranges from $4 to $12 per acre. The Burlington & Missouri River Railroad Company owns 135,000 acres here, for which they ask from $1 to $5 per acre.

POPULATION.—The following is the population of the County by Precincts: Scotia, 282; Adell, 79; Cedar Valley, 146; Spring Creek, 146; O'Connor, 140. Total 753, of whom 436 were males and 317 females. The population of the County in 1878 was 473; increase in last year, 280.

## LAMARTINE,

On the Loup, in the southwestern part of the County, was one of the first points settled. It contains a couple of dozen dwellings, a hotel, two general merchandise stores, a blacksmith shop, school house, etc., and is surrounded by a fertile farming country. The streams in the vicinity are spanned by substantial bridges. On Davis Creek, close at hand, there is a good flouring mill.

## SCOTIA,

On the Loup, four miles north of Lamartine, is the largest town in the County, having about 250 inhabitants. It contains a hotel, blacksmith shop, several stores and other business houses, and a weekly newspaper, the *Tribune*.

### HALIFAX

Is a thriving young village on the Cedar, in the northeastern part of the County. It has a good general merchandise store, hotel, school house, etc.

### O'CONNOR

Is a flourishing young town recently laid out near the geographical center of the County. It was made the County Seat at the general election held in the spring of 1879. The town was settled by an Irish colony, and is improving very rapidly, having at present over 100 inhabitants. A large amount of land has been purchased from the B. & M. R. R. this year, for another Irish colony, who are expected in the early spring of next year.

## GOSPER COUNTY.

Gosper County was organized in 1873. It is located in the southwestern part of the State, on the divide between the Platte and Republican Rivers, and is bounded on the north by Frontier and Dawson, east by Phelps, south by Furnas, and west by Frontier County, containing 468 square miles, or 299,520 acres.

WATER COURSES.—The Platte River touches the northeast corner of the County. Plum Creek, a tributary of the Platte, and the most important stream in the County, being large enough for mill purposes, flows from west to east entirely across the northern tier of townships. Stinking Water, Muddy, Elk, Wild Turkey and a number of smaller Creeks, have their rise in the central part of this County, and flow in a southerly course into the Republican.

TIMBER.—There is very little native timber in the County. Plum Creek and a few of the other streams have a light sprinkling of cottonwood, box elder, ash, elm, etc., along their banks, but no large groves. Young and thrifty artificial groves adorn many farms. No report of the number of forest trees under cultivation.

PHYSICAL FEATURES.—The surface of the country consists mainly of undulating upland, with about ten per cent. bottom and five per cent. bluff. Plum Creek has a very fine valley, and there are wide reaches of beautiful bottom land along the streams in the southern part of the County.

SOIL AND CROPS.—With the exception of a narrow sandy strip along the Platte bottom, the soil throughout the County is generally rich and productive, especially for small grain. The area reported under cultivation for 1879 was 1,735 acres. The yield of the principal crops was as follows: Winter wheat, forty-six acres, 726 bushels; rye, 341 acres, 4,861 bushels; spring wheat, 586 acres, 7,768 bushels; corn, 488 acres, 8,186 bushels; barley, 194 acres, 3,713 bushels; oats, seventy-four acres, 2,642 bushels; potatoes, six acres, 900 bushels.

HISTORICAL.—Otto Renze made the first permanent settlement in the County, in the fall of 1871. He was followed slowly by others, who, leaving the great thoroughfares along the Platte and Republican Valleys, selected choice claims along Plum Creek, in northern part of the County, and on Muddy, Elk, and Turkey Creeks, in the southern part.

The first religious meetings were held at the residence of Rev. T. G. Davis, a Baptist Minister, on Elk Creek.

The organic election was held on the open prairie, near the geographical center of the County, in May, 1873, and resulted in the election of the following officers: Commissioners—G. H. Jones, H. A. Millard, E. G. Vaughan; Clerk, R. G. Gordon; Daviesville, in the southwestern part of the County, was selected as the County Seat.

The first Postoffice was established at Daviesville, in 1874, and a comfortable school house was also erected there the same year.

PUBLIC SCHOOLS.—There are at present eight school districts in the County, six school houses, and 119 children of school age, of whom sixty-six are males and fifty-three females; number of qualified teachers employed, four; wages paid teachers for the year, $138.88; value of school property, $170.

TAXABLE PROPERTY.—Acres of land, 83,318; average value per acre, $1.27. Number of horses, 275, value, $5,616; number of mules, thirty-one, value $879; number of neat cattle, 819, value,

$6,685; number of sheep, 2,313, value, $1,388: number of swine, 234, value, $183; vehicles, 182, value, $1,599; moneys and credits, $225; furniture, $515; property not enumerated, $552.30. Total valuation, $126,131.95.

LAND.—There is a large amount of both railroad and government land in this County. The price of wild lands here ranges from $1 to $5 per acre. The prairies and meadows produce an abundance of the finest grasses, and cattle and sheep thrive well here with but little attention. The Platte River is spanned by substantial bridges, giving the settlers of the County easy access to the shipping stations on the Union Pacific Railroad.

POPULATION.—The County is divided into five voting Precincts, the population of each, in 1879, being as follows: Turkey Creek, 165; Elk Creek, 164: East Muddy, 118; West Muddy, 155; Robb, twenty-two.

Total population 622, of whom 354 were males and 268 females.

### DAVIESVILLE,

The County Seat, is the only town in the County. It is situated on Muddy Creek, in the southwestern part of the County, and has a couple of good general merchandise stores, a hotel, school house, blacksmith shop, etc.

PLUM CREEK, VAUGHAN'S and JUDSON'S Ranches have each a Postoffice, general store, school house, blacksmith shop, and good accommodations for travelers.

## HALL COUNTY.

Hall County was established by an Act of the Legislature, in 1855, and organized in 1859. It is located in the south-central part of the State, and is bounded on the north by Howard, east by Merrick and Hamilton, south by Adams, and West by Buffalo Counties, containing 576 square miles, or 368,640 acres, at an average elevation of 1,850 feet above the sea level.

WATER COURSES.—The County is finely watered by the Platte and Wood Rivers, Prairie Creek, and numerous smaller streams.

The Platte enters the County at the southwest corner, and flows in a northeasterly course, passing out at the middle of the eastern boundary line. Wood River waters the central portion of the County, and joins the Platte near the eastern line. Prairie Creek, with its numerous branches, waters the northern portion of the County. Mill privileges are abundant, and could be utilized at light expense.

TIMBER.—The islands of the Platte are covered with a thick growth of natural timber, and the banks of the stream are also well skirted. Wood River and some of the smaller streams are well wooded. The amount of timber under cultivation in the County is 1,557 acres, or 1,262,294 trees, besides twelve miles of hedging.

The first fruit trees were planted in the spring of 1863. The first cherries were produced in 1867, the first peaches in 1871, and the first apples and pears in 1872.

FRUIT.—The amount of fruit trees reported under cultivation in 1879 was as follows: Apple, 6,266; pear, 169; peach, 4,559; plum, 10,165; cherry, 1,427; and grape vines, ten acre.

CHARACTER OF THE LAND.—Fully forty per cent of the area is valley, and the balance undulating prairie. South of the Platte, there are no bluffs dividing the bottom and upland, but instead, a succession of plateaus or gentle undulations, terminating in broad tables one hundred feet above the level of the river. The valley on the north side of the Platte is very wide, the first three miles being fine, rich bottom. Wood River has wide bottoms and rich undulating prairie on either side. Northward from this, a fertile, low upland prevails for ten or fifteen miles, in the middle of which is the beautiful little valley of Prairie Creek.

CROPS.—The soil is a deep, black sandy loam, and very productive for all kinds of crops. The area reported under cultivation in the County for 1879, was 49,648 acres. The yield of the principal crops was as follows: Winter wheat, thirty-six acres, 329 bushels; spring wheat, 28,390 acres, 278,202 bushels; rye, 1,994 acres, 27,288 bushels; corn, 10,672 acres, 261,179 bushels; barley, 1,247 acres, 24,872 bushels; oats, 4,879 acres, 122,802 bushels; potatoes, 575 acres, 42,584 bushels; onions, $1\frac{1}{4}$ acres, 200 bushels.

HISTORICAL.—The first permanent settlements were made in

the summer of 1857, by a colony from Davenport, Iowa, sent out under the auspices of a Town Company consisting of A. H. Barrows, W. H. F. Gurley and B. B. Woodward. The object of this Company was to locate a town site somewhere in Central Nebraska, in the great Platte Valley, with the expectation that sooner or later a railroad would be built across the Continent, running through the Platte Valley, and that eventually the National Capital would have to be removed from Washington City to a centrally located point somewhere in the Northwest.

This colony consisted of five Americans, twenty-five Germans, six married women, one single woman, and one child four years old, as follows, viz.: R. C. Barnard, Surveyor; Joshua Smith, David P. Morgan, William Seymour, L. Barnard, Henry Shaaf, Matthias Gries, Fred. Landmann, Theodore Nagel, Hermann Vasold, Christian Anderson and wife, Henry Johnk and wife, Mary Stelk, Henry Schoel and wife, Fred. Doll and wife, W. A. Hagge, William Stolley, George Shuls, Fred. Varge, Johan Hamann, Fred. Heddle, Ditlef Saas, William Steir and wife, Peter Stuhr, Hans Wrage, Nicholas Thede and wife, Cornelius Axelson, Anna Stier, Henry Egge, Christ. Menck, and Cay Ewoldt. The Surveyor's party, consisting of R. C. Barnard, all the Americans, Fred. Heddle, and Chr. Menck, left Davenport a few days ahead of the main party, with one mule team. William Hagge and Theodore Nagel were detailed to proceed by river to St. Louis and purchase a supply of provisions, fire-arms, ammunition, blacksmith's tools, etc., and have them shipped up the river to Omaha, in time for the arrival of the main party there.

On the 28th of May, 1857, five heavy-loaded teams, drawn by sixteen yoke of work oxen, and with the remainder of the parties named, left Davenport in charge of William Stolley. This train arrived at Omaha on the 18th of June following; passed through Fremont on the 23d, which town had then only ten log houses; arrived at Columbus, which had then only eighteen log houses, on the 26th; crossed the Loup River, at Genoa, on the 27th of June; and on July 2d Wood River was reached. After reconnoitering the County in the vicinity for one day, the Surveyor selected a place on the 4th day of July, and on the 5th stakes were driven for a town site and adjoining claims.

The location selected covered only partly the present town site of Grand Island, the greater part lying south and southwest from the present town. At a meeting of the settlers it was resolved that four log houses should be first built, each 14x33 feet. At the same time the breaking of prairie had to be attended to, as the season was already far advanced. Only about fifty acres were broken, all told, the first season. On July 12, the work began in earnest. Some chopped logs, others hauled them out, and a few prepared wood for the burning of charcoal to start the blacksmith shop.

Saturday, August 15, some of the settlers could already move into their new houses, and on the 27th of the same month all the houses were occupied. These houses were built on the south half of the northwest quarter of section fourteen, town eleven, range nine.

During the winter months of 1857-58, the settlers underwent many privations and hardships. There were neither candles nor soap in the settlement for a long time, and the washing of clothes was done with home-made lye. Want of food compelled them to kill several work oxen. There was plenty of flour, but everything else was wanting; and so passed the first winter in the first settlement of Hall County.

In June, 1858, the supply of provisions again failing, the settlers had to live for some time on half rations, besides being compelled to work very hard, as the spring season demanded. However, on Thursday, June 24, fresh and ample supplies arrived from Omaha, which ended the trouble.

July 2, 1858, more settlers arrived from Davenport, Iowa, with a train of ten teams, bringing in addition about twenty persons and twenty yoke of work oxen, besides a number of milch cows and young stock, and matters began to look brighter.

On the 27th of August, about 1,500 Pawnee Indians passed through the settlement, and committed trifling depredations by stealing green corn and potatoes, but were otherwise friendly.

Tuesday, January 19, 1859, was a terrible day for the young settlement. Three men, on their return from the gold fields of Colorado, recklessly set fire to the tall, dry prairie grass in the vicinity; and the wind at the time blowing a perfect gale, the fire soon attacked the settlement, destroying, in an hour's time, eight houses and a number of hay and grain stacks. This happening in the midst of a severe winter, was a terrible blow. The citizens of Omaha made up a purse for the sufferers, but the party to whom the money was intrusted for delivery ran away with it.

Colonel May, then in command of Fort Kearney, was a true friend to the settler, and gave many of them remunerative employment at the Fort when their presence on the farm was not needed.

During the year 1859, difficulties arose between the Town Company and settlers, and the result was that the Company soon gave up the idea of carrying the speculation any further. R. C. Barnard, L. Barnard, Joshua Smith, David P. Morgan and William Seymour left the settlement soon after this. Of the first settlers, G. Schulz died a natural death, Fred. Vatge committed suicide, and J. Hamann was killed on the railroad. Twelve of the pioneer settlers remain in the County, and are owners of fine farms.

Of the pioneer women, Mrs. Henry Schoel died many years ago; Mrs. Fred. Doll removed with her husband to Howard County; Mrs. Joehnk and Mrs. Andresen are yet living in this County, with their families; Mrs. Stier returned with her husband years ago, to Davenport, Iowa. Anna Stier, the only unmarried lady who participated in the first settlement of the County, is married to John Thompson, a well-to-do farmer in this County. The first child born in the County was Nellie Stier, daughter of Wm. Stier, on March 3d, 1858.

In the spring of 1858, a lot of Mormons settled on Wood River, and opened up quite a number of farms.

The first newspaper in the County was published by them, and was called the *Banner*. In the spring of 1863, this Mormon colony removed to Salt Lake City, Utah, taking with them the *Banner*.

The first Postoffice was established in the spring of 1859, with R. C. Barnard as postmaster.

The first weekly stage was put on the road from Omaha to Ft. Kearney, October 1, 1858. It was changed to tri-weekly in 1860, and became a daily mail in 1864.

The County was organized in the year 1859, and the first officers elected were as follows: Probate Judge, Fred. Hedde; County Clerk, Theodore Nagel; County Commissioners, Hans Wrage, Jas.

Vieregg, Henry Egge; Justices of the Peace, R. C. Barnard, William Stolley; Sheriff, H. Vasold; Treasurer, Christian Andreson; Assessor, Frederick Doll; Constables, Christian Menck and Mathias Gries.

During the first years of the existence of the settlement, there was no trouble with the Indians.

This friendly state of affairs did not last long, however, and on February 5, 1862, occurred the first massacre of whites by the Indians in this County. Joseph P. Smith and Anderson, his son-in-law, farmers on Wood River, living about twelve miles west of Grand Island, went after some building logs to the north channel of the Platte River, about two and a half miles south of their claims, accompanied by two of Mr. Smith's sons—William, eleven years of age, and Charles, aged nine, and his grandchild, Alexander Anderson, about fourteen years of age. Anderson, who took a load of logs home in the morning, returned to the woods where he had left his father-in-law, Smith, with the above named boys, and two teams (the property of Smith), about 9 a. m., and found them all brutally massacred by a band of Sioux Indians. Mr. Smith had seven arrows in his body, and was lying on the ice with his face down, holding each of his boys by the hand. His son William was still alive when found; he was shot with an arrow, and one of his cheeks was cut open from the mouth to the ear. He soon bled to death after he had been carried home. The other son, Charles, had his skull smashed in and his neck broken, probably with a war club. Young Anderson was found some distance off in the woods with his skull broken. The four horses were taken away by the Indians. A number of the settlers followed in pursuit of the Indians, and captured some, but these proved not to have been implicated in the massacre.

During the summer of 1864, the Sioux were noticed on the bluffs not far from George Martin's ranche, about eighteen miles southwest of Grand Island City, on the south side of the Platte River. Two sons of Mr. Martin, Nat and Robert, at once hurried with a pony to drive the cattle home. While thus engaged, the Indians—about one hundred in number—approached so rapidly that the boys saw they would be unable to secure the cattle, so jumping on the pony, they made for the ranche as fast as possible.

The Indians were soon within shooting distance of them, however, and showered balls and arrows after them, till finally an arrow struck the hindmost boy, and passed through the bodies of both, pinning them together. Notwithstanding being thus badly wounded, the boys stuck to their pony and succeeded in reaching the ranche, when they fell to the ground exhausted, just outside of the inclosure. An Indian approached, knife in hand, to take their scalps, when another of the party remarked, in plain English, "Let those boys alone," which order was heeded. The boys were carried into the ranche, the arrow drawn out; and, after careful nursing, both fully recovered, and are still residents of the County.

On July 24, 1867, the Sioux attacked the ranche owned by Peter Campbell, a Scotchman, on the south side of the Platte, about ten miles from Grand Island. No men being at home to protect the family, the ranche was easily taken. A lady by the name of Mrs. Thurston Warren was killed by a rifle shot, and her little son with an arrow. Two girls, nieces of Mr. Campbell, aged respectively seventeen and nineteen years, and also two little twin boys four years old, were carried away captives. At the same time a German by the name of Henry Dose was killed near the same place. Months afterwards, the government bought the two girls and the two little boys from the Indians, paying for them $4,000.

In August and September, 1864, all sorts of rumors about the hostile Indians were afloat. It was reported that they were coming in great force to take Fort Kearney, and devastate the settlements below; and for a time the wildest panic prevailed. From far up the Platte Valley down to Columbus, the settlers, with very few exceptions, left their homes, and even east of Columbus many abandoned their claims and fled. For a distance of twenty miles, the main traveled road along the Platte River was covered with fugitives on the 13th and 14th days of August, 1864. Heavy-loaded wagons, with household goods and provisions, bedding, droves of cattle and horses, people on foot and on horseback, hurried along in the greatest confusion.

But the settlement at Grand Island was not deserted; here the people made a stand, and resolved to give the Indians a warm reception should they venture to attack them. A fortified log house twenty-four feet square, provided with port-holes, had been built
24

previously by William Stolley, for the protection of his family, in case of an Indian attack. The first star-spangled banner that ever floated in the air in this County was raised over this fortification, which the inmates chose to call thereafter "Fort Independence." Friends gathered in, and soon thirty-five persons had found a place where the scalping-knife of the savage was not very likely to reach them. Sufficient fire-arms (seventy-two shots without re-loading), about fifty pounds of powder, and other ammunition, besides an ample supply of provisions, were stored within the Fort, and a well was dug in one corner. Other precautionary measures were taken, such as the building of a stable eighty-eight feet long, under ground, for horses and a cattle-yard within range of the Fort.

But the fortification afforded protection to only a small portion of the then already numerous settlers; therefore it was resolved to fortify the "O. K." store, established in August, 1862, which was about one and a half miles due south of the Court-house in Grand Island. Mr. Thavenet engineered the work, and Dr. A. Thorspecken was chosen captain. The combined force at this place soon erected a formidable breastwork of sod, which surrounded all the buildings. This breastwork was provided on each corner with a tower, built of green cottonwood logs, projecting out far enough to permit the shooting of any person who should venture to crawl under cover of the breastwork from outside. Sixty-eight men and about one hundred women and children gathered into this fortification, and found there a safe place of refuge.

August 22, 1864, Gen. Curtis arrived here with the First Regular Cavalry, bringing with him one cannon—a six-pounder. The General inspected both fortifications, and praised the settlers for the efficient measures adopted by them for their self-protection. He left the cannon with them, and continued his march the same day to reinforce the garrison at Fort Kearney.

Soon afterwards, Capt. J. B. David, and twenty men of Company E, Seventh Iowa Cavalry, were stationed at the "O. K." store fortification. The Indians, however, never ventured an attack.

In 1863, the second saw-mill was built on Wood River, and the first windmill erected at the Grand Island settlement. A large number of windmills have since been erected in the County, also several steam and water-power grist and saw mills.

The Government Survey of the public lands in this County took place in July and August, 1866.

HALL COUNTY COURT HOUSE, GRAND ISLAND.

The first artificial grove—6,000 trees—was set out in the spring of 1860, on the west half of the northwest quarter of section twenty-eight, and on the east half of the northeast quarter of section twenty-nine, town eleven north of range nine west, and consisted of cottonwood, black locust, ash and black walnut. Some of these trees are now from sixty to one hundred feet high.

The first settlers on Prairie Creek opened up farms in March, 1871.

On the 21st of May, 1870, bonds were voted by the County to the amount of $15,000 for the purpose of bridging the Platte River. The bridge was completed early in March, 1871, in section twenty-nine, town ten, range nine west.

An election for Court-house bonds was held February 15, 1872. The Court House was completed as it now is, June 28, 1873.

PUBLIC SCHOOLS.—The first school taught in the County was in 1862. It was located one mile south of the Court House, Grand Island—Mr. Theodore Nagel, teacher; pupils, six. The present number of school districts in the County is sixty-one; school houses, fifty-one; children of school age—males 1,150, females 1,139; total, 2,289; number of qualified teachers employed—males, forty-one, females, forty-eight; total, eighty-nine; amount of salary paid teachers for the year—males, $6,143.72, females, $4,717.57; total, $10,861.29; value of school houses, $41,825; value of sites, $3,523; value of books and apparatus, $2,057.81.

TAXABLE PROPERTY.—Acres of land, 257,959; average value per acre, $3.51. Value of town lots, $178,225. Money invested in merchandise, $58,812; money used in manufactures, $9,172; number of horses 2,736, value $97,939; number of mules 360, value $14,850; number of neat cattle 8,668, value $82,546; number of sheep 1,409, value $1,411; number of swine 5,134, value $4,401; number of vehicles 1,156, value $28,349; moneys and credits, $50,028; mortgages, $10,323; furniture, $27,852; libraries, $1,623; property not enumerated, $66,388; railroad, $265,369.60; telegraph, $2,176. Total valuation, $1,815,280.60.

RAILROADS.—The County is traversed from east to west, through the central portion, by the Union Pacific Railroad. The Grand Island and Hastings Road, opening up communication with the Republican Valley Counties, was completed in 1879, and is now in running order from Grand Island southward. Bonds have been voted to the Union Pacific Company, to aid in the construction of a branch running from Grand Island up the Valley of the Loup; and the road-bed is now being graded between Grand Island and St. Paul, Howard County. The road is to be in running order between these points by June, 1880. Other lines are also contemplated through this County, and the surveys have been made.

LANDS.—There are no desirable government lands left in the County. The Union Pacific Railroad owns a large amount here, for which they ask from $3 to $6 per acre.

POPULATION.—The following are the names of the Precincts of the County, and the population of each in 1879: Grand Island, 2,200; Prairie Creek, 506; Alda, 913; South Loup, 832; Wood River, 949; South Platte, 704; Mariansville, 271.

Total population of County, 6,375, of whom 3,465 were males and 2,910 females. In 1878, the population was 5,119; increase in last year, 1,256.

### GRAND ISLAND,

The County Seat, is a beautiful town of 2,200 inhabitants, located on a high plateau overlooking the Platte River and surrounding country, in the eastern part of the County. It derives its name from a fertile island in the Platte, about two miles distant, which is sixty miles long and averages three miles wide. The town occupies one of the most desirable locations on the line of the Union Pacific Railway, and here are found the first round-houses and repair-shops of that Company west of Omaha. During the present year, the St. Joe & Denver Railroad was extended to this point, from Hastings, opening up communication with the Republican Valley Counties; and a branch from the U. P. is now being rapidly constructed from here to the Loup Valley Counties. During the past few months, new freight depots, a rolling-mill, an engine-house, large elevator and other improvements have been made, to the estimated value of $300,000.

The first train of cars on the Union Pacific track passed through Grand Island, July 8, 1866, and was drawn by engine "Osceola." A Postoffice was established in November, 1866, with George Schuller, postmaster; and about the same time several stores were opened. The old "O. K." store was removed to the town proper, in 1867. Dec. 6, 1869, the U. S. Land Office for this District was opened here. January 1, 1870, the *Platte Valley Independent*, the first weekly newspaper, was established by Mrs. M. T. G. Eberhart and Seth P. Mobley, and is still conducted by the same parties, under the firm name of Mr. & Mrs. S. P. Mobley. The *Times* was established July 16, 1873. The *Democrat* was started the present year, and both are large, excellent papers.

The city was incorporated in the spring of 1873; R. C. Jordon, first Mayor. The State Central Bank was established in 1871, with a capital of $45,000. The Catholics erected the first Church in the city. It was blown down by a hurricane in 1870. The city now has several handsome Church edifices. Masonic and Odd-Fellows' Lodges were established in 1871, and since then, the Knights of Pythias, Sons of Temperance, Leiderkranz, and numerous other secret and benevolent Societies have been organized. In 1874, a fire company and hook and ladder company were organized.

PUBLIC SCHOOL BUILDING, GRAND ISLAND.

Grand Island to-day is an excellent business point, and offers great inducements to capital and enterprise. It has several fine hotels, an excellent graded school, stores of various kinds, extensive lumber-yards, and one of the largest steam flouring mills in the State. The Platte is crossed here by a series of bridges from island to island, and a good bridge across the Loup gives easy access to the farmers of Howard County and the country on the north.

ADA, WOOD RIVER and DONIPHAN are shipping stations on the railroad, and rapidly growing towns.

Martinsville, Orchard, Junctionville, Zurich, Cameron, and Runelsburgh are villages of recent birth located in different parts of the County.

## HAMILTON COUNTY.

Hamilton County was organized in May, 1870, by proclamation of Governor Butler. It is located in the southeastern part of the State, and is bounded on the north by the Platte River, which separates it from Merrick County, east by Polk and York, south by Clay, and west by Hall County, containing 560 square miles, or 358,400 acres, at an average elevation of 1,800 feet above the sea level.

WATER COURSES.—The County is watered by the Platte and Blue Rivers and their tributaries. The Platte, flowing in a northeasterly course, forms the northwestern boundary of the County, a distance of about thirty-five miles. The West Blue flows from west to east through the lower tier of townships, and furnishes good mill privileges. Lincoln Creek, the North Fork of the Blue, Beaver, and several smaller streams, water the central and northern portions of the County.

TIMBER.—The number of forest trees planted up to date, is 2,157,259. Large, thrifty domestic groves may now be seen on many sections of land, and fuel is abundant. The streams furnish a small amount of natural timber. Forty-three miles of hedge fencing have been planted in the County.

FRUIT.—The number of fruit trees reported under cultivation, in 1879, was as follows: Apple, 9,778; pear, 243; peach, 4,684; plum, 8,246; cherry, 1,792; besides 395 grape vines. There are several very large orchards, and many of them are in bearing.

Limestone abounds in the vicinity of the Blues.

PHYSICAL FEATURES.—The surface consists principally of rolling prairie and nearly level plains, which have a gradual rise to the westward. In the western part of the County, where the Blues and several of their tributaries have their sources, the land is considerably broken, but affording the finest advantages for stock. The Blues and School Creek have fine valleys and wide, rich bottoms.

CROPS.—Acres under cultivation, 83,230. The yield of the principal crops, reported for 1879, was as follows: Winter wheat, sixty acres, 681 bushels; spring wheat, 42,278 acres, 470,250 bushels; rye, 1,938 acres, 21,765 bushels; corn 11,106 acres, 291,644 bushels; barley 6,016 acres, 99,496 bushels; oats 5,095 acres, 117,076 bushels; buckwheat, sixty-five acres, 102 bushels; sorghum, one acre, 106 gallons; flax, forty-five acres, 399 bushels; broom corn, seventy-three acres, 443 tons; potatoes 392 acres, 33,528 bushels; onions, three acres, 502 bushels.

The soil is very productive, and ranges from eighteen inches to two feet deep on the uplands.

HISTORICAL.—The first permanent settlements of which there are any records, were made in 1867 and 1868, by J. D. Wescott, Jarvis Chaffee, John Brown, James Rollo, John Harris, N. M. Bray, John Laurie and Robert Lemont, on the West Blue River.

John Harris, J. T. Biggs, and a Mr. Millspaugh kept ranches on the Overland Freight Road, long before Hamilton County was organized, when the buffalo, elk, deer and antelope roamed the prairies undisturbed.

Lincoln Creek was first settled in October, 1869, by Martin Werth and family, and William and August Werth. In the spring of 1871, a Postoffice was established at Spafford's Grove, on this Creek, with S. W. Spafford as Postmaster.

Beaver Creek was settled, in 1870, by R. M. Hunt, Samuel Yost and S. B. Chapman; and shortly afterward J. W. Jones, H. M. Graham, Henry Newman and Franklin Jacobs arrived.

The Big Blue, in the northern part of the County, was settled in 1871 by B. F. Webb, of Missouri, who located on section twelve, town twelve, range five. W. L. Whittemore settled on section two, town twelve, range five. T. W. Manchester, M. Vanduzen, and others, settled in 1872.

John Danhauer settled in the South Platte Precinct in 1871, and Stephen Platz and James Odell in 1872. About the same time, Mr. Hewitt settled in the extreme northeast corner of the County, and soon afterward J. W. Ward, C. Thurman, James Foster and C. Foster settled in the Bluff Precinct.

Among the older settlers on the extreme western side are Charles Tompkins and family and Mrs. Charlotte Ward, who arrived on the 22d of July, 1872, and located claims on section four, town ten, range eight, and at once began the erection of sod houses.

Hamilton Precinct, which was formerly a part of Deepwell, was settled in the spring of 1872, by G. K. Eaton.

Settlements were made in the central portion of the County, in 1871–72, by James Faris, W. S. Strain, and the Libott family. The southwest part, including Scovill and Union Precincts, was settled about the same time.

The first Church Society was organized at Father Hunt's house, in Beaver Creek Precinct, on the 12th of August, 1871, and was known as the Aurora Baptist Church. Since then, the Farmer's Valley Baptist Church has been organized, also one in the southwest corner, and another in the northeast corner of the County, making four Baptist Churches in all. The Methodists, Presbyterians, Congregationalists, United Brethren, Catholics and other denominations have organized Societies, and hold stated services.

The first sermon preached in the County was by Rev. S. W. Spafford, in the summer of 1871, in the sod house of J. P. Elliott, which stood on the present site of the town of Hamilton. The first Sunday School was organized in this house at the same time. There are at present six Churches in the County.

The first frame house in the County was built in 1870, by T. H. Clark, on the Blue, the lumber being hauled from Grand Island.

The first birth was Orville Westcott, son of C. O. Westcott, after whom Orville City was named. The first death was that of the wife of J. D. Westcott. The first marriage was that of Philip Hart to Elizabeth Ellen Verley, on the 21st of August, 1870, by Robert Lemont, Probate Judge. The first Fourth of July celebration was held in 1870, in a beautiful grove on the west side of the

West Blue, belonging to J. D. Westcott. The oration was delivered by B. D. Brown. The first case tried in the District Court, held at Orville City, in May, 1870, with Hon. Geo. B. Lake as presiding Judge, was a suit for divorce, Mr. E. W. Denio for plaintiff. Mr. Denio, Mr. Darnall and A. Poston were the first practicing lawyers.

The first election was held on the 3d of May, 1870, at the house of John Harris, on the West Blue, eighteen voters being present. The following County Officers were elected: Commissioners, Wm. D. Young, Norris M. Bray, Alex. Laurie; Clerk, Josias D. Westcott; Treasurer, Clarence O. Westcott; Sheriff, Geo. F. Dickson; Probate Judge, Robert Lemont; Surveyor, John E. Harris; Superintendent Public Instruction, John Laurie; Coroner, James Rollo.

PUBLIC SCHOOLS.—Number of districts, eighty-two; school houses, seventy-one; children of school age—males 1,224, females 1,040, total 2,264; number of qualified teachers employed—males, forty-eight, females, sixty-two, total, 110; wages paid teachers for the year, $11,704.95; value of school houses, $21,203.62; value of sites, $722; value of books and apparatus, $1,316.61.

TAXABLE PROPERTY.—Acres of land, 256,954; average value per acre, $3.22. Value of town lots, $32,381. Money invested in merchandise, $14,955; money used in manufactures, $1,872; number of horses 3,567, value $132,786; mules 405, value $20,526; neat cattle 4,258, value $47,799.00; sheep 720, value $967.00; swine 7,027, value $6,670; vehicles 1,346, value $31,935; moneys and credits, $11,157; mortgages, $9,934; stocks, etc., $50; furniture, $26,169; property not enumerated, $62,841. Total valuation for 1879, $1,228,792.

RAILROADS.—During the present year, 1879, the Nebraska Railway, under the control of the B. & M., has been extended westward from York County to Aurora, the County Seat of this County. The Omaha & Republican Valley Railway is also heading this way, and is now in running order to the County Seat of the adjoining County on the east.

LANDS.—Improved lands are worth from $6 to $18 per acre. The U. P. and B. & M. Railroad Companies each own a large amount here, for which they ask from $4 to $7 per acre.

POPULATION.—The County is divided into fifteen precincts, the population of each in 1879 being as follows; Bluff, 342; Monroe, 474; Scovill, 404; Farmer's Valley, 498; Beaver, 628; Hamilton, 372; Union, 455; Valley, 514; Orville, 450; Platte, 304; Otis, 405; Deepwell, 347; Aurora, 796; Cedar Valley, 76; Grant, 418.

Total population of County, 6,478; of whom 3,527 were males and 2,951 females.

### AURORA,

The County Seat, is pleasantly located near the center of the County, in the midst of a fertile farming section. It was recorded as a town on the 21st of December, 1872, and became the County Seat, January 1, 1876. The first house on the town site was a dugout, erected in August, 1871; the next was a frame building, built by David Stone. The first child born in the town was Abbie Aurora Goodman, on December 24, 1871. The first death was a daughter of David and Mary E. Stone, February 14, 1872. Aurora at present contains 800 inhabitants, a $5,000 Court House, an excellent School House and neat Churches, two newspapers, *Republican* and *News*, and business establishments representing all lines of trade. Within the past year, its population and business have about doubled; and now that it has railroad connection, it must become the shipping point and chief business center of the County.

### ORVILLE CITY,

Located on the West Blue, was surveyed and recorded in 1870, and was selected as the County Seat, at the general election held the 3d of May, 1870, which honor it retained until January 1, 1876. It is surrounded by a thrifty farming community, and has several stores, mechanics' shops, etc. A first-class flouring mill is located in the vicinity, and all the streams are well bridged.

### HAMILTON,

Located on the prairie, seven miles southwest of the County Seat, was surveyed in 1874, and the plat filed for record on the 19th of April, 1875. It has about 200 inhabitants, and was a lively contestant with Aurora, in 1875, for the honors of the County Seat.

HAMILTON COUNTY COURT HOUSE.

## LINCOLN VALLEY

Is a village located in the Platte Valley, in the western part of the County. It has a daily mail, good school house, blacksmith shop general store, etc.

## FARMER'S VALLEY

Is located on the West Blue, in the southeastern part of the County. It is one of the oldest settlements in the County, and is where the records were kept before the Court House was erected at Orville City in 1872. It has a good general store, Postoffice, Church and school house.

MIRIMICHI, WILLIAMSPORT, LERTON, SHILOH, STOCKHAM, BUCKEYE, CEDAR VALLEY, OTIS and AVON are all flourishing young villages.

## HARLAN COUNTY.

Harlan County was organized in June, 1871, in accordance with a special Act of the Legislature. It is located on the middle-southern border of the State, and is bounded on the north by Phelps, and east by Franklin County, south by Kansas, and west by Furnas County, and contains 576 square miles, or 368,640 acres.

WATER COURSES.—The Republican River flows from west to east through the south half of the County. It has a large number of tributaries in this County, some of which are of considerable size and excellent mill streams. The principal feeders on the north side are Turkey, Mill, Tipover, Methodist, Foster, Murrin, Rope, Flag and Spring Creeks; on the south, Prairie Dog, Sappa and Beaver Creeks. Small rivulets flowing from never-failing springs, are numerous in the south half of the County.

TIMBER.—There is considerable native timber in this County, the Republican and its numerous branches being generally well fringed along their banks, and the gulleys and hollows through the bluffs are frequently covered with a thick growth. The varieties most common are cottonwood, ash, elm, box elder, hackberry, walnut and oak. On the uplands, the farmers have been active in tree planting, and the artificial groves now afford both shelter and fuel. The quantity reported under cultivation in 1879 was 686 acres, or 260,321 trees. There are also nineteen miles of hedge fencing.

FRUIT.—The amount reported in 1879, was: Apple trees, 780; pear, twenty-nine; peach, 1,618; plum, 142; cherry, 963. Wild fruits are abun ant.

BUILDING STONE.—A good quality of limestone is found in different parts of the County. Quarries have been opened on the south side of the Republican.

CHARACTER OF THE LAND.—One-fourth of the County is valley—the remainder rolling prairie and a small per cent. bluff. North of the Republican, the uplands consist mostly of gently-rolling prairie and table; on the south side it is more broken, although almost everywhere tillable. The soil is well adapted to the growth of all the cereals, and produces largely, as will be seen from the following statement:

CROPS.—Acres under cultivation, 303,393; winter wheat 996 acres, 14,231 bushels; spring wheat 14,961 acres, 233,642 bushels; rye 960 acres, 16,212 bushels; corn 9,863 acres, 132,668 bushels; barley 1,160 acres, 26,320 bushels; oats 1,420 acres, 33,000 bushels; buckwheat, seventeen acres, 280 bushels; sorghum, thirty-six acres, 9,630 gallons; hungarian, 597 acres; potatoes 320 acres, 2,240 bushels.

FIRST SETTLEMENT.—During the summer of 1870, Victor Vifquain, J. W. Foster, H. V. Toephfar, and several others, explored the Republican Valley as far west as the present town of Melrose, where they built a stockade for protection against the Indians. They also laid out a town, which they called Napoleon, but soon after abandoned the enterprise and went away.

Mr. J. W. Foster, however, immediately selected a claim on a beautiful creek which afterwards took his name, near the present County Seat, where he built himself a house, and thus became the first permanent settler of the County. H. V. Toephfar, another of the party who helped to build the stockade at Melrose, crossed the Republican and took a claim on Sappa Creek, but soon abandoned it. Several other settlers located claims during the summer of 1870, among whom were John Talbott and a Mr. Donaldson In March, 1871, a Company which had been formed at Cheyenne Wyoming, sent a number of settlers to the Valley of the Republican. In June of this year, A. C. Robbins and son, and John Skinner located on the Sappa, and were the first permanent settlers in that section. Their families were brought out the following month. Mrs. Kate Reynolds and Mrs. Joseph Gould have the honor of being the first women in the County. In the fall, Judge Thompson and son, J. J. Jones, Gordon Kellogg and L. T. Newell, with their families, located in the vicinity of the Sappa. Although these settlements were on the extreme frontier, they never suffered any serious harm from the Indians, who frequently visited this vicinity to hunt, beg food, and steal what they could, but they never committed any murders.

Among the first to locate on Prairie Dog Creek were James E. Ryder, Gilbert R. Parish, the Woodwards, Drews, and Cabeldieks, the most of whom made permanent settlements.

John Brady and the Whitings were the first to settle on Methodist Creek. The first sermon preached in the County was delivered by John E. Whiting, in June, 1871, in a beautiful grove on the banks of this stream, from which it took the name of "Methodist."

In accordance with the provisions of the special Act of the Legislature organizing the County, James O. Phillips, T. D. Murrin and Marcus Coad were appointed a Board of Commissioners to locate a temporary County Seat and organize the local government.

The first election was held July 3, 1871, at which the following County Officers were chosen, viz: T. Sheffrey, H. Trimble and J. W. Foster, Commissioners; Joseph Gould, Probate Judge; A. J. Burke, Clerk; H. M. Luce, Superintendent Public Instruction; G. R. Parish, Treasurer; James E. Ryder, Sheriff; and W. P. Carr, Coroner. Alma City was selected as the permanent County Seat.

During the summer, claims were taken very rapidly, and several towns were laid out. Companies of U. S. Cavalry from Fort Hays, Kansas, patrolled the Valley to protect the settlements.

In July, L. G. Coon, W. H. Coon, S. D. Main, Elisha Main, and others, settled on the bottom lands below the present Republican City. Later in the same month, Dr. John McPherson and A. Starry, with a party from Brownville, Nebraska, laid out Republican City. The lumber was hauled from Brownville, a distance of 140 miles, and within ten days after its arrival, the first frame house in Harlan County graced the town site of Republican City.

Early in the spring of 1872, Dr. McPherson erected a steam sawmill, which was kept busily at work to supply the great demand for lumber.

Melrose was laid out about the same time as Republican City, and was a Company enterprise. A number of commodious buildings were erected, large stocks of goods brought on, and a newspaper started, called the *Sentinel*.

These two cities at once became rivals of Alma City for the honors of the County Seat. Elections were held, and claimed by one and contested by the other, and thus the controversy was kept up for two years, engendering a bitter feeling, which entered into all business of a public character, till finally the question was decided by the Courts in favor of Alma City.

The Fourth of July, 1871, was celebrated in a beautiful grove on Foster Creek. Fifty-six persons were present—men, women and children—and a sumptuous dinner was served. On the evening of this day, the first death in the County, of which there is any record, occurred. It was that of William McBride, who was shot dead in an altercation with a soldier named Costello, of Capt. Spaulding's Company, Second U. S. Cavalry. Costello was tried for the murder, and acquitted.

The winter of 1871-72 was a terribly severe one to the settlers of this County. Storm followed storm in quick succession; and none but those who have had a like experience can realize the sufferings and privations endured during those long, dreary winter months. Many subsisted on buffalo meat alone during most of the winter. The nearest depot for supplies was at Grand Island, on the Union Pacific Railroad, one hundred and fifty miles distant; but the deep snows made the journey dangerous and almost impracticable.

The first child born in the County was Harlan Parish, on Prairie Dog Creek, November 2, 1871.

In December, 1872, a Church and Sabbath School were organized, with J. M. Grundy, Pastor, and Jabez Cobeldick, Sr., Superintendent of Sabbath School. This Society, in 1874, erected a Church edifice near Mr. Cobeldick's place, which is known as Morristown Chapel. The building is made of sod and such other material as could be found at hand, and was built by the gratuitous labor of the residents of the neighborhood.

PUBLIC SCHOOLS.—The number of school districts in the County, in 1879, was forty-eight; school houses, thirty; children of school age—males 753, females 643; total, 1,396; whole number of children that attended school during the year, 569; number of qualified teachers employed—males, nineteen, females, twenty-seven; total, forty-six; wages paid teachers for the year—males, $1,519, females, $1,930.72; total, $3,449.72; value of school houses, $2,750; value of sites, $178; value of books, $147.66.

TAXABLE PROPERTY.—Acres of land, 55,696; average value per acre, $2.23. Value of town lots, $9,585. Money invested in merchandise, $13,276.47; money used in manufactures, $6,094; horses 1,630, value, $34,757; mules 184, value $6,055; neat cattle, 3,401, value $23,654; sheep 1,007, value $565; swine 2,050, value $1,654; vehicles 711, value $10,077; moneys and credits, $4.674; mortgages, $3,700; stocks, etc., $484; furniture, $4,583; libraries, $221; property not enumerated, $14,096, Total valuation for 1879, $257,897.47.

LANDS.—Wild lands are selling at $1.25 to $5 per acre, and improved from $4 to $12. There is a small amount of government land in this County, which is admirably adapted to stock-raising or farming. Stock-raising is engaging the attention of the farmers generally, and there are now a number of small herds here, ranging from 100 to 300 head.

The Republican Valley branch of the B. & M. Railroad is now in running order to the eastern line of this County, and the grading for its extension westward is now in progress.

There are three flouring mills, two saw mills, and five Churches in the County, and substantial bridges span all the streams at the principal crossings.

POPULATION.—In 1879 the County had a population of four thousand one hundred and ninety-three.

### ALMA CITY,

Situated on Foster Creek, near its junction with the Republican, is the County Seat, and has about 250 inhabitants. It contains a neat Court House, an excellent school house, a weekly newspaper, the *Standard*, general merchandise, grocery, dry goods, hardware, drug and implement stores, lumber yards, grain warehouses, etc.

It is favorably situated for business, and latterly has improved very rapidly, a Church and many new business houses having been established and dwellings erected during the past year.

### REPUBLICAN CITY

Is the largest town in the County, having at present about three hundred inhabitants. It was laid out in the summer of 1871, and is situated on the north bank of the Republican River, on a fine plateau opposite the mouth of Prairie Dog Creek. Mill Creek, a pretty stream, passes through the center of the town. A very fine bridge, two hundred and twenty-six feet long, spans the river at this point and has added greatly to the prosperity of the place, attracting the trade and travel from the southern portion of the County and Northern Kansas. The Methodists erected the first Church here in 1874. A flouring and saw mill are in operation here, and all classes of business are well represented, there being several general merchandise stores, drug, hardware, implement, grocery and feed stores, etc., large lumber yards, grain warehouses, good hotels, livery stable, several attorneys' and doctors' offices, and an able weekly newspaper, the *News*.

### ORLEANS

Is situated on the Republican, near the mouth of Flag Creek, five miles west of the County Seat. It was surveyed in October, 1872, by Mr. A. B. Smith, and in January, 1873, the first house was erected on the townsite. It contains at present two hundred and fifty inhabitants, and has a weekly newspaper, the *Sentinel*, three hotels, good school and Church privileges, and all the stores and business establishments usual to a growing town of its size.

MELROSE, GRAFT, WATSON, BAINBRIDGE, and SCANDINAVIA are close settlements, each having a Postoffice, general store, etc.

## HITCHCOCK COUNTY.

Hitchcock County, named in honor of Ex-U. S. Senator Hitchcock, of Nebraska, was organized in the summer of 1873, by proclamation of Governor Furnas. It lies on the southwestern border of the State, bounded on the north by Hays and by Red

Willow County, south by Kansas, and west by Dundy County, containing 720 square miles, or 460,800 acres.

The County is watered by the Republican River and tributaries. The Republican flows from west to east through the central portion of the County. Frenchman's Fork and Blackwood Creeks, both large streams, water the northern portion of the County, and Driftwood Creek and branches water the southern portion. Excellent water-power.

Timber is abundant along the streams. Building stone is found on the south side of the Republican.

Fifteen per cent of the area is fertile valley land, adapted to the growth of all classes of crops; ten per cent. is bluff, and the balance gently rolling prairie, which possesses a rich soil and with deep plowing will produce excellent returns of small grain. The prairies are covered with the celebrated buffalo, grama and other nutritious grasses affording the finest grazing the year round. Stock raising at present is the leading industry engaged in by the settlers. There is plenty of good Government land here.

HISTORICAL.—G. C. Gessleman, located near the mouth of Blackwood Creek, on section 15, town 3, range 31, in the latter part of Fabruary, 1873, and has the honor of being the pioneer settler of the County. In the latter part of May, following Mr. Gessleman's settlement, his solitude was broken by the arrival of about a dozen other settlers, among whom were W. W. Kelley, and G. E. Baldwin; and a few days later Daniel Murphy arrived, closely followed by J. E. Kleven, E. J. Bakken, and H. H. Hongan, all of whom settled on Blackwood Creek. In June and July the Blackwood settlement was increased by the arrival of W. Z. Taylor, Dr. Reaves, F. Martin, C. A. Gessleman, Dr. A. J. Vanderslice and J. H. Conklin. About the same time a number of families settled on Driftwood Creek.

On the night of the 31st of May, (1873) a great flood came down the Blackwood, sweeping everything before it, and covering the whole bottom to the depth of several feet. The settlers had a narrow escape from drowning, and barely saved themselves by climbing into trees, where they were obliged to remain for twelve hours, till the water subsided. A company of soldiers, encamped about six miles from the mouth of the creek, lost six men and thirty head of horses by drowning.

At the first election for County Officers, held on the 30th day of August, 1873, nineteen votes were polled, and the following officers elected: Commissioners W. W. Kelley, T. G. Le Grande, and F. U. Martin; Clerk, W. Z. Taylor; Probate Judge, A. J. Vanderslice; Treasurer, J. E. Kleven; Sheriff, G. E. Baldwin; Superintendent Public Instruction, W. W. Kelley.

At this election CULBERTSON was selected as the County Seat.

On the 4th day of August, of this year, a big battle was fought between the Sioux and Pawnee Indians twelve miles west of Culbertson, in which the Pawnees were badly beaten, losing sixty in killed.

The first stock of merchandise in the County was opened at Culbertson in 1873, by W. Z. Taylor.

During the year 1874 several families located on Driftwood Creek, among whom were J. H. Sackett, the Burd brothers, and the Beasely family. Good crops were raised in 1875, but the population did not materially increase. Several large herds of cattle were brought into the County this year, and distributed along the river and creeks; and a number of cattle men built houses in Culbertson for their families.

PUBLIC SCHOOLS.—The first school building was erecting at Culbertson, in 1876. Major R. S. Criswell taught the first school. There are at present one hundred and seven school children in the County, and two teachers employed.

TAXABLE PROPERTY.—Acres of land, 1,154, average value per acre, $2.77; value of town lots, $3,584; money invested in merchandise, $2,100; number of horses, 312, value, $6,960; mules, twelve, value, $367.00; neat cattle, 13,312, value $141,762.00; swine, 14, value $28.00; vehicles, 35, value $562.00; moneys and credits, $5,000.00; mortgages, 905.00; other personalty, $631.00; total valuation for 1879, $165,101.00.

The estimated population of the County at the commencement of 1879, 264.

### CULBERTSON,

The County Seat, is located on the Republican, in the northeast part of the County. The townsite was selected in 1873 and surveyed in August, 1875, by D. N. Smith. A large number of cattle men have made this place their headquarters and erected neat dwellings. It is a good business point and has three large general merchandise stores.

## HOLT COUNTY.

Holt County was organized in August, 1876. It is located on the northeastern border of the State, bounded on the north by the Niobrara River, east by Knox County, and south and west by unorganized territory, containing an area of about 1,080 square miles, or about 691,200 acres.

It is watered by the Niobrara and Elkhorn Rivers and their tributaries. The Niobrara flows in a general southeasterly direction on the northern border, a distance of about fifty miles, and receives numerous branches which have their sources in the southern and central portion of the County, the most prominent of which are Red Bird, Turkey, Eagle, Brush, Beaver and Willow Creeks. These streams all furnish sufficient water-power for mills. The southern portion of the County is finely watered by the Elkhorn and tributaries, which are also good mill streams.

Natural timber is plentiful along the Niobrara and many of its tributaries. The Elkhorn also furnishes a considerable quantity. Through the bluffs and canons, elm, oak and other hard woods are found. Several hundred acres of forest timber have been planted in the County; also ten miles of hedge fence.

Twenty-six thousand six hundred and eighty apple trees are reported under cultivation, besides a large number of peach, pear, plum and cherry trees. Wild fruits are abundant.

Twenty per cent. of the area is valley and bottom land, the remainder rolling prairie with bluffs along the streams. The bottoms of the Niobrara are from three to six miles wide, and very productive. The beautiful little valley of the Elkhorn averages about two miles in width, and several of the larger creeks have valleys from one to three miles wide.

The uplands are especially adapted to the growth of small grain, and yield excellent crops. The last report shows the number of acres under cultivation to be 5,300. Rye, 293 acres, 3,891 bushels; springwheat, 1,322 acres, 17,643 bushels; corn, 2,610 acres, 55,878 bushels; barley, 105 acres, 2,940 bushels; oats, 292 acres, 7,491 bushels; potatoes, 140 acres, 12,492 bushels.

For stock raising, dairy farming, or agriculture this County affords every advantage. Stock can subsist the year round on the nutritious grasses which grow here in abundance, and the wooded canons furnish all the shelter necessary for large herds.

The Elkhorn Valley Railroad is now being graded through the adjoining County on the southeast, and no doubt before another year, the citizens of this County will also enjoy all the benefits and advantages of railroad communication with the eastern markets.

There is considerable fine government land in this County, which is being fast taken up by colonies from the Eastern States. Improved lands are worth from $4 to $12 per acre; wild lands, from $1.25 to $6.

HISTORICAL.—The first settler in the County, of whom there is any record, was Wm. H. Inman, who erected a house on the banks of the Elkhorn, in 1872. During the following year, Dr. Wentworth, James Ewing, Tom Kelly and William Dougald located claims in the County. On the 13th of June, 1873, Henry H. McEvony, Eli H. Thompson, Frank Bitney, John T. Prouty, Eli Sanford and John Sanford, from Sauk County, Wisconsin, located claims in range eleven west, near the Elkhorn.

James McFarling, Conrad Mitchell, David Weisgarber, Samuel Wolf, John Develin, Mr. Hoxie and sons, Joe Kreiser, Mr. Gunther, and the Palmer brothers, located here during the summer and fall of 1873.

The above named parties, together with their families, included about the entire population of the County until the spring of 1874, at which time General John O'Neil arrived from the East with an Irish colony, and established the now flourishing town of O'Neil. The members composing this colony were: Patrick S. Hughes, Michael H. McGrath, Neil S. Brennan, Thomas N. J. Hynes, Thomas Connolly, Timothy O'Connor, Patrick Murry, Thomas Cain, Pat. Brannon and Thomas Kelly.

General O'Neil has since brought out many additional Irish families from the Eastern cities, all of whom are much pleased with the country.

The organization of the County was effected on the 26th day of August, 1876, by Messrs. Ewing, Thompson and Berry, special Commissioners appointed by the Governor for that purpose. The first County Officers elected were as follows: Ryland Parker, Probate Judge; Wilson Hoxie, Treasurer; Michael McGrath, Clerk; H. H. McEvony, Sheriff; Herman Strasburg Coroner; T. N. J. Hynes, Surveyor; Patrick Haggerty, Austin Hynes, and Jacob Shrob, Commissioners.

The first Church in the County was erected by the Catholics, at O'Neil, in 1876. Several other denominations now have flourishing organizations. The first clergyman to visit the County was Father J. P. Bedard, from Antelope County. Rev. J. R. Wolfe held a protracted meeting at O'Neil in the fall of 1876.

PUBLIC SCHOOLS.—Number of districts in the County, twenty-one; school houses, three; children of school age—males 190, females, 163; total, 353; number of qualified teachers employed, ten; wages paid teachers for the year, $60; value of school property, $160.

TAXABLE PROPERTY.—Acres of land, 4,568; average value per acre, $2.00. Value of town lots, $7,199. Money used in merchandise, $3,431; money used in manufactures, $2,950; horses 630, value $19,507; mules, fifty-six, value, $2,165; neat cattle 3,344, value $25,190; sheep 215, value $245.75; swine 494, value $1,086.75; vehicles 321, value $6,018; moneys and credits, $1,522; mortgages, $1,870; furniture, $304; libraries, $56; property not enumerated, $3,762. Total valuation for 1879, $84,444.44.

POPULATION.—The following is the population of the County, by Precincts, in 1879: Paddock, 537; Steel Creek, 171; Keya Paha, 241; Inman's Grove, seventy-nine; Atkinson, 176; Center, 660; Ford, ninety-five.

Total, 1,839, of whom 1,063 were males and 776 females. Increase in population since 1878, 539.

## O'NEIL CITY

Is located in the Valley of the Elkhorn, which is here finely timbered. It was surveyed and recorded in the spring of 1874, and the first store in the County was opened here the same year, by Wilson Hoxie. The city at present contains 150 inhabitants, a hotel, school house, three large general merchandise stores, a harness shop, drug store, two blacksmith and wagon-makers' shops, etc. It is favorably situated on the line of travel and immigration to the government lands of the Niobrara region, and commands the trade of an immense stock-grazing country. It was the County Seat until 1878.

### PADDOCK,

The County Seat, is situated on the Niobrara River, at the mouth of Eagle Creek. It was first called Troy; but, in 1875, the name was changed to Paddock, in honor of U. S. Senator A. S. Paddock, of Nebraska. The founder of the settlement was Mr. William T. Berry, who located here in June, 1874. Thomas Berry, J. B. Berry, T. H. Berry, J. W. Ross and C. G. Benner came shortly afterwards. The first marriage in the County was that of Thomas Berry to Sarah Smith; the first death was that of William T. Berry, the founder of the colony, on the 24th of November, 1874; the first birth was that of Cora A. Berry, March 28, 1875.

During the last year, Paddock was made the County Seat, and as a consequence is improving very rapidly. It is the largest town in the County, having 450 inhabitants and a good assortment of stores and mechanics' shops. The surrounding country is closely settled and very fertile.

### ATKINSON

Is a young village on the Elkhorn, twenty miles from O'Neil City. It has a Postoffice, school house, general merchandise store, etc. John O'Connell located here in the spring of 1875, and was the first settler. The first birth in the settlement was that of Sarah Burke.

RED BIRD, LAVINIA, and KEYA PAHA, are close town settlements along the Niobrara, each having a Postoffice and store.

## HOWARD COUNTY.

Howard County was organized by a special Act of the Legislature, approved March 28, 1871. It is located in the central part of the State, and is bounded on the north by Greeley, east by Nance and Merrick, south by Hall and west by Sherman County, containing 576 square miles, or 368,640 acres.

WATER COURSES.—The County is finely watered by the Loup Rivers and tributaries. The main Loup is formed in the north eastern part of the County by the junction of the North Fork, which enters the County at the northwest corner, and the South Fork, which enters at the southwest corner. The Middle Loup joins the South Fork in the southwestern part of the County. The Loups have numerous tributaries in this County, of which the most important are Oak, Turkey, Spring, Munson and Davis Creeks. Water-power unlimited, and springs of pure water are numerous in the vicinity of the larger streams.

TIMBER AND FRUIT.—Cottonwood, ash, elm, box elder, walnut, hackberry and willow, skirt the streams, and the canyons are frequently well timbered with oak. The farmers give more or less attention to forest tree planting, many of the domestic groves being old enough to furnish fuel. Wood can be bought at $2.00 to $3.00 per cord. Many of the farmers have surrounded their places with osage-orange and honey locust hedges, and have also planted orchards of choice fruit trees, which are now in a promising condition.

STONE.—A good quality of limestone crops out along the North Loup River, and is extensively used for building purposes.

PHYSICAL FEATURES.—About forty per cent. of the County is valley and bottom land, and the balance rolling prairie, tables and bluffs. The Loup valleys are from three to seven miles wide, and faultless in face and outline. The smaller streams have valleys from one to three miles wide. The bluffy districts abound in canyons and ravines, and present the finest openings for cattle and sheep ranches. Leaving out twenty per cent. of hilly and sandy lands, the balance, or eighty per cent. of the entire County might be turned into a vast grain field.

SOIL.—Eighty per cent. of the County has a deep and mellow soil, and is especially adapted to the growth of small grains. Spring wheat yields from sixteen to thirty-five bushels per acre; barley and oats from thirty to seventy bushels, and rye from twenty to thirty bushels per acre. Corn has proven a good crop, the yield being from thirty to fifty bushels per acre, but steadily increasing in average as the lands become better subdued and cultivated.

The buffalo, mesquite, and gama grasses, are still abundant in this region, and make excellent winter grazing. The coarser varieties, which are very numerous, are fine for summer pasturage or hay.

HISTORICAL.—On the 9th day of January, 1871, J. N. Paul, accompanied by Major Frank North, Ira Mullen, A. J. Hoge, Joseph Tiffany, Enos Johnson, J. E. North, Luther North, Charles Morse, Gus. Cox, and S. M. Smith, (all of whom afterward settled on Spring Creek, except J. E. and Frank North) entered the present limits of Howard County for the purpose of making an exploration of the North and South Forks of the Loup, and their tributaries, with a view to selecting the most desirable locality for settlement. So well pleased were they with the country, its numerous well-wooded streams, and fine soil, that favorable sites were soon selected and located upon.

On the 31st of March following, thirty-one additional colonists arrived under the escort of Mr. J. N. Paul, and made a temporary camp in a cottonwood grove in section 28, town 14, north, of range 10 west. The next day, April 1, the party crossed the river and located claims in the vicinity of the present County Seat. Among those who settled at this time were T. McNabb, D. Aleshire, A. G. Metcalf, J. Peters, J. C. Lewis, N. Z. Woodruff, H. M. Copeland, F. M. Crowell, R. E. Cockerel, F. Godfrey, N. Baxter and A. Robinson.

Lawrence Fleming brought the first load of pine lumber into the County on the 4th of April, 1871.

Under the provisions of the special Act of the Legislature, approved March 28, 1871, I. N. Taylor, Probate Judge of Platte County, on the 17th day of April following, appointed N. J. Paul, J. C. Lewis, and L. H. North, Commissioners for Howard County. This Board, on the 9th of May, located the temporary Seat of Justice at St. Paul.

The first election was held at St. Paul on the 10th day of October, 1871; fifty-four votes were polled. At the general election in 1874, the permanent County Seat was located at St. Paul by vote of the people.

In May, 1871, a Danish colony from Milwaukee, Wisconsin, made up of Lars Hannibal, John Scehusen, Niel Nelson, Jeus Wilkenson, Fred. Ohlson, Paul Anderson, and Loren Erichson, made a settlement on the South Loup, near the mouth of Oak Creek; and in the following year a large colony of Canadians located on the table land between Turkey Creek and the North Loup.

At an early date, steps were taken for the erection of a substantial bridge across the South Loup, to facilitate the settlement of the country on the west side of that stream, where lay much of the finest land of the County. Subscriptions were solicited at Grand Island and other places, by J. N. Paul, who succeeded in raising $650, of which $392 were paid; and on the 27th of April, 1871, a site for the proposed bridge was selected on sections twenty-one and twenty-eight, town fourteen north, range ten west. On the 4th of May following, Dr. Beebe arrived to superintend its construction; a camp was established at the bridge site, for the accommodation of the workmen; and on the afternoon of the same day, work was formally begun. A week later, Captain Munson arrived at the bridge site with a company of soldiers, who rendered valuable assistance in its construction, and remained until its completion, June 10, of the same year.

On the 2d day of March, 1872, the people voted bonds to the amount of $15,000 for the purpose of bridging the Loups, and on the 10th of May following, additional bonds to the amount of $4,000 were voted for the same purpose. Shortly afterwards, H. P. Handy entered into a contract with the County for the construction of two bridges—one over the South Loup, near Dannebrog, and one over the North Loup, north of St. Paul—both of which were completed according to contract, and accepted by the Commissioners.

The great storm which occurred in April, 1873, will long be remembered by the people of Central Nebraska, and Howard County especially, for its terrible severity and the suffering it entailed. On the afternoon of Sunday, the 13th, a steady rain set in, which continued till late at night; on the morning of the 14th, the people awoke from their slumbers and found that a terrific gale was in progress, from a little west of north. The air was so filled with drifting snow that it was impossible to discern an object beyond a few yards. On Monday night, the gale increased to an alarming height, and the strongest buildings creaked and shook to their very foundations. It continued with unabated fury all the next day, and until the afternoon of Wednesday, the 16th, when it lulled somewhat, and people dared to venture from their houses to look after their stock and ascertain the extent of the damages. Although great loss of property, and perhaps life, was anticipated, yet the people were unprepared for the startling news that the families of Cooper and Haworth had perished in the storm.

On Sunday, before the storm began, James Cooper, of Coatesfield, was unexpectedly called to Grand Island on important business. His only son had in the morning crossed the river to visit some friends for a few hours, and being unaware of his father's absence, did not return on account of the rain, thus leaving the mother and two daughters unprotected. On Tuesday morning, when the storm was at its height, the roof of the unfinished dwelling was blown off. The two daughters volunteered to go for help. Carefully covering their mother with blankets, carpets, etc., and feeding, watering and sheltering the horses, they went out into the storm, not to be seen again till the afternoon of Wednesday, when, as the gale was subsiding, Emma, the younger sister, was seen to fall on the prairie while approaching the house of Capt. Munson, then occupied by W. T. Wyman. On being carried into the house, she informed them of the helpless condition of her mother, and that her sister Lizzie lay dead in a canyon. Search was made, and the body of the sister was found, as described, at the head of a canyon, near the Dannebrog and Cotesfield road. The mother was found the next day, lying dead on the prairie, about a hundred yards from a neighbor's house. Among the sad incidents in the meanderings of the girls, is the fact that on Tuesday night they found a dug-out or cave about a hundred yards from Capt. Munson's house, and tried to force an entrance; but failing in this, they left it, supposing they could safely reach the house. There was exhibited all through the long hours of their mental and physical sufferings, that inflexible and resolute spirit by which the body clung to life with the greatest tenacity. It was actuated by such a spirit that led Emma, in the darkness of the night, while lying in the snow by the side of her dead sister, to exclaim, " I will live! I will live to tell the story!" and then begin anew, bareheaded, barefooted, and almost destitute of clothing, the battle for life with the storm-king, that for suffering and endurance for the next twelve hours— for indomitable determination to conquer, " to tell the story," if then but to die—has few parallels in history.

Meanwhile, diligent search was being made on Spring Creek for the family of Dillon Haworth, son-in-law of M. Crow. On Friday, the 18th, the mother and two children were found lying in a snow-drift. The mother and eldest child were dead; the younger daughter, two years old, was still alive, and after tender care was restored. On Saturday afternoon, the husband was found dead in the hills, about four miles east of the creek.

Allen Cozens, a resident of the North Loup, was also found dead after this storm, making a loss altogether of six lives in the County, besides a large amount of stock and other property.

The first child born in the County was a daughter to Mr. and Mrs. John Ellis, in the summer of 1871. The child died a few weeks after it was born, which was the first death in the County.

The first marriage in the County was that of Mr. Benjamin F. Johnson to Miss Mary T. Thomas, on the 30th of May, 1872.

SCHOOLS.—The first school district was organized at St. Paul on the 29th of April, 1872. Miss Lizzie Cooper—who perished in the storm of April, 1873—taught the first term.

Present number of school districts, thirty-six; school houses, twenty-nine; children of school age—males 620, females 494; total, 1,114; total number of children that attended school during the year, 655; number of qualified teachers employed—males, ten, females, ten; amount of wages paid teachers for the year—males, $1,770.50, females, $1,104; total, $2,874.50; value of school houses, $9,890.75; value of sites, $249; books, etc., $149.50.

TAXABLE PROPERTY.—Acres of land, 155,705, average value per acre, $1.42; value of town lots, $19,603; money invested in merchandise, $11,880; money used in manufactures, $3,105; horses, 1,083, value $33,567; mules, 220, value $8,690; neat cattle, 2,420, value $31,873; sheep, 1,250, value $1,058; swine, 1,786, value $11,415; vehicles, 548, value $1,157; moneys and credits, $9,832; mortgages, $300; furniture, $8,714; libraries, $140; property not enumerated, $28,994; total valuation for 1879, $392,256.00.

LANDS.—There is no desirable Government land left in the County. Improved lands are worth from $3.00 to $15.00 per acre. The Union Pacific and B. & M. Railroad Companies own a large amount of land here, for which from $2.00 to $5.00 per acre is asked.

RAILROADS.—The nearest railroad point at present is at Grand Island, on the U. P., twenty-two miles from St. Paul. Bonds have been voted by the County for the construction of a branch of the U. P., extending from Grand Island up one of the Loup Valleys, via St. Paul, and the grading between these points is now being pushed vigorously. The road is to be in running order to St. Paul, by June, 1880.

POPULATION.—There are six voting precincts in the County, the population of each in 1879 being as follows: First, 974; second, 519; Third, 970; Fourth, 185; Fifth, 170; Sixth, 423. Total population of the County, 3,246, of whom 1,712 are males, and 1,524 females.

### ST. PAUL,

The County Seat, was laid out in 1871, and has at present 400 inhabitants. It is beautifully located on the high bottom of the South Loup, four miles above the junction of the North and South Branches, and by virtue of its commanding position at the gateway to the two valleys, must become a prominent commercial city at an early day. It contains a handsome court house, fine school house, two hotels, a livery stable, lumber yard, a dozen stores and shops, and two weekly newspapers, the *Advocate*, established by J. N. Paul, shortly after the organization of the County, and the *Phonograph*, established within the past year.

### DANNEBROG

Is a flourishing town located on the South Loup at the mouth of Oak Creek. It was laid out in 1871, and is situated in the midst of a large Danish settlement. It contains several general stores and shops, a substantial brick school house, hotel, and the best grist mill in the County. An excellent bridge spans the Loup at this point.

### WARSAW

Is a Canadian settlement established in 1872, on the table land near the center of the County. A Postoffice was established here in 1873, and during the same year a school house and Methodist Church was erected—this being the first Church in the County.

### COATESFIELD,

On Munson Creek, in the northwestern part of the County, was located in 1871. A Postoffice, general store and school were established in 1873.

KELSO, GAGE, VALLEY, LOUP FORK AND FAIRDALE, are small villages with Postoffice, general store, etc.

## HAYES COUNTY.

Hayes County was created by an Act of the Legislature, approved February 19th, 1877. It is located in the southwestern part of the State, bounded on the north by Lincoln and Keith, east by Frontier, south by Hitchcock, and west by Chase County, containing 720 square miles, or 460,800 acres.

The principal water courses are Red Willow, Whiteman's Fork and Stinking water Creeks, tributaries of the Republican. These are all large streams and are fed by numerous small branches.

Hayes County as is yet unorganized. Estimated population, 600. No reports of schools, crops, property or improvements. County nearly all Government lands.

## JEFFERSON COUNTY.

Jefferson County was mapped out by the Territorial Legislature, January 26, 1856, under the name of Jones County. At the same time the adjoining County on the west, now Thayer County, received the name of Jefferson. Eight years after, 1864, Jefferson County organized by holding its first election at Big Sandy. An "Act to Enlarge Jefferson County" passed the Legislature on the 18th of February, 1867, uniting Jones to Jefferson County. This union continued until the Legislature of 1870-71 provided by enactment for the division of Jefferson County, which event was consummated in the fall of 1871 by the election of two sets of County Officers, the Sixth Principal Meridian being the dividing line. The former Jones, in the divorcement, retaining the name of Jefferson, and the former Jefferson assuming the name of Thayer.

Jefferson is located in the southeastern part of the State, in the fourth tier of Counties west of the Missouri River, and is bounded on the north by Saline and east by Gage County, south by the State of Kansas, and west by Thayer County, containing about 552 square miles, or 353,280 acres of land, at an average elevation of 1,200 feet above the sea level.

The Otoe Indian Reservation cuts off about twenty-four square miles from the southeast corner of the County.

The principal water courses are the Little Blue River, Big and Little Sandy, Rose, Cub and Rock Creeks.

The Little Blue River runs diagonally through the County from northwest to southeast, and furnishes splendid water power. It has an average depth of two feet, with a rapid current, flowing over a hard, gravelly bottom.

Big and Little Sandy Creeks water the northwestern portion, and are tributaries of the Little Blue. They afford some good mill privileges.

Rose Creek is a beautiful stream with numerous branches, flowing in an easterly course through the southwestern portion of the County, and emptying into the Little Blue. Cub Creek waters the northeastern portion, and Rock Creek the southeastern portion of the County. Springs are numerous.

TIMBER.—There is considerable native timber in the County, the streams all furnishing a fair supply. The Little Blue is bordered with a fine growth of oak, elm, cottonwood, walnut, ash, maple, etc. Jefferson reports more timber under cultivation than any other County in the State, the number of trees being 3,612,220. Nearly every farm has a large grove, and many of them are enclosed by honey-locust or osage orange hedging.

FRUIT.—The number of trees reported under cultivation was as follows: Apple, 10,601; pear, 216; peach, 13,516; plum, 1,906; cherry, 2,751, and grape vines, fifty-two acres.

STONE AND CLAY.—Limestone of an excellent quality is abundant. It burns readily and makes a fine white lime. Red sandstone is found in certain localities. There are extensive deposits of potters' clay, and brick clay of the very finest quality abounds in large quantities.

CHARACTER OF THE LAND.—The surface of the country is made up largely of undulating prairie, much of it nearly level, but sufficiently porous to effectually absorb the rainfall in a reasonably short time. The soil is fertile and well adapted for wheat, and all kinds of small grain. On the Little Blue there are rich, wide bottom lands, the valley rising in beautiful slopes and undulations toward the low rounded hills which encircle it on either side. In some places there are precipitous ravines through the dark-colored sandstone which crop out on these hills.

Rose Creek flows through a fine rich valley, the surface on the south side being somewhat hilly, but affording an excellent grazing range for stock and sheep. Big and Little Sandy, Cub and Rose Creeks have fine bottoms, and beautiful lands adjacent. The soil is everywhere fertile, the natural grasses rich and abundant, and good water plentiful, except on the uplands, where, for stock purposes, the lack of living water may be compensated by windmills.

HISTORICAL.—The pioneers of Jefferson County arrived within its present limits as early as in 1854—Jack Nye having the honor of being the first—and established themselves along the east bank of the Little Blue on the old overland route to California and Pike's Peak, where they erected rude cabins and made some efforts at tilling the soil; but they were continually harassed by Indians, from whose savage onslaughts they were often obliged to flee to the older settlements for safety, leaving behind and losing all they possessed, and it was not until several years had elapsed that a permanent foot-hold was maintained, and thrifty farms began to make their appearance.

After the departure of the Indians, and when the country had become more tranquil, emigration poured in very rapidly and soon all the best Government land was taken; the Little Blue was well settled, and claims were taken on all the streams; towns were laid out, and in 1871 the organization of the County was effected.

In 1874 a colony of Russo-Germans, numbering 350 persons, located on 27,000 acres of land in town 3, range 3, east, consisting of high rolling prairie, destitute alike of water or timber. Undismayed by these disadvantages, the colonists at once began the improvement of their farms by boring wells for wind mills, and the planting of large quantities of forest and fruit trees, and now their settlement will compare favorably with any in the County. Conspicuous for its size and substantial improvements, is the stock farm of Cornelius Jansen & Sons, which embraces about two sections of land. Under the energetic management of Mr. P. Jansen, good buildings, stables and corrals have been erected, and wells bored and supplied with pumps and wind mills by which a constant supply of good water is obtained. Mr. Jansen has large herds of merino sheep and fine blooded stock, the breeding of which is made a specialty.

A County Agricultural Society was organized in 1874, the first fair being held in October, 1876. The Society has about fifty acres enclosed near Fairbury, which embraces an excellent half mile track.

The St. Joe and Denver City Railroad was built through the County in 1872. It follows the valley of the Little Blue, the length of the road in the County being 27.46 miles.

PUBLIC SCHOOLS.—Number of districts, 64; school houses, 56; children of school age, males, 1,256, females, 1,115, total, 2,371; number of children that attended school during the year, 1,509; number of qualified teachers employed, males, 46, females, 52; wages paid teachers for the year, males, $5,143.08, females, $4,838.32, total, $9,981.40; value of school houses, $27,120; value of sites, $1,948.50; value of books and apparatus, $921.50.

TAXABLE PROPERTY.—Acres of land, 318,063, average value per acre, $2.22; value of town lots, $87.090; money invested in merchandise, $47,415; money used in merchandise, $3,891; number of horses, 3,116, value, $84,265; mules and asses, 309, value, $9,717; neat cattle, 6,197, value, $50,360; sheep, 5,029, value, $4,852; swine, 11,247, value, $13,035; vehicles, 1,068, value $15,264; moneys and credits, $26,218; mortgages, $5,763; stocks,

$68; furniture, $13,492; libraries, $725; property not enumerated, $32,202; railroads, $118,984.18; total valuation for 1879, $1,221,-415.18.

CROPS.—Acres under cultivation, 35,864; winter wheat, 237 acres, 4,493 bushels; spring wheat, 12,771 acres, 126,285 bushels; rye, 1224 acres, 31,363 bushels; corn, 10,650 acres, 376,315 bushels; barley, 2,100 acres, 50,899 bushels; oats, 1,649 acres, 58,693 bushels; buckwheat, 10 acres, 146 bushels; sorghum, 17 acres, 3,845 gallons; flax, 271 acres, 2,510 bushels; potatoes, 170 acres, 18,195 bushels; onions, 2½ acres, 200 bushels.

LANDS.—Improved lands are worth from $6 to $20 per acre. The B. & M. and other railroad companies own several thousand acres here, the price of which ranges from $5 to $8 per acre.

POPULATION.—The following are the names of the precincts and population of each in 1879: Buckley, 494; Meridian, 448; Lincoln, 117; Eureka, 262; Antelope, 446; Fairbury, 1,095; Richland, 488; Washingnon, 334; Newton, 1,108; Rock Creek, 290; Cub Creek, 518; Gibson, 249; Jefferson, 176; Plymouth, 255. Total,—6,280,—males, 3,377, females, 2,903.

### FAIRBURY,

The County Seat, has 1,000 inhabitants, and is a beautiful city. It occupies a fine plateau on the east side of the Little Blue, near the center of the County, and was laid out in 1870, by Messrs. McDowell and Mattingly. The St. Joe and Denver Railway was completed to this point in 1872, since which time the growth of the city has been steady and uniform. Elevators and other conveniences have been erected to facilitate the large shipments of grain and stock. All classes of business are well represented here. It has a commodious Court House, a fine school building, accommodating a graded school, and several handsome Churches, representing the Baptist, Methodist, Christian and Presbyterian Congregations. The *Gazette* and *Telegraph*, two well-managed weekly papers, are published here. The Fairbury Flouring Mills, owned by Messrs. Champlin & McDowell, will rank with the best in the State. They occupy a large three-story building with stone basement, situated on a side track of the railroad, and the power is transmitted from the river by a wire cable, a distance of 730 feet.

The dam built across the river by the mill company affords over 200 horse power, of which only about one-fourth is used at present by the mill.

### STEELE CITY,

Situated in the valley of the Blue, and on the line of the St. Joe and Denver Railway, thirteen miles southwest of the County Seat, is a prosperous town of 400 inhabitants. It was laid out in 1872 by Mr. Abner Baker, and has gradually grown into one of the best business centers and largest shipping stations on the line of the above mentioned railroad. It contains several stores, a flouring mill and other business establishments, a graded school, excellent Church advantages, grain warehouses, etc. The *New West Index,* a first-rate weekly paper, is published here.

### ROSE CREEK CITY

Is a flourishing business town situated on Rose Creek in the southwestern part of the County. A pottery establishment has been in operation here for some years past and turns out large quantities of earthenware. There are also good stores, a Church, large school house and a number of neat dwellings. Mark's Mills, by which name the town was formerly known, are located here. The surrounding country is well settled and fertile, and good building stone is abundant in the vicinity.

ROCK CREEK, GEORGETOWN, BOWER, PLYMOUTH, JEFFERSON, MERIDIAN, and LITTLE SANDY are the centers of close farming communities.

## JOHNSON COUNTY.

Johnson County, named in honor of General R. M. Johnson, U. S. Army, was created by an Act of the first Territorial Legislature, March 2, 1855, and organized in the fall of 1856. It is located in the southeastern part of the State, bounded on the north by Otoe, east by Nemaha, south by Pawnee, and west by Gage Counties, containing 378 square miles, or 231,920 acres.

WATER COURSES.—The Great Nemaha River, the principal stream of the County, flows diagonally through the central portions, from the northwest to the southeast corner, affording superior mill privileges, and having several fine tributaries on either side. The principal creeks are Spring, Deer, Turkey, Yankee and Silver. Branches of the Little Nemaha River water the northeastern portion of the County. Every township has a stream passing through it, fed by never-failing springs. Well water is reached at a depth varying from twenty-five to sixty feet.

TIMBER.—There is plenty of timber in the County for fuel. The larger streams have a fine natural growth on their margins, and domestic groves are everywhere to be seen. 1,400 acres of forest trees are reported under cultivation, besides 647 miles of hedge fencing.

FRUIT.—Apple trees, 46,821; pear, 974; peach, 82,262; plum, 1,957; cherry, 8,024; grape vines, 6 acres.

COAL is found in thin seams at a depth varying from twenty to one hundred feet. Beds have been opened and worked for several years past.

LIMESTONE crops out along the hill sides, and is easily quarried and worked. The Court House and several of the school houses of the County are constructed of this material.

CHARACTER OF THE LAND.—The surface of the country consists principally of gently rolling prairie, about fifteen per cent. being valley, bordered with occasional steep bluffs. The Great Nemaha Valley, which divides the County into two nearly equal parts, averages about two miles in width. Fine bottoms are also found along the smaller streams. There is scarcely any waste land, and the soil is very productive.

CROPS.—Area in cultivation, 70,789 acres. Winter wheat 819 acres, 13,107 bushels; spring wheat 9,219 acres, 165,852 bushels; rye 2,957 acres, 44,485 bushels; corn 38,742 acres, 1,549,697 bushels; barley 3,307 acres, 49,615 bushels; oats 3,933 acres, 117,979 bushels; buckwheat, forty-seven acres, 705 bushels; sorghum, fifty-one acres, 4,500 gallons; flax 107 acres, 748 bushels; potatoes, 158 acres, 11,943 bushels; tobacco, 2,000 pounds; onions, 586 bushels.

HISTORICAL.—The two first permanent settlers in the County were James Riggles and Isaac Irwin, both natives of Indiana. They settled three miles southeast of Tecumseh, early in the spring of 1856; the first house being built on the northeast quarter of section ten, town four, range eleven. These were followed soon after by John Maulding, Price, Corson, Walker, Loomis, Baker Lawrence, W. H. Strong, N. B. Strong, Sharrett, Swallow, Holbrook, Goshen, Darby, Little, Drake, Bentz and Cochran.

The winter of 1856-57 was a terribly severe one on the settlers and in many cases the suffering was extreme. They had to haul their provisions from the River towns, across the trackless snow on hand-sleds, a distance of from twenty-five to thirty-five miles.

Mr. J. C. Lawrence represented the County in the Legislature of 1856-57.

COURT HOUSE BUILDING, TECUMSEH.

At the first election for County Officers, held in the fall of 1856, the following were chosen: W. P. Walker, J. D. Mutchmor J. B. Sharrett, County Commissioners; James Bishop, Probate Judge; Charles A. Goshen, Register; Cyrus Wright, Sheriff; James

. Little, Treasurer; Amos A. Brewer, Surveyor; J. B. Haynes,
uperintendent of Public Schools; Robert Wright and N. B.
trong, Constables; Israel Loomis, Justice of the Peace.

The County Seat was located at Tecumseh, February 13, 1857.

The first saw-mill in the County was built by Maulding &
Ioore, at Tecumseh, in 1856–57. It was replaced in 1867 by a
ouring mill by Alexander and S. W. Bivens, who still own and
un the property. This was the first flouring mill in the County.
Vood & Co., erected a saw-mill at Butler, in 1863, and in 1865 it
as turned into a grist mill by H. B. Strong. A new flouring
ill was built upon the site of the old mill, by Albright & Cody,
a 1872. Solomon Gould erected a saw-mill on section ten, town
x, Helena Precinct, in 1864. Fanning & Hall built a steam saw-
ill at Vesta, in 1866. William Mann erected a first-class flouring
ill at Sterling, on the Great Nemaha River, in 1869–70. Mc-
lure & Root built a saw-mill on the Nemaha, above Sterling, in
860.

The highways of the County are kept in good condition—all
e principal streams being spanned with substantial bridges, sev-
ral of which are of iron. A bridge was erected at Bivens' Mill,
1 1856, which was replaced by a more substantial structure in
866, the City of Brownville donating $800 towards its erection.
Tebraska City donated money to build a bridge at Helena, in 1860,
cross the Little Nemaha River. The first iron bridge in the State
f Nebraska was built across the Nemaha River, at Tecumseh, in
869.

The Southwest Railroad, from Nebraska City to Tecumseh,
as surveyed in 1869. The Atchison & Nebraska R. R. was sur-
eyed and located in 1871. The Brownville & Fort Kearney R.
. was surveyed and located in 1872.

The Atchison & Nebraska—the only good road yet constructed
rough the County—ran the first cars to Tecumseh in April, 1872,
nd gave an excursion to the people of the County to Atchison
nd return—five hundred people availing themselves of the oppor-
inity.

The Catholics erected the first Church building in the County,
t Tecumseh, in 1868. It was dedicated by Father Emmanuel;
ost of building, $700.

A Presbyterian Church was erected at Helena, in the year 1870. This was the first Protestant Church in the County; cost $1,500.

The Christian Church at Tecumseh was erected by voluntary subscription, in 1871; cost, $1,800.

The first Methodist Church in the County was erected at Tecumseh, in 1870, and was dedicated by Rev. T. B. Lemon.

The Lutheran Church, at Helena, was built in 1870.

The First Presbyterian Church, at Tecumseh, and the second in the County, was erected in 1873, and dedicated in February, of that year, by Rev. Cleeland, of Iowa; cost of building, $2,600.

The First Methodist Episcopal Church, at Sterling, was built in 1875, and dedicated by Rev. J. H. Pearson; cost of building, $800.

The Baptist Church of Sterling, was built in 1876, being the first of this Denomination in the County; cost, $1,500.

Church services and Sabbath Schools are now held in every Precinct in the County.

James Price, son of Ansford Price, was the first child born in the County.

Mrs. Radley was the first person interred in the Tecumseh cemetery.

The first newspaper published in the County was the Tecumseh *Gazette*, in 1868, by Presson & Andrews. It was burnt out in 1869. The Tecumseh *Chieftain* succeeded the *Gazette* in 1869. The Tecumseh *Herald* was established in 1872, and afterwards consolidated with the *Chieftain*.

The first banking house in the County was established at Tecumseh, August 1st, 1871, by James D. Russell and Chas A. Holmes. The first brick building in the County was erected by the same parties, at Tecumseh, in 1873, at a cost of $7,000. The lower part of the building is used by the banking house and stores, the upper portion by the Masonic, Odd Fellows, and other Lodge rooms.

The first threshing machine was brought into the County in 1872; the first harvesting machine in 1864; both were owned by Mr. Andrew Cook.

PUBLIC SCHOOLS.—The first frame school house in the County was erected at Tecumseh, in 1856, by J. C. Lawrence. In 1879 there were, school districts, sixty-five; school houses, sixty-two; children of school age—males 1,340, females 1,230, total 2,570; total number of children that attended school during the year, 1,766; number of qualified teachers employed—males, thirty-six, females, fifty-seven, total, ninety-three; wages paid teachers for the year, males, $4,984.66, females, $6,093.10, total, $11,077.76; value of school houses, $28,396; value of sites, $1,325; value of books etc., $935.30.

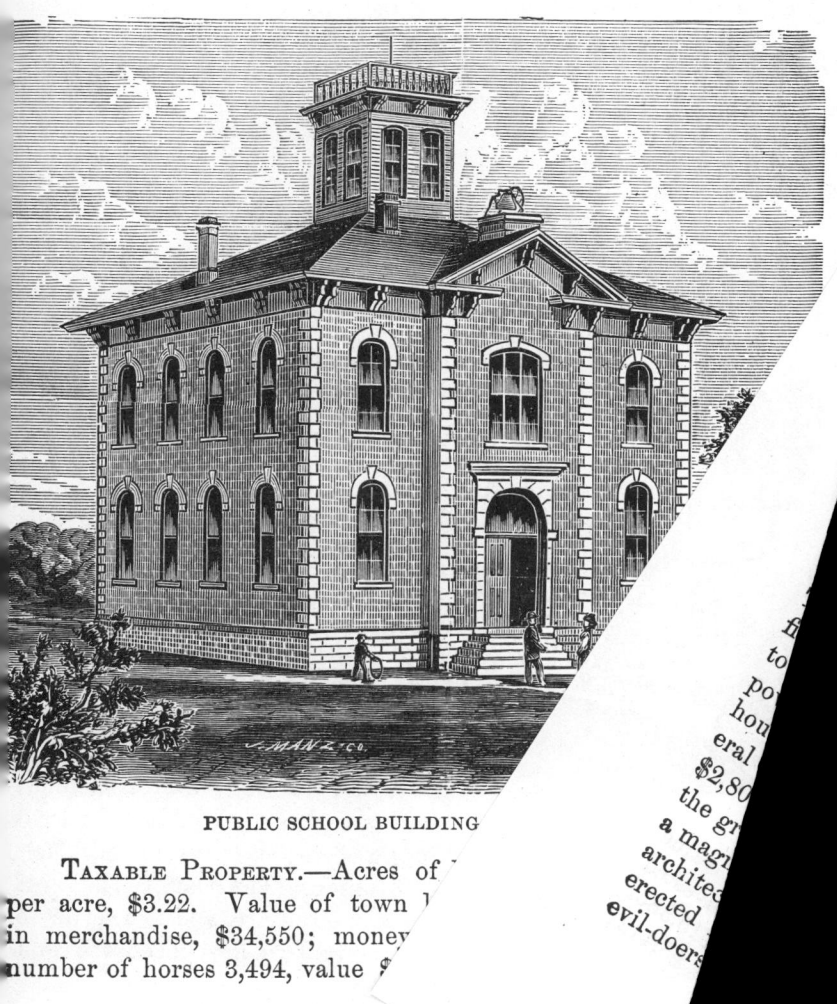

PUBLIC SCHOOL BUILDING

TAXABLE PROPERTY.—Acres of
per acre, $3.22. Value of town
in merchandise, $34,550; money
number of horses 3,494, value

neat cattle 7,280, value $52,181.; sheep 1,334, value $670.00; swine 14,257, value $14,058; vehicles 932, value $11,611; moneys and credits, $10,472; mortgages, $6,830; stocks, $12.00; furniture, $8,909; libraries, $255; property not enumerated, $15,207. Railroads, $128,243.92. Total valuation for 1879, $1,201,164.92.

MISCELLANEOUS.—The price of land ranges from $4.00 to $10.00 per acre, wild, and $5.00 to $25.00, improved. There are twenty-six miles of railway, thirteen Churches, three newspapers, one bank and four flouring mills in the County.

POPULATION.—The following are the Precincts and population of each in 1879: Vesta, 853; Helena, 607; Todd Creek, 929; Lincoln, 529; Spring Creek, 535; Nemaha, 1,695; Sterling, 1,160. Total population of County, 6,302—males, 3,391, females, 2,912.

### TECUMSEH,

The County Seat, has 1,400 inhabitants. It is situated in the valley of the Great Nemaha, near the geographical center of the County, and was located and surveyed in 1856. The town was first christened "Frances," after the wife of General R. M. Johnson, but the name was shortly afterwards changed to Tecumseh, the name of the famous Indian warrior, who is supposed to have been killed in battle by General Johnson.

Tecumseh is the largest city on the line of the Atchison & Nebraska Railroad in Nebraska, south of Lincoln and west of Falls City. Her shipping and general merchandise trade is very large. The general business of the place is represented by an array of as nely fitted up stores and offices as can be found anywhere in a wn of its size in the west. It contains one steam and one water ver flouring mill, two stock yards, large elevators and grain ware-ses, two weekly newspapers, the *Chieftain* and the *Journal*, sev. Churches, etc. The court house was erected in 1868 at a cost of 0. It is built of stone and stands in the center of the city, ounds fenced in and ornamented with shade trees. In 1873 ificent stone school building was erected at a cost of $10,000; t and builder, Mr. W. L. Dunlap. The County jail was in 1873. It is a solid stone structure, and is a terror to . A splendid iron bridge—said to have been the first erected in the State—spans the river at this point, which, besides the great convenience it affords the general public, is the means of drawing an immense trade from the country lying to the southwest.

PUBLIC SCHOOL BUILDING, STERLING

### STERLING,

On the line of the A. & N. Railroad, twelve
cumseh, was surveyed in 1870, and at pres
dred and fifty inhabitants. It is nicely ]
Nemaha and has excellent mill privile
class flouring mill was erected her
is kept running to its full capacity.
river, adding greatly to the busin
Church was erected in 1875, at

was built in 1876 and cost $1,500. The town is building up very rapidly and is now the next best business point on the line of the A. & N. Road after Tecumseh. It contains a couple dozen stores and other business houses, good hotels, fine shipping facilities, large lumber yards, elegant school house and a flourishing weekly newspaper, the *News*.

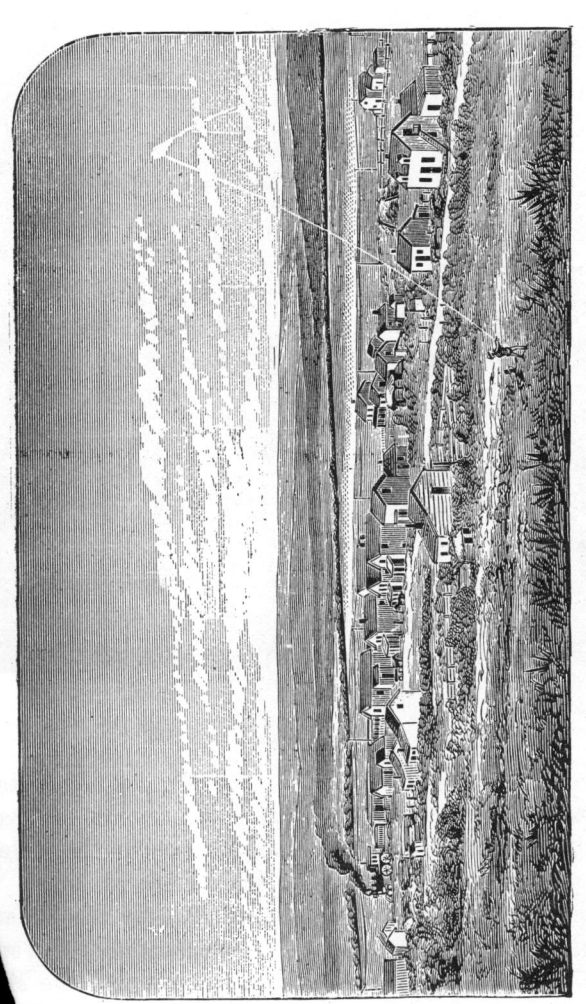

ELK CREEK, IN THE NEMAHA VALLEY.

### ELK CREEK

Is a prosperous town of 300 inhabitants located on the A. & N. Railroad seven miles southeast of the County Seat. It was surveyed in 1873. An excellent water-power flouring mill is in operation here. The town is well provided with stores, has good Church and school privileges, a lumber yard, elevator, stock yards, etc.

### HELENA

Is located on the south branch of the Little Nemaha River in the north eastern part of the County. It was surveyed in 1867 and for a while improved very rapidly. In 1870 the Presbyterians and Lutherans each erected neat houses of worship here. Good bridges span the streams in the vicinity, and make this a center for trade.

### VESTA

Is situated nine miles west of the County Seat, in the midst of a well-settled farming region. It was laid out as a town several years ago and has improved steadily as a business point. Fanning & Hall erected a steam saw mill here in 1866. There are now good stores, several mechanics' shops, fine school house, and other evidences of prosperity.

SPRING CREEK, CRAB ORCHARD, and LATROBE are Postoffices in the County.

## KEITH COUNTY.

Keith County was organized in July, 1873. It is located in the western part of the State, bounded on the north by unorganized territory, east by Lincoln County, south by Hayes and Chase Counties, and west by State of Colorado and Cheyenne County, containing 2,016 square miles, or 1,290,240 acres, at an average elevation of 3,190 feet above the sea level.

The County is watered by the North and South Forks of the Platte River and their tributaries. The North Fork flows in a southeasterly direction, and the South Fork in a northeasterly direction through the County, running nearly parallel and from three to six miles apart for the latter half of the distance.

Timber is scarce in the County. Scattered quantities are found along the Plattes and in the canyons.

With the exception of the valleys of the Plattes, which are here from two to five miles wide, the surface of the country consists of rolling prairie and tables, with high bluff and deep canyons along the streams. The prairies, with the aid of irrigation, may be made to yield excellent crops of small grain and vegetables. Very little attention is given to agriculture, however, stock-raising being the almost exclusive industry engaged in.

Keith is one of the greatest stock Counties in the State, and annually ships thousands of fat cattle to the Eastern markets. There are several ranches established in favorable localities whose herds are numbered by the thousands of head, and no country possesses finer advantages for the business. The high plains and slopes produce nutritious grasses, which, when ripe, dry upon the stock, forming uncut hay superior to that prepared by the most careful curing in the agricultural States, and upon which stock subsist, in excellent condition, the year through. The canyons or hollows among the bluffs skirting the streams furnish protection and shelter to the stock during storms.

The first permanent settlements in the County were made in 1867, at the time of the building of the Union Pacific Railroad, which traverses the County from east to west, following the Valley of the South Platte.

During the building of the railroad through the County, considerable trouble was had with the Indians, every now and then; and even after the road was completed, attempts to wreck the trains were frequent. In September, 1868, a band of Sioux attempted to destroy a train between Alkali and Ogalalla. They fixed the rails the same as at Plum Creek, raising one end of each rail about three feet high, and piling ties under them for support. As the train came up, the rails penetrated the cylinders on each side of the engine, as it was a straight track there; the engine going over into the ditch, with the cars piling up on top of it. The engineer and one of the brakemen who was on the engine at the time, wer' thrown through the window of the cab, and were but little hurt.

The fireman was fastened by the tender against the end of the boiler, and after the train had stopped, there being no draft, the flames of the fire came out of the door to the fire-box upon him, and the poor fellow was literally roasted alive. He was released after six hours in this terrible position, during which he begged the attendants to kill him, but lived only a few moments after his release. All the trains at this time carried arms; and the conductor, with two or three passengers, among whom was Father Ryan, a Catholic Priest of Columbus, Nebraska, seized the arms and defended the train—the Indians meanwhile skulking among the bluffs near the track, and occasionally firing a shot. Word was sent to North Platte, and an engine and men came up, who cleared the wreck. Meanwhile word was sent to Major North, then at Willow Island, to take one company of his scouts and follow the Indians. He came to Alkali and reported to Colonel Mizner, who was marching for North Platte with two companies of cavalry, all of whom started in pursuit. They went over to the North Platte River, crossed that stream, and entered the sand-hills, where the scouts overtook and killed two of the Indians, the whole party going about thirty-five miles, to a little lake, where the main body of the Indians had just left, and camped, finding the smouldering embers of the Indian fires still alive. That night, some of the white soldiers let their camp fires get away into the prairie, and an immense prairie fire was the result. This, of course, alarmed the Indians, and further pursuit was abandoned, much to to the disgust of the scouts.

TAXABLE PROPERTY.—Acres of land, 240; average value per acre, $1.00. Value of town lots, $2,485. Money invested in merchandise, $1,800; money used in manufactures, $11,780; horses 192, value $3,080; mules, six, value $200; neat cattle 19,094, value $115,032; swine, twenty-four, value $46; vehicles, fifteen, value $450; moneys and credits, $450; mortgages, $250; furniture, $590; railroad, $425,006; telegraph, $3,485. Total valuation for 1879, $564,894.

The Union Pacific Railroad Company owns many thousands of acres of land in this County, and the balance is nearly all government land.

The estimated population of the County, in 1879, was 274.

### OGALALLA,

The County Seat, is situated on the Union Pacific Railroad, 351 miles west of Omaha, and near the geographical center of the County. It is the headquarters of an immense cattle trade, Texas and other cattle being driven here for distribution to the various ranches. It is also a great shipping point for stock. It contains two large general merchandise stores, two hotels, a school house, blacksmith shops, etc., and about one hundred and twenty-five permanent inhabitants, although during the shipping season it has a large floating population and business is very brisk.

ALKALI, ROSCOE and BRULE, are small stations on the railroad.

## KEARNEY COUNTY.

Kearney County was created by an Act of the Territorial Legislature in 1859, and named in honor of General Phil. Kearney, U. S. A., who established the military post of Fort Kearney, in 1848. In 1873 the Legislature redefined the boundaries of the County as they exist at present. It lies in the south-central part of the State, bounded on the north by the Platte River, which separates it from Buffalo County, east by Adams, south by Franklin, and west by Phelps County, containing 505 square miles, or 323,200 acres, at an average elevation of 2,100 feet above the sea level.

WATER COURSES.—The Platte River washes the northern border of the County, while the southern and eastern portions are drained by numerous feeders of the Republican and Little Blue Rivers.

CHARACTER OF THE LAND.—The northern portion of the County is included in the wide fertile bottoms of the Platte, which, with the valleys of the smaller streams, comprise about twenty per cent. of the area; the remainder consisting of broad tables, rolling prairie and a small per cent. bluff. A large proportion is very nearly level prairie which drains by percolation to the strata below, while in the southwestern portion of the County there are numerous hollows in which lakelets are formed. Well water can be had almost anywhere on the uplands at a depth of forty to 100 feet. The soil is well adapted to the growth of cereal crops and yields bountifully wherever tested.

TIMBER.—With the exception of the small quantities found along the Platte and on the islands of that stream, there is scarcely any timber of natural growth in the County. The artificial groves are now well grown and present a fine appearance on the broad prairies. 668,944 forest trees are reported under cultivation, besides four miles of hedge fencing.

FRUIT.—The number of fruit trees planted up to 1879, was as follows: Apple, 1,185; pear, 13; peach, 1,696, plum, 255, cherry, 224.

HISTORICAL.—The Fort Kearney Reservation, which occupied a tract of land ten miles square, lying on either side of the Platte River, mostly in Kearney County, was set apart by the general Government for the establishment of a fort thereon for the protection of emigrants traveling across the Continent to California and the Territories. A detachment of Missouri volunteers first erected and occupied a small fort here, which they named Fort Childs, after their commanding officer, and which was also made a depot by the Mormons while crossing the plains to Salt Lake. In 1848, Col. Phil. Kearney arrived here with the Second United States Dragoons, rebuilt the fort, planted shade trees, and made other substantial improvements, and the name of Fort Kearney was given to the Post, after its distinguished commander.

The Fort being located on the main overland road across the plains, in the midst of powerful and hostile tribes of Indians, at once became the central point of rendezvous between the settlements in the eastern part of the State and the Rocky Mountains, and extended its sheltering arms to many a weary pilgrim band to the Far West.

The following troops have guarded at the Fort in the order named, viz.: The Missouri Volunteers, Second United States Dragoons, Sixth United States Infantry, Fourth United States Artillery, Second United States Infantry, Third United States Artillery, Thirteenth United States Infantry, Ninth United States Infantry, Second United States Cavalry, Tenth United States Infantry,

Seventh Iowa Cavalry, First Nebraska Cavalry, Second Nebraska Cavalry, Nebraska Militia, Ninth Ohio Cavalry, Twelfth Missouri Infantry, and Fourteenth Kansas Infantry, besides New York, Michigan, Massachusetts and Tennessee Regiments for short periods each.

The commanding officers have been as follows: Capt. Childs, Col. Phil. Kearney, Capt. E. B. Wharton, Maj. R. E. Morris, Col. C. A. May, Capt. E. McCown, Col. E. B. Alexander, Col. Miles, Gen. Carrington, Gen. Gibbon, Col. Foulke, Major Dallas, Capt. Pollock, Capt. Tenton, Col. R. Livingstone, Col. Baumer, Capt. Gillette, Major Wood, Gen. H. H. Heath, Col. Sumner, Capt. C. L. Tyler, etc.

At first the buildings of the Fort were made of sod and sundried brick, or adobe, but when Col. C. A. May took command, in 1858, he had two saw mills erected, and they were rebuilt with cottonwood lumber sawed from the timber on the islands of the Platte. The trees which tower up so magnificently and shade the grounds around, were planted in 1848.

The winter of 1856-57 was a remarkably severe one at the Fort. About the 9th of February, a terrific snow storm came up which buried all the one story houses under. A young man employed in the sutler's store, having to go from his boarding house in one part of the Fort to his lodging place in another, missed his way in the blinding storm and perished, his remains being found in April following, by some Pawnees, several miles distant.

While Major Morris was in command of the Fort, serious trouble was apprehended with the Pawnees. A Pawnee boy had been killed by a soldier—whether accidentally or in a quarrel it is not known—which greatly excited them, and they came to the Fort in full force, in war-paint and feathers, and fully armed, to demand satisfaction of the Commanding Officer. Every avenue to the Post was lined with Pawnees. The Major, however, in his bold, blunt way, soon disposed of them, and they retired, but night after night the islands of the Platte resounded with their war songs and yells.

At the breaking out of the Rebellion in 1861, Capt. C. L. Tyler, Second U. S. Dragoons, was in command of the Fort. His sympathies were altogether with the South; and under the pretext that a large body of Rebels were coming to take the Fort, he ordered the sixteen brass field pieces on the parade ground to be spiked, so that they might be rendered useless to the enemy. This order caused the greatest excitement among the troops, who, suspecting treachery, threatened to take the life of the Commander, but that officer was soon on his way to the Confederate lines. He afterwards became a General in the Rebel Army, and was captured and confined at Fort LaFayette.

The first settlement near the Fort was made in 1859, by Col. Scott, C. A. Phant, Alex. Constant and others, who put up a house and named the place Central City. John A. Morrow and John Holland soon afterwards bought the house and settled there.

About the same time Dr. Ransom, Dr. C. A. Henry, John Young, J. E. Boyd, L. Miller and others, from Omaha, laid out Kearney City. Several houses were immediately erected, a large hotel built, stores opened, town lots sold, a city government organized, and for a few years it was a very flourishing place, and being situated on the overland road, did an immense trade with the emigrants and soldiers. At one election over 300 votes were polled in the city.

In 1860 Kearney City was made the County Seat, and the County government organized by the appointment of full Board of County Officers by the Governor as follows: Commissioners, J. Tracy, Amos O. Hook and Moses Sydenham; Clerk, C. A. Henry; Probate Judge, J. Talbut; Treasurer, John Holland; Sheriff, Tom Collins.

## VALLEY CITY,

Is another of the early towns of the County, long since abandoned. It was laid out by John Lott and Amos Hook, and was a station on the overland road, situated a mile or two northwest of where Lowell now stands. At one time it was a very promising place, and contained several merchandise stores and hotels, and received a daily mail.

The hostility of the Cheyennes and Sioux during the winter of 1863-4, which culminated in a general Indian war the following summer, put a complete check to the further settlement of the County, in fact most of the settlers abandoned their homes and took their families to places of security in the older settlements further east; the flourishing young towns were mostly destroyed and the County very nearly depopulated—officials and all leaving. All the settlements and ranches in the Platte Valley, west of Fort Kearney, and on the Little Blue and Republican Rivers, were annihilated that summer by the Indians; the overland stage ceased running, and emigrant trains were not allowed to cross the plains by the military, unless there were fifty or more wagons together. Occasionally, however, small trains of a dozen wagons or so would manage to elude the Military by taking a wide circuit around the Fort, and proceed on their journey; but they frequently paid dearly for their temerity.

On the 13th of August, 1864, a mule train of twelve wagons, from Council Bluffs, Iowa, was attacked by the Cheyennes at Plum Creek, about thirty-five miles west of Fort Kearney, and every man belonging to it—thirteen in number—was killed, and two women and one child taken prisoners. The Indians came up to the train in an apparently friendly manner, just as it was about starting, and while the drivers were sitting on their wagons, the signal was given, and in a minute's time every man of the train lay a corpse. After helping themselves to what plunder they wanted, and setting fire to the wagons, the Indians placed the two women captives upon ponies, tying their ankles together underneath, and then hurriedly left the scene of the massacre, going in a southwesterly direction toward the Republican River. A company of soldiers followed their trail, but did not succeed in overtaking them. The mother of the child, during the flight dropped handkerchiefs and articles of the child's clothing, so that their trail might be followed, but to no purpose. The first night of their flight, an Indian took the child from its mother, and that was the last she ever saw of it. She was told that it had been killed. The captives were taken to New Mexico, and a year or two afterwards, through the influence of an Indian trader, at Santa Fe, were bought back from the Indians and restored to their friends.

The ranche next above Hopeville, several miles west of Fort Kearney, was also destroyed that summer, and the man left in charge of it killed by the Indians.

During the construction of the Union Pacific Railroad, the second and permanent settlement of the County was begun, and continued steadily.

In 1872, a re-organization of the County took place and a full Board of County Officers were elected, as follows, viz.: Commissioners, Moses H. Sydenham, N. B. Hamp, and J. Brown; Probate Judge, H. T. Cooper; Clerk, W. S. Morlan; Sheriff, F. Roberts; Treasurer, A. A. Andrews; Surveyor, Chas. Colt. At this election, the County Seat was established at Lowell, a town in the northeastern part of the County, which had just been laid out and surveyed.

Shortly after this, the Burlington and Missouri River Railroad was built in the County, and for a while had its terminus at Lowell, which added greatly to the settlement of this vicinity. A bridge was also built across the Platte, connecting Lowell with Gibbon, a station on the Union Pacific Railroad, and Lowell soon rose to prominence as an outfitting point for the large number of emigrants that came by these roads and crossed the "divide" at Fort Kearney to the Republican valley country.

In 1873, the grading for the St. Joe and Denver City Railroad was completed through the County, to a junction with the Union Pacific at Kearney.

The first newspapers published in the County were the Kearney *Herald*, the Central *Star*, and the *Star of Empire*, all of which suspended after a brief existence.

April 26, 1879, Samuel D. Richards was executed at Minden, the County Seat, for the murder, in December, 1878, of Peter Anderson, a Swede, of this County, with whom he had been living as a hired hand. He killed Anderson with a hammer and buried his body in the cellar under a pile of coal. Richards, although but twenty-three years of age at the time of his execution, was one of the most hardened criminals and fiendish humans of the age. Previous to his execution he confessed to this and several other murders, the most notable being that of the Harolson family, living near Anderson's, and consisting of a mother and her three small children, whom he butchered in the most brutal manner, on the night of November 2, a little over a month previous to the murder of Anderson. At the time this occurred Richards was living with Mrs. Harolson, her husband having fled the country to escape the charge of horse stealing. On the night of the murder, Mrs. Harolson sat up very late fixing her children's clothing, intending to start with them the next day to visit friends in the East. About 2 o'clock, while the tired mother was drowsing on the outside of the bed, undressed, Richards smashed in her skull with a heavy flat iron. He next served the oldest and next oldest child in the same way. The noise awoke the baby which he seized by the ankle and dashed its brains out against the floor. He then wrapped the bodies in bed sheets and buried them in a trench near a hay stack, where they were afterwards found. Richards was six feet two inches in his stockings. He first came to Nebraska in the early part of 1877.

SCHOOLS.—The first schools in the County were conducted at Fort Kearney, the Chaplains of the Post usually acting as teachers. A school house was erected at old Kearney City, in 1865, Mr. R. K. Freeman being the first teacher. The present number of school districts is twenty-eight; school houses, thirteen; children of school age, males, 441, females, 325, total, 766; whole number of children that attended school during the year, 381; number of qualified teachers employed, twenty-two; total wages paid teachers for the year, $1,982; total value of school property, $4,892.35.

TAXABLE PROPERTY.—Acres of land, 159,636; average value per acre, $1.31; value of town lots, $2,975.50; money invested in merchandise, $2,885; money used in manufactures, $50; horses, 1,205, value, $33,406; mules and asses, 173, value, $5,583; neat cattle, 1,483, value, $15,844; sheep, 581, value, $581; swine, 2,723, value, $1,620; vehicles, 591, value, $6,930; moneys and credits, $5,426; mortgages, $2,818; stocks, $30; furniture, $4,403; libraries, $89; property not enumerated, $18,037.30; railroads, $117,909.76. Total valuation for 1879, $428,814.25.

CROPS.—Acres under cultivation reported for 1879, 21,698. Winter wheat, eleven acres, 180 bushels; spring wheat, 834 acres, 95,700 bushels; rye, 350 acres, 4,721 bushels; corn, 2,693 acres, 60,697 bushels; barley, 201 acres, 9,791 bushels; oats, 1,950 acres, 23,181 bushels; sorghum, six acres, 931 gallons; flax, thirteen acres, 109 bushels; broom corn, 1,835 acres, 226 tons; millet, eighty eight acres, 250 tons; potatoes, ninety-one acres, 10,664 bushels.

RAILROADS AND LANDS.—The Burlington and Missouri River Railroad runs from east to west through the northern portion of the County, a distance of 14.68 miles.

The B. & M. and Union Pacific Railroad Companies each own a large amount of land in this County, the price of which ranges from $2 to $6 per acre. There is also some good Government land here. Improved lands are worth from $4 to $18 per acre.

POPULATION.—The population of the County in 1879 was 2,840, being an increase over 1878 of 1,516.

### MINDEN,

Situated on the table land near the geographical center of the County, was made the County Seat in 1877. It is a very promising new town and is growing rapidly. It contains a weekly newspaper, the *Bee*, several good stores, mechanics' shops, Church and school advantages, etc. A $5,000 court house is being erected.

### LOWELL,

Situated on the B. & M. Railroad, in the northeastern part of the County, contains about 350 inhabitants, a weekly newspaper, the *Register*, a $3,000 school house, several stores, grain ware houses, etc. It was surveyed in 1872 by A. B. Smith, and until 1877 was the County Seat. A fine brick court house was erected at a cost of $15,000. The first building erected on the townsite was the Continental Hotel; the first residents were W. W. Patterson, and Mr. White, Mr. Barney, Mr. Kent and Dr. Cooper settled here at an early day; the first family to locate was Mr. T. Munhal's. Lowell is an enterprising town and at present the chief shipping point and business center of the County.

### CENTORIA,

In the northwestern part of the County, was laid out on the proposed line of the St. Joe & Denver Railroad, but the non-completion of that road through the County gave a check to the growth of the town. It has a good school house, store, blacksmith shop, etc.

### KEENE

Is a close farming settlement in the southwestern part of the County. The first improvements were made by Wm. C. Walker, who established a ranch. It has a Postoffice, store, school house and blacksmith shop.

FARM VIEW NEAR SHELTON, BUFFALO COUNTY.

### MIRAGE,

Located in the middle-western part of the County, was first settled by J. Zimmerman, who put up a sod house and stable, dug a well, and did a general ranching business. It is now supplied with a daily mail and has a good store and school house.

### EATON

Is a small village in the northeastern part of the County. Messrs. Huffman, Mather, and Conyer were among the first settlers here.

### OSCO

Is a Postoffice in the southeastern part of the County. Messrs. Mills, Wells, Fountain, Hill, Pressley and Kelley, who now have fine farms in the neighborhood, were among the first settlers of the Precinct.

### FREDERICKSBURG

Is a thriving Danish settlement in the central part of the County. A well stocked general merchandise store is kept here by J. J. Jensen & Brother.

---

## KNOX COUNTY.

Knox County was organized under the name of L'eau qui Court by the Territorial Legislature of 1856-7. In February, 1873, the Legialature changed its name to Knox. It is located on the northern border of the State, bounded on the north by the Niobrara and Missouri Rivers, east by Cedar, south by Pierce and Antelope and west by Holt County, containing 1,075 square miles, or 688,000 acres.

WATER COURSES.—The County is watered by the Missouri and Niobrara Rivers and their tributaries. The Missouri forms about two-thirds of the northern boundary line and receives several fine tributaries, the largest and most important being Bazile Creek, an excellent mill stream, which, with its branches, waters the central portions of the County. The Niobrara joins the Missouri after forming about one-third of the northern boundary. Verdigris Creek, its most important tributary, flows from south to north through the western portion of the County, and furnishes some excellent mill privileges. The North Fork of the Elkhorn River waters the southeastern townships of the County, besides which there are innumerable smaller streams and springs.

TIMBER.—The Missouri and Niobrara are well timbered, as are also the smaller streams, the varieties consisting chiefly of elm, hackberry, boxelder, maple, ash, walnut, coffee-bean, red cedar and willow. Three hundred and seven acres of forest trees are reported under cultivation.

FRUIT.—It is only of late years that fruit culture has received any attention. Eight hundred and thirty apple, and a number of peach, pear, plum and cherry trees are reported.

CHARACTER OF THE LAND.—Ten per cent. of the area is valley and bottom land, the balance consisting of rolling prairie with frequent high bluffs along the streams. Bazile and Verdigris Creeks have very fine valleys, and considerable rich bottom and bench land is found along the smaller streams, The bottoms of the Niobrara and Missouri are very wide and fertile. The soil throughout the County is generally of the best character.

CROPS.—The number of acres reported under cultivation for 1879 was 9,350. Rye, 116 acres, 2,156 bushels; spring wheat, 3,965 acres, 61,871 bushels; corn, 2,367 acres, 72,170 bushels; barley, 378 acres, 9,822 bushels; oats, 1,088 acres, 42,445 bushels; buckwheat, nine acres, sixty-five bushels; sorghum, sixteen acres, 1,064 gallons; potatoes, 153 acres, 19,926 bushels.

HISTORICAL.—June 7th, 1856, Dr. B. Y. Shelley and R. R. Cowan, came to the present site of Niobrara, the County Seat, for the purpose of locating a town. Being well pleased with the location, they marked out claims and then returned by river to Sioux City, Iowa. A town company was formed, called L'eau qui Court Company, which shortly afterwards erected some houses upon the townsite, and built a fort for the protection of the settlers. The Indians soon began to be very troublesome, and during the winter of 1856-7 all the houses and improvements, except the "old fort," in which the settlers had at that time gone for safety, were burned by them. The Indian annoyances continued during the spring of 1857, numerous acts of hostility were committed and nearly all the live stock and other property were destroyed.

During the session of the Territorial Legislature of 1856-7, the L'eau qui Court Company was properly and duly incorporated. In the Act of Incorporation, the town of Niobrara was located, the Company's claim defined, and liberal ferry and bridge privileges granted. The claim of the Company embraced almost the entire Niobrara bottom for a townsite.

The permanent improvements date from about the first of July, 1857, although a small store had been opened a month or two earlier. The steamer "Omaha," from St. Louis, laden chiefly for Niobrara, landed there June 29, greatly to the bewilderment of the six hundred Ponca Indians who swarmed upon the levee. Three days later the first frame building was completed in Niobrara. A steam saw mill was immediately put in operation, and in little more than three months thereafter, a hotel had been built and opened, at that time the largest in Nebraska, being three stories high and costing about $10,000. In August of this year, there were over sixty men living in Niobrara. At the Territorial election held this month— the first election held in the County—there were forty-two votes cast. The first United States mail arrived the same month.

The monetary crisis of 1857 stripped the whole frontier of all available funds, destroyed confidence, and stagnated business generally, and for the next few years but little was done. The L'eau qui Court Company finally failed, and in 1860, "The Niobrara Town Company" was organized. The failure of the old Company took place before they had secured title to the townsite, and the patents were finally issued to the Niobrara Town Company. Among the leading men of the old Company were Dr. B. Y. Shelley, James Tufts, H. W. Harges, J. Austin Lewis, W. H. Benner, Geo. W. Gregg and Henry Thompson. The new Company was composed of a part of the members of the old Company, and some new men, among whom were Dr. Joel A. Potter, J. Shaw Gregory, Robt. M. Hagaman, Walter M. Barnum, F. Weis, and others. The patents to the land were issued to the new Company in 1861.

Of all the old settlers who are now in Niobrara, Wm. Lamont, C. G. Benner and T. N. Paxton, and their families, came in 1858; T. G. Hutchinson and H. Westerman, in 1859; Otto E. C. Knudson, in 1860, and Fritz Bruns, in 1862. In 1859 about seventy-five men left Niobrara for Pike's Peak.

There were three other settlements of some note in the early history of the County, viz: Frankfort, Breckenridge, and Running Water.

Frankfort was first settled in 1856, by S. Loeber, now deceased, who opened an Indian trading post here. Smutty Bear had the camp of his tribe on the other side of the Missouri, making this a good trading point. In the following year Mr. Loeber was joined by his brother Justus. The Town was laid out in 1857, and the plat filed in St. James, then the Seat of Justice of Cedar County, and was afterwards burned with other records of that County. Fifteen or twenty men located here and a number of houses were built during this year, and at one time it was thought that Frankfort would be the town on the Upper Missouri. Of the old settlers now living about the place, Louis Stettner came to this County in 1856, Justus Loeber and Chas. Mischke, in 1857, Leonard Weigand, John Buhrow, John Leder, and Mr. Mettsler, in 1862.

Breckenridge, now Santee Agency, was located in 1857, by Major J. S. Gregory, Dr. Joel A. Potter, the Steinberg Bros., and others. This place has the honor of having the first mill in the County.

The Running Water settlement, now Pischelville, on the Niobrara, was commenced in 1858, by Judge T. N. Paxton. He lived here five years, and was compelled to leave by the Santee Sioux Indians.

Immigration did not come to the County, after the war, in sufficient number to deserve mention, until about 1869 or 1870, when settlements were started in the valleys of the different streams. In 1870-71, Indian depredations became so aggravating that in January, 1871, a detachment of soldiers was sent from Ft. Randall, on the Missouri, under the charge of Sergeant Herko Koster, for the protection of the settlers on the Running Water and at other points.

The first school in the County was taught at Frankfort, in 1871, by Mrs. Clark.

The first natural death among the whites in the County was that of a Mrs. Smith, in 1859. The next was a Mrs. Young, in 1861. In the winter of 1857, Charles Rohe was shot through the heart, at Frankfort, by Rudolph Grasso. The shooting was the result of a quarrel. No arrest was ever made. In 1859, one Frank West, while drunk in Niobrara, deliberately shot and killed a Ponca Indian. No arrest. In 1869, James T. Small was shot and killed at his own door, while alone on his claim, nine miles above Niobrara. The perpetrators of this murder were never discovered. In 1870, Alexander Cook was killed, it is supposed by Indians, while building the Bazil Mill. The same year, two children of Thomas Brobbanec—one a girl of thirteen, and the other a boy about eight years of age—were killed by Indians, supposed to be either Pawnees or Sioux. His wife was shot at at the same time, but feigned death, and thus escaped with her life.

The Santee Sioux Indians, numbering about 800, have a reservation of 115,200 acres in this County, bordering on the Missouri River. They are the most peaceable of all the Sioux, wear citizens' dress, have day schools, farm some, and raise considerable stock.

PUBLIC SCHOOLS.—Number of districts, twenty-one; school houses, eighteen; children of school age—males 349, females, 319; total, 668; number of qualified teachers employed—males, eleven, females, fourteen; total wages paid teachers for the year, $3,024.19; value of school houses, $4,774; value of sites, $388; value of books and apparatus, $606.62.

TAXABLE PROPERTY.—Acres of land, 149,913; average value per acre, $2.09; value of town lots, $34,661; money invested in merchandise, $16,595; money used in manufactures, $9,840; horses, 813, value $22,167; mules, seventy-eight, value $2,820; neat cattle, 2,972, value $33,873; sheep, 447, value $896; swine, 596, value $782; vehicles, 416, value $9,387; moneys and credits, $1,256; mortgages, $2,340; stocks, etc., $150; furniture, $3,625; libraries, $68; property not enumerated, $6,683; total valuation for 1879, $458,222.

LANDS.—There is quite a considerable amount of good government land in this County, which can be secured under the homestead, pre-emption, and timber-culture laws. Wild lands can be bought at $2 to $5, and improved from $7 to $15 per acre.

POPULATION.—The following are names of the Precincts and the population of each in 1879: Niobrara, 642; Creighton, 450; Eastern, 307; Western, 287; Central, 179; Verdigris, 233.

Total population of County, 2,088—males, 1,157; females, 931.

## NIOBRARA,

The County Seat, is an enterprising town of 550 inhabitants, situated on the Missouri River, near the mouth of the Niobrara. It is the seat of the U. S. Land Office for Northern Nebraska, has a printing-office and an old-established weekly newspaper, the *Pioneer*, a number of good stores, three hotels, a large lumber yard, and a number of mechanics and professional men. It is the last settled point on the Missouri River below Bismarck, a distance of 700 miles, the country between these two places being taken up with United States' Forts and Indian Reservations. It is forty miles above Yankton, Dakota, the present terminus of the Dakota Southern Railroad. A daily stage leaves for Yankton, and four routes go to other points. During the season of navigation, passenger steamers make regular trips between Niobrara, Yankton and Sioux City. This town is rapidly coming into public notice as the starting point, after crossing the Missouri River, on the Niobrara Route to the Black Hills, and as the river terminus of the Covington, Columbus & Black Hills Railroad. The Omaha & Northwestern, the Elkhorn Valley, the Chicago, Milwaukee & St. Paul, and the O. C. & B. H. Railroads are now being rapidly constructed to this point.

## CREIGHTON,

On Bazile Creek, in the south central part of the County, was settled in the spring of 1871, by the Bruce colony, from Omaha, consisting of Mr. J. A. Bruce, who matured the enterprise, Miner W. Bruce, C. Lightner, Charles Osborn, Isadore Hammerly, B. Behrens, J. Steele, A. L. Towle, Mr. Hubbard, Ike Hammond, C. Cheatam, W. Cross and J. Lovell. A good merchandise store, hotel, and large school house, are located here. Church services are held every Sabbath.

## BLYVILLE,

In the northeastern part of the County, is composed principally of Americans and Swedes. George W. Bly is one of the first settlers, and has one of the finest dwelling-houses in the County.

## KEMMA,

On a branch of Bazile Creek, was first settled in 1870, by Charles Wittenaben. Good school facilities are at hand.

### PLUM VALLEY,

On Bazile Creek, was settled in 1872. It is one of the best stock-raising settlements in the County. Mr. James Steele has here some of the finest blooded stock in the West.

### MILLERSBORO;

Situated on a branch of Verdigris Creek, was settled in the spring of 1873, by Capt. J. M. Miller and family, John A. Davis, James Hindman, Wm. Crum, and Geo. Edgerton, who were joined in the fall following by Archibald McGill and others. It is a good farming section.

### WALNUT GROVE,

on a branch of the Verdigris, was settled in 1873 by the Chicken brothers, Henry Grim and sons, Groling, Clyde, Bennet and others. Timber and building stone are abundant in the vicinity.

### BAZILE MILLS,

Located in Creighton Precinct, has one of the best grist mills in the County. The mill has four run of burrs. A large general merchandise store and two agricultural implement stores are located here. There is a good school house and Church services are held every Sabbath.

### REIDSVILLE,

On Bazille Creek, was settled in 1871, by Chas. J. Reid and others Some of the best tilled and largest farms are found in this settlement.

PISHELVILLE, DUKEVILLE, VERDIGRIS VALLEY, WELCH, and HERRICK are Postoffices in the midst of close farming settlements.

## LINCOLN COUNTY.

Lincoln County, formerly called Shorter, was created by the Legislature in 1859, and an attempt at organization was made in 1860, but not perfected. In 1866 the County was permanently organized under its present name. It is located in the western part of the State, bounded on the north by unorganized territory, east by Custer and Dawson Counties, south by Frontier and Hayes and west by Keith County, containing 2,592 square miles, or 1,658,880 acres, at an average elevation of 2,789 feet above the sea level.

JUNCTION OF NORTH AND SOUTH FORKS OF PLATTE RIVERS, NORTH PLATTE, LINCOLN COUNTY.

WATER COURSES.—The central and northern portions of the County are watered by the Platte River and tributaries, and the southern portion by tributaries of the Republican River. The North and South Forks of the Platte, flowing nearly parallel with each other and from one to four miles apart, unite and form the main stream near the center of the County.

TIMBER.—Small quantities of natural timber are found along the Plattes and in the canyons adjacent. No report of timber planted.

CHARACTER OF THE LAND.—About eighty per cent. of the area consists of rolling prairie and table land, and the balance of valley and bluff. The valleys of the Plattes are noted for the excellent quality of hay they produce, and for years past thousands of tons are annually put up on these rich meadows to supply the military Posts and country east of the mountains. The yield is from one to three tons per acre. The bluffs, canyons and prairies are covered during the entire year with the famous buffalo grass, affording the finest pasturage summer and winter. Large herds of cattle are wintered here without hay, grain or shelter. The County is admirably adapted to stock-raising and dairy farming. Agriculture is as yet carried on to a very limited extent. No report of crops.

HISTORICAL.—The first permanent settlements were made in 1859, by Messrs. D. L. Smith, W. S. Penniston, Thomas French, Patrick Mullaly, J. P. Boyer, A. J. Miller and others, who located along the Platte, on the overland road.

To accommodate the immense travel to California and the gold fields of the Territories of those days, numerous ranches were established along the main thoroughfare in this County, on the south side of the Platte, and until the completion of the Union Pacific Railroad, they did a very profitable business. Every settler turned his house into a hotel for the accommodation of travelers, and no attention whatever was paid to farming, beyond the cultivation of an acre or two of corn, and perhaps a small garden of vegetables. The majority of the ranches had large stores stocked with groceries, provisions, and wearing apparel. The Indians were troublesome, continually annoying the ranchmen by stealing stock and committing all sorts of depredations; and in 1864 the settlers were all driven from their homes, their ranches burned, stock captured, and in many instances entire families were wiped out of existence by these savages.

The general election for the organization of the County was held in September, 1866, and resulted in the election of the following officers, viz.: Commissioners, W. M. Hinman, J. C. Gilman, J. A. Morrow; Probate Judge, Chas. McDonald; Clerk, Chas. McDonald; Treasurer, Hugh Morgan; Sheriff, S. Baker.

PUBLIC SCHOOLS.—Number of districts, seven; school houses, ten; children of school age, males, 361, females, 392, total, 753; whole number of children that attended school during the year, 397; number of qualified teachers employed, thirteen; value of school houses, $12,400; value of sites, $2,172; value of books, etc., $250.

TAXABLE PPOPERTY.—Acres of land, 73,136, average value per acre, $1.18; value of town lots, $143,151; money invested in merchandise, $34,195; money used in manufactures, $7,757; horses, 1,351, value, $32,621; mules, sixty-nine, value, $1,825; neat cattle, 40,364, value, $241,727; sheep, 5,307, value, $6,295; swine, 146, value, $350; vehicles, 238, value, $4,827; moneys and credits, $10,034; mortgages, $19,560; furniture, $18,727; libraries, $1,065; property not enumerated, $112,560; railroads, $601,228; telegraph, $4,930; total valuation for 1879, $1,327,036.

LANDS.—The Union Pacific Railroad Company owns thousands of acres of land here, for which $2 to $6 per acre is asked; the balance is nearly all Government land.

POPULATION.—There are six Precincts in the County, the population of each in 1879 being as follows: North Platte, 1,593; Brady Island, 72; Gannett, 23; Cottonwood Springs, 178; O'Fallon's, 65; McPherson, 86.

Total population of County, 2,017—males, 1,130; females, 887.

### NORTH PLATTE,

The County Seat, was laid out in the fall of 1866, by the Union Pacific Railroad Company. It is 290 miles west of Omaha, and is located near the center of the County, on a peninsula about three miles from the forks of the Platte. It is the terminus of the first division of the U. P. R. R., and here the Company have erected extensive, well-built brick shops, a round-house with twenty stalls, blacksmith, machine and repair shops, and a fine hotel.

The first building on the town site was put up in 1866, by Messrs. Penniston & Miller, who stocked it with goods to sell to the crowds who were flocking to the then terminus of the railroad. With the advent of the railroad came a motley crowd of laborers, business men, gamblers and roughs. All law, for the time being, was disregarded, and gambling and rowdyism ruled the day. This state of affairs lasted till June, 1867, when the terminus of the road was changed to Julesburg; and with this move, North Platte, which had at the time about 2,000 inhabitants, was nearly depopulated—only some twenty remaining. Early in the fall of 1867, the Railroad Company erected their round-house and numerous other buildings here, since which time the growth of the town has been steady and uniform, and in 1879, the population was about 1,600. The first newspaper, "*The Pioneer on Wheels,*" was started in 1866. At present there are two flourishing weekly newspapers published here—the *Republican* and the *Nebraskian*. The Court House cost $22,500, and an elegant school building, which is supplied with all the modern conveniences and apparatus, cost $17,000. The Knights of Pythias have a fine building, worth about $8,000, which is used for Lodge rooms and general business purposes. The Masons, Odd-Fellows and Good Templars have well fitted up Lodge rooms, and hold regular meetings. The Episcopalians, Unitarians, Baptists and Catholics have Church buildings of their own; and the Methodists and Presbyterians each have organized Societies and resident ministers, and recently erected Churches. There are several general stores, two grocery, two drug, and two jewelry stores, a confectionery, liquor, flour and feed, hardware, furniture, and millinery stores, two blacksmiths' and two wagon-makers' shops, three meat markets, two lumber and coal yards, and a host of smaller establishments. The U. S. Land Office for this District is located here.

This city is the central point of the great cattle business of the Western Plains, and several of the most extensive dealers reside here with their families.

## M'PHERSON

Is a Station on the railroad, about twelve miles east of the County Seat. It is an extensive shipping point for stock, and transacts a large business. A good wagon bridge across the Platte connects it with the settlements on the south side.

WARREN, BRADY ISLAND and GANNETT, in the eastern, and NICHOLS and O'FALLON'S, in the western part of the County, are Stations on the Union Pacific.

### COTTONWOOD SPRINGS

Is a village on the south side of the Platte, in the eastern part of the County. It has a good general store and school house.

## LANCASTER COUNTY.

Lancaster County was organized in the fall of 1859, previous to which it was attached to Cass County, for revenue, judicial and election purposes. It is located in the southeastern part of the State, in the second tier of Counties west of the Missouri River, and is bounded on the north by Saunders, east by Saunders, Cass and Otoe, south by Gage and west by Saline and Seward Counties, and contains 864 square miles, or 552,960 acres, at an averge elevation of 1,114 feet above the sea level.

WATER COURSES.—Salt Creek, the principal stream, rising in the southern part of the County, flows southeasterly through the central portions, and furnishes an ample water supply for manufacturing purposes. It has numerous tributaries on either side, the most important of which are Haine's Branch, from the southwest, Middle Creek, from the west, and Oak, Little Salt, Gar, and Rock Creeks, from the northwest, and from the southeast, Stevens and Camp Creeks. Most of these streams are large enough for mill purposes, a good flouring mill with three run of stone being already erected on Oak Creek. The middle, eastern and southern portions of the County are drained by the headwaters of the Nemahas. Altogether the County is well watered, living streams passing through every township.

CHARACTER OF THE LAND.—The surface of the country consists chiefly of gently rolling prairie, about twelve per cent. being valley. Salt Creek valley, extending through the central portion of the

County, varies in width from two to five miles, and is exceedingly fertile and beautiful. Adjoining the smaller streams there are fine, level bottoms, and back from them the country is rolling, yet rarely too broken for tillage. In the southern portion of the County the surface consists largely of fine table land.

SOIL AND CROPS.—The surface soil is a black loam from one-and-a-half to three feet in depth. The area in cultivation in 1878 was 106,206 acres; in 1879, 125,800; increase, 19,594 acres. Bushels of winter wheat reported, 7,000; spring wheat, 700,000; corn, 1,000,000.

TIMBER AND FRUIT.—The streams are generally fringed with a fine growth of natural timber. There are, on an estimate, 4,000 acres of timber planted, 40,000 apple trees, 4,000 pear, 30,000 peach, 7,000 plum, and 10,000 cherry trees, a large number of grape vines, and 300 miles of live hedge. Wild fruit, such as the plum, grape, gooseberry, etc., grow in profusion along the streams. Many of the domestic orchards are in bearing.

STONE.—Magnesian limestone and sandstone are abundant in the County. They are easily worked and make an excellent building material, both having been largely used in the construction of buildings in Lincoln.

SALT.—The saline deposits of this County will one day afford the material for an important manufacturing interest. The great salt basin near Lincoln covers an area of twelve by twenty-five miles, the brine of which contains by weight twenty-nine per cent. of pure salt.

HISTORICAL.—In the year 1856, several pioneers penetrated within the present limits of the County as far as the banks of Salt Creek, in search of future homes, though no permanent settlements were made until the following year.

The first permanent settlers, it is generally admitted, were John D. Prey and his sons, John W., David, and William, with his wife and daughter, who early in 1857, located at Olathe, on Salt Creek, about fifteen miles south of Lincoln.

Very soon after the settlement of the Prey's, Capt. Wm. T. Donavan located with his family and built a cabin, on the west bank of Salt Creek, near and west of the mouth of Oak branch, not far from the Cahn artesian well. This was the first settlement in Lancaster County, as at that time bounded.

J. L. Davidson, W. W. Dunham, James Eatherton, Jeremiah B. Garret, J. C. Bristol, Solomon Kirk, William Arnold, Ogden Clegg, the Bogus Brothers, and Weeks, Haskins, and Palmer, joined the Preys at Olathe during the summer of 1857, and others took claims along the Upper Salt Creek, extending the settlement from where Hickman station now stands, on the A. & N. Railroad down to Saltillo. At this date, however, and down to 1864, this settlement was in old Clay County.

Shortly after Capt. Donavan's settlement near Lincoln, Wm. Norman and Alexander Robinson built a cabin near the present works on the Salt Basin, but left in the following spring. In 1857, also, John Dee settled on Camp Creek, near Waverly; A. J. Wallingford and his brother, Richard, pitched their cabins on Salt Creek, between Lincoln and Saltillo, and later the same year, Daniel Harrington, James Cardwell, and Abraham Beals, joined Dee at Waverly.

In the spring and summer of 1858, James Moran, John P. and L. J. Loder, and Michael Shea, settled at Waverly; William Shirley, Joseph Brown, Mr. Bottsford, J. D. Main, C. F. Retztoff, John Lemp, Aaron Wood and others, settled on Stevens Creek; Festus Reed, Jeremiah Showalter, and Joel Mason, settled south of the Wallingfords, and John Cadman, John Hilton and others, located near Saltillo.

The gospel was first preached in the County by Rev. Turman, of the Methodist Episcopal Church, at the house of Capt. Donavan, in the summer of 1858.

In 1859, Robert Farmer, J. J. Forest, and Joseph Gilmore settled at Waverly.

The first child born in the County was Morton Donavan, son of Capt. W. T. Donavan, on March 12, 1859. The boy still lives, and in 1867 had the honor of breaking the first ground for the Capitol building at Lincoln. Six days after the birth of Master Donavan, the wife of Michael Shea, on Camp Creek, gave birth to a son, and immediately afterwards a child was born to Wm. Shirley.

In the fall of 1859, the first movement toward County organization was made. A public meeting was held under the "great elm" that stood on the east bank of Salt Creek, near the northwest corner of the present B. & M. R. R. depot grounds in Lincoln. A. J. Wallingford, Joseph J. Forest, and Capt. W. T. Donavan were appointed a committee to select a location for the County Seat, and they chose the present site of Lincoln, which was laid off and named Lancaster.

According to law, the Commissioners of Cass County ordered an election to be held in Lancaster County, on the 10th day of October, 1859, for the purpose of County organization. Said election was held at the house of Wm. Shirley, on Stevens Creek, and resulted in the election of the following officers, viz.: Commissioners, A. J. Wallingford, J. J. Forest, and W. T. Donavan; Clerk, L. J. Loder; Recorder, John P. Loder; Treasurer, Richard Wallingford. No record of this election or of the official proceedings of the officers are on file in the archives of the County, except the certificates of election and qualification of L. J. and J. P, Loder.

At the general election held on the 9th of October, 1860, at the house of W. T. Donavan, twenty-three votes were polled, and the following County officers elected, without opposition : Commissioners, J. J. Forest, A. J. Wallingford, W. T. Donavan; Clerk, J. P. Loder; Treasurer, R. Wallingford; Justices of the Peace, Festus Reed, and R. Wallingford; Constables, C F. Retztoff, and James Coultard.

The settlement of the County from 1859 to 1863 was very slow. The records of the elections of 1860-1-2 show no apparent increase in numbers. But the passage of the homestead law in 1862, gave a great impetus to emigration. The first homestead entry in Lancaster County under this law, was made by Capt. Donavan, just east of the site of the Insane Hospital, at Lincoln, on January 2, 1863.

In the summer of 1863, Elder J. M. Young and others, representing a colony, selected a site for a town which embraced the old town of Lancaster, then destitute of inhabitants, and which still belonged to the Government. Jacob Dawson and John Giles took homesteads adjoining the site. In 1864 Elder Young and sons, Dr. J. McKesson, Luke Lavender, E. W. Warnes, and J. M. Riddle, located here permanently, and J. and D. Bennet entered claims in the vicinity. The next arrivals to this settlement were Phillip Humerick, E. T. Hudson, C. Aiken, Robert Monteith, and sons, John and William; William and John Guy, O. F. Bridges, Cyrus Carter, P. Billows, W. Porter, Milton Langdon and others. Luke Lavender built the first residence on the new town site,—a log house. Elder Young located his dwelling near his present stone house in the eastern part of Lincoln.

In 1864, Silas Pratt, the Crawfords, Mrs. White and daughters, C. C. White and John Moore, settled on Oak Creek, about twelve miles northwest of the Lancaster settlement.

In September, 1864, during the great Indian insurrection, the majority of the settlers abandoned their claims, and sought refuge nearer the Missouri. However, a few stuck to their chances and remained, among whom were Capt. Donavan, J. S. Gregory and E. W. Warnes, in the neighborhood of Lincoln, Richard Wallingford at Saltillo, James Moran and John P. Loder on "Lower Salt," and Aaron Wood on Stevens Creek. Many of the settlers from the Big Blue River, under the leadership of J. J. Davidson, of Seward County, made a stand at the house of Capt. Donavan; but the Indians did not come further east than the Big Blue.

In 1865, Ezra Tuttle, lawyer, located on Oak Creek, and in 1866, S. B. Galey and S. B. Pound settled at Lancaster. In the latter year, the Hardenburghs and Lindermans took possession of the Salt Works in the Big Basin, and erected a portable saw-mill, which was of great use to the settlement. They also erected, this year, in Lancaster, a large stone house, which was used for a hotel, and a frame building, in which they opened a general merchandise store. In 1867, John Monteith and sons erected a building in Lancaster, in which they engaged in the boot and shoe business. Dr. McKesson built a residence in the north part of town, and Jacob Dawson commenced the erection of an elegant stone mansion, in which he afterwards resided and kept the Postoffice.

Ever since the discovery of the Salt Basins near Lincoln, by the government surveyors in 1856, they have attracted much attention as the probable source of great wealth. Capt. W. T. Donavan, when he pitched his cabin near the basin, in 1857, represented the

"Crescent Company," which had been organized previously at Plattsmouth, Nebraska. William Norman and Alexander Robinson, who next arrived and located near the Big Basin, represented another Company; but they soon left the County, and a year later, Donavan abandoned the enterprise also. In 1862, J. S. Gregory, Jr., laid siege to the Basin. Two years later, he had some boilers and solar vats erected, and made salt enough to supply the settlers and overland travel. The place was called "Gregory's Basin," and in 1863, a Postoffice was established there by that name, with J. S. Gregory as postmaster, which was the pioneer letter delivery of the County.

In 1866, E. H. and T. F. George, Jacob Hardenberg, and S. B. and W. Linderman, representing a New Jersey Company, bought out Gregory's claim, and established the "Nebraska Salt Company." They expended several thousand dollars on the enterprise.

All this time there had been entries made on the most valuable of the Basins, and these claims had passed into the hands of J. Sterling Morton and Col. Manners, one of the government surveyors who had made the discovery of the basins. Soon after Nebraska became a State, the Governor leased the Big Basin for twenty years to A. C. Tichenor and J. T. Green, and they expended about $12,000. About this time, however, Messrs. Morton and Manners got their claim into the courts by writ of ejectment, and the work of building ceased. After years of litigation, the State made good its claim to the land, and her title was made perfect by a decision of the U. S. Supreme Court, in 1875.

In 1870, Isaac Cahn obtained a lease of land adjacent to the Big Basin, and sank an artesian well to the depth of 600 feet, striking a vein of saline; but the Legislature refusing to grant the franchises he asked for, he abandoned the enterprise. The artesian well sunk by the City of Lincoln, on the block occupied by the U. S. Government building, pours out a steady stream of salt water, highly impregnated with other minerals, and powerfully magnetic. But at the Big Basin, the supply of water flowing up from the numerous springs is inexhaustible, and it is not difficult to utilize it without sinking wells. Considerable salt of an excellent quality is at present made at the Basin, with the appliances already provided.

Upon the admission of the State into the Union, in March, 1867, the Legislature appointed a commission to select a site for the new Capitol. The commission, consisting of the Governor, David Butler, Secretary of State, T. P. Kennard, and the Auditor, John Gillespie, were directed and empowered by law to select a site from lands belonging to the State within certain boundaries prescribed, which embraced the Counties of Lancaster and Seward, and a part of Butler, Saunders and Saline. The general government had set apart twelve salt springs, and with each six sections of land, for the use and benefit of the new State, and these springs were immediately selected by the Governor, and the lands located. Most of this land was located within a radius of twenty miles of the Great Salt Basin, principally in the County of Lancaster. In July, the Commission selected about a section and a half of land, which embraced within its limits the old town of Lancaster, as a site for the Capitol. Prior to the formal location, the proprietors of the land and lots embraced in the site made deeds of the same to the State, either by way of a gift or in exchange for State lands in the vicinity.

According to the provisions of the Act, the Commission was directed to lay out the new site into lots and blocks, and to sell the alternate blocks at public sale to the highest bidder, and to use the proceeds for the erection of a State House. A. B. Smith, of Plattsmouth, and Hon. Aug. F. Harvey, of Nebraska City, were employed by the Commission to survey and lay out the new city. The streets running north and south, commencing on the west side, were numbered, and the streets running east and west, commencing at the south boundary, were named from the alphabet. "A" and " U " were the boundary streets on the south and north, the First and Seventeenth on the west and east; making thirty-seven streets, with an average length of over one and a quarter miles. The site was, however, cut into by a reservation on the northwest corner of about twenty acres for the Burlington & Missouri River Railroad, and another on the northeast corner, penetrating as far as O street to the south, and Fourteenth to the west. The blocks were 300 feet square, and laid out in twenty-four business, or twelve resident lots each, with a frontage of twenty-five and fifty feet. The streets were 100 feet wide, with the exception of D, J, O, S,

Seventh, Eleventh and Fifteenth, which were called avenues and were laid out with a width of 120 feet. A reservation of four blocks, bounded by H and K and Fifteenth and Sixteenth streets, was made for the Capitol, another of the same size, bounded by R and T and Tenth and Twelfth, for the State University, and another of the same size, bounded by D and F and Sixth and Eighth streets, for a park. Reservations of one block each were made for a Court House, a State Horticultural Society, a market square, and for ward and High Schools. All Churches applying had reservations set out to them of three lots each. Forty acres, three miles south of Lincoln, were given to the State by Messrs. Donovan and Hilton for the site of a Penitentiary, and afterwards eighty acres were received on Yankee Hill, a mile and a half south of the city, for an Insane Asylum.

In October, 1867, the survey was completed, and the even numbered blocks offered for sale to the highest bidder, a minimum price having been first set upon each lot. At the close of the sale on the site, at which $34,000 was realized, two other sales were held one at Nebraska City, and the other at Omaha, and as $53,000 had been realized and only a comparatively small portion of the alternate blocks disposed of, the State still owns a large number of these lots, the Commissioners proceeded to advertise for plans and specification for a Capitol building.

THE CAPITOL.—The plans and specifications for the Capitol were opened at Omaha on the 10th of October, 1867, and those of Mr. John Morris, of Chicago, were selected. Mr. Morris was also appointed superintendent, and at once proceeded to procure material for the foundation of the building, the first ground for same being broken November tenth.

January 11, 1868, the contract for erecting the building was awarded to Joseph Wood, of Chicago, for $49,000. The walls of the building were constructed of magnesian limestone, from the Beatrice quarries in Gage County. The building, as it now stands, except the cupalo, was completed sufficiently for occupation before the close of the year, and on December 3d, the Governor issued a proclamation announcing the removal of the Seat of Government to Lincoln, and ordered the transfer of the archives of the State to the new Capitol.

OTHER STATE BUILDINGS.—By the Act of June 14, 1867, for locating the Seat of Government, the State University and Agricultural College were consolidated, and a reservation for a site for the buildings for the same, also the seventy-two sections of land for the University, and the 90,000 acres for the Agricultural College, were located by the Commissioners, under the direction of the Governor.

The Legislature of 1869, that met in January in the new State House, passed an Act organizing the "University of Nebraska," vesting its government in a Board of Regents, to be appointed in the first instance by the Governor, who was *ex-officio* chairman; the Superintendent of Public Instruction and the Chancellor of the University being also *ex-officio* members of the Board. Under the new Constitution there are only six Regents, who are elected by the people.

By an Act, approved, February 15, 1869, the Governor, Secretary of State, and Auditor, were appointed Commissioners to sell the unsold lots and blocks in Lincoln, and to locate and erect a "State University and Agricultural College, and a State Lunatic Asylum." From the proceeds of the sales, $16,000 were appropriated for the completion of the dome of the Capitol, $50,000 for the erection of the Insane Asylum, and $100,000 for the erection of the State University and Agricultural College building. Fearing that the proceeds of the sales of lots would not amount to the aggregate of these appropriations, the Commissioners were authorized to sell not to exceed forty sections of the Saline land grant to meet any deficiency that might arise.

In pursuance of this Act, the Commissioners advertised on February 24, for plans and specifications for these two buildings. On June 1st following, the plans and specifications received were examined, and the designs submitted by M. J. McBird, of Logansport, Indiana, were accepted for the University and Agricultural College building, and those of Prof. John K. Winchell, of Chicago, for the Lunatic Asylum.

The Commissioners let the contract for the excavation of the basement of the University on the third of June, 1869, to Messrs. D. J. Silver & Son, of Logansport, Indiana, for the sum of $23,520, and for the same work on the Lunatic Asylum to Joseph Ward, of Lincoln, for $18,055.

The work on the Lunatic Asylum was shortly afterwards commenced, and on the University, about the 15th of July; but the walls of the latter were ready for the laying of the corner stone on the 23d of September, and it was put in place on that day with Masonic ceremonies. During the first week of September, the basement was completed. In the meantime the architect had made alterations in the plans for the super-structure, suggested by the Regents, which necessarily increased the expense of the building. The Commissioners, feeling that considerations of public policy demanded that the building should be such as the present and prospective needs of the State indicated, decided to take the responsibility of exceeding the appropriation.

In pursuance of advertisements published July 15th, the contract for completing the University was awarded on the 18th of August, to D. J. Silver & Son, for $128,480, making the total cost of the building $152,000. The contract for the completion of the Lunatic Asylum, was let September 18, to Joseph Ward, for $119,300, making it cost $137,550.

Prior to the commencement of the work on the superstructures, the Legislature, at a call session, passed a joint resolution, March 4, 1870, approving the action of the Commissioners in exceeding the appropriation and letting the contracts, and also passed an Act, approved March 4, providing for the care and custody of State prisoners, and for the erection of a Penitentiary on the site selected by the Commissioners, in 1867. Three Prison Inspectors were elected, who were to act as a Commission in the erection of the Penitentiary, and to sell the 34,000 acres of Penitentiary land granted by the general government for that purpose.

The Inspectors, Messrs. W. W. Abbey, W. W. Wilson, and F. Templin, proceeded to advertise for plans and specifications for a State Penitentiary, to be opened on the sixth of June following; also proposals for the erection of a temporary prison, for which the Legislature had appropriated $5,000, to be opened April 28th. Perkins & Hallowell were awarded the contract for the temporary prison, and the designs of Wm. H. Foster, of Des Moines, Iowa, for the Penitentiary, were adopted, and the proposal of W. H. B. Stout, of Washington County, Nebraska, and J. M. Jamison, of

Des Moines, Iowa, for building the same, was accepted, and the contract awarded to them for $312,000.

The brick work on the University was commenced April 7th, 1870, and the walls were up and the roof nearly completed by the 9th of August following. The Asylum was pushed forward at the same rapid pace, and the buildings were completed and accepted by the Commissioners on the 29th of November, of the same year.

The University was formally opened and dedicated on Wednesday, September 6, 1871, and Chancellor Benton inducted into office by Acting Governor James.

Shortly before the Asylum was completed, it was set on fire in the wood work of the roof, by some unknown person, but the flames were extinguished before any serious damage was done. Dr. Larsh, of Nebraska City, was appointed Superintendent, and the insane of the State were placed there in his charge. On the night of April 18, 1871, it was set on fire again in the roof, and this time it was totally consumed, and two of the patients perished in the flames.

The building had been insured in various Companies for $96,000, but the State received only $72,000. After the usual preliminaries, the diagrams of Wm. H. Foster, of Des Moines, Iowa, for a new building, were accepted, and the contract awarded to Robert D. Silver, for the construction of the main building and one wing. According to the design, the exterior walls were to be faced with limestone ashlar, rough finish, but this was afterwards changed, and Carrol County, Missouri, sandstone, with ruble work finish, with rustic joints, substituted. The building was completed by October 1, 1872, and is a credit to the State.

The Asylum was filled with inmates almost as soon as finished, and the Legislature of 1875, appropriated $25,000 for the building of the second wing, which was completed under the supervision of the trustees.

The Penitentiary was completed in the fall of 1876, under the contract made by the State, and is a substantial structure, well ventilated and heated, and is regarded as perfectly secure. Its walls are built of a hard magnesian limestone taken from the quarries near Saltello, about twelve miles south of Lincoln. With the addition of cells it is large enough to hold all the criminals likely to be sent there for years to come.

RAILROADS.—There are five railroads in the County, as follows:

The Burlington & Missouri River, running from Omaha and Plattsmouth, *via* Lincoln, to a connection with the U. P., at Kearney, Buffalo County.

The Nebraska Railway, running from Nemaha City, on the Missouri River, *via* Lincoln, to a connection with the U. P., at Central City, in Merrick County.

The Atchison & Nebraska, from Atchison, Kansas, to Lincoln.

The Lincoln & Northwestern, now being rapidly constructed to a connection with the U. P., at Columbus, Platte County.

The Omaha & Republican Valley, which has now about completed a branch line from Valparaiso, Saunders County, to Lincoln, a distance of twenty miles.

LANDS.—Improved lands sell from $8 to $30 per acre. The B. & M. Railroad lands, of which there are about 75,000 acres here, sell from $4 to $10 per acre.

TAXABLE PROPERTY.—Acres of land, 475,449, average value per acre, $3.55; value of town lots, $771,919; money invested in merchandise, $110,303; money used in manufactures, $30,752; number of horses, 7,390, value, $181,339; mules and asses, 695, value, $21,311; neat cattle, 15,330, value, $127,698; sheep, 5,406, value, $5,880; swine, 31,487, value, $24,984; vehicles, 2,633, value $41,392; moneys and credits, $24,771; mortgages, $19,477; stocks, etc., $77,745; libraries, $251; property not enumerated, $85,283; railroads, $508,192.45; telegraph, $1,467.45; total valuation for 1879, $3,762,039.90.

PUBLIC SCHOOLS.—Number of districts, 104; school houses, 97; children of school age, males, 3,187, females, 3,090, total, 6,277; whole number of children that attended school during the year, 4,372; number of qualified teachers employed, males, sixty-eight, females, 113; wages paid teachers for the year, males, $8,858.26, females, $15,764.15, total, $24,622.41; value of school houses, $69,720; value of sites, $6,286.50; value of books and apparatus, $1,309.92.

POPULATION.—The following are the names of the Precincts, and population of each in 1879: Olive Branch, 726; Highland, 472; Denton, 219; Middle Creek, 353; Elk, 387; West Oak, 240;

Buda, 427; Centerville, 535; Yankee Hill, 734; Lincoln, 2,285; Midland, 2,221; Capital, 2,813; Oak, 482; Little Salt, 436; South Pass, 819; Saltillo, 648; Grant, 473; Lancaster, 519; North Bluff, 307; Rock Creek, 552; Panama, 442; Nemaha, 832; Stockton, 450; Stevens Creek, 266; Waverly, 520; Mill, 509.

Total population of County, 18,675—males, 10,092; females, 8,583. Population of County in 1878, 15,658; increase in past year, 3,017.

## LINCOLN,

The Capital of Nebraska, and the County Seat of Lancaster County, is a very remarkable and progressive city of some 10,000 inhabitants, and is situated about three miles from the geographical center of the County. It is emphatically "beautiful for situation." The view from the heights of the exquisitely rounded bluffs can scarcely be surpassed. The Capitol Building, which is undergoing extensive repairs and additions, occupies the highest point, and from this the prairie shapes off on all sides, for miles, in gentle waves and undulations, encircled by low, rounded hills, which plainly mark the shore line of an ancient lake, in the basin of which, upon this beautiful elevation, stands the city.

No place can afford a scene of quiet beauty that surpasses this view, when all the hills are covered with the emerald green of the summer months. The slope is dotted all over in every direction with groves and farm-houses that lie nestled in the valleys or crown the gently swelling bluffs that rise on every side and form a landscape of which the eye never tires. To the northwest, a mile or two distant, the Salt Springs come boiling up from the depths below, and yield an inexhaustible supply of pure salt; to the southwest are seen the commodious buildings of the Insane Asylum, with the extensive and attractive grounds surrounding them—an institution fully ranking with the very best in the country; on Yankee Hill, and further to the south, is the State Penitentiary, a model institution. In the northern part of the city, in a large square adorned with shade trees and evergreens, stands the State University and Agricultural College—a fine building of the Italian style. The college grounds are surrounded with elegant residences, handsome Churches, and fine public buildings, among which are the new United States Postoffice and Court House and the City High School building. The latter cost over $40,000, and the former fully $150,000.

There are other buildings of note in the city, including fine business blocks noticeable for solidity and capacity, and showing the confidence of business men and capitalists in the future of the city, and the enterprise and ability to erect structures that are not only ornamental to the city, but profitable to those who seek investment. The Opera House is the finest structure of the kind in the State.

Among the places of business represented in the city are the U. S. land office, the First National, State National and the Lancaster County Banks; the Lincoln Foundry and machine shops; the State Journal Company, printers, lithographers and blank book manufacturers, employing fifty hands; two steam flouring mills, two breweries, two marble cutting establishments, a carriage manufactory, etc. The newspapers are the *State Journal,* the *Globe* and the *Democrat,* published daily and weekly, besides three or four monthly publications.

The first Church erected in the city was by the Methodist Episcopal denomination; there are now twelve Churches, some of them very fine structures.

From small beginnings Lincoln has grown rapidly, in ten years, to its present large proportions. This has been due to several combined agencies, among which are the location there of the Capitol and the public institutions of the State, and the push, energy and enterprise of its citizens. Its excellent social and educational surroundings, its pleasant and central location, its broad agricultural country stretching without limit from its center, with the most fertile soil and delightful climate; and above all, its marked railroad facilities, making it with its present and proposed railroad connections, that will be completed in the near future, the Indianapolis of Nebraska.

It is now the second city of importance in the State, and with the Burlington and Missouri River Railroad crossing its bridge over the Missouri at Plattsmouth, and stretching through the State to the Union Pacific at Kearney, the Atchison and Nebraska running south to Kansas and St. Louis, the Nebraska Railroad

VIEW ONE MILE SOUTH WEST OF LINCOLN, NEBRASKA.

connecting it with Nebraska City, and other projected railroads to span and gridiron the State and join important connections East to the Atlantic, and West to the Pacific, South to the Gulf and North to the British Possessions, it cannot fail to have a magnificent future. It must be our inland central city of wealth, immense agricultural and other resources, and as the Capital, will be as it now is, the pride of the State.

Lincoln illustrates the boundless capacity of the Great West. Little more than a decade since the antelope and deer and wolf, and the retiring red man held full sway over the open prairie where are now all the appliances of comfort, civilization, education and commercial enterprises of a great city. It has no water-courses, no outside influences nor resources, except the railroads and the broad fertile prairies stretching from the Missouri to the Mountains, and yet it is destined to number its tens of thousands in the near future, and become a central power in a great State.

WAVERLY and NEWTON, promising towns on the B. & M. Railroad, east of Lincoln, each have about 200 inhabitants, good school and Church advantages, several stores and mechanics' shops, shipping facilities, etc.

BERKSHIRE, DENTON and HIGHLAND, are fine young towns on the B. & M. Railroad, west of Lincoln.

FIRTH, HICKMAN and SALTILLO, located on the A. & N. Railroad, are rapidly growing into prominence as business centers.

BENNETT,

On the Nebraska Railway, sixteen miles southeast of Lincoln, has about 300 inhabitants. It contains two Churches, an elegant school house, several stores, elevator, mechanics' shops, etc., and is surrounded by an excellent grain and stock producing country.

## MADISON COUNTY.

Madison County was created in 1856, and organized in January, 1868, by proclamation of Governor Butler. It is located in the northeastern part of the State, bounded on the north by Pierce, east by Stanton, south by Platte, and west by Boone and Antelope Counties, containing 576 square miles, or 368,640 acres.

WATER COURSES.—The Elkhorn River flows from west to east through the northern portion of the County, a distance of over twenty-five miles. The North Fork enters the Elkhorn in the northeast corner of the County. Dry, Buffalo, Deer, Battle, Taylor, and Big and Little Union Creeks, tributaries of the Elkhorn, water the central and southeastern portions of the County. Shell Creek, a tributary of the Platte River, waters the southwestern townships. The Elkhorn, Shell, Union and Taylor Creeks afford excellent mill privileges. Well water can be obtained on the uplands at a depth of from thirty to sixty-five feet, and in the valleys, from ten to twenty-five feet.

TIMBER.—There is considerable timber along the banks of the Elkhorn, and on several of its tributaries. On Shell Creek, there is a beautiful natural grove. 1,658 acres, or 1,547,551 forest trees, and twenty-two miles of hedging, are under cultivation. Many of the artificial groves are sufficiently grown to furnish the farmer with all the fuel needed.

FRUIT.—2,718 apple, thirty-three pear, 267 peach, and 758 cherry trees, and thirty-eight acres of grape vines, are reported under cultivation and in promising condition.

THE SURFACE OF THE COUNTRY.—The north half of the County lies in the fertile Valley of the Elkhorn, which here varies in width from three to six miles. Union and Battle Creek Valleys are from one to two miles wide. The uplands are gently undulating prairies, and comprise about forty-five per cent. of the area. There are few steep bluffs, and the surface is rarely too broken for tillage.

SOIL AND CROPS.—The soil is a black vegetable mould, from two to three feet deep on the uplands, and three to six feet deep in the valleys.

The number of acres under cultivation was 39,356. The yield of the principal crops was as follows: Winter wheat, sixty-five acres, 869 bushels; spring wheat, 17,869 acres, 185,045 bushels; rye, 1,871 acres, 30,229 bushels; corn, 12,301 acres, 309,877 bushels; barley, 601 acres, 12,161 bushels; sorghum, fourteen acres, 857 gallons; potatoes, 266 acres, 26,944 bushels.

HISTORICAL.—The first settlements were made in June, 1866, by a small party from Illinois, consisting of L. D. Barnes, Wm. H. Bradshaw, D. L. Allen, Mathias Carr and Wm. A. Barnes, who located near the mouth of the North Fork of the Elkhorn, on the ground now occupied by the town of Norfolk. In the following month, a large German colony from Wisconsin settled in the vicinity of Norfolk. In October of this year, Nicholas Paul surveyed the County. Erastus Jones, of Norfolk, was the pioneer merchant of the County. He was followed by Barney Barnes and a Dane by the name of Nelson, who kept an Indian trading post in the fall of 1866.

May 3, 1867, a settlement was established on Union Creek, near the present town of Madison, by H. M. Barnes, P. J. Barnes, W. J. Barnes and F. W. Barnes. Shortly afterward, Henry Platts and Charles Huylar and family located on this stream; and before the close of the year, Henry J. Severance and a number of others, settled in the vicinity. A substantial bridge was erected over Union Creek in 1867.

S. H. Thatch, A. J. Thatch and many others, settled on the Elkhorn, near Norfolk, during the summer of 1867.

Captain O. O. Austin built a house on Shell Creek, in June, 1866, but did not occupy it. John Bloomfield arrived in 1868, and was the first bona fide settler on this stream. He was soon followed by Lewis Warren, George Whitcher and William Meniece.

In 1869, the Sioux Indians made a raid on the Shell Creek settlements, killed some stock belonging to Lewis Warren and others, and shot a Mrs. Nelson, who afterwards recovered.

January 21, 1868, the first election for County Officers was held, which resulted as follows: Henry M. Barnes, August Raasch, Herman Braasch, Commissioners; Samuel H. Thatch, Clerk; Frederick Wegner, Probate Judge; Fred. Heckendorf, Treasurer; Fielding Bradshaw, Sheriff; August Lentz, Surveyor; Fred. Boche, Assessor; John Allison and William Bickley, Justices of the Peace; Thomas Bickley and Fred. Haase, Constables.

Said election was held at a small frame house located on Taylor Creek. The County was named Madison at the suggestion of the Germans of the Norfolk settlement, who came from Madison County, Wisconsin.

In the summer of 1869, the Commissioners divided the County into two Precincts, designating the north half Norfolk and the south half Union Creek Precinct.

In 1869, L. D. Barnes, John Teigden, John Leucke, A. Eyl and J. W. Risk, settled on Battle Creek. The Hales came in 1870 and settled on Upper Battle Creek. Battle Creek derived its name from the bloodless battle which occurred on its banks between the Territorial militia and Pawnee Indians during the first Pawnee war.

During the summer of 1871, a settler named Fuller was murdered in a field, near Shell Creek. Two cattle dealers, strangers in the County, were arrested on suspicion of being the murderers, but after an examination were released. The mystery of the murder has never been solved.

The first marriage in the County was that of Mr. Frederick Spawn to Miss Frederica Waggener, May 3, 1868. The first natural death was that of Mrs. Carr, in March, 1867.

The first term of the District Court was held in August, 1871; Hon. Lorenzo Crounse, Presiding Judge.

PUBLIC SCHOOLS.—Number of districts, forty-eight; school houses, forty; children of school age, males, 863, females, 761, total, 1,624; total number of children that attended school during the year, 940; qualified teachers employed, males, twenty-four, females, thirty-three; total wages paid teachers for the year, $5,298.56; value of school houses, $11,533; value of sites, $231; value of books, etc., $223.50.

TAXABLE PROPERTY.—Acres of land, 222,967; average value per acre, $1.24. Value of town lots, $26,257. Money used in merchandise, $24,925; money invested in manufactures, $12,132; horses, 2,707, value $59,782; mules, 116, value, $4,193; neat cattle, 5,156, value $41,820; sheep, 789, value, $910; swine, 6,316, value, $5,331; vehicles, 695, value, $9,704; moneys and credits, $8,525; mortgages, $13,325; stocks, etc., $2,000; furniture, $3,109; libraries, $750; property not enumerated, $24,431; total valuation for 1879, $524,710.

RAILROADS AND LANDS.—The Fremont, Elkhorn and Missouri Valley Railroad has been constructed through the County the present year, and is now in running order to Norfolk. The Omaha Niobrara and Black Hills Railroad, is now in running order from Jackson, on the U. P., to Norfolk.

The Burlington and Missouri River Railroad Company owns 60,000 acres of land here, the price ranging from $2 to $6 per acre. All the desirable Government land is taken. Improved farms are worth from $5 to $20 per acre.

POPULATION.—The County is divided into nine Precincts, the population of each in 1879, being as follows: Center, 414, Fairman, 272; Emerick, 143; Deer Creek, 478; Shell Creek, 254; Schoalcraft, 432; Norfolk, 957; Union Creek, 874; Jefferson, 456.

Total population of County, 4,280,—males, 2,288, females, 1,992.

## MADISON,

The County Seat, is a beautiful village of 400 inhabitants. It is located on Union Creek, in the southeastern part of the County; was laid out as a town in January, 1870, and made the County Seat at the general election in 1875. It has just been reached by the O. N. & B. H. R. R., and new buildings are being erected very fast. The *Chronicle*, a weekly newspaper, is published here, and it contains, besides the County offices, two Churches, two hotels, a fine school house, a large flouring mill with three run of burrs, a bank, four dry goods and grocery stores, one drug store, one harness shop, one jewelry store, a lumber yard, broom factory, etc.

## NORFOLK,

Located on the North Fork of the Elkhorn River, in the northeastern part of the County, contains 500 inhabitants. It was laid out in December, 1869, and is the oldest and largest town in the County. The United States Land Office for this district, is located here. It has a good weekly paper, the *Journal*, three Churches, the Methodist, Congregational, and German Lutheran, five general stores, two hotels, a bank, two drug and one hardware store, two furniture and one shoe store, blacksmith and wagon shops, lumber yard, livery stables, a fine flouring mill, large school house, real estate offices, etc. It is also the present terminus of two railroads, the O. N. & B. H. and the F. E. & M. V., and is rapidly becoming a prominent business center.

## BATTLE CREEK,

Located on a creek of the same name, in the central part of the County, contains about 150 inhabitants. The townsite was surveyed in 1873, by J. D. Hoover, who erected houses and opened a store here the following year. At present it has two general stores, one drug store, two blacksmith, wagon and carriage shops, one hotel, harness and shoe shops, and a grist mill with two run of burrs.

### NEWMAN GROVE,

Situated on Shell Creek, in the southwestern part of the County, contains two stores, a fine school house, two blacksmith and one wagon shop, drug store, etc. Excellent water-power for a flouring mill, is close at hand. There is also a fine natural grove of timber on the creek, near the town.

## NEMAHA COUNTY.

Nemaha, in the first organization of the Territory, was called Forney County. It was re-organized by the First Territorial Legislature, under its present name. It lies in the southeastern part of the State, bounded on the north by Otoe County, east by the Missouri River, south by Richardson and Pawnee, and west by Johnson County, containing about 400 square miles, or 256,000 acres.

WATER COURSES.—The County is watered by the Missouri River—which washes the entire eastern boundary—the Little Nemaha River and numerous smaller streams. The Little Nemaha flows diagonally through the central portion of the County from northwest to southeast, and empties into the Missouri near Nemaha City. Muddy Creek, a large tributary of the Great Nemaha River, waters the southwestern portion of the County. Long Branch, Plum and many smaller creeks meander through the County, leaving not a single township without running water. Water-power abundant.

CHARACTER OF THE LAND.—Fifteen per cent. of the area is valley, about five per cent. bluff, and the remainder gently rolling prairie. The valley of the Little Nemaha varies from two to five miles in width. Wide sloping bottoms are also found on Muddy and other streams. The bluffs of the Missouri are here quite prominent, and frequently cut through with deep ravines. The soil everywhere is of an excellent quality and magnificent crops are raised. No returns for 1879.

TIMBER.—There is plenty of timber in the County. Numerous large artificial groves dot the hillside and plain, and there are, besides, many fine natural groves in the valleys and along the bottoms of the Missouri.

FRUIT.—No returns have been made of fruit trees under cultivation, yet this is one of the very best fruit growing Counties in the State, many of the apple orchards returning their owners a yearly revenue of $500 to $2,500. In 1878 the orchard of Ex-Governor Furnas, near Brownville, yielded several thousand bushels of peaches.

COAL.—An excellent quality of coal is mined at Aspinwall, in this County. The seams vary from eighteen inches to two feet in thickness.

BUILDING STONE.—Along the bluffs of the Missouri, limestone of a superior quality for building is abundant.

HISTORICAL.—Richard Brown has the honor of being the first settler in the County. He crossed the Missouri in a canoe August 29, 1854, and laid the foundation of a claim cabin on the land now occupied by the town of Brownville. A number of pioneers quickly followed Mr. Brown, among whom were Rev. Joel M. Wood, Jesse Cole, Newton Kelley, Henry Emerson, Elder Thomas B. Edwards, Talbot Edwards, Josiah Edwards, B. B. Frazer, Houston Russell, James W. Coleman, Allen L. Coate, Israel R. Cuming, Stephen Sloan, A. J. Benedict, Henry W. Lake, O. F. Lake, W. A. Finney, Hiram Alderman, W. H. Hoover, Homer Johnson, R. J. Whitney, Mat. Alderman, Eli Fishburn, B. B. Chapman, Hudson Clayton, Thomas Heady, Sr., Mr. Christian, J. N. Knight,, Dr. Hoover, Wm. Hall, Wm. Hawk, Thomas Jeffries, Wm. Hays, Arch Handley, and others.

The first officers of the County were appointed by Governor Cuming, and are recorded as follows: A. J. Benedict, Probate Judge; H. W. Lake, Register of Deeds and County Clerk; Thomas B. Edwards, Sheriff.

The first election for County Officers, held December 12, 1855, resulted as follows: A. J. Benedict, Probate Judge; W. H. Hoover, Register of Deeds and County Clerk; J. W. Coleman, Sheriff; W. Hobbitzelle, Treasurer, and Allen L. Coate, County Surveyor. Richard Brown was elected to the Council, and Wm. A. Finney and Joel A. Wood, to the House, of the First Territorial Legislature.

Mrs. Thomas B. Edwards was the first white woman to settle in the County. Talbot Edwards erected the first house in Brownville. A daughter was born to Thomas and Mary Fitzgerald, at Brownville, October 20, 1854, this being the first birth in the County. Shortly after this event Mr. Samuel Stiers and Miss Nancy Swift were married by Rev. J. M. Wood. The first death in the County was that of an infant daughter of John Mullis, Jr., near Brownville, in September, 1854.

A. L. Coates surveyed the townsite of Brownville during the spring and summer of 1855. Messrs. I. T. Whyte and Wm. Hobbitszille opened the first stock of goods at Brownville in March, this year. In March, W. A. Finney built for R. Brown, the first flat-boat, to be used as a ferry across the Missouri River at Brownville. During this spring R. Brown, Henry Emerson and S. E. Rogers, built the first steam sawmill in the County. The Christian Church organized a society at Brownville, in January, 1855, Rev. Joel M. Wood, Pastor. H. S. Thorpe, on July 10, opened the first school at Brownville, with a dozen or so of scholars. Dr. A. S. Halliday located at Brownville November 2, 1855, and was the first physician in the County. Richard Brown was the first Postmaster at Brownville, receiving his appointment in the summer of 1855.

Brownville was incorporated and made the County Seat by the first Legislature, in March, 1855. About the same time, and by the same authority, Thos. B. Edwards, W. A. Finney, and H. W. Lake, were appointed Commissioners to locate the first Territorial Road in the County, commencing at Brownville and ending at Marshall's Trading Point, on the Big Blue River.

Daniel L. McGary, the first lawyer in the County, located at Brownville, in February, 1856.

In June, 1856, the first military company was formed in the County, at Brownville, called the "Home Guards;" O. F. Lake, Captain.

The first number of the Nebraska *Advertiser* was issued on the 7th day of June, 1856; R. W. Furnas, publisher and editor.

William Thurbur was the first County Superintendent of Common Schools. The first school district was organized at Brownville, June 21, 1856, with A. J. Benedict, President; R. W. Furnas, Secretary; and Homer Johnson, Treasurer.

The first Fourth of July celebration was held in 1856, at Brownville. Nearly every inhabitant in the County attended. R. J. Whitney was President of the day; Capt. Thurbur, Marshal; and N. Meyers, Assistant. Henry W. Lake read the Declaration of Independence; and R. W. Furnas delivered the oration.

Nemaha Valley Bank was established during the summer of 1856; A. Hallam, Cashier; S. H. Riddle, President.

The town site of Brownville was entered at the Land Office at Omaha, in February, 1857, by the Mayor, A. S. Holliday. At the same time and place, William Ferguson entered the land now known as South Brownville, being the first claim entry in the County.

The Brownville Stone and Stone Coal Company was organized in March, 1857. John Jackey was the first adult to die in Brownville, which occurred March 25, 1857.

In the spring of 1857, the U. S. Land Office for Nemaha District was located at Brownville, and commenced business in September following.

The first school house in the County was erected at Brownville, and was used for several years as a Church also.

The first apple orchard to bear fruit was in 1857, and belonged to John W. Hall, on Honey Creek. The Nemaha County Agricultural Society was organized in 1857. Its first Officers were: J. S. Minick, President; J. W. Coleman, Vice-President; R. W. Furnas, Secretary; and Jesse Cole, Treasurer.

In October, 1857, the first steam ferry-boat, the "Nemaha," arrived at Brownville. The event was hailed with loud rejoicing, and in the evening a cotillion party was held on board the boat.

Brownville Union Sabbath School was organized November 15, 1857.

First meeting for the organization of Nemaha Valley Lodge, No. 4, A. F. & A. M., was held at the residence of Jesse Noel, at Brownville, on the 26th day of September, 1857. Date of Charter, June 2, 1858.

The first County Commissioners were elected in November, 1856. The Board consisted of D. C. Sanders, J. N. Knight, and John W. Hall. First meeting, Dec. 1.

The first city election, under the new Act incorporating Brownville, was held February 9, 1857, and resulted as follows: Mayor, A. S. Holliday; Recorder, B. B. Thompson; Aldermen, J. T. White, J. D. N. Thompson and George W. Bratton; Marshal, Homer Johnson; Treasurer, J. T. Dozier; and A. L. Coates, Surveyor.

The first code of ordinances was adopted February 23, 1857.

The first term of District Court was held in a log cabin, at Brownville, in May, 1856, with Hon. James Bradley, Judge; J. W. Coleman, Sheriff; Wm. McLellan, District Attorney; and W. H. Hoover, District Clerk.

The Methodist Church at Brownville, was organized in February, 1858; Rev. Gordon in charge. At the same time the first protracted meeting was held, Revs. Goode, Cannon, Powell, Gordon and Horn officiating.

The Brownville House, now a part of McPherson's Block, was completed in the spring of 1858, and opened on the 4th of July of the same year, by Robert Morrison and C. W. Wheeler.

In the fall of 1858, the Presbyterian Church of Brownville was erected through the efforts and under the supervision of Luther Headley.

The first Lodge of the I. O. O. F. was organized at Brownville, January 29, 1858.

January 14, 1857, B. F. Lushbaugh and John L. Carson established a Bank at Brownville. This firm dissolved in 1860, and J. L. Carson continued the business of private banker until August 28, 1871, when the private bank was consolidated with, and organized as the First National Bank of Brownville, John L. Carson, President.

The first daily mail commenced from Rockport, Missouri, to Brownville, on July 1, 1858.

In January, 1857, the first number of the *Nemaha Journal* was issued at Brownville; S. Belden, editor and publisher. Shortly after, Langdon & Goff commenced the publication of the *Daily Snort*, which was short lived.

The Baptist Church was organized at Brownville on January 29, 1859.

First Nemaha County Agricultural Fair was held at Brownville, Oct. 6 and 7, 1859. October 10, 1859, the first Church bell arrived in Brownville, for the Presbyterian Church.

R. W. Furnas published the first number of the *Nebraska Farmer*, the first journal of the kind in Nebraska, in January, 1860.

The telegraph line was completed and an office duly opened for business, on August 29, 1860.

On the 1st of November, 1867, Brownville Chapter No. 4, R. A. M., was duly organized.

Brownville High School Building was completed in 1865. The Congregational Church was erected in 1859, and sold to the Methodists in 1861. The Christian Church, erected in 1859, was blown down by a hurricane in 1866, and rebuilt by the Baptists in 1868–69.

The first number of the Brownville *Journal* was issued January 1, 1868. The office was removed to Falls City the same year.

Holladay & Hill commenced the publication of the Brownville *Democrat* on July 11, 1868. The name of this paper was changed to the *Nemaha County Granger* by Holladay & Whitehead, and the first number was issued by them January 23, 1874.

The first railroad train arrived in Brownville, on February 1, 1874, over the route known as the Midland Extension, from Nebraska City, now called the Nebraska Railway.

The corner stone of the Catholic Church in Brownville, was laid July 24, 1870, by Rev. Father Curtis, of Omaha.

The corner stone of the Episcopal edifice, was laid by Rev. Geo. R. Davis, in October, 1857.

Furnas Council, No. 3, R. A. M., was organized April 25, 1871. Ada Chapter No. 2, was organized February 10, 1872.

Brownville Division, No. 19, Sons of Temperance, was organized November 12, 1872. Excelsior Lodge No. 15, Knights of

Pythias, was organized October 21, 1873. The State Bank of Nebraska organized on October 1, 1870.

The State Agricultural Fair was held at Brownville, in September, 1870, and October, 1871. The first graded or high school, was organized at Brownville, during the term commencing April 6, 1868.

PUBLIC SCHOOLS.—Present number of districts in the County, seventy-five; school houses, seventy-four; children of school age—males, 1,906, females, 1,925, total, 3,832; qualified teachers employed,—males, forty-nine, females, eighty-four; total wages paid teachers for the year, $13,849.06; value of school houses, $46,194; value of sites, $3,117; value of books and apparatus, $1,069.

TAXABLE PROPERTY.—Acres of land, 246,762; average value per acre, $4.13; value of town lots, $146,570; money invested in merchandise, $63,935; money used in manufactures, $13,460; horses, 4,892, value $111,050; mules and asses, 630, value $18,146; neat cattle, 13,630, value $130,019; sheep, 591, value $419; swine, 34,739, value $31,267; vehicles, 1,668, value $26,026; moneys and credits, $23,978; mortgages, $35,425; stocks, etc., $,26085; furniture, $36,192; libraries, $1,499; property not enumerated, $76,760; railroads, $62,831.69; telegraph, $676.80; total valuation for 1879, $1,823,002.49.

RAILROADS.—The Nebraska Railway, under control of the B. & M., runs through the eastern portion of the County, a distance of about thirteen miles, Nemaha City being its present terminal point. Track laying for the extension of this road to a connection with the B. &. M. branch at Beatrice, Gage County, sixty-five miles distant, via. Tecumseh, on the A. &. N. road, is now being vigorously pushed forward, and is nearly completed to the latter point. The surveys for several other lines projected through the County have already been made.

LANDS.—Improved lands are worth from $7 to $30 per acre; wild lands from $4 to $10.

The estimated population of the County in 1879, was 10,504.

BROWNVILLE,

The County Seat, is an enterprising city of about 1,500 inhabitants. It has a handsome location on the high ground facing the Missouri

River, near the center of the County from north to south, and is also on the line of the Nebraska Railway. The bottoms and bluffs of the Missouri in the vicinity are well timbered, while the surrounding country on the north, west and south, is highly cultivated, and dotted with numerous large orchards and beautiful artificial groves.

STATE NORMAL SCHOOL BUILDING.

A splendid steam ferry connects the city with the Kansas City, St. Joe and Council Bluffs Railroad, on the opposite side of the Missouri. Two excellent weekly newspapers are published here, the *Granger* and the *Advertiser*, and there are besides, two banks, a large number of stores, representing all the various lines of trade, several handsome Churches, a very fine high school building, accommodating a graded school, etc.

### PERU

Is a beautiful city of 600 inhabitants, situated on the banks of the Missouri, and on the Nebraska Railway, seven miles north of

Brownville. The State Normal school is located here. Business is represented by a weekly paper, the *Herald*, a large three story flouring mill, one manufacturing establishment, several grocery and dry goods stores, two drug stores, a brick yard, harness, boot and shoe, millinery, confectionery and a host of smaller establishments. It has several Church organizations and neat Churches, and an elegant school house, supplied with complete apparatus and all the modern improvements.

### NEMAHA CITY,

Located near the mouth of the Little Nemaha River, about five miles south of Brownville, was one of the earliest towns located in the County. Allen T. Coates came here in the summer of 1854, and in December following, the townsite was surveyed by Drs. Hoover and Wyatt. It was incorporated by the Legislature in 1856, and during the same year a Postoffice was established, with Dr. Jerome Hoover, postmaster. The Methodists organized the first religious Society, Rev. Philo Gordon, Pastor. Joel W. Wells, elected in 1857, was the first Mayor of the city. S. Belden issued the first number of the *Nemaha Valley Journal* here in January, 1858. Geo. W. Fairbrother and T. C. Hacker commenced the publication of the *Nebraska Herald* here in October, 1859. The first white child born in the Precinct was a son of Alex. Weddle, on June 23, 1855.

Nemaha City is at present the terminus of the Nebraska Railway, and has made more substantial progress during the past year than ever before. The railroad has put new life into it and new buildings are going up very fast. It contains about 250 inhabitants, two Churches—Methodist and Episcopal—a good school house, stores, grain houses, etc.

### ASPINWALL,

Situated on the Missouri, in the southeastern part of the County, was surveyed in 1857. Hobbitzill & Co., opened the first store in the town. Among the first settlers of the place were Darius Phipps, Wm. Thurman, Henry Hart, Hegler and Paulin. Miss Clara Parker taught the first school here in the fall of 1861. The town was incorporated in 1870. At present it contains several mercantile stores and other business establishments, good school and Church advantages &c. Extensive coal mines are being worked at this place.

### SHERIDAN

Is a flourishing town of two hundred inhabitants, situated near the geographical center of the County. It was surveyed and recorded in 1869, and the first store was opened the same year by Wesley Dundas. Dr. A. Opporman located here in May, 1871, and was the first physician. The first hotel was erected in 1874 by A. W. Morgan. The first school was taught by E. E. Savage, in November, 1874, and during the same year the Methodist Church was organized. Sheridan is located on the Branch of the Burlington and Missouri River Railroad now building through the County, and is improving very rapidly. The railroad will make it one of the best business centers in the County. All classes of business are represented and well sustained. It has excellent Church and school facilities, and a weekly newspaper, the *Post*.

### ST. DEROIN

Is an old village located in the southeast corner of the County. It was laid out in 1854, and surveyed by Greever, Nuckolls and others. Judge A. J. Ritter opened a general merchandise store here in 1859. A Postoffice was established in 1861. It contains a fine brick school house, a first class flouring mill, two blacksmith and one wagon shop, stores, and other places of business.

### HOWARD.

Located on the Little Nemaha, in the northwestern part of the County, is a new town and contains a grist mill, hotel, tin shop, wagon and blacksmith shop, grocery and dry goods stores, two physicians, etc.

### LONDON,

Three miles west of Brownville, has two Churches a fine school house and several business establishments.

DRATTON, JOHNSON, GRANT, SHERMAN, HILLSDALE, FEBING, ST. FREDERICK, POPENS, CLIFTON and LOCUST GROVE, are promising young towns.

## MERRICK COUNTY.

Merrick County was organized by the Legislature in the winter of 1858-9. It lies between the Platte and Loup Rivers, in the middle-eastern part of the State, bounded on the north by Nance and Platte Counties, east and south by the Platte River,—which separates it from Polk and Hamilton Counties, and west by Hall and Howard Counties, containing about 400 square miles, at an average elevation of 1,686 feet above the sea level.

WATER COURSES.—The County is finely watered by the Platte River and tributaries. The Platte washes the southeastern border, a distance of about fifty miles. Prairie Creek, a very fine stream, flows from southwest to northeast through the central portion of the County. Silver and several smaller creeks meander through different portions of the County. Well water is obtained almost anywhere at a depth of from 15 to 25 feet.

TIMBER.—Native timber is scarce. Along the banks of the Platte and on the islands, there is a small amount. A very large amount of timber has been planted in the County, however, and fuel is no longer a scarcity. The reports for 1879, show the number of forest trees under cultivation to be 2,107½ acres, or 1,301,390 trees, besides 11¾ miles of hedging.

FRUIT.—2,264 apple, sixty-four pear, 1,773 peach, 2,811 plum, and 616 cherry trees, and 284 grape vines are reported. Many of the orchards are in bearing.

CHARACTER OF THE LAND.—The surface of the country consists almost entirely of fertile valley land, the Platte River being on the southeastern boundary, and the Loup River just beyond the northern boundary of the County, while through the central portion, midway between the two, extends the fine valley of Prairie Creek. At least seventy per cent. of the area is valley and bottom, and the remainder low, undulating prairie.

SOIL AND CROPS.—The soil is a deep, black sandy loam of inexhaustible fertility, and almost everywhere yields abundant crops. The area in cultivation reported for 1879, was 78,270 acres. Rye, 2,503 acres, 36,485 bushels; spring wheat, 16,606 acres, 206,520 bushels; corn, 9,168 acres, 239,633 bushels; barley, 595 acres, 15,094 bushels; oats, 4,041 acres, 128,220 bushels; sorghum, thirty-six acres, 2,958 gallons; flax, 121 acres, 1,195 bushels; millet, fifty-three acres, 912 tons; potatoes, 318 acres, 31,014 bushels.

HISTORICAL.—James Vieregg, a returned Californian, has the honor of being the first settler in the County, locating on the south-east quarter of section five, town eleven north, range eight west, on Thursday, September 15, 1859. Later on the same day, Charles Eggerton and Jesse Shoemaker, selected a site for a ranche within a few rods of the original "lone tree" on the left bank of the Platte River, three miles southwest of where Central City now stands. Here they built a large sod house and stabling, which soon became widely known as the "Lone Tree Ranche." A few months later the co-partnership of Eggerton & Shoemaker was dissolved, the latter going eight miles farther west, to the banks of Wood River, where he established "Shoemaker's Point Ranche."

On the first of January, 1860, Jason Parker staked his claim upon the land where he still resides, about two miles southeast of Central City, and on the first of March following, he brought his family out, being the pioneer family of the County.

Many of the Pike's Peak gold seekers, upon their return, settled permanently in this County, among whom were James G. and Wells Brewer, who located in 1860.

John L. Martin, who had been living at Silver Creek for a year and a half previously, settled upon a claim about a mile and a half southeast of Chapman, on Tuesday, May 21, 1861. Mrs. Martin was for five years the only physician between Columbus and Fort Kearney.

On Tuesday, July 15, 1862, Mrs. Jason Parker was buried, being the first death among the settlers.

The first marriage ceremony in the County, was performed by Judge James G. Brewer, at his residence, between John M. Hyes and Viola Parker, on Sunday, December 25, 1864, in the presence of Charles Combs and Wells Brewer.

According to the provisions of an Act of the Legislature, the Commissioners of Platte County issued an order for an election to be held in Merrick County, on the 18th day of April, 1864, for the purpose of County organization. At this election the following

County officers were elected, viz.: Commissioners, George Gilson, Jason Parker, and Jesse Shoemaker; Probate Judge, James G. Brewer; Clerk, Wm. H. Mitchell; Treasurer, Wells Brewer; Prosecuting Attorney, Henry Latrop; Sheriff, Frank Parker; Coroner, Robert Mitchell.

All the County business was transacted at the house of James G. Brewer for several years.

The first jury trial held in the County was on a civil suit before Jas. G. Brewer, Probate Judge, wherein Henry Twitchell was plaintiff and William Haylen and Jesse Shoemaker, defendants. Counsel for plaintiff, John L. Martin; for defendant, Wells Brewer.

The first criminal trial was before the same, on June 16, 1867, the People against Matt Vertz, charged with shooting Isaac Berry.

During the year 1868 the Indians made several raids into the County, but the greater part of the mischief done by them was in stealing stock. However, a son of Claus Gottesh, and a hired man, was killed by Indians in 1868, and in June, 1869, Wm. Shoulders and John Sanford were also killed by them while trying to recapture stolen animals.

At an election held on the 12th of October, 1869, Lone Tree was selected as the permanant County Seat.

The first term of the District Court of Merrick County was held at Lone Tree, November 24, 1869; Hon. Lorenzo Crounse, presiding Judge; E. F. Gray, District Attorney; Ira Prouty, Clerk, and G. W. Moore, Sheriff.

The first bonded indebtedness of the County was created on June 4, 1870, when the citizens, at a special election, voted bonds to the amount of $18,000 for the erection of a court house and jail at Lone Tree. The contract for its construction was awarded, March 21, 1871, to Charles Lightfoot, for $16,000. The building, however, was finished by Q. B. Skinner, and owing to changes made in the plans, cost about $20,000. It is brick, fifty by sixty, and thirty feet high; offices and jail below, and court room above.

A tornado crossed the County, from west to east, on the afternoon of the 5th of July, 1871, destroying everything in its path for a width of about 200 feet. It lifted the roof from the depot at Lone Tree, destroyed part of Bryant's Hotel, demolished a blacksmith shop and several small buildings, and scattered Traver &

May's lumber yard in every direction. About a mile east of town, the house of a Mr. Phelps, in which he and his four children were eating supper at the time, was lifted bodily from the ground, and carried some eighty yards. making a complete wreck of it. Mr. Phelps was instantly killed, his body being found partially hanging in a cottonwood tree, while around him, in the *debris*, lay his children, stunned and bleeding; but, strange as it may seem, they all eventually recovered.

MERRICK COUNTY COURT HOUSE BUILDING.

County bonds, to the amount of $6,000, were voted January 9th, 1872, to aid James G. Brewer in the construction of a water-grist mill in the County.

In 1872–73 peace and prosperity reigned in Merrick County, and its growth and improvement was substantial and great. And it so promised for 1874, but in July vast swarms of grasshoppers visited the County, and swept all cultivated vegetation from the land.

In February, 1875, the citizens of Lone Tree petitioned the District Court to change the name of that town to Central City, and it was so changed.

CHURCH MATTERS.—Elder T. B. Lemon, of the Methodist Church, conducted services at the residence of James G. Brewer, June 24, 1866, taking his text from Daniel, 6th Chapter, 10th verse; and during five days of the following week, held a protracted meeting in the log school house, at the close of which a class was formed, with Jacob Rice, as leader.

The first Church in the County was erected at Silver Creek, by the Episcopalians, in 1870, and dedicated in 1872.

The first Baptist Church was built at Lone Tree, in 1872, and dedicated in August, of that year.

The Presbyterian and Union Churches at Clarksville were erected in 1873. The Presbyterians also have a Church at Central City. At the present time there are seven Churches and several Church organizations in the County, and services are held in the school house, also.

PUBLIC SCHOOLS.—Miss Ella Abbott, now Mrs. Dodge, taught the first school in the County in the winter of 1866-7. The number of districts in 1879 was forty-eight; school houses, forty-six; children of school age, males, 848, females, 799, total, 1,647; whole number of children that attended school during the year, 1,303; number of qualified teachers employed, males, forty-one, females, thirty-three; total salary paid teachers for the year, $9,418.44; value of school houses, $29,990; value of sites, $1,789.25; value of books and apparatus, $1,599.76.

TAXABLE PROPERTY.—Acres of land, 222,763, average value per acre, $2.25; value of town lots, $47,748; money invested in merchandise, $44,325; money used in manufactures, $10,585; horses, 2,434, value, $47,177; mules, 189, value, $4,532; neat cattle, 7,340, value, $35,341; sheep, 1,189, value, $598; swine, 3,621, value, $350; vehicles, 918, value, $13,720; moneys and credits, $13,489; mortgages, $12,139; stocks, $37.00 furniture, $12,013; libraries, $514; property not enumerated, $39,380: railroads, $462,323.60; telegraph, $3,791; total valuation for 1879, $1,386,999.60.

RAILROADS.—The Union Pacific Railroad passes through the County from east to west, a distance of 44.60 miles. The Nebraska Railway, under control of the B. & M., is now being extended from Aurora, Hamilton County, to a connection with the Union Pacific at Central City. The track is being laid as fast as men and money can do the work, and the road will be in running order between these points before the close of the present year.

LANDS.—The Union Pacific Railroad Company owns about 20,000 acres in this County, for which $3 to $6 per acre is asked. Improved lands are worth from $5 to $25 per acre.

POPULATION.—The following are the names of the Precincts and the population of each in 1879: Silver Creek, 368; Clarksville, 831; Lone Tree, 977; Chapman, 406; Prairie Island, 56; Mead, 328; Prairie Creek, 406; Loup, 365; Central, 144; Vieregg, 456; Midland, 288.

Total population of County, 4,625—males, 2,480; females, 2,145.

THE KETCHUM AND MITCHELL MURDER.—In December, 1878, the sheriff of this County, assisted by the sheriff of Buffalo County, arrested Luther Mitchell and A. W. Ketchum, homesteaders, of Custer County, for the murder of Sheriff Stevens, of that County, who with two comrades went to the place of Luther Mitchell, to arrest Ketchum on a warrant charging him with cattle stealing from the ranche of I. P. Olive, in Custer County.

It is claimed that Mitchell and Ketchum were out doors handling stock, when Stevens and companions rode up and commenced firing. Mitchell and Ketchum returned the fire; and Mitchell shot Stevens, who died a few days afterward. On the other hand, it is claimed that Ketchum was resisting arrest, and was aided by Mitchell.

Stevens, it is claimed, was a brother of I. P. Olive, and was passing under an assumed name, on account of crimes committed in Texas. Shortly after he was killed, Olive sent out notices offering a reward for the capture and delivery to him of Mitchell and Ketchum—$500 for Mitchell and $200 for Ketchum. They were arrested, as before stated, by the Sheriffs of Merrick and Buffalo Counties, and taken to Kearney, and from there were taken by Barney J. Gillen, Sheriff of Keith County, to Plum Creek, Dawson County, arriving there December 10, in the afternoon. Gillen, accompanied by a young man named Dufrand, and with the two prisoners shackled together, left there the same afternoon in a wagon, for the County Seat of Custer County, forty miles north. Before reaching their destination, they were met on the road by Olive and a dozen or fifteen "cow boys," who took the prisoners from the Sheriff, and murdered them in the most atrocious manner. Their bodies were found the next day, in a canon three miles south of Olive's ranche. Ketchum's body was hanging to a tree, with a rope around the neck, and Mitchell's was lying partly on the ground, nearly upon the knees, and held in this position by shackles to the body of Ketchum. The tall, dry prairie grass had been set on fire, which burned the bodies in the most horrible manner, the flesh falling from the limbs of Mitchell while being raised from the ground.

I. P. Olive, W. H. Green, John Baldwin, Pedro Dominicus, Phil. Dufrand, and Barney J. Gillen, were surprised and captured soon after, at and near Plum Creek. Dennis Gartrell, one of the party, escaped.

Custer County being unorganized, the Judge of the Fifth Judicial District set the trial of the case at Hastings, in Adams County. The Legislature appropriated $10,000 to carry on the prosecution.

The District Attorney, T. D. Scofield, was assisted by Attorney-General Dilworth. Hon. J. M. Thurston, of Omaha, and C. W. McNamara, of Plum Creek, were employed by the Governor.

The defence was made by John Carrigan, of Blair, Hinman & Neville, of North Platte, Conner, of Fillmore County, James Laird, of Juniata, and Warrington, of Plum Creek.

The trial was had in April, 1879, and including disposition of technical points, lasted nearly three weeks, resulting in the conviction of Olive and Fisher of murder in the second degree, and sentence to penitentiary for life, by Judge Gaslin. Ten of the jury stood for murder in the first degree. Bion Brown turned State's evidence.

Immediately after the conviction of Olive and Fisher, Baldwin and Green were tried, the jury disagreeing. The defence made the point that they were at most only spectators and not participants. In their trial the Mexican, Dominicus, turned State's evidence.

The other prisoners have not yet been tried, and will not be till the case of Olive is passed upon by the Supreme Court.

Gillen and another prisoner, name not ascertained, escaped from Plum Creek jail.

### CENTRAL CITY,

Formerly called "Lone Tree," is the County Seat, and has about 500 inhabitants. It is situated in the valley of the Platte, and on the line of the U. P. Railroad, 132 miles west of Omaha. Mr. Ed. Parker, and a Mr. Mills, erected the first house on the townsite in May, 1866. At present it contains a fine brick court house, two story school house, three Churches, a weekly newspaper, the *Courier*, two hotels, several stores, a bank, two elevators, lumber yards, etc., and the prospects of the town are very flattering. There is a fine wagon bridge across the Platte at this point, making this the trading and shipping center of a number of villages on the south side of the river.

### CLARKSVILLE,

Named after S. H. H. Clark, manager of the Union Pacific Railroad, has a population of 400. The first house on the townsite was completed October 30, 1871, by Mr. L. B. McIntyre. The city is located on the line of the U. P. Railroad, ten miles east of the County Seat, and contains a weekly paper, the *Messenger*, several fine stores, large lumber yards and implement stores, a hotel, three grain elevators, two Churches, fine school house, etc. This is an extensive shipping point, and in 1876 a bridge was completed across the Platte here, at a cost of $11,000, for the convenience of the farmers of Hamilton and York Counties.

### SILVER CREEK,

On the Union Pacific, eleven miles east of Clarksville, has about 200 inhabitants. It contains several business houses, an Episcopal Church, school house, grain elevators, etc. A wagon bridge across the Platte connects it with Polk County, and draws a large trade.

VIEW NEAR CENTRAL CITY, MERRICK COUNTY.

CHAPMAN,

On the Union Pacific, in the southwestern part of the County, is a flourishing village of about 150 inhabitants. It does a large shipping and general merchandise trade. The first house erected here was completed June 19, 1872, by Leake and Read.

## NUCKOLLS COUNTY.

Nuckolls County was organized early in the summer of 1871. It is located on the south-central border of the State, and is bounded on the north by Clay and east by Thayer County, south by the State of Kansas, and west by Webster County, containing 576 square miles, or 368,640 acres, at an average elevation of 1,600 feet above the sea level.

WATER COURSES.—The County is finely watered by the Republican and Little Blue Rivers and tributaries. The Republican flows through the southwestern portion, and is supported by numerous fine tributaries, which have their source in this County. The Little Blue flows diagonally through the northeastern portion, and has several large tributaries, the most important of which is Elk Creek, a splendid mill stream flowing through the central portion of the County. Every township has a living stream. Water power is unlimited.

TIMBER.—The larger streams are all well skirted with timber, much of it being hardwood; 215,779 forest trees have been planted in the County up to date, and fuel is already abundant. Six and one-half miles of hedging are reported.

FRUIT.—4,222 apple, 79 pear, 5,618 peach, 118 plum, and 854 cherry trees, are returned, besides 928 grape vines. Various wild fruits are found along the streams.

BUILDING STONE of an excellent quality is found in different localities.

CHARACTER OF THE LAND.—About twenty per cent. of the area is valley and bottom land, and the balance rolling prairie, with prominent bluffs in occasional places along the streams. The Republican valley averages six miles in width. The valley of the

Little Blue, which extends a distance of about fifteen miles through this County, varies from three to five miles in width. Elk and Spring Creeks also have beautiful valleys. The general average of the surface soil of the uplands is from one and a half to three feet in thickness. The following statement will show the principal productions as reported for 1879:

CROPS.—Area under cultivation, 24,730 acres. Winter wheat, seventy-five acres, 1,148 bushels; spring wheat, 8,549 acres, 80,871 bushels; rye, 479 acres, 6,694 bushels; corn, 7,361 acres, 220,638 bushels; barley, 761 acres, 17,333 bushels; sorghum, twenty-six acres, 2,823 gallons; hungarian, forty-four acres, 172 tons; potatoes, 132 acres, 14,867 bushels.

HISTORICAL.—As early as in 1858, a few hardy pioneers located upon claims in this County, but for the next several years scarcely any progress was made toward its permanent settlement, even as late as 1871 the population numbering only eight, according to the State census returns. From that date onward, however, the tide of immigration has continued steadily, and close settlements have sprung up in all parts of the County. A few years ago, a large body of Danes and Norwegians located in the southeastern part of the County. In the northwestern part, in the neighborhood of Liberty Creek, there is a thrifty settlement of Germans.

The first election for County Officers occurred on the 27th of June, 1871, and resulted as follows: Commissioners, A. Simonton, and J. Hannum; Probate Judge, A. E. Davis; Clerk, E. L. Downing; Treasurer, Willis Henby; Sheriff, R. J. Harmon; Superintendent Public Instruction, D. W. Montgomery; Coroner, F. Naylor; Surveyor, D. W. Montgomery.

The St. Joe & Denver City Railroad was built through the northeastern part of the County in 1872. The Burlington & Missouri River Railroad Company have made their surveys through the County for a branch line running from Beatrice, Gage County, to Red Cloud, Webster County, and the road is to be constructed as rapidly as possible.

LANDS.—A large amount of the land in this County is owned by the Railroads and non-residents. The price of wild lands is from $2 to $8 per acre; improved from $5 to $18.

Five flouring mills and two Churches are among the recent improvements in the County.

PUBLIC SCHOOLS.—Number of school districts, thirty-four; school houses, twenty-eight; children of school age—males, 588, females, 469; total, 1,057; qualified teachers employed—males, twenty-four, females, twenty-six; wages paid teachers for the year—males, $3,554, females, $2,753.81; total, $6,307.81; value of school houses, $12,985; value of sites, $302; value of books, etc., $602.

TAXABLE PROPERTY.—Acres of land, 325,854; average value per acre, $2.15; value of town lots, $14,398; money invested in merchandise, $11,200; money used in manufactures, $8,453; horses, 1,862, value, $31,902; mules, 211, value, $5,186; neat cattle, 2,995, value, $26,953; sheep, 999, value, $825; swine, 7,776, value, $7,307.55; vehicles, 578, value, $7,536; moneys and credits, $5,489; mortgages, $8,654; stocks, $66; furniture, $5,560; libraries, $164; property not enumerated, $19,945.45; railroad, $25,088.07. Total valuation for 1879, $880,908.07.

POPULATION.—The following is the population of the County in 1879, by Precincts: Alban, 99; Beaver, 377; Bonhard, 319; Elk, 488; Liberty, 313; Nelson, 707; Sherman, 404; Spring Valley, 65; Spring Creek, 192.

Total, 2,964—males, 1,615; females, 1,349.

## NELSON,

The County Seat, is a rapidly growing town of 600 inhabitants. It is situated on a gentle slope on the north side of Elk Creek, near the geographical center of the County, and was surveyed in December, 1872. It contains a good court house, secure jail, fine new school house, Church, grist mill, weekly newspaper, the *Herald*, several stores and shops, real estate offices, lumber yards, agricultural implement stores, etc. Excellent bridges span the Elk and other streams in the vicinity, adding greatly to the convenience of trade, and making this a fine business center.

## SUPERIOR

Is a prosperous town of about 400 inhabitants, located on the Republican River, twelve miles south of Nelson. The town site was surveyed in February, 1875. It has a weekly newspaper, the

*Guide*, an elegant school house, hardware, drug, grocery, dry-goods, furniture, implement, and various other stores and business places. A substantial bridge, 480 feet long, costing $10,000, spans the Republican at this point, and draws large travel and trade from northern Kansas.

ELKTON, HENRIETTA, SPRING VALLEY, BEACHAMVILLE, OX BOW, OAK and NORA are prosperous young towns of fifty to 250 inhabitants each.

## NANCE COUNTY.

Nance County, formerly the Pawnee Indian Reservation, was organized by proclamation of Governor Nance, after whom it was called, June 16, 1879. It lies near the center of the State from north to south, in the fifth tier of Counties west of the Missouri River, and is bounded on the north by Boone and Platte, east by Platte and Merrick, south by Merrick, and west by Merrick and Boone Counties, containing 450 square miles, or 288,000 acres.

The Loup River flows from west to east through the entire length of the County, and receives several fine tributaries from the north, of which the most prominent are Beaver, Plum and Cedar Creeks. The southeastern portion of the County is watered by Prairie Creek. There are numerous fine mill privileges on the tributaries of the Loup.

The surface of the country consists of about eighty per cent. undulating prairie, and the balance valley and bottom. Almost every acre is rich tillable land. The Loup Valley is from three to seven miles wide. Cedar, Plum and Beaver Creeks each have beautiful valleys, varying in width from two to five miles, and well fringed with forest timber along the banks of the streams. Taken as a whole, Nance County embraces as fine a body of lands as there are to be found in the State.

In the spring of 1857, three colonies of Mormons, comprising together over one hundred families, located on the Loup, near the mouth of Beaver Creek, where they established the town of Genoa.

They enclosed, with a ditch and sod fence, 2,000 acres of rich land, and put 1,200 acres under cultivation.

In 1862, the U. S. Government surveyed the territory now comprising this County, and confirmed it by treaty to the Pawnee Indians, for a Reservation. This displaced the Mormons, and they removed to other localities. The Indians afterwards cultivated the land which had been broken up by the Mormons. In 1875, the Pawnees were removed to their reservation in the Indian Territory, and these lands were appraised for sale and opened for settlement.

The first election for County Officers and location of County Seat, occurred in November, 1879, under the supervision of D. E. Stearns, George McClusey and J. W. Whitney, special Commissioners appointed by the Governor for that purpose. The results of the election are not yet fully assured, Genoa had a small majority, but it is contested on illegal votes, by its rival town Fullerton. The Governor located the temporary County Seat at Fullerton.

The old village of Genoa, in the northeastern part of the County, is building up very rapidly since the organization of the County. At present it contains forty or fifty dwellings, good stores and a school house. The Omaha, Niobrara and Black Hills Railroad, now being constructed from Jackson, on the Union Pacific to Albion, in Boone County, will pass through Genoa and assure its prosperity.

### FULLERTON

Is a town recently established on Cedar Creek, fifteen miles west of Genoa. It has already three stores, two livery stables, one hotel, lawyers and doctors offices, a newspaper, the *Journal*, and other improvements.

The estimated population of the County in 1879, was 1,000.

THE BEAVER VALLEY, NEAR ALBION, BOONE COUNTY.

## OTOE COUNTY.

Otoe County was organized by an Act of the first Territorial Legislature, approved March 2, 1855. It is located on the southeastern border of the State, bounded on the north by Cass County, east by the Missouri River, south by Nemaha and Johnson Counties, and west by Lancaster County, containing about 575 square miles, or 368,000 acres.

WATER COURSES.—The County is most excellently watered by the Missouri and Little Nemaha Rivers, and several large creeks. The Little Nemaha River, affording fine mill advantages, flows diagonally through the central portion from northwest to southeast, its chief tributaries being the North and South Forks, Muddy, Porter, Deer, and Fox Creeks. The eastern portion of the County is watered by the Weeping Water, North and South Table, Dunbar, Stanton, Rock, and Camp Creeks. There are but very few quarter sections of land which do not furnish good stock water.

CHARACTER OF THE LAND.—The surface of the country consists chiefly of rolling prairie, about fifteen per cent. being valley and bottom. The Missouri bottom is exceedingly fertile, yielding from fifty to eighty bushels of corn per acre, and the bottoms of the other streams are equally as productive. The bluffs of the Missouri are high, cut through with innumerable draws, or ravines, and are admirably adapted for grape growing. From the valleys of the streams in the interior, the land rises and falls in gentle undulations, gradually blending in long stretches of nearly level prairie. The area in cultivation in 1878, was 94,247 acres, and in 1879, 104,439 acres. Bushels of spring wheat returned, 300,000; corn, 1,200,000.

TIMBER.—The bluffs of the Missouri and banks of the other streams of the County are well clothed with timber, the varieties most common being oak, ash, elm, maple, cottonwood, box-elder and hackberry. The estimated number of acres of timber planted is 11,000. Well developed groves gladden the eye on every hand,

and many of the farms are surrounded with honey-locust and osage hedges.

FRUIT.—Otoe has more vineyards and orchards than any other County in the State. Hon. J. Sterling Morton, of Nebraska City, has a fine orchard of forty acres. Ex-Chief Justice Mason has an orchard near the same place, containing some 15,000 choice fruit trees. Apples, pears, plums, grapes and all the minor fruits grow to perfection. A few years ago an apple was grown in the orchard of Perry & Walker, near Nebraska City, which weighed twenty-nine and a half ounces.

BUILDING MATERIAL.—Limestone abounds throughout the middle and eastern portions of the County. Sandstone also crops out in several places. Good building sand and fine clays for the manufacture of brick are abundant.

COAL, in thin seams, has been discovered in several localities.

HISTORICAL.—The first settlements in the County were made where Nebraska City now stands. In 1844 the United States Government occupied a portion of the present townsite for a Military Post, which was named Fort Kearney. The Fort proper, a blockhouse, was built in 1846. It stood in what is now Fifth Street. A log cabin, used for officer's quarters, barracks, or hospital, stood about 150 feet easterly of the block-house.

A Mr. Hardin was put in charge of the government buildings, when, in 1848, the Military Post was removed to New Fort Kearney, on the Platte River.

Col. John Boulware, who came to the Fort in 1846, and established a government ferry, was appointed in Mr. Hardin's place, in 1849; and Hiram P. Downs, formerly a sergeant in the United States army, was, in 1850, put in charge, instead of Col. Boulware.

The original settlers and claimants of the ground embraced by Nebraska City, were John Boulware, Hiram P. Downs and John B. Boulware. John B. Boulware built, in 1852, a ferry house, and the first permanent habitation on the townsite, on the river bank, at the foot of Commercial street. His father's claim was the present Kearney Division of the city, and was staked off in the spring of 1853. Hiram P. Downs claimed 320 acres, and in the fall of 1853, Charles W. Pierce surveyed the claim, running the north line from the river nearly along North Table Creek, to Tenth Street, the west line along Tenth Street, and the south line south of the present Kansas street. John B. Boulware claimed 320 acres from the south line of Down's claim to South Table Creek, and from his father's, on the east, nearly to the west line of what is known as Hail & Co's Addition. West of Tenth Street, Mr. Pierce also surveyed 160 acres for a Mr. Fawks.

Hiram P. Downs sold his claim—which embraced the greater part of the land now occupied by Nebraska City—to the Nebraska City Town Company, which was composed of S. F. Nuckolls, A. A. Bradford, H. P. Bennett, Wm. B. Hail, Lafayette Nuckolls, John Doniphan, L. D. Bird, Jas. Doniphan, S. E. Frazee, Marshall & Woodward, N. B. Giddings, C. F. Holly, J. W. Kelly, W. S. Van Doren, Robert Cook and J. Sterling Morton.

The Town Company, as aforesaid, employed Chas. W. Pierce, to survey the land and make it into streets, alleys and lots. On May 5, 1855, the first grand sale of town lots was held. The three lots where the Nebraska City National Bank now stands, on the corner of Main and Sixth streets, were sold for twenty dollars each; the lot on Sixth street, now Hawke's Hall, was donated to Conrad Mullis for a blacksmith shop. At figures ranging from fifty to sixty-five dollars, almost any "claim" within a distance of four miles from Nebraska City, could have been readily purchased.

The survey of the original plat of Nebraska City was made by Chas. W. Pierce, assisted by Dr. Wm. Dewey, Cornelius Schubert, Samuel Saunders, and others, in the fall of 1854.

By Act of the Territorial Legislature, approved March 2, 1855, Nebraska City was declared to be the seat of justice of Otoe County. The charter was amended in 1867.

In 1857 a small patch of corn was grown where the court house now stands.

Chas. H. Cowles erected the first, and Chas Pierce the second frame house on the town site. The former stood on the corner of Fifth street, and the latter next door to where the *Press* office stood. The first brick house was built by Mr. Nuckolls, upon the northwest corner of Main and Fifth streets. The first hotel was built by Mr. Downs, in the fall of 1854, and called the City Hotel. A few years later Mr. Simpson Hargus erected a four story brick hotel upon the site of the old City Hotel, which he named the Morton House, and now called the Seymour House.

The first stock of goods brought to the city was by Charley Cowles. The next store was opened by Joel Deneen, in Kearney, and the third by Nuckolls & Hail, afterwards Nuckolls, Hail & Van Doren. The Platte Valley Bank was esthableshed at an early day, by S. F. Nuckolls, Joshua Garside and N. S. Harding, and maintained its credit by the redemption of its whole issue.

The first Postoffice was called Table Creek; it was established in 1852, with John Boulware as Postmaster. In 1854 the name of the office was changed to Nebraska City.

The first regular preaching in the city was by Wm. D. Gage, a local preacher of the Methodist Church. The first building for religious services was erected in 1854, by the Baptists. The first Methodist Episcopal building was commenced in 1855. The walls were thrown down by the wind the following winter, but were rebuilt and the house finished in 1856. The Presbyterian Society was organized not long after the founding of the city, with Rev. Henry Giltner as Pastor. Their Church was completed in 1857, and the bell which adorns it was taken from the wreck of the steamboat "Genoa," which was sunk in 1856. The Protestant-Episcopal Church (St. Mary's Parish,) was organized in April, 1857, with Henry B. Bartow, as Rector.

The first newspaper, now the oldest in the State, was the *Nebraska City News*. The press-work of the first number was done in Sidney, Iowa. It was dated November 14, 1854. The office was first opened in the old Block-House; Thos. Morton was the printer.

The second United States land office in the State was located at Nebraska City.

The first and only slaves that were ever brought into the Territory, were owned in Nebraska City, in 1857. There were eleven in all.

The *People's Press* was established in 1858, by O. H. Irish and L. L. Lurvey. It still flourishes as the *Daily Nebraska Press;* W. A. Brown, publisher and proprietor.

The first steam ferry boat—the "Nebraska"—was brought to Nebraska City by Mr. McLennan, in May, 1854. The next was the "Comet," brought from Ohio, in 1857.

Game, which before the winter of 1856-7, had been abundant, perished from cold and hunger that winter. Deer run through the streets seeking safety from wolves, which followed them on the ice-crusted snow, making them an easy prey. Herds of deer frequently passed from the north between J. Sterling Morton's house and the court house square.

The population in the early days was made up of emigrants from Michigan, Ohio, Illinois, Indiana and Missouri. The Campbellites and Methodists were the largest of the religious denominations. The Old School Presbyterians were also quite strong.

During the early spring of 1856, immigration was unusually heavy. While this continued, the price of lots steadily advanced, and a number of additions were made to the town plat.

The first election in Otoe County was held on the first Monday in November, 1854. Henry Bradford, Hiram P. Bennett and Charles H. Cowles, were elected to the Territorial Council, and Jas. H. Decker, Harvy C. Cowley, Wilson M. Maddox, Gideon Bennett and Wm. B. Hail, to the House of Representatives.

The first city election was held in April, 1855, and the following officers were elected: Mayor, Dr. Henry Bradford; Aldermen, Wm. R. Craig, John W. Pearman, Wm. B. Hail; Recorder, Martin W. Riden; Treasurer, W. D. Gage; Marshal, Smith McManus, and Assessor, Alfred B. Wolston.

The first election for County officers was held October 8, 1855, and resulted as follows: Wm. B. Hail, Probate Judge; Wm. Birchfield, Sheriff; J. W. Pearman, Treasurer, and C. C. Hail, Recorder.

On March 31, 1857, Mayor Bradford "entered" Nebraska City as a town site, in the land office at Omaha.

In 1858, Nebraska City and the suburban cities of Kearney, South Nebraska City and Prairie City, were consolidated and organized into Nebraska City, as it now stands.

In the winter of 1856-7 the corporation of Kearney was organized by the election of Mills S. Reeves, Mayor; Henry C. Norton, Recorder; Byron Sanford, Marshal; Councilmen, David Lindley, John Boulware, and J. C. Campbell.

Kearney was surveyed as a town in June, 1854, and was entered at the land office in Omaha, under the town site law, by Mayor Reeves, on April 13, 1857.

On the first Monday in May, 1857, the corporation of South Nebraska City, comprising the old survey, and Hail & Co.'s addition, was organized by the election of John B. Lull, Mayor; Recorder, Fountain Pearman; Marshal, Henry Brown; Treasurer, Samuel W. Burnam; Attorney, Chas. F. Halley; Councilmen, Wm. W. Saper, Simon Hooper, and Geo. Allen. It was surveyed in 1854-5, and entered by Mayor Lull, on the 25th of June, 1857.

#### PRAIRIE CITY

Was organized in August, 1858, by the election of Benjamin F. Hayward, Simpson Hargus, John H. Croxton, H. M. Giltner, and James F. Hoffman, Trustees. It was surveyed by John A. Goodlette, and entered as a town site by John H. Croxton, for the Trustees, on the 7th of October, 1857.

Besides the towns named already, there was up to 1857, ground adjacent to the present city, surveyed and staked off in Marietta, McLennan's Addition to Marietta, Anderson's first and second Additions, Cambridge, Belmont, Elmwood, Greggsport, Gregg's Addition to Greggsport, Cowles Addition to Greggsport, and Condit, while the island rejoiced in two towns under the euphonious titles of Woodlawn and Woodville.

Russell, Majors & Waddell, government freighting firm, established themselves in Nebraska City, in the spring of 1858. The Government had made this its point for the transhipment of army stores destined for the plains and mountains. The next few years witnessed scenes of great activity. The levee and several great warehouses were constantly filled with immense piles of merchandise. The streets and byways were filled with a multitude of heavy freight wagons drawn by six to ten yoke of oxen each. Hundred of millions of pounds of army stores were transferred from here prior to the completion of the Union Pacific Railroad.

The following statement taken from the books of Mr. Majors of the firm of Russell, Majors & Waddell, will illustrate the immense amount of freighting done by a single firm, over the great Central Route leading from Nebraska City across the Plains to Pike's Peak, Utah and the Forts: "From April to October, 1859 Number of pounds transported, 2,782,258; number of oxen used 5,682; number of wagons, 517; number of mules, seventy-five number of men employed, 602." There were a great many other heavy freighters, among whom were Robert Hawks, S. F. Nuckolls, and A. & P. Byram.

The first child born in the County was the son of George H. Benton, in August, 1854. The first death was that of — Clemons, in January, 1855. The first marriage was that of George W. Nuckolls to Sarah Kennedy. The first marriage license was issued August 11, 1856, to Francis Berger and Mary Ann Jameson.

The first term of District Court was held in March, 1855, beginning on the 19th of the month; Edwin R. Hardin, Judge; M. W. Riden, Clerk.

The first case of murder in Nebraska City, was committed on April 23, 1856, by Simpson Hargus, who shot Benjamin Lacey, during a claim quarrel. Hargus was indicted, and had two or three trials, but finally escaped.

In 1860, the great fire occurred. On Saturday, the 12th of May, at a few minutes past 12 o'clock, noon, a fire was kindled in a butcher's shop in the rear end of the bank building where Hawk's store now is. A strong, hot south wind was blowing, and in less than three hours the business part of the city—forty buildings—was in ashes. The sun which rose that morning upon a young city full of life and promise, set behind a cloud of blackest gloom and disaster. But with a will of iron, the people rallied and commenced life anew. The calamity of the fire, however, closed the youthful days of the city, and became the foundation of the strength of its manhood. The insurance on the property destroyed by the great fire amounted to more than sixty thousand dollars; but out of that entire sum, less than three thousand dollars was re-invested in the city. The era of speculation, its fallacies and its fever, had passed away.

September 18, 1860, a telegraph office was opened in Nebraska City.

In April, 1861, the First Nebraska Cavalry, afterwards the Fifth Iowa Cavalry, was partially organized in Nebraska City. Lieut. A. Mathias, editor of the *Press*, recruited one of the companies, and afterwards became its Captain.

Company F, second Nebraska Cavalry, was recruited in Nebraska City; Lieut. D. P. Rolfe, recruiting officer. Its Officers were: D. Laboo, Captain, Nebraska City; Robert Mason, First Lieutenant, Nebraska City; C. W. Hail, Second Lieutenant, Peru, Nebraska.

Company B, First Nebraska Infantry, was recruited in Nebraska City, in 1861. Allen Blacker, Captain; Lee P. Gillette, First Lieutenant. J. C. Potts, a corporal at the organization, became a captain after the regiment veteranized.

On the 4th of July, 1860, the corner stone of the Methodist Church was laid. Rev. Isaac Chivington performed the ceremony. Copies of the *People's Press* and Nebraska City *News*, sketch of Nebraska City, and Act of Consolidation, etc., were placed in a tin box and deposited in the foundation of the building.

The erection of the Catholic Church, on Kearney Heights, was commenced in October, 1860.

The first exhibition of the Otoe County Agricultural Society was held in September, 1861.

J. A. Ward's new banking house, the finest in the Territory at that time, was completed in 1861.

In 1861, when the "burnt district" was being rebuilt, a board of trade was organized.

The "Nebraska Staats Zietung," edited by Dr. F. Renner, made its appearance in April, 1871.

The first annual session of the M. E. Conference for Nebraska, was held at Nebraska City, in March, 1861. Bishop Morris, of Cincinnati, presided. H. T. Davis was appointed Presiding Elder, and T. B. Lemon, Pastor for this station.

At this time there were the following Churches in the city: Baptist, Rev, J. M. Taggart, Pastor; Duer's Hall, Rev. J. Stickney Haskell, Pastor; Episcopal, Rev. Eli Adams, Pastor; United Presbyterian, Rev. Wm. M'Cartney, Pastor; Protestant-Methodist Church, Rev. J. M. Young, Pastor; Methodist-Episcopal Church, Rev. T. B. Lemon, Pastor; Lutheran, Rev. Mr. Muhlenbrook, Pastor; Roman-Catholic, Father Phillip, Pastor; First Presbyterian, Rev. H. W. Giltner, Pastor.

In September, 1866, a lad named Hamilton, while herding, cattle, was riddled with buck-shot and killed by a man named Dirks, who afterwards stripped the body and threw it into a creek near by. The crime was soon detected, and Dirks was arrested, tried by a jury of twelve citizens, found guilty, and was hung the same day in the court house yard.

The court house, Nebraska City, was finished in December, 1866. It is a fine building, eighty-two by forty-six feet, two stories high, and cost, with furniture, about $35,000.

The Union School House, on Ferry street, was completed in 1866, and cost upwards of $38,000. It is a model of architectural neatness and beauty.

In 1866, the citizens voted $40,000 to aid in the construction of the St. Joe & Council Bluffs Railroad, which runs along the east bank of the Missouri River. The first train of cars on this road reached Nebraska City station in 1867.

In 1867, the County voted bonds to the amount of $150,000 for the construction of a railroad running from Nebraska City westwardly to a connection with the Union Pacific, and on the 15th of November, 1867, the Midland Pacific Railway Company was organized at Nebraska City. On the second day of March, 1868, the first spade full of dirt was turned at Nebraska City to make smooth the bed for the iron highway. It was a joyful occasion; cannons were fired and speeches and processions were the order of the day.

Hawk's Hall, and one of the finest Church buildings in the city—the Methodist Episcopal—were erected in 1868.

The Nebraska College and Divinity School, formerly Talbot Hall, was established by Bishop Talbot, of the Episcopal Church, in 1867. Cost of building, $20,000.

The Opera House, formerly called Turner Hall, was finished in 1869, at a cost of $20,000.

The Nebraska City Gas Light Company was organized in March, 1869.

The Third Ward School House was completed late in the summer of 1869, and cost $10,000, exclusive of the grounds.

The County having voted two hundred thousand dollars in aid of an Eastern railroad connection, and the Burlington & Missouri River Railroad Company having proposed to build a railroad from Red Oak, Iowa, making Nebraska City its terminus, a contract was entered into in May, 1869, Otoe County paying $150,000 in bonds drawing eight per cent. interest, payable semi-annually from

January 1, 1870, for the building of the said road from Red Oak to that city. The road was finished in 1870.

In 1871, Mr. Jacob Shoff, an old and wealthy citizen, began the erection of the Shoff House. The name was afterwards changed to Grand Central Hotel. The building cost $50,000, and is an ornament to the city.

The city was illuminated with gas, for the first time, early in the year 1872.

The Nebraska City Elevator Company was organized in the spring of 1871, by T. Ashton, J. Metcalf, W. E. Hill, O. Stevenson and B. J. Newsom. The Elevator was built at a cost of $22,000.

The city voted $100,000 in bonds for a bridge across the Missouri River at this point. Ten thousand dollars were expended by the Bridge Company, James Sweet, J. Sterling Morton and others, in surveys, soundings, etc. The Trustees, Messrs. Tuxbury, Horace Monroe and Gen. Coe, turned over the balance of the bonds, $90,000, to the City Council, which body, on the 25th of August, 1873, destroyed them.

The Congregational Church was dedicated in January, 1873.

Work was commenced on the distillery at the foot of Main street, May 2, 1873. Capacity of the building, six hundred bushels per day, and the cost about $50,000.

At a special election on the 6th of December, 1873, $75,000 in bonds were voted for an extension of the Midland Pacific south, in accordance with their amended charter, to Brownville; and in the following year the road was completed.

On the morning of the 24th of February, 1874, the Third Ward School Building burned to the ground. The building was insured for $10,000, and was immediately rebuilt.

The High School Building was erected in this year (1874) Cost of grounds and building, $50,000.

The State Institution for the Blind is located in this city. The State appropriated $10,000; Otoe County, $3,000; total, $13,000. The ground was purchased of John M. Gregg for $2,400; cost of building, $9,795.

March 20, 1875, the Third Ward School House for the second time was burned down. The insurance, $7,000, paid for the rebuilding of the present handsome edifice.

The "City Mills," of Messrs. Pinney & Thorp, are one of the best mills in the State.

The "Star Mills," located on South Table Creek, are owned by Messrs. Schminke & Reiber. Their mill building is one of the finest in the County.

Frontier Lodge No. 3, I. O. O. F., was organized March 24, 1856. Two other Lodges have been organized from the members of this Lodge—Golden Era, No. 16, and Nebraska Lodge, No. 1.

Eureka Lodge No. 7, Knights of Pythias, was organized in May, 1871.

Mount Olivet Commandery No. 2, Knights Templar, was organized in February, 1869.

Early in December, 1878, Henry Martin, Henry Jackson, colored, and Wm. Givens, a white man, broke into the house of Charles Slocum and wife, at Nebraska City, an aged couple, killed the husband, outraged the wife, and robbed the house of a small sum of money. They were promptly arrested and indicted; their trial begun inside of a week after the crime was committed; Judge Wm. Gaslin, of the Fifth District, occupied the bench; the evidence was circumstantial until Givens offered to turn State's evidence on condition of being released from arrest for being accessory to the murder. His offer was accepted, and it was on his testimony that Martin and Jackson were convicted of murder in the second degree only, for which Judge Gaslin sentenced them to the penitentiary for life—the heaviest penalty the statutes allowed him to impose. But confinement for life was deemed to be insufficient punishment; and in the still hours of the night of December 10, a number of citizens of Nebraska City, went to the jail, took the prisoners Martin and Jackson therefrom, and hung them.

PUBLIC SCHOOLS.—Present number of districts, eighty-five; school houses, eighty; children of school age, males, 2,840, females, 2,345, total, 5,185; wages paid teachers for the year, males, $8,264.21, females, $7,615.60, total, $13,879.81, value of school houses, $38,725; value of sites, $2,820; value of books and apparatus, $1,032.

TAXABLE PROPERTY.—Acres of land, 369,527; average value per acre, $4.27. Value of town lots, $638,232. Money used in merchandise, $128,575; money invested in manufactures, $15,820;

horses, 5,994, value $137,814; mules, 725, value, $21,487; neat cattle, 18,460, value $169,081; sheep, 5,649, value, $4,244; swine, 31,742, value, $30,709; vehicles, 1,967, value, $32,278; moneys and credits, $34,329; mortgages, $40,903; stocks, etc., $80,075; furniture, 60,565; libraries, $2,510; property not enumerated, $92,424; railroads, $208,911.82; telegraph, $2,250.45; total valuation for 1879, $3,279,104.77.

RAILROADS.—The Nebraska Railway, now operated by the Burlington and Missouri R. R. Company, runs westward from Nebraska City through the center of the County, and it has recently been extended from Nebraska City southward along the Missouri River to Nemaha City, in Nemaha County. This road also connects with the Chicago, Burlington and Quincy, St. Joe and Council Bluffs Railroads, on the east side of the Missouri, opposite Nebraska City.

LANDS.—The price of improved lands ranges from $7 to $30 per acre. The Burlington and Missouri River Railroad Company owns 10,000 acres in this County, for which they ask from $6 to $10 per acre.

POPULATION.—The following will show the population of the County by Precincts, for 1879: Hendricks, 328; South Branch, 258; Osage, 493; McWilliams, 407; Rock Creek, 720; Otoe, 949; Four Mile, 564; Nebraska City, 4,551; Belmont, 693; Delaware, 369; Syracuse, 919; Russell, 903; Palmyra, 1,137; North Branch, 420; Berlin, 504; Wyoming, 648.

Total, 13,863,—males, 7,412, females, 6,451.

### NEBRASKA CITY,

The County Seat, is the third largest city in the State, having about 8,000 inhabitants. It is an enterprising, well built city, situated on the banks of the Missouri, near the center of the County from north to south, and contains seventeen Churches, three elegant school buildings, an Episcopal College, the State Blind Asylum, a fine court house, an opera house, several good hotels, commodious brick business blocks, several manufactories, machine shops, a well-appointed steam ferry, excellent railroad advantages, three first class flouring mills, large steam grain elevators, two newspapers, the *Press*, daily and weekly, and the weekly *News*, etc. The streets are broad, and in the resident part of the city planted with shade trees. The open plain to the south and west, is divided up into highly cultivated farms, while large orchards and vineyards, bearing the choicest fruits, dot the surface in every direction.

## SYRACUSE

Is a prosperous town of 800 inhabitants, located in the central part of the County, on the line of the Nebraska Railway, and on the north bank of the Little Nemaha River. The first stake was driven in the ground toward laying off the town site on September 18, 1871, and the first house was erected thereon by T. E. Sensabaugh. The town was incorporated on the 6th of January, 1875. It contains a $4,000 school house, two Churches, a weekly newspaper, the *Journal*, several stores, three grain warehouses, a flouring mill, lumber yard, and all the general branches of trade are represented. The County fairs are usually held here on account of its central location. A thriving trade is carried on with the surrounding country, which is a well settled farming section, and the shipments of farm products are extensive.

## PALMYRA,

Located on the Little Nemaha and on the line of the Nebraska Railway, in the northwestern part of the County, contains some 500 inhabitants. It was laid out in 1870 by J. M. Taggart, and is situated on a beautiful slope facing the river, thirty-four miles, by rail, west of Nebraska City, and twenty three miles east of Lincoln. The surrounding country is well settled by an industrious class of farmers. The Presbyterians and Methodists have each comfortable houses of worship here, and the Baptists are well organized. In 1874, a $3,500 school house was erected, and in the following year the Masons and Odd Fellows, together, built a fine Hall. There are an excellent steam flouring mill, two grain elevators, two hotels, several general merchandise stores, hardware and drug stores, mechanics' shops, lumber yards, etc., and the shipments of hogs, cattle and grain are very large.

DUNBAR, UNADILLA, MINERSVILLE and BARNEY, are prosperous young towns on the railroad.

HENDRICKS, SALON, BURR OAK, OSAGE, NORTH BRANCH, ELA and WYOMING, are Postoffices with general stores, etc. In the County there are seven flouring mills and three cheese factories.

## PLATTE COUNTY.

Platte County was organized by an Act of the first Territorial Legislature, in 1855, and was composed of the twenty-four miles square included in townships seventeen, eighteen, nineteen and twenty north, of ranges one, two, three and four east of the Sixth Principal Meridian. In 1858, it was made to include, in addition, all of Monroe County, on the west, which was not comprised within the Pawnee Indian Reservation. In 1868, the County of Colfax was created, taking from Platte all of the three east ranges. Subsequent legislation fixed the boundaries of the County as they exist at present. It is located in the middle-eastern part of the State, in the fourth tier of Counties west of the Missouri River, bounded on the north by Madison and Stanton Counties, east by Colfax County, south by the Platte River, Merrick and Nance Counties, west by Merrick, Nance and Boone Counties, containing 684 square miles, or 437,760 acres.

WATER COURSES.—Platte is a finely-watered County, and possesses numerous excellent mill privileges. The Platte River washes the southern border, a distance of about twenty miles. The Loup River flows from west to east through the southern portion of the County. Shell and Looking Glass Creeks, both large, beautiful streams, water the western and central portions of the County. Union Creek waters the northeastern townships, and there are besides a large number of rivulets and springs.

TIMBER is in fair supply along the streams, and in the northern part of the County are found some fine natural groves, consisting principally of hardwood. The amount of timber reported under cultivation is 1661¾ acres; hedging, 15¾ miles.

FRUIT.—The amount returned is as follows: Apple trees, 4,936; pear, fifty-one; peach, 714; plum, 2,345; cherry, 557; grape vines, forty.

SANDSTONE is found in several localities.

CHARACTER OF THE LAND.—One-third of the County is valley and bottom land, and the balance gently rolling prairie. The wide valleys of the Platte and Loup embrace about one-sixth of the area. Shell Creek has a magnificent valley, extending directly through the central portion of the County, from northwest to southeast. Eastward from this, the surface consists of undulating prairie, with an occasional small valley. The soil is composed of a deep, vegetable mould, and is the same throughout the County. No crop returns have been received.

HISTORICAL.—Early in the spring of 1856, Fred. Gotteschalk, Jacob Lewis and George Roush marked the site of the present town of Columbus, and returning shortly afterward to Omaha, the Columbus Town Company was organized, and a committee of exploration sent out, consisting of Vincent Kummer, in charge; Charles Turner, Surveyor; John C. Wolfel, carpenter; Fred. Gottschalk, Jacob Lewis, Jacob Guter, Carl Rienke, Henry Lusche, Michael Smith, Adam Denk and John Held.

On the 28th day of May, 1856, the outlines of the town were determined, and the whole was soon blocked out. A rough building of logs was erected, and roofed with grass and sod, which answered all their purposes for dwelling, storage and fortification, and was long known as the "Old Company House." On the 7th day of October, 1856, other settlers arrived, among whom were J. Rickley, J. P. Becker, John Browner, Anthony Voll, Charles Bremer, John H. Green, William Distlehorst, Jedediah Mills, George Berni, Martin Heintz, the Quinns, Haney's and Mrs. Walfel. To Mrs. Walfel, as the first lady adventurer, the Company afterwards gave one share in the capital stock of the Company—equal to ten lots in the town. In December, came J. M. Becker and D. Hashberger, the latter driving his stake where the town of Schuyler is now located; and thus was completed the immigration to Platte County in 1856—twenty-five souls, all told.

During the autumn, a change was made in the town plat. A Messrs. Burtch & Mitchell, who had established a ferry on the Loup, laid out a town extending from the ferry and interfering with the other. Finally a compromise was effected, and "Pawnee City"—Burtch & Mitchell's town—was abandoned, and Messrs. Kummer and Rickley were appointed to lay out a new plat. Under their superintendence, Col. Loren Miller, of Omaha, surveyed the town site of Columbus.

During the winter of 1856-7 the whole plain was covered with snow to the average depth of three feet, while the drifts on low ground were from ten to twenty feet deep. The situation of the little colony was not only trying, it was perilous. In December, a few of the settlers went to Omaha and purchased ox teams and provisions, but on their return the deep snow stopped them at the Elkhorn River, where they had to leave their teams; so equipping themselves with snow shoes, they hauled the provisions to Columbus on hand sleds, a distance of about seventy-five miles. Wolfel, Bremer and Hashberger made a second trip to Omaha that winter, bringing back provisions on hand sleds. They followed the frozen channel of the Platte River, and made the round trip in ten days.

Early in 1857, Dr. Chas. B. Stillman, Geo. H. Hewett, Patrick Murray and Patrick McDonald, arrived at Columbus. Michael Kelly, Thos. Lynch, Pat. Gleason and John Denean soon afterwards located on Shell Creek. On the first day of May, L. Gerrard located claims for himself and his father's family on Looking Glass Creek.

Two and a half to three miles northwest of Columbus was laid out, in 1857, on a magnificent scale, the town of Cleveland. George W. Stevens, Wm. H. Stevens and Michael Sweeny were the active workers, and for a while occupied the premises.

Three or four other towns were started in 1857, all of which were short lived. But while these cities faded out of sight, farms came into view, and during this, and the next two years, valuable accessions were made to all the neighborhoods.

To the German settlement came Held, Erb, Marohn, Will, Wettner, Rickert, Ahrens, Hengeller, Matthis, and the Losekes. To the Irish came Hays, Doody and the Carrigs. To the eastern end came Nelson Toncray, William Davis, Robert Corson, and farther up, Rolfel, Russell, Skinner, Kemp, Clough, Spaulding and Fayls. In September, 1859, came the Salt Lake emigrants, also Father James Galley and his three sons, Geo. W., James H. and Samuel, and his two son-in-laws, William Draper and John Barrow. Later came M'Allister and Anderson. Beyond the Loup, in this County, settled Barnum, Clother, the Beebe brothers, Stevens, Morse, Perry, Clark, Cushing, Curtis and Witchie.

During the years 1860-1, the line of ranchmen that filed out on the military road was much extended, in order to accommodate the surging tide of emigration and through travel to and from Colorado, Utah and California. The hotel business and ranching was then at its height, and all shared in it to some extent—every house was a ranche, and every floor a lodging, and every table a cake and pie stand.

In the month of May, 1866, the construction trains of the Union Pacific Railroad entered the eastern border of the County, and on the first day of June the track was laid through the town of Columbus, under the management of the Casement Brothers. The whole city—men, women and children—turned out to witness the wonderful spectacle of a line engine slowly creeping along as the rail were laid, a pair at a time, by a gang of disciplined men, all moving with the harmony of a clock, and completing the tracklaying at the rate of ten feet per minute. This event was to Columbus and Platte County the beginning of a new life.

The lower Platte Valley is well settled by English and Scotch, mostly of the Mormon faith. The Germans possess the lower Shell Creek Valley, with all its tributaries, and are mostly Lutherans. The northeast and Tracy Valley are New Englanders and are largely Presbyterians. The Irish have got the upper Shell Creek Valley, and the lower north shore of the Loup, and are Catholics. The Scandinavians possess the upper Looking Glass and Lost Creek, and are mostly Lutherans. The upper north shore of the Loup Valley is pretty well settled by Quakers, from Pennsylvania. Stearns' Prairie, in the center of the County, is a mixture of all denominations—Jew and Gentile, Catholic and Protestant.

In August, 1857, the Counties of Platte and Monroe were organized. Judge Smith, of Fremont, issued a proclamation calling elections for County Officers and the location of County Seats. In Platte County, the result was as follows: Probate Judge, Isaac Albertson; Clerk, George W. Hewitt; Recorder, J. P. Becker; Treasurer, V. Kummer; Sheriff, Cyrus Tollman; Justice of the Peace, C. B. Stillman; Constable, J. Guter; County Commissioners, Gustavus Becher, George Spaulding, and Abram Root. And in Monroe County: Probate Judge, Charles H. Whaley; Clerk, George W. Stevens; Recorder, G. E. Yeaton; Treasurer, C. Whaley; Sheriff, N. Davis; Representative, Leander Gerrard; Surveyor,

P. Kimball; County Commissioners, H. Peck, C. H. Pierce, and H. J. Hudson.

The first election in Monroe County was also the last; for in the winter session of the Territorial Legislature of 1858-9, on joint petition of the two Counties, Monroe was consolidated with Platte County.

The first store in Columbus was kept by Mr. Becker; the first postmaster was John Rickley; the first mail came July 4, 1857. The first boy born in the County was Lewis Erb, on Shell Creek; the first girl born was Mary Wolfel, at Columbus. The first wedding was that of John Will and Marie Rickart; the second wedding was between J. E. North and Nellie Arnold, who were married on horseback in the streets of Columbus. First blacksmith, Jacob Ernst; first house-builders, Wolfel and Becker; first shoemaker, Louis Phillippi; first lawyers, L. Gerrard and A. B. Pattison; first doctor, C. B. Stillman; first school teacher, G. W. Stevens; first Catholic Priest, Father Fourmont; first death and burial was that of J. M. Becker.

In 1857, the mammoth steam mill of Rickley & Co. was erected. It was a grist, saw, lath and shingle mill. In 1868, a steam flouring mill was built by F. A. Hoffman. In 1869, Becker's mill on Shell Creek came into operation.

The Churches of the County, in the order of their organization, are as follows:

The Catholic Church of Columbus (St. John's), organized in 1860; Church property, $4,000.

The Congregational, organized September, 1866; Church property, $1,000.

The Protestant Episcopal Church, organized Oct. 19, 1868; Church property, $2,000.

The Methodist Episcopal Church; first class formed in 1867, by Rev. David Hart; good edifice.

The Presbyterian Church, organized Jan. 30, 1870; neat house of worship.

Shell Creek Catholic Church, established in 1872; value of Church property, $1,200.

Congregational Church, of Monroe, organized in 1868.

German Reformed Church, Columbus, organized December 25, 1875; value of Church property, $3,000.

Shell Creek Lutheran Church, organized September, 1873.

Stearns' Prairie Catholic Church, organized in 1875; value of Church property, $1,000.

Church of Latter Day Saints, organized July 30, 1865; Church property, $600.

Tracy Valley Presbyterian Church, organized in 1875; value of Church property, $900.

The fraternal Lodges and Societies are: Lebanon Lodge No. 58, A. F. & A. M.; charter, June 30, 1875. Eastern Star or Degree of Adoption Right; chartered June 15, 1872. The Wildey Lodge No. 44, I. O. O. F.; chartered May 5, 1874. Daughter of Rebekah, Columbia Degree No. 11; chartered February 18, 1876; Sons of Temperance; chartered February 22, 1873. Knights of Pythias Lodge, started in August, 1875. Good Templars' Lodge 176; chartered June 16, 1876.

The first newspaper published in the County was the Columbus *Golden Age*, by C. C. Strawn, commencing June 21, 1866, and ending with its twelfth number. Next came the *Platte Valley Journal*, by O. T. B. Williams. It was maintained one year, and was followed by the Columbus *Journal*, by M. K. Turner & Co., the first number bearing date May 11, 1870.

The Columbus *Era*, under the management of W. A. Hensley, commenced in February, 1874.

In May, 1875, the Columbus *Republican* was established.

The first settlers of Platte County were more or less harassed by the Indians. The Pawnees, in the early days, when they were strong and the settlements weak, begged and stole, insulted and threatened, until their insolence became unbearable, and the Governor of the Territory sent the militia to chastise them. Platte County furnished over fifty of the little army of 300 that pursued the fugitive tribe and overtook them at Battle Creek, where they surrendered without a battle, and were permitted to return to their homes upon promise of good behavior.

In the summer of 1864, Pat. Murray had a hay-making camp on Looking Glass Creek, near Genoa. One evening, about sunset, while Mr. Murray was absent, a squad of twenty-five Sioux rode into camp from the hills. They demanded food and were supplied by Mrs. Murray. This done they began to untie the teams from their fastenings, which the men of the camp resisted, and in the twinkling of an eye the weapons of savages were in play. An old man was instantly brained and scalped. Adam Smith, Murray's brother-in-law, fell pierced with eight arrows, and others in a like manner yielded to the fatal poisoned arrows. Mrs. Murray, with hay fork in hand, defending the property, was badly wounded with arrows. Only one escaped—a boy who hid underneath a pile of hay. The noise of the fight being heard at a distant farm, parties came in the darkness and carried away the dead and dying. Mrs. Murray had crawled away in the tall, damp grass, and spent the lonely night in agony of pain and horror. She afterwards recovered. The Indians made off with $2,500 worth of property.

PUBLIC SCHOOLS.—Number of districts, 62; school houses, 51; children of school age, males, 1,507, females, 1,301, total, 2,808; qualified teachers employed, males, thirty-one, females, thirty-nine; wages paid teachers for the year, males, $5,343.50, females, $4,909.30, total, $10,252.30; value of school houses, $21,335; value of sites, $1,151; value of books, etc., $3,660.

TAXABLE PROPERTY.—Acres of land, 315,191; average value per acre, $3.54; value of town lots, $272,718; money invested in merchandise, $80,025; money used in manufactures, $13,085; horses, 3,313, value $113,204; mules and asses, 288, value $9,835; neat cattle, 9,123, value $98,517; sheep, 3,173, value $4,238; swine, 7,206, value $7,111; vehicles, 1,820, value $22,569; moneys and credits, $25,958; mortgages, $22,815; stocks, etc., $1,015; furniture, $37,470; libraries, $3,095; property not enumerated, $63,819; railroads, $201,100.40; telegraph, $1,649; total valuation for 1879, $2,103,888.40.

RAILROADS.—The Union Pacific traverses the southern portion of the County from east to west. The Omaha, Niobrara and Black Hills Railroad runs from Jackson, on the Union Pacific northward through the County. Six miles north of Jackson a branch of the Omaha, Niobrara and Black Hills Railroad is now being constructed, running up the valley of Beaver Creek through Boone County.

LANDS.—Improved lands are worth from $8 to $30 per acre. The Union Pacific and Burlington and Missouri River Railroad Companies each own a large amount of land here, the price of which ranges from 12 to 16 per acre.

POPULATION.—There are sixteen Precincts in the County, the population of each in 1879, being as follows: Granville, 202; Creston, 205; Looking Glass, 275; Woodville, 226; Pleasant Valley, 309; Humphrey, 324; Sherman, 356; Monroe, 430; Lost Creek, 510; Bismarck, 501; Butler, 622; Columbus, 2,210; Stearns, 340; Walker, 312; Burrows, 392; Shell Creek, 373.

Total, 7,587,—males, 4,125, females, 3,462.

## COLUMBUS,

The County Seat, is a prosperous city of 2,000 inhabitants, located on the Union Pacific Railroad, ninety-two miles west of Omaha. It is situated on a wide plateau at the junction of the Loup valley with the Platte, the ground being sufficiently sloping to afford good drainage. It is an excellent business point, and contains many good stores, an elevator, a bank, three hotels, several lumber yards, foundry and machine shops, a fine brick court house, elegant school buildings, seven Churches, and four newspapers—the *Journal*, the *Era*, the *Independent*, and the *Democrat*. The adjacent country is exceedingly fertile and well settled. The first bridge built across the Platte River is located at this point, and an extensive trade is derived from the country south of that stream.

## JACKSON

Is a station on the Union Pacific Railroad, eight miles west of Columbus. It has a very promising future, having been selected during the present year as the starting point of the Omaha, Niobrara and Black Hills Railroad. The railroads are making extensive improvements here, and new dwellings and business houses are going up very rapidly. A good wagon bridge spans the Platte here also, and makes this a convenient shipping and trading center for the settlements on the south side of the river.

## PLATTE CENTER

Is a new town established during the present summer at the forks of the Omaha, Niobrara and Black Hills Railroad, six miles north of Jackson. A large elevator, stock yards, depot, several dwelling houses and stores, are now in course of construction here.

### ST. BARNABAS,

Situated in the north-central part of the County, was laid out in 1876, by a German colony. It has about 200 inhabitants, three or four stores, and one of the finest school houses in the County.

MONROE, HUMPHREY, METZ, GLEASON, LOOKING GLASS, STEARNS' PRAIRIE, NEBO, CRESTON, ST. MARY'S, WOLF, LINDSAY, FARRALL, and WOODVILLE, are small villages in the County, having from fifty to 200 inhabitants each.

## PAWNEE COUNTY.

Pawnee County was created by an Act of the first Territorial Legislature, early in the spring of 1855, and attached to Richardson County for election, judicial, and revenue purposes, until the 4th day of November, 1856, at which time it was regularly organized. It is located in the southeastern part of the State, in the second tier of Counties west of the Missouri River, and is bounded on the north by Johnson and Nemaha Counties, east by Richardson County, south by the State of Kansas, and west by Gage County, containing 432 square miles, or 276,480 acres of land.

WATER COURSES.—The three principal streams of the County are the North and South Forks of the Great Nemaha River, and Turkey Creek. The North Fork runs diagonally across the northeast corner, cutting off about a township and a half; the South Fork passes northeasterly across the southeast corner; and Turkey Creek flows in a general southeasterly direction through the central portion, each furnishing sufficient water-power for manufacturing purposes. The principal tributaries of the North Fork are Dry Branch and Taylor Creeks; of the South Fork, Jake's Run, and Nigger Branch; and of Turkey Creek, Rock, West Branch, and Johnson Creeks. Ball's Branch, in the central part of the County is a tributary of the West Branch of Turkey Creek. Mission Plum, and Wolf Creeks are streams draining the western portion of the County, and flowing southwesterly into the Big Blue River. Tipp's Branch and Art-Oceoto, are small streams in the middle-western part of the County, emptying into Plum Creek.

CHARACTER OF THE LAND.—Ten per cent. of the County is valley, and the balance rolling or undulating prairie. The larger streams have fine smooth valleys which are separated from the upland, usually, by a range of low rounded hills. The per cent. of untillable land in the County is exceedingly small, and the soil is everywhere of the highest order for the production of all the general crops grown in the State.

CROPS.—Area under cultivation reported for 1879, was 48,580 acres. Winter wheat, 882 acres, 1,656 bushels; spring wheat, 8,908 acres, 68,941 bushels; rye, 1,656 acres, 19,552 bushels; corn, 25,583 acres, 995,207 bushels; barley, 1,241 acres, 30,059 bushels; sorghum, 131 acres, 13,068 gallons; flax, 17 acres, 191 bushels; millet, 425 acres, 1,393 tons; tobacco, 1¼ acres, 1,479 pounds; potatoes, 235 acres, 22,418 bushels.

TIMBER.—There is an abundance of timber for fuel in the County, the banks of the streams being skirted with a fine natural growth, and almost every farm having a well grown domestic grove. 598,520 forest trees and 425¼ miles of hedging are reported under cultivation.

FRUIT.—42,515 apple, 474 pear, 71,237 peach, 1,454 plum, 15,839 cherry trees, and 17,889 grape vines are reported. The orchards are very prolific, and have been in bearing for several years past.

STONE.—Excellent building stone is abundant along the streams and in the hill sides. A beautiful cream-colored limestone found here is extensively used for building. Sand stone is also plentiful.

COAL.—South of Pawnee City coal of good quality is mined in a seam from twelve to eighteen inches thick. It is preferred to any other coal in the market.

HISTORICAL.—Mr. Christian Bobst, Robert Turner, Jacob Adams, and Robert Archer, the first settlers of the County, arrived at a point on the South Fork of the Great Nemaha, on the 4th day of April, 1854, where they selected claims and located permanently that spring. Mr. Bobst selected one of the best timber claims in the County—the north west quarter, section twenty-five, town one, range twelve; Mr. Turner located on the south east quarter, section twenty-five, town one, range twelve; Mr. Archer on the south west quarter, section twenty-five, town one, range twelve, and Mr. Adams on the south west quarter, section twenty-four, town one, range twelve. George T. Bobst, arriving shortly after, took the remaining quarter section twenty-five, town one, range twelve.

Mr. Christian Bobst's was the first house erected in the County. After making the necessary preparations, the party returned to St. Joseph, Mo., where they had left their families and effects, to bring them to their new homes, and before their return Joseph Fries, William Barnes, and a Mr. Dragoo, arrived in the same neighborhood with their families, and located. In the same year, John Morrison, Martin Fisher, Henry Shellhorn and family, and E. J. Shellhorn settled on the South Fork, and James M. Hinton on the North Fork. Mr. Hinton originally held the land now occupied by the Table Rock mill. He first projected the mill, which was ultimately erected by other parties.

In July of this year, James O'Loughlin, and Charles and Arthur McDonald, ascended Turkey Creek, from the South Fork of the Nemaha, as far as the present location of Pawnee City, and going upon the high ground where the house of J. S. Davenport now stands, they saw a large party of Indians, with ponies grazing, just beyond where the cemetery now is, and deeming discretion the better part of valor, they quietly made their way back to the Nemaha.

Christian Bobst was appointed Probate Judge for Richardson County, by the Governor, in the fall of 1854. His jurisdiction extended over all contiguous settlements west of the Missouri River, no lines at that time having been established. At the same time and by the same authority, Joseph Fries was appointed Justice of the Peace, and Robert Turner, Constable.

In 1855, H. G. Lore, W. S. Lore, and J. P. Lore, with their families, settled on the South Fork, and L. G. Jenkins, Elijah Markee, Daniel Powell, and Elisha Kirkham, on the North Fork of the Nemaha. A. A. Jordan, L. D. Jordan, Eben Jordan, and Charles McDonald, settled on Turkey Creek.

In the spring of this year, the first sermon was preached in the County, by Rev. David Hart, of the Methodist Episcopal Church, at the house of Henry Shellhorn, on the South Fork of the Nemaha. In the fall following, a class was organized by Mr. Hart.

Mr. Henry Shellhorn died on the 4th day of May, 1855, after a short illness; and in the fall following, Mr. John Barnes died, being the first deaths among the settlers.

During 1856, many families located in the County, among whom were P. M. Rogers and family, on Turkey Creek; Joseph Steinauer, and others, on Upper Turkey Creek; John Williams, and several families, on the North Fork; and the Thallimers, Dr. A. F. Cromwell (the first physician in the County), and family, on the South Fork; Wm. McClintock, and several others, on Taylor's or Hogan's Branch; John Jordan and Branick Cooper, on the West Branch of Turkey Creek; James B. Robertson, on Jake's Run; and the Messrs. Buckner, two colored men, on Nigger's Branch.

Hon. John C. Miller, Probate Judge of Richardson County, in accordance with the provisions of the Act creating Pawnee County, issued an order, in 1856, for an election to be held in Pawnee County, on the 25th of August of that year, for the purpose of County organization.

At this election, three localities entered the contest for the County Seat, but neither received a majority of all the votes cast, consequently neither was chosen; but notwithstanding this, when the returns were sent to Archer, the County Seat of Richardson County, the Clerk of that County, N. J. Sharp, declared the southwest quarter of section twenty-six, town two, range eleven, duly chosen as the seat of Justice of Pawnee County. This point was then called Enon.

Considerable dissatisfaction existing in regard to the election, the matter was brought before Judge Miller, who declared the certificate issued by the Clerk null and void; that no choice of County Seat had been legally made; and ordered a new election to be held on the 4th day of November, 1856.

With the prestige of the certificate already issued in favor of the above named place for the County Seat, immigration rapidly changed to that point; and when the election of the 4th of November came off, it was found to have a majority of sixteen votes over its competitors, and was therefore duly declared the County Seat.

At this same election, the following County Officers were elected, to-wit: Commissioners, John C. Peavy, E. W. Fowler and Joseph Fries; Probate Judge, H. G. Lore; Clerk, G. G. Thallimer; Treasurer, W. B. Arnett; Sheriff, Rufus Abbott; Superintendent of Public Schools, Rezin Ball; Surveyor, John J. Lebo; Register, William S. Lore; Justices of the Peace, C. Huntley, H. Billings, A. A. Jordan and J. Adams; Constables, Wm. McClintock, L. F. Roges, J. O'Loughlin and — Bedgood.

The first Commissioners' Court was held on the 5th day of January, 1857, at the house of Rufus Abbott, at which time the County was divided into three Commissioners' Districts.

The name of Pawnee City was chosen for the County Seat. The town site was surveyed and platted by John J. Lebo; and a public sale of town lots was held by Sheriff Abbott, between January and July, 1857.

During the year 1857, many settlers arrived with their families. In the spring of this year, John Fries' grist and saw mill commenced operation. P. M. Rogers' saw mill, just beyond the west line of Pawnee City, and a mill by J. S. Woods and Eben Jordan were erected; and in the fall the Table Rock water-power saw mill commenced operation. During this fall the most destructive prairie fire ever known in this County, occurred, many of the settlers being burnt out of house and home.

On the 6th day of July, 1857, two mills were levied upon the taxable property of the County for the building of a court house, and in the following year a contract for its erection was entered into with E. W. Fowler. This enterprise, however, was carried no further than the raising of the frame, which so stood until leveled to the ground, in 1860, by a severe storm.

Rev. Mr. Copeland, of the Methodist Church, organized a class, in the fall of 1857, at Ball's Branch.

The first marriages in the County were those of James O'Laughlin to Lydia Adamson, and Richard Clency to Priscilla Adamson, on the 13th of March, 1856, by Joseph Fries, Justice of the Peace. These were the first and only marriages within the limits of the County previous to its organization.

The first house erected on the town site of Pawnee City, except Mr. Galligher's blacksmith shop, was that of F. F. Linning, in the spring of 1857. The next was Joseph B. Morton's. Messrs. Linning & Morton were also the first merchants in the town, and Morton was the first hotel-keeper.

The first child born in Pawnee City, was Andrew Perry Linning, son of F. F. Linning, in October, 1857.

The first school house erected (frame) was in the District west of Pawnee City, which afterwards received the classic name of "Rosin Weed Seminary." The first teacher in this building was Miss Sarah H. Ball, now the wife of Hon. J. L. Edwards.

In 1859, the first camp meeting in the County was held at Table Rock.

The first District Court held in the County was on September 8, 1859; Hon. Joseph Miller, Presiding Judge; Wm. McLennan, District Attorney; Allen Blacker, Clerk, and Eben Jordan, Sheriff.

In the year 1860, Independence day was celebrated at Pawnee City for the first time in the County. A general table was set in the grove above Turkey Creek bridge, then only a ford. Judge E. W. Fowler was the orator of the day.

The first building that was burned in Pawnee City was the dwelling of Hon. David Butler, in 1861.

In 1861, Table Rock had obtained a Postoffice, and within the next year Pawnee was blessed with a tri-weekly mail.

During the years 1861-2, bands of horse-thieves were organized throughout the west, including in their numbers men in Pawnee County who long had had the confidence of the people. These bands were popularly known as Jay-hawkers. By the year 1863 this organization had laid their plans with such shrewdness and cunning, that Pawnee County seemed to be within their grasp and at their mercy. This state of affairs ultimately culminated in a determination of the people to protect themselves, and if necessary, take the law into their own hands. Near the close of the rebellion, a fine span of horses, belonging to Mr. Andrew Fellers, was missing. Mr. Fellers and several others, under the leadership of John

C. Peavy, pursued and captured the thieves, with the horses, in Iowa. They were brought back as far as Table Rock, where the next night a disguised mob took the thieves from the guards by force, and hung them. The leader of the thieves, Catteran, escaped with two or three gunshot wounds in his body, only to be recaptured next day and hung. Many of the citizens of Table Rock, among whom was Elder Giddings, used their utmost efforts to prevent this terrible violation of the law. The effect of this summary mode of dealing with thieves was salutary, and increased the security of life and property a hundred fold. The confession of these men involved several men in Pawnee County hitherto of good standing, who at once left the country.

In 1861, the M. E. Church commenced the erection of their present fine building at Pawnee City, which cost, when completed, near $7,000.

The Christian Church was organized in the fall of 1865, by Elder D. R. Dungan.

In the summer of 1856, the Presbyterian Church at Pawnee City was organized.

The first Baptist Church in the County was organized on the West Branch, in the fall of 1866, by Elder Robert Turner.

The Dunkards, or German Baptists, have a flourishing organization five or six miles southeast of Pawnee City. The Methodists also organized a Church on the South Fork, at an early day.

The people of the County having voted $15,000 for the erection of a Court House, the Commissioners, in February, 1869, advertised for bids for its erection, the building to be built of white limestone, forty by sixty feet, and two stories high. The plans and specifications for the building were prepared by Mr. J. L. Edwards, and it was erected in accordance therewith.

Contracts were also entered into the same year, with W. Wheeter, of Nemaha County, for the construction of bridges across the three principal streams of Pawnee County, to-wit: one across Turkey Creek, south of Pawnee City; one across the South Fork, near Fries' Mill, and one across the North Fork, near Table Rock Mill.

PUBLIC SCHOOLS.—The number of districts in the County, in 1879, was fifty-eight; school houses, fifty-three; children of school age—males, 1,186, females, 1,220, total, 2,406; qualified teachers employed,—males, thirty, females, fifty-seven; total wages paid teachers for the year—males, $3,361.10, females, $5,268.30; total, $8,629.40; value of school houses, $42,826; value of sites, $2,054; value of books and apparatus, $1,254.10.

TAXABLE PROPERTY.—Acres of land, 259,423, average value per acre, $2.80; value of town lots, $50,432; money invested in merchandise, $25,390; money used in manufactures, $3,550; horses, 3,282, value, $90,506; mules, 162, value, $5,040; neat cattle, 8,216, value, $91,318; sheep, 6,604, value, $6,480; swine, 10,246, value, $13,850; vehicles, 935, value, $20,641; moneys and credits, $22,948; mortgages, $14,455; stocks, etc., $4,500; furniture, $1,384; libraries, $775; property not enumerated, $14,490; railroads, $52.210.76; total valuation in 1879, $,1,144,506.76.

RAILROADS.—The Atchison & Nebraska Railroad, following the Nemaha Valley, traverses the northeastern portion of the County, a distance of about eleven miles. The surveys for other lines have been made through the County.

MISCELLANEOUS.—The price of lands ranges from $3 to $10, wild, and $5 to $25, improved. There are fifteen Churches, three flouring mills, two saw-mills and one cheese factory, in the County.

POPULATION.—The following is the population of the County, in 1879, by Precincts: Mission Creek, 290; Plum Creek, 328; Turkey Creek, 156; West Branch, 344; Miles, 266; Steinauer, 417; Clay, 631; Pawnee City, 1,042; South Fork, 745; Sheridan, 366; Table Rock, 1,314.

Total, 5,899—males, 3,102; females, 2,797.

### PAWNEE CITY,

The County Seat, is a beautiful little city of 900 inhabitants, situated on Turkey Creek, near the geographical center of the County. It is surrounded by a fine rolling country, and has considerable natural timber in the vicinity. There are also a number of large orchards and vineyards in the neighborhood. It contains several neat Churches, a $12,000 school house, an excellent court house, two newspapers—the *Enterprise* and the *Republican*—a bank, two hotels, several good stores and minor business places. A substantial bridge spans Turkey Creek just south of the city.

SCHOOL BUILDING, PAWNEE CITY.

TABLE ROCK,

On the A. & N. Railway, in the northeastern part of the County, is a rapidly growing town of about six hundred inhabitants. The town site was selected in 1875, by the Table Rock Town Company, of which Robert W. Furnas, James Hinton and John Fleming were active members. The town is pleasantly situated in the Valley of the North Fork of the Nemaha, and was reached in 1872 by the railroad, which made it the chief shipping point for the County and an excellent business center. It is well supplied with stores and grain houses, and has excellent school and Church advantages. The first Church in the County, it is claimed, was organized here in 1857, by Rev. C. V. Arnold, of the Methodist denomination.

CINCINNATI, MISSION CREEK, STEINAUER, WEST BRANCH, TIP'S BRANCH and NEW HOME, are flourishing young towns in the County, of fifty to 200 inhabitants each.

## PIERCE COUNTY.

Pierce County was created in 1859, and organized in 1870. It is located in the northeastern part of the State, in the third tier of Counties west of the Missouri River, and is bounded on the north by Knox and Cedar, east by Cedar and Wayne, south by Madison, and west by Antelope County, containing 540 square miles, or 345,600 acres.

WATER COURSES.—The North Branch of the Elkhorn River, a fine, large stream, affording some excellent mill privileges, flows through the central portion of the County, from northwest to southeast, supported on either side by numerous small branches.

TIMBER.—Considerable natural timber is found along the streams and in the adjacent ravines. Tree planting—both forest and fruit—has received a large share of attention. The groves are thrifty and growing rapidly.

CHARACTER OF THE LAND.—The surface of the County consists chiefly of undulating prairie, about ten per cent. being valley and bottom. The valley of the North Fork varies in width from two to five miles, and there are also wide bottoms on several of the tributaries. The uplands are especially adapted to the growth of small grains, and large crops are raised wherever tested. The prairie grasses are nutritious, and afford a wide range of pasturage. Good well water can be obtained on the prairies, at a depth of thirty to sixty feet.

CROPS.—Acres under cultivation, 54,470. Rye 1,712 acres, 26,725 bushels; spring wheat 26,692 acres, 372,997 bushels; corn, 13,900 acres, 545,553 bushels; barley, 626 acres, 16,068 bushels; sorghum $2\frac{3}{4}$ acres, 170 gallons; flax, 181 acres, 993 bushels; broom corn, twenty-five acres, $6\frac{1}{4}$ tons.

HISTORICAL.—The first settlements in the County were made in the spring of 1867, by a colony of Germans from Wisconsin, consisting of Christian Heubner, A. J. Heubner, August Nenow, Jacob Bernhardt, and others, who located on the North Fork, in the southeastern part of the County. Many others came soon afterward; and during 1870–71, most of the choice land along the

Fork and its principal tributaries was taken. In the summer of 1870, R. S. Lucas and J. H. Brown, from Iowa, settled in the Valley of Willow Creek, at the confluence of that stream with the North Fork. They erected a substantial log house on the south side of Willow Creek, near the present bridge crossing, which soon became the general headquarters for the County, serving as a hotel, Postoffice and Court House.

The first regular County election was held on the second Tuesday in October, 1870, and resulted as follows: Commissioners, R. S. Lucas, August Nenow and T. C. Verges; Probate Judge, R. S. Lucas; Treasurer, H. R. Mewis; Clerk, J. H. Brown; Sheriff, John Tietz.

The County Seat was located on the south half of the northeast quarter and north half of the southeast quarter of section twenty-seven, township twenty-six, range two west.

The first Postoffice in the County was established at the County Seat, in October, 1870.

In the spring of 1871, Pierce—the County Seat—was laid out on land belonging to Messrs. Lucas and Brown. That same spring, the people of the County voted bonds to the amount of $15,000, for the erection of a brick Court House, which was completed the following year.

In June, 1871, a large number of settlements were made in Dry Creek Valley, in the northwestern part of the County. The succeeding winter was one of unusual severity, and the settlers in this section of the country were poorly prepared to meet it. Their houses were mostly built of prairie sod, and at times they were entirely covered up with the snow drifts, a column of smoke issueing from the snowy surface, being the only indication of life beneath. This part of the County also suffered to a greater extent than any other from the ravages of the grass-hopper, yet the people manfully clung to their homes, and to-day they have farms to be proud of.

The first death in the County was that of John Teitz, who was drowned in the North Fork on the 26th of July, 1870.

There is no record of the first marriage and first birth in the County, but both of these interesting events occurred in 1871.

The first term of the District Court for Pierce County, was held at the Court House on the 20th of August, 1873; Hon. Samuel Maxwell, presiding. Twelve cases were on the calendar,— one criminal, one for divorce, and the balance civil actions.

On the 27th of March, 1876, the people voted bonds to the amount of $85,000 to aid in the construction of the Covington, Columbus & Black Hills Railroad through the County.

This County has furnished two representatives to the State Legislature—Hon. R. S. Lucas and Hon. C. H. Frady.

PUBLIC SCHOOLS.—The first school districts were organized in 1871. At present there are ten districts, nine comfortable school houses, and 224 children of school age; qualified teachers employed, males, seven, females, seven; total wages paid teachers for the year, $2,591.52; value of school houses, $6,799; value of books, etc., $275.50.

TAXABLE PROPERTY.—Acres of land, 203,150, average value per acre, $2.90; value of town lots, $3,458; money used in merchandise, $,791; money used in manufacture, $75; horses, 421, value $11,290; mules, 22, value $730; neat cattle, 1,323, value, $8,855; sheep, 685, value $670; swine, 926, value, $812; vehicles, 154, value, $2,308; moneys and credits, $790; mortgages, $900; furniture, $198; libraries, $100; property not enumerated, $5,809; total valuation for 1879, $634,653.00

RAILROADS.—The nearest railroad point at present is at Norfolk, in Madison County, three miles from the south line of this County. The Omaha, Niobrara & Black Hills Railroad which has just reached Norfolk, is to be extended northward through this County early in the Spring of 1880.

LANDS.—The price of improved lands ranges from $5 to $12 per acre. The B. & M. R. R. Company owns 13,000 acres of land here, the price ranging from $1.25 to $6 per acre.

POPULATION.—The following are the Precincts and population of each in 1879: Dry Creek, 113; Pierce, 87; Slough, 168; South Branch, 260; Willow Creek, 56.

Total, 684,—males, 357; females, 327.

### PIERCE.

The County Seat, is located on the North Fork of the Elkhorn, at the mouth of Willow Creek. It contains several dwellings, two stores, a hotel, blacksmith shop, large school house, a weekly paper—the Pierce County *Call*—and a fine brick Court House, surrounded by a beautiful grove of cottonwood. Mrs. A. M. Lucas was the first school teacher. The German Lutherans and Methodists are well organized and hold services every Sabbath.

### PLAINVIEW

Is a small village in the northwestern part of the County. It has a Postoffice, store, blacksmith shop, school house, etc.

## POLK COUNTY.

Polk County was created in 1856 and organized in 1870. It is located in the middle-eastern part of the State, and is bounded on the north by the Platte River—which separates it from Merrick and Platte Counties,—east by Butler, south by York and west by Hamilton County, containing about 425 square miles, or 272,000 acres, at an average elevation of 1,600 feet above the sea level.

WATER COURSES.—The Platte River flows on the northwestern border of the County, a distance of about thirty-five miles, and receives several small creeks. The central and southern portions of the County are watered by the North Fork of the Big Blue River and tributaries. The Blue affords good mill advantages.

TIMBER.—1,865 acres, or 1,124,610 forest trees are reported under cultivation. Large domestic groves adorn almost every quarter section of land that is improved. Considerable natural timber is found along the streams. Twelve miles of hedging are reported.

FRUIT.—10,567 apple trees, 221 pear, 7161 peach, 2,259 plum, 1,227 cherry, and 2,764 grape vines are returned.

CHARACTER OF THE LANDS.—About fifteen per cent. of the County is valley, the balance consisting of broad tables and gently rolling prairie, with occasional high bluff along the rivers. The valley of the Blue is very fine and can be cultivated to the water's edge. The soil is everywhere exceedingly rich and productive.

CROPS.—Acres under cultivation, 65,994. Winter wheat, 506 acres, 7,541 bushels; spring wheat, 32,131 acres, 398,540 bushels; rye, 2,817 acres, 37,692 bushels; corn, 17,840 acres, 601,484 bushels; barley, 1,196 acres, 28,524 bushels; sorghum, four acres, 339 gallons, flax, twenty six acres, 212 bushels; broom corn, 286 acres, eighty two tons; potatoes, 275 acres, 32,190 bushels.

HISTORICAL.—The first settlements are here given by Precincts as follows:

HACKBERRY PRECINCT is the oldest and one of the best settled. The North Blue runs through it from west to east. Thomas Donolly has the honor of being the first settler. He located in 1867, and was followed in the same year by Albert Seaver. In 1868, Mr. John Patterson and wife, with their sons, Richard, James and William, James Clark, John H. Mickey, and W. W. Maxwell made settlement. In 1869 Messrs. James Query and V. P. Davis settled on what is now known as Davis Creek, this creek taking its name from Mr. Davis.

The first child born in the Precinct, and, in fact, in the County, was Edgar Roberts, son of Mrs. Louisa Roberts, born November 30, 1868. School district No. 1, was organized in 1871, with thirty-eight scholars; John A. Giffin, teacher. In the fall of 1872 and winter of 1873 the Methodists organized the first Church, under the charge of Rev. James Query, Polk County's pioneer preacher. In the winter of 1873-4 the Church of God was organized in the Hoffer settlements, and in the spring of 1876, Rev. Mr. Earnhart, organized a Baptist Church. Wayland Postoffice is located in the southern part of the Precinct. At the end of the year 1871 about 100 acres of land were under cultivation.

ISLAND PRECINCT lies in the north-eastern part of the County, and is so named from its being located between the two channels of the Platte River. Mr. Bouker Beebe made a settlement in this Precinct in the summer of 1870. In the spring of 1871 Rudolph Kummer, Dr. H. M. Mills, Wm. Thomas, Henry Augustine, and Alex. T. Simmons, located here. The first school district organized was No. 17, with Miss Jennie Osterhaut, as teacher. Seventy-five acres of land were under cultivation at the end of the year 1871.

CLEAR CREEK PRECINCT derives its name from a beautiful stream of the same name that runs through the northern part of it.

The first settlers in the Precinct were Geo. D. Grant, G. E. Barnum, Guy C. Barnum, and Levi Kimball, who all came about the same time. School district No. 4, was organized in 1871, and a school house was built in the spring of 1872; Miss Vandercoff, first teacher. About ninety acres of land were under cultivation at the end of the year 1871.

CANADA PRECINCT is one of the largest and best improved. James W. Snyder located in this Precinct in 1871, and has the honor of being the first settler. Closely following him were Peter Bull, William Jarmin, Geo. Bull and family, S. O. Whaley, M. H. Whaley, J. A. Palmer, Rufus Burnett, William Fosbender, H. W. Chase, M. W. Stone, and D. D. Bramer. School district No. 14 was organized with twenty-six scholars. Cyclone Postoffice was organized in 1873; Albert Cowles, postmaster. Rev. A. G. Whitehead organized a Methodist Church in the fall of 1873, at what is known as the Burly School House. A building was erected by this organization in the spring of 1876, called WESLEY CHAPEL. Number of acres of land under cultivation in 1871, 100.

OSCEOLA PRECINCT derives its name from the County Seat. James Query and V. P. Davis settled in this Precinct in October, 1868. II. C. Query came in 1869, and was followed shortly afterward by J. R. Stewart, Geo. Kerr, John A. Beltzer, Henry Hilderbrand, Geo. W. Kenyon, J. F. Campbell, William Query, Lumin Van Hoosen, H. T. Arnold and others. About fifty acres of land were in cultivation in 1871.

STROMSBURG PRECINCT was first settled in the fall of 1869, by Wm. H. Records. B. F. Smith, Thomas Records, J. P. Smith, A. P. Buckley, P. T. Buckley, J. C. Smith and A. L Larson came in the spring of 1870. The town of Stromsburg is located in this Precinct. School district No. 10 was organized in the winter of 1872, with six scholars; Mr. J. A. Palmer, teacher. The Baptists formed an organization in the summer of 1873; the Lutherans organized in the fall of 1874. The Congregational Church of Pleasant Prairie, in this Precinct, was organized in the fall of 1873; the Methodist Episcopal Church formed a society in the winter of 1875-6. The Baptists and Lutherans have each a Church building, worth together over $3,000. In 1871 there were about fifteen acres of prairie under cultivation.

PLEASANT HOME PRECINCT is in the southwestern part of the County; and S. C. Davis has the honor of being its first settler. He came here on the 29th of October, 1870. Shortly afterward, Milo Barber, Wm. Maston, J. N. Nickell, John and Henry Marty, J. D. Darrow and J. N. Skelton settled in the Precinct. In the fall of 1872, School District No. 6 was organized with fifteen scholars; Jay N. Skelton, teacher. In the summer of 1872, Pleasant Home Postoffice was established, with S. C. Davis, postmaster. The United Brethren formed an organization in the fall of 1872; the Methodists in the fall of 1875. There is also an organization of Adventists. In 1871, there were about sixty-five acres of prairie broken.

PLATTE PRECINCT is situated in the northern part of the County. Messrs. P. C. King and W. T. Dodge located claims in March, 1871, and Guy, Faustus and Beebe, in April following. J. A. Powers, A. J. Sherwood, G. W. Cadwell, Oliver Scott, and others, came in shortly afterward. School District No. 7 was organized in the fall of 1871, and a school house was built in 1872. The school consisted of eight scholars; John P. Heald, teacher. Thornton Postoffice was established in August, 1874; J. N. Hurd, postmaster. The United Brethren formed an organization in December, 1872; the Methodists organized in March, 1875; and the Lutherans (Swedish), in 1876. The last named have erected a neat Church edifice in the southeastern part of the Precinct.

VALLEY PRECINCT was first settled by B. H. Keller, who located in the spring of 1871. He was soon followed by Charles R. Clarke, J. W. Sheldon, Levi Kelley, James Bell, Wm. B. Daymude, James Harmon, William Stevens, D. C. Place, Andreas Horst, John and Joseph Curran, M. C. Stull, John Benson, Collin and Robert Beebe, and Thomas Clarke. School District No. 5 was organized in June, 1871, with James Bell as teacher. The first Church organized was the Methodist. In 1871, there were about 200 acres of prairie under cultivation. There are about 100 acres of natural timber in this Precinct.

The first election for County officers was held on the 6th day of August, 1870, and resulted as follows: Commissioners, S. Stone, C. A. Ewing, Jonathan Crockett; Clerk, Frank Reardon; Probate Judge, James Query; Treasurer, John H. Mickey; Sheriff, Ole Bredeson.

On the 14th of December, 1870, F. M. Stone was appointed County Surveyor, and John Fox Superintendent of Public Schools.

At the same date, the County was divided into two Precincts—Hackberry and Clear Creek. In April, 1871, Platte Precinct was formed.

On the 10th of November, 1871, the question of the permanent location of the County Seat was voted upon by the people, and on the 14th day of November following, the County Commissioners issued a proclamation declaring the County Seat located on the southeast one fourth of section sixteen, township fourteen north, of range two, west, in accordance with the vote at said election. The name selected for the seat of justice was Osceola.

On the 16th day of November, 1871, bids for the construction of a Court House were advertised. The contract was awarded to M. W. Stone, who completed the building, and it was accepted by the Board of Commissioners, March 20, 1872.

A large Swedish colony was established in the western part of the County, mainly by Lewis Headstrom. The town of Stromsburg is its chief trading point. The Canadian settlers are mostly settled in Canada Precinct, in the eastern part of the County. The German element is well distributed throughout the County; and their thrifty, well-improved farms may be seen in almost every township.

The first newspaper in the County was the *Polk County Times*, W. D. Ferree, editor, established at Stromsburg in the summer of 1872. It lasted only six months. The Osceola *Homesteader* was established a few months later, at Osceola. In January, 1876, its name was changed to the Osceola *Record*, and it is still a live, prosperous paper.

PUBLIC SCHOOLS.—Number of districts, fifty-six; school houses, fifty-two; children of school age—males 995, females 840; total, 1,835; total number that attended school during the year, 1,293; qualified teachers employed—males, thirty-one, females, forty-six; wages paid teachers for the year—males, $4,104.77, females, $4,725.67; value of school houses, $22,649.95; value of sites, $638.50; value of books and apparatus, $1,262.20.

TAXABLE PROPERTY.—Acres of land, 215,523, average value per acre, $3.33; value of town lots, $17,116; money invested in merchandise, $9,470; money used in manufactures, $4,570; horses, 2,423, value $75,646; mules and asses, 290, value $9,833; neat cattle, 3,696, value $31,359; sheep 217, value $217; swine 10,284, value $9,889; vehicles, 980, value, $15,582; moneys and credits, $3,627; mortgages, $15,441; stocks, etc., $474; furniture, $3,352; property not enumerated, $35,867; total valuation for 1879, $950,295.

RAILROADS.—The Omaha & Republican Valley Railroad enters the County near the middle of the eastern border, and is now in running order to Stromsburg, in the south-central part of the County. A branch line from this road has just been completed, from Arcadia, in this County, to Jackson, on the Union Pacific.

LANDS.—Improved lands range in price from $6 to $25 per acre. The Union Pacific Railroad Company owns some 25,000 acres in this County, the price ranging from $2 to $6 per acre.

POPULATION.—The following are the Precincts and population of each in 1879: Hackberry, 695; Canada, 608; Clear Creek, 339; Island, 269; Stromsburg, 746; Osceola, 807; Valley, 439; Pleasant Hill, 664; Platte, 456.

Total, 5,023—males, 2,725; females, 2,298. Increase in population over 1878, 1,092.

### OSCEOLA,

The County Seat, is located on the line of the Omaha & Republican Valley Railway, in the middle-eastern part of the County. It is pleasantly situated near the North Blue River, and contains about 700 inhabitants—its population having fully doubled within the past year, or since it has been made a railroad town. Business is flourishing, and is represented by a full line of stores, offices and shops. The Osceola *Record*, a weekly paper, is issued here.

The town site of Osceola was purchased and surveyed in June, 1872, by Wm. F. Kimmel and John H. Mickey. The Court House, completed in January, 1872, was the first building on the town site; the first store was opened by W. H. Waters. During the same year, a school house was erected, and the Methodist Episcopal and Congregational Churches organized. The first child born in the town was Evan Mickey, on January 26, 1874.

### STROMSBURG,

Located on the North Blue, in the south-central part of the County, is the present terminus of the Omaha & Republican Valley Railroad. It contains about 400 inhabitants, and is at present a very prosperous and brisk business place. The town site was surveyed in the summer of 1872, by Lewis Headstrom, who acted for the Stromsburg Town Company. The first building was erected in the fall of 1872. The Baptists organized a Society in 1873, and the Lutherans in 1874; both have neat Churches. The surrounding country is thickly settled by Swedes, who have some of the finest and largest farms in the County.

PLEASANT HOME, WAYLAND, CYCLONE, REDVILLE, and THORNTON, are young towns, with stores, Postoffices, school house, etc.

## PHELPS COUNTY.

Phelps County was organized in 1873. It is located in the south-central part of the State, bounded on the north by the Platte River, east by Kearney, south by Harlan, and west by Gosper County, containing 500 square miles, or 320,000 acres.

Ninety per cent. of the area consists of undulating prairie. The bottoms of the Platte, extending across the northern portion of the County, are from two to six miles wide. Several Creeks, tributaries of the Republican River, water the southern portion of the County, along which there are some fine bottom lands. Good water is obtainable on the prairies, at a depth of thirty to seventy feet. The soil is well adapted to the growth of small grain. No returns have been made of crops, timber, or fruit. The Platte River is spanned with bridges affording easy access to the shipping stations on the Union Pacific Railroad. There is still a large amount of good government land in this County. The Union Pacific Railroad Company own some 50,000 acres here, ranging in price from $2.50 to $5.00 per acre.

PUBLIC SCHOOLS.—Number of districts, ten; school houses, four; children of school age—males 195, females 150; total, 345; qualified teachers employed, six; amount of wages paid teachers for the year, $387.50; value of school houses, $1,675.50; value of sites, $200; value of books, etc., $136.54.

TAXABLE PROPERTY.—Acres of land, 130,239; average value per acre, $1.88. Money used in merchandise, $1,505; money used in manufactures, $648; horses 496, value $19,315; mules 111, value, $5,948; neat cattle 916, value $12,255; sheep 190, value $197; swine 315, value $387; vehicles 248, value $5,723; moneys and credits, $3,673; furniture, $3,879; total valuation for 1879, $300,842. The population of the County in 1879 was 1,275.

### WILLIAMSBURGH,

The County Seat, is located on the Platte bottom, near the center of the County from east to west. It contains 250 inhabitants, the County Offices, a school house, good general stores, and a weekly newspaper.

HOPEVILLE and SHERWOOD are small villages located on the Platte bottom, in the eastern part of the County. ROCK FALLS is a new town established on Spring Creek, in the southwestern part of the County.

## RICHARDSON COUNTY.

Richardson County, named in honor of Wm. A. Richardson, of Illinois, third territorial Governor, was created by proclamation of Acting Governor Cuming, in 1854, and re-organized by the first Territorial Legislature in the spring of 1855. It is located in the south-east corner of the State, bounded on the north by Nemaha County, east by the Missouri River, south by the State of Kansas, and west by Pawnee County, containing 550 square miles, or 352,000 acres.

WATER COURSES.—The County is finely watered by the Missouri and Great Nemaha Rivers and small streams. The Missouri washes the entire eastern border. The Nemaha flows in a general easterly direction through the southern portion of the County. The North Fork waters the northwestern townships, and the South Fork the southwestern portion of the County. The principal tributaries of the Nemahas are Pony, Walnut, Contrary, Wild Cat, Rattle Snake, Easley, Sardine, Deer, Half Breed, Rock, Long Branch and Muddy Creeks, the last two being fine large streams. Water-power is abundant.

CHARACTER OF THE LAND.—About fifteen per cent. is valley and bottom land, and the remainder rolling prairie, with a small per cent. bluff. The valley of the Nemaha is three miles wide on an average. Muddy Creek also has a beautiful valley extending through the central portion of the County, and wide sloping bottoms are found along several of the other streams. Altogether Richardson is one of the finest and richest Counties in the State. The prairies have a deep rich soil, and there is but little waste land in the County.

CROPS.—Area under cultivation, 109,179 acres. Winter wheat, 4,756 acres, 89,637 bushels; spring wheat, 22,944 acres, 188,130 bushels; rye, 2,485 acres, 31,700 bushels; corn, 61,182 acres, 2,215,810 bushels; barley, 2,644 acres, 57,169 bushels; buckwheat, 77 acres, 709 bushels; sorghum, 213 acres, 18,886 gallons; flax, five acres, forty-two bushels; broom corn, ten acres, three and a half tons; millet, 240 acres, 195 tons; potatoes, 552½ acres, 45,-167 bushels; onions, six and one eighth acres, 1,085½ bushels.

TIMBER.—This is one of the very best timbered Counties in the State, the streams being skirted with a heavy growth, and beautiful natural groves are frequently met with, while large thrifty domestic groves adorn every farm. The total number of forest trees planted is 2,827,816, or 14,742 acres; hedging 949½ miles.

FRUIT.—Large orchards have been in bearing here for several years past and fruit is now abundant. The following statement will show the number of trees in the County: Apple, 101,229; pear, 2,365; peach, 118,466; plum, 2,901; cherry, 13,944; grape vines, 13,618.

COAL is found in thin seams and is mined to some extent.

BUILDING MATERIAL.—Limestone and sandstone abound, and many fine quarries have been opened. Good brick and fire clays are plentiful.

HISTORICAL.—-The first settlement by whites in the County was in August, 1854, although Stephen Story, Charles Martin and F. X. Dupuis, white men who had intermarried with the Indians, came shortly before that time, and settled upon what has since been called the "Half Breed Tract." Story, still residing in the County, laid out, platted and surveyed the town of St. Stephen, which was up to 1865, a thriving village, but is now nearly vacated. Dupuis lived with the widow of the great Iowa Chief, "White Cloud," whose remains are interred in the Rulo Cemetery.

The first white settler outside of the "Half Breed Tract," was a man by the name of Level, who in the spring of 1854, dug a hole in the side of a hill near the townsite of ARCHER, and kept whiskey to sell to the Indians, until the Chiefs came in and emptied his whiskey barrel.

In the summer of 1854, Jesse Crook, Wm. G. Goolsby, John A. Singleton and J. C. Lincoln, passed through the County, making a survey, naming the streams, and taking claims—Crook and Goolsby, near ARCHER, and Singleton and Lincoln, near SALEM, to which they returned with their families in the fall. They were soon followed by Isaac Crook and J. F. Harkendorff, who settled near ARCHER, John Crook and Wm. Roberts near SALEM, and Thomas F. Brown and Wm. Withrow, who located in the west end of the County.

The County when first organized, comprised what is now known as Richardson, Pawnee and Johnson Counties, there being but little settlement in the territory of the two last named Counties, and they were detached and organized by themselves some two or three years later.

Richardson County, in 1855, consisted of two election Precincts—SALEM and ARCHER.

The following is a list of the first County officers, as appointed by Governor Cumming, to wit: John O. Miller, County Judge; F. L. Goldsberry, Clerk; Louis Misplais, Treasurer; and — McMullin, Sheriff.

At the election in 1856, there were ninety-eight votes polled in the County.

The first Court was held at ARCHER, then the County Seat, in 1856, at Judge Miller's large log house, which served as Court House, jail, and tavern, all in one. Archer was then quite a busy little place, with two stores, two hotels, a blacksmith's shop and quite a number of dwellings.

At the election in 1857, there were 320 votes polled in the County, and the following County officers elected, to wit: W. H. Mann, Clerk; Isaac Crook, Treasurer; Samuel S. Keefer, Sheriff; and Joseph Yount, Arnet Roberts and George Coffman, County Commissioners. At the election in 1859, the election Precincts were Rulo, St. Stephenson, Falls City, Salem, Spizer and Franklin; 800 votes were polled.

In the winter of 1857, the Half Breed Line was run, and the land east of it to the Missouri River, reserved by the U. S. Government to be divided, 320 acres each, between certain Half Breeds or mixed Indians, according to the treaty of PRAIRIE DU CHEIN, WIS., made in 1831. Archer being supposed to be on the Half Breed Track, the County Seat was removed to SALEM in 1857, where it remained until 1860, when it was removed by Act of the Legislature to FALLS CITY, the present County Seat.

The first death in the County was that of the wife of Francis Purkett, who died in child-birth, near Archer, in the fall of 1854.

The first birth in the County was that of Frank Luchman, born near Archer, in the spring of 1855.

The first marriage in the County, was in May, 1855, at St. Stephen, between N. J. Sharp, Esq., and Miss Tramel (daughter of Esquire Tramel, afterwards Probate Judge of the County.)

The first saw mill run by water power was built in 1856, by Chas. Rouleau, Wm. Kencelear, E. Bedard, E. H. Johnson, E. Plant, and others, at the mouth of Muddy Creek where Thacker & Jones' grist mill now stands. The first steam saw mill run in the County was put up at Rulo, in the spring of 1858, by Israel May.

E. H. Johnson, residing at Rulo, was the first practical surveyor and engineer who came to the County. In the fall of 1856, Mr. Johnson surveyed the townsite of Rulo (named from Charles Rouleau, one of its proprietors) for Charles Martin, Charles Rouleau, Wm. Kencelear and Eli Bedard, proprietors of the town.

In 1858, the Rulo *Western Guide,* published by a man by the name of Barret, was commenced at Rulo, and also the Falls City *Broad Axe,* published at Falls City, by J. E. Burbank and S. R. Jamison, and these were the two first newspapers published in the County.

Dr. Whitmeyer, of St. Stephens, Dr. Johnson, and Dr. H. O. Hanna, of Falls Bity, John R. Brooks, of Salem, and A. Godfrey, of Rulo (the last now dead) were the first practicing physicians in the County.

The first practicing attorneys in the County were Hon. E. S. Dundy, now U. S. District Judge for Nebraska, Hon. Isham Reavis, late U. S. Judge in Arizona, and Hon. Augustus Schoenheit, of Falls City; A. D. Kirk, and A. M. Acton (killed while a Colonel in the Confederate army) of Rulo, and Hon. J. J. Marvin, of Falls City.

The oldest living explorer of this County, or of Nebraska, is a Frenchman named Zephyr Rencontre, now nearly one hundred years old, living at the White River Indian Agency, in Dakota Teritorry, as interpreter. He accompanied Lewis and Clark in their world famed tour of discovery to the Pacific Ocean, and passed through Richardson County, to which he returned in a few years, and residing there for several years, drew land for his children as Half Breeds, from the Government.

Henri Goulet, who came to the County in 1854, and laid out the town of Yankton, and Antoine Barrada, who first passed through the County in 1816, and from whom Barrada Precinct takes its name, are two of the old French pioneer settlers, who still live in the County.

In 1855 and 1856 the County was filled with wild game; gangs of fifteen or twenty deer could be seen any day, and wild turkeys and prairie chickens were abundant. In 1856, Wm. G. Goodsby, had during the winter, a cabin filled with venison which he had slaughtered himself, and gave away to his neighbors when they came after it.

The first sermon preached in Richardson County was in St. Stephen Precinct, two and a half miles south of St. Deroin, in the spring of 1855, by Rev. David Hart, a Methodist minister, now dead; the next sermon was delivered near Archer, in the summer of 1855, by Rev. L. D. Gage, also a Methodist.

There are at present from twenty-five to thirty Church buildings in the County, costing from $200 to $3,000, and upwards each.

In 1858, the greatest inundation ever known in the County took place, commencing on the 12th day of July, the rain falling for ten days and nights until the Nemaha and its tributaries burst over their banks and inundated all the bottom land in the County. The bridges upon all the streams were swept away, and Falls City left isolated and cut off from connection with the rest of the County, and the farmers and their families were compelled to leave their inundated homes, in skiffs or by swimming.

The two first murder trials in the County, were that of one Clifford, for the murder of a young man in his employ, and the suspected murder of his wife, and one Moran for the murder of Hudgins. These murders took place in 1858 and 1859,—and singularly enough, Hudgins, just before he was killed, was one of the Grand Jury who indicted Clifford; both murderers escaped, being found Not Guilty by the Juries who tried them.

A most remarkable change of weather occurred in the County in January or February of 1871—upon a Sunday morning. At ten o'clock, there being some little snow upon the roofs of the houses, the eaves were dripping; at half-past ten a dark cloud came up from the west, with a howling wind, and at eleven o'clock it was as dark as night, and the thermometer had sunk from 30 degrees above zero, to 10 degrees below—a change of forty degrees in one half hour.

The first Court House in the County was built by subscription, at Falls City, in 1863, and cost $2,500, upon a block donated by Falls City to the County. The County jail was built in 1871, at a cost of $11,000. The present Court House was built upon the site of the old one and cost about $30,000.

PUBLIC SCHOOLS.—The first school in the County was taught near Archer, in the spring of 1856, by Mrs. Samuels. The present number of districts is ninety-five; school houses, ninety-four; children of school age, males, 3,073, females, 2,790, total, 5,863; total number that attended school during the year, 3,816; qualified teachers employed, males, fifty-six, females, sixty-five; wages paid teachers for the year, males, $9,275.45; females, $8,871.56; total, $18,147.21; value of school houses, $73,374.55; value of sites, $4,270; value of books and apparatus, $1,810.40.

TAXABLE PROPERTY.—Acres of land, 325,563; average value per acre, $4.70; value of town lots, $179,483; money invested in merchandise, $67,894; money used in manufactures, $8,193; horses, 7,221, value $171,830; mules and asses, 696, value $19,095; neat cattle, 18,091, value $142,575; sheep, 3,162, value $2,390; swine, 34,690, value $25,206; vehicles, 2,195, value $30,519;

moneys and credits, $57,244; mortgages, $6,820; stocks, etc., $1,585; furniture, $32,790; libraries, $1,560; property not enumerated, $65,837; railroads, $211,473.43; total valuation for 1879, $2,556,705.43.

RAILROADS.—The Atchison and Nebraska was completed through the County in 1871. It follows the valley of the Great Nemaha, a distance of 42.95 miles, in this County.

LANDS.—The price of wild land ranges from $5 to $12, and improved, $7 to $35 per acre.

POPULATION.—The following are the precincts and population of each in 1879: Arago, 799; Barada, 1,137; Falls City, 2,651; Franklin, 447; Grant, 739; Humboldt, 1,253; Liberty, 622; Muddy, 721; Nemaha, 546; Ohio, 855; Porter, 443; Rulo, 1,205; Salem, 807; Spicer, 644; St. Stephens, 464.

Total, 13,433,—males, 7,227, females, 6,206.

### FALLS CITY,

The County Seat, is located in the southeastern part of the County, on the high ground overlooking the Nemaha Valley and about two miles north of the river. The County Seat was removed to this place from Salem, in 1860, by an Act of the Legislature. At the election held in the spring of 1860, upon the location of the County Seat, the contest between Falls City and Rulo was very spirited, two men being shot and killed at the former place on election day —Doctor Davis, of Rulo, and a Mr. Meeks, of Falls City. The Atchison and Nebraska Railroad was completed to Falls City on the 4th day of July, 1871, and to-day this is one of the best business centers and most prosperous towns on the line of that road. The population of the city is 2,200. It contains five handsome Churches, two parsonages, a $20,000 school house, an elegant Court House, substantial jail, two flouring mills, two banks, one pork packing establishment, large grain elevators and stock yards, and a multitude of fine stores and minor places of business. The newspapers published here are the *Globe-Journal*, and the *News*, both able papers.

### HUMBOLDT

Is the second largest town in the County, having at present a population of 1,000. It is located on the Atchison and Nebraska Railway, twenty-one miles west of Falls City, and is surrounded by a very fertile and beautiful country. Business of all kinds is well represented here. There are two grist mills, a bank, several dry goods and grocery stores, two drug and two hardware stores, two grain warehouses, two hotels, large lumber yards, and numerous other business enterprises. It has a fine graded school and excellent Church facilities. The *Sentinel*, a weekly newspaper, is published here. This town is only seven years old and already many elegant residences and fine business blocks of brick have been erected.

### SALEM,

Situated at the confluence of the North and South Forks of the Great Nemaha, in the south-central part of the County, has a population of 550. It is also a station on the A. & N. Railroad, seven miles west of Falls City, and is one of the best trading points in the County. It contains two elevators, a grist mill, several general assortment stores, one hardware, one drug, one agricultural implement, and one furniture store, a good hotel, good school and Church advantages, etc., and a weekly paper, the *Advertiser*. Fine limestone quarries have been opened here.

### RULO

Is a town of 800 inhabitants, situated on the banks of the Missouri, in the southeastern part of the County. The A. & N. runs a side-track up to the town, and a large amount of grain and stock is shipped from here. It contains a steam flouring mill, steam saw-mill, a bank, hotel, grain warehouse, stock yards, a brickyard, and several large mercantile establishments.

### ARAGO,

Situated on the banks of the Missouri River, near the center of the County from north to south, has about 300 inhabitants. Business is represented by three general assortment stores, one hardware, one drug, and one implement store, a hotel, cooper-shop, blacksmith and wagon shop, and a pork-packing establishment.

### DAWSON'S MILL

Is a village of 100 inhabitants, located on the Railroad, sixteen miles west of Falls City. It contains a Church, school house, flouring mill, grain elevator, hotel, two general assortment stores, a drug store, lumber yard, wagon and blacksmith shop, and two physicians.

ARCHER, ST. STEPHEN, YANKTON, WINNEBAGO, and GENEVA, were flourishing villages in the early days of the County, but are now entirely abandoned.

BARRADA, WILLIAMSVILLE, ELMORE, MIDDLEBURGH, ATHENS, and FLOWERDALE, are villages having a Postoffice, general store, school house, etc.

The reservation of the Sacs and Foxes, and the Iowa Indians, is located in the southeast corner of this County, extending over into Kansas, and comprises a body of rich and beautiful land, well timbered. The Postoffice of NOHART is on this reservation.

## RED WILLOW COUNTY.

Red Willow County was organized in May, 1873. It is located on the southwestern border of the State, bounded on the north by Frontier and east by Furnas, south by the State of Kansas, and west by Hitchcock County, and contains 720 square miles, or 460,800 acres.

WATER COURSES.—The County is watered by the Republican River, Beaver, Red Willow, and other large Creeks. The Republican flows from west to east through the central portion of the County. Red Willow Creek, from which the County takes its name, is a fine stream about seventy-five miles long, which flows from the northwest, and empties into the Republican near the center of the County. The Beaver flows through the southern portion of the County, and is one of the largest tributaries of the Republican. Driftwood, Coon, Dry, and many smaller streams meander through the County. Water power is abundant.

TIMBER.—25,170 forest trees are reported under cultivation. The streams are generally well skirted with natural timber.

FRUIT.—Wild fruits are abundant. A large number of fruit trees, embracing all the choice varieties of apple, peach, pear and plum, have been planted in the County within the past two years, and are reported as growing finely.

BUILDING STONE of an excellent quality is found in several localities.

34

CHARACTER OF THE LAND.—Fifteen per cent. of the County is valley, and the balance rolling prairie, with bluffs along the Republican and other large streams. The Valley of the Republican is here from three to six miles wide. The Red Willow, Beaver and Driftwood, each have fine valleys varying in width from one to three miles. The blue-stem and gramma grasses abound on the bottoms, and the buffalo grass on the uplands and divides. The soil is fertile and easily tilled.

CROPS.—Area under cultivation in 1879, 2,990 acres. Winter wheat, 45½ acres, 485 bushels; spring wheat, 331½ acres, 4,814 bushels; rye, 343½ acres, 4,653 bushels; corn, 1,631 acres, 32,064 bushels; barley, seventy-three acres, 1,403 bushels; sorghum, 17¼ acres, 982 gallons; broom corn, 13½ acres, two tons; potatoes, 17½ acres, 1,132 bushels; onions, one-half acre, 114 bushels.

HISTORICAL.—The first actual settler in the County was John S. King, who took a claim on the Republican, near the east line of the County, in the fall of 1871.

On the 22d of November, 1871, various claims were staked out near the mouth of Red Willow Creek, and the town site of Red Willow located by a party of gentlemen representing a Town Company, which had been organized in Nebraska City that fall. This Company was regularly organized under the laws of the State, and had a President, Vice-President, Secretary, Treasurer and Board of Directors. An exploring party, consisting of Hon. Royal Buck, President of the Company; Latrop Ellis, Surveyor; and John Roberts, John F. Black, W. W. W. Jones, John Longnecker, L. R. Sitler, Wm. Byfield, Frank Usher, Wm. McKinney and J. M. Davis, left Nebraska City in the fore part of November, with two wagons loaded with provisions sufficient for a thirty-days' trip; and after a very trying journey over roads made almost impassable by deep snows, they arrived at Red Willow Creek on the 22d of the same month, and went into camp in a grove near its mouth. One week was spent at this camp in selecting claims and locating the town site, which they named RED WILLOW, after the beautiful stream near by; and here also, on the 28th, was held the first religious meeting in the County. On the 29th, they broke camp, and retraced their steps to Nebraska City, where they arrived on the 10th of December following. On the 10th of January,

1872, the town site was filed at the Land Office at Beatrice, and at the same time homestead entries were made by Messrs. Black, Longnecker, Jones, Byfield, Davis, and a Mrs. Shaw.

The first arrivals in the spring of 1872, were Messrs. Hunter, Hill, Korns, H. Madison, and W. Weygant and son, on the 29th of April. A few days later, L. H. Lawton and family, Mr. Young and family, Henry Burger, and several other single men, arrived. In May, quite a number of families came, viz: Royal Buck and family, Mrs. Shurvinton and family, Mrs. Shaw and family, and T. P. Thomas and family, who brought with him a fine herd of cattle.

Early in May, 1872, a Company of U. S. Cavalry and one of Infantry established a camp near Red Willow, and guarded the settlement until November following.

The first election for County Officers and the location of the County Seat, was held on the 27th of May, 1873, at the house of Willburn Morris, on section fifteen, township three, range twenty-eight, west. Sixty-three votes were polled, and the following officers elected, viz: W. H. Burger, W. S. Fitch and W. B. Bradbury, Commissioners; G. A. Hunter, Sheriff; E. S. Hill, Probate Judge; I. J. Starbuck, County Clerk; J. E. Burger, Treasurer; P. F. Francis, Surveyor; Edward Lyon, County Superintendent.

At this election, Indianola received a majority of seven votes for the County Seat, over Red Willow. The latter, however, contested the election on the ground of fraud, claiming that a number of votes greater than the majority, had been cast for Indianola, by men not citizens of the County. A long and tedious litigation followed, which ended in the final triumph of Indianola.

The first Postoffice in the County was established at Red Willow in April, 1872; Royal Buck, postmaster. In the summer of 1873, a Postoffice was established at Indianola, and later in the same year, at Canby, Lebanon, and Danbury on the Beaver.

The first session of the District Court for Red Willow County, was held at Indianola, on the 28th and 29th days of April, 1875; Judge Gaslin presiding.

During 1872, there were no deaths in the County, of record; in 1873, there were two; in 1874, none; in 1875, six, of whom two were killed by lightning, and one was drowned.

The first stock of goods brought into the County was by T. P. Thomas, late in the summer of 1872. John Byfield also opened a store on his homestead, adjoining Red Willow town site, in the same year.

The Christian denomination organized a Society at Red Willow, in 1873; and another has since been organized on the Beaver. In 1875, the Congregationalists organized Societies at Indianola and Valley Grange; and since then, a Society of the same denomination has been organized at Red Willow. In 1876, the M. E. Church organized a Society at Indianola, and the United Brethren a class at Red Willow. A Union Bible class and prayer-meeting was organized at Red Willow in the summer of 1872, and early in 1873 a regular Sabbath school was organized at the house of Royal Buck. There are now several Church buildings in the County, and flourishing Sabbath schools are conducted at Indianola and at different points on the Beaver.

PUBLIC SCHOOLS.—The first school districts were organized in December, 1873, at Indianola and Red Willow. The present number of districts is fifteen; school houses, eleven; children of school age, males, 162, females, 141, total, 303; qualified teachers employed, males, six, females, seven; total wages paid teachers for the year, $792.80; value of school property, $525.

TAXABLE PROPERTY.—Acres of land, 18,775; average value per acre, $1.50; value of town lots, $2,457; money invested in merchandise, $1,330; money used in manufactures, $200; horses, 544, value, $11,764; mules, 51, value, $2,132; neat cattle, 2,817, value, $19,778; sheep, 1,375, value, $1,222; swine, 284, value, $351; vehicles, 192, value, $2,783; moneys and credits, $2,506; mortgages, $175; furniture, $258; property not enumerated, $623; total valuation for 1879, $73,741.

RAILROADS.—The nearest railroad point at present is at Bloomington, Franklin County, sixty miles distant. The grading for the extension westward of the Republican valley branch of the B. & M. road is now in progress, and the road is to be completed through this County before the close of 1879.

LANDS.—There is some good Government land still left in this County. The price of wild lands ranges from $1.25 to $7 per acre.

POPULATION.—The following are the precincts and population of each, in 1879: Indianola, 420; Red Willow, 207; Driftwood, 108; Beaver, 125; Danbury, 103.

Total, 963,—males, 544, females, 419.

### INDIANOLA,

The County Seat, is located on the east bank of Coon Creek, near its junction with the Republican, and five miles northeast of the geographical center of the County. The town site was surveyed and recorded in the fall of 1873. It has a population of 300, and contains a newspaper, good school and Church facilities, the County offices, several general stores, hotel, blacksmith shop, lumber yard, etc.

### RED WILLOW,

Beautifully located on the west bank of Red Willow Creek, within a mile of the Republican, was the first town laid out in the County. It contains 150 inhabitants, a good school house, three well-stocked general assortment stores, a flouring mill, etc. It is surrounded by a magnificent fertile country, and the streams are well timbered and bridged.

VALLEY GRANGE, on the Driftwood, and DANBURY and LEBANON, on the Beaver, are flourishing young towns.

---

## SAUNDERS COUNTY.

Saunders County, formerly called Calhoun, was created in 1856. By an Act of the Legislature, approved January 8, 1862, its name was changed to Saunders, in honor of Hon. Alvin Saunders, the last Territorial Governor and present United States Senator from Nebraska. By an Act approved February 8, 1865, it was attached to Cass County for election, revenue and judicial purposes. The organization of the County was effected in October, 1866. After several changes by the Legislature in the boundaries of the County, they were fixed as they exist at present by an Act approved February 25, 1875.

Saunders is located in the middle-eastern part of the State, in the second tier of Counties west of the Missouri River, bounded on the north and east by the Platte River, which separates it from Dodge, Douglas, and Sarpy Counties,—south by Cass and Lancaster, and west by Butler County, containing about 756 square miles, or 483,840 acres, at an average elevation of 1,150 feet above the sea level.

WATER COURSES.—Besides the Platte River, which forms the County boundary from the northwest to the southeast corner, there are many beautiful streams flowing through the County in every direction, among which are the Salt, Wahoo, Sand, Cottonwood, Dunlap, North Fork, Miller's Branch, Silver, Upper Clear, Lower Clear, Rock and Oak Creeks, making this one of the best watered Counties in the State, every township having one or more living streams passing through it. Several of the creeks afford excellent mill privileges.

TIMBER.—The native timber is limited, being found chiefly in the bluffs, on the islands of the Platte, and along the banks of the creeks. The amount reported under cultivation is 2,538 acres, or 1,451,358 trees. Of hedge fencing, 130 miles are returned.

FRUIT.—4,762 apple, 1,059 pear, 14,938 peach, 8,035 plum, and 8,716 cherry trees are returned, besides six and three-fourths acres of grape vines.

LIMESTONE and sandstone of fair quality are found in several localities.

CHARACTER OF THE LAND.—Twelve per cent. of the County is valley, and the remainder plain and rolling prairie, with high bluffs skirting the valley of the Platte. The flood plains of the Platte River, Salt, Wahoo and Rock Creeks are extensive, being broad and beautiful expanses of natural meadow, clothed with nutritious grasses growing upon a deep alluvial soil of great fertility.

CROPS.—The area under cultivation reported for 1879, was 152,354 acres. Winter wheat, 400 acres, 5,059 bushels; spring wheat 64,695 acres, 723,206 bushels; rye 3,790 acres, 39,598 bushels; corn, 59,794 acres, 1,578,366 bushels; barley, 2,301 acres, 36,006 bushels; oats, 11,209 acres, 120,033 bushels; buckwheat, ten acres, seventy-nine bushels; sorghum, nine acres, 687 gallons; flax, 660 acres, 3,204 bushels; broom corn, 409 acres, eighty-eight and three-fourths tons; potatoes, 437 acres, 38,226 bushels.

HISTORICAL.—Mr. Joseph Stambaugh, who located upon Section thirty-five, of town thirteen, range nine, of the Sixth Principal Meridian, September 6, 1856, has the honor of being the first white settler of Saunders County. Mr. Stambaugh and his heroic wife are entitled to much credit for perseverance, fortitude and heroism in enduring the privations, hardships and annoyances of frontier life. The murauding and thieving Pawnees were a constant source of annoyance to them during the first years of their stay in the County. Scarcely were they settled upon their homestead—ere they were compelled to leave it and seek shelter and protection among the settlers of Cass County. Their first house was destroyed by the Indians soon after their departure. Early in the spring of 1857, however, a new house was erected, and the brave parents with their little ones returned to their chosen home. With not a Postoffice, store, or even a blacksmith shop, nearer than the town of Plattsmouth, over thirty miles distant, with numerous unbridged streams intervening, requiring days to make the trip, the loneliness and hardship of their lives during the first three years cannot be imagined by the uninitiated. But victory perched upon their banner, and has crowned their efforts with success. A brick house now occupies the place of their original "sod mansion," and is surrounded with a fine grove of forest trees, a thrifty orchard and several barns for the protection of stock. John Stambaugh, their second son, was the second white child born in the County, April 9, 1858.

Reuben L. Warbritton and family, and John Aughe, accompanied Mr. Stambaugh on his return to the County in the spring of 1857. In June, Mr. Ramsey settled upon the south side of Wahoo Creek, about one mile above Mr. Warbritton's, where his widow still resides. She has the honor of giving birth to the first white child born in the County, March, 1858.

Thomas K. Chamberlain also came in 1857, and located near the junction of Musquito Creek with the Wahoo.

In 1860, came Austin Smith, John Smith, Henry Howe, Stephen Brown, Solomon Henry, and a Mr. Aldrich, all from Wisconsin. They settled upon the table land north of R. L. Warbritton. Perry Tarpenning came in 1861, and settled between Warbritton and Smith.

In 1858, Samuel Hahn settled upon section one, town twelve, range nine, then a part of Cass County, but now a part of Saunders. In 1861, Charles Richart settled on the Platte bottom, town seventeen, range six; near him settled, in the fall of the same year, John Garrett and a Mr. Anderson. W. H. McCowan and Doctor Wood settled upon the table land just above Pohocco headland, in 1863, and Perry Reed on the headland bluff, in 1865.

This noted headland merits a brief notice in this place. Having in a former geological period occupied the position of an island in a lake of considerable magnitude, it now stands as a bold headland, against which the waters of the Platte impinge with violence, at least 150 feet beneath its surface. Across its smooth bosom the fierce Red Man laid his trail, and from its higher elevations stood and gazed over the beautiful landscape—beneath, the rushing, turbid waters of the Platte, and around, a sea of verdure; in the distance, to the northeast, the valleys of the Elkhorn River and Maple Creek; on the other hand, the immense Platte bottom, stretching far to the northwest—presented a scene of softened loveliness seldom surpassed. Near the close of 1856, this lovely spot was selected by a party of speculators residing in Nebraska City, Plattsmouth, and Glenwood, Iowa, as the site for a town, which was to become *the city* of the Territory, and Capital of the future State. NEOPOLIS was laid off with imposing proportions. Broad avenues and spacious streets crossed each other at right angles; public squares and parks were numerous; and a saw-mill was purchased and set to work to cut out lumber for the building of the future Capital of Nebraska. But, alas! all these visions of future greatness came to naught. The great Capital City was never built; and the operators, after losing considerable money, abandoned the enterprise.

At the general election held October 8th, 1866, for the purpose of County organization, Ashland was selected as the County Seat, and the following County Officers elected: Commissioners, Wm. Reed, Austin Smith, and Thompson Bissell; Hobart Brush, Clerk; J. Richardson, Treasurer; Loomis Nickwin, Sheriff; Andrew Marble, Probate Judge; S. E. Wilson, Surveyor; Marcus Brush, Prosecuting Attorney.

The first Commissioners' Court was held at Ashland, November 10, 1866.

A. B. Fuller was the first Superintendent of Public Schools—appointed by the Commissioners in April, 1867.

COURT HOUSE BUILDIMG, SAUNDERS COUNTY.

The first tax was made July 8, 1867. The first license to sell spirituous, vinous, and malt liquors within the County, was granted April 6, 1868.

At an election held on the 8th of May, 1869, the County voted bonds to the amount of $40,000 to the B. & M. Railroad in Nebraska, to aid in the construction of that road.

The first marriage in the County occurred November 7, 1866, between Mr. Samuel V. Bumgarden and Miss Lucinda Hooker.

CHURCHES.—The religious denominations in the County are: Episcopalian, Presbyterian, Congregational, Lutheran, Baptist, Reformed Church, Baptist Missionary, Presbyterian-Reformed, Methodist, Disciples, Catholic, and Universalist. The Methodists erected the first house of worship in the County. There are now twelve Church buildings altogether.

PUBLIC SCHOOLS.—Number of school districts, 100; school houses, ninety; children of school age—males, 2,523, females, 2,435, total, 4,958; whole number of children that attended school during the year, 3,412; qualified teachers employed,—males, sixty-five, females, ninety-four, total, 159; total wages paid teachers for the year, $18,763.60; value of school houses, $51,518; value of sites, $3,314; value of books, etc., $1,014.60.

TAXABLE PROPERTY.—Acres of land, 430,860, average value per acre, $2.67; value of town lots, $120,636; money invested in merchandise, $59,497; money used in manufactures, $3,235; horses, 6,379, value, $142,712; mules and asses, 599, value, $15.615; neat cattle, 11,847, value, $79,328; sheep, 2,979, value, $2,016; swine, 29,512, value, $21,751; vehicles, 2,303, value, $26,632; moneys and credits, $19,750; mortgages, $14,666; stocks, etc., $51; furniture, $22,891; libraries, $2,407; property not enumerated, $76,652; railroads, $179,583.59; total valuation for 1879, $1,938,734.59.

RAILROADS.—The Omaha and Republican Valley Railroad runs through the central portion of the County from northeast to southwest. The Burlington and Missouri Railroad crosses the southeast corner of the County at Ashland.

LANDS.—The price of improved lands ranges from $7 to $30 per acre. The Union Pacific and Burlington and Missouri Railroad Companies each have several thousand acres for sale in this County at from $3 to $7 per acre.

MILLS.—There are eight flouring mills in the County, all water-power except one; one is located at Valparaiso, two at Ashland, two at Wahoo, two near Clear Creek, and one at Ithica.

POPULATION.—The following are the Precincts and population of each in 1879: Oak Creek, 414; Newman, 484; Elk, 783; Chester, 461; Bohemia, 485; Rock Creek, 466; Chapman, 507; Mariposa, 676; Douglas, 858; Richland, 557; Stocking, 1,460; Center, 569; Cedar, 687; Green, 470; Wahoo, 532; Marietta, 492;

Pohocco, 714; Ashland, 1,012; Clear Creek, 551; Marble, 692; Union, 658.

Total, 13,528,—males, 7,119, females, 6,409. Population of County in 1878, 12,514; increase, 1,014.

SCHOOL BUILDING WAHOO, SAUNDERS COUNTY.

## WAHOO,

The County Seat, occupies the site of a former Indian town, upon beautiful ground between the Wahoo and Sand Creeks, and is near the geographical center of the County. It was made the County Seat in the fall of 1873, and was then a village of only a few houses, since which time its growth has been most remarkable, it now being a city of the second class, with a population of 1,250. The Omaha and Republican Valley Railway was completed to Wahoo in the fall of 1876. The United Presbyterians, Reformed Presbyterians, Catholics and Baptists, have comfortable Church buildings here. The Methodists, Congregationalists and Lutherans hold regular services. An elegant Court House was erected in 1874, and a fine school house, accommodating a graded school, in 1875. Business is generally well represented, there being two flouring mills—one steam and one water-power,—two weekly newspapers—the *Times* and the *Independent*, three grain elevators, three lumber yards, three hotels, one bank, eight general merchandise, three grocery, four hardware, four drug, two furniture, three harness and three shoe stores, five agricultural implement dealers, thirteen lawyers, six doctors, three brokers, numerous mechanics' shops, etc. Among the Societies represented here are, the Masonic, Odd Fellows, Knights of Honor, Grand Army of the Republic, Sons of Temperance, Merchant's and Business Men's Club, and Bohemian Benevolent. Near the city are the Fair Grounds, with an extensive floral hall, stables, and an excellent half-mile track.

## ASHLAND,

Located in the southeast corner of the County, on the line of the Burlington and Missouri Railway, has 950 inhabitants. It is beautifully situated on both sides of Salt Creek, about two miles from its junction with the Platte River. Ashland is the oldest town in the County, and was until 1873 the County Seat. Archibald Wiggins located here in 1857, and was the first settler upon the town site. Samuel Hahn, Martin Hall and Wm. B. Warbritton, located here at an early period. Fuller & Moe erected the first frame building, in which they opened a store in the spring of 1863. During the same year Joseph Hume and a Mr. Border built a dam across the creek and erected a saw mill. In 1864 Dennis Dean erected a large saw mill, and also a grist mill with one run of burrs. Ashland now contains two first-class flouring mills, one windmill manufactory, one machine shop, ten general merchandise, three grocery, two hardware, two drug, two book, two boot and shoe, two furniture, and three agricultural implement stores, five grain warehouses, one bank, two meat markets, stock yards, and numerous other business establishments. The Saunders County *Reporter*, an old established weekly newspaper, is published here. An elegant school house was erected in 1871, which cost, with furniture, $16,500. There are four handsome Church buildings in the city, viz.; Methodist (the first in the County erected,) Episcopal, Baptist and Congregational.

ASHLAND HIGH SCHOOL BUILDING, SAUNDERS COUNTY.

### VALPARAISO

Is a prosperous and growing town of 350 inhabitants, located on the Omaha & Republican Valley Railroad, in the southwest corner of the County. It contains several stores, and transacts a large grain and stock business. The extension of the railroad between

Valparaiso and Lincoln is now about completed, and new dwellings and business houses are springing up rapidly.

### CLEAR CREEK,

The first Station on the Omaha & Republican Valley Railroad, in Saunders County, has a population of 200. Various branches of mercantile business are represented.

ALVIN and WESTON are small villages on the railroad, the former east, and the latter west of Wahoo.

Ithaca, Rose Hill, Ceresco, Bradford, Milton, Swedeburgh, Headland, Isla, Colan, Esteina, Sand Creek, Platteville, Clayton, Cedar Bluffs, Benton, Cedar Hill, Willow Creek, Rescue, Newton, and Chowder, are Postoffices in the County.

## SARPY COUNTY.

Sarpy County, named in honor of Col. Peter A. Sarpy, was organized by Act of the Territorial Legislature, approved February 7, 1857, previous to which it was a part of Douglas County. It lies on the middle-eastern border of the State, and is bounded on the north by Douglas County, east by the Missouri River, and south and west by the Platte River, which separates it from Cass and Saunders Counties, and contains about 275 square miles, or 176,000 acres.

WATER COURSES.—The Missouri River washes the eastern border of the County, and the Platte River, flowing in a general southeasterly course, the western and southern borders. The Elkhorn River empties into the Platte in this County, after passing through the northwestern township. Big Papillion River, a very fine stream furnishing sufficient water for mills, drains the eastern portion of the County, flowing in a general southeasterly direction into the Missouri. Little, or West Papillion Creek, a tributary of the Big Papillion, with its branches, drains the northern tier of townships. Numerous small creeks, having their rise in the central portions of the County, flow in a southerly course into the Platte, the most prominent being Buffalo Creek.

TIMBER.—There is a great deal of fine native timber in this County. Through the central portion, running from east to west, there are several large, beautiful groves, the varieties consisting principally of hardwood, such as hickory, oak, walnut, ash, elm, and hackberry. Considerable cottonwood, ash, elm, willow, and other varieties, are found along the Missouri bottoms and ravines adjacent; also in the Platte bluffs, and on the large islands of that stream. 872 acres of forest trees, and $131\frac{3}{4}$ miles of hedge fencing, are reported under cultivation.

FRUIT.—27,512 apple, 810 pear, 6,297 peach, 1,127 plum, and 4,305 cherry trees, are returned, besides 9,834 grape vines.

BUILDING STONE.—There is an abundance of the best quality of limestone in this County. Extensive quarries have been worked here for many years.

TOPOGRAPHY.—Twelve per cent. of the County is valley, and the remainder rolling prairie, with high bluffs skirting the rivers. The first mile or two westward from the Missouri, the surface is broken in wave-like ridges which gradually give place to gently undulating prairie, extending to the south and west until the wide bottoms of the Platte and Elkhorn Rivers are reached. The Big Papillion, in the eastern portion of the County, has a beautiful valley varying from two to five miles in width.

CROPS.—Area under cultivation, 43,521 acres. Winter wheat, twenty-five acres, 366 bushels; spring wheat, 7,440 acres, 85,782 bushels; rye, 792 acres, 8,418 bushels; corn, 27,786 acres, 1,062,210 bushels; barley, 937 acres, 20,171 bushels; oats, 5,576 acres, 266,-633 bushels; buckwheat, eleven acres, ninety-five bushels; sorghum, $15\frac{1}{4}$ acres, 1,401 gallons; flax, five acres, fifty bushels; potatoes, 413 acres, 31,334 bushels.

Large quantities of hay are annually put up on the broad meadow lands of the County. The soil on the uplands is a rich loam, the same as in Douglas County, and is seldom less than two feet in depth.

HISTORICAL.—The Expedition of Lewis and Clarke reached the mouth of the Platte River on the 21st of July, 1804, and on the evening of the 22d, it encamped on the beautiful plateau on which the old town of Bellevue now stands. In 1805, it is stated, Manuel Lesa, a Spanish adventurer, visited this site, and upon viewing the magnificent panorama spread out before him, exclaimed with a burst of admiration, "Bellevue!" (or beautiful view), a name by which it has since been recognized.

In 1810, the American Fur Company established a trading post at Bellevue, and appointed Francis De Roin, Indian Trader, who was succeeded by Joseph Robideaux, who served a term of six years, when his place was supplied by John Carbanne, until superseded, in 1824, by Col. Peter A. Sarpy, the distinguished Indian Trader of the Upper Missouri, who continued in that capacity for about thirty years.

In 1823, the Council Bluffs Indian Agency, at Fort Calhoun, was removed to Bellevue, and included in its limits the Omaha, Otoe, Pawnee, and Pottowattamie tribes. In 1834, Rev. Moses Merrill, a Baptist Missionary, erected a Mission House among the Otoes. Mr. Merrill died at his post in 1835, and was buried on the Iowa side of the river. In the fall of 1834, Samuel Allis and Rev. John Dunbar, under the direction of the Presbyterian Board of Missions, arrived at the Agency at Bellevue, in Company with Major John Dougherty, Indian Agent to the Otoes, Omahas, and Pawnees. Messrs. Dunbar and Allis opened a school among the Pawnees, at Council Point, a short distance up the Platte River, and when that village was abandoned on account of the hostility of the Sioux, they returned to Bellevue, and taught the children of the Pawnees at the Agency.

General Fremont's exploring party stopped at Bellevue, in 1843, on their return from the West, when they sold their mules and wagons at auction, and then descended the Missouri in boats to St. Louis.

In 1846, Rev. Edward McKinney, acting for the Presbyterian Board of Foreign Missions, selected a site on the southeast part of the plateau at Bellevue, for a Mission house and school for the Pawnees. The buildings were commenced in the fall of 1847, and completed in 1848.

In 1847, the Mormons, under Brigham Young, reached the Missouri River nearly opposite Bellevue, afterwards called Old Trader's Point, on their journey to Salt Lake, in a weak and destitute condition, but were relieved by the generosity of Col. Sarpy, who furnished them supplies, sheltered them from the storms of winter, and in the spring crossed numbers of them over his ferry free of charge.

In 1849, the Nebraska Postoffice, at Bellevue, was established. This year, Col. Sarpy's ferry-boat from St. Mary's to Bellevue was constantly employed in crossing over gold-hunters on their way to California.

In 1852, Major Barrows, Stephen Decatur, and others, projected a town organization at Bellevue, which seems to have existed only in name.

June 6, 1853, Rev. William Hamilton arrived with his family, and took charge of the Presbyterian Mission House. During this year, the Agency buildings and blacksmith shop were erected on the plateau south of the Mission lands, under the direction of Major Gatewood, Indian Agent.

On the 9th of February, 1854, the Bellevue Town Company was formally organized, with Col. Peter A. Sarpy, Stephen Decatur, Hiram P. Bennett, George Hepner, James M. Gatewood, Geo. F. Turner, P. J. McMahon, A. W. Hollister, and A. C. Ford, as the original proprietors.

The 4th of July, 1854, was observed with much enthusiasm at Bellevue. An immense vine-clad arbor was erected near the Agency buildings; the star-spangled banner floated in the breeze; and a salute was fired for each State in the Union, including one for the new Territory of Nebraska.

Bellevue has the credit of publishing the first newspaper in the Territory, which appeared on the 15th of July, 1854, and was entitled the *Nebraska Palladium;* Dr. E. Reed, editor and proprietor. It was printed at St. Mary's, Iowa, until the middle of November, 1854, when the office was transferred to Bellevue. Dr. E. N. Upjohn struck off the first paper, and Thos. Morton set up the first column of type. It died a natural death in April, 1855.

The first Claim Club north of the Platte River was organized at Bellevue, in the fall of 1854, with Judge William Gilmer, as President.

At the first Session of the Legislature, Bellevue was incorporated as a city. In the latter part of January, 1855, D. E. Reed was appointed Postmaster. The Postoffice was held at the Mission

35

House, where the Doctor's wife taught the first white school in the Territory.

Nebraska Lodge No. 1, of A. F. &. A. M., was instituted at Bellevue, in March, 1855, although meetings were held at the old trading post in 1854.

It was not until June, 1855, that the Omaha Indians left for their new reserve, about a hundred miles further up the Missouri. They were loath to leave their old hunting grounds, and expressed dissatisfaction with the Government in sending a weak and defenceless tribe of less than one thousand souls, to a country where they would be at the mercy of their hereditary foe, the Sioux, having thousands of warriors.

Hon. S. D. Bangs, in his Centennial history of Sarpy County, in speaking of Logan Fontenelle, the celebrated Chief of the Omahas, says: Logan Fontenelle was a half-breed, his father being French. He was educated in St. Louis, spoke English fluently, and was at this time about thirty years of age; of medium height, swarthy complexion, black hair, and dark, piercing eyes.

"In the middle of the summer of 1855, a procession might have been seen winding its way toward the old home of Logan Fontenelle, on the bluffs overlooking the Missouri, above the stone quarries at Bellevue. It moved slowly along, led by Louis Sanso-see, who was driving a team with a wagon, in which, wrapped in blankets and buffalo robes, was all that was mortal of Logan Fontenelle, the Chief of the Omahas. On either side the Indian Chiefs and braves, mounted on ponies, with the squaws and relatives of the deceased, expressed their grief in mournful outcries. His remains were taken to the house which he had left a short time before, and now, desolate and afflicted, they related the incidents of his death. He had been killed by the Sioux on the Loup Fork, thirteen days before, while on a hunt with his tribe. Having left the main body with San-so-see in pursuit of game, and while in a ravine that hid them from the sight of the Omahas, they came in contact with a band of Sioux, on the war-path, who attacked them. San-so-see escaped in some thick underbrush, while Fontenelle stood his ground, fighting desperately, and killing three of his adversaries, when he fell, pierced with fourteen arrows, and the prized scalp-lock was taken by his enemies. The Omahas did not recover his body until the next day. It was the wish of Col. Sarpy to have it interred on the bluffs fronting the house in which he had lived, and a coffin was made which proved too small without unfolding the blankets which enveloped him, and as he had been dead so long this was a disagreeable task. After putting him in the coffin, his wives, who witnessed the scene, uttered the most pitious cries—cutting their ankles until the blood ran in streams. The impressive funeral service of the Episcopal Church was read over the grave by Stephen Decatur."

On the afternoon of April 20, 1855, Geo. Hollister, a young man of considerable promise, while engaged in surveying on a high piece of ground overlooking Bellevue, was shot and killed by Dr. C. A. Henry. It appears that Dr. Henry and a man named Butterfield, had been out hunting along the Papillion that afternoon, and coming up with the surveying party, he had some angry words with Hollister in regard to claim lines, during which his gun was discharged, shooting Hollister in the abdomen, from the effects of which he died shortly after. Dr. Henry claimed that the shooting was wholly accidental, that the hammer of his gun caught in the heavy binding of his coat and was discharged. He gave himself up, and was confined in Sheriff Peterson's house at Omaha to await trial, but the grand jury failing to find an indictment against him, he was discharged. During the Doctor's confinement he frequently visited and prescribed for the sick of the city, in company with Sheriff Peterson, and upon his liberation he became one of Omaha's most active and influential citizens.

In January, 1856, the Mission Reserve was incorporated within the limits of Bellevue by Act of the Legislature, being a section of land reserved in the treaty with the Omahas to the Presbyterian Board of Free Missions, and for which the Government afterwards granted a patent. The Presbyterian Church was completed this year, and Rev. Wm. Hamilton installed as minister.

The Fontenelle Bank was incorporated in 1856, and transacted business at Bellevue until the financial crash of 1857.

During the year 1856, the Benton House was completed and kept as a hotel by Geo. Jennings, and the old Mission House was also converted into a hotel, known as the Omaha House, which was kept by Jos. Allen. A city organization for Bellevue was effected by the election of Reuben Lovejoy, Mayor, and W. D. Rowles, J. T. Allen, and A. H. Burtch, Aldermen. The *Young America* newspaper figured about this time, but was short lived. It was succeeded by the Bellevue *Gazette*, edited by Hon. Silas A. Strickland, which launched its first number to the public October 23, 1856.

At an election held in November, 1856, Gen. L. L. Bowen, and J. S. Allen, were elected Councilmen of the election district, and S. A. Strickland, C. T. Holloway, John Finney, and Joseph Dyson, Representatives; and through their exertions Sarpy was set off from Douglas County by Act of the Legislature, approved February 7, 1857.

Messrs. Bowen, Holloway, and Strickland were the Commissioners appointed to locate the County Seat, and Bellevue was selected.

The first election after the organization of the County, was held May 25, 1857. Wm. H. Cook was elected Probate Judge; C. D. Keller, Register of Deeds; S. D. Bangs, County Clerk; W. F. Wiley, Treasurer; H. A. Longsdorf, Superintendent Public Schools; W. H. Harvey, Surveyor; John M. Enoch, Sheriff; and John B. Glover, Robert McCarty, and Philander Cook, County Commissioners.

At this election, Hon. Fenner Ferguson, of Sarpy County, having received the highest number of votes, was elected delegate to Congress. Judge Ferguson resided at Bellevue until his death, which occurred November 11, 1859.

The original town of La Platte, laid out in 1855, on the Missouri, between the Platte and Papillion Rivers; Papillion City, laid out in 1857, at a point about two and a half miles northeast of the present town of Papillion; and Plattford and Hazleton, towns organized at an early day, have long since been abandoned.

PUBLIC SCHOOLS.—The number of districts is thirty-six; school houses, thirty-five; children of school age, males, 858, females, 706, total, 1,564; whole number of children that attended school during the year, 1,183; qualified teachers employed, males, twenty-eight, females, thirty; total wages paid teachers for the year, $8,800.10; value of school houses, $35,383; value of sites, $1,710; value of books and apparatus, $1,508.25.

TAXABLE PROPERTY.—Acres of land, 142,528; average value per acre, $5.17; value of town lots, $60,343; money used in merchandise, $15,954; money used in manufactures, $1,420; horses, 2,734, value $78,842; mules and asses, 165, value $5,369; neat cattle, 7,176, value $70,545; sheep, 438, value $247; swine, 11,013, value $11,357; vehicles, 701, value $13,817; moneys and credits, $12,724; mortgages, $19,017; furniture, $12,152; libraries, $115; property not enumerated, $36,450; railroads, $218,883.28; telegraph, $1,071; total valuation for 1879, $1,295,780.28.

RAILROADS.—Two railroads traverse the County, the Union Pacific, through the northeastern townships, a distance of 12.60 miles, and the Burlington and Missouri River, from north to south along the Missouri River, a distance of 10.99 miles.

LANDS.—Improved lands range from $8 to $35 per acre. The Union Pacific Railroad Company owns several thousand acres in the western part of the County for which they ask from $5 to $10 per acre.

POPULATION.—The following is the population of the County in 1879, by Precincts: Bellevue, 905; Papillion, 1,048; La Platte, 374; Forest City, 416; Richland, 496; Fairview, 622; Plattford 531.

Total, 4,392,—males, 2,431, females, 1,961.

### PAPILLION,

The County Seat, is a prosperous town of 800 inhabitants. It is finely located on the Little Papillion Creek, in the northeastern part of the County, and is a station on the Union Pacific Railroad. The valley of the Papillion at this point is beautifully undulating and about a mile wide. The first building on the town site was erected in November, 1869, by Dr. D. E. Beadle, who also opened the first store in January following. The town site was surveyed and platted in January, 1870. Papillion is now an excellent market center, and contains several well stocked stores, a hotel, flouring mill, grain elevators, etc., and an able weekly newspaper,—the *Times*, established in November, 1874. The Court House and school house are both handsome brick structures. There are five Church buildings, viz.: Methodist Episcopal, Catholic, Presbyterian, Episcopal and Baptist.

### BELLEVUE,

The oldest town in the State, which at one time boasted a population of over 2,000, has now only about 200 inhabitants. It is located on the Missouri River, near the center of the County from north to south. The County Seat was removed from here to Papillion, by vote of the people in 1875. It contains at present three or four general merchandise stores, a hotel, grain warehouses, two Churches, a school house, and some elegant private residences.

### LA PLATTE,

A village on the line of the B. & M. Railroad, in the southeastern part of the County, was laid out in 1870. It contains a hotel, grist mill, general store, blacksmith shop, etc. Near the town, a splendid limestone quarry gives employment to a large number of men.

### SARPY CENTER

Is a village situated near the geographical center of the County. The town site was surveyed and platted in 1875. It contains a hotel, two merchandise stores, a drug store, harness, and blacksmith shop etc.

### GILMORE

Is a small town on the Union Pacific Railroad, in the northeastern part of the County. It is the shipping and trading point of a well-settled farming country.

FOREST CITY, PLATTFORD, XENIA, and NASBY, are Postoffices.

## SALINE COUNTY.

Saline County was created in 1855, and organized in 1862. It is located in the southeastern part of the State, in the third tier of Counties west of the Missouri River, and is bounded on the north by Seward, east by Lancaster and Gage, south by Jefferson, and west by Fillmore County, containing 576 square miles, or 368,640 acres.

WATER COURSES.—The Big Blue River flows from north to south, through the eastern tier of townships, and furnishes most excellent water-power. The West Blue River joins the Big Blue in the northeastern part of the County. Turkey Creek, also a good mill stream, flows in a southeasterly course entirely through the County; besides which there are Swan, Walnut, Plummers, Dry, Brush, Spring, Johnson, Squaw, and many smaller Creeks and rivulets. The splendid water-power of this County is an element of great wealth, and only awaits development. Six grist mills are now in operation.

TIMBER.—The Big Blue and its tributaries are well timbered along their banks, with oak, cottonwood, ash, walnut, etc. Large artificial groves adorn almost every farm, while many are surrounded with honey-locust and Osage-orange hedges. The amount of forest timber planted is 1,835 acres; hedge fence, 174 miles.

FRUIT.—There are many thrifty orchards and vineyards in the County, bearing the choicest fruits. 32,128 apple, 854 pear, 28,659 peach, 3,509 plum, 9,135 cherry trees, 5,564 grape vines, are returned.

BUILDING MATERIAL.—Magnesian limestone of the finest quality is abundant. Large quarries are being worked near the center of the County, where there are also extensive kilns for burning lime, much of which is shipped abroad. Building sand, and clay for the manufacture of brick, are plentiful.

TOPOGRAPHY.—In the northern portion of the County, there are broad stretches of nearly level prairie; in the central and southern portions, the surface is gently undulating, with a gradual rise to the westward, the eastern border of the County being about 1,330 feet, and the western border 1,550 feet above the sea level. The streams all have wide bottoms on each side, the land being rich and dry, and not subject to overflow. The Valley of the Big Blue, which runs a distance of about twenty miles through this County, is famous for its beauty and fertility. The Valleys of the West Blue, Turkey and Swan Creeks, are also very fine throughout their whole length.

CROPS.—The area under cultivation, reported for 1879, was 100,986 acres. Winter wheat, 281 acres, 5,500 bushels; spring wheat, 47,720 acres, 579,602 bushels; rye, 1,759 acres, 28,699 bushels; corn, 35,101 acres, 1,491,850 bushels; barley, 7,648 acres, 189,573 bushels; oats, 7,295 acres, 138,403 bushels; buckwheat, twenty-eight acres, 2,789 bushels; sorghum, thirty-seven acres,

3,700 gallons; flax, 108½ acres, 911 bushels; broom corn, fifty-one acres, twenty-one tons; millet and Hungarian, 363 acres, 869 tons; tobacco, five acres, 3,783 pounds; potatoes, 556 acres, 70,707 bushels.

HISTORICAL.—General Victor Vifquain, who located with his family near the Fork of the Blue, on the first of May, 1858, has the honor of being the first settler in the County. For nearly a year, his house was the only habitation in all that region of country. Among the first settlers to follow him were E. Frink, W. Remington, C. Haynes, T. Stevens, J. Bickle, Tobias Castor, Wm. Stanton, and James Johnson.

From 1858 to 1860, the country was very much overrun by Indians. In August, 1857, the Comanches and Kiowas, under command of Yellow Buffalo, had a great fight with the Pawnees, commanded by Peternasharrow. The Pawnees were defeated and driven to their reservation; the Comanches and Kiowas fell back on General Vifquain's farm, where, after hostile demonstrations, they were pacified by the gift of an ox. For two years, General Vifquain had his house mined, ready to blow up in case of Indian capture; but fortunately the occasion never arose. The General was a great friend of Peternasharrow and other head Chiefs of the Pawnees; and that tribe used to make his farm their headquarters on their trips to the buffalo grounds—as many as 1,900 camping in his timber at one time, but never doing him any injury.

A panic occurred among the settlers in 1862, on account of Indians; and the only farm not deserted was Vifquain's, where Mrs. Vifquain and hired help remained, the General being in the army at the time.

The following are the first County Officers elected at the first general election held in the County, in 1862: Commissioners, P. Caldwell, T. Cline, and A. Duval; Clerk, Th. Freeman; Treasurer, — Tucker; Sheriff, W. Remington; Judge, J. S. Hunt; Surveyor, Tobias Castor.

At the same time, SWAN CITY, at the junction of Swan Creek with Turkey Creek, in the southeast corner of the County, was selected as the Seat of justice.

The first birth in the County was that of Victor Emmanuel Vifquain, on October 21, 1859. The first death was Thomas Duncan's, in 1860. The first marriage was that of Orion Johnson to Isabella West, on the 25th of March, 1861. The first school house was built on Vifquain's farm, in 1864; Miss Mollie Hess being the first teacher. The first sermon was preached at the same place, by S. Caldwell.

First Representative from Saline County to the Legislature, J. E. Hunt (Democrat), in 1869; first Senator, J. W. Davis (Republican), in 1877: Delegate to Constitutional Convention, in 1871, Victor Vifquain.

A County agricultural society was organized in 1873. Fairs were held at Crete in 1873-74-75-77.

PUBLIC SCHOOLS.—The number of school districts is 107; school houses, ninety-eight; children of school age; males, 2,325, females, 2,162, total, 4,487; whole number that attended school during the year, 2,980; qualified teachers employed, males, sixty-nine, females, eighty-seven; value of school houses, $42,756.65; value of sites, $2,096.75; value of books, and apparatus $1,974.35.

TAXABLE PROPERTY.—Acres of land, 335,192, average value per acre, $3.37; value of town lots, $262,233; money used in merchandise, $87,253; money invested in manufactures, $18,322; horses, 5,527, value $139,168; mules and asses, 412, value $11,780; neat cattle, 8,397, value, $73,841; sheep, 2,029, value $1,932; swine, 26,289, value, $25,387; vehicles, 2,119, value, $32,850; moneys and credits, $30,533; mortgages, $15,840; stocks etc., $21,385; furniture, $11,730; libraries, $876; property not enumerated, $74,276; railroads, $339,281.68; total valuation for 1879, $2,284,943.68

RAILROADS.—The Burlington & Missouri River Railroad runs from east to west through the northern portion, and from north to south through the eastern portion of the County.

LANDS.—Improved lands range from eight to thirty-five dol- per acre. The B. &. M. Railroad Company own about 40,000 acres in this County at from four to ten dollars per acre.

POPULATION.—The following are the Precincts and population of each in 1879: Crete, 2,022; Dorchester, 673; Lincoln, 616; Johnson Creek, 1,062; Turkey Creek, 607; Monroe, 489; Pleasant Hill, 918; Big Blue, 818; Wilbur, 1,388; Brush Creek, 756;

North Fork, 626; Atlanta, 446; Oliver, 234; South Fork, 562; Swan, 487; DeWitt, 713.

Total, 12,417, males, 7,271, females, 5,146. The population of the County in 1878, 10,453; increase in last year, 1,964.

### WILBER,

The County Seat, is located in the valley of the Big Blue, and on the B. & M. Railroad, near the center of the County from north to south. It was laid out in 1872 and is growing rapidly, having at present 900 inhabitants. Within a radius of seven miles there are four grist mills, the mills at Wilbur having a capacity of 1,000 bushels daily. There are two newspapers—*Record* and *Opposition*, one bank, three grain elevators, five general stores, three hardware, three furniture and three drug stores, two lumber yards, three hotels, two livery stables, four blacksmiths, etc., a good Union school, and five Church societies, viz: Congregational, Methodist, Christian, Catholic and United Brethren.

### CRETE

Is a beautiful city situated on the east bank of the Big Blue River, in the northeastern part of the County, and is also on the line of the B. & M. Railroad, a branch from which runs south from here to Beatrice, in Gage County. The town was laid out in 1870 and now has a population of 1,700. All lines of business are well represented, among which are four hotels, six general merchandise stores, five grocery, three drug, three hardware, five agricultural implement, three harness, four boot and shoe, and three furniture stores, three elevators, one grain house, three lumber and coal yards, one bank, two newspapers—the *Union* and *Standard*, one grist mill, one brewery, one windmill and pump manufactory, one brick yard, eleven lawyers, eight doctors, five real estate agents and six ministers. There are six Church buildings and three school houses. Doane College, conducted under the auspices of the Congregationalists, is located here. This institution is now erecting a beautiful brick edifice, costing $10,000, to be called Merrill Hall. A number of other fine brick buildings are about to be erected here, among which are a three story hotel, to cost $6,000, and a bank building, to cost $7,000.

### DEWITT

Is a thriving town of 400 inhabitants, situated on the Beatrice Branch of the B. & M. Railroad, and in the valley of the Big Blue, at the mouth of Turkey Creek. It contains a weekly newspaper, —the *Free Press*, an excellent water-power flouring mill, grain elevator, and warehouses, several stores, fine school house, etc.

### DORCHESTER

Is an enterprising town on the B. & M. Railroad, eight miles west of Crete. It was laid out in 1871 and contains at present about 300 inhabitants. There are here, four general stores, two drug and one grocery store, one coal and lumber yard, one steam elevator, one livery stable, one hotel, etc., a graded school, and two Church buildings, the Christian and Congregationalist.

### FRIENDVILLE,

Located on the B. & M. Railroad, in the northwestern part of the County, was laid out in 1871, and now has a population of 500. It contains four general merchandise, three grocery, three hardware, two drug, one furnitute, two agricultural implement, two harness, three millinery and one shoe store, one newspaper, the *Telegraph*, two lumber yards, three grain warehouses, one jeweler, and many other business establishments. It also has three Churches and a large new school house.

### PLEASANT HILL

Is located on Spring Creek, about five miles northeast of the geographical center of the County. It was laid out in 1868 and contains at present about 400 inhabitants. In 1870 Pleasant Hill was made the County Seat, which honor it retained until 1878. Business is generally well represented here. Near the town there are extensive limestone quarries, and large kilns for making lime. On Turkey Creek, within a mile of the town, there is a good grist mill.

EQUALITY, FAIRVIEW, ATLANTIC, GOLDRINSEY, VARNEY, SAXON, GIRARD, RICEVILLE and TABOR, are Postoffices in the County.

## SEWARD COUNTY.

Seward, formerly Green County, was created in 1855 and organized in 1865. Its name was changed by an Act of the Legislature in 1862, in honor of Hon. Wm. H. Seward, the distinguished statesman. It is located in the southeastern part of the State, in the third tier of Counties west of the Missouri River, and is bounded on the north by Butler, east by Lancaster, south by Saline, and west by York County, containing 576 square miles, or 368,640 acres.

WATER COURSES.—The County is finely watered by the Big Blue, and West Blue Rivers and tributaries. The Big Blue flows from northwest to southeast through the central portion of the County, and furnishes excellent mill advantages. The West Blue and tributaries water the southwestern townships; Lincoln Creek and branches, the northwestern townships, and Plum Creek, the northeastern townships of the County, besides which there are numerous smaller creeks and springs.

TIMBER.—Along the banks of the Blues and tributaries there is considerable native timber. The amount of forest timber planted in the County is estimated at 4,000 acres.

FRUIT.—No returns have been made. There are a large number of fine orchards, however. The number of trees planted is estimated at 42,900.

BUILDING STONE of fair quality is found in several localities.

CHARACTER OF THE LAND.—About twelve per cent. of the County is valley, and the remainder rolling prairie and broad tables. Every stream has its wide, fertile bottoms, and from these the land rises gently, and mostly in even slopes, until the high, level tables, or undulating prairie are reached, the highest elevation, however, seldom exceeding sixty feet from the bottoms. The soil throughout the County is a rich black loam, easily tilled, and very productive for all kinds of grain and vegetables.

CROPS.—In 1878 the wheat product was 578,588 bushels; rye, 51,320; barley, 166,860; oats, 257,290; flax, 14,050; corn, 1,863,360; potatoes, 70,356; broom corn, 62 tons.

HISTORICAL.—The first settlements in the County were made in 1859, by a number of persons who were on their way to Pike's Peak, but hearing adverse reports from the new Eldorado, they became discouraged and started across the country from the Platte River, in Butler County, to explore the Valley of the Blue.

Following that stream down to the junction of the West Blue, they located claims upon the beautifully timbered banks of the latter at what is now called West's Mills. In the following year a few more claims were located on the Big Blue, about half way between the present towns of Seward and Milford. This was the beginning of the settlement of what was then called Green County.

In 1861, J. L. Davison, Esq., of Milford, was appointed by the Legislature one of the Commissioners to locate a Territorial road between Nebraska City and Fort Kearney. This road crossed the Big Blue near where Camden now stands, and was a great convenience to the through travel and heavy freight trains traversing the plains to the western posts.

Very few settlements were made during the years 1862–63. In 1864, the first flouring mill was erected in the County, on the West Blue, by Mr. Thomas West. The Camden Mills were built the same year, by Messrs. Parker & Roper. In 1865, the County settled up rapidly, and in all directions could be seen the breaking plow turning over the virgin soil, where to-day are many of the best improved farms in the State. In 1867, Messrs. Reed & Davidson erected flouring mills at Milford; and in 1868, H. L. Boyes began the erection of his mill at Seward.

PUBLIC SCHOOLS.—The number of districts is eighty-three; school houses, seventy-nine; children of school age—males, 1,842, females, 1,622, total, 3,464; whole number of children that attended school during the year, 2,390; qualified teachers employed—males, forty-three, females, eighty; wages paid teachers for the year—males, $4,947.60, females, $6,384.40; total, $10,432; value of school houses, $35,982; value of sites, $2,846; value of books and apparatus, $1,657.05.

TAXABLE PROPERTY.—Acres of land, 334,429; average value per acre, $3.20; value of town lots, $94,284; money used in merchandise, $36,435; money used in manufactures, $6,635; horses,

4,740, value $118,101; mules and asses 453, value $12,009; neat cattle 6,648, value $57,212; sheep 1,855, value $1,810; swine 19,611, value $18,357; vehicles 1,557, value $23,802; moneys and credits, $6,101; mortgages, $25,388; stocks, $3,461; furniture, $5,890; libraries, $360; property not enumerated, $36,697; railroads, $107,-532.69; total valuation for 1879, $1,628,492.99.

RAILROADS.—The Nebraska Railway passes through the County from east to west, a few miles north of the center line. The Lincoln & Northwestern Road, completed in 1879, enters the southeastern part of the County, and runs northerly through the central portion.

LANDS.—Improved lands are held at $7 to $25 per acre. The B. & M. R. R. Company have 40,000 acres for sale here, at $5 to $10 per acre.

POPULATION.—In 1870, the County had a population of 2,953; in 1875, 6,601; in 1878, 7,991; and in 1879, it was estimated at 9,389.

### SEWARD,

The County Seat, is a prosperous city of 1,500 inhabitants. It is located on a fine plateau in the Valley of the Big Blue River, near the geographical center of the County, and at the intersection of the Nebraska and Lincoln & Northwestern Railways. At this point, Lincoln Creek on the west, and Plum Creek on the east, empty their waters into the Blue. The town site was laid out and surveyed in 1868, by T. Graham, Esq.; and during the summer of that year several buildings were erected, In 1870, the Nebraska *Atlas*, the pioneer journal of the County, was established here by Hon. O. T. B. Williams. One square of the town was set apart for a Court House, another for a market place, and a third for a high school. In addition to these, a public park, extending over five blocks, was laid out, which is now beautified with shade trees and shrubbery, and surrounded with a thick hedge of Osage orange.

Seward is surrounded with a splendid and thickly-settled farming region, and is one of the best grain markets and commercial centers in the Valley of the Blue. It has many commodious brick business blocks, and nearly all branches of trade are represented.

The State Bank building is an elegantly finished structure. The High School building, constructed of brick and stone, is a model of beauty and elegance. Walker's Opera Hall, one of the best arranged places of amusement in the State, has a seating capacity of 1,000. The Church Societies represented are the Methodist, Presbyterian, Baptist, Episcopalian, Catholic, and United Brethren. Four newspapers are published here, the *Reporter*, *Advocate*, *Blade*, and *Atlas*.

### MILFORD,

Situated in the Valley of the Big Blue, about ten miles south of Seward, contains several hundred inhabitants. It was the recognized County Seat from 1865 until 1871, when the offices and records were removed to Seward. A substantial iron bridge, costing $10,000, spans the river at this point. For a distance of one mile above and four miles below Milford, the waters of the Blue roll over a bed of solid rock, and afford the finest advantages for manufacturing enterprises. A large flouring mill is already in operation here. An excellent white and blue limestone, easily worked and susceptible of a high polish, is quarried near the town, on the south. The religious organizations are the Methodists, Congregationalists, Baptists and Presbyterians. The Lincoln and Northwestern Railroad was built to Milford in the fall of 1879, and grain elevators, depots and many other substantial improvements are now under way.

### BEAVER CROSSING

Is a promising village, situated on the West Blue, near the mouth of Beaver Creek, in the southwestern part of the County. A good flouring mill is located here.

### CAMDEN

Is a small village located on the Big Blue in the southeastern part of the County. It was settled in 1864. A good flouring mill is in operation here.

### UTICA,

Located on the Nebraska Railway, in the western part of the County, has 300 population, and is a rapidly growing town.

WEST'S MILL, GERMANTOWN, GLENDALE, STAPLEHURST, ORTON, MARYSVILLE, BATESVILLE, and OAK GROVES, are Postoffices in the County.

There are eight flouring mills in the County and ten Churches.

## SHERMAN COUNTY.

Sherman County was organized by proclamation of Governor Furnas, January 13, 1873. It is located in the central part of the State, in the seventh tier of Counties west of the Missouri River, and is bounded on the north by Valley, east by Howard, south by Buffalo, and west by Custer County, containing 576 square miles, or 368,648 acres.

WATER COURSES.—The Middle Loup River, from four to five hundred feet wide, flows through the central portion of the County, from northwest to southeast. Its tributaries are Brown, Cobb, Moon, Coal, Chapman, Wiggle, Cook, Hays, Dead Horse, Davis, Oak and Turkey Creeks. The Sweetwater and tributaries, Dry, Clear and Red Run Creeks, water the southern portion of the County. Mill privileges are numerous.

TIMBER.—Small quantities of native timber are found along the streams and in the ravines and gulches. 183 acres, or 106,300 forest trees are reported under cultivation.

FRUIT.—Various wild fruits grow in profusion along the streams. During the present year a large number of fruit trees have been planted.

CHARACTER OF THE LAND.—Twenty-five per cent. of the County is Valley and bottom; forty-five per cent. is made up of tables, parks, and undulating prairie; and the balance is considerably broken, but admirably adapted to grazing. The Valley of the Loup averages about three miles in width. The tables are from three to ten miles in extent, and are as level as a plain. The broken districts are coursed by hundreds of gulches and canons, affording perfect winter shelter for herds. The buffalo and mesquite grasses cover the hills and plains. The soil on the uplands is a vegetable mould, and ranges from fifteen to thirty inches in depth.

CROPS.—Area under cultivation reported for 1879, 6,535 acres. Winter wheat, forty acres, 423 bushels; spring wheat, 2,422 acres, 34,643 bushels; rye, 318 acres, 3,356 bushels; corn, 1,633 acres, 34,781 bushels; barley, 195 acres, 4,812 bushels; sorghum, eleven acres, 803 gallons; potatoes, sixty-four acres, 8,091 bushels; tobacco, one-fourth acre, 220 pounds.

HISTORICAL.—The first permanent settlements in the County were made on the Middle Loup, near the County Seat, in 1872. Among the first to take claims were O. S. Brown, Ed. Neilson, M. W. Benschoter, H. W. Humes, T. N. Johnson, P. Carlton, C. E. Webster, and Wm. Young, who nearly all arrived early in 1872, and taking their choice of lands in the fertile Valley of the Loup, at once began the erection of houses for themselves and shelter for their stock. Before the close of the year, many additional settlers had arrived, some taking claims lower down on the Loup, others on Oak Creek, while a few pushed still further west, to the fertile bottoms of the Beaver, in the southwestern part of the County. By the following spring the settlements were numerous.

The first election for the organization of the County was held on April 1st, 1873, and resulted in the selection of Loup City as the County Seat, and the election of the following Board of County Officers: Commissioners, M. W. Benschoter, Ed. Neilson, Matt. Coleman; Probate Judge, R. W. Russell; County Clerk, W. Walt; Sheriff, M. A. Hartley; Treasurer, C. E. Rosseter; Superintendent of Public Instruction, T. N. Johnston; Coroner, Peter Keitges.

Good school houses were among the first improvements made in the County. Wherever the settlements came closely together, a comfortable school house was erected for the education of the children; and the educational interests of the County have since kept pace with its growth. At present, the number of school districts is twenty-one; number of school buildings, eleven; number of children of school age, 438. Total value of school property, $3,965.

Religious services have been regularly held in the County since its organization. Various Church Societies have been organized, representing the several denominations, the majority of which hold regular weekly meetings and Sunday schools in the different school houses. There are at present six flourishing Sunday schools in the County, and two Church buildings—the Methodist Episcopal and United Brethren.

Indians from the Agencies in the northwestern and northern parts of the State, were in the habit of roaming through this country in bands, and about the time of the first settlement of the County, committing depredations and annoying the settlers greatly, but seldom doing any serious mischief. In 1872, E. Neilson was shot in the face, and seriously, though not fatally injured, by some Indians on the Loup River, near the present location of Loup City.

The first death in the County was the infant son of William Davis, in July, 1873.

The first birth was Alexander Dewooddy, son of Nelson Dewooddy, in November, 1873.

The first marriage was Mr. Frank Ingram to Miss Fannie I. Taylor, December 18, 1873.

The first term of the District Court held in the County, was commenced on March 3d, 1876.

TAXABLE PROPERTY.—Acres of land, 151,865; average value per acre, $2.96. Value of town lots, $9,159. Money invested in merchandise, $5,840; money used in manufactures, $100; horses, 382, value $17,082; mules, sixty-five, value, $3,957; neat cattle, 1,283, value $16,282; sheep 169, value $253; swine 658, value $1,127; vehicles 181, value $4,883; moneys and credits, $2,708; mortgages, $430; furniture, $3,431.50; libraries, $37; property not enumerated, $4,819.50; total valuation for 1879, $156,903.75.

LANDS.—There is still a large amount of good Government land in this County. The Burlington and Missouri Railroad Company owns 80,000 acres here, for which they ask from $1 to $5 per acre.

POPULATION.—The following are the Precincts and population of each in 1879: Upper Loup, 456; Lower Loup, 187; Oak Creek, 129; Hayestown, 145; Clear Creek, 203.

Total, 1,120,—males, 652, females, 468.

LOUP CITY,

The County Seat, is situated on the east bank of the Middle Loup, near the geographical center of the County. It contains about 250 inhabitants, has a weekly paper—the *Times*, an excellent hotel, Court House, school house, two Churches and several business houses. A good bridge crosses the river here.

ROCKVILLE, HAYESTOWN, CEDARVILLE, FITZALON, and AUSTIN are new towns, each having a Postoffice, general store, blacksmith shop and school house.

## STANTON COUNTY.

Stanton County was created in 1861 and organized in 1866. It is located in the northeastern part of the State, in the third tier of Counties west of the Missouri River, bounded on the north by Wayne, east by Cuming, south by Colfax and Platte, and west by Madison County, containing 432 square miles, or 276,480 acres.

WATER COURSES.—The Elkhorn River enters the County on its western border, about seven miles from its north line, and flows in a southeasterly direction several miles when it bends to the northeast and passes out of the County, almost due east from where it enters; or in other words, its course through the County resembles in shape the letter V. Tributary to the Elkhorn on the north are Humbug, Indian, Muskatine and Pleasant Run Creeks, while on the south are the Union, Cedar and Butterfly Creeks, having their source from a system of springs mostly within the borders of the County. There are several excellent water-powers.

TIMBER.—Along the Elkhorn and its tributaries there are considerable belts of timber embracing the cottonwood, elm, ash, oak, box-elder and hackberry varieties. There are 754 acres, or 1,100,500 forest trees, and twelve miles of hedge fence reported under cultivation.

FRUIT.—Very little has been done as yet in the way of fruit culture. 468 apple, three pear, thirty-four peach, twenty one plum, thirty-five cherry trees, and seven acres of grape vines, are returned.

CHARACTER OF THE LAND.—Thirty per cent. of the County is valley and bottom, and the balance gently rolling prairie, with occasional bluff along the river. The Valley of the Elkhorn at this point ranges from three to five miles in width. The larger tributaries also have fine bottoms. The south half of the County consists chiefly of undulating prairie, possessing a rich soil, well adapted to the growth of the different cereals, vegetables and fruits.

CROPS.—The area under cultivation reported for 1879 was, 14,976 acres. Winter wheat, ten acres, sixty bushels; spring wheat, 7,745 acres, 88,828 bushels; rye, 363 acres, 4,935 bushels; corn, 4,756 acres, 136,730 bushels; barley, 424 acres, 9,747 bushels; oats, 1,571 acres, 13,888 bushels; sorghum, four and three-eighth acres, 437 gallons; potatoes, seventy-nine acres, 6,715 bushels.

HISTORICAL.—Among the first permanent settlers of the County, were C. F. Sharp, M. B. Sharp, F. M. Scott, and Jacob Hoffman, who, in September, 1865, located homesteads on Humbug Creek, near the present town of Stanton. After selecting their claims, the Sharps returned to their former homes, where they remained until the spring following, when they returned with their families. Scott and Hoffman remained on their claims, and employed their time, during the winter of 1865-6, in building log houses for their families, and in making other preparations for improving their lands.

At the first election for County Officers, held in the fall of 1866, Paul Heyse was elected Clerk; Jacob Hoffman, Treasurer; Joshua Maltby, Probate Judge; M. B. Sharp, Sheriff; and F. M. Scott, J. R. Layton, and W. D. Whalen, Commissioners; the number of votes cast being seventeen.

From its organization till the close of 1870, Stanton County received its share of the immigration into the State. Since then, there has been very little increase in its population, owing to the fact that a very large portion of the land not being taken at the public land sales prior to 1870, were subject to private sale, and being very desirable, they were rapidly secured by speculators and railway companies, who at the present time own nearly or quite three-fourths of all the land in the County. These lands being held at prices considerably above the views of buyers, served to divert immigration in other directions; and as a result, actual settlers turned their attention to the Counties adjoining, where homesteads were secured at more advantageous terms.

RAILROADS.—The Fremont, Elkhorn & Missouri Valley road runs through this County from east to west, while the Omaha, Niobrara & Black Hills road runs from south to north, near its west line.

LANDS.—Improved lands are held at $5 to $25 per acre, while unimproved range at $2.50 to $10.

PUBLIC SCHOOLS.—The number of districts is twenty-two; school houses, twenty-one; children of school age—males 309, females 290; total, 599; qualified teachers employed—males, twenty, females, nine; total wages paid teachers for the year, $4,064.86; value of school houses, $10,631.08; value of sites, $405; value of books, etc., $700.50.

TAXABLE PROPERTY.—Acres of land, 250,951, average value per acre, $2.11; value of town lots, $6,915; money invested in merchandise, $3,925; money used in manufactures, $1,279; horses, 775, value, $18,703; mules, twenty-seven, value, $825; neat cattle, 1,833, value, $15,671; sheep, 2,440, value, $2,510; swine, 1,830, value, $1,074; vehicles, 280, value, $2,245; moneys and credits, $1,425; mortgages, $3,735; stocks, $700; furniture, $1,582; libraries, $95; property not enumerated, $2,994; total valuation for 1879, $608,320.

POPULATION.—The following are the Precincts into which the County is divided, and the population of each in 1879: Stanton, 1,106; Humbug, 217; Kingsberry, 163.

Total, 1,486—males, 788; females, 698.

## STANTON,

The County Seat, is situated on the banks of the Elkhorn River, upon a beautiful elevation commanding a fine view of the surrounding country, and is nearly in the center of the County. It was laid out in September, 1870, and now contains a thrifty and intelligent population of 300; and its industries are expanding as the country developes through the influences of immigration.

The industries represented consist of one banking house, three general merchandise stores, one hardware, one drug, one millinery, and one furniture store, three carpenter shops, one harness, two blacksmiths', one carriage and one wagon shop, two hotels, one livery stable, three real estate offices, one weekly newspaper—the *Register*—three physicians, four attorneys, etc.

The different religious denominations are well represented, although at the present time there are but two Church buildings here—Methodist and German Lutheran. The Baptists, Congregationalists, and Presbyterians also hold services in the two Churches mentioned, and in a public hall built for that purpose.

CLINTON, KINGSBERRY, CANTON, DONAP, ORION, and SCHWEDT, are villages having only a Postoffice, store, etc.

## SIOUX COUNTY.

Sioux County was created by an Act of the Legislature, approved February 19, 1877. It is located in the northwest corner of the State, bounded on the north by Dakota Territory, east by unorganized territory, south by Cheyenne County, and west by Wyoming Territory, and contains about 7,344 square miles.

Sioux County is as yet unorganized and unsurveyed. Its population in 1879 is estimated at 550. A stage road from Sidney, on the Union Pacific Railroad to the Black Hills in Dakota, traverses this County from south to north, on the line of which, in this County, situated on White River, is Camp Robinson, garrisoned by United States troops.

## THAYER COUNTY.

Thayer County was created in 1856 and organized in the fall of 1871. It is located on the southern border of the State, in the fifth tier of Counties west of the Missouri River, bounded on the north by Fillmore and east by Jefferson County, south by the State of Kansas, and west by Nuckolls County, containing 576 square miles, or 368,640 acres.

WATER COURSES.—The Little Blue River, affording numerous fine mill advantages, flows from west to east through the central portion of the County. Big Sandy Creek, also a good mill stream, enters the County at the northwest corner, flows southeasterly, and joins the Little Blue near the middle of the eastern line of the County. Rose Creek and branches water the southeastern portion of the County, besides which there are Little Sandy, Spring and a dozen smaller creeks tributary to the above mentioned streams There is not a township in the County without running water.

TIMBER.—Along the Blue and tributaries there is a very considerable amount of native timber, a large per cent. of it being hardwood. 21,798 forest trees and twenty-two miles of hedge fencing are reported under cultivation.

BUILDING MATERIAL.—Limestone of an excellent quality is extensively quarried in various portions of the County. Potters,' brick and fire clays are abundant.

FRUIT.—5,996 apple, seventy-two pear, 13,930 peach, 1,690 plum, and 2,494 cherry trees, and 1,641 grape vines are returned.

CHARACTER OF THE LAND.—Ten per cent. of the County is valley, and the remainder mostly rolling prairie with bluffs in occasional places along the river. The beautiful valley of the Blue varies from two to four miles in width in this County, and the valleys of the Little Sandy, Rose and Spring Creeks, from one to three miles. The soil is everywhere rich and mellow.

CROPS.—The area returned as under cultivation in 1879, was 32,285 acres. Winter wheat, 264 acres, 6,126 bushels; spring wheat, 11,124 acres, 146,634 bushels; rye, 2,026 acres, 16,960 bushels; corn, 8,006 acres, 317,432 bushels; barley, 2,740 acres, 76,709 bushels; sorghum, eighteen acres, 854 gallons; tobacco, three and three-fourths acres, 262 pounds; potatoes, 143 acres, 16,572 bushels.

HISTORICAL.—The first permanent settlements in the County were made along the Little Blue River, in 1869. Among the earliest to take up claims were Isaac Alexander, A. T. Hobbs, Amasa Stevens, and J. Ball, who, however, did not remain long alone— other settlers flocking in so rapidly that in the next two years, the best locations along the Blue and most of its tributaries were taken.

The first County election was held in October, 1871, and resulted in the election of the following Officers: Commissioners, W. P. Wilson, J. C. Pluss, and G. D. Proctor; Clerk, Ed. S. Past; Treasurer, James B. Smith; Probate Judge, Newton Clarke; Sheriff, Tracy E. Ross; Superintendent of Public Instruction, B. F. Young; Surveyor, C. E. Barton; Coroner, James Knox.

The first term of the District Court for Thayer County was held in June, 1873; Judge Gantt presiding.

The Methodist, Christian, United Brethren, Baptist, Lutheran, Catholic, and Universalist denominations, have organized Societies and hold regular services. At present, there are five Church buildings in the County.

There are also six flouring mills, several saw-mills, and two cheese factories in operation in the County.

The St. Joe & Denver City Railroad traverses the County from east to west, following the Valley of the Big Sandy Creek, a distance of 25.55 miles.

Wild lands vary in price from $3 to $7 per acre; improved, from $6 to $25.

PUBLIC SCHOOLS.—Number of school districts, fifty-two; school houses, forty-six; children of school age—males, 755, females, 710, total, 1,465; whole number of children that attended school during the year, 937; qualified teachers employed—males, thirty-four, females, thirty-five; total wages paid teachers for the year, $8,675.33; value of school houses, $23,748; value of sites, $987.75; value of books and apparatus, $2,281.65.

TAXABLE PROPERTY.—Acres of land, 327,908; average value per acre, $2.10. Value of town lots, $39,182. Money used in merchandise, $51,821; money invested in manufactures, $11,700; horses 2,076, value $54,928; mules and asses 186, value $6,169; neat cattle 3,733, value $33,182; sheep 3,156, value $4,308; swine 8,921, value $10,984; vehicles 806, value $11,722; moneys and credits, $10,531; mortgages, $8,861; furniture, $4,286; property not enumerated, $29,222; railroad, $110,708.15; total valuation for 1879, $1,074,905.15.

The population of the County in 1874, was 1,781; in 1875, 2,139; in 1876, 2,410; in 1878, 3,391; and in 1879, 4,535.

## HEBRON,

The County Seat, is located in the Valley of the Little Blue, near the center of the County, and about seven miles south of the St. Joe & Denver Railroad. It contains a $6,000 Court House, a fine brick school building, costing $8,000, a $20,000 stone flouring mill, a fine stone Church, two newspapers—the *Journal* and *Sentinel*—

a cheese factory, plow factory, wagon and carriage shops, etc., and several well-stocked stores. Large quantities of grain from the southern part of the County and northern Kansas pass through Hebron to the railway stations, the farmers on their return purchasing most of their supplies at this point.

ALEXANDRIA, BELVIDERE, and CARLETON, are thriving towns of about 200 inhabitants each, situated on the St. Joe & Denver Railroad. Alexandria has a good weekly paper—the *News*.

DAVENPORT, SICKLER MILL, DRYDEN, FRIEDENSAU, KIOWA, GAZELLE, and PRAIRIE STAR, are Postoffices in the County.

## VALLEY COUNTY.

Valley County was organized in 1871. It is located in the central part of the State, bounded on the north by Wheeler, east by Greeley, south by Sherman, and west by Custer County, containing 576 square miles, or 368,640 acres.

WATER COURSES.—The North Loup River flows southeasterly through the northeastern portion of the County, its principal tributaries being the Myra, Haskels, Ireland, Weaver, Terrapin, Clear, Davis, Dane, Shepherd, Messenger, Spring, Elm and Hawthorn Creeks. The Middle Loup River and branches water the southwestern portion of the County. There are several good mill privileges in the County.

TIMBER.—A limited supply of timber is found on the streams and in the canyons, embracing the cottonwood, ash, elm, cedar and oak varieties. Three hundred and sixty-one acres, or 165,985 forest trees, and two and a half miles of hedging are returned.

FRUIT.—627 apple, 575 peach, 211 plum, and fifty-four cherry trees are reported under cultivation.

CHARACTER OF THE LAND.—About thirty per cent. of the County is valley and bottom, fifty per cent. rolling prairie, and the balance broken and bluffy. The Loup Valleys range from three to seven miles in width, and the smaller valleys from one-half to two miles. Through the broken region run deep gulches and canyons in which water and the finest pasturage are usually found.

CROPS.—Acres reported in cultivation, 7,350. Winter wheat, twenty-eight acres, 360 bushels; spring wheat, 3,042 acres, 39,568 bushels; rye, 360 acres, 4,214 bushels; corn, 1,123 acres, 28,781 bushels; barley, 281 acres, 7,997 bushels; oats, 877 acres, 49,309 bushels; sorghum, eleven and three-fourth acres, 1,348 gallons; potatoes, seventy-six and a half acres, 9,963 bushels.

LANDS.—There is a small amount of good Government land in this County. The Burlington and Missouri Railroad Company owns 120,000 acres here, ranging in price from $1 to $5 per acre.

PUBLIC SCHOOLS.—Number of districts, nineteen; school houses, fourteen; children of school age, males, 251, females, 225, total, 476; qualified teachers employed, males, six; females, ten; total wages paid teachers for the year, $1,341; value of school houses, $5,126.35; value of sites, $115.

TAXABLE PROPERTY.—Acres of land, 154,980; average value per acre, $1.66; value of town lots, $3,405; money invested in merchandise, $4,157; money used in manufactures, $585; horses, 681, value, $19,338; mules, sixty-eight, value, $2,503; neat cattle, 1,909, value, $20,568; sheep, fifty-four, value, $52; swine, 522, value, $509; vehicles, 320, value, $4,529; moneys and credits, $1,562; mortgages, $2,222; furniture, $2,959; property not enumerated, $6,814; total valuation for 1879, $326,768.

POPULATION.—The County is divided into eight voting Precincts, the following being the population of each in 1879: First, 268; Second, 261; Third, 187; Fourth, 107; Fifth, ninety-two; Sixth, 125; Seventh, 292; Eighth, 208; total, 1,540,—males, 838, females, 702.

### ORD,

The County Seat, is located on the North Loup near the geographical center of the County, and has a population of 150. It contains a hotel, good school house, the County offices, several stores, a grist mill, blacksmith shop, and a lively weekly paper—the *Journal*. A Howe truss bridge spans the river here.

### NORTH LOUP

Is a small village situated on the Loup, ten miles south of the County Seat, at the mouth of Myra Creek. It contains a hotel, store, blacksmith shop, and a good school house. A bridge spans the river at this point also.

VINTON, ARCADIA, SPRINGDALE, ADAIR, CALAMUS and IDA, are the names of Postoffices in the County.

## WAYNE COUNTY.

Wayne County was organized in the fall of 1870, by proclamation of Governor David Butler. It is located in the northeastern part of the State, in the second tier of Counties west of the Missouri River, bounded on the north by Cedar and Dixon Counties, east by Dixon County and Omaha Indian Reservation, south by Cuming and Stanton, and west by Madison County, containing 448 square miles, or 286,720 acres.

WATER COURSES.—The central and northern portions of the County are finely watered by Logan Creek and its numerous branches, which flow in a general easterly direction and furnish several fine mill privileges. The southern portion of the County is watered by Plum, Humbug, Spring and other tributaries of the Elkhorn River.

Well water is found at a depth of twenty to sixty feet.

TIMBER.—Along the Logan and branches there is a limited supply of native timber. $325\frac{1}{4}$ acres, or 126,637 forest trees, and seven and three-fourth miles of hedging have been planted.

FRUIT.—657 apple, eleven pear, 325 peach, 663 plum, 243 cherry trees, and thirty-two grape vines are reported.

CROPS.—About ten per cent. of the County is valley, ten per cent. broken, and the balance gently rolling prairie. The Logan has a beautiful and fertile valley, with bottoms frequently four miles wide. Several of its tributaries have fine valleys ranging from one to two miles in width. In the vicinity of the sources of the several creeks, the land is considerably broken by deep ravines and gulches, in which stock find excellent shelter from the storms of winter. The soil is well adapted to the growth of the different cereals.

CROPS.—Acres in cultivation, reported for 1879, $5,114\frac{1}{4}$; spring wheat, 1,344 acres, 16,420 bushels; rye $265\frac{1}{4}$ acres, 4,132 bushels;

corn 1,589 acres, 52,898 bushels; barley, 117 acres, 2,161 bushels; sorghum 2¾ acres, 266 gallons; potatoes 33⅞ acres, 3,435 bushels; tobacco ⅝ acre, 800 pounds.

HISTORICAL.—The pioneer settler of the County was Mr. B. F. Whitten. His house, completed in April, 1869, was the first erected in the County. A month later, a small colony from Illinois located homesteads in the eastern part of the County, mostly along Coon Creek. In the spring of 1870, a colony of Germans located on Spring Branch, in the southwestern part of the County.

The first election for County Officers was held on the 5th of September, 1870, at the house of George Scott, on Coon Creek, and resulted as follows: Commissioners, W. E. Durin, M. T. Sperry, and Isaac Miner; Clerk, C. E. Hunter; Treasurer, B. F. Whitten; Sheriff, A. D. Allen; Probate Judge, A. A. Fletcher; Surveyor, Wm. G. Vroman; Superintendent of Public Instruction, R. B. Crawford; Coroner, Nathan Allen.

Mr. B. F. Whitten failing to qualify for Treasurer, George Scott was appointed to fill the vacancy.

The first Postoffice in the County was established September 8, 1870, near the Logan bridge, and was called Taffe; Wm. Agler, postmaster. The second Postoffice was established at Laporte, Feb. 21, 1871; C. E. Hunter, postmaster.

The first child born in the County was a son to Mr. and Mrs. Charles Phillips, near Logan Bridge, on June 1st, 1869.

The first death was that of a son of William Vroman, August 6th, 1870.

The first marriage occurred on the 14th day of May, 1871, between M. T. Sperry and Miss Sarah Eayrs.

The first sermon was preached by Mrs. M. B. Richardson, at the residence of Alexander Scott, in December, 1870.

The first practicing physician in the County was Dr. R. B. Crawford, who located June 1, 1869.

On the 4th of July, 1871, a grand celebration was held near LaPorte.

The first store was opened in June, 1872, by C. E. Hunter and Solon Bevins, near LaPorte. The first school district was organized on February 11, 1871; first school teacher, Miss Jane Olin. The first school house was erected in October, 1871. The first newspaper established in the County, was the *Wayne County Review*, by C. E. Hunter, August 5, 1876.

On the 24th of February, 1874, at a special election, County bonds to the amount of $15,000 were voted for the erection of a brick Court House at Laporte, forty by fifty feet in size. The building was completed by Sawyers & Leach, December 8, 1874, and cost $11,983.

PUBLIC SCHOOLS.—The number of districts is eleven; school houses, eight; children of school age, 169; qualified teachers employed—males, seven, females, six; total wages paid teachers for the year, $1,674; total value of school property,$6,334.

TAXABLE PROPERTY.—Acres of land, 239,267; average value per acre, $1.92; value of town lots, $2,420; money invested in merchandise, $875; money used in manufactures, $100; horses, 288, value, $6,908; mules, ten, value, $275; neat cattle, 675, value, $5,649; sheep, 1,439, value, $1,314; swine, 878, value, $515.40; vehicles, ninety-two, value, $975; moneys and credits, $310; stock, $38.55; furniture, $201; property not enumerated, $2,580.50; total valuation for 1879, $482,059.88.

LANDS.—There are about 5,000 acres of Govenment land in this County. The B. & M. Company owns about 20,000 acres here, for which they ask from $1.25 to $6 per acre. Improved lands vary from $4 to $15 per acre.

POPULATION.—There are three Precincts in the County, the population of each in 1879 being as follows: La Porte, 228; Spring Branch, 119, and Leslie, 134; total, 481,—males, 269, females, 212.

## LA PORTE,

The County Seat, is situated in the middle-eastern part of the County, and was laid out on the 22nd of May, 1874, by Mr. Solon Bevins. It contains a fine Court House, good school house, hotel, two general stores, blacksmith shop, grain warehouses, lawyers,' doctors' and real' estate offices, and a weekly paper—the *Review*. Divine services are held every Sabbath in the school house.

## LESLIE

Is the name of a Postoffice four miles southeast of the County Seat.

A fine flouring mill is now being erected on Logan Creek. It is 26x60 and three stories high, and will contain a four and a half foot Turbine wheel and four run of burrs.

## WASHINGTON COUNTY.

Washington County was organized by an Act of the first Territorial Legislature, approved February 22, 1855. It is located on the middle-eastern border of the State, bounded on the north by Burt County, east by the Missouri River, south by Douglas County, and west by Dodge County and the Elkhorn River, containing about 400 square miles, or 256,000 acres.

WATER COURSES.—The County is finely watered by the Missouri and Elkhorn Rivers and tributaries. The Missouri washes the entire eastern border, and the Elkhorn the southwestern border for a distance of about two townships. Bell Creek, a beautiful tributary of the Elkhorn, flows from north to south through the western portion of the County. Among the smaller streams are Fish, Long, New York, Stewart, North, South, Turkey, Deer, Moore, Little Bell, Brown, Walnut, and Papillion Creeks. Every township in the County has running water.

TIMBER.—There is an abundance of timber for fuel in this County. On the Missouri bottoms and along several of the streams there is a fine native growth. The amount of timber planted is 1,840½ acres; hedging, twenty-four and a half miles.

FRUIT.—59,629 apple, 1819 pear, 3,287 peach, 3,277 plum, 9,960 cherry trees, and 19,013 grape vines are reported under cultivation.

TOPOGRAPHY.—Thirty per cent. of the County is valley and bottom, sixty per cent. rolling prairie, and ten per cent. broken and bluffy. The bottoms of the Missouri at this point are very wide, ranging from three to seven miles. The bottoms of the Elkhorn, on the southwestern border of the County, vary from three to six miles in width, while the beautiful valley of Bell Creek, extending through the County from north to south, is from one to three miles wide, with fine level table lands adjoining. Everywhere in the County the soil is of an excellent character.

CROPS.—The area in cultivation, reported for 1879, was 77,657 acres. Winter wheat, forty-two acres, 893 bushels; spring wheat, 23,057 acres, 259,241 bushels; rye, 1,857 acres, 28,002 bushels; corn, 34,084 acres, 1,308,486 bushels; barley, 1,597 acres, 17,856 bushels; oats, 7,772 acres, 36,662 bushels; buckwheat, sixty-six acres, 585 bushels; sorghum, 106 acres, 10,357 gallons; flax, 211 acres, 1,772 bushels; broom corn, $1\frac{1}{2}$ acres, nine tons; onions, five acres, 910 bushels; potatoes, $543\frac{1}{4}$ acres, 39,706 bushels.

HISTORICAL.—The first permanent settlement was made in the southeastern part of the County, upon the beautiful plateau upon which old Fort Calhoun stood. The buildings of the old Fort consisted of about sixty small brick structures, arranged in four lines inclosing about ten acres of ground. Outside of this inclosure, to the north, were a number of other buildings supposed to have been used by officers and Indian traders. The brickyard was southeast of the Fort, at the foot of the bluff. Some eighty rods to the west was a spring, where was erected a spring-house for dairy purposes, and still further to the north was a large cultivated field where grain and vegetables were raised to supply the fort. The stone magazine building was still standing in 1854. This site was selected as a claim early in the summer of 1854, by John Goss, Sr., who, however, soon after donated it, with the exception of two shares, to a Town Company consisting of Casady & Test, Addison Cochran, and H. C. Purple, of Council Bluffs, Iowa; and Mark W. Izard, A. J. Poppleton, and Hadley D. Johnson, of Omaha.

This Company built a cabin on the site of the old Fort, near the magazine; and in March, 1855, the town was surveyed and platted by E. H. Clark.

Several families came to the new town immediately after it was located, and a number of others settled on claims near by.

By Act of the Legislature, approved February 22, 1855, Fort Calhoun was made the County Seat; and at the same time the County was fully organized by the appointment of Stephen Cass, Probate Judge; George W. Newell, Recorder; and Thomas J. Allen, Sheriff.

During the spring of 1855, an immense immigration came into the County, and many settled at Fort Calhoun.

The first District Court in the County was opened here in June of this year, in the claim cabin of the Town Company. It was presided over by Hon. Fenner Ferguson, with Major J. W. Paddock, as Clerk; Gen. E. Estabrook, U. S. Prosecuting Attorney; and Thomas J. Allen, Sheriff. The attorneys present were A. J. Poppleton, E. H. Clark, Jonas Seeley, and J. McNeal Latham. The first case tried was that of Elias Wilcox *vs.* James M. Taggart for claim-jumping; verdict for the defendants.

About the 10th of August, the Calhoun town site was jumped by Charles D. Davis, who moved into the town house, where he and his friends fortified themselves. The Town Company and citizens undertook to put him off, which resulted in the killing of Mr. Goss, the shooting of Mr. Purple through the shoulder, and the wounding of Mr. Thompson in the thigh—all being of the Town party. Thus matters rested until November, when Davis made sale, or pretended sale, of his interests; and a new Town Company was formed, taking in several new members, including the widow of Mr. Goss.

During the summer of 1855, E. H. Clark built a hotel for the Town Company, which was opened to the public the following spring, by Col. Geo. Stevens.

A court house was built in 1856, in which Hon. E. Wakely presided as judge, with Hon. Geo. M. Doane, prosecuting attorney, Roger T. Beal, clerk, and Orrin Rhodes, sheriff.

During this summer, Rev. Collins, a Methodist minister, residing at Omaha, preached in the court house once a month.

In 1857, the town was entered at the land office by Hon. Elam Clark, Mayor.

In 1858, the Fort Calhoun flouring mills were erected by Z. Vanier & Brother, and in 1861, they passed into the hands of Hon. Elam Clark & Co., the present proprietors. These mills soon became widely celebrated, and during the days of freighting across the plains they manufactured thousands of sacks of flour for shipment to Colorado and Utah. Many of the early settlers came a distance of seventy-five to one hundred miles to these mills.

FORT CALHOUN,

On the O. & N. road, has about 400 inhabitants, several stores, two Churches, a good school house, etc. The old Fort Calhoun steam flouring mills, which gained such wide notoriety in the early days of the Territory, are still running to their full capacity.

### FONTENELLE,

Situated in the middle western portion of the County, on a fine piece of table land commanding a splendid view of the Elkhorn and Platte Valleys, was settled in the summer of 1854, by a company from Quincy, Illinois, called the "Nebraska Colonization Company," of which Jonathan Smith was President, and Rev. W. W Keep, Secretary, and including as members, J. W. Richardson, J. C. Barnard, O. C. Barnard, H. Metz, John Evans, J. Armor, James, A. Bell, and others.

Before the close of the year many additional settlers had flocked to the town and surrounding country. The first stock of goods at Fontenelle was opened early in 1855, by Wm. H. Davis, who also kept the first hotel in a double log house, called the "Fontenelle House."

The first child born in the town was Mattie Francis, daughter of Samuel Francis, October 2, 1855. A few hours later, on the same night, a daughter was born to Mr. and Mrs. Wm. H. Davis, and named Fontenelle. In May, 1856, Rev. Reuben Gaylord, organized a Congregational Church, with about twenty-five members, and Rev. Thomas Waller as pastor. A Sabbath School was organized at the same time. The new Church was presented with a handsome communion service by the First Congregational Church cf Quincy, Illinois. In 1856 a college was erected under the auspices of the Congregationalist Church, and was a flourishing institution for a number of years, Professor Burt being the first teacher. The first saw mill was brought in by Thos. Gibson in 1856, and run by Samuel and Silas Francis. The first marriage was that of Henry Whitter to Miss Emily Strickland, in the fall of 1856. Miss Strickland taught the first school the winter previous. On the evening of the 15th of July, 1855, a Mr. and Mrs. Porter, and a young man named Demaree, came up from Bell Creek, where they had been breaking prairie, and encamped on Sam Francis' lake, a mile north of Fontenelle, intending to go up into the settlement on Sunday morning. As they were about to leave camp on Sunday, a party of Indians rode out of the willows and approached Porter's wagon. One of them snatched Demaree's hat off his head and was riding away with it, when the owner called to him to stop, or he would shoot him, picking up his rifle as he spoke. The Indian turned, saw this demonstration on the part of Demaree, called out "Pawnee!" and shot him instantly, the ball passing through Porter also, killing both men. The Indians then rode off, leaving Mrs. Porter alone with the dead. This double murder caused the greatest excitement in Fontenelle, all the settlers in the neighborhood flocking thither for safety, and it was many months before they considered themselves safe from assault and massacre by the Indians.

Fontenelle is now a village of some 150 inhabitants. It contains a Church, school house, blacksmith and wagon shop, and a large general merchandise store. The adjoining country is well settled and fertile.

### DE SOTA,

On the Missouri River, was laid out in the fall of 1854, by Dr. John Glover, Gen. J. B. Robinson, Potter C. Sullivan, E. P. Stout, Wm. Clancy and others. It was incorporated by an Act of the Legislature, in March, 1855. During the summer of 1855, thirty frame and log houses were built in the town. Dr. A. Phinney opened the first store, and Chas. Seltz the second. P. C. Sullivan was the first postmaster. Judge Jesse T. Davis located there in the fall of 1855. The first child born in DeSota, and probably the first in the County, was John Critz, in June, 1855. The first marriage was that of Thomas M. Carter to Miss Sullivan. In 1856 the Kennard Brothers established themselves in the mercantile business here, and the Bank of DeSota entered upon a career of brilliant, but short lived prosperity, with Samuel Hall as president, and Geo. E. Scott, cashier. In the same year the Waubeek Bank was established, and the following spring the Corn Exchange Bank opened for business.

Rev. Jacob Adriance, of the Methodist Church, was the first regular minister. In 1857, the town had fifteen or twenty business houses, and between six and seven hundred inhabitants, and prosperity was the order of the day, until the Pike's Peak excitement broke out in 1859, when it was almost entirely deserted.

DeSota which at one time boasted several hundred inhabitants, is now a mere village of half a dozen houses.

HAYES, KENNARD, MILLS, WASHINGTON, AMHERST, MEADS, NERO and ADVANCE, are Postoffices in the County.

### CUMING CITY,

Was "claimed" in September, 1854, by P. G. Cooper, and two others, and in the spring of 1855, it was laid out as a city, and named in honor of the Acting Governor, T. B. Cuming. For a while it grew very rapidly, but the financial crash of 1857, gave it a check from which it never recovered, and it was soon afterwards abandoned entirely. Among the first settlers were Jacob Pate, Lorenzo Pate, J. Zimmerman, J. Gall, E. Pilcher, P. G. Cooper, J. S. Stewart, L. M. Kline, T. C. Hungate, and O. W. Thomas. In 1857, it had fifty-three dwellings, several business houses, and a weekly newspaper.

MURDERS.—In April, 1856, one Isaiah Peterson jumped the claim of a Mr. Coon, near Ft. Calhoun, and built a house upon it in an out-of-the-way place. Mr. Coon went to see him, and was there found dead soon afterward, with a bullet through his heart.

In 1858, a man named Blackwood, living near DeSota, was arrested for cutting a man named Lamb, with an axe. He broke jail and returned to his house, where he barricaded himself, and Wm. Frazier, Deputy Sheriff, in endeavoring to arrest him, shot him dead. Frazier was tried and acquitted.

In 1859, Henry Seevers, while under the influence of liquor, stabbed a man named Povie, in a saloon at DeSota, killing him. Seevers was arrested, but the Grand Jury failing to find an indictment against him, he was released.

In 1861, Hiram Frazier, a boy thirteen years old, shot a German who had said the boy stole a whip, the man dying within a few hours from the effects of the wound. The boy was sentenced to be hanged, but the Governor commuted the sentence to imprisonment for life. He was subsequently pardoned.

In the winter of 1869–70, one McAuley, a clerk at the Quimby House, at Blair, was killed by John Jones, head cook of the hotel. McAuley was running away from Jones, when the latter threw a butcher's cleaver at him, which severed the main artery of the arm, causing him to bleed to death in a few minutes. Jones was tried in June, 1870, when the Jury disagreed, standing eleven to one. At the second trial he was sentenced to ten years' imprisonment, and was pardoned at the end of two years.

On the 8th of February, 1875, Mrs. Phillip Kleinburg, living on the Brainard farm, a mile north of Fontenelle, was brutally murdered by having her throat cut, while her husband was absent, hauling wheat. Willard Randall, a young man, nineteen years of age, who occupied a house alone about a half mile distant, was arrested on suspicion of being the murderer. He was tried at Blair, in November, 1875, and the jury disagreeing, a change of venue to Douglas County was obtained. At the second trial, in March, 1876, a verdict of murder in the second degree was returned by the jury, and the prisoner was sentenced to ten years' imprisonment.

In May, 1876, Henry Koing, a German, was killed by Minor Milton. It was the result of a feud which existed between Milton and two Swedes, named respectively, John Christian, and Jans Jensen, on the one side, and Henry and Edward Koing, brothers, on the other. The parties all lived in the same neighborhood, some ten miles south of Blair. On the day of the killing, the Koing brothers were overtaken on their return home from Blair, by Milton and the two Swedes, who immediately commenced an assault. The Koings jumped out of their wagon and started to run into a farm house. Henry was pursued by Milton, who struck him over the head with a heavy club, breaking his skull, and knocking him senseless to the ground. Edward Koing was also knocked down by either Milton or Christian, while Jensen held the team. Henry Koing died from the effects of his injuries, but his brother recovered. Milton was found guilty of murder in the first degree at the special term of court held by Judge Savage, in the latter part of May, and was sentenced to be hanged, September 22, 1876. Christian was tried and acquitted, and a *nolle* was entered by the State in the case of Jensen. The case of Milton was appealed to the Supreme Court, which granted him a new trial. At the second trial he was sentenced to ten years' imprisonment.

PUBLIC SCHOOLS.—The number of school districts in the County is forty-five; school houses, forty-six; number of children of school age; males, 1,481, females, 1,402, total, 2,883; qualified teachers employed, males, twenty-three, females, fifty-six; value of school houses, $43,470; value of sites, $2,935; value of books and apparatus, $2,355.

RAILROADS.—The Omaha & Northern Nebraska Railroad runs through the County from south to north, passing up the Missouri Valley. Length of road in the County, 24.47 miles.

The Sioux City & Pacific Railroad, connecting with the Union Pacific at Fremont, in Dodge County, runs through the central portion of this County, from east to west, a distance of 19.60 miles.

LANDS.—Improved lands range in price from $7 to $35 per acre. The Union Pacific R. R. Company owns 5,000 acres in this County, the price ranging from $5 to $10 per acre.

TAXABLE PROPERTY.—Land, 231,834 acres, average value per acre, $3.66; value of town lots, $136,271; money used in merchandise, $27,960; money used in manufactures, $3,690; number of horses, 3,666, value $85,154; mules and asses, 469, value $14,317; neat cattle, 10,656, value, $84,363; sheep, 1,313, value $1,323; swine, 18,408, value, $1,8153; carriages and wagons, 1,311, value, $14,710; moneys and credits, $16,209; mortgages, $11,799; furniture, $26,045; libraries, $1,050; other personalty, $26,976; railroad property, $167,902.89; telegraph property, $855; total valuation for 1879, $1,481,733.89.

POPULATION.—The population of the County in 1855 was 207; in 1860, 1,249; in 1870, 4,452; in 1875, 6,114; in 1878, 7,116; and in 1879, 8,361.

### BLAIR.

Thirty miles to the north of Omaha, about three miles west of the Missouri River, on a beautiful plateau in the Missouri Valley, at the junction of the Omaha & Northwestern and Sioux City and Pacific Railways, is situated the thriving little town of Blair —the County Seat—containing a population of 1,589. The town was surveyed and laid out in 1869, and on the 10th of March in that year, town lots to the amount of over $100,000 were disposed of at auction.

BLAIR HIGH SCHOOL BUILDING, WASHINGTON COUNTY.

Few towns in the State have developed more rapidly, or present a more inviting appearance, or offer larger inducements to business industries, than this. Possessing ample railroad advantages, and surrounded by a well-cultivated, rich farming country,

Blair offers inducements to commercial and manufacturing industries that may be looked for in vain in many other sections of the West. The buildings, including both business houses and residences, are as a rule commodious, substantial, and attractive. The streets are wide, and outside of the immediate business center, shade trees have been planted to a large extent, while the public squares are supplied with fine and well-developed groves of maple, cottonwood, and other favorite varieties. To the south and southwest, the city is flanked by a crescent-shaped range of hills, all under a high state of cultivation, and from which a most charming view of the town is obtained. Having direct rail communication with all the prominent market centers at the East and South, it is an important shipping point for grain, live stock, and other farm products.

The first business house established there, was that of Herman Bros., dry goods, and the next, that of Clark & Donavan, dealers in general merchandise. In 1879, there were six stores that handled dry goods and groceries, three hardware, three drug, two that handled groceries exclusively, three agricultural implement depots, two millinery stores, one boot and shoe store, two confectionery stores, two meat markets, four blacksmith shops, four livery stables, one foundry, two elevators, one large flouring mill (steam), two lumber yards, three hotels, and two excellent weekly papers—*Pilot* and *Times*.

Religious and educational interests are also well represented, there being several fine Churches, a number of common school buildings, and one very attractive high school structure that was erected in 1872, at a cost of $15,000. Except the jail, which is a fine structure, the County buildings are rather modest in their appearance. The town also has one bank, several loan agents, and a full complement of lawyers, doctors, and insurance agents. In brief, Blair is a pleasant, thriving city, and its geographical position insures for it a prosperous future.

### BELL CREEK

Is a flourishing town of 550 inhabitants, situated on the Sioux City and Pacific Railroad, and near the mouth of Bell Creek, in the southeastern part of the County. It was laid out in 1869.

The first improvements on the town site were made by the railroad Company, by the erection of a fine depot and store building, which were soon followed by several dwellings, a lumber yard, by Samuel Francis, a grain warehouse, by L. H. Jones, and a general merchandise store, by A. C. Mansfield. At present all branches of business are well represented. A good water-power grist mill is located near the town. In the fall of 1876, a fine school house

BELL CREEK SCHOOL BUILDING, WASHINGTON COUNTY.

was erected at a cost of $5,000, and in the following year a neat Methodist Episcopal Church was erected. The surrounding country is most beautiful and fertile.

### HERMAN,

Located on the Omaha and Northwestern Railway, in the northern part of the County, was laid out in 1870. It contains about 150 inhabitants, has two grain elevators, and transacts a large grain and stock business, being the principal shipping station between Blair and Tekamah.

## WEBSTER COUNTY.

Webster County was organized in the spring of 1871. It is located on the southern border of the State, in the seventh tier of Counties west of the Missouri River, and is bounded on the north by Adams and east by Nuckolls County, south by the State of Kansas, and west by Franklin County, containing 576 square miles, or 368,640 acres.

WATER COURSES.—The Republican River flows from west to east entirely through the southern portion of the County, its principal tributaries on the north being Beaver, Guide Rock, Willow, Elm, Crooked, Indian and Farmer Creeks; on the south, Runakin, Hake, Cedar, Penny, State and Walnut Creeks. The northern townships of the County are watered by branches of the Little Blue River. Several of the creeks are fine mill streams.

CHARACTER OF THE LAND.—Fifteen per cent. of the County is valley, five per cent. broken and bluffy, and the balance rolling prairie. The prairies have a gradual rise west by north of about eight feet to the mile, the eastern border of the County being about 1,800 feet and the western border 1,990 feet above the sea level. The fertile valley of the Republican is from two to six miles wide. South of the river the land rises into low hills, and sinks into little valleys, each with its stream. The buffalo grass grows on the uplands and the blue stem in the valleys. The surface soil is from one-and-a-half to three feet in depth. Corn and wheat and all the small grains grow to perfection.

CROPS.—The returns for 1879 show the number of acres under cultivation to be 52,277. Winter wheat, 205½ acres, 2,128 bushels; spring wheat, 17,680 acres, 157,934 bushels; rye, 513½ acres, 4,805 bushels; corn, 11,843 acres, 377,122 bushels; barley, 1,370 acres, 18,920 bushels; oats, 1,870 acres, 15,526 bushels; buckwheat, four acres, fifty-seven bushels; sorghum, 79$\frac{3}{8}$ acres, 5,983 gallons; flax, twelve acres, sixty-eight and a half bushels; broom corn, 886 acres, 173 1-6 tons; potatoes, 281 acres, 32,525 bushels; tobacco, 2$\frac{1}{4}$ acres, 158 pounds.

TIMBER.—Ash, elm, oak, walnut, box elder, cottonwood, cedar, and other varieties of natural timber are found along the streams. 1,519$\frac{3}{4}$ acres, or 860,609 forest trees and ten miles of hedging are returned.

FRUIT.—8,369 apple, 112 pear, 10,083 peach, 683 plum, and 1,034 cherry trees have been planted up to 1879. Many of the orchards are in bearing. Wild fruits are abundant.

LIME STONE of a fair quality is found in various parts of the County.

HISTORICAL.—The first settlements within the present limits of Webster County were made in the fall of 1870, by a small colony under the leadership of Capt. Silas Garber, (ex-Governor of Nebraska.) The party at once erected a stockade on the banks of Clear Creek, near its confluence with the Republican, for their protection against roving bands of hostile Indians. It was named the Guide Rock Stockade, from a bold rock bluff on the river, which had long been a land mark for hunters and trappers. In this stockade the colonists spent the winter in safety, and some of them located permanently in its vicinity.

In the spring of 1871, Captain Garber, with a part of the colonists from the stockade, and a few others who had arrived in the meantime, ascended the Republican till they came to Crooked Creek, near the mouth of which they selected a townsite, which was surveyed by Capt. Garber, and the name of Red Cloud given to it, after the illustrious Sioux Chief from whom they daily expected a visit.

In April, this year, the County was formally organized, a full board of officers elected, and the seat of justice located at Red Cloud.

During the summer the mail was brought from Hebron by private carrier whom the settlers paid five dollars per trip; and in the fall the government established offices at Guide Rock and Red

Cloud, Andrew Talbut being the first postmaster at the former, and Wm. E. Jackson at the latter place.

RAILROADS.—The Republican Valley Railroad runs south through the center of the County to Red Cloud, on the Republican River, and thence along the valley of the river, west through the County. Other lines also have been surveyed through the County.

LANDS.—Improved lands are held at from five to twenty dollars per acre. The B. & M. Railroad Company own about 10,000 acres here, the price ranging from two to five dollars per acre.

PUBLIC SCHOOLS.—The number of districts is seventy; school, houses, forty-eight; children of school age—males, 1,207, females, 1,011, total, 2,218; whole number of children that attended school during the year, 1,523; qualified teachers employed—males, thirty-four, females, forty-two; wages paid teachers for the year—males, $1,717.05, females, $1,304.00; total, $3,021.05; value of school houses, $11,857; value of sites, $902.50; value of books $95.

TAXABLE PROPERTY.—Acres of land, 198,895; average value per acre, $1.51; value of town lots, $42,027; money invested in merchandise, $56,725; money used in manufactures, $6,581; horses, 2,681, value $61,840; mules 413, value $11,660; neat cattle 5,032, value $36,166; sheep 3,922, value $2,732; swine 12,450, value $9,174.85; vehicles 1,074, value $13,683; moneys and credits, $12,968.50; mortgages, $16,807; furniture, $15,286.35; libraries, $712; property not enumerated, $37,658.95; railroads, $123,302.61; total valuation for 1879, $774,669.09.

POPULATION.—The following are the Precincts and population of each in 1879: Oak Creek, 403; Glenwood, 335; Stillwater, 451; Batin, 249; Harmony, 449; Walnut Creek, 333; Elm Creek, 331; Inavale, 430; Guide Rock, 721; Pleasant Hill, 287; Potsdam, 345; Red Cloud, 1,613. Total, 5,947—males, 3,233, females, 2,714.

### RED CLOUD,

The County Seat, is situated on Crooked Creek, near the Republican River, in the south-central part of the County. It was located in April, 1871, and at present contains 900 inhabitants. The Republican River is here spanned by a fine bridge. Four miles east, on Elm Creek, there is a good water-power flouring mill, and another is located south of the town, on the Republican, to which a saw mill is attached, The Republican Valley Railroad was completed to Red Cloud during 1879, and has made it a considerable trade center, not only for this County, but for the northern Counties of Kansas also. Two newspapers are published here—the *Chief* and *Argus*; the mercantile interests are well represented, and the school and Church privileges excellent.

### GUIDE ROCK

Is an old village situated on the north side of the Republican, in the southeastern part of the County. It contains about 200 inhabitants, has three or four large general merchandise stores, and enjoys a fine trade from a wide scope of country.

INAVALE, WHEATLAND, WELLS, CATHERTON, CLOVERTON, BATIN, THOMASVILLE, STILLWATER, ECKLEY, NEZUNDA and SCOTT are Post-offices in the County.

## WHEELER COUNTY.

Wheeler County was created by an Act of the Legislature, approved February 17, 1877, and is as yet unorganized. It is located in the north-central part of the State, bounded on the north by unorganized territory, east by Antelope and Boone Counties, south by Greeley and Valley Counties, and west by unorganized territory, containing 1,152 square miles, or 737,280 acres.

Cedar Creek flows southeasterly through the central portion of the County. Beaver Creek, and branches of the Elkhorn River, water the northeastern portions, and the North Loup and branches, the southwestern portions of the County. No report of schools or crops.

The estimated population of the County in 1879 was 700.

## YORK COUNTY.

York County was organized early in the spring of 1870. It is located in the southeastern part of the State, in the fourth tier of Counties west of the Missouri River, and is bounded on the north by Polk, east by Seward, south by Fillmore, and west by

Hamilton County, containing 576 square miles, or 368,640 acres, at an average elevation of 1,600 feet above the sea level.

WATER COURSES.—The County is finely watered by the West Blue River, Beaver, and Lincoln Creeks, all of which flow from west to east through the County, and are fine mill streams. Three flouring mills are located upon the West Blue, one on the Beaver, and one on Lincoln Creek, with many excellent sites remaining unimproved. Besides the above streams there are numerous creeks and rivulets in the County. Well water is obtainable anywhere at a depth varying from twenty to sixty feet.

CHARACTER OF THE LAND.—Ten per cent. of the County is valley, and the balance mostly undulating prairie. There is scarcely any land too rough for tillage. The table lands of the County are fine, and drained by gentle draws or ravines. The larger streams have wide, fertile valleys through their entire length. The soil is a black vegetable mould, everywhere deep, rich and productive.

CROPS.—The area in cultivation, reported for 1879, was 103,208 acres. Winter wheat, 152 acres, 2,428 bushels; spring wheat, 60,025 acres, 708,599 bushels; rye, 2,995 acres, 46,970 bushels; corn, 26,535 acres, 739,516 bushels; barley, 5,153 acres, 132,931 bushels; oats, 5,323 acres, 176,482 bushels; sorghum, seventeen acres, 938 gallons; flax, 311 acres, 2,953 bushels; broom corn, forty acres, eight tons; potatoes, forty-two acres, 5,612 bushels.

TIMBER.—One thousand nine hundred and fourteen acres of forest trees have been planted in the County, and the groves are now sufficiently grown to furnish fuel. There is a light growth of natural timber along the streams.

FRUIT.—13,692 apple, 402 pear, 8,720 peach, 1,642, plum, 3,180 cherry trees, and 3,068 acres of grape vines are reported in a thrifty condition.

BUILDING STONE in fair supply.

HISTORICAL.—Among the pioneers of the County, some of whom located homesteads as early as in 1863, are Elias Gilmore, John H. Parker, James H. Stewart, and Edward Bates. These were followed by others in such rapid succession that anything like a correct list could not well be given.

The first election for County officers was held on the 26th day of Aril, 1870, and resulted as follows: Commissioners, S. V. Moore, David Bussard, and L. F. Wyman; Clerk, Edward Bates; Treasurer, J. W. Frost; Sheriff, Geo. Flock; Probate Judge, D. T. Moore; Superintendent Public Instruction, W. H. Armstrong; Coroner, Randolph Fairbanks; Surveyor, Frank Manning.

At this election York was selected as the County Seat.

CHURCHES.—There are at present sixteen Church buildings in the County, and in the Precincts where Churches have not yet been erected, religious services are regularly held in the school houses.

PUBLIC SCHOOLS.—The number of districts is eighty-four; school houses, sixty-nine; children of school age, males, 1,702; females, 1,583, total, 3,285; whole number that attended school during the year, 2,358; qualified teachers employed, males, forty-seven, females, seventy-five; wages paid teachers for the year, males, $4,283.50, females, $6,618, total, $10,901.50; value of school houses, $21,495.72; value of sites, $840; value of books and apparatus, $994.50.

TAXABLE PROPERTY.—Acres of land, 319,991; average value per acre, $2.30. Value of town lots, $86,416. Money invested in merchandise, 39,530; money used in manufactures, $2,420; horses, 4,755, value $146,994; mules and asses, 434, value $17,449; neat cattle, 5,647, value $44,167; sheep 1,383, value $1,151; swine 17,-262, value $10,118; vehicles 2,389, value $20,559; moneys and credits, $8,978; mortgages, $13,078; stocks, etc., $18,220; furniture, $21,400; libraries, 1,257; property not enumerated, $55,955; railroads, $52,278.07; telegraph, $562.95; total valuation for 1879, $1,278,953.02.

RAILROADS.—The Nebraska Railway runs from east to west through the central portion of the County, a distance of twenty-four miles.

LANDS.—Improved lands are held at from $6 to $25 per acre, according to location. The Burlington and Missouri Railroad Company owns 30,000 acres here, for which from $4 to $10 per acre is asked.

POPULATION.—The County is divided into nine voting Precincts, the population of each in 1879, being as follows: Stewart,

885; Houston, 737; North Blue, 776; Baker, 905; Beaver Creek, 952; York, 1,879; West Blue, 1,035; Woodruff, 930; Henderson, 1,070.

Total, 9,112,—males, 4,944, females, 4,168.

## YORK,

The County Seat, is handsomely laid out on a well-drained and gently sloping stretch of land on the north bank of Beaver Creek, and at the geographical center of the County. The Nebraska Railway was completed to this point in the fall of 1877, since which time the population and business of the town have increased more than 100 per cent., it having at present 1,200 inhabitants. It contains three school houses, four Churches, two newspapers— the *Tribune* and *Republican*, four dry goods, four grocery, three hardware, four drug, five agricultural implement, three furniture, two harness, two boot and shoe, two clothing and six millinery stores, five hotels, two bakeries, three meat markets, five livery stables, five blacksmith and two wagon shops, one foundry, two lumber yards, one flouring mill, four grain elevators, etc.

## WACO

Is a promising new town of 250 inhabitants, located on the Nebraska Railway, six miles east of the County Seat. It contains a grain elevator, several stores and other business establishments.

## ARBORVILLE

Is a flourishing village of about 100 inhabitants, situated on the North Fork of the Blue, in the northwestern part of the County.

PLAINFIELD, WESTFIELD, BLUE VALLEY, MCFADDEN, INDIAN CREEK, SEELEY, DANA, LONG HOPE, PALO, THAYER, CRESWELL and EUREKA, are Postoffices in the County.

# MID-AMERICAN FRONTIER

An Arno Press Collection

Andreas, A[lfred] T[heodore]. **History of Chicago.** 3 volumes. 1884-1886

Andrews, C[hristopher] C[olumbus]. **Minnesota and Dacotah.** 1857

Atwater, Caleb. **Remarks Made on a Tour to Prairie du Chien:** Thence to Washington City, in 1829. 1831

Beck, Lewis C[aleb]. **A Gazetteer of the States of Illinois and Missouri.** 1823

Beckwith, Hiram W[illiams]. **The Illinois and Indiana Indians.** 1884

Blois, John T. **Gazetteer of the State of Michigan,** in Three Parts. 1838

Brown, Jesse and A. M. Willard. **The Black Hills Trails.** 1924

Brunson, Alfred. **A Western Pioneer:** Or, Incidents of the Life and Times of Rev. Alfred Brunson. 2 volumes in one. 1872

Burnet, Jacob. **Notes on the Early Settlement of the North-Western Territory.** 1847

Cass, Lewis. **Considerations on the Present State of the Indians,** and their Removal to the West of the Mississippi. 1828

Coggeshall, William T[urner]. **The Poets and Poetry of the West.** 1860

Darby, John F[letcher]. **Personal Recollections of Many Prominent People Whom I Have Known.** 1880

Eastman, Mary. **Dahcotah:** Or, Life and Legends of the Sioux Around Fort Snelling. 1849

Ebbutt, Percy G. **Emigrant Life in Kansas.** 1886

Edwards, Ninian W[irt]. **History of Illinois, From 1778 to 1833:** And Life and Times of Ninian Edwards. 1870

Ellsworth, Henry William. **Valley of the Upper Wabash, Indiana.** 1838

Esarey, Logan, ed. **Messages and Letters of William Henry Harrison.** 2 volumes. 1922

Flower, George. **The Errors of Emigrants.** [1841]

Hall, Baynard Rush (Robert Carlton, pseud.). **The New Purchase:** Or Seven and a Half Years in the Far West. 2 volumes in one. 1843

Haynes, Fred[erick] Emory. **James Baird Weaver.** 1919

Heilbron, Bertha L., ed. **With Pen and Pencil on the Frontier in 1851:** The Diary and Sketches of Frank Blackwell Mayer. 1932

Hinsdale, B[urke] A[aron]. **The Old Northwest:** The Beginnings of Our Colonial System. [1899]

Johnson, Harrison. **Johnson's History of Nebraska.** 1880

Lapham, I[ncrease] A[llen]. **Wisconsin:** Its Geography and Topography, History, Geology, and Mineralogy. 1846

Mansfieid, Edward D. **Memoirs of the Life and Services of Daniel Drake.** 1855

Marshall, Thomas Maitland, ed. **The Life and Papers of Frederick Bates.** 2 volumes in one. 1926

McConnel, J[ohn] L[udlum.] **Western Characters:** Or, Types of Border Life in the Western States. 1853

Miller, Benjamin S. **Ranch Life in Southern Kansas and the Indian Territory.** 1896

Neill, Edward Duffield. **The History of Minnesota.** 1858

Parker, Nathan H[owe]. **The Minnesota Handbook, For 1856-7.** 1857

Peck, J[ohn] M[ason]. **A Guide for Emigrants.** 1831

Pelzer, Louis. **Marches of the Dragoons in the Mississippi Valley.** 1917

Perkins, William Rufus and Barthinius L. Wick. **History of the Amana Society.** 1891

Rister, Carl Coke. **Land Hunger:** David L. Payne and the Oklahoma Boomers. 1942

Schoolcraft, Henry R[owe]. **Personal Memoirs of a Residence of Thirty Years With the Indian Tribes on the American Frontiers.** 1851

Smalley, Eugene V. **History of the Northern Pacific Railroad.** 1883

[Smith, William Rudolph]. **Observations on the Wisconsin Territory.** 1838

Steele, [Eliza R.] **A Summer Journey in the West.** 1841

Streeter, Floyd Benjamin. **The Kaw:** The Heart of a Nation. 1941

[Switzler, William F.] **Switzler's Illustrated History of Missouri, From 1541 to 1877.** 1879

Tallent, Annie D. **The Black Hills.** 1899

Thwaites, Reuben Gold. **On the Storied Ohio.** 1903

Todd, Charles S[tewart] and Benjamin Drake. **Sketches of the Civil and Military Services of William Henry Harrison.** 1840

Wetmore, Alphonso, compiler. **Gazetteer of the State of Missouri.** 1837

Wilder, D[aniel] W[ebster]. **The Annals of Kansas.** 1886

Woollen, William Wesley. **Biographical and Historical Sketches of Early Indiana.** 1883

Wright, Robert M[arr]. **Dodge City.** 1913